MAZAR

STUDIES ON ISLAMIC SACRED SITES IN CENTRAL EURASIA

INTERNATIONAL WORKSHOP, STUDIES ON THE MAZAR CULTURES OF THE SILKROAD.
AUGUST 26-29, 2008, XINJIANG UNIVERSITY, URUMQI, XINJIANG, CHINA.

Mazar

Studies on Islamic Sacred Sites in Central Eurasia

مزار

Edited by SUGAWARA Jun, Rahile DAWUT

Tokyo University of Foreign Studies Press
Fuchu, Tokyo
MMXVI

Cover: "Shrine of Sultan Satuk Boghra Khan at Artush, North of Kashgar" in Thomas Douglas Forsyth (ed.), *Report of a Mission to Yarkund in 1873.* Calcutta, 1875, no.82.

Design: Sasaki Tomomi

First published in March 2016 by Tokyo University of Foreign Studies Press,
3-11-1 Asahi-chō, Fuchū-shi, Tokyo 183-8534 Japan

Printed in Japan by Shinano Co. Ltd., Ikebukuro, Tokyo, Japan

ISBN 978-4-904575-51-2

This publication is a final product of the research project
"Preservation, Compilation, and Annotation of Mazar Documents in Ferghana and Xinjiang:
Sharing Research through an International Conference and Scholarly Publishing"
headed by Jun Sugawara, research fellow of ILCAA, Tokyo University of Foreign Studies,
sponsored by The Toyota Foundation (Research Grant "Special-Subject Research:
Preservation, Compilation, and Annotation of Indigenous Documents
in Peripheral Regions of Asia," 2007, Grant Number: D07-SQ-003)

本書は、財団法人トヨタ財団 2007 年度研究助成特定課題
「アジア周縁部における伝統文書の保存、集成、解題」助成課題「新疆・フェルガナ両地域
におけるマザール文書の調査・集成・研究：成果普及へ向けた国際会議開催と論集出版」
（助成番号：D07-SQ-003、研究代表者：菅原純、東京外国語大学
アジア・アフリカ言語文化研究所研究員）の最終成果である。

Contents

Illustrations and Tables — page iii
Preface — v
Introduction — vii
Notes on transliteration — xii

Chapter One: Contemporary Mazars — 1

Mazar Pilgrimage among the Uyghurs — 3
Rahile Dawut

Transition and Transformation— Healing Rituals and Mazar Worship — 21
Zhou Xijuan

Kirghiz Bakhshi and the Mazar — 35
Gulbahar Ghojesh

"Ziyara" and the Hui Sufi Orders of the Silk Road — 47
Wang Ping

The Saint Mausoleums of Sufi Order Lingmingtang — 55
Wang Jianxin

Pilgrimages to Mazars in Contemporary Kazakhstan—The Processes of Revivalism and Innovation — 63
Aitzhan Nurmanova

Chapter Two: Iranian Elements — 73

A Cultural Layer in Relation to Hazrat-i Ali—A Preliminary Approach to Mazars of "Imams" in Khotan — 75
Ablimit Yasin

Sacred Sites Associated with Hazrat 'Ali in Central Asia — 95
Nodirjon Abdulahatov

Chapter Three: Document Studies — 125

The Waqf System and the Xinjiang Uyghur Society from the Qing Dynasty to the Republic of China Period — 127
Zhang Shicai

A Holy Place and Its Shaykh in the XIX Century History of Southern Kazakhstan page 141
Ashirbek MUMINOV

Opal, a Sacred Site on the Karakoram Highway—A Historical Approach Based on Mazar Documents 153
SUGAWARA Jun

CHAPTER FOUR: STORIES OF CHILTÄN 175

The Historical Significance of Chiltän Mazar in Yarkand City 177
SHINMEN Yasushi

A Few Remarks on Muḥammad Ṣiddīq Zalīlī and His Tadhkira-i Chihiltan 189
Abliz ORXUN

Mazar Pilgrimage— In the Footsteps of Swedish Missionaries in East Turkestan 193
Patrick HÄLLZON

CHAPTER FIVE: VOICES OF TADHKIRA 225

The Tale of Jānbāz Khoja—Pilgrimage and Holy War in a 19th-Century Tadhkira from Xinjiang 227
Devin DEWEESE

A Sufi Travelogue as a Source for the History of Mazars in the Tarim Basin 253
Alexandre PAPAS

Untangling the Bughrā-Khān Manuscripts 275
Rian Thum

The Genealogy of Makhdūm-i A'ẓam and the Cultural Traditions of Mazārs 289
SAWADA Minoru

The Mazar of Imām Mūsā Kāẓim of Khotan —A Quest for Legends and other Cultural Elements 301
Omerjan NURI

Remarks on the Tazkira-yi Awliya in the Uyghur Script 321
SUGAHARA Mutsumi

INDEX 330
CONTRIBUTORS 344

Illustrations and Tables

Illustrations, Map and Facsimiles

01. Fig. 1. Shrine pilgrimage in Xinjiang 13
02. Fig. 2. Praying at the mazar in Khotan 14
03. Fig. 3 Ordam Mazar 14
04. Fig. 4. Büwi Märyäm Mazar in Kashgar 15
05. Fig. 5. Mazar in desert, Khotan 15
06. Fig. 6. Baghdad Mazar in Khotan 16
07. Fig. 7. Toyoq Mazar in Turpan 16
08. Fig. 8. Kohmarim Mazar in Khotan 17
09. Fig. 9. Hanging the scarf on mazar 17
10. Fig. 10. The Habib Ejem Mazar in Atush 18
11. Fig. 11. Epic singers at mazar in Khotan 18
12. Fig. 12. Sheep stuffed offerings on Baghdad Mazar, Khotan 19
13. Fig. 13. Flags on mazar, Khotan 19
14. Fig. 14. Women prayer in Imam Aptah Mazar in Khotan 19
15. Fig. 15. Miniature cradle in Sultan Uwayis Mazar, Ghulja 20
16. Fig. 16. A doll placed around the mazar in Kashgar 20
17. Fig. 1. Trace of wondering sufis live at a mazar in Yarkand 26
18. Fig. 2. The sacred spring and tree at the mazar of Mahmud Kashgari 26
19. Fig. 3. Worshippers pause & pray at a turn of the path to the Imam Jaffar Sadiq Mazar .. 30
20. Fig. 4. Blessing the food and water 32
21. Fig. 5. Rocks with healing power found at Sultan Sutuq Bugrakhan Mazar 33
22. A *Bakhshi* calling on mazars during her healing ritual 44
23. *Bakhshi* performing a healing ritual in a yurt (*aq uy*) 44
24. A Kirghiz *bakhshi* practicing healing by incantation 44
25. Qambar Atam Mazar in Qarajul Village 45
26. Qoyjol Mazar in Tegirmeti Village 46
27. Qoyjol Mazar in Tegirmeti Village 46
28. Qazan Bulaq Mazar in Tegirmeti Village 46
29. Suiding Gonbei in Ili 51
30. The entrance of Wuxingping Gongbei, Lanzhou City 58
31. Notification Board of Imami(*sic*) Äskär Mazar 85
32. An offered flag with the text of Quranic *sura* at Imam Mahdi Mazar 91
33. Imam Mahdi Mazar in Chira, Khotan 94
34. Mazar Hazrat 'Ali. Sokh (Uzbekistan) 100
35. Mazar-i Sharif (Afghanistan) 104
36. Shahi Mardan, Khiva (Uzbekistan) 105
37. *Gazatname-i Shah Jarir*, copied in 1906 109
38. Door of the Mazar Shah-i Mardan (Ferghana) 114
39. The Mazar of Shah-i Mardan (Ferghana, 1905) 115
40. Mazar Shah-i Mardan (Ferghana, 2001) 119
41. Bakhtiyār-Khwāja Ṣābir-Khwājayev and his family 143
42. Mausoleum and tomb of Zhalang Ayaq Qozha 145
43. Seals 146
44. General view of the Document 148
45. Upper part of the Document with the Seals 149
46. Part of the document with the *khwāja* genealogy 150
47. Section added to the first text with the names of Kazakh tribes, their *biys* and *batirs* 151

48. Lower part of the document with the other Kazakh names 152
49. Map: Opal Township and the mazars 154
50. A view of the Ḥaḍrat-i Mollām Mazar from a distance (2004) 156
51. The Imamlirim Mazar (2004) 160
52. Qondāq Atam Mazar (2004) 163
53. *CKWD* No.6 (p.11) "The tauliya on Ḥaḍrat-i Mollām of Opal" 167
54. *CKWD* No.5(p.10) "The tauliya on Ḥaḍrat-i Mollām Buzrūgwār of Opal" 167
55. *CKWD* No.4 (p.8-9) "The tauliya on Buzrūgwār Ḥaḍrat-i Mollām of Opal" 168
56. *CKWD* No.7 (p.12-14) "The tauliya on Imāmlarim of Opal" 170
57. *CKWD* No.9 (p.16) "The tauliya on Khwāja Qondāq Buzrūgwār of Opal" 173
58. *CKWD* No.10 (p.17) "The tauliya on Khwāja Qondāq Mazār of Opal" 173
59. *CKWD* No.8 (p.15) "The tauliya on Buzrūgwār Khwāja Qontāq(*sic*) of Opal" 174
60. Internal view of the shrine (Lundahl 1917: 212) 178
61. Chiltän Mazar (Lundahl 1917: 209) 183
62. Chiltän Mazar (photographed by Shinmen Y., Aug. 2011) 183
63. The manuscript of "comparison", *Tadhkira-i Haft Muḥammadān*, fol 80b-81a 192
64. Häzret Afaq, Photographer: missionary John Törnquist 223
65. Pilgrims on their way to Odäm > Ordam Padisha, Photographer unknown 224
66. Unidentified mazar, Photographer: John Törnquist 224
67. The external appearance of the mausoleum of Makhdūm-i A'ẓam in Samarkand 300
68. The tomb of Makhdūm-i A'ẓam 300
69. Fig. 1. *Tadhkira-i tort imām*, fol.72a 302
70. Fig. 2. *Tadhkira-i tort imām*, fol.146b 302
71. Fig. 3. The Mazar of Imām Mūsā Kāẓim in Khotan 303
72. Fig. 4. The Grave of Imām Mūsā Kāẓim's Mother 304
73. Fig. 5. The Main Gate of the Friday Mosque 305
74. Fig. 6. *Sümä* 307
75. *Tadhkira of Imām Mūsā Kāẓim*, fol. 36b 314
76. *Tadhkira of Imām Mūsā Kāẓim*, fol. 37a 315
77. *Tadhkira of Imām Mūsā Kāẓim*, fol. 37b 316
78. *Tadhkira of Imām Mūsā Kāẓim*, fol. 38a 317
79. *Tadhkira of Imām Mūsā Kāẓim*, fol. 38b 318
80. *Tadhkira of Imām Mūsā Kāẓim*, fol. 39a 319

Tables and Lists

01. Table 1. List of Lingmingtang's Saint Mausoleums 59
02. The glossary of special terms used by "Ata Zholï" 71
03. Table: The Khotan Twelve Imams and the Mazar 78
04. Table A: Allotments from the revenue of *waqf* land in 1285 Ḥ.(Ḥaḍrat Mollām Mazar) 159
05. Table B: Allotments from the revenue of *waqf* land in 1285 Ḥ.(Imāmlarim mazar) 162
06. List: The genealogies of Makhdūm-i A'ẓam and Kashgharian *khwājas*, etc. 296
07. Table 1 Spelling in different manuscripts 323

Preface

The beginning of our work goes back to the research project "Preservation, Compilation, and Annotation of Mazar Documents in Ferghana and Xinjiang," which was conducted over a period of three years beginning in 2005. This research project was sponsored by the Toyota Foundation, and included the excavation and collection of written sources related to mazars and Islamic sacred sites through collaboration with scholars from Xinjiang, Kazakhstan, Uzbekistan, and Japan. The ultimate aim of this project was to contribute to the preservation and continuation of cultural traditions and customs centered on the local mazar through establishing a systematic preservation framework of mazar documents. This volume, based largely on the proceedings of a 2008 academic meeting entitled "Studies on the Mazar Cultures of the Silkroad: an International Workshop" (国际学术研讨会：丝绸之路上的麻扎文化研究; hereafter "Mazar 2008") and held at Xinjiang University (Urumqi, Xinjiang, China) from August 26–29, 2008, is the final product of this collaborative work.

The editors would first like to extend a deep apology to the contributors to the volume and to other friends involved in the project for delay of its release. This volume is being published only after overcoming a series of obstacles, including horrible social incidents and natural disasters alongside the personal issues of people involved.

Our workshop itself also faced serious hardships from the beginning. It was the time of the Beijing Olympic Games in summer 2008, and while resplendent air prevailed over China, at the same time the mass media broadcasted news of a series of bomb incidents that had taken place in Xinjiang. Once we visited and saw Urumqi with our own eyes, we knew that the city was stable and peaceful as usual. However, the whole of Xinjiang looked very horrible and dangerous from abroad. A number of participants backed out of the meeting, and we heard cries of worry from every direction. Eventually, the ever-positive Rahile DAWUT, one of the volume's co-editors, encouraged us all to press ahead with the meeting.

Although the workshop and its organizers were in a "tightrope situation" at all steps, the event turned out to be a great success. Many Urumqi-based researchers, intellectuals, and students gathered and engaged in lively discussions with foreign students, scholars, and other guests. After the two-day meeting, participants enjoyed a one-day excursion to the Toyoq Khojam Mazar in the Turpan prefecture. All of our plans proceeded without any problems, and we completed the meeting successfully.

We began the work of compiling and editing this volume immediately after the meeting. The translation and editing of many papers originally not written in English, however, was a complicated task. Furthermore, it was also hard work to lead twenty authors in the direction of our reviewer's opinions. Editing these papers took considerably more time than we anticipated.

The Urumqi riots of July 5, 2009, also had a damaging effect on our editing process. Internet communication between Xinjiang and the outside world was cut off for ten months, such that it was impossible for us, the co-editors, to correspond with the contributors and even one another. Then, five months after the restoration of communication, the Great East Japan Earthquake of March 11, 2011 occurred. Co-editor Jun SUGAWARA, a native of Iwate, was deeply affected by this shocking disaster. Moreover, his teaching and research commitments, along with personal issues, impacted his work on this volume. This is no place to make excuses, though, and we accept full responsibility for the delays in publishing this volume.

We owe many thanks to our sponsor, the Toyota Foundation, for their help and understanding. As a distinctive non-governmental foundation, they appreciated both the academic and social value of our project and offered unstinting support. Here the editors express our full gratitude to this fund as well as to the members of the selection committee headed by Christian DANIELS. We would also like to say sincerest thanks to the reliable and smart program officers, HONDA Shiro and KUSUDA Kenta. Without their very instructive committment to our work, this volume would not have come to fruition.

We also thank the contributors of this volume for enduring an odyssey of editing; we feel greatly indebted to them. SUGAHARA Mustumi, a contributor and a member of the Mazar Document Project, was instrumental in starting and completing this editing. A faculty member of the Tokyo University of Foreign Studies, he took on the role of publishing this volume through the University Press (TUFS Press), and he helped a lot in the final check of drafts.

The kind support of friends in Urumqi to our research activities and to Mazar 2008 were invaluable, strengthening our attachments to this land and people. We extend heartfelt thanks to Tashpolat TEYIP, Manze, Arslan ABDULLA, and the helpful students of Xinjiang University's Humanities Institute. We thank MA Pinyan of the Xinjiang Academy of Social Sciences for his invited lecture at the meeting. Joshua FREEMAN and Margaret SUN deserve many thanks for interpreting between several languages at the meeting; their skillful translations are included in this volume.

Many other friends and colleagues assisted in our further work. Daniel PRIOR, Nathan MONTGOMERY, and Elise ANDERSON all helped at various stages of translating and/or revising papers. YAJIMA Yō'ichi and SAWAI Mitsuo served as primary peer reviewers for this volume. Their careful work definitely improved this volume's academic value.

We also thank our young, new academic publisher, the Tokyo University of Foreign Studies (TUFS) Press, for whom this volume is their first commercial publication in English. Their staff members have played a consistently active and professional role while dealing with new tasks. Finally, we would like to express our gratitude to IWASAKI Minoru, the ex-chief editor of TUFS Press, editor OH'UCHI Hironobu, and designer SASAKI Tomomi .

There is a popular Uyghur proverb that reads *baliliq öy bazar, balisiz öy mazar*, or a home with children is a bazaar; a home without, a mazar. Though the mazar is invoked in the proverb as a solemn and lonely place, we have come to know it instead as a lively one, where we have learned much and made many wonderful friends. THANK YOU ALL.

JS & RD

Introduction

SUGAWARA Jun & Rahile DAWUT

> The shrine is marked by four tall masts decorated with *yak* tails (*tugh*) and flags inscribed with Arabic texts, and by numerous huge horns of the *Ovis Poli* (or rather *Ovis Karilini*) found in the neighbouring mountains. These are ranged along the top of the walls surrounding the shrine, and the finest are formed into two heaps, in front of a little pavilion where pious worshippers sit and meditate on the virtues of the saint. These fluttering *yak* tails and heaped-up horns are strange features for a Musulman holy place . . .
>
> —Robert Barkley Shaw[1]

One winter day in 1874, a 34-year-old British tea-planter in Kangra, Robert Barkley Shaw, was riding forth from the city gate of Kashgar. They climbed up a gentle ascent after crossing a wooden bridge over the Tümän River and went through the vast graveyards connected to a large shrine. On this day, Shaw visited one of the most celebrated Islamic sacred sites in this region, a mazar of Khwāja Hedāyat Allāh Āfāq. Shaw was received well by the *shaykh* of the mazar, and there he observed the resting place of the Khwāja clans, which centered on the famous Khwāja Āfāq, as well as a newly-built school and *khaniqa*. Later on Shaw wrote about this visit, concluding by remarking that the *shaykh*'s polite reception at the mazar, "which one might suppose to be a refuge for the conservative and religious sentiment of the country, rather belies the usual idea of Musulmān fanaticism and intolerance in Central Asia" in that era. He went on emphasize how positive an experience he had, stating that this good treatment had been "of a piece with all [his] experience" there.[2]

Mazars, or Islamic sacred sites, have played important roles in various dimensions of the Central Eurasian world. For over a millennia the mazar was the central source of spiritual strength and guidance for local communities, and it has played a substantial social role in the large-scale intersection and contact of various peoples through the act of pilgrimage. Moreover, the mazar sometimes functioned as a kind of landmark that recalled local history, or what Alexandre Papas, in his chapter in this volume, calls a *lieux de mémoire* ('memory space'). The cultural, social, economic, and historical values of the mazar are indispensable, and thus studies of the mazar have an academic significance in that they help us to develop an in-depth understanding of Central Eurasian history and society. It is for this reason that we believe that Shaw's account is suggestive for the way that it demonstrates some of the mazar's most extant features.

---

[1] Shaw & Elias 1897:61.

[2] *Ibid.*:63.

Here, for descriptive purposes, we use the word mazar (*mazār*, a verbal noun from the Arabic *zaur*, meaning visiting; a place of visitation; a shrine, sepulchre, tomb, grave; visitation, a visit) to refer to a broader cultural phenomenon, employing it as a generic term for a wide variety of Islamic sacred sites.[3] This volume aims to shed light on various aspects of mazars from the points-of-view of twenty different specialists, aiding readers in imagining new intellectual horizons for and about the Central Eurasian world, a welcome counterpoint to some of the tired tropes that have long defined debates about the region.

Although explorations of and research about mazars have been conducted constantly up through the present, only a limited number of people have left fragmental records of mazars in the historical record. The contents of this volume build in various ways on the on these previous fragments. We would like to open this volume by looking briefly at the history of the description and study of mazars in historical and present-day Xinjiang, which we have understood in four groupings.

The first grouping of descriptions could be labeled as pre-nineteenth century fragmental records by local historians. Generally speaking, these written sources are limited in number,[4] and their records of mazars typically lack detailed information. The earliest such record of a mazar in this region appears to be that left in the fourteenth century by Jamāl al-Qarshī, who gave an account of the Sulṭān Satūq Bughrakhān Mazār in his *Mulḥaqāt al-ṣurāḥ*.[5] In the sixteenth century, Mīrza Muḥammad Ḥaydar left brief descriptions of several mazars, such as the tombs of Imām Ja'far Ṣādiq and Imām Ja'far Ṭayrān, in his historiographical work *Tārīkh-i rashīdī*.[6] In the seventeenth century, Shāh Mahmūd Churās also mentioned a couple of local mazars, such as Qūchqār Ata, Quṭb al-'Ālam, and Sūt-Bībī, in his *Tārikh*.[7] And Zalīlī also mentioned numerous mazars in the Kashgar and Khotan regions in his poetic travel account *Safarnāma*, which was written in the beginning of the eighteenth century.[8]

A second grouping of mazar records, a series of legendary accounts related to mazars, are found in the genre of *tadhkiras*, or hagiographic works. Hamada Masami has suggested that these *tadhkiras* can be divided into two categories. The first is "classical hagiographies," which describe mazars through fragmental quotes and the miraculous episodes of saints, focusing very little on the specific profiles and daily lives of those saints. The second category of *tadhkira* is that which provides biographical accounts of one saint, similar to the *manāqib nama* in Anatolia. Many Xinjiang *tadhkiras* belong to this category.[9]

According to Rian Thum, "at least twenty-eight different works" of *tadhkiras* were produced in Altishahr, and the earliest "indigenous" *tadhkira* was the *Tadhkira-i Khwāja*

---

[3] For the definitions of the word mazār, *see* Steingass 1970:1221.

[4] On the general situation of local, Turkic-language sources, *see* Hamada 1983; Hamada 2006.

[5] Hamada 1991:90.

[6] Elias & Ross 1972:289, 298.

[7] Akimushkin 1976:388.

[8] Tursun 1985. Alexandre Papas's paper in this volume (253–74) deals exclusively with this work.

[9] Hamada 2006:8–9.

Muḥammad Sharīf, "written sometime between 1559 and 1724."[10] This work itself is a legendary biography of a saint whose mazar exists in Yarkand, and, as Hamada has demonstrated, also includes a miraculous episode relating to a mazar of Sulṭān Satūq Bughrakhān.[11] These *tadhkiras* are, to quote Thum's attractive phrasing, the "primary textual vehicle of popular local history" and can be recognized as indispensable resources to approach a comprehensive picture of the mazars.

A third grouping of mazar records includes those observations made in administrative records, gazetteers, and travelogues. In the middle of the eighteenth century, this region came to be ruled by the Qing Empire, thus beginning their indirect rule. For a century the Qing officials were satisfied only with charging taxes as well as stationing their garrisons in this new dominion. They were not deeply committed to indigenous social issues, but rather to practical, administrative matters, and thus compiled comprehensive geographical records, which included mazars as essential landmarks. As Saguchi Tōru has described in detail, some Chinese gazetteers such as *Xiyu tuzhi* and *Huijiang zhi* contain certain accounts related to mazars.[12] With the expansion of the so-called Great Game by Western imperial powers in the late-nineteenth century, many travelers, journalists, and academic explorers visited the region, leaving various accounts and records behind, including valuable photos of mazars.[13]

The fourth grouping of resources on the mazar, which is still very much alive in the present, is of those works that are the product of contemporary scholarly research. Until the People's Republic of China's policy of "reform and opening-up" (*gaige kaifang*) was implemented in the 1980s and 1990s, mazars could not be a scholar's primary interest but were studied instead as a part of text-based research on history or philology.[14] Any studies that focused specifically on mazars were primarily conducted by the Xinjiang Academy of Social Sciences (XASS); Ma Pinyan's 1983 *Nanjiang de Maza he Maza Chaobai* ('Mazar and mazar worship in Southern Xinjiang') was published in this context. Rahile Dawut's comprehensive *Weiwuerzu Maza Wenhua Yanjiu* ('A study on Uyghur mazar culture'), based on her doctoral dissertation, set the stage for intensive fieldwork-based studies of mazar outside the auspices of the XASS.[15] Since then, a series of other works about mazars have been published. They include works by Shinmen *et al.* (2002), Zarcone *et al.* (2002), and Sawada (2007), among others.

The years 2005 to 2008 saw the launching of an international research project headed by Jun Sugawara, sponsored by the Toyota Foundation, and titled "Preservation, Compilation, and Annotation of Mazar Documents in Xinjiang and Ferghana." The many participants in this project conducted various research activities on documentary

---

[10] Thum 2014:41, 43.

[11] Hamada 2006:142–43.

[12] Saguchi 1995 (*see* especially chapters 1–3). Saguchi's work can be seen as an exhaustive study in its use of rich Chinese sources as well as travelogues in Western languages.

[13] For example, Le Coq 1928; Stein 1903; Jarring 1986. For general information on the travels of Westerners in Xinjiang, *see* Dabbs 1963; Saguchi *op.cit.*

[14] For example, Hamada 1978; Kim 1993; and Gürsoy-Naskali 1985.

[15] Dawut 2001.

sources related to mazars, eventually releasing three volumes of facsimile works, including those by Sugawara and Kawahara (2006), Orxun and Sugawara (2007), and Muminov et al. (2007). The final program of the project, an international workshop organized by Rahile Dawut, Arslan Abdulla, and Jun Sugawara, titled "Studies on the Mazar Cultures of the Silk Road," was held at Xinjiang University in August 2008. Scholars from five countries and various disciplinary backgrounds participated in this meeting, a meaningful opportunity to show some possible directions for the future of mazar studies.

About this volume

This volume includes twenty papers. The majority of papers are based on those that were presented in the 2008 workshop, and the concept of the chapters basically follows the program of the meeting.

Chapter One, "Contemporary Mazars," includes six papers dealing with contemporary issues based on the results of each author's fieldwork. Rahile Dawut and Zhou Xijuan discuss pilgrimage and healing rituals in Uyghur mazar culture. Gülbahar Ghojesh looks at the *bakhshi*, the important player in mazar worship rituals among the Kirghiz. Wang Ping and Wang Jianxin's papers deal with mazar worship among the Hui, and with social brotherhoods (*menhuan*) under Hui mazars (*gongbei*). Aitzhan Nurmanova's paper reports on new religious trends in Kazakhstan that have close connections with mazar worship.

Chapter Two, "Iranian Elements," consists of two papers by Ablimit Yasin and Nodirjon Abdulahatov, which deal with influences from Iran-Shi'ite cultures in both Xinjiang and Central Asia proper.

Chapter Three, "Document Studies," includes three papers. Zhang Shicai and Jun Sugawara both address the issue of Islamic endowments (*waqf*). Ashirbek Muminov introduces a newly discovered private archive, which shows a glimpse of Qoqand–Southern Qazāq relations in the nineteenth century.

The three papers in Chapter Four, "Stories of Chiltän," address different aspects of the Chiltän Mazar in Yarkand. Shinmen Yasushi tries to describe this mazar from a comprehensive historical perspective. Abliz Orxun deals with the hagiography of the mazar written by Zalīlī. And Patrick Hällzon attempts to show this mazar through the eyes of Western missionaries from the late-nineteenth to early-twentieth centuries.

Chapter Five, "Voices of Tadhkira," includes six papers, all of which engage in the close analysis of one or more *tadhkiras*. Devin DeWeese's paper deals with the *Tadhkira-i Jānbāz Khwāja*, Alexandre Papas's with the *Safarnāma*, and Rian Thum's with manuscripts related to Bughrā-Khān. Sawada Minoru tries to draw a genealogy of Makhdūm-i A'ẓam by comparing ten different hagiographies, Omerjan Nuri gives a general account of the mazar of Imām Mūsā Kāẓim of Khotan with facsimile and translations, and Sugahara Mutsumi uses the *Tadhkirat al-awliyā* for a historical linguistic approach to mazars.

In the process of preparing the volume, the editors paid special attention to "material richness": that is to say, we have tried our best to supply facsimiles, transliterations, and translations of the written sources, especially *tadhkiras,* as much as we can. We all expect that this volume will be a useful and fundamental source of literature in the study of mazars, and that students of the phenomenon of religious holy sites in Central Eurasia and elsewhere will continue to use it for many years to come.

References

Akimushkin, O. F. (ed. & tr.) 1976. *Shāh Maḥmūd ibn Mīrzā Fāẓil Churās, Khronika.* Moscow: Nauka; Pis'mennye pamiatniki Vostoka, XLV.

Dabbs, Jack A., 1963. *History of the Discovery and Exploration of Chinese Turkestan* (Central Asiatic Studies 8), The Hague: Mouton & Co.

Dawut, Rahile (Reyila Dawuti) 热依拉・达吾提 2001. *Weiwuerzu Maza Wenhua Yanjiu.* 维吾尔族麻扎文化研究 [Study on Uyghur Mazar Cultures], Urumqi: Xinjiang Daxue Chubanshe.

Elias, N. & E. Denison Ross 1972. *A History of the Moghuls of Central Asia. Being the Tarikh-i-Rashidi of Mirza Muhammad Haidar, Dughlat.* London: Curzon Press, New York: Barnes and Noble, 1972 (first published 1895, second edition 1898).

Gürsoy-Naskali, Emine (ed. and tr.) 1985. *Aṣḥābu'l-Kähf: A Treatise in Eastern Turki.* Helsinki: Suomalais- Ugrilainen Seura; Suomalais-Ugrilaisen Seuran Toimituksia/Mémoires de la Société Finno-ougrienne.

Hamada Masami 1978. "Islamic Saints and Their Mausoleums." *Acta Asiatica*, 34: 79-98.

Hamada masami 濱田正美 1983. "Jyūkyū seiki Uiguru rekishi bunken josetsu" 19 世紀ウイグル歴史文献序説 [Satuk Boghra Khan's Mausoleum in History] , *Seinan Ajia Kenkyu*, 34: 89–112.

Hamada Masami 濱田正美 1991. "Satoku Bogura Han no bobyō wo megutte" サトク・ボグラ・ハンの墓廟をめぐって [Satuk Boghra Khan's Mausoleum in History] , *Seinan Ajia Kenkyu*, 34: 89–112.

Hamada Masami 濱田正美(ed.) 2006. *Hagiographies du Turkestan Oriental: Textes čaġatay édités, traduits en japonais et annotés avec une introduction analytique et historique* 東トルキスタン・チャガタイ語聖者伝の研究, Kyoto: Graduate School of Letters, Kyoto University.

Jarring, Gunnar. 1986. *Return to Kashgar: Central Asian Memoirs in the Present.* Translated from the Swedish by Eva Claeson. Durham, N.C: Duke.

Kim, Ho-dong 1993. "The Cult of Saints in Eastern Turkestan: The Case of Alp Ata in Turfan," in *Proceedings of the 35th Permanent International Altaistic Conference (September 12-17, 1992, Taipei, China)*, Taipei: Center for Chinese Studies Materials/United Daily News Cultural Foundation, 199-226.

Le Coq, Albert von., 1928. *Buried Treasures of Chinese Turkestan.* London: George Allen

Ma Pinyan 马品彦 1983. "Nanjiang de maza he maza chaobai" 南疆的麻扎和麻扎朝拜 [Mazar and Mazar Worships in Southern Xinjiang], *Xinjiang shehui kexue*, 1983-3.

Mumiov, Ashirbek, Nadirbek Abdulahatov and Kawahara Yayoi (eds) 2007. *Mazar Documents from Xinjiang and Ferghana (facsimile)* vol.3, Studia Culturae Islamicae No. 88, Tokyo: Research Institute for Languages and Cultures of Asia and Africa, TUFS.

Orxun, Abliz, and Sugawara Jun (eds) 2007. *Mazar Documents from Xinjiang and Ferghana (Facsimile)*, vol. 2 Studia Culturae Islamicae No. 87, Tokyo: Research Institute for Languages and Cultures of Asia and Africa,TUFS.

Pucha ziliao: Zizhiqu wenwu pucha bangongshi, Kashi diqu wen wu pucha dui 自治区文物普查办公室，喀什地区文物普查队(eds), "Kashi diqu wenwu pucha ziliao huibian" 喀什地区文物普查资料汇编[Collection of Materials by General Survey on Cultural Assets of Kashghar District], *Xinjiang wenwu*, 1993:3, 1-112.

Saguchi Tōru 佐口透 1995. *Shinkyō musurimu kenkyū.* 新疆ムスリム研究 [Studies on muslims in Xinjiang], Tokyo: Yoshikawa Kōbunkan.

Sawada Minoru (ed.) 2007. *Islamic Sacred Places in Central Asia : the Ferghana Valley and Kashghar Region.* (Silk Roadology (*sic*) : bulletin of the Research Center for Silk Roadology vol.28). Nara: Silkroad Foundation

Shaw, Robert Barkley, & Ney Elias 1897. "The History of the Khojas of Eastern Turkistan", Supplement of *Journal of Asiatic Society of Bengal*, vol LXVI, Part 1:61-63.

Shinmen Yasushi *et al.* 2002. *Shinkyō Uiguru no bazāru to mazāru* (The Bazaars and Mazaars of the

Xinjiang Uighur.) Studia Culturae Islamicae No.70, Tokyo: ILCAA.
Stein, M. Aurel.1903. *Sand-buried Ruins of Khotan. Personal Narrative of a Journey of Archaeological & Geographical Explorations in Chinese Turkestan.* London: T. F. Unwin.
Steingass, F., 1970. *A Comprehensive Persian-English Dictionary*. Beirut: Librarie du Liban.
Sugawara Jun and Kawahara Yayoi (eds) 2006. *Mazar Documents from Xinjiang and Ferghana (facsimile)* vol.1, Studia Culturae Islamicae No. 83, Tokyo: Research Institute for Languages and Cultures of Asia and Africa, TUFS.
Thum, Rian, 2014. *The Sacred Routes of Uyghur History*, Cambridge (Mass.) and London: Harvard University Press.
Tursun, Imin 1985. *Zälili Diwani.* Beijing: Millätlär Näshriyati.
Zarcone, Thierry *et al.*(eds) 2002. *Saints and Heroes on the Silk Road* (= *Journal of the History of Sufism* 3), Paris: CNRS.

******

Notes on Transliteration

In transliterating, we have generally followed the system used by Komatsu Hisao *et al.*(eds), *Chūō Yūrashia wo Shiru Jiten* ('Cyclopedia of Central Eurasia'), Tokyo: Heibonsha, 2005, 592–593. On the other hand, this volume respects each each author's preference for spelling personal and place names based on the academic conventions of various disciplines.

(1) For Perso-Arabic: *a/i/u, ā, b, p, t, th, j, ch, ḥ, kh, d, dh, r, z, zh, s, sh, ṣ, ḍ, ṭ, ẓ, ', gh, f, q, k, g, l, m, n, h, y/i*

(2) For New Uyghur: *a, ä, b, p, t, j, ch, kh, d, r, z, zh, s, sh, gh, f, q, f, q, k, g, ng, l, m, n, h, o, u, ö, ü, w, e, i, y*

(3) For Uzbek: *a, b, v, g, d, e/ye, yo, j, z, i, y, k, l, m, n, o, p, r, s, t, u, f, x, ts, ch, sh, shch, ', e, yu, ya, o', q, g', h*

(4) For Kazakh: *a, ä, b, v, g, gh, d, e, e, j, z, i, y, k, q, l, m, n, ng, o, ö, p, r, s, t, u/w, ŭ, ü, f, kh, h, ts, ch, sh, shch, ", ï, í, ', e, yu, ya*

(5) For Russian: *a, b, v, g, d, e, e, zh, z, i, i, ķ, l, m, n, o, p, r, s, t, u, f, kh, ts, ch, sh, shch, ", y, ', e, yu, ya*

(6) For Kirghiz, the paper by Gozjesh employs the following sytem:
a, b, p, n, t, j, ch, kh, f, q, gh, k, g, ng, l, m, o, ö, u, ü, w, s, sh, d, r, z, e, ï, i, y

(7) For Chinese, we adopt the Chinese *pinyin* transliteration system.

(8) For Japanese, we adopt the Hepburn romanization system.

Chapter One

CONTEMPORARY MAZARS

Mazar Pilgrimage among the Uyghurs

Rahile DAWUT

The practice of shrine pilgrimage has long been prominent on the global Islamic landscape. Its significance has been noted by many scholars (Hawley 1987; Werbner 2003; Kieckhefer and Bond 1988; Tyson 1997). People across the Islamic world go on pilgrimages to fulfill a wish expressed in the name of a saint or to seek the blessing of a particular mazar [Fig. 1].

In Xinjiang, there are numerous such mazars, some of the earliest evidence about mazars in Xinjiang is that left by foreigners from various European countries and Japan in the 19th and early 20th centuries. They came to this area as travelers, scholars, diplomats, and missionaries and have provided us useful information related to the historical situations, shapes, locations and legends of some of the mazars of that time. Also, under the Qing Dynasty, Chinese scholars or rulers recorded important information on mazars.

However, since 1949 there have been few ethnographic studies of shrine–centered religious activities in Xinjiang (for recent publications in Western languages see Harris and Dawut 2002; Sawada 2001a, 2001b; Zarcone 2001, 2002). Chinese scholars have tended to be more interested in the historical aspects of Islam among the Uyghurs, while researchers from other countries have often encountered difficulties in gaining access to rural areas in Xinjiang. An examination of current Uyghur pilgrimage practices, coupled with knowledge of religious behavior in the region from a historical perspective, will demonstrate that shrines have long been critical focal points of Islamic practice among the Uyghurs (cf. Tyson 1997).

In this paper, I shall draw on information obtained from fieldwork and written resources to provide insight into the mazar culture among the Uyghurs by exploring the classification, distribution and physical evidence for rituals of worship at mazars. Of particular interest is the way this material suggests a relationship between Islamic mazar culture and pre-Islamic traditions, including those of Buddhism and shamanism.

In the Uyghur language, mazar means "tomb" or "shrine." It often refers to the burial place of a saint or a place where miracles are believed to have occurred. Mazar pilgrimage refers to the practice of making journeys to the tombs of saints, which are scattered around the deserts and towns of Xinjiang. The mazars are the sites of pilgrimage in part because they are believed to have the power to cure infertility and diseases and avert natural or other disasters. In principle, mazar worship involves the activities of worship: reading of the Quran, prayers, offerings of sacrifices and other rituals for the purpose of securing the divine protection of the mazar [Fig. 2]. Mazar worship is popular among the broad masses of the Uyghur people, and has become an inalienable part of their religious belief. Worshippers at the mazars pour out the sorrows and bitterness of their hearts and use different forms to express their needs and wishes. Some pray for revenge on people who had done them wrong, some for protection from disaster or for material wealth. Still others pray for harmony in marital relationships, or for an ideal marriage partner. Others pray for financial security in old age, or for relief from extended drought. People look on the mazar as a place which can protect them from disaster, where they can pour out their innermost feelings, where they can seek cure for diseases, where their souls can be saved, and also as a place where they can seek pleasure. Therefore, whether in extreme cold or heat, regardless of how dangerous or difficult the journey, people will make pilgrimage to mazars. Some will not stint their fortune to offer sacrifices at the mazar in order to gain its divine protection. There are individuals who hold mazar worship to be of equal importance to a pilgrimage to Mecca. Many local cemeteries have a shrine around which people of the community are buried. In the course of several years' fieldwork I have documented more than seventy in the Khotan Prefecture alone (Dawuti 2001).

The Types and Geographical Distribution of Mazars

The most common pilgrimage sites, which attract the greatest number of worshippers, are the tombs of kings, Islamic missionaries and Islamic martyrs (*shehit*) killed in holy war (*jihad*) against the Buddhist kingdoms of Xinjiang. Major sites of pilgrimage include the tomb of the founder of the Qarakhanid Dynasty[1] Sultan Satuq Bughra Khan[2], and the Ordam Padishah, "Court of the Emperor" (located about 24 km. southeast of Harap Township in Yengishähär County)[Fig. 3], which is reputed to be the shrine of Sultan Äli Arslan Khan, grandson of Satuq Bughra Khan. Shrines of sufi leaders are also quite common, but their rituals are more localized. The most widely known are the tombs of the Khoja rulers of Kashgar including that of Apaq Khoja and the "Fragrant Concubine" Ipar Khan.[3]

Although they are considered an Islamic phenomenon, many sites of worship are

---

[1] The Qarakhanid Dynasty was established in the mid-9th century and lasted for 150 years. In 1041 the Khanate divided into a western and an eastern part. The western part occupied the territory between the Amu Darya in modern Uzbekistan eastwards to the Ferghana Basin, with the capital at Bukhara. The eastern part was ruled by Hasan Bughra and his descendants from Balasaghun, while Kashgar served as an important religious and cultural center. The Qarakhanid Dynasty was the first Muslim state of the Turkic peoples.

[2] Satuq Bughra Khan is reputed to have been the first convert to Islam among the Central Asian Turkic peoples. His shrine is located 3 km. southwest of Atush city. For details on his mausoleum and cult, see Hamada 2001.

[3] Ipar Khan is considered by many Uyghurs to be a Uyghur heroine. There are controversies around this historic figure. Chinese historians call her Xiang Fei, the "Fragrant Concubine" of the Manchu Emperor Qianlong. For a discussion of the way her history has been treated, her tomb and its political implications see Millward 1994 and Zarcone 1999.

not directly linked to Islam. The tombs of philosophers and writers have in the past been important sites of pilgrimage for students at Islamic schools. Most famous of these are the tombs of the prominent 11th century Uyghur scholars, Yusuf Khass Hajib, author of "Wisdom of Royal Glory" (*Qutadghu Bilig*), and Mahmud Kashghari, author of the "Compendium of the Turkic Dialects" (*Divanu Lughat-it-Türk*). The tomb of the first is in Kashgar city, the second in the village of Opal some 50 km to the west. Other sites of pilgrimage are the tombs of craftsmen, which are believed to be effective in healing specific ailments such as skin diseases. Many tombs of female historical figures are sites of pilgrimage for women, especially those who seek to have a child. The most famous of these is the tomb of Büwi Märyäm (located in Bäshkeräm Township near Kashgar) [Fig. 4], also of the Qarakhanid dynasty. According to local legend, Büwi Märyäm was a sister of Äli Arslan Khan, and grand-daughter of Sultan Satuq Bughra Khan, founder of the Qarakhanid Dynasty.

Most mazars in Xinjiang are concentrated in the south and east, although there are some in the north, in the Ili River valley. The distribution of the mazars is uneven; some mazars are situated in traffic hubs and densely populated areas, while others are in remote areas [Fig. 5]. Especially in the Khotan area some mazars are located on the edges of the Taklamakan Desert or even farther out in the desert. Although such mazars are far from any community, their surroundings are scenic, with a water source and shady trees, and mosques, *khaniqas*, inns, and similar affiliated constructions.

Travel on the ancient Silk Road meant following paths which led from one oasis to another in order to reach a remote destination, the mazars often serving as road markers. Between the oases are either the barren gobi, mountainous paths or dense forests. In the southern parts of Xinjiang, many mazars have the name of "längär" which literally means "station" or "inn" in Uyghur. Mazars located at traffic hubs and way-stations usually have caretakers and adjoining inns and are situated in quiet and elegant surroundings with springs and trees. While resting there, travelers can recover from the weariness of the journey and can also pray at the nearby mazars for blessings and protection for the remainder of their trip.

However, most mazars do not have caretakers or inns to shelter the travelers, but rather are mainly burial sites even if the sites of some mazars are not really suited for burials. They may be marked by piled up stones or earth and the usual mazar sign of poles with colorful flags on them. On the poles and the trees near the mazar will be found many strips of cloth, and on the graves will be placed the horns of cows or sheep [Fig. 6].

The geographical location and form of such mazars suggest that they have the obvious characteristics of the shamanist *obo*. Sacrificial activity at an *obo* is an integral part of shamanist religious rituals, and played a very important role in the religious life of the ancient nomadic peoples of northern China. However, for the Uyghurs, probably in conjunction with the concept of worshipping saints in Islam, in certain sacrificial rituals the *obo* continues to play a role in mazars. Indeed, there is much evidence to suggest that the shrine tradition is not purely Islamic but has roots in a variety of pre-Islamic beliefs and practices (Dawuti 2001). Many shrines are named after animals and plants, such as Üjmä (Mulberry) Mazar, and Ghaz (Goose) Mazar.

Some sites of pilgrimage were also formerly Buddhist sites of worship (Dawuti 2001). It is well known that after the advent of Islam, in Central Asia and other regions local Buddhist and Zoroastrian temples and Christian churches were converted into mosques. However, it was rare that Buddhist temples and caves be transformed into Islamic sacred ground such as mazars. Some mazars which we can document today are near the locations of Buddhist sacred sites recorded by Buddhist monks such Faxian (early 5th century) and Xuanzang (7th century). When Aurel Stein was looking for Buddhist ruins in Khotan, he first looked for local mazars. He believed that if one wanted to look for ancient Buddhist or Hindu holy sites, all he needed to do was to look for an Islamic mausoleum (Stein 1994, p. 129; 1904, pp. 180-181).

An example is Toyoq Mazar near Turpan [Fig. 7]. The Toyoq Ravine was one of the important holy lands of Buddhism and Manichaeism before the advent of Islam. Not far from the eastern side of the mazar and on the left bank of the stream are the famous Toyoq Thousand Buddha Caves. The ninety-four caves contain some of the earliest and most significant Buddhist murals in the Turpan area and are the location of important discoveries of early Buddhist manuscripts. Worship at the mazar here centers on a cave as it does in Khotan's Kokhmarim (Snake Mountain) Mazar, where people go to pray for rain [Fig. 8].[4] The local population combined local history and custom with the legend of the Seven Sleepers (Äshab al-kähf) in order to transform the Buddhist holy land into an Islamic one and in the process greatly increase the influence of the mazar.

Even before the advent of Islam, the worship of saints was central to the religious system of the local people, because Buddhism, in which their world outlook was anchored, began with the worship of a holy one. Buddhists not only worshipped the saint himself but also worshipped any holy article connected with him — his remains, articles that had been used by him, and so on. In addition, places which had once housed the holy one or any of the saints, individual buildings, the places to which they traveled, bushes and groves, trees, etc., are all revered by devotees. Analogous to this phenomenon of saint worship are local beliefs in ancestor worship.

The activities at mazars not only adapted their form and content from Buddhism but also adapted the form of the offerings. Excavation of Xinjiang Buddhist ruins has uncovered small flags, strips of cloth, copper coins and other items left by worshippers as offerings. To pray to the gods for their protection, the devout believers placed such offerings in the base of the stupas or nearby, and also offered oil to light the lamps of the temple. Similar forms of offerings are commonly seen in mazar worship, where flags or strips of cloth hung near or on burial sites to mark Islamic sacred ground have become symbols of mazars in the southern parts of Xinjiang [Fig. 9]. The offerings and ritual practice will be discussed in greater detail below.

Even the architecture of the mazars may reflect the influence of Buddhism. The most prominent feature of mazar architecture of Central Asia, Xinjiang, and Turkey is

---

[4] This was a famous Buddhist site before Islam. Here too, Buddhist ruins can be seen near the shrine. For detailed discussion see Dawuti 2001.

the domed top and *gumbäz*, and most of the exterior of the construction is carved with niche-like decoration [Fig. 10]. The most likely source for these architectural forms is the Buddhist stupa. However, Buddhist architecture has considerable regional variation in Uyghur territory, where the Gandharan and Bamiyan styles were of particular importance. Mazar architecture in its turn displays regional variations and changed over time, adapting the styles of local ancestral graves and temples to create a new synthesis.

Apart from the connection of mazar location and worship with pre-Islamic Buddhist traditions, many scholars have emphasized the importance of Shiite religious practices among the Sunni Uyghurs. After the advent of Islam, Shiite worship of saints was rapidly accepted by the Uyghur people, and consequently many pseudosaint mazars appeared, a phenomenon closely related to the local people's traditions. Almost every county in the Khotan Prefecture boasts tombs of one or another of the twelve Shiite imams, who historically never came close to Xinjiang. There are many mazars which are worshipped mainly because a certain saint had stopped there for a rest. Some mazars even have rocks with symbolic footprints. The worship of a saint's footprints was especially popular in Buddhism.

The Calendar of Mazar Visitation

In the southern part of Xinjiang most villages have mazars, and the bigger mazars usually have an attached mosque. In the villages, people usually pray at the mazar mosques on the two important traditional Islamic holidays a year. On the 17th and 27th day of the month of Ramadan, people will go to the nearby mazars to pray through the night. Following longstanding tradition, many Muslims go to the mazars to pray on the 15th day of the 8th month according to the Islamic calendar, the month of *Barat*, which means Atonement. On that day, which falls before the month of Ramadan, Muslims pray to Allah that he forgives the sins which they have committed in the past year; angels in heaven write down the charitable and sinful doings of the people on earth. In the evening children will hold a lighted gourd lamp hung from a pole, singing religious songs in a parade or singing songs while begging from door to door. Some will pour oil into a gourd lamp, light it, and hang it on a tree near the mazar where they gather for prayers. The most influential mazar activity is called the Ordam, which is held in the month of *Barat* and on the day of *Ashura*. *Ashura* falls on the 10th day of the month of Muharram, according to the Islamic calendar. On that day the Shiite Muslims remember the martyrdom of Husayn in the battle of Karbala. And Ordam is remembered for the martyrdom of the Qarakhanid general, Äli Arslan Khan, in the battle with the Khotan Buddhists.

Aside from special occasions, more people than usual go to the mazars to worship on Thursdays. For example, major mazar activities of the Khotan area are held on Thursdays. Many people gather at the mazars for activities that day, stay overnight, and then participate in the mazar mosque worship on Friday before returning home. According to legend, Thursday is a day of rest in Paradise; so all the souls of the buried dead return to their resting place on earth that day to hear the prayers and supplications of the people. The worshippers can pray directly to the dead, thus assuring that their prayers will be answered (Ma 1983).

While some Uyghur visits to mazars take place according to a regular calendar of important dates, there are also irregularly scheduled visits for important events or personal needs. My data indicate that the mazar activities of the Khotan and Kashgar areas are of the former kind while those of the Turpan and Qumul areas belong to the latter. Given the deep roots of mazar locations in popular tradition, an interesting question concerns why there has developed a tradition of fixed itineraries of worship at certain mazars. There are two major "circuits," one centered around Kashgar, the other around Khotan. Each year, at fixed dates, people worship in sequence at mazars which are mutually connected along the route. Indeed, because of its many mazars and the prominence of the rituals at them, Khotan is sometimes referred to as the "Holy Land". The mazar activities of Khotan are connected specifically with local seasonal changes and are usually held between the months of March and October.

Before the 1950s, the majority of the Uyghurs in the Kashgar Prefecture participated in largescale mazar visiting activities such as the *häzrät säylisi* at the Apaq Khoja Mazar in the city of Kashgar and the *Ishqol säylisi* at the Uchtur Khälipä Mazar of Yarkand County. Such activities, usually held in Spring and Autumn, were mass gatherings of people to pray for good fortune and protection from disaster, for favorable weather, and also for a bumper harvest [Fig. 11].

Prior to the advent of Islam, regular and fixed dates for sacrificial activities and prayer rituals had already existed amongst the Uyghurs (Geng and Ayup 1980). So it is reasonable to assume that the timing of mazar visits not only manifests the different Islamic memorial activities, but also would have a close connection with local primitive religious activities. Whether there may also be a connection with patterns of pre-Islamic Buddhist pilgrimage is an interesting question deserving of further study. Quite apart from any specific religious tradition and practice, such activities also express the people's wishes in life, in combination with their physical and psychological need for entertainment, leisure, and relaxation.

The Offerings at Mazars and Their Significance

In Uyghur folk belief, many material objects are used to express ideas; there are specific regional characteristics, all of which have symbolic meanings. The use of symbolic material things to give expression to people's various needs and wishes is especially evident in Uyghur mazar worship. Several important questions arise in examining this phenomenon: What is the origin of these symbolic objects? What kind of cultural data can they impart? And what are their regional characteristics? To answer these questions, let us examine the objects which are placed around the mazars, either as expressions of faith or with a utilitarian purpose.

One of the most conspicuous phenomena of the mazar is the different sacrificial offerings which are placed around it. Some of these objects have become the symbols, or markers, of certain local Islamic sacred places, the mazars. Some objects express the wishes of the pilgrims or are the expressions of gratitude for prayers answered, while other objects are expressions of the continuation of traditional rituals. These sacrificial offerings are objects hanging on poles and objects with figurative meanings, such as a cradle, a piece of stoneware, a lantern, a doll, and others. To hang some sacrificial offerings on poles erected around a mazar is a custom most commonly found in the Khotan area of Xinjiang. It also exists in different degrees in the neighboring areas of Kashgar, but is hardly ever seen in the eastern or northern parts of Xinjiang.

In Khotan, there are generally three different types of mazar structures: 1) a simply built mazar inside a flat-roofed house, with the poles erected outside the house; 2) a mazar surrounded by a wall or a fence, with the poles erected inside the wall or fence (or the sacrificial offerings hanging from the wall or fence); 3) a mazar constructed of earth to form a distinct hill or a sand dune surrounded by a barren landscape. In this third type, poles for hanging the sacrificial offerings are erected next to the mazar.

The objects hung from such poles are varied, including strips of cloth, banners, chicken or bird heads, tails of a sheep, cow or horse, ram and cow horns, or a sheep or chicken that is stuffed with hay, carved wooden decorations, and triangles sewn with colored cloth and filled with cotton or hay and strung together. The number of erected poles and selection of objects will differ at different mazars. If there are trees around the mazar, one or more of the trees may be viewed as "sacred" and used instead of a pole to hang the various offerings. The most expressive of the hanging objects is the sheep or chicken which is stuffed with hay [Fig. 12]. From afar, it seems that the object is flying in the air. According to the local inhabitants, immediately after a religious ritual at the mazar they will hang the skin, head, wool or tail of the sacrificed animal on a tree or on an erected pole, and place the head and horns of the animal on the mazar or on the wall or fence surrounding the mazar. It is more common to see flags, or banners strung on the erected pole or poles which surround the mazar or directly on the mazar itself [Fig. 13]. The flags are usually of bright, solid colors such as red, white, black, blue, or green. Many are edged with saw-toothed designs of very brightly contrasting colors: for example, a black flag might have white edging.

If erecting the poles and hanging some of the objects on them are the efforts of the men, then the objects decorating the surroundings of the mazar are the artistic creations of the women. Among those making vows at the mazars are many women who want children [Fig. 14]. They pray before the mazar, pour their hearts out, tie strips on cloth on the erected poles or trees, embrace the "sacred tree" and scatter grain on the mazar, throw coins and agate in the spring near the mazar, light lanterns around the mazar and give alms in the hope that the holy one in the mazar will grant them their wish. The mazars known for granting children to the barren are especially sought after by women who long for offspring. In the Ghulja area there is the custom of offering a simulated cradle to the mazar to pray for offspring [Fig. 15]. Women leave a symbolic doll in the cradle and put it near a mazar or hang it from a "sacred tree". This custom is rare in the southern parts of Xinjiang where there are mazars with names like Cradle Mother (*Böshük ana*). Local inhabitants think that objects from caves called Cradle Mother not only have the power to grant children to women, but also have the power to cure sickness and grant physical health and are especially effective for the healing of sick children. In southern Xinjiang, those praying for offspring frequently put a doll near the mazar [Fig. 16]. Among the Uyghurs there is a close connection between the belief in mazars which specifically grant fertility and the age-old belief in the "God of Reproduction" and "God of Protection" of pre-Islamic times (Dawuti 2004).

The desire for a happy marriage is also a prominent reason for offering sacrifices at a mazar. In the Khotan and Kashgar Prefectures we often see symbolic stoves made with small pieces of stone or bricks and containing firewood, leaves and kindling. Placing at a mazar two pieces of stone which have been tied together expresses the wish of becoming a pair with someone whom the heart desires. A custom in Yengisar and Yarkand counties of Kashgar is to make a small symbolic arrow and place it at a mazar in the hope that the arrow will hit the heart of one's beloved. Such customs which reflect the idea of "using similar behavior to achieve similar results" are to a great extent very much like a practice in magic (*Voodoo*).

The custom of offering sacrifices in mazar worship has very deep historical and cultural roots. Mazar worship can be traced back in history at least to the times of the Turk Khaganate. According to Legends of the Turks, recorded in *Zhou Shu* 周书(annals of the Northern Zhou Dynasty, 557-581 CE) and *Sui Shu* 隋书(annals of the Sui Dynasty, 581-618 CE), after a Turk's death, the relatives of the deceased slaughter sheep and horses for sacrifices. "After the burial, stones are erected as markers. The number of stones depends on the number of people the deceased had killed during his lifetime. The heads of the sacrificed sheep and horses are hung on the stone pillars" (Wu 1991). The Uyghur historical epic *Oghuznamä* records that at the hero's triumphal return from war, the cheering crowds welcomed him at the square where two poles had been erected. On one was hung a golden cock and tied a white sheep; on the other was hung a silver cock and tied a black sheep (Geng and Ayup 1980, p. 39). The scene bears a remarkable resemblance to the Khotan custom of hanging a chicken from a pole.

Obviously, the Uyghur custom of hanging sacrificial objects from an erected pole is closely connected with a custom of their Huihu ancestors and other nomadic tribes of the steppe who practiced shamanism. Erecting a pole on which to hang sacrificial objects is a legacy from shamanism which the Uyghur people have embraced for a long time. The appearance of this custom is closely connected to the worship of sacred trees, the worship of Tengri and many other kinds of beliefs. Although these beliefs appeared in pre-Islamic times when the slaughtering of animals for sacrifice was forbidden by Buddhism, even in Khotan where Buddhism had a stronghold this custom was not eradicated. The fact that this custom has continued to the present demonstrates that the dissemination and acceptance of foreign religions very much depends on the degree to which they accommodate local beliefs which are maintained even in the face of substantial pressure to accept an alien culture.

Another kind of offering at shrines is a flag. According to local inhabitants, the origin of the custom of erecting flag poles can be connected with the religious wars of the Qarakhanid Dynasty, with the flags seen to symbolize the military banners of its army. The custom of erecting flag poles is quite common in Khotan and the Ordam Mazar of the Kashgar area — that is, the main battlegrounds where the Qarakhanid army fought the infidels of Khotan. In Islam, those martyred in a holy war are accorded very high positions. When members of the Qarakhanid army died in battle, it was possible that they were buried locally, and a flag which represented their army was erected on their burial ground as a symbol of respect for the dead and as a grave marker for the martyrs.

It is quite common for the believers in shamanism, Buddhism and Islam to mark a holy place with flags. The believers in shamanism and Lamaism among the Mongols, Yugurs and Tibetans hang flags at *obos* and as sacrificial offerings in other activities.

Conclusion

In short, analysis of the various sacrificial offerings at the mazars demonstrates that mazar worship of the Uyghurs is not merely an Islamic religious activity. Studying it from another point of view shows that it is a blend of many different cultures and religions, the most important influence being that of shamanism. Although the Uyghurs had at different times embraced Buddhism, Manichaeism, Nestorian and Islam, and there were great differences between these religions and shamanism, shamanism had always remained a part of Uyghur life and customs. Its undiminished vitality is especially evident in the *obo*-like forms of many mazars and in the rituals of mazar worship involving sacrificial objects hanging from poles. Belief in shamanism and magic (*Voodoo*) transcends time. It has continued throughout history even down to the present. Later, "artificial" religions such as Buddhism, Islam and others, all treated shamanism with tolerance; in fact, those religions even blended their own beliefs with shamanism in order to facilitate the spread of their own beliefs among the local people.

Prior to the advent of Islam into Central Asia, including Xinjiang, idol worship was a well-established religious tradition. Therefore, it was difficult for the converts to Islam to accept the worship of an abstract, formless concept of Allah. When their existing idols (Buddhist statues) were destroyed and the temples were torn down, they searched in their traditional culture for something that would make Islam more concrete and nearer to their former belief, and yet not clash with Islam. Thus they turned their attention to the mausolea of their ancestors. Ancestor worship has always been an important part of the shamanist belief in spirits which was either passed down individually or in combination with other religious forms. In various pre-Islamic religions, a belief that the soul does not die combined with the social custom of praying to the ancestors for blessings. After the conversion to Islam, the people combined the worship of Islamic Shiite saints with the local ancestral veneration and thus created a mazar worship with local characteristics. The concept of the worship of saints in Buddhism and other religions, its form, and rituals of offering helped to promote the integration of mazar worship into the practices of the new faith.

According to Islamic belief, worshipping any person other than God is unacceptable; there is no intermediary between man and God. Muslims must express their hopes, requests, and confessions directly to God. In Islamic law the creation of grand tombs, the worshipping of graves, and the holding of large ceremonies in graveyards is forbidden. For this reason, the original Arabic meaning of the word "mazaret" is "a place that is visited", not "tomb of a saint" or "place of worship". Nonetheless, religious activities intended to meet one's needs are held at mazars in many Islamic countries. People believe those buried at mazars to be close to God, and think the dead will convey their hopes and requests to God. The formation of this concept of "saints" and "sages" in Islam is in fact related to comparable ideas in Buddhism, Christianity, and Judaism. After the formation of Islam, the creators, disseminators, and martyrs of Islam took on a saintly character. This is especially evident in the development of mazar beliefs among the Uyghurs, a process in which Shiite and Sufi Islam played an important role.

References

Dawuti, Reyila 热依拉•达吾提 2001. *Weiwuerzu maza wenhua yanjiu* 维吾尔族麻扎文化研究 [Research on Uyghur Mazar Culture]. Urumqi: Xinjiang Daxue Chubanshe.

——— 2004 "Cong maza chaobai kan weiwuerzu funui de shengyuguan" 从麻扎朝拜谈维吾尔族妇女的生育观 [Mazars and Women: A Study of Birth Rituals among Uyghur Women]. *Xibei Minzu Yanjiu* 2004/1: 181- 189.

Geng Shimin and Tursun Ayup (eds.) 1980. *Oghuznamä: Qadimqi uyghurlarning tarikhiy dastani* [Oghuznamä: An Ancient Uyghur Historical Epic]. Beijing: Millätlär Näshriyati.

Hamada Masami, 2001, "Le mausolée et le culte de Satuq Bughrâ Khân." *Journal of the History of Sufism* 3: 63-87.

Harris, Rachel and Rahilä Dawut, 2002. "Mazar Festivals of the Uyghurs: Music, Islam and the Chinese State." *British Journal of Ethnomusicology* 11/1: 101-118.

Hawley, John Stratton(ed.), 1987, *Saints and Virtues.* Berkeley and London: University of California Press.

Kieckhefer, Richard and George D. Bond (comp.) 1990. *Sainthood: Its Manifestations in World Religions.* Berkeley and London: University of California Press.

Ma Pingyan 马平彦, 1983. "Nanjiang de maza he maza chaobai" 南疆麻扎和麻扎朝拜 [Mazar and Mazar pilgrimage in Southern Xinjiang]. *Xinjiang Shehui Kexue Yanjiu*, 1983/3.

Millward, James A. 1994. "A Uyghur Muslim in Qianlong's Court: The Meanings of the Fragrant Concubine." *Journal of Asian Studies* 53/2: 427-458.

Sawada Minoru 2001a. "A Study of the Current Ordam- Padishah System." *Journal of the History of Sufism* 3 (2001): 89-111.

——— 2001b. "Tarim Basin Mazars: A Fieldwork Report." Journal of the History of Sufism 3: 39-61.

Stein, M. Aurel 马克•奥里尔•斯坦因 1994. *Shamai Hetian feixuji* 沙埋和田废墟记. Urumqi: Xinjiang Meishu Chubanshe (tr. of *Sand-Buried Ruins of Khotan: Personal Narrative of a Journal of Achaeological and Geographical Exploration in Chinese Turkestan*. London: Hurst and Blackett, 1904).

Tyson, David 1997. "Shrine Pilgrimage in Turkmenistan as a Means to Understanding Islam Among the Turkmen." *Central Asia Monitor*, No. 1. Accessed May 2, 2009 from *Central Asia Monitor—On-line Supplement* <www.uga.edu/islam/turkmen.html>.

Werbner, Pnina, 2003, *Pilgrims of Love: The Anthropology of a Global Sufi Cult.* London: C. Hurst, 2003.

Wu Jingshan 吴景山 1991. "Tujueren de sangzang xisu shulun" 突厥人的丧葬习俗述论 [Some Thoughts on the Funerary Customs of the Turks]. *Xibei Minzu Yanjiu* 1991/1: 240.

Zarcone, Thierry, 1999, "Quand le Saint légitime le politique: le mausoleée de Afaq Khwaja à Kashgar." *Central Asian Survey* 18/2: 225- 242.

——— 2001. "Le Culte des saints au Xinjiang de 1949 à nos jours." *Journal of the History of Sufism* 3: 133-172.

——— 2002. "Sufi Lineages and Saint Veneration in 20th Century Eastern Turkestan and Contemporary Xinjiang." *The Turks.* Istanbul: Yeni Türkiye Publications: 534- 541.

Fig. 1. Shrine pilgrimage in Xinjiang.

Fig. 2. Praying at the mazar in Khotan.

Fig. 3. Ordam Mazar.

Fig. 4. Büwi Märyäm Mazar in Kashgar.

Fig. 5. Mazar in desert, Khotan.

Fig. 6. Baghdad Mazar in Khotan.

Fig. 7. Toyoq Mazar in Turpan.

Fig. 8. Kohmarim Mazar in Khotan.

Fig. 9. Hanging the scarf on mazar.

Fig. 10. The Habib Ejem Mazar in Atush.

Fig. 11. Epic singers at mazar in Khotan.

Fig. 12. Sheep stuffed offerings on Baghdad Mazar, Khotan.

Fig. 13. Flags on mazar, Khotan.

Fig. 14. Women prayer in Imam Aptah Mazar in Khotan.

Fig. 15. Miniature cradle in Sultan Uwayis Mazar, Ghulja.

Fig. 16. A Doll placed around the mazar in Kashgar.

Transition and Transformation

Healing Rituals and Mazar Worship

ZHOU Xijuan

Mazar worship (or *ziyarat*) is a common ritual among local Muslims in Central Asian Regions. In Xinjiang, Mazar worship normally takes variety of ritual forms and includes many different activities. In general, these rituals and activities can also be divided mainly into two large categories: Islamic devotional practices, especially Sufi mystic ceremonies, and healing rituals that reflect more folk cultural elements, specifically shamanic beliefs. The present paper will focus on examining the rituals and ceremonies take place in the frame of mazar worship, and the function and goals of these rituals in Xinjiang. I propose that two types of religious activities and beliefs not only co-exist in the phenomenon of mazar worship but also share a common element of ritual transition and transformation.

Many scholars in the past have reported various sites of important mazars and various kinds of rituals took place at mazars in Xinjiang region. However, more systematic studies about mazar worship activities in Xinjiang are only started in recent years, notably, the impressive books by Dr. Rahile Dawut,[1] articles by Prof. Ma Pinyan, Li Jinxin and other scholars.[2] The important works by these scholars provide first hand information about the history, distribution of mazars in Xinjiang, types of rituals and pilgrimages related to various mazars and religious beliefs reflected in mazar worship activities.

The current study in this paper will be based mainly on two types of sources: the first-hand information and analysis of the above-mentioned scholars and the field works I have conducted from 2004 to 2008 in Xinjiang. In the past few years, I have visited various mazars in Turfan, Hami, Ili, Kucha, Aksu, Kashgar, Khotan and Yarkand areas and observed some *ziyarat* ceremonies in these areas. I have also interviewed some local scholars as well as some local Islamic leaders and some local practitioners. I will use my observations and some of the information I have obtained in my trips in the discussions in this paper. Mazar worship is also common among different ethnic groups in Xinjiang. However, I will focus the discussion in this paper mainly on mazar worship activities among the Uyghurs. I intend to show that Islamic devotion practices and folk

---

[1] Rahile Dawut 2001.

[2] Li Jinxin and Nurmaimaiti Tohuti 1999: 51-56; Maimaiti Sailai and Ma Pinyan 1986: 30-38.

healing rituals co-exist on many mazars in the region, and that these two types of activities share a common element of ritual transition and transformation. I plan to briefly discuss various types of mazars and types of activities that take place in *ziyarat* in Xinjiang first. Then I will examine the common understanding about mazar worship shared by Islamic practitioners and folk culture. Finally, I will look at the key elements shared by both Islamic and folk rituals.

Types of Mazars and *Ziyarat* Rituals in Xinjiang

Orthodox Islamic spiritual leaders, strictly speaking, do not accept Mazar worship as a standard Islamic practice. However, mazar worship is one of the most important religious rituals in Xinjiang. Sometimes it is considered even more essential than the Friday *namaz* in mosques. Sufi practitioners consider performing *namaz* at mosque is only to fulfill a religious duty but rituals at mazar are for salvation of one's individual soul. Furthermore, it provides blessing, protection and healings to the practitioners.[3] Apparently *ziyarat* occupies the essential part of local Uyghurs' religious life. There are numerous examples reflect such understanding about *ziyarat*. For instance, at Yarkand, a local scholar told the author that one of the khans in the local history once commented that one should not focus entirely on mazar worship but on other things such as economy or prayer at mosques, which reveals that this understanding about the significant functions of *ziyarat* in local people's life does not only exist today but also in early local Islamic history. The importance of *ziyarat* in local Muslims' view even surpasses that of more orthodoxy rituals. When visiting mazars at Khotan, I was told that if one performs seven times of pilgrimage to Imam Jaffar Sadiq Mazar it is considered equal to one hajj to Mecca. However, one can become a real Hajji if s/he visits the Imam Jaffar Sadiq mazar seven times but one cannot be called a real Hajji if one only visited Mecca without at least one pilgrimage to this mazar. Aurel Stein has noted the same zeal of local Khotanese to the worship of these sacred Imam mazars in the early twentieth century. According to him, crowds of pilgrims from all parts of Xinjiang region come to pay respect to the mazars.[4]

There are several different types of mazars that are popular in Xinjiang today. In general, they could be divided into two large categories: those with close ties to Islamic beliefs or legends and those of non-Islamic natures. The first group includes mazars of famous Islamic religious figures, including those of transmitters of Islam such as Arshdin Khoja Mazar at Kucha, those of Islamic saints and spiritual teachers such as Muhammad Sherip Mazar in Yarkand or the Apaq Khoja Mazar at Kashgar, and those of Islamic heroes and martyrs such the Ordam Padshah Mazar near Kashgar. The second group includes mazars of famous historical figures or scholars such as the mazar of Mahmud Kashghari, the author of the "Compendium of the Turkic Dialects" (*Divanu Lughat-it-Türk*), mazars of sacred trees, such as Üjmä Mazar in Khotan, mazars for sacred

---

[3] Information obtained from interviews at Yarkand. It is also mentioned by Prof. Rahile Dawut in her books. See Rahile Dawut 2001: 28.

[4] Stein, M. Aurel 1907: 140.

springs or river, such as Kohmarim Mazar in Khotan Prefecture, and other types of mazars related to important locations, such as Qondaq Mazar in Kashgar.[5] The second group often includes sacred religious sites in pre-Islamic traditions as well.

However, function wise, mazars in Xinjiang can be divided into the following two types: the important religious sites that attract Islamic pilgrims and Sufi practitioners and the ones that attract people seeking solutions for various individual needs such as healing, blessing or protection from evil forces. Many small mazars, especially those belong to the category of non-Islamic natures, are only visited by those who seek healing power for specific family or personal problems. Many mazar sites, on the other hand, often serve both functions of Sufi religious practice and more pragmatically needs. In fact, one can find mixed types of rituals on most of the major mazar sites in Xinjiang region. In general, the most common rituals that take place on many mazars are these two types: Islamic rituals (mainly Sufi practices) and folk healing rituals.

Islamic rituals mainly include weekly *zikr* at the *khanaqah*, major celebrations in local religious holidays and pilgrimages. For instance, in south Xinjiang, the White Mountain Sufi order holds major mazar worship rituals twice a year, in the time period of May to June and August to September. Usually, there is no specific date during these two periods but people would travel to the famous mazars during these months from various regions of Xinjiang. Sometimes even Hui Muslims from Gansu and other provinces would travel here and pay homage to the Islamic saints. I have observed several times that buses loaded with pilgrims from Gansu Province visiting famous mazars, even those located in very remote dessert area in south Xinjiang. The rituals performed by the Hui Muslims are slightly different from those by Uyghurs. The Hui Muslims' ceremony carries a strong element of ancestor worship, which is another interesting phenomenon to study but it is beyond frame of discussion in the current paper.

The other type of rituals often found at *ziyarat* activities are folk healing rituals. These healing rituals are often performed by different religious specialists, which vary from *sheykhs* or *mollas* to *bakhshi* who are generally recognized as shamans. *Sheykhs* or *mollas* often chant prayers for those in need or write charms for protection, while *bakhshi* usually performs more typical shamanic ritual such as divination or exorcism. People come to mazars seeking solutions for various personal problems in life, such as seeking for sons, cure for illness, charms against evils, or blessing for career success.

In many occasions, the two types of rituals are actually mixed in the same mazar worship activities: formal religious worship often combines religious devotions with more practical functions such as healing and blessing. This is especially true with celebrations involving community worship during major Islamic religious holiday, which often attract large groups of participants. Community worship often relates to agricultural need such as blessing, protection against disasters or requests for rain. This type ritual reflects more influence from shamanic traditions. One good example of this is the *Zara Khatime* festival that is an agricultural ceremony that takes place at mazars in

[5] Rahile Dawut 2001: 48.

the spring and fall.[6] At Yarkand, I noticed that people often request for communal blessing or help during a Sufi *zikr* ceremony. Practitioners often stand up during the ritual chanting and request the participants pray for a sick relative or for some specific needs of a certain community member.[7]

On the other hand, one usually could find these two types of rituals co-exist but performed separately at the same site and often at the same time as well. For instance, at the major festivals at the Ordam Mazar, while some Sufi practitioners perform *zikr* in a circle, other pilgrims sitting right next to them are busy burying themselves in the heated sand, hoping that sand therapy at this sacred site would help to heal their ailments.[8] At the same site, after prayers and chanting rituals at the mazars, some women would try to dig up some insect in the sand hills and eat them, which is believed to cure infertility or certain ailments.[9]

Sometimes, Islamic *sheykh*s and folk shamanic healers such as *bakhshi* would share different duties in one ceremony. For instance, at the main festival of Ordam Mazar, the climax of the celebration is to change the banners on the poles at key site on the mazar. Worshippers march into the mazar with banners from all directions. After people seat down in a circle around the poles, *sheykh* who guards the mazar will start to pray. After the prayer, *bakhshi* will take the banners, climb up the ladders or ropes and tie the banners on top of the poles. This is considered by *bakhshi* as the most honored and a privileged duty that can only pass down to the next *bakhshi* through family heritage. Besides tying the banners, *bakhshi* also play drums and trumpets at this most important religious ceremony of a key Islamic leader in the local history. In addition to participation of these Islamic rituals, they would also provide services such as divination and healing to the pilgrims.[10] Apparently, local *sheykh*s not only tolerate the existence of folk rituals at *ziyarat* but also actually would share duties with folk healers such as *bakhshi* in major rituals. *Bakhshi*, on the other hand, consider this important mazar of an Islamic martyr as the source of their power. One of the *bakhshi* I have talked with in Kashgar told me how important for him it was to visit this site and participate the religious rituals here because the spiritual power at this mazar would enable him to heal patients more efficiently.

Sacred Places and Saints

The unique phenomenon of mixed functions and that of the strong interests in mazar worship in Xinjiang has its historical root both in the process of religious development and conversion to Islam in the region, and in the beliefs in the powers of the sacred locations and saints among the local people. The process of religious development and conversion to Islam in Xinjiang, though being an important topic for studying the

[6] Rahile Dawut, 2001: 81-3.
[7] Observations from my field trip to South Xinjiang in 2005.
[8] Observations from home-made videos in the 1990s at Kashgar.
[9] Rahile Dawut, 2001 : 54.
[10] Li Jinxin, 1999: 51-56.

mazar culture, is beyond frame of the discussion of the current paper. I would like to point out, however, that Islam, just like any other new religions spreading in a foreign culture, adapted many local cultural elements in the course of its development in Xinjiang. In the following discussion, I will only focus on how the belief in the power of sacred locations and saints makes the mixture of the above-mentioned two types of rituals possible in mazar worship.

First of all, both Sufi and folk tradition believe in the sacred power of saints or spiritual leaders. The belief in sacred geographic locations and saints plays significant roles in many religions. Essentially, one of the key elements of the importance of the sacred places and saints is the sacred or supernatural power they possess, be it the power to transform or the power to interact between humans and the Divine. In Xinjiang, the belief in the sacred power of locations or saints is shared both by Sufi practices and the folk shamanic tradition. Sufi practitioners believe that saints or imams have a sacred power that is above ordinary humans and could intermediate on behalf of humans with the Divine. The power of a saint is called *baraka*, which is imagined as almost intangible.

> "Whatever his origin, the saint has, for an essential attribute, the *baraka*, the sacred emanation. Through it he brings to those who worship him, prosperity, happiness, all the good things of this world; he can bestow his gifts, passing beyond the individual, upon a whole district, and even beyond the confines of this world, through his powers of intercession with Allah."[11]

Sufis in Xinjiang apparently share this understanding. In Xinjiang, the beliefs in this power, however, are not only limited to that of legendary Islamic saints or *imams* but also extended to that of spiritual leaders and founders of certain Sufi orders. In general, Uyghurs consider that saints or spiritual leaders still possess and emanate sacred powers in their tombs. Therefore, mazars become the central locations for worshipping and performing various Sufi rituals. For Sufi followers, mazars are ideal locations for meditation and spiritual cultivation. *Ishan*s and *sheykh*s often adopt some famous mazars as their teachers and stay there to meditate for a long period of time. Some even live on mazars of famous Sufi leaders. They believe in this way they could reach the highest spiritual status. Often, after staying and meditating for a certain period of time at a famous mazar, the *ishan*s and *sheykh*s became famous and are acknowledged to possess sacred power themselves.[12] In my visit to various mazars, I often found many mazars showing traces of human residency and was told that Sufi practitioners sometimes live in these places (see Fig. 1).

Sufi followers prefer to meditate and hold their rituals at mazars not only because of their beliefs in the power of the saints but also because of their understanding in the

[11] Gaudefroy-Demombynes, Maurice 1968: 56.
[12] Maimaiti Sailai 1986: 33.

Fig. 1. Trace of wondering Sufis live at a mazar in Yarkand.

Fig.2. The sacred spring and tree at the mazar of Mahmud Kashgari.

sacred knowledge about the unity with the Divine. They believe in the transcendence of the Divine. Sufism emphasizes the final or the highest religious goal is to become one with the Divine, through various methods, including meditation, chanting God's name, ritual dance, music and other activities to reach transcendence. To be closer to the saints, who are the intercessors of humans and the Divine, even to their burial grounds, would help greatly to speed up their progress to achieve unity with the Divine. It is no surprise that Sufi practitioners prefer holding their weekly rituals at mazars.

On the other hand, folk traditions in Xinjiang hold very similar understanding about magic power of spiritual leaders such as shamans or heroes. Part of this belief originates from ancient practice of ancestor worship. *Huijiang zhi* mentions that Uyghurs would go to the cemeteries to pray and light lumps in order to worship their ancestors during the *Duva* festival.[13] Part of this understanding comes from shamanic beliefs in the power of deceased shamans. It is a common view in shamanic cultures in Central Asia that deceased shamans usually become tutelary spirits to initiate new shamans. A shaman's tomb is often feared by common folks due to its potential dangerous power to possess people and turn them into shamans. Even a shaman's costume, after its owner is passed away, has to be dealt with carefully. Whoever encounters it will be possessed by the shaman's spirit.[14]

Turkic epics are also full of examples about supernatural power of heroes. One of the oldest Uyghur stories regarding their early history is the legend of Bögü Khan. The story portrays the supernatural power the heroic khan possesses.[15] The *Oghuznama*, the epic of Oghuz Khan that was formed during the fourteenth and fifteenth century C.E., tells a similar story about the magic powers of the hero Oghuz Khan. According to the epic, Oghuz Khan started to go on various quests, including defending his tribes and killing monster animals ever since his youth. Just like Bögü Khan, he was bestowed with

---

13 Chen Guoguang 1985: 44.

14 Eliade, Mircea 1964: 79-99, 145-180.

15 'Ala-ad-Din 'Ata-Malik Juvaini 1958: 54-61. Also see Huang Wen-bi 1964: 34-40.

magic superhuman powers by spirits.[16] This belief is adopted eventually into local legends about Islamic heroes. For instance, in the legend about the Ordam Mazar, the hero Ali Arslan Khan is believed to be invincible warrior. No one can hurt him during the fight. His only weakness is that when he was performing *namaz* he became vulnerable. According to the story, his enemy took advantage of this and killed him and many of his followers during the time when they were praying.[17] However, even after his death, the hero's head still led the army fought against the infidels all the way back to Kashgar. This is why the local tradition portrays him to be buried in two locations today: his body at the Ordam Mazar and his head at Kashgar. It is only natural that his burial place became one of the most famous mazars with great healing powers in Xinjiang that attracts tens of thousands of pilgrims.

Secondly, the shared faith in the sacred locations by both Islamic culture and the folk tradition plays an important role in the popularity of *ziyarat* in Xinjiang. The importance of the Islamic saints' tombs in connection Sufi practitioners' goal of unity with the Divine is already discussed above. However, this interest in mazars by Sufi followers is strengthened by the folk beliefs in sacred geographic locations. Pilgrims regularly journey to mazars to pray and to make offerings, because they believe that mazars are charged with supernatural power and that spirits dwell in them. Worship the sacred locations has long history in Uyghur folk traditions. Qing source *Huijiang zhi* volume two mentions local Muslim rituals as the following: "First, heaven, earth, the sun, the moon and all things that circulate should be worshipped; Second, mountains, rivers and anything that is nurturing and beneficial to humans should be worshipped; and lastly, ancestors and tombs that are the root for humanity and possess the power of protection, should be worshipped".[18] This explains why mazars other than Islamic saints are also popular in Xinjiang. The non-Islamic types of mazars are usually those located in either noteworthy or unusual geographic locations. People belief these significant locations are also charged with sacred healing powers and have close ties to the spirit world. In times of crises people turn to the *ziyarat* at such locations for assistance. They tie ribbons to the flagpoles or trees at mazars which would bring their wishes to the spirits. I have even found a small chamber at Altun Mazar at Yarkand named "Wish Granting Room." Evidently people believe the spirits of saints buried at this mazar possess the power to grant their wishes or cause changes in their lives.

This kind of belief of sacred locations is also originated in shamanic cultures. shamanic cultures venerate various significant geographic locations. It considers the world is divided into different cosmic zones. These cosmic zones are connected by a certain kind of path, known as the *axis mundi*. The *axis mundi* could be represented by the world tree, a mountain, a cave, a spring, a river and etc. Shamans travel to the spirit world to bring back teachings or healings.[19] Many popular mazars at Xinjiang reflect their associate with such beliefs. For instance, at the Mahmud Kashghari mazar, legend

[16] Wei Cuiyi, 1998: 63-73.

[17] Maola Hajji, 1988: 1-9.

[18] Chen Guoguang, 1985: 42.

[19] Eliade, Mircea, 1964: 269-273.

has it that when Mahmud Kashghari rested at this location, his walking stick stuck into the ground, where a spring appeared and the stick became a tree. To this day, locals trust the water from this spring can cure eye diseases and the barks from this tree have power of protection against evils. As the result of such beliefs, one of the stems of the tree is completely tripped off. People take small pieces of the tree barks away to use them as charms (See Fig. 2). When visiting the Apaq Khoja Mazar, I noticed similar fate happened to some older trees there as well. Many small mazars in south Xinjiang are actually mazars of single trees, which are believed to have healing power for infertility. This kind of belief in trees reflects the shamanic understanding that trees are akin to living spirits. Many mazars also mirror shamanic beliefs in the sacred well or springs. For instance, sacred wells exist both at Ordam Mazar and at Dost Bulaqim, a small mazar located on the path to Ordam Mazar.[20] The continued faith in their healing powers reflects pre-Islamic beliefs with connection to shamanic views about sacred locations.

Similar connections to shamanic beliefs in the significance of caves and mountains can also be found in many mazars in Xinjiang. In the north of Kashgar, a cave in Mount Tushuqtagh is believed by locals is the place that Mohammad Emin's disciple Rohman meditated and entered heaven from. Today, it is said that if the worshippers are sincere and pious, they may still see the saint in the cave. This mountain is also known as the Great Snow Mountain. It is considered as the sacred mountain because it provides the sacred water that nurtures the land and people here. In the fall, locals would gather donations to make offering to the mountain.[21] When visiting the caves at the Toyoq Mazar, where legend tells seven Islamic saints had meditated, the *sheykh* told the author a similar theory: if one is sincere and pious, one can still see the saints meditating inside the cave. While talking with the author, the *sheykh* was busy copying the saints' names with a prayer on a piece of paper. Later, he gave this paper to the woman who was waiting there to use it as a protective charm for her son who was leaving for college in the fall. Another famous cave the author visited is at the Kohmarim Mazar. This site is located right next to the Qaraqash River. The cave is located at the foot of a hill, facing the river. Many scholars, such as Aurel Stein and Prof. Dawut have discussed the connection of this mazar to the ancient local tradition of river worship in the symbol of dragon.[22] Today, locals believe if a woman meditate and chant prayers here for three days, her wish for children would be granted. The faith in caves in important geographic locations apparently has its root in shamanic understanding of *axis mundi*.

Many mazars in Xinjiang are located on the sites that were center for religious worship during pre-Islamic times. Kohmarim is not the only site that reflects the longevity of the sacred locations from ancient folk tradition and pre-Islamic religions. At the Qirmish Ata Mazar at Wensu County, numerous ancient trees are growing here due to its rich underground water resource. However, this mazar is located in the middle hill of a mountain that is surrounded by lifeless desert. The very existence of this tiny oasis is a miracle in nature. Even though local legend connects this site to the

[20] Jarring, Gunnar, 1935: 352.
[21] Chen Guoguang, 1985: 43.
[22] Rahile Dawut, 2001: 54-55.

martyrs of Islamic holy war that supposed to take place here, there is no doubt that this was a sacred place in pre-Islamic traditions with connections to worshipping the mountain, the spring and the ancient trees. This practice of adopting ancient religious sites into Islam reflects the importance of these sacred locations in local folk beliefs. The meanings and stories about these sacred sites change when the locals convert to the new religion. However, faith in the power of these sacred sites remains the same.

There are many more similar examples of connections of the mazars in Xinjiang with shamanic beliefs in the power of mountains, trees, springs and rocks. It is noticeable that many mazar locations have very old trees and springs. Both are essential life resources in a dry and arid region such as Xinjiang. It is no wonder that such places are considered as sacred ground with various supernatural powers and that many Uyghurs would seek both spiritual and practical help from pilgrimage to these places despite the heat and difficulty of traveling.

Transition and Transformation in Rituals at Mazars in Xinjiang

Now let us look back at the two types of rituals performed during *ziyarat* in Xinjiang. As mentioned above, the more traditional Sufi devotional rituals and the folk healing rituals not only co-exist at the same site but are often mixed and even complementary to each other. One is geared to the transcendental functions of mystic religion and the other to the more pragmatic needs in daily life. This phenomenon is not unique in Xinjiang mazar worship but also found in many other cultures.[23] While the Sufi rituals are more concerned with spiritual unity with the Divine, the folk healing rituals deal with more individual practical needs. The key element that makes the goals of both types of ritual achievable is the ritual transition from the profane to the sacred at mazars. The result of such transition is to transform the practitioner from an ordinary human to the sacred and therefore transform the troubled person spiritually or physically into a health being. While devote Sufis obtain sacred knowledge of being one with the Divine with the help of the power of the saints, patients obtain healings by stepping into the sacred location that loaded with sacred power. In the end, *ziyarat* fulfills both the spiritual and the practical need of the practitioners.

Many examples found at *ziyarat* rituals in Xinjiang reflect conscious or unconscious actions to make the transition from the profane to the sacred and therefore achieve the result of transformation. For instance, before entering the proper ground of many mazars, there is always a section specifically set up for the purpose of ritual purification. When the author visited Imam Jaffar Sadiq Mazar near Niya, the visitors are requested by the *sheykh* in charge to perform purification first. Then the *sheykh* would lead the group to offer a prayer at each turn along the path to the main chamber of the mazar (see Fig. 3). Similarly, at one of the festivals at Apaq Khoja Mazar, pilgrims lined up in groups and marched into the mazar. Along the way, they would stop several times to offer prayers during the March. Another example for this kind of ritual transition is

[23] Mandelbaum, David G. 1966: 1174-1191.

reflected in the famous Ordam holidays. Pilgrims visiting the Ordam Mazar would stop at several smaller mazars along the way before they reach the main site of the mazar. At each stop, there are ritual callings and prayers to mark their stages in the pilgrimage. [24] All these examples demonstrate steps of ritual transition from the ordinary daily life into solemn religious rituals or from profane world to the sacred ground.

Fig. 3. Worshippers pause and pray at a turn of the path to the Imam Jaffar Sadiq Mazar.

Another example shows element of ritual transition is reflected by the key component of the festivals at the Ordam Mazar. According to the local legend, Ali Arslan Khan, the first Uyghur khan to lead Islamic holy wars in Xinjiang, was killed here while carrying out a holy war against Buddhists from Khotan Prefecture in the tenth century. Ordam Mazar worship normally takes place twice a year: one on the tenth day of the month of Muharram, the other on the fifteenth day of Shaban month (the 1st and 8th month). The second one is also known as *Barat* night when it is believed that this is the night angles start a new book to record each individual's deed in a year. This is the night for asking Allah for forgiving. Muslims come to Ordam Mazar to chant Qur'an, to perform confession, to ask forgivingness and to pray for souls of the deceased relatives.[25] The significance of the second festival clearly lies in the meaning of transition to a new leaf in one's life book. In fact, the very legend of Ali Arslan Khan's death demonstrates elements of transition and transformation in *ziyarat* rituals. Legend portrays Arslan Khan as an invincible warrior. As mentioned above, weapons can harm him only when he is performing namaz because during the ritual his body became as soft as water. His tragic death is actually caused by the fact that religious ritual transformed his body!

According to Victor Turner, ritual affords a creative 'anti-structure' that is

---

[24] Information obtained from videotapes recording rituals took place in early 1990s.

[25] Rahile Dawut 2001: 52-3.

distinguished from the rigid maintenance of social orders, hierarchies and traditional forms.[26] Same transition from the orderly to the 'anti-structure' also happens at *ziyarat*. At mazar festivals many practices normally considered immoral are permissible. Mazar worship provides a place where people can step out of normal social restrictions. People from different social background, trades, regions or class can associate freely here. Women are allowed to participate public events at mazars.[27] They may even remove their veils. Activities such as story-telling, singing, dancing, smoking hashish and gambling are all permissible within the special ritual space of the mazar.[28] At the Imam Asim Mazar near Khotan, the author was told that during main festivals, anything is possible here: wrestling, chicken fights, story-telling, Sufi *zikr* rituals, etc. Almost any kinds of activities or entertainments can be found here. Transition that took place here is from ordinary strictly regulated social life into a temporary ritual space.

Ritual transitions can also take place in the middle of ritual. One good example for this again can be found during the main celebration festival at Ordam Mazar. As mentioned above, this festival is for the commemoration of the martyrdom of Ali Arslan Khan.[29] During the highlight of Ordam Mazar festival, the pilgrims would erect banners (*tugh*) on the high poles marking the sacred site of the hero.[30] The ritual is said to enact the bringing together of the head and body of Ali Arslan Khan after he was decapitated in battle.[31] The culminating ritual of the Ordam Mazar involves a procession of flags to the tomb and erects the banner to the highest poles. This action symbolically marks the ritual transition from separation to unity, which is an essential aspect of Sufi practice.

Ritual transition leads to both symbolic physical and spiritual transformation. *Ziyarat* rituals are fundamentally based on the element of transformation. Only through spiritual and physical transformation can practitioners achieve either spiritual transcendence or healing. Pilgrims believe the souls of saints or the sacred location possess supernatural power that can perform miracles. They believe if they pray at mazars, they would be transformed by the sacred power of saints or the location, and thus be protected and blessed. For the Sufis, the transition from the profane world into the ecstasy of *zikr* and *sama* dance transforms their souls to embrace the temporary unity with the Divine. For them, a *ziyarat* ritual is a spiritual journey to the transformation of the self. One of the participants at a *zikr* at Yarkand told the author that the weekly ritual transforms him to such happiness that gives him strength to endure difficulties in life for the rest of the week.

Mazars are the sacred ritual grounds that not only have the power to transform and heal a person, but also are believed to have the power to transform the pilgrims and things at the site to be the carriers of sacred powers. For instance, some *bakhshi* initiates, after being caught by *jin* (or received callings from spirits), often are found wondering

---

[26] Victor W Turner 1969. Bell, Catherine 1992: 21.

[27] Rahile Dawut 2001: 95-6.

[28] Rahile Dawut 2001 : 112.

[29] Li Jinxin 1999: 51- 56.

[30] Rahile Dawut, 2001: 24-6.

[31] Harris, Rachel and Rahilä Dawut 2002: 101-118.

around at mazars, which they consider as the sources of their spiritual power. One of the *bakhshi* told the author that he needs to perform *ziyarat* at mazars at least once a week to recharge his power so that he could continue to help people.[32] Sometimes, folk healers consciously use this understanding about the transformation power of mazars. A *bakhshi* near Kashgar usually diagnoses his patients' problem at home. However, he would group them together and go to the Mahmud Kashgari Mazar on Thursday nights to perform the healing rituals. They would light up a fire under the sacred tree and spring, then they would perform ritual dance until daylight.[33] The healing rituals performed at the sacred site, is understood in this case to transform the patients and therefore help them cure the ailments.

This kind of ritual transformation is even reflected in normal Friday namaz at mosques. I encounter an interesting phenomenon at the Eidgah Jami in 2004 which illustrates this type of power of ritual transform. Even though this happened at a mosque but it essentially shows the same understanding about what happens at mazars. Outside the Eidgah Jami, women often would line up outside the entrance, some holding bottles of water, some carrying some food in their hands. They hold the water or food in front of them, waiting. Worshipper eventually walking out of the mosque after the Friday *namaz*, they pass the lines of women and blow gently on the water, food or fruit (See Fig. 4). The blessed food, water or fruit then is given to patients at home to drink or eat because they are now transformed and carry healing powers!

Fig. 4. Blessing the food and water.

[32] Information from interviews at Aksu in 2007.
[33] Information from interviews at Kashgar in 2007.

Fig. 5. Rocks with healing power found at Sultan Satuq Bugra Khan Mazar.

Not only pilgrims are transformed by the sacred mazars. Objects at the mazars are also considered to have been transformed. Gunnar Jarring mentioned that pilgrims frequently take away with them a little dust from these shrines, using it as a charm against evil spirits. They may also take with them a few leaves plucked from a nearby tree, which later they use to make potions said to be capable of curing illness.[34] When I visited mazars at Kashgar, I noted that some ancient trees show cuts by small knives. I was told that people often take a small piece away to use either as charms or cure for illness. I also found two pieces of rocks at a mazar that apparently have been robbed frequently. I was told that people with ailment would carry them and circle around the saint's tomb, which wound help to cure their problems (see Fig. 5).

Sometimes, pilgrims would offer sacrifice, usually chickens, or pay small donation at mazars in order to make a change in their life. Pilgrims would burn a kind of herbal plant called *adrasman* at the mazar. It is used to achieve a variety of goals such as asking for offspring, for good luck, for success in business, for boy/girl friend, or getting rid of bad luck from a dream. The act of burning herb or offering sacrifice is again aimed to obtain transformation – changes things from bad to good-- in daily life.

Another aspect of ritual transformation is reflected in the communal meal after mazar worship. This communal meal is to share sacrificed food with the saints or heroes in order to gain spiritual transformation. Gunnar Jarring noted on his journey to Xinjiang: "It is a popular belief in Eastern Turkistan that the ghost of a dead man remains in or about the grave until the day of resurrection, and that he must be provided with food at least for some time after his death. The smell of boiling cauldrons is considered sufficient to satisfy the ghost".[35] Sharing the food with the spirits at the ritual ground would evidently allow the participants benefit from the sacredness of the sacrifice and become transformed.

In conclusion, Islamic ritual ceremonies and folk healing ritual activities co-exist and

[34] Jarring, Gunnar, 1935: 287.

[35] Jarring, Gunnar, 1935: 353.

are even mixed together in mazar worship in Xinjiang. This is possible because local Sufi followers and folk culture share the same belief in the supernatural power of saints/heroes and sacred locations. Both types of rituals also share the same elements of ritual transition from the profane to the sacred and the goal of ritual transformation. The transformation in mazar worship resembles more to regeneration of a spiritual connection with the saint/hero or spiritual world, which brings both religious mystic experience of oneness with the Divine and healing for individual problems.

Bibliography

Bell, Catherine 1992. *Ritual Theory, Ritual Practice*, New York/Oxford: Oxford University Press.

Chen Guoguang 陈国光 1985. "Yishanpai kaolun" 依禅派考论 [On Ishaniya orders], *Xinjiang Zongjiao Yanjiu Ziliao Lunwenji.*

Reyila Dawuti 热依拉·达吾提 (Rahile Dawut) 2001. *Weiwuerzu Maza Wenhua Yanjiu* 维吾尔族麻扎文化研究 [Study about Uyghur Mazar Culture], Urumqi: Xinjiang Daxue Chubanshe.

Eliade, Mircea, 1964, *Shamanism: Archaic Techniques of Ecstasy*. Princeton: Princeton University Press.

Gaudefroy-Demombynes, Maurice 1968. *Muslim Institutions*. London: George Allen & Unwin.

Maola Hajji 毛拉·哈吉 1988. "Bugelahan zhuan" 布格拉汗传 [Hagiography of Bughra Khan], *Xinjiang zongjiao yanjiu ziliao* No. 16, 1-9.

Harris, Rachel and Rahilä Dawut 2002. "Mazar Festivals of the Uyghurs," in *British Journal of Ethnomusicology*, Vol. 11, No. 1, 101-118.

Jarring, Gunnar 1935. "The Ordam-padisha-systerm of Eastern Turkistan Shrines" *Geografiska Annaler*, Vol. 17, Supplement: Hyllningsskrift Tillagnad Sven Hedin.

Huang Wen-bi 黄文弼 1964. "Yiduhu Gaochangwang Shixunbei Fuyuan bin Jiaoji" 亦都護高昌王世勳碑復原並校記 [The Reconstruction and Commentaries on the Inscription of Iduk Kut, the King of Gaochang], *Wenwu*, no. 2, 34-40.

'Ala-ad-Din 'Ata-Malik Juvaini 1958. *The History of the World-Conqueror*, tr. by J. A. Boyle, Cambridge (Mass.): Harvard University Press, vol. 1.

Li Jinxin and Nurmaimaiti Tohuti 李进新，努尔买买提·托乎提 1999. "Odang Maza zongshu"奥当麻扎综述 [Survey about Ordam Mazar], *Kashi Shifan Xueyuan Xuebao*, Vol. 20, No. 2, 51-56.

Mandelbaum, David G. 1966. "Transcendental and pragmatic aspects of religion." *American Anthropologist*, New Series, Vol. 68, No. 5. (Oct., 1966), 1174-1191.

Maimaiti Sailai and Ma Pinyan 买买提 ·赛来，马品彦 1986. "Xinjiang de maza he maza chaobai" 新疆的麻扎和麻扎朝拜 [Mazars and Mazar Worship in Xinjiang] *Xinjiang zongjiao yanjiu ziliao neikan*, 30-38.

Stein, M. Aurel 1907. *Ancient Khotan*, New York: Hacker Art Books.

Turner, Victor W. 1966. *The Ritual Process: Structure and Anti-Structure*, Chicago: Aldine.

Wei Cuiyi and Karl W. Luckert 1998. *Uighur Stories from Along the Silk Road.* New York: University Press of America, Inc.

Kirghiz Bakhshi and the Mazar

Gulbahar GHOJESH

Introduction

The Kirghiz of Northern China, as other minority ethnic groups in the region, practice a unique form of shamanism. Although shamanism as practiced among other ethnic minorities in northern China has received attention from scholars around the world, there remains a lack of research on the subject of Kirghiz shamanism. Only a handful of books published in China provide us with a few valuable insights into the topic, including the following: Keerkezizu Jianshi Bianxiezu 2008; Du Rongkun, Ainiwaer 1991; and Ömürbay 2004 on Kirghiz oral literature, including incantations of Kirghiz shamans. Some mentions of Kirghiz shamanism can be found in books on shamanism among China's northern ethnic minorities in general, such as the work by Aomaer 1995, however, to date there has been no systematic work addressing the topic. Today, shamanism persists among the Chinese Kirghiz and Xinjiang Uyghur Autonomous Region's (XUAR) Kizilsu Kirghiz Autonomous Prefecture continues to have practicing Kirghiz shamans.

The Kirghiz are one of the 56 ethnic groups officially recognized by the People's Republic of China and have a population of approximately 160,600. In Chinese the Kirghiz are known as *Kēěrkèzī zú* (柯尔克孜族). Approximately 90% of China's Kirghiz population is located in Xinjiang's Kizilsu Kirghiz Autonomous Prefecture with smaller groups scattered throughout the Ili Kazakh Autonomous Prefecture, Aksu, Kashgar, and Khotan Prefectures. Several hundred Kirghiz whose ancestors moved east over 200 years ago now reside in Wujiazi Village of Fuyu County in Northwestern China's Heilongjiang Province. The Kizilsu Kirghiz Autonomous Prefecture (*Qizilsu Qirghiz Aptonom Oblasti*) of the People's Republic of China was established in 1954 and is located on Xinjiang's western border and has an area of 69,112 km^2; the prefectural capital is located in Artush. In the Kirghiz language *Qizilsu* means "red water". As of 2007, the prefecture had a population of 500,007 139,141 of them Kirghiz, 317,540 Uyghur, and 36,758 Han.[1]

Among the Kirghiz it is the shamans themselves who represent and preserve shamanism. Their beliefs in magic, the spirits of mountains, trees, water and their ancestors embody their worldview and their cultural meaning is embodied through

[1] Li Shixiang 2008: 36.

their shamanic practices. There are several types of shamans among the Kirghiz:

jaychï	shaman responsible for calling down rain by using a sacred stone known as a *jada tash*
darïmchï	shaman who cures people bitten by poisonous snakes or insects, and sometimes uses incantations
emchi	shaman who cures sickness by chanting an incantation and patting the afflicted individual's body
domchu	shaman who cures sickness through the chanting of incantations alone
sïnchï	shaman who practices divination
jönchü	shaman who practices divination
tölgöchü	shaman who practices divination using 41 small stones
dalïchï	shaman who practices divination using a sheep's shoulder blade
baqshï	shaman who practices divination, cures sickness, and casts out evil using prayers to his/her patron saints

The different types of shamans listed above heal by different means and make use of distinct incantations, songs, and chants. This preliminary categorization of Kirghiz shamans is based on personal fieldwork and requires further research.

Materials collected through fieldwork prove that the practices of Kirghiz shamans exhibit a mixture of Islamic and pre-Islamic practices in spite of the fact that most of the Kirghiz shamans today associate their special powers with Islam. The practices of the shamans, their tools, and incantations clearly show their strong connection to pre-Islamic values and practices. In Kirghiz society, shamans are the bearers of Kirghiz shamanic culture and possess an abundant cultural heritage in their spiritual worldview, their healing songs and chants, and in their shamanic practices. There are deep meanings associated with the shamans' beliefs in magic, the spirits of mountains, trees, water and ancestors. Therefore, research on Kirghiz shamans is of special significance to the study of the society, history, religion, and culture of the Kirghiz people as well as other Turkic peoples and even other ethnic minorities in northern China. Thus, the Kirghiz shaman is an ideal representative of Kirghiz culture and religion.

Mazars are one of the primary features of Kirghiz culture. For the Kirghiz, the mazar is a place apart and is usually located in a sacred place like a mountain, a spring, a special tree, a cave, or the burial grounds of a great ancestor. In the spring, residents make pilgrimages to mazars in many of the villages of Kizilsu to ask the spirits for sufficient water and good fortune; such pilgrimages are often performed collectively by entire villages. People also visit mazars to pray for health and happiness because of their belief that mazars can drive away evil spirits, cure disease, provide protection from misfortune, and grant safety and well-being.

During my fieldwork in Kizilsu, the relationship between *bakhshi* (in Kirghiz *baqshï*) and mazar attracted my attention. The *bakhshi* plays the role of medium between physical and spiritual realms while the mazar is the residence of the spirits that protect, lead and help the *bakhshi*. Because of the lack of research on the shamanic culture of the

Kirghiz in China, the relation between *bakhshi* and mazar has yet to attract the attention of scholars. Among the Kirghiz, the *bakhshi* is a type of shaman who practices divination, cures disease, serves as an intermediary between God and man, and drives out evil spirits with prayers and incantations; all done with help from his/her patron saints. *Bakhshi* visit mazars in order to maintain their relationship with the good spirits there as it is through this relationship that the spirits endow the *bakhshi* with the power to tell the future, to heal the sick, locate lost objects, and solve a range of other problems. I propose that the relationship between the Kirghiz *bakhshi* and the mazar affords us with excellent material for further research on the religion among the Kirghiz.

In this article, I draw on material collected during my fieldwork carried out in Kizilsu from 2006 to 2009 to reflect on the special relationship between *bakhshi* and mazar, and use this relationship as a window into religious practice among Chinese Kirghiz to illuminate its synthesis of shamanism and Islam.[2]

1. Mazars, *Bakhshi* and Liminal Experiences

Most Kirghiz *bakhshi* have liminal experiences prior to becoming *bakhshi*. In some cases, these experiences involve a spirit appearing in the guise of a sheep, an old man with a white beard, a wild goat, hare or camel. Others became *bakhshi* after recovering from an illness they thought was fatal after being cured by a *bakhshi*. Yet others became mute and recover their ability to speak when they are healed by a shaman. Some *bakhshi* report having been lost for days, or even months, before suddenly returning to recount their experiences of visiting mazars while their families had been looking for them.

In the case of Döletkhan Bakhshi, a sudden two-day bout of insanity was followed by her complete disappearance.[3] 41 days later, however, she returned, claiming to have visited a large number of mazars.

> "There were mazars everywhere in front of me. The whole time I walked, but felt as if I were flying because I was being blown by the wind. I don't remember eating anything but do remember that I drank water twice. I fainted a couple of times, but heard a voice telling me to "keep going". In this way I visited the Aq Mazar and Qizil Jilghin Mazar in Juluqbash; the Eziret Bigim Mazar (burial place of Mahmud al-Kashghari) in Opal; the Ezsultunum Mazar (burial place of Sultan Satuq Bughrakhan) in Artush; the Qizil Khoroz Mazar and the Jilanjay

---

[2] This paper is a research report based on my fieldwork performed from 2006 to 2009 in Xinjiang's Kizilsu Kirghiz Autonomous Prefecture. Through visiting the shamans and participating their shamanic practices, particularly in Qarajul and Tegirmeti Village in Artush, Boston Terek and Börtoqoy Village in Uluuchat county, Juluqbash village in Aktaw County (now administrated by Boston Terek Village in Uluuchat County), and in Kizilsu's Aqchi County. I obtained rich first-hand materials on Kirghiz shamans, including definitions, categorization, information on their social function and status, the tools and other items used in their shamanic practices, as well as texts of their incantations and prayers used to communicate with their protective spirits. This paper only focuses on the special relationship between *bakhshi* and mazars alone.

[3] Informant: Döletkhan, female, 69 years old, peasant and *bakhshi*. Interviewer: Gulbahar Ghojesh, time of interview: 23 August 2006, interview location: Döletkhan Bakhshi's house, Juluqbash Village, Uluuchat, Kizilsu, Xinjiang, China.

> Mazar in Aktaw's Qarakutke; the Alip Ata Mazar in Aktaw's Qarakichik; the Padichim Mazar in Tashmiliq located in Kashgar's Toquzak County; the Qïrghïz Mazar in Yengisar's Aqqash......"

Altogether she visited 23 mazars. Her husband relates that when Döletkhan Bakhshi returned, she was emaciated and so dirty that when he saw her, he was terrified and ran to a neighbor's house, staying there for three whole days before returning home. Döletkhan recalls that each of the mazars she visited during her liminal experience and claims that the mazars are the abodes of her patron saints. It was these saints and other good spirits dwelling in the area that she claims protected her and left her with the ability to communicate with the spirit world.

Töraqun Bakhshi is a famous shaman in Artush's Qarajul Village who as a child struggled with epilepsy.[4] He told me that the illness tortured him, causing him to frequently succumb to illness. After his parents' divorce, he was left homeless and began to live at the Jay Döbö Mazar. At the time, he claimed he could see a group of camels that no one else saw and an old man and woman who would speak to him and lead him to do things. It was also during this time that he encountered a girl named Zumur. When his condition deteriorated he was taken to a hospital where his health continued to deteriorate. Töraqun Bakhshi later stated: "At the time the only thing before me was Jay Atam Mazar; that was the only place I wanted to go".

After this he began to visit and perform pilgrimages to mazars. He reports that after staying at Jay Atam Mazar for 41 days, he finally began to feel better. After this he visited many mazars, including Kökönïshïq Mazar in Aqchi County, the reputed burial place of Muzburchaq, who was one of the Qans (kings) of the Manas cycle. He went to the Baq Sögöt Mazar, Chilantoo Mazar and Tabïlghï Mazar in Qarajul Village as well as Kükürt Mazar and Qalday Mazar in Uluuchat County. After visiting these mazars, Töraqun Bakhshi completely recovered from his illness. Through worshipping at these mazars, he was able to win over three mighty mazars, and the hosts of these mazars became the patron saints who help and protect him.

Zura is a young woman living in Qarajul Village who became a *bakhshi* only recently.[5] She considers herself a *moldo,* however, and not yet a *bakhshi.* She states that she once had a heart condition and went to the hospital where she discovered that she would need to pay 300,000 yuan for the necessary operation. She left the hospital because of her lack of funds to cover the procedure and began visiting mazars. She related that she prayed and presented offerings at 12 mazars. She started at the Jay Atam Mazar in Tegirmeti Village where she sacrificed a male sheep (*irik*) and then proceeded to the Kökönïshïq Mazar in Aqchi County where she offered a kid. At Baq Sögöt Mazar she sacrificed another kid; at Jilanduu Mazar in Qarajul Village, she sacrificed a cock; at

---

[4] Informant: Töraqun, male, 58 years old, herder and *bakhshi.* Interviewer: Gulbahar Ghojesh, time of interview: 27 July 2008, interview location: Töraqun Bakhshi's house, Qarajul Village, Artush, Kizilsu, Xinjiang, China.

[5] Informant: Zura, female, 37 years old, herder and *bakhshi.* Interviewer: Gulbahar Ghojesh, time of interview: 25 February 2009, interview location: Zura Bakhshi's house, Qarajul Village, Artush, Kizilsu Autonomous Prefecture, Xinjiang, China.

Chilantoo Mazar in Qarajul Village she sacrificed a cock; at Shorbulaq Mazar in Qarajul Village she sacrificed a kid; at Jay Döbö Mazar in Qarajul Village she sacrificed a kid; at Satuq· Bughrakhan Mazar in Artush's Meyshet Village she sacrificed a ram; at Appaq Khoja in Kashgar she donated 50 yuan; at Qarajul Atam Mazar in Qarajul Village she sacrificed a hen; at Toroq Bulaq Mazar in Qarajul Village she sacrificed a hen. Lastly, she worshipped the Jilu Suu Mazar in the pasture of Aqchi County, and sacrificed a male sheep.

Zura's mother and husband accompanied her on each of her mazar visits. Zura's mother stated that at each mazar where they sacrificed, Zura's husband made a fire, and she [the mother] fried flat cakes while Zura prayed. Zura claims that she prayed at the mazars with the sole hope of recovering from her illness. It was her supporters who encouraged her in becoming a *moldo* and curing illnesses. She states that it was Allah's will that she do this: "I went to the mazars and saw their spirits. I also gained the help of the spirits at the mazars to protect of spirits and bless of the people in Qarajul who were concerned about her." After visiting the mazars, Zura recovered from her heart disease and also gained the favor of the mazars' spirits, and through their power became a healer herself.

Just as mentioned above, the spiritual powers of many Kirghiz *bakhshi* are connected with mazars. *Bakhshi* believe that the spirits that inhabit mazars can help and protect them.

2. Mazars and *Bakhshi* Patron Saints

Each Kirghiz *bakhshi* has his/her own patron saints: the *pirs* who serve as guides and protectors. *Pirs* may appear in the form of a white camel, a wild goat, an old man with a white beard, an eagle, a tiger, a swan, a lion, or even a dragon. The Kirghiz *bakhshi* believes that all *pirs* are the masters (*eesi*) of the mazars they dwell in. Mamilang Bakhshi stated:

> "Our patron saints are the masters of mazars, and each *bakhshi* can occupy one or more mazars where his/her pirs dwell. The more mazars a *bakhshi* can occupy, the more powerful he or she becomes. My mazars are all in Tegirmeti: Suunun Bashï Sulayman Mazar, occupied by the Prophet Sulayman; Kiyiktuz Atam Mazar, occupied by a wild goat; Kekilik Mazar, occupied by a boy riding a camel; Qazan Bulaq Mazar, occupied by a horse; Jay Atam Mazar, occupied by a boy with a copy of the Quran in his hand; and Qarasuu Mazar, occupied by an old man, a pony and a camel." [6]

Abdureshit Bakhshi stated that he has 74 mazars,[7] among them the Ordam Mazar in

[6] Informant: Mamilang, male, 52 years old, herder and *bakhshi*. Interviewer: Gulbahar Ghojesh, time of interview: 14 September 2006, interview location: in Mamilang Bakhshi's house, Tegirmeti Village, Artush, Kizilsu, Xinjiang, China.

[7] Informant: Abdureshit, male, 86 years old, peasant and *bakhshi*. Interviewer: Gulbahar Ghojesh, time of interview: on 13 November 2006, interview location: Abdureshit Bakhshi's house, Arghi Village, Artush, Kizilsu, Xinjiang, China.

Kashgar's Yengisar; Appaq Khoja Mazar and Ezsultunum Mazar, both occupied by a copy of the Quran; Jiluu Suu Mazar in Sheyit located in Artush's Qarajul, occupied by water; and Aqtash Boqoy Mazar, occupied by a white rock.

Töraqun Bakhshi told me that he possessed Jay Döbö Mazar, Jay Atam Mazar, and Kökönïshïq Mazar. His patron saints occupy three mazars and include the girl named Zumur, whom he saw when the old man and the old woman appeared to him. He said that the spirits occupying Jay Atam Mazar were a woman with a baby and men riding horses; the spirit at Jay Döbö Mazar was a camel; and the spirits of Kökönïshïq Mazar were strong men riding horses. In fact, *bakhshi* were frequently reticent to reveal their patron saints to me as they believe it is bad for them because their patron saints do not like being spoken about with others. Only after more persuasion were a handful of *bakhshi* willing to disclose their patron saints.

The more mazars a *bakhshi* can occupy, the more *pirs* he or she will have. Thus, the greater the number of mazars a *bakhshi* can occupy, the more influential he or she becomes.

3. Mazars and a *Bakhshi*'s Communication with Spirits

A *bakhshi* begins to communicate with spirits before he or she begins to perform shamanistic rituals. A *bakhshi* must call on his/her patron saint or pir for instruction, guidance and assistance. If a *bakhshi* is invited to a place outside of the area where his/her mazar is located, the *bakhshi* will call upon the mazar in the area. For example, Abdïqadïr Bakhshi will call upon the Ezsultunum and Appaq Khoja Mazars when he performs healing in Artush, but when he is summoned to Uluuchat County to perform a healing, he will notify the local mazars there.

This portion of my interview with Gülü Bakhshi may serve to elucidate the process of summoning spirits among Kirghiz *bakhshi*.

Q. What kind of place is a mazar?

A. Places that the elders told us were mazars. There have wild roses (*itmurun*) tied with pieces of cloth. The elders say that places like that are ancient mazars and have their own spirits. We kindle oil candles to worship at mazars and pray to the spirits for their blessing.

Q. Where do you kindle oil lamps (*sham*)?

A. At the healing gathering.

Q. Have you seen the bakhshi summoning a mazar's spirit?

A. Yes, I have. They just call to the hosts or spirits of the mazar, like calling to Sulayman of Suunun Bashï. The spirits at mazars can cure illness. In fact, we pray to Allah; the particularity of mazars is that we call upon mazars' spirits. Qara Suu Mazar, Chekende Mazar, Jay Atam; there are many mazars. Each mazar has its own spirit, the person whose eyes are open (those who can see the spirits) can see them. The spirit of one mazar is an old man with white beard and another is a camel. We call the spirits of mazars to drive away the illness and evil afflicting patients together. My hometown is Maydan Village where the Qara Suu Mazar is located. Its host is a child riding atop a white camel and wearing an overcoat made of camel's hair. It was destroyed to build a road; it was a mighty mazar before, though.[8]

Kirghiz *bakhshi* call upon the mazars they possess by singing to contact the spirit of the mazars to obtain the information or help they need. Orozbübü Bakhshi calls a mazar's spirit by singing the following song aloud:

Oy, bendeler qudaydan(gho) tilek qïlghïla,	Oy, people, please pray to God,
Oy, Sögöt (bir) bulaq tenggetar,	Oy, Sögot Bulaq tengitar,
Oy, maneke özungdön (gho) medet tileymin.	Oy, I pray to you for help.
Oy, Kiyiktuz Atam,	Oy, Kiyiktuz Atam
Oy, pirim(gho) jolbors(gho) keldi jïyïngha.	Oy, my patron saint, the tiger, has come to this gathering.
Oy, Toghuz (bir) Bulaq,	Oy, Toghuz Bulaq,
Oy, maneke gertayghan keldi jïyïngha,	Oy, the hound has come to this gathering too,
Oy, tayghanïm özüngden medet tileymin	Oy, my hound, I pray to you for help.
Oy, Jaydöbö Atam	Oy, Jaydöbö Atam,
Oy, maneke aba enem keldi jïyïngha ,	Oy, Mother Eve, came to the gathering
Oy, aba enem özüngdön(gho) medet tileymin.	Oy, Mother Eve, I pray to you for help.
Oy, Baq Sögöt Atam ,	Oy, Baq Sögöt Atam,
Oy, tulparïng keldi jïyïngha ,	Oy, the horse has come to the gathering,
Oy, aqsaqal özüngdön medet tileymin .	Oy, aqsaqal, I pray to you for help.
Oy, mana bardiq pirler keldi jïyïngha,	Oy, now, all my patron saints have come to this gathering,
Oy, köpchülük qudaydan(gho) tilek qïlalï ,	Oy, let us pray to God,
Oy, maneke tilekti(gho) berer qolubuzgha .	Oy, May our prayers will be answered.

This song includes references to multiple mazars and spirits. According to this song, Kiyiktuz Atam refers to Father Ibex, the spirit of a mazar in Tegirmeti Village, its host is a tiger; Toghuz Bulaq, also a mazar in Tegirmeti, means a spring with nine mouths, its host is a hound; Jaydöbö Atam, a famous mazar in Qarajul Village, its host is Mother Eve; Baq Sögöt Atam, means Willow Garden Father, also a famous mazar in Qarajul, its host is a horse.

The spirits are called together by the song of the *bakhshi*'s and the gathering of spirits gives power to the *bakhshi* so that he or she can perform his/her shamanistic rituals with full confidence.

Mamilang Bakhshi's song for calling the spirits of mazars is as follows:

Suunun bashï Sulayman,	Sulayman of headstream water,
Aqsaqal senden medet tileymin.	Aqsaqal, I pray to you for help.

---

[8] Informant: Gülü, female, 51 years old, herder and *bakhshi*. Interviewer: Gulbahar Ghojesh, time of interview: on 14, January 2009, interview location: in Gülü Bakhshi's house, Tegirmeti Village, Artush, Kizilsu, Xinjiang, China.

Jay Atamdan jashbala, *Chari kitep qolunda,* *Dabager qïlchu özüngüz.*	The child of Jay Atam, with Quran in his hand, You can cure illness.
Kiyiktuzdan aq bürküt, *Qasidengdi ayta kel,* *Sen daba qïlchü kishiler osholor.*	White eagle of Kiyiktuz, please come reading your elegy, These are the patients who need your cure.
Teshik Tashta Chinar Mazar boz bala, *Aptiyeging qolungda,* *Sho kelgen keselge,* *Daba bir qïlchu ongunan.*	The child of Teshik Tashta's Chinar Mazar, with prayer book in your hand, for these patients, please give your help.
Kekilikte jash bala, *Aruulardïn pirising,*	The child of Kekilik, You are the patron saint of sick children with aruu.
Jashbaldar keldi daba qïl, *Özüngdön medet tileymin.*	the children come, please cure them, I pray to you for help.
Chekende Mazarda aqsaqal, *Top jïyïngha kelekör,* *Shu turghan keseldin,* *Dabasïn achïq bilekör.*	White beard elder of Chekende Mazar, please come to this gathering, tell the patients the state of their illness.
Qazan Bulaqta gerqula, *Aybandardïn pirising,* *Shu turghan keselge,* *Derdin aytïp bilip ber.*	The brown horse of Qazan Bulaq, you ate the patron saint of animals, tell the patients their suffering.

(Mamilang Bakhshi then said) "After the healing ceremony ends, we should send off the spirits of the mazars whom we have called by saying: Oh, spirits, thank you so much, please return, sorry to bother you all. We call you for the patients alone and pray that you cure their illness and bless them. May Allah bless the people and keep them far from illness and disaster. And say 'Oomin'".[9]

Many mazars are mentioned in this song, including that of Suunun Bashï, meaning "headwaters" and located at the headwaters near Tegirmeti Village. Each spring, villagers perform a ritual there to pray for a better year. The spirit of this mazar is the prophet Sulayman. Other patron saints of Mamilang Bakhshi include the child spirit of Jay Atam, the white eagle of Kiyiktuz, the white-bearded elder of Chekende Mazar, and the brown horse of Qazan Bulaq. Mamilang Bakhshi's purpose in summoning the spirits of the mazars is obvious; to gather the spirits to obtain their help in healing patients.

[9] Informant: Mamilang, male, 52 years old, herder and *bakhshi*. Interviewer: Gulbahar Ghojesh, time of interview: 30 October 2006, place of interview: a house in Qarajul Village, Artush, Kizilsu Autonomous Prefecture, Xinjiang, China. Mamilang Bakhshi and Gülü Bakhshi were called to drive away evil spirits, because of two divorced girls. I recorded Mamilang Bakhshi's song after the shamanic ritual had ended. At my strong insistence he chanted the song for me.

Concluding Remarks

In short, a *bakhshi* communicates with spirits, which, in turn, instruct, guide, help, and protect the *bakhshi.* This explains the close relationship between Kirghiz *bakhshi* and the mazars where the spirits dwell, and also reveals shamanistic values such as beliefs in the spirits of nature and ancestors that are preserved among the Kirghiz people. The existence of such remnants is even clearer in the relationship between Kirghiz *bakhshi* and mazars. For example, mountains, peaks, springs, and trees are seen as sacred places and called mazars. It is also said that burial sites of ancient heroes or those who have lived long lives have magical powers, and that ancestral spirits dwelling in mazars can give power to *bakhshi.*

We can also see that mazars occupied by *bakhshi* and their patron saints display Islamic characteristics. For Kirghiz, a sacred place is called a mazar, and at mazars occupied by *bakhshi* people not only display their belief in nature, but also in Islam, as in the case of the grave of Satuq Bugrakhan, the first king converted to Islam. Ordam, the most influential mazar in south Xinjiang, is also associated with a Qarakhanid who was martyred in the wars with the Buddhists of Khotan. The spirit of these mazars is the Quran, Islam's holy book. Among the patron saints of *bakhshi* there is a boy clutching the Quran in his hand. When *bakhshi* summon the spirits of mazars, they first pray to *Huda* (God) and then pray to Mother Eve for help. This practice is very Islamic and conforms to Islam's monotheism by upholding that there is no god but Allah, restricting the worship of an individual or object. But the belief of Kirghiz *bakhshi* in nature does not clash with their belief in Islam. Indeed, there are no contradictions between the existence of multiple spirits and Allah, on the contrary, it reveals a harmonious relationship between the two, reflecting the blend of shamanistic and Islamic values in the worldview of Kirghiz *bakhshi.*

The close connection between the Kirghiz *bakhshi* and mazars provides living material for the study of the coexistence between Kirghiz folk beliefs and Islamic faith in a developed society. It also reflects the current state Kirghiz popular religion characterized by shamanism and Islam.

Bibliography

Dimulati Aomaer 迪木拉提·奥玛尔 1995. *Aertai Yuxi Zhuminzu Samanjiao Yanjiu* 阿尔泰语系诸民族萨满教研究 [Research on the shamanisim of Altaic people]. Urumqi: Xinjiang Renmin Chubanshe.

Du Rongkun and Ainiwaer 杜荣坤，安瓦尔 1991. *Keerkezizu* 柯尔克孜族 [The Kirghiz]. Beijing: Minzu Chubanshe.

Keerkezizu Jianshi Bianxiezu《柯尔克孜族简史》编写组 2008. *Keerkezizu Jianshi* 柯尔克孜族简史 [The Brief History of Kirghiz]. Beijing: Minzu Chubanshe.

Li Shixiang 李世祥 (ed.) 2008. *Kezilesu Keerkezi Zizhizhou Nianjian 2008* 克孜勒苏年鉴 2008 [Annals of Qïzïlsuu Kyrgyz Autonomous Prefecture 2008] . Atush: Kezilesu Keerkeziwen Chubanshe.

Ömürbay, Makelek 2004. *Qïrghïz adabiyat tarïkhï (1)* [The History of Kirghiz Literature (1)] Urumqi: Xinjiang El Basmasï.

Reyila Dawuti (Rahile Dawut) 热依拉·达吾提 2001. *Weiwuerzu maza wenhua yanjiu* 维吾尔族麻扎文化研究 [A Study on the Mazar Cultures of Uyghurs]. Urumqi: Xinjiang Daxue Chubanshe.

A Bakhshi calling on mazars during her healing ritual.

Bakhshi performing a healing ritual in a yurt (aq uy).

A Kirghiz bakhshi practicing healing by incantation.

Qambar Atam Mazar in Qarajul Village.

Qoyjol Mazar in Tegirmeti Village.

Qoyjol Mazar in Tegirmeti Village.

Qazan Bulaq Mazar in Tegirmeti Village.

"Ziyara" and the Hui Sufi Orders of the Silk Road

WANG Ping

Introduction

There are numerous sacred Islamic tombs found throughout China, particularly in the northwestern provinces of Gansu, Ningxia, Qinghai and Xinjiang where numerous of Hui communities are located. Unlike Uyghur Muslims, Hui Muslims call these sacred tombs "*gongbei*" (拱北).[1] *Gongbei* is a transliteration of the Arabic word *kubba* which originally meant "a domed structure", an architectural feature popular in Arab countries. In China, however, the term refers to the tomb of a *murshid* (穆勒师德; master) of a Sufi order, and also the center of particular order's activities. Sometimes the word is used to refer to the tombs of the early Islamic missionaries and sages. The *gongbei* is the most important religious site for a Sufi order and often viewed as the order's "sacred site". Each order has its own *gongbei* which its followers visit; some orders have only one or two, while others may have several dozens.

There has been little research on the historical and current situation of the majority of *gongbei* located in Gansu, Ningxia, Qinghai and Xinjiang provinces. For example, Ma Tong's historical research on the Chinese Hui Sufi *gongbei* (Ma Tong 1983); Ma Hangong's historical origin and general survey of the religious activities of the *gongbei* in the different places of Qinghai (Ma Hangong 1997); Liu Wei and Hei Fuli on the historical and current condition of *gongbei* in Guyuan (固原) region of Ningxia (Liu Wei and Hei Fuli 2002). Wang Jianxin uses the example of the Lingmingtang (灵明堂) branch in Guyuan to point out how Sufis spread their influence among the Hui migrant communities through the leadership of designated officials and blood lineage. He continues to show how these institutions reinforced the leadership network through the rebuilding and repair of *gongbei* and *daotang* (道堂) (Wang Jianxin 2007).

Ziyara (则亚拉) differs from the other two kinds of pilgrimages; *hajj* (麦加朝觐) and *'umra* (副朝), in that Islamic law (*shari'a*) does not contain specific regulations concerning it. Due to their geographical and historical differences, Sufi orders and *gongbei* possess distinct characteristics. The distribution pattern of the Hui Muslims in Gansu, Ningxia, Qinghai, and Xinjiang is characterized by small communities. For most

[1] The Uyghurs refer to these sites as mazars. Mazar is the phonetic transliteration of the Arabic word *mazār*, and the site typically contains a gate, surrounding wall, courtyard, and a room where the graves lie; some also incorporate domes "*gongbei*".

Hui Muslims, the mosque plays a central role in the community, as especially in villages. Because *ziyara* is primarily performed in Gansu's Lanzhou (兰州) and Linxia (临夏), as well as Ningxia Hui Autonomous Region's Guyuan and Wuzhong (吴忠), and even provinces like Yunnan and Jilin, organization can be extremely complicated. In the organized activities, the function of the mosques is of decisive importance. Unfortunately there has been little research that discusses the importance of these events for the *murid* (穆里德; pupil of *murshid*, or high-ranked Sufi) and *qawm* (高目; ordinary members of a Sufi order) as well as how the activities have influenced them.

Ziyara is an important channel through which to study Hui culture. For several years, the author, in cooperation with the Gansu Nationalities Research Institute, the Ningxia and Qinghai Academies of Social Sciences, the Gansu Bureau of Religious Affairs, the Xinjiang Bureau of Religious Affairs and figures from religious communities, has made several social surveys of Hui *ziyara*. In the process, the author interviewed Hong Yang (洪洋), the *murshid* of the Hong sect of the Khufiyya order (虎非耶洪门) and the elderly Wang Shoutian (汪守天), *murshid* of the Lanzhou Lingmingtang sect of the Qadiriyya order (嘎德林耶灵明堂). The author also participated in mediating a dispute over two *gongbei* in Xinjiang belonging to the Jahriyya order (哲和林耶). This article is the result of my findings during this period of research.

A General Survey of Hui Sufi Orders and the *Gongbei*

Starting in the 12th century, Sufi mysticism gradually began to take form and permanent organizations appeared. Muslim usually refer to these organizations as *tariqa* (pl. *turuq)* while Western scholars typically use the term "order".

The word *tariqa,* meaning "road", "path" or "method", is used by Muslim mystics when speaking about spiritual meditation and practical methods of attaining oneness with Allah. Under the specific direction of a teacher (*murshid*), a practitioner of *tariqa* goes on a spiritual journey, performing all rituals stipulated by religious law and abiding by certain special rules, and then progresses through different psychological stages while seek the hidden truth providing access to the highest spiritual realm. Therefore, the term *tariqa* means a way of religious life to which a certain group of people commonly adhere to and that mystics use as a name for religious organizations following this method.

In the latter half of the 17th century, some Sufi orders, such as the Khufiyya (虎夫耶), Kubrawiyya (库布林耶), Qadiriyya (嘎的林耶), and Jahriyya (哲赫忍耶), spread from Arabia through Central Asia and Xinjiang to Gansu, Ningxia, and Qinghai by both sea and land. Under the influence of traditional Chinese culture, new types of organizations formed. But, for a long time, these organizations were not identified by any one term such as *tariqa* nor "order". Although the large orders were known by names such as Khufiyya, Qadiriyya, Kubrawiyya and Jahriyya, the subbranches were often known by their geographical location, such as Bijiachang (毕家场) and Beizhuang (北庄); some even derived their order's name from the surname of their founder, such as *Liumen* (刘门; Liu family), *Yangmen* (杨门; Yang family) and *Zhangmen* (张门; Zhang family); while still others were named after a particular characteristic of their founder, such as *Humen* (胡门; the bearded), and *Fengmen* (疯门; the mad man).

In the middle of the Qing Dynasty, Ma Xianzhong (马显忠, 1736-1795), the 6th *mufti* (religious leader) of Lintiao Beixiang (临挑北乡) in Gansu Province, received the title of "Supreme Leader (统领)" of the various sects of Hezhou (河州), from the Qing local government for meritorious actions such as donating funds to build schools and improving the relationship between local Hui and Han people. The masses refer to this phenomenon as the "seven sects and eight officials (七门八宦)" that would later became the term "*menhuanjia*" (门宦家; family of officials). In the 3rd volume of the *Ping Huizhi* (平回志), we find the following:

> ....The three old centers of the area are the Hua Mosque (华寺) in the north of the town, as well as Bijiachang (毕家场) and Qijiachang (祁家场), commonly known as *gongbei*, which also means mosque. Its leader is called *mufti* (牟费谛). The three centers are the refuge for the Hui, and even followers in Shaanxi and other provinces obey his commands.[2]

The term *menhuan* (门宦; Sufi order) first appeared in March of the 23rd year of the Guangxu Emperor in a document submitted to the throne entitled *Chengqing Caigu Huijiao Menhuan* (呈请裁革回教门宦) [Beseeching the Removal of the Muslim *Menhuan*] by Yang Zengxin (杨增新), the governor of Hezhou. In recent years, however, most Chinese scholars have decided that the Sufi organizations are primarily social organizations which serve to strengthen religious ties. In this case, referring to these organizations as *menhuan* is not accurate, since Sufi Muslims rarely use the name in referring to themselves. I propose the use of the Sufi term *tariqa*, as there are no substantial differences between these Sufi organizations and *tariqa*. Although these groups do display are strong regional characteristics, they are not unique to Chinese Hui Muslims. Hui Sufi orders are part of the tradition of Sufi mysticism within Islam and such organizations are a common phenomenon in the historical processes that contribute to the development of Sufism.

Of the multitude of Sufi orders, the four main groups that spread into Gansu, Ningxia, Qinghai and Xinjiang were the Khufiyya, Qadiriyya, Kubrawiyya, and Jahriyya. During their expansion in these provinces these four groups established nearly forty sub-sects. These sub-sects follow the doctrine and rituals contained in the Quran and the Hadith and adhere to the five pillars of Islam. In addition, they follow a *murshid*, whom they encourage to serve as elders who lead their followers on the right path; Followers must submit to the *murshid*'s leadership. The *murshid* should frequently spend time in quiet meditation, reciting the *zikr* (齐克尔) as well as build a *gongbei* over the tomb of a *murshid* so that the faithful can go there to pray. The post of *murshid* in most of the larger orders is hereditary or passed down to reliable senior disciples. A *murshid* usually has several mosques under his charge and is responsible for appointing *akhun*, or imam, to run them. The religious activities of the order are usually supported by funds from the *murshid*'s business profits and the donations from the faithful.

---

2 Bai Shouyi 2000, vol.3, p.107.

In addition, each sub-sect usually has several special rules that the believers must follow: Khufiyya adherents must affirm the principles "the *tariqa* and the *shari'a* are equally important", "seeking calmness in the midst of chaos" and "quietly saying the zikr". This sub-sect is primarily located in Gansu Province's Hezhou, Lanzhou, and Chinzhou (秦州); in Qinghai Province's Xunhua (循化), Hualong (化隆), and Xining (西宁); in Ningxia Hui Autonomous Region's Yinchuan (银川), Tongxin (同心) and Xihaigu (西海固), as well as Xinjiang and other places. Although these sub-sects all fall under the Khufiyya order, when it comes to preaching there is no direct contact between them. Qadiriyya order holds to the principle of "path before religion" and a portion of the believers remain celibate, sit in silence and meditate for enlightenment, perform the silent *zikr*, live in the *gongbei*, promote the idea that "a moment of enlightenment is more valuable than ten thousand years of accumulating merit" in their quest for virtue. This order is primarily located in Gansu Province's Linxia, Dongxiang (东乡), Kangle (康乐) and Lanzhou; Qinghai Province's Datong (大通), Minhe (民和), and Xining; Ningxia Hui Autonomous Region's Haiyuan (海原), Shaanxi Province's Xixiang (西乡), and Langzhong (阆中) in Sichuan Province. The widely distributed sub-sects are in communication with each other and submit almost exclusively to Huazhe Abdu Donglaxi (华者·阿布都·董拉希) and his disciples. Sub-sects of the Kubrawiyya order maintain their adherence to the Five Pillars of Islam and the silent *zikr*. The group has only one *daotang* in Dawantou (大湾头) but each of its fourteen elderly preachers has a sub-sect of his own; different sub-sects do not discriminate against each other. Sub-sects of the Kubrawiyya are primarily found in Gansu Province's Dongxiang and Kangle. The Jahriyya *menhuan* adheres to the principle of "religion before path," collective and vocal *zikr*, and the simplification of rituals. Sub-sects of the Jahriyya are primarily located in Gansu Province's Zhangjiachuan (张家川) and Pingliang (平凉); Ningxia Hui Autonomous Region's Xiji (西吉), Ningxia Hui Autonomous Region's Guyuan and Wuzhong; as well as various location in Xinjiang, Yunnan, Hebei, Jilin, and Shandong.

A *daotang* was originally a place for the *murshid* and other clerics to perform meditation. In Chinese these sites were called "houses of silence" while in Arabic they were known as *khaniqa* or *zawiya* and were typically located in remote, crude, and dark rooms or caves. With the secularization of the Sufi orders, the *daotang* underwent substantial changes and became a center for a *menhuan's* preaching and a sacred site and their size expanded to include *gongbei*, arches, quiet rooms for meditation, pavilions to house stone tablets, facilities for the performance of ablutions, dining halls, gardens, reception halls, residences for the principal preacher, mosques, slaughterhouses, and other facilities. There were also changes in architectural forms and styles used in these constructions; longer monotonous dome-shaped buildings were no longer the only constructions used to house tombs, being replaced by traditional Chinese architectonic elements such as hexagonal pavilions, heightening the solemn and dignified atmosphere of the religious complex.

Historically, the largest *gongbei* in Gansu, Ningxia and Qinghai are the Huasi Gongbei (花寺拱北), Da Gongbei (大拱北), Mufti Gongbei (穆夫提拱北), Bijiachang Gongbei (毕

家场拱北) in Hezhou, Xuanhuagang Gongbei (宣化岗拱北) in Zhangjiachuan, and Dongchuan Gongbei (东川拱北) in Lanzhou. Among the larger Hui *gongbei* located in Xinjiang are the Dawan Gongbei (大湾拱北), Ergongjinjiao Laorenjia Gongbei (二工金脚老人家拱北) in Urumqi, Toudaohezi Gongbei (头道河子拱北) in Turpan, Suiding Gongbei (绥定拱北) in Ili (伊犁), and Erliugong Gongbei (二六工拱北) in Changji (昌吉). The earliest *gongbei* have been destroyed by fire and rebuilt many times. Some of the most magnificently constructed *gongbei* are the Bijiachang Gongbei (毕家场拱北), Humen Gongbei (胡门拱北), Dongchuan Gongbei (东川拱北) in Lanzhou, Lingmingtang Gongbei (灵明堂拱北), Mufti Gongbei (穆夫提拱北), and Honggangzi Gongbei (洪岗子拱北) in Ningxia. These *gongbei* are usually administrated by the successors or relatives of the figures buried inside. Although a majority of the *gongbei* do not have personnel responsible for their daily upkeep, account management, or logistics. They are responsible for receiving believers, accepting of donations, maintaining the mausoleum, and entertaining visitors. The *gongbei* is the property of all believers, but the rights of allocating funds and limiting usage belong to the administrator.

Suiding Gongbei in Ili.
(Photographed by Rahile Dawut, 2008)

The Performance of the *Ziyara*

According to my research, the scale of a *ziyara* depends on the size of an order's membership. Since most orders have large numbers of *gongbei* distributed over a very large geographical area, it is frequently difficult for many *qawm* to participate in the activities. A *qawm's* financial situation is a decisive factor in the number and frequency of *gongbei* it visits. For the *qawm* based in Xinjiang, traveling expenses a limiting factor and mosques must raise funds to send only representatives to participate whenever there are large-scale *ziyara*. Because of the improvement in the financial situation of many *qawm* members, it is now possible for these groups to participate in *ziyara* with the help of travel agencies. Between 2005 and 2006, the author met Hui Muslims from Fukang City (阜康市) and Yining County (伊宁县) who were participating in *ziyara* to Chengdu (成都) and Lanzhou. Their trip was organized by a travel agency which arranged for their food and lodging, as they visited Lanzhou, Tianshui (天水) and Pingliang in Gansu Province, Guyuan and Wuzhong in Ningxia Hui Autonomous Region, Kaifeng (开封) in Henan Province, Jilin Province in Northeast China, and Mojiang (墨江) in Yunnan Province to participated in *ziyara* with expenses totaling around 10,000 yuan per person.

An important component of *ziyara* is *ermanli* (尔曼里), a transliteration of the Arabic word *amal* meaning "alms giving", that in a Sufi context refers to the remembrance of sages and the founders of the order. This ritual is performed often as Sufis consider this to be an activity that accumulates merit.

In the days leading up to the memorial days of the order's founder, such as the first, tenth, or twentieth anniversaries, mosques of the order, regardless of geographical location, make preparations for *ziyara*. The necessary funds are primarily raised by the mosques and individual *qawm* members who contribute as they are able. Except for the mosques' responsibility to cover the expenses of an individual *murid* and religious scholars, all other *ziyara* expenses are borne by the individual. Since most of those who participate in these activities are well advanced in age they are typically funded and accompanied by their children. Although some travel by train to the event, the majority travels by hired coach.

Through my own participation in the *ermanli* events held by the Khufiyya Honggangzi Gongbei (洪岗子拱北), Qadiriyya Da Gongbei (大拱北), Lingmingtang Gongbei (灵明堂拱北), and Jahriyya Dongchuan Gongbei (东川拱北) I have observed that the events are all very similar and generally follow the following order:

1) Ablutions: Men and women enter their respective ablution halls to perform either major or minor ablutions. Most select the latter although some choose to perform the former.

2) Audience with the current *murshid*: Participants take their turns meeting the *murshid* and other *gongbei custodians* according to region or mosque. *Akhun* and the *qawm* will lead other participants in reading the *tasbih* (泰斯比哈) and donations are presented to the chief religious leader. The size of the donation varies according to the individual's financial ability and willingness to give. Many *qawm* members that are unable to attend have a representative present a donation on their behalf.

3) Incense Offering: The burning of incense is common religious ritual among the Hui Sufi Muslims and most larger *gongbei* are equipped with large censer. The representative of the *qawm* offers a large handful of incense and places it in the censer while the other *qawm* offer smaller handfuls.
4) Collective Quran Recitation: Participants sit in an oblong formation in the main hall and *akhun* and *qawm* begin to perform the *zikr*. Those who cannot read sit at the back and listen. As the ceremony concludes, all join together in prayer. The *qawm* members who cannot read make donations to those who can. During the reading, each group reads from its own prayer books.
5) Tombs are approached in order while participants pray and some recite the *zikr*. After this, representatives from different regions and mosques place shrouds over the tombs. Shrouds are usually lengths of silk or flannel, measuring from just a few meters up to 20 meters in length.
6) At the appointed time, organizers provide participating groups with a free communal meal consisting of stew and a piece of fried cake in one of the *gongbei* dining halls.

Characteristics of *Ziyara*

The purpose of the Hui Sufi Muslim participation in *ziyara* is not unlike that of other Muslims around the world and can be very complex.

1) Good Fortune: One of the main purposes of the *ziyara* is to seek good fortune. *Qawms* see this as "benefiting from good luck", "benefiting from the atmosphere" and "benefiting from *barakat* (白勒科提)", an Arabic word meaning good fortune. In the *ermanli* events held at Hui *gongbei* in Qinghai, there are Han and Tibetan visitors who come to pray, give alms, burn incense, and to make wishes.
2) Meeting the *murshid*: According to custom, when members of a Sufi *qawm* meet the *murshid*, they should share with him all of their thoughts and desires, be they good or bad, so that the *murshid* can show them the difference between right and wrong. The *murshid* should not be deceived as meeting him brings one into proximity with the spirits of past *murshids*. This is seen as a means to directly obtain religious respite and also the gaining merit.
3) Prayer for one's own peace after death or for the salvation of deceased loved ones.
4) Entertainment: An important part of these events is meeting and talking with relatives and friends from other mosques and exchanging news as well as happily shopping at the stalls around the *gongbei*.

Mosques play an important role in *ziyara*. Organizers plan the dates of *ermanli* events and all other religious rituals, and also will hire similar means of transportation to take groups of participants to the *ziyara* events and dining facilities. Mosques that have *qawm* members with religious knowledge will lead the rituals and *qawms* who participate in *ermanli*, in spite of their lack of formal learning to fulfil their purpose there. Through participation in *ziyara*, *qawm* members renew their understanding of their own order and the meaning of Islamic knowledge, thus reinforcing their sense of belonging to their mosques and their own identity as Muslims.

This is a brief introduction to the *ziyara* in which the author has taken part. In fact many Hui Muslims belonging to groups such as the Ikhwani (伊赫瓦尼) and Qadim (格底木) sects hold entirely different views on *gongbei* and *ermanli* events. Indeed, there are *qawm* members who would sell their means of production or even real estate in order to raise funds to participation in *ermanli*. However, in Gansu, Ningxia, Qinghai, and Xinjiang, Hui communities and Sufi *gongbei* are widespread and so many Hui Sufi Muslims in those regions hold magnificent *ermanli* ceremonies at *gongbei* located there. Therefore, the study of the performance of *gongbei ermanli* is of great importance meaning for the understanding of the religious culture and psychology of Hui Muslim communities.

References

Bai Shouyi 白寿彝 2000. *Huimin Qiyi* 回民起义 [The Muslim Rebellions] 4 vols, Shanghai: Shanghai Renmin Chubanshe.

Liu Wei and Hei Fuli 刘伟, 黑富礼 2000. *Guyuan Huizu* 固原回族 [The Hui People of Guyuan], Yinchuan: Ningxia Renmin Chubanshe.

Ma Hangong 马翰龚 1997. "Qinghai Yisilanjiao Gongbei Shulue 青海伊斯兰教拱北述略 [A Brief Narration of the Islamic Gongbei of the Qinghai]", in *Qinghai Minzu Yanjiu*, 1997(3).

Ma Tong 马通 1983. *Zhongguo Yisilanjiaopai yu Menhuanzhidu Shilue* 中国伊斯兰教派与门宦制度史略 [A Brief History on the Chinese Islamic Sects and the Menhuan System], Yinchuan: Ningxia Renmin Chubanshe.

Wang Jianxin 王建新 2007. "Zongjiao Wenhua Leixing 宗教文化类型：中国民族学·人类学理论新探 [Religion and Culture Type: Chinese Nationalities Study New Explorations on Anthropological Theory]", in *Qinghai Minzu Yanjiu*, 2007(4).

The Saint Mausoleums of Sufi Order Lingmingtang

WANG Jianxin

Introduction

In China, there are about twenty million Muslim populations composed of ten ethnic minority groups. Based on language origins, they can be divided into two main groups: the Turkic and Indo-European speaking one including Uyghur, Kazakh, Kirghiz, Uzbek, Tatar, Salar and Tajik, the Chinese-Mongolian speaking one contains Hui, Dongxiang and Bao'an. In addition to their languages, their different historical experiences and geographic locations are also critical factors contributing to the diversity of their cultural traditions.

Though Islam is a core part of the religious life of all these Muslim minorities, it functions differently in relation to the diversity of Muslim societies and cultures. For example, among the Hui people, who have closer relations to the Han people in their social structures and folk traditions, the role of Islam has different significance depending on the variety of their local traditions. In the southeastern coastal areas of China, the Hui people have their education systems, kinship relations and ritual customs parallel with that of the Han people. Islam is a cultural source significant in recognizing the genealogical decent of the Hui people from their Muslim ancestors (Gladney 1991). But in the northwestern corner of China, the Hui people are strongly influenced by Islamic Sufi teachings and Islam contributes to the ritual perfection and organizational integration of numerous mystic orders (Ma 1983, Zhang 1993). In the case of other Muslim groups who have closer relations to Muslims in Central Asian areas, such as the Uyghur people, Islam intertwines deeply with various popular beliefs, exorcist and magic practices (Wang 1996, 2004a).

Other than the different Islamic traditions, which based on a transcendental body of religious doctrines and disciplines, Muslim minorities in China are also sharing a grass-rooted bottom stream of their religious life, the worship of saint mausoleums, especially in those Muslim groups who take Islamic Sufism as their leading part of religious traditions. Some research mentions the existence of about 2,000 mausoleums in only the Khotan Prefecture in Xinjiang Uyghur Autonomous Region,[1] many others pay attention to the different characteristics of Islamic saint mausoleums in the area, depending on their religious origins, social functions and symbolic meanings, and

[1] Xinjiang Shehui Kexueyuan Zongjiao Yanjiusuo 1989: 193.

divide them into three groups:

1) the mausoleums without clear names and with their Islamic origins suspect, 2) the mausoleums of the imams of Shia sects, and 3) the mausoleums of great Muslim military leaders (Hamada 1978, Ma 1987, Shimen 2002).[2] A recent research also makes two-groups classification between Islamic and non-Islamic saint Mausoleums (Dawut 2001: 5-11).

Similar cases exist also among the Chinese-Mongolian speaking Muslims, especially in those Sufi orders, so called as *menhuan*(门宦)in Chinese, there is a high popularity of the worship of Islam-related mausoleums. However, different from those Turkic and Indo-European speaking Muslim groups, the worship seems to concentrate on only the human souls of those great Sufi leaders who have important positions on the genealogical trees of those patrilineal saint families. One source undertakes the ethnographic mapping on the distribution and functions of those saint mausoleums of "four great menhuan" (四大门宦, Ma 1983), and another makes analyses on the symbolic meaning of various Sufi calligraphies and architectural styles of the saint mausoleums (Yang 2007), and also some source investigates the key role of the mausoleums in the process of the socio-cultural construction of some specific Sufi order (Wang 2004b 2007).

All the above facts show the popularity and different versions of the saint worship and their important socio-cultural functions in Muslim minority groups in China. In this paper, I will report on a unique case from the Chinese-Mongolian speaking Muslims, a series of saint mausoleums , owned by a Sufi order called *Lingmingtang*. One salient characteristic of *Lingmingtang*'s saint mausoleums is that though they belong to the male leaders of the order but the buriers have not necessarily to have genealogical relations to their patrilineal families, because the particular institution of the order that its top leaders do not marry and have family. However, these mausoleums still function well as theological bases to the legitimacy of the Sufi teachings of the order and effective devices to integrate different social groups, including those patrilineal kinship organizations.

I believe that the study of *Lingmingtang*'s saint mausoleums will no doubt provide us with a precious case for achieving richer insights into the nature and function of the saint worship existing among Muslim minorities in China.

The Formation of the Order and its Mausoleums

Lingmingtang is the youngest Sufi order among those Sufi groups of the Chinese-Mongolian speaking Muslim minorities. It was established by Ma Lingming in 1915 in a street courtyard called *Xiaxiyuan* (下西苑) in the western suburb of Lanzhou City. After the establisher of the order died in 1925, the second leader of the order, Shan Zijiu, started actions to construct a great tomb for his teacher Ma Lingming, then the

[2] Ma's classification makes little difference to the Hamada's one with only the second item, saint descendants, different from imams of Islam Shia sect, the one Hamada gave.

first saint mausoleum of the order came to exist in Xiaxiyuan. When Ma Lingming was alive, he had even sent disciples two times to Xinjiang area for missionary activities, the first one was Kao Futang and the second was Sha Baoqing, both had been active in Hami area and succeeded in expanding the religious teaching of the order. It was said that Kao Futang died before his teacher and was buried as a saint disciple according to the order of Ma Lingming. Then in the period of the leadership of the second leader Shan Zijiu, the tomb of Kao Futang was made a saint mausoleum in the eastern suburb of Hami City after the mausoleum of his teacher in Lanzhou.

In the period of Shan Zijiu's leadership (1925-1953), the order had once separated into two factions, "the east courtyard" (东院) and "the west courtyard" (西院), taking respectively a part of Xiaxiyuan's courtyard as their religious centers. Following the separation that happened at the headquarter, the Hami branch of the order split also into two: the adherents of Kao Futang gathered at the religious center where their mausoleum exists and formed "the Huochezhan group" (火车站, since the location is near the Hami Railway Stantion) following the east courtyard faction, and the sympathizers of Sha Baoqing established their own religious center in a street called Xiheba (西河坝), therefore formed "the Xiheba group" standing close to the west courtyard faction.

In later years under the leadership of the third generation leader Wang Shoutian, especially entering the period of religious revitalization after 1980, the east courtyard group has been coming to lead in the rapid development of the order. In 1984, the east courtyard faction donated their part of the courtyard to a neighboring government-owned factory, and got a wasteland on the top of the south mountain near the Wuxingping (五星坪) street area, which was about three kilometers from Xiaxiyuan, as the compensation for their part of the courtyard. There, they started their historic step to construct a new headquarter called Wuxingping Daotang (五星坪道堂). Until the present, after more than 25 years hard efforts, the Wuxingping Daotang of the order has already become a huge well-decorated, Chinese-styled castle, attracting a great number of adherents as well as travelers from inside and outside of China.[3]

During the beginning years of 1990s, a branch of Wuxingping Daotang in Sanying Town, Guyuan County of Ningxia Hui Autonomous Region became Guyuan Fentang (固原分堂) and got its late leader Ma Renpu, who was one of the students of the second generation leader Shanzijiu, approved as a saint disciple by the third generation leader Wang Shoutian. In 1996, under the economic assistance of Wuxingping Daotang, Guyuan branch built the mausoleum of Ma Renpu in the branch courtyard. In the same time, Wuxingping Daotang also supported its Hami Fentang (哈密分堂), the Huochezhan group, to have built up the branch's castle-styled center.

In contrast to the great integration and development of the east courtyard faction, the west courtyard faction withered and split further into several small groups, the adherents of these groups began to scatter in the surrounding areas outside of Lanzhou City, for instance in Guanghe, Linxia areas. In Linxia, the adherents of its group leader,

[3] See a related report by Ma Qiang (2001).

The Entrance of Wuxingping Gongbei, Lanzhou City.

Ma Hasan made a mausoleum for their leader some years after his death in a village called Beishangen (北山根). Since the greater number of the adherents and stronger influence comparing with those mausoleums at the branch centers, the Mausoleum of Ma Hasan became well-known among the believers of the *Lingmingtang* order.

At the present, *Lingmingtang*, the Sufi order of a 95 years history, has already entered its mature period with about 250 thousands believers[4] and six centers having respectively their own saint mausoleums. Wuxingping Daotang is the largest center led by the third generation leader Wang Shoutian, with two mausoleums of the first and second generation leaders, under the Chinese styled pagodas with octagonal roofs in its center courtyard. The Hami and Guyuan branches are two local centers of Wuxingping Daotang, the east courtyard faction, and their mausoleums were built with hexagonally roofed pagodas.

The saint mausoleums in the present Xiaxiyuan Lanzhou, Beishangen Linxia and Xiheba Hami are taken as belonging to the west courtyard faction, but actually they have no tight relationship each other as the former three mausoleums have. It was said that the east courtyard faction removed the bones of the first and second generation leaders to Wuxingping Daotang's mausoleums when they changed their center to the mountain area. However, the adherents of the west courtyard faction still take the mausoleum in Xiaxiyuan as the most important center to make religious sacrifices and undertake routine ceremonies. (Table 1)

---

[4] Since there is no statistic data of the population existing now, I use the number got in several interviews to concerning members of the order. The exact number of the order's believers remains a problem to be dealt with in the coming researches.

Table 1: List of Lingmingtang's Saint Mausoleums*

Fraction	Name	Place	Burier	Establish Time
The East Courtyard	Wuxingping Daotang Gongbei	Wuxingping, Lanzhou City	Ma Lingming Shan Zijiu	1984
	Hami Fentang Gongbei	Huochezhan, Hami City, Xinjiang	Kao Futang	1920s?
	Guyuan Fentang Gongbei	Sanying, Guyuan Ningxia	Ma Renpu	1996
The West Courtyard	Xiaxiyuan Xiyuan Gongbei	Xiaxiyuan Street, Lanzhou City	The old headquarter	1915
	Hami Xiheba Gongbei	Xiheba Street, Hami City, Xinjiang	Sha Baoqing	1950?
	Linxia Beishangen Gongbei	Beishangen, Linxia City, Gangsu	Ma Hasan	1990?

**Sources: Field interviews to the concerning members of the order. Still there are some suspect points have to be made clear in the coming research, for instance the establish times of some mausoleums.*

Theological Significances of the Saints and Mausoleums

Here, I have to take a space to make clear the theological reasons of the saint worship of the Sufi order Lingmingting. According to a mosque preacher of Guyuan branch, Ma Ximing, to whom I made several interviews during 2000-2004, the Prophet Muhammad once got two bunches of sacred rays from Allah, the only God. One of the rays he got had already been sent to Muslims as the teachings of the Islamic legal system *shari'a* (教) included in Quranic sentences and Sunna traditions, while the other sacred ray by the God sent only to those saint disciples who had special ability to catch it and understand its meaning. Since the second ray contains the more important messages about being Muslims and going on Islamic way, the *tariqa* (道), Muslims have to learn it following those saint disciples.

The preacher talked to me also about the qualification of the saint disciples. The founder of Lingmingtang, Ma Lingming, was a Sufi saint, who created the religious teaching of the order by combining the religious teaching of three origins: the Sufi order Qadiriyya, Khufiya, and Bab, an Iranian Islamic sect. His successors and the successors' students can also be such great man. They first have to learn hard from a great Sufi teacher, and then get religious attestation (usually some religious scriptures) for undertaking missionary activities (a research source tells us also that Ma Lingming once learned Qadiriyya from a India born Sufi missioner called Daxiangbaba when he was 25 years old, and he learned Khufiya from an Arab born Sufi missioner called Salim when he was 33, and later got influences from the religious teaching of the Bab sect [Ma Tong 2000: 98-99]).[5]

Though these events of religious learning can hardly be taken as historical facts, they tell us about the theological significance of the saints, and the reason of the saint worship among the believers of the order. That is, those great religious leaders of the order are special persons, who have the intelligent power to understand the messages from the Prophet and play the role of religious mediator between ordinary Muslims and

[5] See also my recent paper on the order's history, organization and theological traditions (Wang 2009).

the God. They have a kind of mystic ability to telepath with their predecessors, just as in the way of Sufi Uways tradition (the mystic conduction to communicate with the souls of late Sufi leaders). Such ability and nature of the Sufi leaders provide believers not only with a lot of miracle happenings, which can raise the possibility of personal salvation, but also the legitimacy for the religious teachings of the order. It can be said that the existence of Sufi leaders, the saints, is a theological base for the existence of the order itself and its religious traditions.

The saint mausoleums of the order have a similar theological significance. For example, the east courtyard faction of the order has three centers (see Table 1), Wuxingping headquarter, Guyuan and Hami branches, and several dozens of mosques scattered in the central and northwest parts of China as local bases for religious activities. The mosques are the places to observe ordinary prayers and religious routines, where mosque preachers teach ordinary believers to learn and obey Islamic disciplines provided by Islamic legal regulations. In contrast, the three religious centers are taken as *daotang* or *fentang* which have the meaning of temple or shrine. They are religious combinations containing saint mausoleums, prayer halls, classrooms and dormitories. Other than observing religious routines, the key characteristics of the centers are providing believers with a sacred circumstance and the opportunities of undertaking Sufi meditation and communication with the souls of the late saints.

The disciples of the leaders have to stay there for many years to receive Sufi training until becoming mosque teachers, religious representatives, *rayyis*, to local branches, and even the successors of the leaders. As a rule of the order, they should not marry and have family all life, but concentrate on religious routines in day times and Sufi rituals at saint mausoleums at night. For them, their ritual performances and ability of making spiritual exchanges with the souls of the saints are social facts to evaluate their learning and working results. Therefore, the Sufi meditation and mystic practices at saint mausoleums are the paths to their success. However, for ordinary believers, the saint mausoleums are the sources of numerous religious miracles, the evidences of the religious legitimacy of the order, the sacred places to comfort the souls of their saints, and therefore worth to worship.

Socio-cultural Functions of the Saint Mausoleums

The saint mausoleums of the order are firstly religious centers, providing circumstances and necessary conditions for ritual activities and mystic meditation. For example, the Wuxingping Daotang in Lanzhou is composed of three main parts: a square surrounded by high walls used for undertaking religious gatherings and ritual activities, a large courtyard with a huge praying hall, classrooms and dormitories, a smaller courtyard in which the mausoleums of the first and second generation located. The courtyard with the saint mausoleums is the core part of the center, since all important ritual activities should be taken or completed with mystic prayers at tomb sites. Different from mosques whose functions are limited for only routine prayers, religious centers with the saint mausoleums are places free to visit and stay for various religious reasons. In day times, many believers come to visit the center for making prayers to the buriers at the purpose of getting help in achieving good fortunes or dealing with deceases. Some people may be there for only a moment to pray, but other people may stay there for some days making communication with the saints. At night, the order leader, his students, mosque preachers will undertake religious rituals and meditation at tomb sites.

Secondly, the saint mausoleums are taken as ideal places for educating young people and providing life supports to elders without family, orphans and handicapped people. The economic supports of the mausoleums are partly based on the donation of the order's believers, but in return, the religious centers with the mausoleums are shelters for their believers. For example, Wuxingping Daotang has a management system which makes the sacred place almost economically self dependent. Other than the maintenance of the mausoleums and surrounding courtyards, its management committee runs farmlands to cultivate vegetables and flowers, raise cows, sheep, fowls and plant trees. Many believers coming from local places may stay there for a permanent period, from several months till a year, working voluntarily in groups to serve the different purposes of farming. Some young people are sent there by their parents for getting ethic and religious education, also elders without children, handicapped without help come to live there both offering their own contributions to the construction of the mausoleums and getting life supports.

Finally, the mausoleums of the order are becoming sightseeing spots and therefore the resource of local traveling enterprise. Since the mausoleums attract more and more visitors from inside and outside of China, especially those religious centers such as Wuxingping Daotang, Hami and Guyuan branches, with luxuriously constructed tomb sites and beautifully decorated Chinese-styled courtyards, provide visitors with a kind of landscape combining Sufi spirit of religious meditation and the beauty of Chinese geomancy together. Since Lingmingtang is taken as a good model in supporting the ethno-religious policy of the state, its construction plan of the saint mausoleums got approved by local governments. In the end of April 2005, a celebration ceremony of the 90th anniversaries of the order was held at Wuxingping Daotang, and I was fortunately invited to attend the ceremony and stayed there for two days. I saw more than ten thousands of believers coming from local places, Hui, Dongxiang and even some Uyghurs from Xinjiang, undertook prayers in the courtyards and observe the religious rituals at the mausoleum. In addition to that, many lay visitors, Muslims as well as non-Muslims came to see the scene, and even government officials came to attend the ceremony and made speech to praise the order's contribution to the peace and consolidation of the ethno-religious causes of the country.

Conclusion

By this short paper, I mean to report on the general conditions of the saint mausoleums of the Sufi order Lingmingtang, about their theological significances and socio-cultural functions. These mausoleums represent a typical mode of the saint worship existing among mainly Chinese-Mongolian speaking Muslims, which are different from the ones in the Turkic and Indo-European speaking Muslims in China. No doubt, the research of the Muslim worship of the saints and their mausoleums forms a very important realm of academic studies which can provide deep insights to the essence and diversity of the Islamic culture and Muslim societies in China.

References

Dawut, Rahile 2001. *Uyghur Mazarliri* [The Uyghur Mazars], Urumqi: Shinjang Khäliq Näshiriyati.

Gladney, Dru C. 1991. *Muslim Chinese: Ethnic Nationalism in the People's Republic*. Cambridge (Massachusetts) and London: published by Council on East Asian Studies and distributed by Harvard University Press.

Hamada Masami 1978. "Islamic Saints and Their Mausoleums" in *Acta Asiatica*, No. 34: 79-98.

Ma Pinyan 马品彦 1987. "Nanjiang de maza he maza chaobai" 南疆麻扎和麻扎朝拜 [Mazar and Mazar pilgrimage in Southern Xinjiang] in *Zhongguo Yisilanjiao Yanjiu.* Xining; Qinghai Renmin Chubanshe.

Ma Qiang 马强 2001. "Lingmingtan gongbei de jueqi" 灵明堂拱北的崛起 [The Rise of the mausoleum of Lingmingtan] in *Shijie Zongjiao Wenhua* 2001/4: 22.

Ma Tong 马通 1983. *Zhongguo Yisilan jiaopai menhuan zhidu shi* 中国伊斯兰教派门宦制度史 [History of jiaopai and menhuan in Chinese Islam], Yinchuan: Ningxia Renmin Chubanshe.

Shinmen Yasushi, Sanada Yasushi and Wang Jianxin 新免康, 真田安, 王建新 2002. *Shinkyō Uiguru no bazāru to mazāru* 新疆ウイグルのバザールとマザール [Baazars and Mazars in Xinjiang Uyghur] (*Studia Culturae Islamicae* No.70), Tokyo: Research Institute for Languages and Cultures of Asia and Africa, Tokyo University of Foreign Studies.

Wang Jianxin 1996. "Religious Legitimation in the Healing Practice of an Uyghur Preacher in Rural Turpan" in *Journal of Asian and African Studies*, No. 52: 35-55.

——— 2004a. *Uyghur Education and Social Order: The Role of Islamic Leadership in the Turpan Basin* (*Studia Culturae Islamicae* No.76), Tokyo: Research Institute for Languages and Cultures of Asia and Africa

——— 王建新 2004b. "Chūgoku Isuramu no shinzoku to chi'iki shakai; Reimeidō Kogen bundō no jirei wo chūshin ni" 中国イスラムの親族と地域社会—霊明堂固原分堂の事例を中心に— [Kinships and Regional Society of Chinese Islam: Centering on the case of Guyuan subbranch of Linmingtang], in *Gengo, Bunka, Komyunikēsyon* 32: 21-43.

——— 王建新 2009. "Reimeidō ni okeru shūkyō kyōgi no shisō teki keihu" 霊明堂における宗教教義の思想的系譜 [Ideological Lineage of the Religious Doctrine of Linmingtang], in *Chūgoku no Isramu shisō to bunka.* Tokyo: Bensei Shuppan, 106-122

Xinjiang Shehui Kexueyuan Zongjiao Yanjiusuo 新疆社会科学院宗教研究所 1989. *Zhongguo Zonngjiao* 中国宗教 [Religions in China]. Urumqi: Xinjiang Renmin Chubanshe.

Yang, Wenjun 杨文炯 2007. "Yi mai san xian yu he er bu dong: Gan Ning Qing diqu Yisilanjiao 'gongbei' fuhao de renleixue jiedu" 一脉三弦与和而不同-甘宁青地区伊斯兰教"拱北"符号的人类学解读 [Three Flows from One Route and Plurality in Harmony: An Anthropological Study on the Symbols of Islamic Saint Mausoleums in Gansu, Qinghai and Ningxia] in Wang Jianxin and Liu Zhaorui 王建新、刘昭瑞(eds.) *Diyu shehui yu xinyang xisu: Liuzu tianye de renleixue yanjiu.*地域社会与信仰习俗-立足田野的人类学研究 [Local Societies and Folk Beliefs: Anthropological Studies Based on Field Investigations] Guangzhou: Zhongshan Daxue Chubanshe, 154-174.

Zhang, Chengzhi (張承志著・梅村坦編訳) 1993. *Junkyō no chūgoku isuramu: Shinpi shugi kyōdan jahurīya no rekishi.* 殉教の中国イスラム－神秘主義教団ジャフリーヤの歴史 [Martyred Islam in China: A History of the Sufi Order Jahriya]. Tokyo: Akishobō.

Pilgrimages to Mazars in Contemporary Kazakhstan

The Processes of Revivalism and Innovation

Aitzhan NURMANOVA

The Formulation of Problem

After receiving independency (in 1991) five republics of the Central Asia announced themselves as secular states, the freedom of religion, toleration, inter-confessional concord and cooperation were guaranteed.

The Kazakh clergy became separated from the Central Asian Muslim Religious Board (SADUM, 1943-1992), and in 1991 it was founded the Independent Muslims' Board of Kazakhstan (DUMK).

Complicated processes of shaping Muslim community started under conditions of influence from the side of the Muslims Board of Kazakhstan as well as from that of unofficial Islamic groups. New concept of "pure or true Islam" was born, and Muslim missionaries from Turkey, Saudi Arabia, Pakistan and other Muslim countries began energetic re-Islamization activity. Different Muslim movements such as Tablighi Jama'at, al-Takfir wa'l-Hijra and others are very active in recruiting and missionary work.

Sufi brotherhoods like Yasawiya, Naqshbandiya became active too, they are considered as "local" Islam asserting that Kazakh ancestors were followers of certain *tariqa*, each Kazakh tribe had its *pir* and mainly practiced Sufism.

If the fundamentalists deny all traditional and announce local Muslims' rituals and ceremonies, formed during several centuries out the Islamic law, in the contrary the "Local" Party declares and treats them as "Wahhabis".

In mass media hard discussions are taking place on the subject of these movements and trends - which of them is "right" or "not right", about rules of prayer, ablution, appearance, clothing, other ritual ceremonies.

And in this background as counterbalance to new trends "Folk" Islam is strengthening, shaped in the cult of holy mazars and pilgrimage to these places. Number of mazars and cult places are increasing each year. Special groups or unions are founded which are involved in organization of pilgrimage, creating special rites and instructions for *ziyarat*, sacrifice and recovery, in finding and construction of new mazars, announcement or canonization of previously famous public figures and their graves (*batïrs*, poets, political and cultural men), new "holy persons" or "new prophets" are appearing. "People's" Islam does not require from its followers either knowledge of

Arabic language, or five times prayer, or special forms of clothing. They do their work fully in Kazakh, everything is explained at place and there isn't any particular difficulties – this is the main reason for most of its followers to join them.

At present time when Islam has got a political slant and "pure" Islam declares saints and holy places "without the law", pilgrimage to holy places is spread as "people's" Islam and is very popular among population. That's why problems of pseudo-religious activities realization require objective assessment in the example of non-traditional Muslim movements and trends

Material's Outline

One of such new movements in the religious life of Kazakhstan is *ziyarat* – pilgrimage, organized by «Ata Zholï» (Ansector's path). «Ata Zholï» started its activity in February 1997.

Founder

Its founder is Qïdïrali Tarïbayev, called by holy ancestors (or called himself) as "Aq ul" (White or pure, saint sun). Sometimes he is called as "Prophet", if Muhammad is Allah's Prophet, Qïdïrali Tarïbayev is Arwahs' Prophet.[1]

At the end of 1996 he fell hard sick and dreamt saint old men "Bes Ata" (Five ancestors) – Tuktibay, Suyinbay, Sarïbay, Zhambïl and Qaynazar. They told him to go to holy places and pass the night in Arïstan-Bab, there they came to his dreams again and gave "ayan" to take a white flag into his hands and lead his nation to the ancestors' path. He was advises that after nine years of ordeal he would get a happiness of two worlds, the whole world would worship Kazakhs' ancestors (Take a White Flag and start a White Path, serve to Allah and ancestors' Arwahs. Nine years long we will be giving you hard ordeals, and then you will get a satisfaction in both worlds. All people in the world will worship Kazakh Arwahs). Nine years he divides to 5 stages: 3 years of hesitations, doubts; after 3 years believing ancestors' power; after 5 years everything in his life goes up and improves; after 7 years getting what is desired, praising Allah; after 9 years getting happiness in both worlds.[2]

Legitimating

«Ata Zholï» followers claim that Nostradamus himself predicted Aq Ul's birth.[3]

In 1999 Aq Ul visited the mountain Qazïghurt with 500 people and hoisted the White Flag of Aysha-Bibi.

---

[1] "Ata Zholï", Where is leading "Aq Orda". "Zhas Alash" newspaper, No. 45 (15295), dd. June 05, 2008.

[2] Interview with head of Ata Zholï – Mr. K. Tarïbayev, by Mr. O Tazhiqululy. "Ata Zholï" magazine, No. 3, dd. February, 2006.

[3] *Ibid.*

Aq Ul has a stamp on his right palm and he opens heart by blowing person's back in frond of heart. Then women become "aqqu" and men – "sunqar". Only after this ritual they can transfer saints' epistle – "bata" through their hearts. They are transmitters between the world of dead ancestors and alive "pende".

After "heart opening" ceremony "aqqus" and "sunqars" are sent to open new branches in regions not enveloped by "Ata Zholï" members, it can be other regions of Kazakhstan. They are given an official order issued by local administration. E.g. Order No. 94-P dd. March 13, 2007 issued in Ust-Kamenogorsk about opening and appointment of supervisor of "Information center of religious and moral revival and pilgrimage "Ata Zholï" named after Tolebi Ata" in Petropavlovsk city (copy of the Order is available). This task is considered as "sïnaq" – ordeal.

Purpose of «Ata Zholï» is first of all, to bring all Kazakhs to the way of faith, i.e. open them doors of «Ata Zholï», break them of alien, external rites. Returning lost people influenced by alien religions to this religion, fighting with them is a priority.

- To teach people rules of pilgrimage to ancestors' graves;
- To ask all the best for their state, our families by making sacrifice;
- To educate people about their ancestors;
- To put monuments over graves of forgotten ancestors;
- To send pilgrims to Mecca from «Ata Zholï»;
- To help poor families;
- To break of people from alcohol, smoking and drugs;
- To call to god-fearing – "Imandïlïq";
- To pray for 21 ancestors: 7 – from father's side, 7 – from mother's side and 7 – from wife's ancestors.
- To purify Kazakh from filth.

The main idea is to visit graves of Arïstan-Bab, Qoja Ahmed Yasawi, Baydibek-Baba, Domalaq-Ana, Aysha-Bibi and others and get "bata".[4]

With the course of time and in accordance with priorities of the Republic of Kazakhstan issued by the President, «Ata Zholï» paraphrased its purposes, e.g. in temporary rules "About informational center of religious and moral revival and pilgrimage "Ata Zholï" they declare their purposes as follows:

- Revival, development and strengthening of religious and moral values;
- Succession of traditional connections with moral and historical past, present and future;
- Development and strengthening of patriotic sense;
- Worshiping and increasing number of ancestors' traditions;

[4] Interview with chief imam of «Ata Zholï» community Mr. Kozhahmet-Qazhi Dosïmbayev and one of heads Mr. Talghat Kayranbekov, by Mr. O. Tajikulï. «Ata Zholï» magazine, No. 1, dd. July 2005.

- Careful and respective approach to parents, elder people, young generation, motherland and environment;
- Propagation of healthy mode of life among population of the Republic of Kazakhstan;
- Confrontation to distribution of immorality, religious extremism and terrorism.

Also they declare that «Ata Zholï» neither follow any political purposes, nor finance activity of political parties, professional unions and other organizations with political aims. All activity of the organization is carried out on a voluntary basis, while pilgrimage to holy and historical places is carried out with the means received from voluntary contributions and sacrifices of pilgrims. Transportation, catering and accommodation during pilgrimage are laid on representatives and supervisors of «Ata Zholï».

From 2005 the magazine "Ata Zholï" took a start, special brochures named as "Introduction to Ata Zholï (alphabet)", "Start your way from Arïstan-Bab ...", route books, posters with portraits of saint men and "Ata Zholï" founder are published.

Joining the Way

A person who is joining "Ata Zholï" is to visit "orda" fist and during "shïraq" he receives a "bata".

Before entering "orda" it is necessary to do ablution (*taharat*), and while entering one is to welcome by putting his hand to heart and bowing his head to "Bes Ata" – portraits of them are hanging in front of the door, above is Aysha-Bibi's portrait and posters representing Arïstan-Bab's and Yassawi's *mazars* – this is a duty – "parïz".

In the corner there is Holy book Coran, near is "*sadaqa*" – money. It is required to pronounce or read words written on a white paper hanging on the nearest wall, these are transcriptions of formulations of *tawhid, kalima*.

"Shïraq" is a special candle made of wool thread and fat, when it is lighted; it purifies and cures souls and bodies of followers.

Then Qur'an is read, at the end names of all *arwahs* are enumerated. Only afterwards "aqqu" or "sunqar" calls on soul of *arwahs*. With putting his hand to heart he calls a name of ancestor who will be speaking through him. Not only distant ancestors but recently dead public figures, politicians, artists, singers etc. may come to calling. When *arwah* (through "aqqu" or "sunqar") calls his name, a person sitting there must stand, greet and listen to his "bata" on his feet. And then he must act accordingly to what was said in "bata", which can describe events-symbols (dreams, diseases and recovery, past and future), give special task how to bring definite people to his community, visit a definite grave, make a sacrifice etc.

And he is to make small pilgrimage to local "five or seven ancestors".

After doing it, in "bata" or in "ayan" a way to big pilgrimage is opened, i.e. to the south of Kazakhstan, there are four main routes: Ukkasha-Ata, Baydibek-Baba,

Qara-Bura-Ata, Aq-Bura-Ata. All routes start from visiting and passing night in Arïstan-Bab, next morning visiting "Besik-Tau", further is Yasawi's *mazar* and from this point *keruens* are divided by their routes.

Stop in "Keruen-sarays" or "Orda". Buses usually come to keruen-saray at 10 or 11 p.m., then ablution (*taharat*) and dinner take place. About 1 a.m. "bata" ritual starts and this is for 2.5 or 3 hours long at least. Several "aqqus" or "sunqars" in turn give "bata" from the names of *arwahs*. All 40 or 50 men and women pass the night in one room; this is not more than 2-3 hours of sleep. At 5 a.m. keruen continues its trip. At daytime bus twice stops for breakfast and lunch in special canteens.

In Shïmkent keruen-saray before Arïstan-Bab young people offer their services to shoot video. If shooting is ordered by not less than 10 people, they follow the bus in their own cars and shoot video of pilgrimage in full (it costs 4 000 tenge from each person).

Ambitions

In future the same number of people will be visiting Arïstan-Bab as Mecca, descendants of Kazakh saints must carry Way of Truth to the whole mankind. "Ordas" of "Ata Zholï" have been already opened abroad, and citizens of Austria, Germany, Bulgaria, Cyprus, France and Russia, even Ethiopia have been in pilgrimage here.

Routes

In Shïmkent the routes lead to Ibrahim-Ata, Qarashash-Ana, Mariyam-Ana, Abdulaziz-Bab, Essenqoja-Ata, Miralï-Ata and Zhanïs-Ata.

In Taldïqorgan it is "Bes-Ata": Yeskeldi-Bi, Balpïq-Bi, Aytu-Bi, Qabïlissa-Ata, Zholbarïs-Ata.

In Qustanay: Baraq-Ata, Shoqay-Aulie, Ïbïray Altïnsarin, Zhazï-Bi, Yesbol-Ata.

Currently new routes are being developed. Every year visited are in July graves of Qarasay and Aghïntay *batïrs* in North Kazakhstan, in August cave of Qonïr-Aulie in Eastern Kazakhstan, also Abay Qunanbayev's, Shakarim's, Kengirbay-Bi's graves and others as well. If in "bata" visiting Beket-Aulie is given as a task, one goes to Western Kazakhstan. Keruen path to Ulïtau is being opened.

Rites

At the food of Qazïghurt three saint springs are visited and praying is made. Each spring has its own curative features. After slaking thirst, everyone come to two crags standing separately called "Adam" and "Eve". Two "breathing stones" stand very close to each other between them is a narrow long passage. It is a kind of ordeal-passing between the crags. If a person has a pure soul and mind, in spite of his constitution he can go through the passage without any difficulty, while sinner even being the thinnest person can stick between the stones – either the stones hold them or a snake is met.

Ukkasha-Ata is a legendary associate of the Prophet Muhammad. He distributed Islam and neither arrow nor saber could take him, his force was growing from day to day. He lived in the suburbs of Yasï. His enemies even sent a witch to his wife. But he had only one weak spot – neck. Once in the morning during praying his enemies cut his head, it rolled a while and fell through the earth. Further his head was found in Mecca. His body was buried in 40 kilometers from Turkestan in the Qaratau Mountains. In the place where his head fell a well appeared. Here pilgrimages are checked for purity of their minds. Pilgrims take saint water from his well, but there were cases when instead of water Ukkasha-Ata put into the bucket stones, rings, flowers, some of them received nothing.

Who Joins Them?

Worsening of living standards and crash of common ideological system were reasons for arising of sense of lost. People are in hard social stress and this is no wonder that under these conditions they are looking for some guidance, definiteness and believe in better future and they find consolation in religion. Most of people show passive and traditionalistic approach to Islam and do not want to study it deeply, considering it as a duty of religious people and search for easy ways of "being Muslim". At this stage pseudo-Islamic organizations like "Ata Zholï" come to the forefront, offering the way to be pure Muslim without fulfilling five obligatory rules of Islam. Reading definite *suras* while visiting *mazars* is enough, but if you can you should pray five times a day, *taharat* is obligatory. Mecca pilgrimage can be replaced by *ziyarat* to holy places. Though several people are sent to Hajj every year for the means of the organization.

Influence on People's Mind

Members of the "Ata Zholï" group attract people by several means:

1) by persuasions – newcomer start to persuade his relatives, friends and acquaintances to join saying that after "opening the way" and visiting "Shïraq", "Bes-Ata" and big *ziyarat*, all their problems and diseases will go away and they will go up in the world.

2) by trick – in the street they can come close to any person and say: "I see that you have a special gift, and to reveal this gift you must come to us, we will open your heart.

3) by intimidation – if they learn that in some family there is a hard sick person or somebody has recently died, they come or send a letter summoning people to join "Ata Zholï", otherwise "their way will be closed and they will be punished by "arwahs".

4) Also, newcomers in "Ata Zholï" are given "sïnaq" (ordeal), a task to bring a definite number of people to "orda" – the more, the higher his status will be. By what means he will bring people does not matter.

5) When a person passes some stages in the "Ata Zholï" structure, he is given a special task – "amanat", which he is to fulfill anyway, e.g. if there is a person holding good position among his acquaintances or relatives, it is asked to bring this very person

to "Ata Zholï". Otherwise his status will be lowered.

As it was told before, mainly people who experienced social stress join such organizations. Some of them find themselves, become leaders – in our case "aqqu" or "sunqar", but some of them become ascertained in their groundlessness and retire into themselves. There are several cases ended with suicide.[5]

What People Think about Them?

There are two different opinions:

1) Good. People joint "Ata Zholï" give up smoking, drinking, live a healthy mode of life, study history of places, tell religious stories about saints, batïrs fighting for independency of Motherland.

2) Bad. By joining "Ata Zholï" followers are seldom at their own homes, too much time spending to serve for the organization and too much money contributing for is purposes. They agitate their relatives, friends and acquaintances to join "Ata Zholï" otherwise breaking off any relations with them.

Polemics with the Muslims' Board of Kazakhstan, with Salafis

In mass media disputes about competence of "Ata Zholï" are taking place. If the Muslims' Board of Kazakhstan declares that "Ata Zholï" convicts to Islamic law, call it "shirk" by declaring *ayats* from *suras*, e.g. *sura* A'raf – ayats 6-17, Isra – ayats 22-23, Qaf – ayat 16, Fatr – *ayat* 14, Rum – *ayat* 52, etc. "Ata Zholï" says that our ancestors have been always applying for the help of arwahs while protecting motherland, in fights and curing different diseases. They say that the Prophet himself told that visiting graves is a reminder about that world and even in Qur'an in 21 *suras* arwahs are told about.[6]

Financial Issues

In mass media financial activity of the organization is being discussed a lot even by "Ata Zholï" followers, as pilgrims give 20 000 tenge for *ziyarat* (it is from Almatï, accordingly from regions amounts twice or three times more are collected), this amount contains cost of sacrifice (1 sheep for 14 000 tenge) and transport fee. Also 2 000 tenge is collected for stops in keruen-sarays and for using plates and dishes. Moreover, each pilgrim should have at least 10 000 tenge for catering. This is all not including purchase of piece of white cloth called "aqtïq" which are bound to or cover stones over graves in mazars and voluntary charity, besides each pilgrim is to take sweets for having tea – dried apricots, raisins, cakes, sweets etc. by 1 kilo each. In general, pilgrimage costs 35 000 – 40 000 tenge. For those coming from regions it is about 65 000 – 70 000 tenge. There were cases when for going to pilgrimage people sold their last cow, took a bank

---

[5] What way is "Ata Zholï" worshipping *arwahs*. "Qostanay tangï" newspaper, No.19-20, dd. February 15, 2008.

[6] Ancestors are giving "Bata". "Ata Zholï" magazine, No. 1, 2005.

loan or debt from relatives.

Here we need to mention that each *keruen* contain 40-45 pilgrims, among them 10-12 are "aqqu" or "sunqars", it means that pilgrimage is paid by about 33. For the 5 days of *ziyarat* only 3 sheep is knifed, so cost of other 30 sheep are gone to net profit.

There were some pilgrims who just asked about financial side of pilgrimage, but they were frightened and advised that it is a big sin to ask about it, it means that he does not believe in arwahs and his pilgrimage will not be reckoned and "arwahs" will give him negative "Bata" and his way will be closed. Some answered that this money is given for construction and improvement of mazars, new mosques are built, but in fact no construction is erected with the aid of "Aq Zhol". However there are keruen-sarays and canteens specially built for pilgrim servicing but they are used to bring rather good income by themselves.

Specialization of Saints, Duties

"Ata Zholï" members do medicinal activity, for this purpose during "shïraq" they call "arwahs" and with their help cure different diseases. E.g. for heart diseases they summon Suyinbay ata's spirit, for osteopathic diseases – Zhambïl Zhabayev's spirit and so on, each "arwah" has its own "specialization".

Also during *ziyarat* they hold a ceremony of "Alastau" – "genie ousting". At the food of Tuktibay-Ata's grave they lay and roll him forth and back on the ground, it is considered that the dead's ashes purifies a person from filth. In the "Orda" they hold "Alastau" with the help of fire – "shïraq", also a rite of "dem salu" – "giving breath" is held – "aqqu" or "sunqar" can cure by their "saint" breathing.

Mass Media

In republic, regional and district mass media there are a lot of publications devoted to "Ata Zholï" activity. Rites and methods of this organization are described in detail, heads of the Muslims' Board of Kazakhstan; scientists who study religions, psychologists are interviewed. In internet also discussions for and against such organizations are held, articles are published.

But this information is not available for the most part of perspective followers of "Ata Zholï" as currently the official press is rarely subscribed by common people in villages, while "Ata Zholï" penetrates to the most distant places with their ideas.

Conclusion

In general, on the one hand, "Ata Zholï" is similar to the institute "Otin" in Uzbekistan; on the other hand, it's a kind of net marketing.

Popularity of "Ata Zholï" among population can be explained, first of all, by the fact that cult of holy places and *ziyarat* plays an important role in the Kazakh's social life and even in Soviet regime *ziyarat* existed as a tourist trip to historical places.

Secondly, the population needs a faith, worshipping. Representatives of official religion like imams of the Muslims' Board of Kazakhstan are not able to meet demands of population. E.g. most of religious Kazakhs raise an objection to declaration of their most reverenced ceremonies, e.g. funeral, as something incorrect and replacing them with more orthodox rites. Or they object for the statement that *ziyarat* to graves of their ancestors is without the Islam law too.

Here appear people who propagate "traditional or local" Islam, which reflects all national and local preferences of population, rites are easier and adapted to local demands, no need to pray five times a day, and instead of Hajj to Mecca, several trips to Turkestan are enough. Of course, they will be very popular.

At present, "Ata Zholï" has its branches all over Kazakhstan, in every oblast and regional centers, but not all of them are registered and houses are open as "Orda" attracting more and more people. There are branches in Omsk and Orenburg oblasts of the Russian Federation, pilgrims from these places also come to *ziyarat*.

Notwithstanding to counter-propagation in mass media had explanatory works in mosques, "Ata Zholï" has already taken its place in religious life of Kazakhstan. They are developing new routes, but in many places, especially in the South Kazakhstan they have a big net with material basis (keruen-sarays, canteens, buses, personnel, shïraqshï). Currently they are in the process of setting ritual ceremonies for visiting definite mazars, but not all of them have shaped in dogmas. Hierarchy structure of the organization is being set too, statuses are under consideration.

I think in future their activity will be more closed and they will be accepting only proved and checked people. All the more, keruen-sarays are built in the outskirts of villages with high inaccessible fences.

The Glossary of Special Terms Used by "Ata Zholï"

amanat a duty, special task, e.g. to build *mazar* to a definite ancestor or to bring to the way of truth "Ata Zholï" "this or that village people", a neighbor, brother, husband etc.

aqtïq each pilgrim must leave in saint's grave "aqtïq" – a piece of white cloth of 1 or 2 meters, it is defined at first night in "Bata" how many meters are to be left to which saint. A list is made and "Aqqus" and "Sunqars" take a control over fulfillment of the rite. A pilgrim is to wear one "aqtïq" on his neck all the way of pilgrimage.

arbakesh a pilgrimage bus driver.

keruen a bus going in the route the pilgrimage.

keruen-basï a senior "aqqu" or "sunqar" leading *ziyarat*-pilgrimage.

keruen-saray a special guest house located in the route of pilgrimage, they are usually kept by people – followers of "Ata Zholï" living in the pilgrimage way. This duty is sent by *arwahs* as an ordeal – "sïnaq". They must keep these houses and canteens for pilgrims 3, 5, 7 or 9 years subject to the "bata" sent. Members of "Ata Zholï" are employed for servicing as well. "keruen-saray" accepting pilgrims are built specially for this purpose - with the assistance of the central administration of "Ata Zholï" a land plot is bought, usually in the outskirts of settlements in order not to draw unwanted attention, a big house is built and enclosed by high fence, and its yard can hold up to 20 buses. House has 7, 9 or more large rooms for 40-45 pilgrims (one *keruen*). A canteen, bath-house and shower-rooms, water closets, spaces for doing *taharat* are obligatory. In the season of pilgrimage these "keruen-saray" can accept 20 and more buses a night (each bus can seat 20-25 pilgrims in average).

Nine years' ordeal after receiving "bata" in a big *ziyarat*, a person enters a "nine years' ordeal". This means that he must neither use foul language, nor offend and cheat anyone, nor drink alcohol and smoke, but must give alms, devote Quran to saint ancestors, cook seven flat cakes and distribute them. Only then he can get happiness of both worlds, i.e. in his life everything will be ok and after death he will go to heaven. These nine years he can spend lying at home, but better to help others to come to the way of truth "Ata Zholï".

orda a special holy place, considered as a home of saints "arwahs" (usually a room in the house) where "aqqu" or "sunqar" conducts a ceremony of "shïraq-lighting" and gives "Bata", there newcomers are taught to do *taharat*/ablution and pronounce kalmia. Each "aqqu" and "sunqar" must have its own "orda", each "orda" is given a name of a saint, e.g. "Arïstan-Bab's Orda", "Suyinbay-Ata's Orda" etc.

qaralïq danger, this can be somebody's damnation or evil eye thus closed the way.

sarbaz assistants of "aqqus" and "sunqars", mainly their husbands or wives.

shïmïldïq (curtain) if during "bata" this word is met, it means that this is warning for caution, e.g. "one day shïmïldïq" means one day a person should be very careful and even not go out of home.

shïraq, shïraq lighting a ceremony held in "Ordas" for purifying and receiving arwah's "bata". "shïraq" is lighted only after Quran is read for the soul of *arwahs*. Also it purifies houses, cars, people, for this purpose 1, 3, 7, 21 "shïraqs" are lighted.

zhol ashu way opening, only after making *ziyarat* to holy places a person's way is opened. Only *arwahs* can open the closed way.

Chapter Two

Iranian Elements

A Cultural Layer in Relation to Hazrat-i Ali

A Preliminary Approach to Mazars of "Imams" in Khotan

Ablimit YASIN

Introduction

Xinjiang's Khotan Prefecture possesses one of the region's richest collections of cultural relics and historical places with over one hundred sites, including ancient cities, tombs, Buddhist temples and Islamic buildings.[1] Of all of these, the places in relation to 'Ali and his sons is considered the most sacred and holds a special place in the hearts of the people of Khotan. There are many sacred tombs of "Imams", or saints related to 'Ali and his descendents, found there that are distinct to mazars found in other regions.

Although the historical value of some of those sacred tombs have been officially recognized through recognition as protected cultural sites (文物保护单位) at the county (*nahiyä*) and provincial levels, the fields of archaeology, history and anthropology have produced few studies of the subject.[2]

Khotan's uniqueness in this respect has been noticed and is addressed in several early written works. In the 16th century, the remarkable Moghul historian, Mirza Muhammad Haydar, wrote that there were sites associated with "Imám Zabiha [or Zabija]", "Imám Tayyár"(< Tayrān?), "Imám Jafar Sádik" and "several others of the Companions [of the Prophet]" in Khotan, and declared their "falsehood" to be "evident".[3] In the late 19th and early 20th century, local historian Molla Musa Sayrami also discussed the mazars of Khotan and saw them as suspicious just as Mirza Haydar had.[4] The well-known archeological explorer Aurel Stein also visited the mazars and left behind short accounts of them as well.[5] More recent studies conducted by scholars such as Ma Pinyan and Rahile Dawut have also noted the existence of the tombs of Imams . Ma critically called these tombs "fake mazars (*jia maza*)" vis-à-vis the "genuine"

---

1 Nizamidin Tokhti 2002: 2-3.

2 For example, Imam Zayn al-'Abidin Mazar, Imam Jafar Sadiq Mazar, Imam Aptah Mazar have been appointed as the Historical and Cultural Sites Protected at the County Level (县级文物保护单位), and Imam Musa Kazim Mazar has been appointed as the Historical and Cultural Sites Protected at the Autonomous Regional Level(自治区级文物保护单位).

3 Elias-Ross 1898: 298.

4 Sayrami 1986: 643.

5 Stein 1903: 345-349.

ones located in Middle East.[6]

As Ma correctly insists, the existence of Khotan's Imam mazars runs contrary to commonly accepted facts of the history of the Islamic World. In order to situate aspects of this region's religious culture correctly, however, it is first necessary to approach the sites descriptively, asking questions such as; what Imam-related mazars do exist, and how people maintain their belief in mazars, instead of simply ending the discussion with the assertion that they are all fake.

Thus, in this chapter, I address the fundamental aspects of Imam-related mazars through the results of my own fieldwork as well as descriptions found in earlier accounts. In particular, I organize these mazars into three separate categories: (1) sacred sites related to the "footsteps" (*qadam-jay*) of 'Ali, (2) mazars of the so-called Twelve Imams (*On ikki Imamlar*) revered by local Muslims, (3) mazar of the Imam Mahdi and other 'Ali-related mazars. I provide basic information, describe the condition of beliefs as they exist today, and the legends associated with each site. Finally, I examine the way in which cultural elements appearing in mazars linked to 'Ali characterize the religious culture of the region.[7]

Ali's Footsteps

The history of Islam states that 'Ali died in 661 A.D., and during the following 50 years, Amir Qutayba ibn Muslim (661-750) held the governorship of Khorasan and the eastern regions (705-715). For the first time ever, he established stable Arab control over Mawarannahr and conquered the Central Asian cities of Bukhara, Penjkent and Samarqand. Only 200 years later did Islam reach Kashgar from the Central Asia. Although 'Ali never visited Central Asia or Khotan, there are many mazars dedicated to him throughout in the Central Asia and Xinjiang. For example, tombs said to be 'Ali's are located not only in the city of Najaf in Iraq, but also Afghanistan's Mazar-i Sharif, which takes its name from the reputed resting place of 'Ali located there. The local Afghan population (including Uzbeks, Tajiks and others, the majority of them are Sunnis) believe that 'Ali 's tomb is located there giving rise to the city built around the tomb. The majority of visitors to 'Ali 's mazar in Najaf are Shiite, while those who visit 'Ali 's mazar in Mazar-i-Sharif are primarily Sunni, many of them are Uzbeks. In addition, there are signs of a mazar associated with 'Ali 's horse in Khwarezm in present day Uzbekistan, and the mazar of Shah-i Mardan in Khiwa.[8] In addition, there are two sacred sites located in Khotan region, that although not tombs, mark 'Ali's legendary footsteps (i.e. *qadam-jay*), that may be understood in same context.[9]

---

[6] Ma Pinyan 1993: 570; Rahile Dawut 2001: 15.

[7] I carried out fieldwork in July of 2006 at Imam Asim Mazar in Jiya Village, Lop County, Khotan Prefecture, and in January of 2008 at Imam Äptäh Mazar in Saybagh Village, Imam Äskär Mazar in Tüwet Village, and Yalghuz Oghul Mazar in Urchi Village, all in Qaraqash County of Khotan Prefecture.

[8] Abudulahatov's chapter in this volume also focuses on this matter.

[9] *Ibid*. 124.

The first of these is Mazartagh located in Qaraqash County. Mazartagh ("mazar mountain"), also known to locals as "Red Mountain" or "White Mountain", is located on the west bank of Khotan River, lies from west to east in the south area of Taklimakan desert. The south side of the mountain, which also contains Buddhist artifacts, has a reddish hue while the north side appears white. 45 meters from the south side of the mountain is the mazar known as Mazartagh. According to the local legend, Imam 'Ali had attended a religious service at this location that the marks the place where the Imam prostrated and worshiped and has been preserved until today.[10]

The second *qadam-jay* is the "ancient sacred tree" associated with a legend regarding 'Ali. There is a thousand-year-old plane tree in Chinar Village (*känt*) of Aqsaray Township (*yeza*), Qaraqash County. In Uyghur, the word "chinar" means plane tree and this particular tree is sacred to the local Uyghur population because according to local legend the origin of this tree is related to Imam 'Ali:

> In the past there was a war between the Muslims and Jews in the city of Medina. The Muslim army could not breach the Jews' fortress. Brave Imam 'Ali, a son-in-law of the Prophet, said "I can open the door of the fortress". Many people did not believe what he said, and replied, "if you can uproot the big plane tree next to you, we will let you attack the city, otherwise, don't talk about it any more". Imam 'Ali at once took the tree trunk in his handsand using all his strength, uprooted the tree. He lifted it above his head, broke it into two pieces, and then threw them into the air. One piece landed in Aqtam Village in present day Qaraqash, and survived until it was cut down in 1960; the other half fell in Aqsaray Township and remains to this day.This is the ancient plane tree in Aqsaray Township's Chinar Village.[11]

As we observe similar stories regarding 'Ali's military success in the early Islamic period, this local legend should be seen as a local version of an original.[12]

On August 5, 2001 and again on January 28, 2007 I visited Aqsaray Township to examine this sacred tree. Locals told me that before 1950, this plane tree had been sacred to the local people, but with the changes in politics, the economy and culture, traditional practices related to the tree have been in constant flux. Since 2000, the garden where it is located has been rented by businessman and has become a tourist spot because of the plane tree. Now people rarely come to the tree to pray and 10 RMB is charged just to see it.

The Twelve Imams in Khotan

It is said that 'Twelve Imams' (*Ithna-'ashariyyah*) are the descendants of the Khalifa 'Ali and Fatimah, the daughter of the Prophet Muhammad, and starting from the second generation, they are all descendants of Imam Husayn. In Khotan, however, there are different opinions regarding the order and number of Imams. Most of the differences are based on local mazar legends and the explanations given to visitors to mazars.

---

[10] Memetimin Qurban 2006: 46.

[11] Interview of local people of Aqsaray township, in January 2007.

[12] Muhammad Husayn Haykal 2003: 509.

Table: The Khotan Twelve Imams and the Mazar

	Name	Location of the Mazar
1	Hasan and Husayn	
2	Zayn al-'Abidin	Iza bagh Village, Baghchi Township, Khotan County, 15 kilometers away from the county town.
3	Muhammad Baqir	
4	Jafar Sadiq	Qapaq Asqan Villagein Niya Township, Niya County, 90 kilometers away from the county town
5	Musa Kazim[13]	Aznebazar Village in Buzaq Township, Khotan County, 8 kilometers away from the county town.
6	Ali Riza	
7	Muhammad Taqi	Buya Mazar Village, Buya Township, Lop County, 3 kilometers away from the county town
8	Muhammad Naqi	
9	Hasan Eskeri[14]	Imam Eskeri Village, Yengiyer Township, Qaraqash County, 20 kilometers away from the county town
10	Qasim	
11	Aptah[15]	Karuk Village, Saybagh Township, Qaraqash County, 26 kilometers away from the county town.
12	Töt Imam	Jighde Bostan Village, Bostan Township, Chira County, 152 kilometers away from the county town.

The local practice of worshipping these *Imams* together can be traced to a hagiographic work of poetry known as the *Täzkiä-i Töt Imam* dating from the late 18th century. In this work, the author Molla Niyaz Khotani mentions the geneology of the *Imam.*[16] The local epic narraive of *Abdurahman Khan*, originating in the late 19th century, also mentions the names of Twelve Imams.[17] Thus we can see that local traditions regarding the Twelve Imams in Khotan have a relatively long history.

Mazars dedicated to the Twelve Imams have a special place in Khotanese mazar culture. Such mazars can be found in Khotan, Keriyä, Lop, Qaraqash, and Niya Counties; dates of their initial establishment are not known. All of the sites are located in the desert in simple mudbrick constructions or flat-topped dugouts supported by wooden beams sometimes surrounded by an earthen wall. Each site also contains from one to three other constructions such as a mosque or *khaniqa.*[18]

These Imam were all Arabs, and since none of them visited Khotan, these mazars are in fact "memorial sites" associated with their names. That said, all of the folk legends

---

13 About the hagiography of Imam Musa Kazim mazar, see Omerjan Nuri's chapter in this volume.
14 About the legend of Imam Häsän Äskäri mazar, see Muhämmät Imin Qurban 1996: 406-407.
15 *Ibid.* 144-146.
16 Molla Niyaz 1984: 88-105.
17 Mämtili Sayit and Abdulla Majnun, n.d.: 13.
18 Ma Pinyan 1993: 570.

and biographical records preserved at each mazar state that the Imam associated with the mazar came to Xinjiang to spread Islam and was martyred. For hundreds of years, individuals in the position of *khoja*, *ishan*, or *shaykh* as well as local feudal officials have promoted these sites and thus, the mazars have gained good reputation among Muslims in Xinjiang, attracting a continuous stream of visitors who come to worship. The mazar of Imam Jafar Sadiq in Niya County has a particularly large and devout following. Professor Ma Pinyan asserts that the Twelve Imams as represented in Khotan are a valuable topic of research to learn more about the effect of Shi'ite on Xinjiang and its mazar culture.[19]

To this very day, local residents believe that eight of the Twelve Imams visited Khotan and died there as martyrs. They also believe that the "Imams" that descended from 'Ali were not Shiite and died as martyrs bringing Islam to the region. For example, 72 year old Aqram Akhun (living in Qaraqash County's Saybagh Township) recounted the story of Imam Aptah as follows:

> "Imam Aptah had reached the peak of perfection in Islamic laws and customs. Both he and his son,Töt Imam, are buried in Nur Township located in Chira County. Imam Aptah is the son of Imam Qasim who died in Medina but was also buried here. Imam Qasim is the son of Imam Häsän Äsqäri; his tomb is located in Imam Häsän Äsqäri Village in Yengiyär Township of Qaraqash County. In addition to these, the tombs of Imams Zayn al-'Abidin, Jafar Sadiq, Musa Kazim, Muhammad Taqi, and Muhammad Naqi are also located in Khotan".[20]

Nurmuhämmät Akhun, the *shaykh* of the Imam Häsän Äsqäri Mazar in Qaraqash County and a group of worshippers described their opinions on the biographies of the Twelve Imam as follows:

> "'Ali is one of the four Khalifas, but he is not an Imam. We believe that the Twelve Imams are martyrs, and since the Imam Mahdi is not a martyr, so is not a Imam either".[21]

The above statement confirms that certain groups of Muslims in Khotan do not consider the Imam Mahdi as one of the Twelve Imams, but instead see him as an independent saint. In the following section we will examine other "Imams" associated with 'Ali in Khotan including the Mahdi.

The Imam Mahdi and Mazars of Other Saints Associated with 'Ali

The mazar of the Imam Mahdi is located in Qizilboy Village, Chahar Township, Chira County in Khotan, 94 kilometers from the county town and 23 kilometers from the township government. The site has a total area of 18 *mu* and is located on a hill believed to be the site of the Imam Mahdi's seclusion. There are several poplars on this hill with sheep skin and pieces of cloth hanging from them as well as several fresh water springs.

[19] *Ibid.*

[20] In the interview in Jan., 2008, at Imam Häsän Äsqäri Mazar in Qaraqash County.

[21] Interview on Jan. 29, 2008, at Imam Häsän Äsqäri Mazar in Qaraqash County.

There is also a mosque located nearby where local Muslims go for Friday prayers and to celebrate the two major festivals of the year.

In January 2007, while conducting fieldwork in Khotan, I was able to record a legend about Imam Mahdi that is not mentioned in historical records. In October, 2010, with the help of Shaykh Yasin Akhun, the *shaykh* of the Imam Aptah Mazar, I collected a *täzkirä* of Imam Mahdi, which was secretly distributed among a group of people in 1980. The text is written in modern Uyghur and has a total of 66 pages; each page is 15×18cm large and containing 12 lines of text.

According to the *täzkirä* and legends among the people of Khotan, Imam Mahdi, 'Ali, and his two sons Imam Häsän and Husayn, are considered to be people living among us. The Mahdi is said to be a son of 'Ali and a princess of Machin. Unlike other Islamic traditions, his mission was not to save the world and he is not the last of the Twelve Imams. This Imam Mahdi does, however, dwell in seclusion similar to the Imam Mahdi of the Shiites.

According my research findings and analysis, the figures of the Imam Mahdi and 'Ali in local tradition have been influenced by the *Shahname*. It is widely known that this heroic epic spread throughout Central Asia, including Xinjiang. In the hagiography, the figure of the Imam Mahdi is very similar to that of the young general Suhlab in the *Shahname* and the figure of the Imam 'Ali resembles the great hero Rustam. Likewise, the other personages found in the hagiography and the general plot of the work resemble this Persian literary masterpiece.[22]

Both Iranic and Turkic peoples love the myths, legends, as well as the heroic and historical stories found in the *Shahname*. Professor Äsäd Sulayman has discussed the history of literary exchange between the Persian and Uyghur peoples: Uyghurs and other Turkic peoples in Central Asia have long had a close contact with Persia since ancient times. The Silk Road bound these two cultures closely together and during its development, Uyghur literature has been influenced by literary exchange with neighboring regions, and especially by medieval Persian literature. They share similar applications of literary themes, forms, subjects, and motifs as well as much of the same content and forms. The phenomenon of cultural exchange and synthesis between the Persian and Uyghur peoples is very distinctive not only for literature but also for the religion.[23]

In addition to those already mentioned, there are other five sacred sites in the Khotan region that are associated with 'Ali. These sacred sites and the legends about them are also good examples of "Imam mazar beliefs" in the region.

(1) Yalghuz Oghul Mazar (also known as the Imam Muhammad Hanifa Mazar located in Qaraqash County's Urchi Township, 16 km away from the county town): 'Ali's son.[24]

(2) Imam Asim Mazar (located in Khotan's Jiya Township, approximately 10 km from Khotan city): son of Imam Muhammad Hanifa, grandson of 'Ali[25]

[22] *Shahnamä*, 143-145.

[23] Äsäd Sulayman 2001: 71-76.

[24] Mämätimin Qurban 2006: 146.

[25] Rahile Dawut 2001: 156.

(3) Kohmarim Mazar (located in Khotan county's Layka township, 26 km to the southwest of Khotan City): a *qadam-jay* of Khoja Mu'ip, grandson of 'Ali, son of Imam Husayn.[26]
(4) Imam Jafar·Tayran Mazar (located in Chira Township's Mazarqul Village, 4.5 km away from the county town): brother of Imam 'Ali
(5) Imam Muhamamd Ansari Mazar (Keriyä County's Längär Township, 30 km away from the county town): grandson of 'Ali.

Discussion

To start, the role of the title *Imam* cannot be undervalued when examining the formation of Imam mazars in Khotan and should be assigned different definitions and explanations depending on the context of beliefs related to each mazar. In other words, the concept of *Imam* in Khotan has unique ethnic and regional characteristics.

Imam (*al-Imam*) is an Arabic term meaning 'leader', 'model', or 'director' and is used in reference to a person possessing a degree of intellectual authority. It has many uses, including the following: (1) used by Sunni Muslims to address the political and religious leaders of the country in the early Islamic period, synonomous with the term *Khalifa*. It is inferred that an *Imam* should openly exercise the power in the fields of religion, politics and military affairs and avoid withdrawl from society, an interpretation agreed upon by Ibadiya Muslims as well. (2) used by Shiites to address their spiritual leaders and representatives of the judiciary. This definition is accepted by Twelver, Sevener, and other Shiite groups. Supporters of this interpretation propose that all *Imams* are infallible and rightly guides their believers. (3) Used in reference to religious leaders who direct Muslims in the performance of *salat* in a mosque (*masjid*), also referred to as a *Masjid Imam*. This defnintion is synonomous with the term Akhun used in Chinese Mosques. (4) Used in reference to the founders or religious authorities of religious sects and schools of jurisprudence, *al-fiqh*, the science of *hadith*, the study of the explanatory notes of the Quranic philosophy.[27] Shiites are usually very cautious with their use of the term *Imam* as the concept is particularly important for them. Only Sunni Muslims use the term with the meanings given under definition 3 and 4.

As we have seen above, both Sunni and Shiite Muslims have different definitions and understandings of the concept of *Imam* which are reflected in their religious practice. Additionally, special beliefs regarding *Imams* are not part of basic Sunni belief (*iman*) or religious doctrine. Sunni Muslims believe that the faithful should respect all members of the Prophet's family and have the right to choose their political, religious and military leaders (*Imam*). In Shiite religious doctrine, the position of *Imam* has a unique position, and is an essential part of their basic doctrine. Shiite believe that the position of *Imam* is closely related to the family of the Prophet Muhammad which Shiites maintain includes the following five members: the Prophet Muhammad; his

[26] *Ibid.*: 155.
[27] Ma Zhongjie 1993: 660.

daughter, Fatimah; the Prophet's son-in-law, 'Ali; and the prophet's grandsons Häsän and Huseyn. Shiite doctrine states that these five individuals were created by divine light and so '*Imams*' must be members of this lineage. They also claim that before his death, the Prophet Mohammad appointed 'Ali as his successor. 'Ali and all subsequent *Imams* were also directly appointed by the person they were to succeed. Each *Imam* also inherits special knowledge from the *Imam* he succeeds. Shiites believe that *Imams* should not be selected by the people, but instead appointed by Allah in advance. Thus, the the only legitimate Muslim political and religious leaders are those who are descendants of 'Ali and Muhammed's daughter Fatimah. The final *Imam* is the Imam Mahdi who lives in seclusion in an invisible world and will return to save mankind when the world is filled with injustice and wickedness.[28]

According to my research, beliefs regarding the *Imams* in Khotan stray far from the term's meaning. Although most of the patron saints of *Imam* mazars are seen as the descendants of 'Ali, their existences is not mentioned in basic Sunni or Shiite doctrine or history, but instead rely on local hagiographies that have survived to the present day.

Secondly, in my observation, pilrgrims to the *Imam* mazars of Khotan do not attach little or no importance to the religious sect an *Imam* belonged to, the number of *Imam* mazars in Khotan, genealogies associated with a mazar, or whether the figure had visited Khotan at all. They do believe, however, that all of the buried saints are the descendants of the Prophet Muhammad, 'Ali, and their descendants and that these figures devoted their lives in order to spread Islam and help the local people overcome their hardships in life. Local residents believe that the souls of these saints are able to save people from material and spiritual adversity and thus continue visiting their burial sites in droves. In addition, the political and economic system have continuously strengthened the mazars' influence, and hagiographies have played an important role in forming the ideas associated with them.

The *Imams* discussed in the hagiographies possess the following characteristics: (1) The legendary characteristics of *Imams* mentioned in hagiographies is strong and reduces the prominence of religious and historical features which lack an authoritative textual basis. (2) All of the *Imams* mentioned in the hagiographies are related to 'Ali, and thus descendants of Prophet Muhammad. Of these, the Twelve Imams have unique position. (3) The *Imams* of the hagiographies are not central to the religious beliefs of the Uyghur population and their religious doctrines and principles, but are the foundation of local mazar culture. (4) The hagiographies never mention if the *Imams* they discuss are Sunni or Shiite, but simply state that they came to Khotan to spread Islam and died a heroic martyrs death. (5) The *Imams* mentioned in the hagiographies have unique social standing in that there are general historical, doctrinal, and literary works discussing them as well as local beliefs with special regional features such as those found in the Uyghur mazar culture in Khotan.

[28] Albiri Babatahir 2001: pp.135-153.

Conclusion

The cultural structure of the beliefs related to mazars dedicated to *Imams* in Khotan is very complicated. Here, 'Ali is not seen as an *Imam*, but is instead one of the four great Caliphs. The Shiites' twelveth *Imam*, the Mahdi, is not listed among the Twelve Imams of Khotan while Imam Qasim, Imam Aptah and Töt Imam hold a clear place among their number. In the formation of the beliefs associated with these mazars Sunnis, Shiite, and Sufi doctrine have played an important role just as Uyghur folktales, folk arts, Persian literature,and the imagination of the Uyghur people.. Although we have a general understanding of the development of *Imam* mazar culture in Khotan from other analogous cases in the Islamic world, we see that it clearly focuses on 'Ali and his descendants, who possessed the religious charisma that was strong enough to develop regional and ethnic characteristics and allow related legends to continue to grow.

References

Äsäd Sulayman 艾赛提·苏来曼 2001. "Bosi wenxue yu Weiwuer wenxue jiaoliushi duanxiang" 波斯文学与维吾尔文学交流史断想 [Brief Commentary on the History of Literal Exchanges between Persian and Uyghur], in *Minzu Wenxue Yanjiu*, 2001-3: 71-76.

Elias, Ney and Denison Ross 1898. *A History of the Moghuls of Central Asia : being the Tarikh-i-Rashidi of Mirza Muhammad Haidar, Dughlát.* London.

Albir Babatahir 2001. *Iran The Great Islamic Encyclopaedia* 10 vols, Tehran: The Centre for Iranian and Islamic Studies.

Ma Pinyan 马品彦 1993. "Yimamu maza" 伊玛目麻扎 [Imam Mazars] in *Chinese Encyclopedia of Islam* 中国伊斯兰百科全书. Chengdu: Sichuan Cishu Chubanshe, 570.

Ma Zhongjie 马忠杰 1993 "Yimamu" 伊玛目 [Imam], in *Chinese Encyclopedia of Islam.* Chendu: Sichuan Cishu Chubanshe, 660.

Mämtili Sayit and Abdulla Majnun, n.d. *Abdurahman Khan (Khotän Khälq Dastanliri Toplimi).* Khotan : Khotän Wilayätlik Az Sanliq Millätlär Qädimiy Äsärlirini Rätläsh Ishkhanisi.

Muhämmät'imin Qurban 1996. *Qaraqashni Chüshinäyli.* [Let's understand Qaraqash], Khotan: Khotän Mämuriy Mähkimä Qädimki Äsärlär Ishkhanisi Qaraqash Nahiyilik Khälq Hökümiti Ishkhanisi .

Mämätimin Qurban 2006. "'Mazartagh' häqqidä ikki riwayät" [The Legend of 'Mazartagh'], in Abdulla Sulayman(ed.) *Dunyada Birla Khotän Bar. 8 Äpsanä-Riwayätlär, Chöchäklär.* Urumqi: Shinjang Uniwersiteti Näshriyati, 46-49.

Molla Musa Sayrami 1986. *Tarikhi Hamidi.* näshrgä täyyarlighuchi, Änwär Baytur, Beijing: Millätlär Näshriyati.

Muhämmäd Husäyin Häykäl (Misir) 2003 *Muhämmäd Äläyhissalamning Hayati.* [The Life of Muhammad], tr. into Modern Uyghur by Tokhti Haji Tilla, Haliq Awut , Shihabidin Abdulähäd, Urumqi: Shinjiang Khälq Näshiryati.

Nizamidin Tokhti 2002. *Khotändiki Qädimi Izlär.* [Ancient Tracks of Khotan], Urumqi: Shinjiang Khälq Näshiryati.

Rahile Dawut 热依拉达吾提 2001. *Weiwuerzu Maza Wenhua Yanjiu* 维吾尔族麻扎文化研究 [Studies on the Cultures of Uyghur Mazars], Urumqi: Xinjiang Daxue Chubanshe.

Shahnamä : Obulqasim Firdewsi (Iran) 1998. *Shahnama* tr. into Modern Uyghur by Abdushukur Muhämmäd'imin and Abduwäli Khälpät, Urumqi: Shinjang Khälq Näshriyati.

Stein, Aurel, 1903 *Sand-Buried Ruins of Khotan.* London.

Appendix 1

The Legend of Imam Äskär, the 9th *Imam* of 'Twelves'

This legend was composed by Ablimit Yasin and is based on the information given on the notification board of a mazar located in Tüwät Township of Qaraqash County. The dialogue is by Shäykh Nurmuhämmäd, the shäykh of the mazar. Translated from Modern Uyghur by Jun Sugawara.

[Original Modern Uyghur Text]

ئىمام ئەسكەر پادىشاھىمنىڭ نەسەبى ھەزرىتى پەيغەمبىرىمىز مۇھەممەد ئەلەيھىسسالامغا تۇتىشىدۇ. شۇنىڭ ئۈچۈن"سەييىد" دەپ ئاتىلىپ كەلگەن مۆتىۋەر ئەزىزدۇر. ھەزرىتى مۇھەممەد ھەسەن ئەسكەر پادىشاھىمنىڭ ئاتىسى ھەزرىتى ئىمام مۇھەممەد نەقى، ھەزرىتى ئىمام مۇھەممەد نەقىنىڭ ئاتىسى ھەزرىتى ئىمام مۇھەممەد تەقى، بۇ زاتنىڭ ئاتىسى ھەزرىتى ئىمام ئەلى مۇسا رىزا، بۇ زاتنىڭ ئاتىسى ھەزرىتى ئىمام مۇسا كازىم، بۇ زادنىڭ ئاتىسى ھەزرىتى ئىمام جەئفىرى سادىق پادىشاھىمدۇر، بۇنىڭ ئاتىسى ئىمام مۇھەممەد باقىردۇر، بۇنىڭ ئاتىسى ئىمام زەيدىن ئابىددۇر، بۇ زادنىڭ ئاتىسى ئىمام ھۇسەيىن رەزىياللاھۇ ئەنھۇدۇر، ھەزرىتى ئىمام ھۇسەيىن رەزىياللاھۇ ئەنھۇنىڭ ئانىسى ھەزرىتى مۇھەممەد مۇستافا سەللاللاھۇ ئەلەيھى ۋە سەللەمنىڭ قىزى ھەزرىتى فاتىمە رەزىيەللاھۇ ئەنھادۇر.ئاتىسى ئەلى كەرىمەللاھۇ ۋەجھۇدۇر.

ھەزرىتى ئىمام ھەسەن ئەسكەر پادىشاھىمغان بىر كۈنى رەسۇلىللاھ ھەزرەتلىرىدىن شۇنداق بىشارەت بولدىكى «ئى بالام، ئىمام مۇھەممەد ھەسەن ئەسكەر سىز ھازىرنىڭ ئۆزىدە دەرھال چىن ماچىنغا بېرىپ، ماچىن دىيارىدىكى شاھادەت شەربىتىنى ئىچكەن ئاتىلىرىڭىزنىڭ قەبرىگاھىنى تېپىپ، زىيارەت قىلىپ، قۇرئان ئوقۇپ دۇئا ئالغاچ، ماچىن ئەجەملىكلەرنىڭ توققۇز خاقان شەھرىنى پەتىھ قىلىپ، ئىسلامغا كىرگۈزگەيسىز، غەلىبە نۇسرەت سىزگە يار بولغاي" . بۇ بىشارەت بىلەن ئىمام ھەسەن ئەسكەر پادىشاھىم ئىنتايىن خۇرسەنلىك ۋە ھەسرەتلىك ئىچ ئاغرىق ئىچىدە سەپەرگە چىقتى. شۇ ۋاقىتتا مەككىنىڭ ماۋرائۇننەھرىنىڭ چوڭلىرى ئۈچكۈنلۈك، بەزىلىرى يەتتە كۈنلۈك يەرگىچە ئەگىشىپ بېرىپ ئۇزۇتۇپ قويدىلەر. شۇنىڭ بىلەن ئۇ زادنىڭ ئۆزى 9 مىڭ كىشىلىك زور قوشۇن، ياراغ-جابدۇقلىرى، سەككىز زەئىپ ئايال، يەتتە قېرى چال، تۆت نەپەر ناراسىدە بىلەن كېچە-كۈندۈز يول يۈرۈپ، كۆپ جەبىر-زۇلۇم چېكىپ، ئاخىرى ھەزرىتى ئىمام جەئفىرى سادىق پادىشاھىمنىڭ مەنزىل قەبرىگاھلىرىنى تاپتىلەر، ئاندىن قۇرئان تىلاۋەت قىلىپ دۇئا قىلىشتى. بۇ چاغدا ھەزرىتى ئىمام جەئفىرى سادىق پادىشاھىمدىن بىشارەت بولدى. يا ھەزرىتى ئىمام مۇھەممەد ھەسەن ئەسكەر بىز سىزگە مۇنتەزىرىمىز(ئىنتىزارمىز). بىز سىزدىن شۇنى ئۈمىد قىلىمىزكى، بىز 32 ئىمام، ئالتە سۇلتان، 30 مىڭ لەشكىرى ئىسلام بىلەن توققۇز خاقان شەھرىدە ئىسلام ئاۋادىغا (ئىسلامىي شەھەرگە) كەلتۈرىمىز دەپ شاھادەت تاپتۇق. شۇنىڭ ئۈچۈن سىلەر ماچىنغا بېرىپ بۇزرۇكۋار ئاتىلىرى ئىمام مۇھەممەدە نەقى ۋە ئىمام مۇھەممەد تەقىنىڭ شاھادەت مەنزىلىنى تېپىپ دۇئا قىلىپ، ئىسلامنى ئۈستۈنلۈككە ئىگە قىلىش ئۈچۈن ئۇرۇش قىلغايسىزلەر دېدىلەر. شۇنىڭ بىلەن، ھەزرىتى ئىمام مۇھەممەد ھەسەن ئەسكەر زور غەيرەت شىجائەت بىلەن ئاتىسىنىڭ مەنزىلگاھىنى تېپىپ دۇئا قىلىپ تۇرغان ئىدى. بۇ چاغدا توققۇز خاقان سۇلتانلىقىغا شۇنداق بىر خەۋەر يەتتىكى فالانى جايغا نۇرغۇنلىغان لەشكىرى ئىسلام يېتىپ كەپتۇ. پات پۇرسەت ئىچىدە ھايال بولماي، توققۇز خاقان ئۇستىگە باستۇرۇپ كەلگۇدەك، بۇ خەۋەرنى ئاڭلىغان توققۇز خاقاننىڭ كۆز ئالدى قاراڭغۇلىشىپ، بىر ئاز قورقۇپ، ئاندىن تەرەپ-تەرەپكە ئادەم بۇيرۇپ، 80 مىڭ چېرىك خۇنخورنى جەمئىي قىلىپ ئىمامنىڭ بارگاھىغا تۇيۇقسىز باستۇرۇپ كەلدى. بۇ چاغدا ھەزرىتى ئىمام ئەسكەر پادىشاھىم سەككىز زەئىپ ئايال، يەتتە

قىرى چال، تۆت ناراسىدىلەرنى دۇئا قىلىپ تۇرۇش ئۈچۈن ئاياغ تەرەپكە ئورۇنلاشتۇرۇپ قويۇپ كېلىپ بىر خىلۋەت جايدا سەجدىگە باش قويۇپ تۇرغان ئىدى. توساتتىن تاشقىرىدا قىر چاپ قىيا چىيا ئاۋازلىرى ئاڭلاندى. بۇ چاغدا توققۇز خاقاننىڭ 80 مىڭ ئەسكىرى ھۇجۇمغا ئۆتۈپ بولغان ئىدى. ئۇرۇش قوزغۇلۇپ كەتتى. ئىمام لەشكەرلىرى ئۆزلىرىنى تۈزەشتۇرۇپ، قورال ياراغلىرىنى تەييارلاپ بولغۇچە، نۇرغۇنلىغان لەشكىرى ئىسلام قىرىلىپ كەتتى. ئاندىن ئىمام باشچىلىقىدا لەشكىر ئىسلام تەكبىر سالاۋات ئوقۇپ دەريا ياقىلاپ ئۇرۇش قىلدىلەر. لەشكىرى ئىسلامدىن نۇرغۇن كىشى شېھىت بولدى. ھەزرىتى سۇلتان غوپۇر ئاتا، سۇلتان ھىدايەت ئاتا قاتارلىق يەنە بىر قانچىلىغان ئەزىزلەر شاھادەت تاپتى. ھەزرىتى ئىمام ھەسەن ئەسكەر پادىشاھىم قەھرى غەزەپكە كېلىپ ھىممەت كىمىرىنى بېلىگە مەھكەم باغلاپ، قاتتىق ئۇرۇش قىلغان بولسىمۇ، ئاخىرى شاھادەت مەرتىۋىسىگە يەتتىلەر. شۇ زامان ئالەم قاراڭغۇلىشىپ، ئاسمان زېمىن ماتەم تونىنى كەيدى. چۆل جەزىردىكى ھايۋاناتلار يىغا زارە قىلىشتى. ئارقىدىن قاتتىق بىر بوران چىقىش بىلەن زېمىن قۇم ئاستىغا كۆمۈلۈپ كەتتى. قالۇ ئىننا لىللەھى ئىننا ئىلەيھى راجىئۇن (قۇرئان 2-سۈرە 156- ئايەت، بىرەر مۇسۇلماننىڭ ۋاپات بولغانلىقىنى بىلگەندە ئوقۇلىدۇ مەنسى: بىز ھەقىقەتەن ئاللاھنىڭ ئىگىدارچىلىقىدىمىز، بىز چوقۇم يەنە ئاللاھنىڭ دەرگاھىغا قايتىمىز) ھەر بىر بەندە مۆمىن بۇ تەزكىرىنى ئوقۇپ، كۆز يېشى قىلسا، ھەزرىتى ئىمام ھەسەن ئەسكەر پادىشاھىمنىڭ قەبرىسىنى زىيارەت قىلسا، قۇرئان تىلاۋەت قىلسا، ھاجەتلىرىنى خۇادىيتاالادىن تىلىسە ھاجەتلىرى راۋا بولغاي. بۇلۇپمۇ مۇشۇنداق ئاجايىپ باتۇرلۇق بىلەن شېھىت بولغان مۆتىۋەر سەييىد ئەۋلادلىرىنىڭ بېشىنى زىيارەت قىلىپ، ھايات كىشىلەر ۋاپات تاپقان كىشىلەر ھەققىدە قۇرئان تىلاۋەت قىلىپ دۇئا قىلسا ياكى خەير ئېھسان قىلسا ۋاپات تاپقان كىشىلەر ئۇنىڭ بەراكاتىدىن تېخىمۇ يۇقىرى دەرىجىگە ئېرىشكەي. ھەر مۆمىن پەيغەمبىرىمىزنىڭ ئەۋلاتلىرىنىڭ قەبرىسىنى زىيارەت قىلىپ، قۇرئان ئوقۇپ دۇئا قىلسا، ئۇلار بۇنىڭدىن خۇرسەن بولغاي. قىيامەت كۈنى شۇ كىشىلەرنىڭ گۇناھىنى تىلەپ، شاپائەت قىلغۇسىدۇ.

Notification Board of Imami(sic) Äskär Mazar, Tüwät Township, Qaraqash County.

[English Translation]

The bloodline of Imam Äskär Padishah begins with our Prophet Muhämmäd (*Peace be upon him!*). His sacred ancestry is the reason that he bears the title of "säyyid." Saint Häzriti Häsän Äskär's father was Häzriti Imam Muhämämd Näqi, Häzriti Muhämämd Näqi's father was Häzriti Muhämmäd Täqi, is the son of Häzriti Imam Äli Musa Riza, the son of Häzrät Imam Musa Kazim, the son of Häzrät Imam Jä'firi Sadiq Padishah, the son of Häzriti Imam Muhämmäd Baqir, the son of Imam Zäydin Abid, the son of Imam Hüsäyin (*May God be satisfied with him!*). The mother of Imam Hüsäyin (*May God be satisfied with him!*) was Häzriti Fatimä, daughter of the Prophet Muhämmäd (*Peace be upon him!*). And his father was Äli (*May God glorify him!*).

One day, Häzriti Imam Häsän Äskär Padishah recieved a sign (*bisharät*) from God saying: "Oh my son Imam Häsän Äskär! Go the land of Chin-Machin immediately, and find the graveyard of your father who tasted the nectar of the martyrs. Visit and revere themwith the Qur'an, and [then]conquer the nine cities of infidel khaqan and bring them into Islam. May a victorious wind aid you!" With this *bisharät,* Imam Häsän Äskär Padishahim set out with both great pleasure and great sorrow.

At that time, some of the leading figures of Mecca and Mawarannahr followed Imam Häsän Äskär Padishahim for three days and some for seven as he left Mecca. Accompanied by 9,000 soldiers, a large amount of equipment, eight weak women (*zäyp ayal*), seven old men (*qeri chal*), and four children(*narasid*), he braved great hardships as he marched day and night. At last they found the grave of Imam Jä'firi Sadiq and there they read the Qur'an and prayed.

It was then that they received the following revelation from Imam Jä'firi Sadiq: "Oh Häzriti Imam Muhämmäd Häsän Äskär! We have been expecting you. We, are 32 Imams, six sultans, and a 30,000 strong army of of Islam. [We] fought and were martyred so that the cities of the Khaqan accept Islam. For our sake, please go Machin and find the burial site of Muhämmäd Näqi and Muhämmäd Täqi. Pray there and fight to further the cause of Islam."

Thus with his extraordinary bravery and courage Häzriti Imam Muhämämd Häsän Äskär found his father's grave (*mänzilgah*) and prayed.

At this time, the sultans of the nine cities of the Khaqan received word of the arrival of the forces of Islam. The force fell upon the Khaqan's nine [cities] quickly and with no delay. When they heard this, the [Sultans of the] Khaqan's nine [cities] panicked and dispatched people in all directions; they marshalled a force of eight thousand soldiers and immediately sent it against the Imams.

At this time, Häzriti Imam Äskär Padishah, put eight weak women, seven old men and four children into the direction of his feet, and worshipped at the obscure place. Suddenly, the sounds of bloodshed and battle were heared outside. The eighty thousand troops from nine [cities] of the Khaqan approached and the battle began. The Imam's troop naturally formed ranks, prepared their weapons, and many soldoers of Islam were killed. They recited the *teqbir-salawat* (=*Alla-hu äkbär !*) and fought their battle next to the river and many soldiers of the forces of Islam were martyred. Their leaders, Häzriti Sultan Ghopur Ata and Sultan Hidayät Ata met a martyr's end there also. In the end, Häzriti Imam Häsän Äskär Padishahim also entered martyrdom, although he blazed as he fought bravely, girding his belt with the highest attention. It was then that the world turned dark and the sky and the earth donned the robes of mourning. [Even] the animals of the desert wailed in unison and the land was filled with sand blown strong storms.

"To Allah we belong, and to him is our return" (*Qur'an* 2: 156). The faithful who read this legend, shed tears, make a pilgrimage to the grave of Häzriti Imam Häsän Äskär Padishah and [there] read the Qur'an, God will grant them their requests. This is especially true if you make a pilgrimage to the resting place ofbody of the descendants of respectable sayyids who had been martyred with tremendous braveness, pray or present offerings, the martyrs will pour upon you highest blessings. If you make a pilgrimage to the tombs of the descendants of our faithful prophet and pray as well as read the *Qur'an*, you may gain their favour. Likewise, the sins of these will be forgiven and mercy accorded to them on Judgement Day.

Appendix 2
A Folk Tale Regarding the Imam Mähdi

Informant: Äkräm Akhun, 72 years old, farmer and resident of Tokhula Village of Qaraqash Bazar, Qaraqash County. Interviewed by Ablimit Yasin at the Imam Äftäh Mazar in Aqsaray, Qaraqash County on Jan. 1, 2008. Translated from Modern Uyghur by Jun Sugawara.

[Original Modern Uyghur Text]

ئىمام مەھدى ھەققىدىكى رىۋايەت ، ئېيتىپ بەرگۈچى: ئەكرەم ئاخۇن، 72 ياش، دېھقان، قارىقاش ناھىيە قارىقاش بازىرى توخۇلا كەنتىدە ئولتۇرىدۇ. خاتىرىلىگەن ۋاقىت: 2008-يىل 1-ئاينىڭ 28-كۈنى، خاتىرىلىگەن ئورۇن : ئىمام ئەفتەھ مازىرى

كۈنلەرنىڭ بىر كۈنى، ھەزرىتى ئەلى چۈشىنى ئاالالمايدىغان(ئەسلىيەلمەيدىغان) بىر كېسەل بولاپ قالدى. ھەزرىتى ئەلى بۇ كېسەلگە داۋا ئىزدەپ، رەسۇلىللاھنىڭ قېشىغا بېرىپ:

—— يا رەسۇلىللاھ مەن چۈشۈمنى ئاالايمايدىغان بولاپ قالدىم، دېدى. رەسۇلىللاھ ھەزرىتى ئەلىنى ئەبۇ تالىپنىڭ قېشىغا بېرىشقا بۇيرىدى. ھەزرىتى ئەلى ئەبۇ تالىپنىڭ قېشىغا باردى. ئەبۇ تالىپ ئۆيدە يوق ئىدى. ھەزرىتى ئەلى شۇنداق بىر قارىسا، ئۆينىڭ يېنىدا تۇمشۇقلىرى زۇمرۇجەتتىن(چىرايلىق يېشىل سۇزۇك تاش)، پۇتىنىڭ چەمەكلىرى(بارماق) ئالتۇندىن، 72 رەڭلىك ئەدەسسىز(ناھايتى) ئۇز(چىرايلىق) بىر قۇش تۇرغىدەك. ھەزرىتى ئەلى كۆڭلىدە « بۇ جانىۋار ئەجەب ئۇزكەن، ئاستا بېرىپ تۇتىۋالايىيا» دەپ ئويلاپ، قۇشنىڭ يېنىغا ئاستا كېپ(كېلىپ)، قۇشنىڭ پاچىقىدىن كاپ(تەقلىد سۆز) تۇتىشى بىلەن تەڭ ئۇ قۇش ھەزرىتى ئەلىنى تارتقان پېتى ئاسمانغا ئۇچۇپ چىكەتتى(چىقىپ كەتتى). ئەلى كەرىمەللاھۇ ۋەجھۇ قۇشقا:

— سېنى قوپ بىيەي دېپتى(قويۇپ بېرەي دەپتى).

قۇش:—— يا ئەلى پۇتۇمنى قوپ بەمە(قويۇپ بەرمە)، سەن پۇتۇمنى قوپ بەسەڭ پارە-پارە بولاپ كېتىسەن. مەن ھازىر ئاسماننىڭ تۆپىدە، دېدى.

ئەلى كەرىمەللاھۇ ۋەجھۇ ئاسماندىن قانداق چۈشۈشنى بىلمەي تۇرىتتى(تۇراتتى). جەبرائىل ئەلەيھىسسالام ھەزرىتى ئەلى كەرىمەللاھۇ ۋەجھۇنى ماچىن ۋىلايىتىدىكى بىر تاغنىڭ ئۈستىگە قويدى. بىر ئازدىن كېيىن ناماز پېشىن بولدى. ھەزرىتى ئەلى دەييانىڭ(دەريانىڭ) تېگىگە چۈشتى. پېشىن نامىزىغا تاھارەت ئېپ(ئېلىپ) تۇرىشى، بىر ساندۇق دەييادىن ئېقىپ كەلدى. ھەزرىتى ئەلى« ئۇ ساندۇقنىڭ ئىچىدە نىمە باتۇ(باردۇ)، خۇدايا ئۇ ساندۇقنى مېنىڭ ئالدىمغا يەتكۈزسەڭ» دەپ خۇداغا ئىلتىجا قىلدى. بۇ ساندۇققا مۇئەككەل بولغان مەلائىكلەر بۇ ساندۇقنى ئەلى كەرىمەللاھۇ ۋەجھۇنىڭ ئالدىغا ئاپادى (ئېلىپ باردى). ھەزرىتى ئەلى ساندۇقنىڭ ئاغزىنى ئاچتى، ساندۇق ئىچىدە چۆچۈرىگە توغرىغاندەك توغرالغان بىر كىشىنىڭ جەسىتىنىڭ تۇرغانلىقىنى كۆردى. ئاندىن ھەزرىتى ئەلى دەييانىڭ بويىدىكى بىر ئۇجمە تۈۋىگە بادى. ئۇجمە شېخىنى تۇتۇپ، ئەي شاخ ئامانەتنى تۇت، دېدى. شاخنىڭ قانى(قارنى، قورسىقى) يېرىلدى. جەسەت قاچىلانغان ساندۇقنى شاخنىڭ قانىنىڭ ئارىسىغا قويدى.

بۇنىڭ مۇنداق بولىشىدىكى سەۋەپ شۇكى، بۇ ساندۇقتىكى جەسەت ماچىن شاھىنىڭ قىزىكەن. قىرىق كۈن ئىلگىرى بۇ قىز چۈشىدە « پەيغەمبەر ئەلەيھىسسالامنىڭ ئۆزىنى ھەزرىتى ئەلىگە نىكاھلىغانلىقىنى» چۈشەپتىكەن. قىز دادام ئۇقسا قوشۇلىدۇ، دەپ ئويلاپ دادىسىغا دەپتىكەن، لېكىن، قىزنىڭ دادىسى ئىسلام دىنىغا ئۆچلىكىدىن قىزىغا :

—— سەن ئىسلام دىنىدىن يانغىن، ئۇ مۇھەممەد ۋە ئەلى دېگەنلەرنى ئۇنۇتقىن، ئۇنداق قىلمايدىكەنسەن، سېنى قىيما-چىيما قىلىپ، دەيياغا تاشلايمەن، دەپتۇ. قىز ئىسلام دىنىدىن قەتئىي يانماپتۇ. شۇنىڭ بىلەن دادىسى:

—— سېنى مۇھەممەد ئەلەيھىسسالام قۇتقىزىۋالسۇن، دەپ قىزىنى چاناپ دەيياغا قوپ بېرىتكەن.

پادىشاھنىڭ بۇ دۇنيادا شۇ بىرلا بالىسى بار ئىكەن. ئوغلىمۇ شۇكەن، قىزىمۇ شۇكەن. بىر نەچچە كۈن ئۆتكەندىن كېيىن، ئالاھ تائالا پادىشاھقا قىزىنىڭ ئىشقىنى (مۇھەببىتىنى) سېلىپ قويدى. پادىشاھ قىزىنى ئەسلەپ كېچە-كۈندۈز ئاش-نان يېمەي يىغلىغىلى تۇدى. شۇ كۈنلەردە ھەزرىتى ئەلى ماچىن شەھرىگە كىيدى (كىردى). ھەزرىتى ئەلىنىڭ كەلگەنلىكىنى ئۇققان پادىشاھ ئۇنى ئوردىغا چاقاتتى (تەكلىپ قىلدى). ئەلى كەرىمەللاھۇ ۋەجھۇ پادىشاھنى ئىسلام دىنىغا دەۋەت قىلدى. پادىشاھ ئۇنداق بولسا مېنىڭ بىر قانچە سۇئالىمغا جاۋاپ بېرىڭ دەپ، ھەزرىتى ئەلىدىن سۇئال سودى:

— يا ئەلى سىز مۇھەممەد ئەلەيھىسسالامنىڭ دامادى(كۈيئوغلى) بولا بوسىڭىز، مېنىڭ دىلىمدىكى مەقسەتنى تېپىڭ؟ دېدى. ئەلى كەرىمەللاھۇ ۋەجھۇ پادىشاھقا:

—— سەن بىر قىزىڭنى چاناپ دەيياغا قوپ بېرىپسەن، دېدى. پادىشاھ:

—— ئەمدى ئاشۇ قىزىمنى تەپ بېرىڭ، ئاندىن مەن ئىمان ئېيتىمە (ئېيتىمە)، دېدى. ھەزرىتى ئەلى:

—— ئەمىسە ماڭا ئىككى قوشۇپ دەيياغا يولغا سال، دېدى.

پادىشاھ ئىككى كىشى قوشتى، ھەزرىتى ئەلى ئۇلارنى باشلاپ دەييا بويىدىكى ئۇجمە تۈۋىگە كەلدى. ھەزرىتى ئەلى ئۇجمە شىخىغا قاراپ:

— شاخ ئامانەتنى بە، دېدى. شاخ ئارىسىدىن ساندۇق كۆرەندى. ساندۇقنى تاتىپ ئالدى. ھىلىقى ئىككى كىشى ساندۇقنى كۆتۈرەپ پادىشاھنىڭ قىشىغا كەلدى. پادىشاھ بۇنى كۆرەپ:

—— ئەمدى بۇ قىزىمنى تىرىلدۈرۈپ بەسىڭىز ئىمان ئېيتىمەن، دېدى. ئەلى كەرىمۇللاھۇ ۋەجھۇ ئاللاھنىڭ 99 ئىسمىنى ئوقۇپ، 11 زىكىرنى تاماملىدى. ئان(شۇندىن كېيىن) ساندۇققا قاراپ، «قۇم بى ئىزنىللاھى تەئالا (ئاللاھنىڭ روخستى بىلەن ئورنىڭدىن تۇر) »، دېدى. ساندۇقتىن 17 ياشلىق بىر قىز ئورنىدىن قوپتى.قىز قوپاپلىكىن (ئورنىدىن تۇرۇشى بىلەن تەڭ) تاققىدە (دەرھال) ئەلى كەرىمەللاھۇ ۋەجھۇغا كەيىنى قىلدى. قىز:

—— يا ئەلى بۇ يالىڭاچلىقىم بىلەن ئۆزلىرىگە قالاشقا تاقىتىم يوق، دېدى. شۇ زامان بۇ قىزغا لاباس(كېيىم -كىچەك) كېيگۈزدى. شۇنىڭ بىلەن پادىشاھ ئىمان ئېيتتى. قىزىنى ھەزرىتى ئەلىگە نىكاھلاپ بەدى(بەردى). ھەزرىتى ئەلى بۇ شەھەردە ئالتە ئاي تۇرۇپ قالدى. ھەزرىتى ئەلى چۈشىدە رەسۇلىللاھنىڭ "سىز بىر شەھەرگە باسىڭىز شۇنداق ئۇزۇن تۇرىۋالامسىز، مېنىڭ سىزنى كۆگۈم كەلدى" دېگىنىنى (دېگەنلىكىنى) كۆدى. ھەزرىتى ئەلى چۈشتىن ئويغىنىپ، ئايالىغا:

—— مەن مەدىنىگە قايتىدىغان بولدۇم. سىز مەن بىرگە بارامسىز يا قالامسىز، دېپتى. قىزنىڭ دادىسى قويمىدى. قىزىم مىشەدە قىلىڭ دېدى. ھەزرىتى ئەلى ئايالىغا :

—— ئەگەر قالا بوسىڭىز ئەمىسە مېنى يولغا سېلىپ قوياڭ، دېپتى. قىز: — مېنىڭ بويۇمدا قالدى، دېدى. ھەزرىتى ئەلى:

— نەچچە ئايلىق بولدى، دېدى. ئايالى:

— ئالتە ئايلىق بولدى، دېدى. ھەزرىتى ئەلى :

— ئەگەر ئوغال تۇغسىڭىز ئېتىنى ئىمام مەھدى ئاخىر زامان قوياڭ، قىز تۇغسىڭىز ئۆزىڭىز چاغلاپ(ئۆزىڭىز بىلىپ) قوياڭ، دېدى. ئاندىن بىر تۇمار قىپ بۇ خېنىمغا بەردى. ھەزرىتى ئەلى مەدىنىگە كەتتى.

ھەزرىتى ئەلى كېتىپ ئۈچ ئاي ئۆتتى. ئۇ خېنىم ئوغۇل تۇغدى. ئوغلىغا «ئىمام مەھدى ئاخىر زامان» دەپ ئات

قويدى. بۇ ئوغۇل تۆت ياشتا بارلىق ئىلىمنى تۇگەتتى، يەتتە يېشىدا 72 سىپاھگەرلىكنى (جەڭ ماھارەتلىرى) تۇگەتتى. لېكىن ئىمام مەھدى دادىسىنىڭ كىم ئىكەنلىكىنى بىلمەيتتى، باشقىلارمۇ ئۇنىڭغا ئېيتمايتتى. ئىمام مەھدى توپبازلىق قىلاتتى (توپ ئويناتتى). بىر كۈنى ئىمام مەھدىنىڭ توپى بىر تۇل خوتۇننىڭ يىپ ئىگرىۋاتقان چاقىنى چۇۋەتتى. بۇ تۇل خوتۇن « ئانىسى يوقنىڭ ئەمچىكى چوڭ، دادىسى يوقنىڭ بېشى چوڭ دەپتىكەن، ھۇ يېتىم ئوغلاق» دەپ تىللىدى. ئىمام مەھدىنىڭ ئاچچىقى كېلىپ، ئانىسىنىڭ قېشىغا كەلدى. ئانىسىدىن:

—— مېنىڭ دادام كىما ، دەپ سودى. ئانىسى:

—— سىزنىڭ دادىڭىز پادىشاھ دېدى. ئىمام مەھدى:

—— ئەمىسە سىزنىڭ دادىڭىز كىما، دېيتى. ئانىسى شۈك (جىم) بولاپ قالدى. ئىمام مەھدى:

—— مېنىڭ دادامۇ، سىزنىڭ دادىڭىزمۇ پادىشاما، سىزنىڭ ئەدىپىڭىز(راس گەپ قىلغۇزىدىغان نەرسە) مۇشۇ دەپلا قىلىچنى سۇغادى. ئىمام مەھدى خوجام:

—— سىز چىپىباتىتقان (قىلىچ بىلەن پارچىلىۋېتىدىغان) ئانىكەنسىز، تۇل خوتۇن مەزلۇمنىڭ دېگىنىدەككەنيا مەن، دېدى. ئانىسى:

—— بالام توختاڭ، مېنى چىپىباتسىڭىز ئانىنىڭ قاغىشىنى ئالغانلارنىڭ قاتارىدا كېتىسىز، توختاڭ مەن قىسسەمنى دەپ بېيەي(دەپ بېرەي). سىزنىڭ دادىڭىز مەككە مەدىنىدە داڭ كۆتەگەن (نامى چىققان، مەشھۇر) ھەزرىتى ئەلى، خۇدانىڭ شىرى، تۆت يانىڭ(تۆت خەلىپە: ئەبۇ بەكرى،ئۆمەر،ئوسمان،ئەلى) بىرى، بىر ئىسمى ئەلى، بىر ئىسمى ئەسئەدۇللاھۇ غالىپ (ئاللاھنىڭ غالىپ شىرى) دېدى. ئىمام مەھدى:

—— ئۇنداق بوسا مەن دادام قېشىغا بارىتمەن، دېدى. ئانىسى ھەزرىتى ئەلى بەرگەن تۇمارنى ئوغلىنىڭ ياقىسىغا تىكىپ بەدى. ئىمام مەھدى چۆل جەزىرلەرنى ئارىلاپ، قىرىق كۈن يول مېڭىپ، قارىسا يەنىلا پادىشاھنىڭ زېمىنىدىن چىقىپ بولالمىغانلىقىنى كۆدى. شۇنداق قالىسا بىر قويچى تۇغىدەك، مەكە (بۇ يەرگە كەل) دېيتى. قويچى كەلدى. ئىمام مەھدى ئۆزىنىڭ ئالتۇن تاج، شىر چورۇق(ئۆچكە ۋە قوي تېرىسىدىن ئىشلەنگەن ئۆتۈك) ۋە ئۆشنىسىدىكى (ئۇستىدىكى) شاھانە لىباسلىرىنى (كېيىم) قويچىنىڭ ئەسكى كېيىملىرى بىلەن تىگىشتى. ئىمام بىر قويچىنىڭ سۈرىتىدە يەنە قىرىق كۈن يول يۈرۈپ مەككە مەدىنە ئارىسىدىكى ئوھۇد تېغىغا كەلدى. ئىمام مەھدى تاغنىڭ ئاستىغا قالىسا، ئۈچ كىشىنىڭ، بىيسى خورمىنىڭ ئۇستىدە، ئىككىسى ئاستىدا خورما يەۋاتقانلىقىنى كۆدى. ئىمام مەھدى« خۇدايا شۈكرى نەچچە كۈن بولاپتى ئاچ قالغىلى ، مۇشۇ باغقا كېيىپ، بىر قوساق خورما يەپ چىقمايما» دەپ، بۇ باغقا كىيدى.

باغدىكى ئۈچ كىشىنىڭ بىيسى ئىمام ھەسەن، بىيسى ئىمام ھۇسەيىن، يەنە بىيسى ئىككى ئىمامنىڭ تەربىيەتچىسى قەمبەر ۋەلىيۇللاھ ئىكەن. قەمبەر ۋەلىيۇللاھ خورمىنىڭ ئۇستىدە خورما قاقتى. شۇنداق يوغان بىي خورما چۈشتى. ئىمام ھۇسەيىن ئاكام ئىمام ھەسەن يېسۇن دەپ، ئىمام ھەسەن ئۇكام ئىمام ھۇسەيىن يېسۇن دەپ، ئىككىسى بىر -بىرىگە ھۆرمەت قىپ ئامىدى. ئىمام مەھدى ئاچلىقتىن كېپىلا خومىنى ئېپلا ئاغزىغا كوم (تەقلىد سۆز) سالدى. شۇنىڭ بىلەن، ئىمام ھۇسەيىن:

—— سەن ئاكام يېسۇن دېگەن خورمىنى يېۋالدىڭ، سەن قانداق قويچى دىسە، ئىمام ھەسەن:

—— سەن ئۇكام ئىمام ھۇسەيىن يېسۇن دېگەن خورمىنى يېۋالدىڭ، سەن قانداق قويچى دەپ، ئىككىسى ئىمام مەھدىگە ياماشتى. ئىمام مەھدى ئىككى ئىمامنى ئىككى قولىدا دەس(تەقلىد سۆز) كۆتۈرەپ:

—— سېنى ما(بۇ) تاغقا، سېنى ما (بۇ) تاغقا بىر ئۇراي دېيتىم، خەر (بولدى، مەيلى) ئون گۈلۈڭنىڭ بىرسى ئېچىلماپتۇ(كىچىك يىگىتكەنسەن) سەنمۇ بىر ئەرنىڭ ئوغلىكەن، مەنمۇ بىر ئەرنىڭ ئوغلى، دەپلا يەدە قويدى. ئاندىن قەمبەر خورما ئۇستىن سەكلەپ چۈشۈپ: —— گېپىڭ بولسا ماڭا قىل، دېدى. قەمبەر ۋەلىيۇللاھ بىلەن

تۆتۈشتى. قەمبەر ۋەلىيۇللاھ ئىمام مەھدىگە ئۈچ ھەربە (ھۇجۇم) قىلدى. ئىمام مەھدى رەت قىلدى. ئاندىن ئىمام مەھدى قەمبەر ۋەلىيۇللاھنى بەلدىن كۆتۈرەپ يەرگە بىر قوياپتى، قەمبەر ۋەلىيۇللاھ بىي مېتىر توپىنىڭ ئاستىغا پېتىپ كەتتى. ئان(شۇندىن كېيىن) قەمبەر ۋەلىيۇللاھ ئەشەدىن قوپاپ، ئىككى ئىمامنى ئەگەشتۈرۈپ رەسۇلىللاھنىڭ قېشىغا كەلدى، ئۇ يەردە ھەزرىتى ئەلى با(بار) ئىدى. ئىككى ئىمامنىڭ يېغلىغانلىقىنى كۆرگەن ھەزرىتى ئەلى، زۇلفىقارىنى ئېلىپ ۋەلىيۇللاھلىق (ئاللاھنىڭ دوستى) سۈپىتى بىلەن ماڭماقچى بولدى. رەسۇلىللاھ ئەلىگە:

—— يا ئەلى زۇلفىقارنى ئاماڭ ھىلى پۇشمان قىلىسىز، باكا پۇشمان پايدا بەمەيتۇ، توختاڭ دېپتى، ھەزرىتى ئەلى ئاڭلىماي ئاچچىغىدا چىكەتتى. شۇنىڭ بىلەن ھەزرىتى ئەلى ئىمام مەھدى خوجام بىلەن ئون تۆت كېچە-كۈندۈز جەڭ قىلدى، ھەر ئىككىسىنىڭ 72 تۇرلۇك ياراغلىرى (جەڭ قورالىرى) كاردىن (ۋەيران بولدۇ)چىقتى. ئاندىن ئىككىسى بەلمۇ بەل چىلىشتى، ئىمام مەھدى ئاخىر زامان بىر زور(كۈچەش) بىلەن ھەزرىتى ئەلىنى تىزىغا ئېلىۋالدى. شۇئاندا (شۇ ۋاقىتتا) ھەزرىتى ئەلى خۇداغا «ئى ئاللاھ سەن مېنى شىرىم دەپ ئاتىدىڭ، مەندىن شىرلىق نىسبەتنى (خۇسۇسىيەت) كۆتۈرۈۋەتتىڭمۇ، ماڭا نۇسرەت(غەلىبە) بەمەمسەن » دەپ يىغلاپ دۇئا قىلدى. ئاللاھتەئالانىڭ ئالەمۇل غەيبىدىن (كۆرگىلى بولمايدىغان ئالەم) ھەزرىتى ئەلىگە« مەدەت (ياردەم) تىلىمەك سەندىن، نىجاتلىق بەمەك مەندىن » دېگەن بىر نىداكەلدى. شۇ زامان ھەزرىتى ئەلى بىر زور بىلەن ئىمام مەھدىنىڭ تىزىدىن چۈشۈپ كەتتى. ھەزرىتى ئەلى ئىمام مەھدىگە:

— سۇ ئىچىۋېلىپ ئاندىن چىلىشايلى، دېدى. ئىمام مەھدى سۇ ئىچتى، ھەزرىتى ئەلى تۇمشۇقىنى سۇغا تىقتى، لېكىن سۇ ئىچمىدى. ئىمام مەھدى سۇ ئىچكەندىن كېيىن ئىزىلدى (بوشاپ كەتتى). شۇنىڭ بىلەن ھەزرىتى ئەلى بىر زور بىلەن ئىمام مەھدىنى كۆتۈرۈپ يەرگە ئۇردى. ئىمام مەھدى ھەزرىتى ئەلىگە قالاپ، بىر يىغلاپ بىر كۇلدى. ھەزرىتى ئەلى بۇنىڭ سەۋەبىنى سوردى. ئىمام مەھدى:

—— مەن هازىرغىچە بىر كىمگە يېڭىلمىگەن، بۇگۇن ساڭا يېڭىلدىم، شۇڭا يىغلىدىم، مەن ھەزرىتى ئەلىنىڭ ئوغلى، دادام بىر كۈنى سىنى چوقۇم يېڭىدۇ، شۇڭا كۇلدۇم ، دېدى. ھەزرىتى ئەلى:

—— ۋاي سېنىڭ داداڭ كىم، دەپ سودى. ئىمام مەھدى:

—— مېنىڭ دادام ھەزرىتى ئەلى كەرىمۇللاھۇ ۋەجھۇ، دېدى. ھەزرىتى ئەلى:

—— نىشانەڭ باما، دېدى. ئىمام مەھدى ياقىسىدىكى تۇمانى كۆسەتتى، ھەزرىتى ئەلى ۋاي جېنىم بالام، دەپ ئىمام مەھدىنى قۇچاغلاي دېيىشىگە، ئىمام مەھدى :

— ۋاي مەن دادامغا گۇستاخلىق(تەكەببۇرلۇق) قىپتىمەن، دەپ دەرھال قاچتى. ھەزرىتى ئەلى قوغلىدى، ئىمام مەھدى قاچتى. ئىمام مەھدى قاچا-قاچا(قېچىپ-قېچىپ) چىرا ناھىيىسىدىكى تاغ تۈۋىگە كەلدى.ئىمام مەھدى تاغقا قالاپ:

— ئى تاغ ئاللاھنىڭ ئىزنى(روخسىتى) بىلەن ماڭا پاناھلىق بەگىن، مەن دادام تەرىگە (يۈزىگە) قايدا قالايتمە، دېدى. تاغ يېرىلدى، ئىمام مەھدى تاغنىڭ قانىغا (قارنىغا، قورسىقىغا) چىكەتتى. تاغ يېپىلدى. ئەلى كەرىمەللاھۇ ۋەجھۇ تاغنىڭ ئىككى تەرىپىنى تۇتۇپ تاتتى:

—— ئى تاغ بالامنى چىقىرىپ بە، دەپ نىدا قىلدى. شۇ چاغدا تاغ:

—— يا ئاللاھ ئىمام مەھدىنى قانىڭغا ئال دېدىڭ، ئالدىم، ھەزرىتى ئەلى ئىچىل دېدى، سېنىڭ ئەمرىڭنى تۇتامتىمەن، ھەزرىتى ئەلىنىڭكىنىمۇ؟ دېدى. ئاللاھتىن:

— مېنىڭ ئەمرىمنى تۇتىسەن، ساڭ ئېچىلماققا ئىجازەت يوق، دەپ نىدا كەلدى. ھەزرىتى ئەلى پۇشايمان قىپ(قىلىپ) قاتتىق يىغلىدى. شۇڭا، بۇ يېغا سەۋەبلىك بۇ تاغدىن هازىرغىچە توختىماي سۇ چىقىپ تۇرىتۇ. بۇ سۇ تۇرلۇك كېسەللەرگە شىپا بوتۇ.

An offered flag with the text of Quranic sura (al-baqara 154) at Imam Mahdi Mazar, Chira, Khotan. Photographed by Rahile Dawut, 2009.

[English Translation]
One day Häzriti Äli fell gravely ill and became unable to dream. Seeking a cure, he went to God and said: "Oh God, I can no longer dream!" God ordered Äli to approach Äbu Talip.

When Häzriti Äli sought Äbu Talip, he found [Äbu Talip] was not at home.. Häzriti Äli looked around and noticed a very beautiful bird of 72 colours with a beak more beautiful than an emerald, and feet are more beautiful than gold was standing at the side of the house.

Häzriti Äli thought to himself: "This animal is absolutely beautiful. I should approach it slowly and catch it." He approached to the bird slowly, but when he tried to catch hold of the bird's leg, the bird flew away squaking. Äli (*May God glorify him !*) said to the bird "I will catch you !" The bird replied: "Oh Ali, don't hold my feet , if you do it, you will be smashed. I am high in the sky now". Äli (*May God glorify him !*) can do nothing to me.

Shortly after, during the *pishin.* (*namaz*) Häzriti Äli came to the river to make sacred ablutions (*taharät*) for the service. At this time a box (*sanduq*) floated down from up stream. Häzriti Äli said "What could be inside of the box? God must have sent it my way." The princesses who became angels have brought the box before Äli (*May God glorify him !*). Häzriti Äli opened the box and found a corpse that had been minced like stuffing prepared for dumpling-soup (*chöchüre*). He went to the foot of a mulberry tree that stood at the side of the river. Then he held branch of the tree and said, "Ey branch, take this !" Then, body of the tree was opened, and the coffin was placed in it.

The reason for this is as follows. The body in this coffin was a daughter of the king of Machin. Forty days earlier the girl saw in a dream that the Prophet Muhämmäd was leading her marry Häzritii Äli. She woke up believing that her father would agree [to the marriage] if she told him. Her father was ignorant of Islam and said, "You turn from the religion of Islam and forget the Muhämmäd and Äli. If you do not listen my words, I will dice you and dump you in the river!" But she remained firm in her belief and so her father said "Let Prophet Muhämmäd relieve you!" andthrew her body in the water after he killed her.[But] son or daughter, she was the king's only child .

A few days after, God reminded the king to his love for his daughter. The king missed his daughter, cried and was unable to eat anything, day or night. At this time, Häzriti Äli entered the city of Machin. The king was informed of his coming and called him to his court (*orda*). Äli (*May God glorify him!*) advised the king accept Islam. Then the king asked Äli to answer these questions first:

"Oh Äli! You are son-in-law(*damad*) of Prophet Muhämmäd. Can you read what is in my heart? " Äli replied: "You diced your daughter and dumped her into the river." The king replied: "Well, find and return my daughter to me and I will profess faith [in Islam]. Häzriti Äli said "Please dispatch two people to go with me on the road to the river." The king dispatched two people, and Häzriti Äli went to the mulberry tree by the river-bank. Häzriti Äli looked at the mulberry and said: "Branch, give me what I have entrusted to you!" At this, the coffin appeared from the branch. Äli picked it up and opened the coffin. The two fellows that accompanied him shouldered the coffin and brought it before the king. The king saw it and said: "Will this girl now rise from the dead? If so, I will make a confession of faith." Ali (May God glorify him !) recited the 99 names and performed 11 *zikrs*. After this, he faced the coffin and cried "By the name of God, arise!" With this, the 17 year old girl rose from the coffin. The girl immediately ducked behind Äli and said, "Oh Äli, as I am naked, I cannot stand before you!" Äli dressed her in new clothing (*labas*) and the king made his confession of faith [in Islam] and married his daughter to Äli. Häzriti Äli remained in the city for six months but then in a dream he saw the Prophet saying: "You have remained in this city for long time. I would now like to see you." Häzriti Äli woke and said to his wife: "I must return to Medina. Will you come with me, or remain here?" Her father would not agree to let her go, and said, "Oh my daughter! Please stay here!" Häzriti Äli told his wife: "If you are not pregnant, please let me go." [The king's] daughter said: "I am pregnant." Häzriti Äli then asked: "How many month have passed?" His wife replied: "I am now in my sixth month." Häzriti Äli said "If you give birth to a son, please name him Mähdi Akhir Zaman, if you give birth to a girl, name her as you see fit.". He made an amulet (*tumar*) and gave it to his wife and then left for Medina.

Three months after Häzriti Ali's departure, his wife gave birth to a son and named him "Imam Mähdi Akhir Zaman." The child completed his studies by the age of four and mastered 72 forms of martial arts (*sipahgerlik*) by age of seven. But Imam Mähdi did not know who is his father and no one ever raised the matter to him. Imam Mähdi loved to play with balls and one day his ball hit a woman's spinning-wheel and broke it. The woman blamed him saying "It is said 'Breast of the girl without a mother is big and the penis of the boy without father is big', oh orphan goat!" Imam Mähdi then became angry and went to his mother, asking: "Where is my father?" His mother replied: "Your father is a king." Imam Mähdi retorted: "So who is your father?" This mother then fell silent.. Imam Mähdi again questioned her, saying: "Is my father a king and yours as well? I will draw my sword if you lie to me. You are a mother that should be diced to death! Am I the boy what the widow called me?" His mother replied: "Wait, my son. If you killed me, it shall be you who has cursed your mother. Wait, I will now tell you the story. Your father is Häzriti Äli. Famous in Mecca and Medina, he is the lion of God and one of the four companions (*töt yan*). His name is Äli but he is also known as *äs'ädullahu ghälip* (God's victorious Lion)." Imam Mähdi said "I shall go to be with my father." His mother then placed an amulet which had been given to her by Häzriti Äli around the neck of her son,.

Imam Mähdi traveled through the desert for 40 days but had still not left the territory of the king [of Machin]. When he saw a shepherd (*qoychi*) he called "Come here!" When the shepherd came, Imam Mähdi exchanged his gold crown, fine staff, and many luxurious clothes that he had brought on horseback for the shepherd's poor garments. Imam Mähdi then disguised himself as a shepherd and having traveled another 40 days, arrived at Mt.Uhud which is located between Mecca and Medina. Imam Mähdi looked down at the foot of the mountain and saw three people, one was sitting on [a mound of] dates (*xorma*) and two others were eating the dates [the other sat upon]dates. Imam Mähdi said: "Thanks be to God! How many days have passed since I became hungry? Let me go into this orchard (*bagh*) and eat dates!" Thus he entered the orchard..

Inside of the orchard there were several people: one was Imam Häsän, another was Imam Hüsäyn, and yet another one was Qämbär Wäliyullah, a disciple (*tärbiyatchi*) of the first two. Qämbär Wäliyullah was striking dates on the [mound of] dates. And very big date has came out. The elder brother, Imam Hüsäyn, said "Please eat it, Imam Häsän!" The younger, Imam Häsän, said in turn "You eat it, Imam Hüsäyn!" They showed their respect for each other. Then Imam Mähdi came and because of his hunger, threw that date into his mouth directly. Imam Hüsäyn then said:

"You ate the date that my brother gave me! What sort of shepherd are you?" Imam Häsän also replied: "You the ate date that my brother gave me ! What sort of shepherd are you?" Both Imams reproached Imam Mähdi. Imam Mähdi then lifted the two Imams in his hands and said "I could throw one of you to this mountain, and the other to that mountain. Well, both of you are still young. You are the son of one, and so am I. " Having said this he placed them back on the ground. Then Qämbär leapt down from the atop dates and said: "If you have something to say, tell me!" Then Imam Mähdi wrestled with Qämbär Wäliyullah. Qämbär Wäliyullah attacked Imam Mähdi three times, but Imam Mähdi fended him off.

Imam Mähdi threw Qämbär Wäliyullah to the ground and Qämbär Wäliyullah became stuck one meter in the earth. After this Qämber Wäliyullah became regained consciousness and went to the prophet with his two Imams. Häzriti Äli was there and seeing the weeping of the two Imams, Häzriti Äli set out with a double-edged sword (*zulfiqar*), as a friend of God (*wälliyullah*). The Prophet said to Äli: "Oh Äli, don't take the sword. If you take it you will surely regret it. Wait!" Häzriti Äli did not listen and became angry. Häzriti Äli then battled with Imam Mähdi Khojam for four days and nights. Each of them used their 72 weapons. Finally, they began wrestling wildly with each other and Imam Mähdi took hold of Häzriti Ali by knee. Häzriti Ali then cried our and prayed: "Oh God! You made me to your lion and gave me the attributes of a lion, but still you did not let me win!" God's reply came from far off: "Certainly, you asked for my help and indeed I gave you salvation!" Then, Häzriti Ali fell down from Imam Mähdi's knee with all of his power. Häzriti Ali said to Imam Mähdi "Let's drink water and wrestle." Imam Mähdi drank water, but although Häzriti Ali's lip touched the water, he did not drink. Imam Mähdi relieved from his strain after taking a drink of water, so Häzriti Ali, with all of his power lifted Imam Mähdi and threw him to the ground. Imam Mähdi looked to Häzriti Ali weeping and laughing and whenHäzriti Äli asked why he was acting this way, Imam Mähdi replied: "I have never lost to anyone, but today I have lost to you. Thus I weep. I am a son of Häzriti Ali. My father will defeat you one day. Thus I laugh." Häzriti Äli then asked: "Who is your father?" Imam Mähdi replied: "My father is Häzriti Äli (*May God glorify him!*)" Häzriti Äli then asked: "Do you have any proof of this?" Imam Mähdi then produced the amulet around his neck and [recognizing it]Häzriti Äli said "Oh my son! My heart!" and tried to embrace him.

Imam Mähdi said "Oh! I have been very rude to my father!" and ran away. Häzriti Äli chased him, but Imam Mähdi moved father and farther away from his father, finally coming to the top of a mountain located in Chira County. Imam Mähdi took a look at the mountain and said "Hey mountain, by the Sign of God, give me shelter (*panahliq*). I do not wish to see my father again." The mountain shook, and Imam Mähdi was swallowed up insie of it and was covered.

Äli (*May God glorify him !*) took the two sides of the mountain and cried: "Oh mountain, give my son back to me!" The mountain then replied: "Oh God, just as you ordered that I catch Imam Mähdi in my blood, so I caught him. But Häzriti Ali commands that I open for him. I will obey your command, but what abou Häzriti Ali's request?" God's edict (*nida*) then came: "Obey my command. You shall not open." Häzriti Äli felt regret and cried. Thereafter, throughout the land it was known that this is the reason that the waters that flow from this mountain cure all disease.

Imam Mahdi Mazar in Chira, Khotan.
(Photographed by Rahile Dawut, 2009)

Sacred Sites Associated with Hazrat 'Ali in Central Asia

Nodirjon ABDULAHATOV

This paper is an exploration of the sacred geography of the inhabitants of the Ferghana Valley. As the cultural heritage and values of a people must be treated with care and caution, the use of an anthropological approach to the description of beliefs and religious practices may be the most beneficial for this paper. Oftentimes the personages of the world appear before us in historical, mythicized and ideal hypostases and making it impossible to isolate a single element from the involved complex.

The fact that the fourth caliph 'Ali ibn Abu Talib ibn 'Abd al-Muttalib (656-661) was a cousin and son-in-law of the Prophet Muhammad (d. 632) is well-known. Over time, he was canonized as the fourth in a line of "saint like caliphs" (*al-khulafa' ar-rashidun*; ruling from 632-661). In Islamic literature Hazrat 'Ali is shown as a true supporter (*sahabah*) of the Prophet Muhammad, a great and brave warrior, and a devoted propagator of Islam (*fatikh*), becoming known as the "Asad Allah" (Arabic: 'The Lion of Allah') and "Shah-i Mardan" (Persian: 'The King of Humankind').

Hazrat 'Ali met a martyr's (*shahid*) end on January 21, 661 while praying in a mosque: he was 63 years old. He was later interred in Najaf, located in the modern state of Iraq. According to local legends, it was the dying man's will that he be buried in a place of little renown, ordering that his body be placed on a camel and buried where the camel came to stop.[1]

The legend states that according to the final instructions of Hazrat 'Ali, seven identical coffins (*tabut*) were made, placed on seven camels, and then sent out to each of the seven climes. The order stated that he be interred wherever the camels stopped.[2] In so far as the true resting place of Hazrat 'Ali was unknown, seven different points in Iraq, Syria, Iran, Afghanistan, as well as in the ancient cities of Central Asia became known as the tomb of Hazrat 'Ali.[3]

The Arab military campaigns into Central Asia brought battles for territory and the establishment of Islam and the cult of the *shahid*, i.e. martyr for the faith, began to grow

---

[1] Rakhman 2000: 44.
[2] To'khtiev 2006: 53.
[3] Usmonov 1995: 38.

in popularity. In the initial years of the Caliphate, the influx of preachers of Islam who brought warriors with them, caused the number of graves of Muslims who had perished in battles with non-Muslims - "Mashhads", i.e. the mazars of *shahids* increased.[4] Visiting the tombs of *shahids* and circumambulating them became common practice in pilgrimages to Islamic holy sites. In the *Quran* the following is said regarding *shahids*: "And do not say about those who are killed in the way of Allah , "They are dead." Rather, they are alive, but you perceive [it] not"(2:154).[5]

In all likelihood, the *Quran*'s assertion that the *shahids* are not dead inspired hope for deliverance from hardship in the visitors to the graves of the *shahids*. A *hadith of the Prophet* states that, "The people died for faith are granted protection of 70 persons from among his relatives".[6] Indeed, it was saying such as this that strengthened the faithful's belief in the power of the *shahids'* mazars.

In fold narrations, Muslims martyred for the faith by non-Muslims are depicted as ideal heroes and even venerated as examples. Another *hadith* states that, "The Prophets and *shahids*, died in the field of battle, waging a holy war on their divine way, do not decay in tombs. The Most High God has made 'eating' of their dead bodies forbidden for the ground". It is for this reason that the idea that *shahids* were not truly dead and would come to the aid of their descendants spread throughout the population. This belief implies that "the great figures who approved themselves in life and renowned heroes do not vanish without leaving a trace, however, in order to show their proper spirit again in extremely desperate and dangerous moments, they temporarily hide their force. When the due time comes, the great names of history participate in the role of deliverers and saviors".[7]

The above quote makes clear that Muslim holy places have centered around the graves of martyrs since very early on. In most cases, these graves are known to the local population as "Mashhad" (holy warriors) or "Shahid" mazars.

Data on the first Muslim holy places in the Ferghana Valley are presented in an-Narshakhi's work "History of Bukhara" written in 944. According to an-Narshakhi, the tomb of the well-known Arabian commander and conqueror of Mawarannahr, Qutaybah ibn Muslim, (d.715), was located in Ferghana.[8] A contemporary of an-Narshakhi, al-Makdisi (947-1000) in his work *The Most Excellent Guide to the Study of Climates* mentions a certain spring of Ayyub (Job) in the Ferghana Valley (located in today's Jalalabad Oblast in Kyrgyzstan).[9] In his work *Al-Mulhakat bi-s-surah*, the scholar Jamal Qarshi (later 13th-early14th century) mentions the names of several sacred sites in the Ferghana Valley Isbid Bulan (now Safed Bulan) contained the graves of 2,700 companions of the Prophet and his followers who died for faith while on *ghazawat*

---

[4] Nemtseva 1995: 128.

[5] *Koran*: 43.

[6] *Muhammad payghambar qissasi. Hadislar*: 121.

[7] Imomov 1989: 27.

[8] Narshakhiy 1991: 132.

[9] Bartold 1931: 110.

(raids) against disbelievers.[10] Qarshi also provides information concerning the tombs of Asaf ibn Burhiya in Osh and of Imam Husayn's grandson, Imam Abdulla ibn 'Ali, buried near the city of Kokand.[11]

It is important to mention that over time, the term "Mashhad" began to be understood as a sacred site associated with Hazrat 'Ali's descendants. The 16th century Turkish scholar of the Seydi 'Ali Raisas mentions this in his work *The Mirror of the Nations*.[12]

For centuries the local population has honored sacred sites bearing the name Mashhad, holding them in high regard. In written sources from the medieval period there is also information on sacred sites associated with the term Mashhad or Mashad in the territory of Central Asia.[13] The same can be said in regards of the sacred Mashhad Maydan Mazar in the Besharyk District of Ferghana Oblast which has not survived. In various 19th century documents produced in the Khanate of Kokand, there was a qishlaq known as Shahid Maydan and Mashhad Maydan, and for this reason the sacred site located there was known by the same name.[14]

According to certain sources, the memorial complex of the sacred site included a mosque and madrasah known by the same name. Informants claim that the dome of the Mashhad Maydan Buva mausoleum was approximately 12-15 meters high and contained two tombs. Now the only remaining construction from the complex is the gatehouse - *darvazakhana* dating from the beginning of the 20th century. Unfortunately, the inscriptions on the *peshtak* of the *darvazakhana* were covered with plaster and only with great difficulty can a single *ayat* be made out.

In-depth research on the Mashhad Maydan has revealed a *waqf* document issued in the beginning of the 19th century to the mazar and *madrasah* of Imam Abdullah Bahir. This rare document provided information regarding the individual to which the sacred site is dedicated. According to Jamal Qarshi, the grandson of Hazrat 'Ali ibn Abu Talib Imam Zayn al-'Abidin (d. 713) had children named Sulayman, 'Abd ar-Rahman, 'Umar, al-Husayn, Muhammad Baqir, 'Abdallah al-Bahir, 'Abdallah al-A'raj, al-Hasan, al-Aftas, al-Husayn al-Asgar.[15] Hence, we find the historical basis for the association of the shrine of Imam Bahir, i.e. Mashhad Maydan Buva with Imam 'Abdullah al-Bahir, a great-grandson of Hazrat 'Ali who lived in the first half of the 8th century, and is mentioned among the names of Imam Zayn al-'Abidin's children. It is for this reason that the local population asserts that the Mashhad-Maydan-Buva located in the Besharyk is very ancient.

Special emphasis should be placed on the fact that the site of worship of Imam Abdullah Bahir is known as Mashhad Maydan Buva among the local population. In a

[10] Diakonov 1948: 14.
[11] Bartold 1965: 535.
[12] Seydi Ali Rais 1963: 103.
[13] See Buryakov *et al.* 1973; Mirboboev 1974; Abu Tokhirkhozha 1991; Nemtseva 1995; Abdulakhatov - Eshonboboev 2007.
[14] Nabiev 1973: 372.
[15] Dzhamal al-Karshi 2005: 67.

document preserved in the Central State Archives of Uzbekistan, this sacred site is referred to as the "Mashhad Maydan Mazar".[16]

Locations associated with Hazrat 'Ali and with his descendants such as the mazar of Imam Abdullah and Muhammad Baqir, occupy a special place among the sacred sites in the Ferghana Valley.[17] Thus it is evident that since antiquity there have been *mashhads*, i.e. places where Ali's descendants died for faith in the valley, such as the mazar of Hazrat Shah in Charkukh Qishlaq located 21 km south of Isfara (Republic of Tajikistan, Sogd Oblast). The mausoleum was first constructed with wood in the 10th century and today remains in good condition, having withstood the ravages of time.[18] According to folk narrations, the prince Abulqasim, a descendant of Imam Huseyn, the son of Hazret 'Ali, was buried here.[19] The well-known researcher, S. Khmelnitskiy, noted that one of 'Ali's descendants and victim of the struggle for Islam at the end of the 7th - the beginning of the 8th century was buried at this place of worship.[20]

Mazars similar to these, such as those of Sayyid Battal Gazi, the Qara Yazi baba, Khoja Hasan Nuri, and Imam Ata (Zayn al-'Abidin) can be found not far from the Besharik Uchkuprik (Ferghana Oblast) and Pap (Namangan Oblast) regions. The folk tales associated with these mazars are almost identical and tell of a descendent of the Prophet who arrives from Medina to spread Islam and disappears during a battle. The famous Shah-i Zinda 'Ali Mazar in Chadak Qishlaq in the Pap District of Namangan is one such place. Legends tell of a holy man who entered a cave and was never seen again. The legends claim that the man was Shahi Zinda 'Ali, a descendent of Hazrat 'Ali and disseminator of Islam and science in the beginning of the 9th century.[21]

In our opinion, the use of the names of well-known Muslim missionaries, especially those claiming authority through descent from Hazrat 'Ali and the events associated with him in the Ferghana Valley as well as the Arab invasion in the first half of the 8th century, became the pretext for places of worship associated with them to emerge. Later these stories were continued in oral traditions and historical epics such as *The story of Safed Bulan.*[22]

According to the Russian scientist V.L. Ogudin, in the valley there are 18 natural monuments associated with Hazrat 'Ali in the Ferghana.[23] However, this data is tenuous since the precise number of sacred sites associated with Hazrat 'Ali in the Ferghana Valley has not yet been determined. That said, while carrying out fieldwork in 2001-2006, we managed to identify over ten such monuments in the Ferghana Oblast alone.

The sacred sites associated with Hazrat 'Ali , his son Muhammad ibn al-Hanafiya,

---

16 TsGA Uz. Fund № I – 19. Op. № 1, D. 13965. l. 2.

17 Saidboev 1984: 118.

18 Based on the author's field research, 2005. Republic of Tajikistan, Sogd Oblast, Isfara District, Charkukh Qishlak.

19 Khasanov 2001: 38.

20 Khmelnitskiy 2002: 132.

21 O'lmas Bahromzoda 2000: 17.

22 Abdulakhatov et al. 2003: 23.

23 Ogudin 2006: 182.

his grandson Imam Zayn al-'Abidin, the horseman Qambar Ata and his nephew Akhtam Sahaba in the Ferghana Valley, this day are reputed to be places where the holy men walked. These sites can be classified as follows:

1. Sacred sites associated with Hazrat 'Ali (Shah-i Mardan, Sokh, Qadamjay).
2. Sacred sites associated with Hazrat 'Ali's son Muhammad ibn al-Hanafiya, his grandson Imam Zayn al-'Abidin, and great-grandson 'Abdallah ibn 'Ali (Khoja Turab, Mashhad Maydan Mazar, Khoja Ilgar, Imam Ata, the Baba-yi Khorasan, Shah Talib).
3. Sacred sites associated with the attendants of Hazrat 'Ali - Qambar, Ahtamom Sahaba, 'Umar Umiya: (Baba Qambar, Qambar Ata, Baba Akhtam, Shah Akhtam, Umar Umiya).
4. Sacred sites associated with Hazrat 'Ali's mule, Duldul (Duldul Ata, Pa-yi Duldul, Qushnaguch Ata).
5. Sacred sites associated with a white camel owned by Hazrat 'Ali: (Qara-Tash, Tash-Salar, Aq-Mazar, Tuya-Tash);
6. Sacred sites associated with the descendants of Hazrat 'Ali.[24]

Unfortunately, this article only permits us to discuss a handful of the sacred sites located in the region. Although each sacred site associated with the descendants of Hazrat 'Ali merits a book, here we will only present a brief introduction.

Through our research we have established that the majority of the sacred sites in the Ferghana Valley are associated with the followers of the Prophet Muhammad and Hazrat 'Ali. We have observed that informants see each saint as related to other holy men in the area, either by blood (father - son, mother - daughter, husband - wife, brother - sister, distant relatives, *yetti-oghayni*-'seven brothers') or spiritual transmission (the master- servant, the leader, fellow-fighter, flagman, the warrior). All of these saints, including the descendants of Hazrat 'Ali, are seen as historical figures that came during one of the "Great campaigns". The idea "Great campaign" is known throughout Central Asia – in the Dasht-i Qipchak (led by the Caliph Abu Bakr as-Siddik),[25] in the Syr-Darya Basin (led by three descendants of Imam Muhammad ibn al-Hanafiya),[26] and in Eastern Turkestan (led by Imam Ja'far as-Sadiq).[27] In the second and third cases, the campaign routes are directly connected with the Ferghana Valley. The last two legends differ from the others in that they took place in different historical and cultural contexts. Here we will pay particular attention to the analysis of legends about "Great campaign". It is worthwhile to note that sites associated with Hazrat 'Ali are often located near pools of water, trees and rocks. For example, the *hauz* (pond) located at the mazar of Hazrat-i Shah in Istaravshan (Ura-tyube) is said to have issued from Hazrat 'Ali's staff.[28]

A mazar in Kabr-Kul Qishlaq, 20 km from Arslan-bab (Kyrgyzstan), is associated with

---

[24] Abdulakhatov 2006: 44.
[25] See DeWeese 1994.
[26] DeWeese 1990: 119; Muminov 2000. 385-428, Russian edition: Muminov 2003: 117-153.
[27] Blochet 1925-1926: 12-129.
[28] Rahimov 2002: 7.

Hazrat ʻAli by the local population even though they also associate the name of Paytug Qishlaq in Andijan Oblast's Izbaskan District (Uzbekistan). The legend, recorded by V.P. Nalivkin (1852-1918), states that this place received its name because Hazrat ʻAli was said to have stopped and erected a banner after one of his victories.[29] People say that the upright stones known as the "Sang-i La'nat" (Damned stones) in Namangan Oblast's Gava Qishlaq rose with a blow of Hazrat ʻAli's sword, and the hills in the Kukim Bay farm in Kasansay rose from the dirt that fell from hooves of Duldul, the horse ʻAli rode.[30] In Namangan, people associate with Hazrat ʻAli the Zirk Mazar located in the Yangiqurgan District.[31]

The place-names "Solikur" and "Katput" in the Ferghana Oblast's Altyaryk District are also associated with Hazrat ʻAli and his horse Duldul by local residents. For example, the term *katput* is said to be derived from *katta put* (a big foot) and is associated with the foot of Hazrat ʻAli.[32]

Yet another sacred site, a mazar associated with the name of Hazrat ʻAli, is located in the Sokh District's Sarikanda Qishlaq. Up until the end of the 19th century it was the location of a grave said to be Hazrat ʻAli's and a mosque of the same name; both mazar and the mosque were destroyed during the Soviet era.[33]

Mazar Hazrat ʻAli. Sokh (Uzbekistan).

In Sokh there are several sacred sites associated with the name of Hazrat ʻAli. According to an informant, Rakhman-ʻAli Makhmudov, the name of the Tul Qishlaq is

[29] Nalivkin 1886: 8.
[30] Saksonov 1986: 14.
[31] *Ipak yo'li afsonalari*, 74.
[32] Abdulakhatov - Azimov 2005: 20.
[33] Dzhahonov 1989: 68.

linked with Hazrat 'Ali. In many Turkic languages the word "tul" means "widow". A legend reports that once when Hazrat 'Ali was lost, his wife wept and wailed because she believed she would be left a widow or "*tul.*" Thus people believe this was the reason that the qishlaq started to be refered as Tul.[34]

A sacred site in Devayron Sokha Qishlaq and the Duldul Ata Mazar in Voruh Qishlaq also hold associations with Hazrat 'Ali. Another informant, Rayimdjan Tashbaev, reported that local residents had long held that the grave of Hazrat 'Ali was located nearby in the mountains at the confluence of two rivers. The tomb of Hazrat 'Ali was built in Sokh, a place surrounded with mountains and watered by the rivers Sokh, Tagabi, and Abishir. According to the historian A. Juldashev, one of the motivations for constructing a mazar was to facilitate pilgrimage to the burial place of Hazrat 'Ali in Najaf. Having erected the mazar in this place, people believed that "our prayers will be accepted even in this mazar".[35] A similar explanation is given in narrations about the fortress Janadil-Makatil located in the Pakhtaabad District of Andijan Oblast.[36]

Such legend can also be heard in practically any mountain district in Tajikistan. In A. A. Bobrinskiy's collection of folktales about Hazrat 'Ali compiled in the 20th century during his research on the life of the residents of the Pyandz River's upper reaches, there is mention of a battle between 'Ali and Kakhkakha during the conquest of the fortress of Ishkashim.[37] According to reports, there is a fortress known as Kakhkakha with a mazar named "Shah-i Mardan" located just across from it. It is also said that Iskander Zulkarneyn (Alexander the Great) managed to seize the entire Pamir region in three hours.[38]

Although he conquered the Pamir in just three years, it was above all Hazrat 'Ali reasonable actions that made him of the embodiment of perfection in people's mind over the centuries. Just as his boldness received the people's approval, his virtues of generosity and valor earned him respect Hazrat 'Ali's battles in the name of religion, however, caused his reputation to grow more than any of his other accomplishments. It is this reputation that left people unable to imagine that Hazrat 'Ali was not in some way related to the unusual things surrounding them or wars of old. It is for this very reason that increasingly people began to claim that if an old *tut* (mulberry tree) grew crookedly it was because Hazrat 'Ali had leaned against it to rest or if there were marks on a stone they were from Hazrat 'Ali's sword.[39]

Even ancient cities or hills with unusual shapes began to become associated with Hazrat 'Ali in the eyes of local people.[40] In our ancestors' mind, the image of Hazrat 'Ali was with the very embodiment of love and reliance, and they had no doubt that Hazrat 'Ali had been able to perform feats that ordinary people were unable to do. The names

---

[34] Fieldwork, performed by the author in 2004 . Fergana Oblast, Sokh District, Qishlaq Tul.

[35] Field research of the author 2004 . Fergana Oblast, Sokh District, Qishlaq Sarikanda.

[36] Mamadaliev -Abdumalikova 1997.

[37] Bobrinskiy 1908: 16.

[38] Gornenskiy 2000: 113.

[39] Snesarev 1983: 66.

[40] Mandelshtam - Rozenfel'd 1960: 97.

of ancient cities too were associated with Hazrat ʻAli. Here we shall focus on the city of Shahqadam in Turkmenistan (Krasnovodsk in the Soviet Era, currently known as Turkmenbashi). The name Shahqadam was for alleged rock in the vicinity that bore the marks of a *shah* (ʻAli).[41] Although in reality these marks appeared as a result of geological processes, in the eyes of local people they were the footprints of Hazrat ʻAli. According to the research of N. G. Mallitskiy (1873-1947), the origin of the place-name Margelan was, in local legends, refered as Hazrat ʻAli.[42]

The Russian scholar V. V. Bartold (1869-1930), when studying ancient monuments in the village of Shahristan Ura-Tyube (modern Istaravshan) in 1893, reported that the structure known as Chilkhujra, was associated with Hazrat ʻAli by the local population.[43] To this very day the people of the city cherishes the legends stating that Hazrat ʻAli had lived in Chilkhujra.[44]

Kh. Khasanov noted that the name of the archaeological monument Ulkan-Toytepa located in the Sredne-Chirchik District of Tashkent Oblast has associations with terms such as "fortress", "fortified hill", or "a hill with an army."[45] Local residents, however, believe that the hill is related to Hazrat ʻAli. Professor M. E. Masson (1897-1986), in his 1928 visit to the place stated mentioned the existence of legends associated the place with Hazrat ʻAli. He writes:

> "Half an hour later ... all of us, sitting on the *koshma* (felt pad) at the evening meal with *kokchay* (green tea), listened to the interesting variant of a legend about the origin of the name of Toytyube (literally "Bugor toya", i.e. a celebratory feast). It was vastly and fascinatingly narrated by an elderly and skilled *sartarash* - the barber Sultan Pirimkulov.
>
> The plot lay in that during the old times the ruler of Kashgar, Turkestan, Afghanistan and Caucasus was a certain sovereign Zarkul. He was strongly disturbed with rumors of successes of the caliph ʻAli in spreading Islam with the help of a wonderful sword Zulfikar and a famous horse Duldul. He summoned a brave and strong man Kabil, and he gave his word to kill ʻAli, for what in reward Zarkul promised to give him in marriage his beautiful daughter Gumayunruy by name. By mistake Kabil killed another person, brought his head and received the promised bride. The joyful celebrating lasted many days on the hill dumped for a wedding feast *toy*, the hill - "*tyube*" (whence supposedly was originated the modern name – "Toytyube"). Unexpectedly appeared genuine ʻAli had demonstrated a number of feats, then sustained a heavy fight against pagans, and, eventually had won them. Both the ruler himself, and Kabil, and many other strong warriors had fallen smite in the battle-field; as for inhabitants they were converted in Islam. Evident traces of these events have remained the settlement Ulkan Toytyube and numerous gullies. There are lots of them in the vicinities of the settlement, and they are admitted to be the rests of pitfall traps in which the Zarkul warriors tried to entrap the tireless Duldul and Arabs".[46]

In Tashkent Oblast the sacred sites related to Hazrat ʻAli are located in Khojikent

[41] Qoraev 1970: 138.
[42] Pisarchik 1956: 146.
[43] Bartold 1966: Vol. IV, 90.
[44] Pulatov 1975: 7.
[45] Khasanov 1965: 53.
[46] Masson 1976: 35.

Qishlaq, at the bank of the Chirchik River. The local legends regarding the place were published by the Russian researcher S. Lidskiy in his article "The Mountainous Vicinities of Tashkent", in the *Turkestani Gazette*.[47]

The scholar-archaeologists who carried out archaeological research in Tajikistan's Karategina Valley from 1954 to 1955 confirmed the existence of local legends connecting archaeological monuments such as Kala-i Imlak, Kala-i Jamahur, and Kala-i Dev-i Safid with Hazrat 'Ali.[48] Yet, the orientalist A.V. Stanishevsky in one of his works describing his travels in Tajikistan presented his findings on the connections of the "Shahr-i Barbar" fortress located in the Pamirs with Hazrat 'Ali.[49]

The academic G. A. Pugachenkova (1915-2007) who researched the archaeological site located in Dalverzintepa in the Denau District, Surkhan-Darya Oblast (Uzbekistan) from 1959 to 1960, mentioned that among the local inhabitants there were available folk tales about Dalverzintepe associating it with Hazrat 'Ali among the local inhabitants and provides us with a legend about Dal Zal. Another related legend states that in order to seize the ancient city of Dalverzin, Hazrat 'Ali waged war against the king of the fire-worshippers, Dal Zal, for three months.[50]

There are also similar legends about the Erkurgan monument near Qarshi[51] and the ancient Bukharan city of Paykend (Uzbekistan) has a legend associated with Hazrat 'Ali as well:

> "When Hazrat 'Ali was unable to take Paykend, he built a construction of masts and ropes on which tight-ropewalkers could pass, and then held a tight-rope walking exhibition. The residents of Paykend had never seen such a thing and opened the gate to come out. Hazrat 'Ali saw the people coming outside the gates and proceeded to kill them all. After pulling the city gate down, he threw it and the place where it fell is today a mountain. When Hazrat 'Ali let his horse graze, the horse would always return when he called him. But that once, no matter how many times he called the horse, it did not return. There was an abundance of grass in the steppe and the horse was so busy grazing that it did not return when called. When this happened, discontented Hazrat 'Ali cursed it all and the steppe turned to stone and grass never grew there again".[52]

As we have noted above, the sacred sites associated with Hazrat 'Ali are numerous in Muslim countries. The sacred tombs of Caliph can be found in Najaf (Iraq), Mazar-i Sharif (Afghanistan), the Ferghana Valley's Shah-i Mardan Qishlaq have been regarded as sacred sites since early on, with mausoleums later built by the Abbasids, Timurids and the Khanate of Kokand. Thus, it is possible to glean information from these monuments dedicated to Hazrat 'Ali. For example, there is an inscription in Arabic on a marble plate kept in the archives of the State History Museum of Uzbekistan that states:

---

[47] Lidskiy1886: 184. Fond rukopisey i dokumentov Ferganskogo kraevedcheskogo muzeya. KP № 5858.

[48] Mandelshtam - Rozenfeld 1960: 98.

[49] Abaeva 1975: 279.

[50] Pugachenkova 1963: 55.

[51] Sulaymonov 2004: 37.

[52] Zhoraev - Saidova 2002: 73.

"... If this world is a city, its gate is 'Ali ...". On a jade gravestone found in the Gur-i Emir Mausoleum in Samarqand, Amir Timur's genealogical tree is presented as follows:

> "Amir Timur Kuragan ibn Amir Taragay ibn Amir Burkul ibn Ilangiz ibn Amir Iyjil ibn Amir Karachor-noyon ibn Amir Sogu-chesan ibn Amir Erdamchi-Barlas ibn Amir Kachuli ibn Amir Tumanay". This list is then followed by the lineage of Genghis Khan: "Genghis Khan ibn Amir Yasugey Bakhadir ibn Amir Burtan Bahadir ibn Amir Kabul-khan ibn Amir Tumanay ibn Amir Baysungur ibn Amir Kaydu ibn Amir Tutumanin/Dutumanin ibn Amir Buga Amir Bozunjar; "Dutummanin Khan, the father of this noble person, is not known. His mother was Alankuva; which according to legend, ... happened by means of a true ray, and this ray belonged to descendants of the Lion of Allah, 'Ali ibn Abu Talib."[53]

The final part of the genealogy recorded on the inscription, the legend associated with the name of Hazrat 'Ali, is not mentioned in the family tree in the work by Hafiz-i Abru *Zubdat at-Tavarih* or in the *Zafarname* by Sharaf ad-Din 'Ali Yazdi. In A. Buriev's opinion, this legend, was added when this inscription was engraved on the stone.[54]

The renowned orientalist, A. A. Semenov, scrupulously examined this gravestone at Amir Timur tomb and stated that the reason for the inscription on the gravestone of the sahibkiran was Amir Timur's for Hazrat 'Ali.[55] This is true and can also be seen in the lineage of Qarakhanid. In the above lineage, Amir Timur is reputed to be among the descendants of Hazrat 'Ali.[56]

Mazar-i Sharif (Afghanistan).

---

[53] *Amir Temur azhdodlari*, 6.

[54] *Ibid.* 7.

[55] Semenov 1948: 53.

[56] Rodoslovnaya Karahana 1899: 8791.

In Charjuy (present day Turkmenabad, Turkmenistan) and on the bank of the Gunt River in the Pamirs there are pilgrimage sites associated with 'Ali. Kazakhs would offer sacrifices to "The Sacred Stone" (*Aulie Tas*) on the bank of the Bagsan River (Kazakhstan) the revering it as a place where Hazrat 'Ali had taken a step. Residents near Baku on the Caspian Sea held similar beliefs about a stone known as "'Ali's foot".[57] In the valley region of the Hindu Kush, known until recently as Kafiristan (Afghanistan), there was a mazar located in Namatgul Qishlaq bearing the name of Hazrat 'Ali. Inside the mazar, there were some candlesticks and two spherical black stones, each weighing 1.5 poods placed on the *sufa*. According to legend, when Hazrat 'Ali came to conquer the Pyanj River Valley he, effortlessly, as if it were a child's play, practiced with them.[58]

In 1939, during the construction of the Great Ferghana Canal, archaeologists examined numerous historical monuments in the areas through which the canal passed. In his diaries, the researcher A. Zayniddinov provided information on a stone known as "Sanga 'Ali" (2x2.5x2) located in the Asht District (Tajikistan) as well as the folk tales related to it. Folk tales tell that the stone had belonged to Hazrat 'Ali, and thus the local population referred to it as "Sangi 'Ali" or 'the stone of 'Ali'.[59]

Shahi Mardan, Khiva (Uzbekistan).

Not far from the city of Ferghana on the banks of the Isfayram *say* (mountainous

[57] Klimovich 1962: 272.

[58] Sheraliev 1993: 8.

[59] See Zayniddinov 1939.

stream) there was once a mazar known as "Qara-Tash". It is said that here Hazrat 'Ali had rested while returning from Osh-Takht-i Suleyman (Solomon's Throne). It was also here that his camel turned to stone.[60]

In the city of Khiva (Uzbekistan) near Ichang Kala there was once known as Shahi Mardan where Hazrat 'Ali is said to be buried,[61] and had once been recognized as one of the seven graves of Hazrat 'Ali in the land of Turan.[62]

Gazgan Qishlaq in Navoi Oblast's Nuratin District also contains a mazar associated with Hazrat 'Ali.[63] A folk storyteller, *bakhshi* Rahmatulla Yusuf Oghli, says the following about the site:

> "A short distance from Gazgan's marble mines stands the sacred site of Shah-i Mardan. As people say, inside one of the shrine's rooms stands a statue made of white marble resembling a kneeling camel. The camel's head has been cut off and lies near a spring-fed well. Some people worship the statue, believing that it had been the very camel on which 'Ali's body was placed, and turned to stone after arriving here".[64]

In Karatepa Qishlaq of the Bukhara's Shafirkan District there is another sacred site known as Hazrat 'Ali Shah-i Mardan.[65] It should be noted that according to Ya. S. Akhmetgaleeva, the events reflected in the epic *Kisek Bash Kitaby*, were likely also associated with Nur Ata as the cycle's main hero reports that he was from the fortress Nur before the appearance of the Prophet Muhammad and his followers.[66]

There are reports that in the mid-19th century there was a mazar dedicated to Hazrat 'Ali and to his horse Duldul in Uch Turfan, located in Eastern Turkestan.[67] N. N. Pantusov's (1849-1909) article concerning the site first published in 1909 states that in ancient times a ruler named Barbar reigned in Uch Turfan. After Hazrat 'Ali stood against him, and defeated him in battle, the local population built a mazar in Hazrat 'Ali's honor.[68]

When considering sites associated with the name 'Ali, it is necessary to bear in mind the possibility that these places took their name from a different figure with the same name. There are stories and folk tales that make reference to several holy men and warriors in the region of Turan that also bear the name 'Ali.[69]

Take, for instance, the well-known mazar of saint Abu 'Ali Dakkak in Turkmenistan. The legends associated with Abu 'Ali Dakkak are very similar to those of Alexander the Great.[70] Local legends about this figure were published in an article by M. E. Masson

---

60 Alimukhamedov 1966: 28.
61 Abdurasulov 1997: 48.
62 Mankovskaya - Bulatova 1978: 177.
63 Abashin 1999: 109-111.
64 *Bobolardan qolgan naqllar*, 41.
65 Salim Muhtor, Karim Bobomurod 1998: 191.
66 Ahmetgaleeva 1979: 34.
67 Klimovich 1962: 272.
68 See Pantusov 1894; Molla Musa Sayrami 2007.
69 Alisher Navoiy, 1968, 155.
70 Imomov 1989: 26.

who writes:

> "In reference to the origins of 'Ali Abu Dakkak the current inhabitants of Bagir ... only provide variants of a legend first recorded as told by a certain Sultan Muhammad who worked on a collective farm. According to the legend, 'Ali Abu Dakkak, the only son of a poor widow, was already a giant and muscular by the age of seven when Hazrat 'Ali took noticed him in Medina. Intending to go to Khorasan, Hazrat 'Ali persuaded the boy's mother to let the boy go with him to struggle against the disbelievers. In Nisa, while the Arabs were praying in the Namazgoh Mosque just outside of the city, the disbelievers attacked the group and killed almost everyone. By will of Allah, Hazrat 'Ali was enveloped in a cloud which hid him from his enemies until he finished his *namaz* (prayer). After this, he called to the young 'Ali Abu Dakkak telling him to remain hidden in the room, and then rushed to fight the disbelievers. When the boy looked out and noticed that dozens of unbelievers about to attack his master, he lept out to help him and was killed. Having crushed the disbelievers, Hazrat 'Ali ordered that a large gravestone be placed at the grave of the young warrior and a *gumbäz* (dome) erected to cover it.
>
> Later, when 'Ali Abu Dakkak's mother met Hazrat 'Ali in Medina and told her the truth what had happened, she wanted to see her son's grave with her own eyes to confirm that the story was true. The magical horse, Duldul, galloping at full speed quickly brought her to Nisa. Stopping at a tomb, the widow called her son: "Oh, 'Ali!". Her call was answered by 72,000 of voices from under the ground (variants of the story say that the response came from sixty places). The sheykhs explained that tens of thousands of Muslims named 'Ali had already become *shahids* and suggested that the mother call her son's full name. When she called "Oh, Abu 'Ali Dakkak!" Her deceased son responded that told her that he entered paradise and was happy. Having ensured that her son had been placed in a good mausoleum, the mother returned safely to Medina, and from then on miracles began to happen at her son's tomb".[71]

Over time, because of the people's respect for Hazrat 'Ali, all sacred sites bearing the name 'Ali became associated with Hazrat 'Ali. This is likely the reason for the large number of sacred sites named after Hazrat 'Ali in our area. Take, for example, the legends related to the Shah Qutayba Mazar in Andijan's Jalaladuk District. Though the mazar is related to the Islamic commander Qutayba ibn Muslim al-Bahili (660-715), many people still believe that in reality Shah Qutayba was Hazrat 'Ali himself, something confirmed by the author in conversations with local residents.[72] When compared with data from the genealogy of *The Shah Qutayba Kuk-bulaki Andijani* preserved by the descendants Shah Qutayba we see that Qutayba ibn Muslim was a descendant of 'Ali ibn Abu Talib.[73] Although the assertions of the genealogy are tenuous at best, the military operations carried out by Qutayba ibn Muslim in the Ferghana Valley over the years probably began to be credited to Hazrat 'Ali. Over time, this likely developed into claims of kinship between Qutayba and Hazrat 'Ali. Informants claim that they had heard elderly people claim that "Qutayba is 'Ali himself." Regardless of the veracity of their claim, it seems evident that Arab military campaigns in the Ferghana Valley during the early Islamic period legends and folk tales about Hazrat 'Ali

---

[71] Masson 1949: 104.

[72] Field research of the author. 2004. Andijan Oblast, Jalakuduk District, Qishlaq Shah Qutayba.

[73] This genealogy is kept at the family library of Nusrullakhan Khasanov, residing in the Akhunbabaev Town, Jalakuduk District, Andijan Oblast .

are given special regard.

Sacred Sites in Shah-i Mardan Associated with Hazrat 'Ali

The qishlaq of Shah-i Mardan (Uzbekistan) is one of the most beautiful places in the Ferghana Valley. Located 60 km south of the city of Ferghana in the foothills of the Alay Mountains, Shah-i Mardan is home to several mazars such as "Archa Mazar", "Tal Mazar", "Tash Mazar", "Bel Mazar", and "Zirk Mazar", the most famous among them being associated with Hazrat 'Ali.

Here people tell stories about a white camel (*oq tuya*) that transported his body – in each of the seven places where it stopped, sacred sites appeared bearing the name of the hero who lost his life for religious faith. People also speak of how after Hazrat 'Ali's death, his followers prepared seven coffins (*tobut*) which were brought by his followers to different regions - resulting in several places bearing the name of the same figure. The second possibility is *qadam-jay* (footprint) of Hazrat 'Ali. Its location was identified by a pious local person who either had received a vision revealing the site's location or read about it in a book. The multiple variants and amorphous nature of such legends make them difficult for Muslims scholars to critique. Other features that characterize these legends are their simplicity and accessibility for the local people who have not been educated in history and philosophy and frequently employ "wandering" plots (in most places there are not more than 10 plot variants).

The *Gazatname-i Shah Jarir*, written by Shah Hakim Halis and copied in 1906, includes a poem devoted to this mazar dedicated to Hazrat 'Ali in Ferghana. The works of Russian geographers and the historians published at the end of the 19th and beginning of the 20th century contain descriptions of the Ferghana Valley that pay particular attention to Shah-i Mardan, which is mentioned as one of the most sacred places for the local people.[74] A. F. Middendorf stated that the Shah-i Mardan Mazar was known to locals as "Hazrat Shah-i Mardan".[75]

In addition to the information on the Shah-i Mardan Mazar presented by these researchers, there has been a complete lack of information on the site. These Russian researchers did not confine themselves when writing on the Hazrat 'Ali Mazar and provided fascinating descriptions of its exterior. In particular, V. I. Massalskiy's *Turkestani Territory* provides a general description of the exterior of the mazar in the late 19th century.[76]

After arriving at the natural barrier of a mountain range, L. Kostenko wrote an article entitled "Expedition to the Alay Mountains" which was published in the newspaper *The Russian Invalid* in 1876. Regarding Shah-i Mardan he wrote:

> "... its best features are the mosque and the tomb of a holy man by whose name a small village is also called. In Persian, Shah-i Mardan means "the King of Humankind

---

[74] *Zemlya i lyudi*, 1892: 407.
[75] See Middendorf 1882.
[76] Masalskiy 1913: 707.

(Shah-i-Mardan)". Under this assumed name, as the local *mullahs* assured, the son-in-law of the great Prophet, the fourth caliph of the Muslims 'Ali masquerades. According to the *mullahs*, tombs of this Muslim saint are located in seven other places".

Gazatname-i Shah Jarir, copied in 1906.

Shah-i-Mardan is considered the most popular saint in the entire Khanate of Kokand and is the first among the patrons of Ferghana, bearing the same significance as Bogouddin for the Khanate of Bukhara and Palvan-Ata for Khivans.

The shrine is picturesquely located on a ridge with its façade facing the edge of the slope. There is a mosque at a tomb located in the small building constructed in the typical Central Asian style that serves as a monument and contains the tomb of a saint.

This building is rectangular with the front representing a wall. In the middle of the wall a niche formed with pear-shaped vaulting. This niche contains two wooden folding doors decorated with intricate carvings. In a niche above the door there is a large Arabic inscription reading: "Allah, Muhammad, Abu-Bakr, Omar, Osman, 'Ali". Under the inscription there are painted representations of various sacred sites in Mecca and Medina. At the entrance into the building tower several *tughs*, the high wooden poles with copper tips and horse or yak tails.

The outside door leads into a small room with a ceiling of adequate height that is illuminated by light from two windows covered with carved lattices. Horns of rams and goats lie at the windows. The next room is the same size as the first and is partitioned lengthwise by a wooden lattice, which is covered with colored drapes, completely enclosing "the tomb of a saint". This drape is lifted only for special occasions such as large scale prayers offered at the site.

The holiness of "The King of Humankind" not only attracts dozens of pilgrims which generously provide for the mullahs living near the tomb, but even supports the entire small village by paying tithes to maintain the mosque.

Concerning the origins of the tomb, I managed to hear the following legend at the shrine:

> "The local mullahs stated that 'Ali was the Prophet's son-in-law. After his death he was not buried, but instead his body was placed on a white camel's back, and released to the four winds. Soon after, the camel left: where, no one knows. After this a good deal of time passed when the following happened at the place where the tomb is now located. While playing, children at digging up little mounds of dirt, each time the children dug a white camel would emerge and destroy the mounds the children had just made by leveling the surface of the ground.
>
> Such an unusual and miraculous event could not but attract the attention of the neighboring population. The learned men opened their books and found references to a white camel that had carried the ashes of a great hero; these books also stated that the camel would stop in a place located between the two mountains and two waters, and that it would be here the ashes of 'Ali would be committed to the earth.
>
> As the place where the white camel had appeared matched the indications given in the wise books, it was determined that this must be the location of 'Ali's resting place. Many miracles performed at the site convinced the faithful of the veracity of their suspicions and for the inhabitants of Ferghana the claim became incontrovertible".[77]

Data on the Shah-i Mardan Mazar given by the Russian researchers represent facts and each newly enthroned khan never failed to make a pilgrimage to Shah-i Mardan. According to historical records, during his rule joint rule with his family, Khudayar Khan frequently made pilgrimages to Shah-i Mardan.[78] Trips by such important figures led to increasingly larger numbers of pilgrims visiting the site.

It is important to note that Hazrat 'Ali's name played a significant role in the lives of the khans of Kokand khans as recorded in written sources. It had become a tradition for the khan to utter the words: "Let 'Ali the Lion of Allah, always be with us" when sitting on the throne or at the beginning of a battle. The *History of the Khans of Ferghana*, a work by the 19th century historian Ziyavuddin Makhdum (Makhzuni), also attests to the practice.[79]

For over a millennium, the qishlaq of Shah-i Mardan has been regarded as a sacred site by the residents of the Ferghana Valley. Its reputation as a sacred site had already been established in the pre-Islamic era and continued through the first centuries after the arrival of Islam. Drawings found in Katta Kamar cave, located 12 km to the south from the qishlaq of Shah-i Mardan, on the banks of the Aqsu River at an altitude of 2,100 meters above sea level in 1969, attest to in the fact that Shah-i Mardan has been inhabited for thousands of years and that people had regarded the cave as a sacred site since the Neolithic Age (between the 5th and the 3rd millennia B.C.). Ancient drawings on stones in the cave indicate the performance of ceremonies associated with hunting.

77 See Guliyanc 2002.

78 Troitskaya 1968: 374.

79 See Magzuni, 2007.

This provides visible evidence in support of our opinion that sacred places of worship already existed in Shah-i Mardan in the pre-Islamic era. The fact that the cave lost its status as a sacred site for the performance of religious practice was explained by V.L. Ogudin:

> "The cave lost its position as a sacred site not in the 20th century, but in the earlier period. The reason for this was the appearance of places of sacred sites associated with Hazrat 'Ali and Yardan Ata adjacent to the cave in the 17th century".[80]

Corroborating that opinion, the ethnographer S.N. Abashin corroborates this opinion in stating that rise of the above mentioned sacred sites associated with Hazrat 'Ali dates from the 17th and 18th centuries.[81] However, our most recent research in the area provides evidence for a sacred site located at an altitude of 1,540-1,570 meters above sea level in the qishlaq of Shah-i Mardan even earlier. Although that sacred site did not bear the name of Hazrat 'Ali, it was certainly revered by the local population. Were it not for this fact, the sacred site would have gained such a large reputation as a sacred site in such a short period of time.

Inscriptions on tombstones found in the present day cemetery of Shah-i Mardan have shown that these lands have been sacred sites since the Middle Ages. It should be noted that in the modern cemetery, the first burial places date from 1949. Previously, the cemetery had been located near the Hazrat 'Ali Mazar. During excavation of grave sites ceramic vessels dating from the Middle Ages were found.

The discovery of the burial sites dating from the 7th and 8th centuries belonging to Turkic tribes in Okhna Qishlaq near Shah-i Mardan also indicates that there had been dynamic settlements in the location for a long time. Before becoming known as Shah-i Mardan, the qishlaq was referred to as "Parsin" (now the name of the qishlaq's main street). A manuscript entitled *Nasabname-i Turki*, contains information concerning the word "parsin." The manuscript gives a genealogy of the children of Muhammad ibn al-Hanafiya (637-700), the son of Hazrat 'Ali, Shah Abdurahman, Shah Mansur and Hazrat Parsinshah as well as the Prophet's warriors and followers that arrived here to convert the people of Mawarannahr to Islam. It reports that Hazrat Parsinshah died a martyr for the faith and was laid to rest in the mountains of Margelan.[82]

It is known that people also refer to Shah-i Mardan as the "Mountains of Margelan." This indicates that the qishlaq received the name Parsin it was the resting place of Hazrat Parsinshah, and, after centuries its origin was forgotten. The small mazar of Shah Talib near the mazar of Hazrat 'Ali likely the site of the grave of Hazrat Parsinshah. Regardless, the mazar in Shah-i Mardan has existed for centuries and is authentic.

Constructed in Shah-i Mardan at the end of the 19th century, the mausoleum and mosque dedicated to Hazrat 'Ali have long amazed pilgrims with their beauty. Who, then, led the construction of the mazar of Hazrat 'Ali and built this architectural

---

80 Ogudin 2002: 53.

81 Abashin 2006: 460.

82 Muminov A. K., 2003: 136.

monument so rare this era? Unfortunately, this architectural monument and its restorer, Shakir Mingbashi, both met tragic ends. Shakir Mingbashi was shot as an enemy of the state in the first years of the Soviet power (1918) and the mazar and mosque he constructed were destroyed at the end of the 1930s. Shakir Mingbashi was born Muhammad Shakir, the son of Mirza Qalandar, in 1834 in Rishtan Qishlaq. His father, Mirza Qalandar, held the post of *sarkar* (tax collector) during the reign of the Kokandi khan, Khudayar.[83] After Mirza Qalandar's death, this position was occupied by Mullah Shakir from 1881 to 1907, who also held post of *mingbashi* and was known to the people as Shakir Naib, or Shakir Mingbashi.

Between 1894 and 1898, Shakir Mingbashi personally donated 60 thousand roubles for improvements to the mazar and mosque of Hazrat 'Ali in Shah-i Mardan[84]. His generosity surprised even the officials in the tsarist administration since at that time not every *mingbashi* was capable of making such a donation for the improvement of sacred sites. For this reason the poet Mulla Niyaz (1823-1896), a native of Shah-i Mardan, wrote: "I have never met such noble and courageous person as Shakir".[85]

In the beginning of 1909 the combined population Shah-i Mardan and Yardan numbered 1,818.[86] At that time in Shah-i Mardan there were six mosques, including the mosque Hazrat 'Ali which was distinguished as a rare example of the architecture of the era. L. Kostenko says that the mazar of Hazrat 'Ali in Shah-i Mardan was destroyed by a large earthquake around 1826.[87] Our data indicates that the mazar was destroyed by earthquakes in 1822 and again in 1894.

As Hazrat 'Ali was seen as the saint patron of brave young warriors, Madaminbek (1892–1920), one of members of the independence movement, frequently visited the mazar of Hazrat 'Ali in Shah-i Mardan.[88] It was only after the death of such a well-known representative of the movement such as Madaminbek that the Bolsheviks dared enter Shah-i Mardan.

In December, 1921, not even a year after Madaminbek's death, the mazar and the mosque were burnt down in fights between the Bolsheviks and Normat Mahsum.[89] In the beginning of the 20th century, each year Shah-i Mardan was visited by over 15 thousand pilgrims in July and August alone. Because of the large influx of pilgrims, money 80,000-100,000 roubles were gathered each year by the *sheykh*s of the mazar of Hazrat 'Ali and this had drawn the special attention of the Soviet government.[90] In 1921 an armed detachment of Bolsheviks was sent to Shah-i Mardan to confiscate the accumulated wealth held there.

---

[83] Abdulakhatov N U., 2006: № 4, 44.

[84] *Zolotaya kniga Rossiyskoy imperii.* Moskva, 1905. Fond rukopisey i dokumentov Ferganskogo kraevedcheskogo muzeya (FOKM). KP №5998. ПД 912.

[85] Mollo Niyaz 1993: 82.

[86] Spisok naselennih mest Ferganskoy oblasti. Ot Ferganskogo oblastnogo staticheskago komiteta. Skobelev. 1909. 77.

[87] Guliyanc 2002.

[88] Suhareva 1960: 25.

[89] Hatamov 1979: 62.

[90] Klimovich 1962: 118.

According to informants, a large number of rare manuscripts, endowment credentials, and *waqf* documents granted by khans were kept in the mosque. When the Red Army men entered Shah-i Mardan, the local population assumed that since the mosque was the house of God the troops would not enter it, and therefore, they brought all their valuable things to the mosque.[91] Before long their mistake became obvious and because almost all major events in the area took place inside the mosque, the fighting between the Red Army and Normat Mahsum's men gradually moved towards the mosque. As a result of the gunfire, a fire was ignited in the mosque that lasted several days. The fire consumed the entire architectural monument and its portals fell in.[92]

During the fire the Red Army is said to have suffered 47 casualties but further investigation is required to clarify several points that remain unclear.[93]

According to V. V. Bardadin, commander of the 1st-squadron of the 13th Cavalry Regiment who came the day after the fighting at Shah-i Mardan for gathering provisions he noted that the armed detachment commanded by Kaplin included 47 cavalrymen as a total of 48 soldiers had been sent. Of them, 41 Red Army soldiers perished in the mosque fire and the remaining five died of their wounds in a hospital in the city of Ferghana.[94] According to information collected by V. V. Bardadin, during the fire, three Red Army soldiers had managed to survive by taking shelter in the mazar. The names of the survivors were Shoshist, a machine gunner and Kuznetsov, a sergeant. The way they survived is of particular interest. When the soldiers left the burning mosque, they ran into the mazar and moved the stone plate over the tomb of Hazrat 'Ali and hid inside for some time. When they began to choke from the smoke, they climbed out of the grave and abandoned the mazar.[95] They noticed that inside the grave of Hazrat 'Ali there were human bones instead of the "ordinary stones and clay lumps of various sizes" as the Soviet historians later wrote. These two soldiers who saw human bones inside the tomb and later served in World War II, returned to Ferghana before the 40th anniversary of the end of World War II and confirmed the veracity of what they had seen in the mazar of Hazrat 'Ali in Shah-i Mardan 64 years earlier. As these two individuals had no incentive to lie about the matter, there is no doubt that the mazar is the individual buried in the mazar is in fact Hazrat 'Ali.

The dome of the mazar that was destroyed during the fire was restored in 1924. According to some reports, however, the repair work was completed in 1926 and included a new door approximately 4m x 2m in size that represented a unique sample of ornamental art. On the door there is an inscription amid the relief carvings that reads "1345 *amali* Usta Umrzak Marginani" from which we can know that the door was made in 1926 by the renowned Margilan Usta (craftsman) Umrzak. The ethnographer A. K. Pisarchik wrote that during her stay in Margelan in 1939 she met with Usta Umrzak. She

91 Field research of the author. 2003. Fergana Oblast, Fergana District, kishlak Shakhimardan.

92 Ermoliev - Kovalev 2004: 36.

93 Alimukhamedov 1966: 17.

94 Vospominaniya komandira kaveskadrona 13 kavpolka 7 otd. Turk. Kavbrigadi Bordadina V.V. (FOKM). KP. № 3235: 3.

95 Gorshunova 2000: 39.

stated that at the time, *usta* Umrzak was approximately fifty years old and had made the door for the government building of Uzbekistan (SovNarKom).[96]

Door of the Mazar Shah-i Mardan. (Ferghana).

Credit for producing this masterpiece cannot be given to Usta Umrzak alone, but also the master of chain production, Usta Abulqasim Khodja, son of Jamal Khodja who demonstrated his skill in the use of metal fragments used for ornamentation on the door. Therefore, the name "Abulqasim Khodja Jamal Khodja" can be found on the door handle. Today, this door is the only part of the mazar that has managed to survive the turbulence of the region.

Until the end of the 1920s, Ismail Khodja, son of Sayid Ishan, was the key bearer of the mazar of Hazrat ʻAli, representative of the *sheykhs* of Shah-i Mardan, and chief *mutavalli*. According to V. A. Parfentiev, Ismail Khodja's father, Sayid Ishan, had many *murids* (disciples) in vicinity of Vuadil and Shah-i Mardan.[97] This indicates that he was a man of high standing in Shah-i Mardan. After Sayid Ishan's death his son, Ismail Ishan, was chosen to succeed him as chief *mutavalli*. As the *mutavalli*-treasurer there was a representative of the Margilan *hajji* Buzrukhan Ishan the son of Langar Khoja Ishan. The Kokandi *hajji* had transferred the management of the third mazar to Giyaskhodja, the son of Salahiddin Ishan.[98]

A petition written in 1886 to the military governor of the Ferghana Oblast by the Shah-i Mardan *hajji*, Mahmud Khoja, the son of Langar Khoja and Baba Khodja, the son of Kalan Khodja, is kept in the Central State Archives in Uzbekistan on the behalf of

[96] Pisarchik 1938: 38.
[97] Parfentiev 1904: 64.
[98] Khatamov 1979: 9.

Shah-i Mardan *hajji*. This document states that Deybner, the former chief administrative authority of the *uyezd* (canton), appointed Padsha Khodja Ishan, the son of Zakir Khoja Ishan, to the post of *mutavalli* of the mazar of Shah-i Mardan instead of the above mentioned persons in his order №5 issued in 1883. This irritated the Shah-i Mardan *hajji*. The petition states that despite the writs of protection and letters of privilege regarding the position of *hajji* of Shah-i Mardan that were granted to their ancestors by Genghis Khan, Amir Timur and other Muslim khans reigned in Mawarannahr, and in spite of all the decisions issued by the *qadis* (judges) of Margelan and Chimion, Deybner, the former *uyezd* chief, appointed a person to the post of *mutavalli* of the mazar Shah-i Mardan who was not qualified to fill it. On that account, the *hajji* of Shah-i Mardan sent the petition to the military governor requesting that the post of *mutavalli* be filled by a *hajji* they had elected themselves. It is unknown what decisions were made regarding the petition however, for our research the fact that this document contains the names of all of the *hajji* in Shah-i Mardan is of great importance. Until this point, we had no evidence of the existence of the position of *hajji* of Shah-i Mardan. The mention of the names of the *hajji* in the document provides new data about Shah-i Mardan.[99] The letter contains a list of over 200 names of the *hajji* of Shah-i Mardan. It certainly took a considerable amount of time to settle down in the qishlaq of Shah-i Mardan, making the idea of a newly arrived *hajji* becoming a *sheykh* of the mazar difficult to accept. On the contrary, it is obvious that they had lived in the area for several centuries.

The Mazar of Shah-i Mardan (Ferghana, 1905).

The famous Kazakh scholar Chokan Valikhanov (1835-1865) presented interesting data on sacred sites located in the Ferghana Valley. Pleasant memories and recollections of the mazar of Hazrat 'Ali in Shah-i Mardan are of particular interest.

[99] TsGA Uz. Fund № I– 19. Op. № 1, D. 1821. l. 3

Valikhanov mentions that the *sheykhs* of the mazar in Shah-i Mardan were *hajji* from the Mashhad Mahalla of the city of Margilan.[100]

There is also information indicating that the pilgrimage to Shah-i Mardan started with visits to sacred sites near the qishlaq of Vuadil and Avval and then proceeded to Qadamjay.

The sacred site of Qadamjay is located in the eponymous district of Qadamjay in Kyrgyzstan. This sacred site contains stones that ostensibly contain the prints of Hazrat 'Ali's hand (including marks for five fingers) and his knees known as "'Ali*ning Qadamjayi*", i.e. "the place where the 'Ali's feet stepped". One of the site's peculiarities is that it is reminiscent of Hazrat 'Ali's exploits in his fight with a dragon in Barbar's city as described in the novel *Baba Ravshan.*

On one side of the *say* there is a sacred stone with marks left by Hazrat 'Ali's knees, while on the other side there is a rock resembling a dragon with its head cut off. How, then, is this place connected with Hazrat 'Ali? The cities of Shahr-i Barbar and Shahr-i Khaybar were not forgotten by historians. The first city was situated in the vicinity of Balkh,[101] and the second was located eight *barids* (about 250 km - N.A.) from Medina in the direction of Sham (Syria).[102] These two cities are mentioned in the legends about Hazrat 'Ali; in the Ferghana Valley, there are also ancient fortresses known by names Shahr-i Barbar (Marqamat) and Khaybar (Eylatan).[103] For this reason, the local population believes that Hazrat 'Ali had visited these places. The "Baba Ravshan" legend states: "Hazrat 'Ali led Baba Ravshan to Shahr-i Barbar located six months journey from Medina".[104] Written sources indicate that the mountains containing the water-source of the city of Margilan are in fact located six months journey from Medina.[105] It is for this reason that local people identify Qadamjay as the site of Hazrat 'Ali's battle with a dragon, and cite the sacred stone with marks of Hazrat 'Ali's knees on one side of the *say*, and the rock with the shape of a beheaded dragon as proof.[106]

Another site associated with Hazrat 'Ali's footprints is the qishlaq of Shahr-i Kalach Khojend. It is said that before entering Ferghana, Hazrat 'Ali knelt here to pray and the traces of his knees remained on the stone; today the site is marked with a mausoleum .[107]

The qishlaq of Shah-i Mardan proper contains the following sacred sites:

1. the stone at Ellik Paysaki
2. Koktash (sacred site)
3. the Small or *Kichik Mazar* (Mazar-i Shah Talib)

---

[100] Valikhonov 1986: 157.
[101] Makhmud ibn Vali 1977: 23.
[102] Abd ar-Rashid al-Bakuvi 1971: 26.
[103] Latinin 1961: 111.
[104] *Bobo Ravshan qissasi*, 153.
[105] This manuscript is held in the Qishlak Buvimazar, Buvaydan District, by the family of Shermatova Adinakhon.
[106] Field research of the author. 2004. Republic of Kyrgyzstan, Batkent Oblast, Kadamdzhay District.
[107] Field research of the author. 2005. Republic of Tajikistan, Sogd Oblast, Khojend City, Kishlak Kalacha.

4. the Great or *Katta Mazar* (Mazar Hazrat 'Ali)
5. the mazar of Umar Umiya
6. Chakka Tamar (sacred site)

The Ellik Paysaki Stone (a stone weighing fifty *paysas*) located near the Ellik Paysaki bridge on the approach to the qishlaq of Shah-i Mardan is known as "the tree-pound stone of Hazrat 'Ali". As a "*paysa*" weighs approximately 50 grams, fifty *paysas* would come to a total of 2.5 kg. This stone in Shah-i Mardan, however, weighs several tons. How then, did the stone come to be known as "Fifty *Paysas*"? A story explaining this states that in order to inspire fear in the hearts of his enemies, Hazrat 'Ali lifted the huge stone, said "Only fifty *paysas*", and then cast it aside. Next to the Fifty-*Paysa* stone there is another stone known as the "camel-stone" as people feel it resembles the camel that bore the coffin of Hazrat 'Ali.[108]

People who visit the Hazrat 'Ali Mazar should first read the Quran in honor of all the sacred souls resting in peace in Shah-i Mardan before proceeding up the stairs. This place is known as Mazarbashi (the beginning of the mazar) and according to a cultural informant, Saltanat Ergasheva, this was once a sacred site known as Aq Mazar. At the beginning of the 20th century people would ascent from here on a direct set of spiral stairs made of *archa* (cedar red juniper). After coming up the stairs, pilgrims would then proceed to enter through the *darvozakhana*, (the room directly adjoining to the gate).

The Lesser Mazar (Kichik Mazar)

In the early era, *sheykhs* would first lead pilgrims who came to the *darvozakhana* to the Lesser Mazar. The mazar of Hazrat 'Ali was known as the "Great Mazar", and the mazar of Shah Talib, one of 'Ali's fourth generation descendants, located 150m to the northwest was referred to as "Lesser Mazar."

It is said that the mazar of Hazrat 'Ali in Ferghana was first erected by Shah Talib. According to legend, Shah Talib governed from the city of Mecca and at the end of his life made a vow to restore the seven mazars of Hazrat 'Ali. When he was in Ferghana during the construction of the mazar there, he heard the voice of his grandfather, Hazrat 'Ali, call from the tomb. After that, he became the *sheykh* of the mazar and later he was buried there.[109] Informants claim that Shah Talib was a true descendant of Hazrat 'Ali. When examining genealogical records, the sixth descendant of Hazrat 'Ali, Imam 'Ali Riza (killed in 818), had a son by the name Sayyid Shah Talib. This indicates that Shah Talib lived in the 9th century, but since Sayyid Shah Talib did not rule in Mecca or Medina, in our opinion, Shah Talib and Parsinshah actually represent a single person. It appears that Parsinshah had also been known by the name Shah Talib.

Unfortunately, popular legends give only limited data about the mazar. Regardless, since ancient times the popularity of the figure of Shah Talib and Hazrat 'Ali has been widespread, as is proved by the multiple sacred sights associated with these figures.

108 Field research of the author. 2003. Fergana Oblast, Fergana District, Kishlak Shakhimardan.
109 Field research of the author. 2003. Fergana Oblast, Fergana District, kishlak Shakhimardan.

The Great Mazar (Katta Mazar)

After making a pilgrimage to the Lesser Mazar, pilgrims would continue on to the Great Mazar, passing under the gate to the mazar facing the qishlaq. In front of the Lesser Mazar, there was a stone known as the "cradle-stone" or a "holed stone", which was also visited by pilgrims. In 1947, the photographer P. Panchenko photographed pilgrims arriving in Shah-i Mardan as they visited a sacred stone. This photo is now kept in the Ferghana Regional Ethnographic Museum (No. 5611).

Five more burial sites were situated on the path between the Lesser and Great Mazars.[110] In our opinion, these graves belonged to Shah-i Mardan *hajji*. After visiting these graves, pilgrims would continue on towards the Great Mazar (the mazar of Hazrat 'Ali). Each pilgrim saw visiting this mazar as obligatory.

Descriptions provided by the ethnographer R. Ya. Rassudova concerning the matter are even more interesting:

> "The following seven mazars were considered the Ferghana Valley's most sacred; 1. Osh (Takht-i Suleyman); 2. Jalalabad (Hazrat Ayyub); 3. Aravan (a place where 'Ali walked and the mazar of Duldul Ata); 4) Kampir Ravat (a place where 'Ali walked); 5. Haydarkan-Qadamjay (a place where 'Ali walked); 6. Shah-i Mardan (mazar of 'Ali); 7. Sokh (Yigit - 'Ali-Pirim, a place where 'Ali walked)".[111]

Rassudova also stated that:

> "five of the above mentioned sacred sites are associated with Hazrat 'Ali. According to legend, each Muslim should make a pilgrimage to the above mentioned seven mazars at least once. The first of these should be made at the age one (accompanied by relatives), and the last made at the age of 63 (the age of the Prophet Muhammad when he died)".[112]

Considering the fact that Hazrat 'Ali was the *pir* and patron of young men, pilgrimages performed by youth to his mazar continued year round. Young male pilgrims brought a large number of sacrificial animals, especially during the *sayil* (popular festival). For example, having taken some water flowing out of the holy spring found at the shrine of Hazrat 'Ali in Sokh, they would sprinkle it onto the boys wishing them to be as brave as 'Ali was.[113]

According to informants, if possible, each person should make an animal sacrifice as part of the pilgrimage to the Shah-i Mardan Mazar. Part of the meat from the burnt animal was used for cooking a meal. The remaining parts of the animal would be divided into portions and distributed as offerings to the *sheykhs* of the mazar. Women who made the pilgrimage would primarily offer prayers from in front of the mazar in the evening as the large number of pilgrims in the afternoon prevented them from

[110] Vospominaniya komandira kaveskadrona. 113 kavpolka. 7 otd. Turk. Kavbrigada Bordadina V.V. (FOKM). KP. № 3235. p.2.

[111] Rassudova 1985: 96.

[112] *Ibid.* 97.

[113] *Ibid.* 97.

performing their ceremonies.

The Mazar of Shah-i Mardan (Ferghana, 2001).

In the beginning of the 20th century, pilgrims were met near the mazar of Hazrat 'Ali by approximately fifty-sixty *sheykhs*. The *sheykhs* would lead the way for the pilgrims and tell them to kiss innumerable polls with the yak tails hung upon them, horns of animals, old trees, and the bricks of each of the gateways. Those who did not follow the *sheykhs'* instructions they would be warned that they were inviting misfortune upon themselves. Only after performing these rituals were the pilgrims brought to the primary sacred site, the mazar's *qibla*. As pilgrims entered this space they would present the *mutavalli* with the gift-offerings intended for him, and thus conclude the pilgrimage.

The local residents of Shah-i Mardan believe that any person who questioned the sanctity of the Mazar of Hazrat 'Ali or dared somehow abuse or offend it, would inevitably be punished (*qarghish, teskari fotiha, du'o-yi bad*). Local people tell thousands of stories about how during the period of atheist ideological domination it was not possible to destroy that sacred site. According to informants, the Shah-i Mardan can push forward to attack by putting the doubting individual (*shukkak*) to the test. For example, at the sacred site of Aq-Mazar in Shah-i Mardan pilgrims must count the number of stairs in the ascent and the sinful will inevitably make a mistake while counting.

The older individuals in the qishlaq still remember that at the beginning of the last century, during winter a deer and a sole performed the rounds made by pilgrims at the Shah-i Mardan Mazar. After that, without harming anyone, they continued on to Yardan. The scholar M. E. Masson's says the following about such stories :

> "In former times among the local population the belief was spread that the fierce and fearless kinglike predator tames only near the tombs of especially esteemed Muslim saints, and it was admitted a true attribute of their spiritual greatness. Thus, the staff providing services to the mausoleum of Hakim Termezi located nearby the Amu-Darya group of ruins of Old Termez, assured me that the tigers who went in winter time following the wild boars to the lower reaches of the Amu-Darya, passing by way of pilgrimage nearby the mazar, made annual worship to the tomb of Termez Ata ... According to the Tajiks from the mountain village of Zarkent in the Tashkent Oblast, as early as the end of the last century the tigers (one at a time) came in the late autumn to worship to the located a little bit above this qishlaq esteemed mazar of some Imam Muhammad, better known under the nickname of "Bobo-i Muradbakhsh" (i.e. 'Father granting the fulfilment of desires'). Predators, visiting a mazar, as befits the pious *ziyaratchi*, ostensibly "abstained from a sin", did not cut the horses grazed in the mountains and allowed themselves to do that only on their return way. Coming nearer to the place of burial of Imam Muhammad, where in that season remained to live only one of the foolish - *divana*, each tiger allegedly performed the ceremony obligatory for pilgrims, three times came around the mazar, and at the end was it put its muzzle to the threshold of the construction erected above a "sacred" tomb".[114]

Epilogue

As we have discussed above geographical location plays an important role in sacred sites associated with Hazrat 'Ali by virtue of the fact that sites dedicated to the saint can be found in caves, high mountains, water-springs, *says* and rivers, as well as in large trees. The local population's persistent association of natural monuments with Hazrat 'Ali is a distinguishing characteristic. On this account, the cult of Hazrat 'Ali is particularly widely spread in mountainous regions and in places located close to springs, says, and rivers. In our opinion, one of the primary reasons for this is the references to mountainous areas associated with acts of Hazrat 'Ali in literary works. As mountains, stones, and running water are convenient ways to depict the bravery and courage of 'Ali, they have enabled people to represent his heroic exploits not as mythical but as real events. It is for this very reason that each natural sanctuary was seen as connected to the miraculous force and power of Hazrat 'Ali. In due course gave way to identifying these places directly with Hazrat 'Ali. Thus place names from books were attributed to local places. As Hazrat 'Ali also personified pre-Islamic cults of heroes and saints, his cult among the local population continued from century to century in traditional form. Hazrat 'Ali managed to embody the images of renowned legendary and historical figures in Central Asia such as Iskander Zulkarnayn (Alexander the Great), Rustam, and the Prophets Khizr, Er Hubbi, Suleyman (Solomon).

Although many texts have been produced concerning Hazrat 'Ali , there are still numerous folk tales, epics, and oral traditions that people have preserved but have not yet been collected, commented on, edited, or compared with ancient and modern texts and traditions. In this article we have primarily addressed sacred sites located in the Ferghana Valley while making only brief reference to other sites located in other

[114] Masson M.E., 1963: 151-152.

regions of Uzbekistan, as well as in other countries in Central Asia, and the Near East.

Until recently, research on this subject has been carried out according to two contrasting paradigms: the religious and the scientific/atheistic. Internal antagonism and strong contrasts were shown not only in their methodology, but also in their approach to historical facts, events, and individuals. In particular, if in the first case data from written sources and oral traditions were treated critically and ironically, while in the latter, there was an attitude of mistrust toward the research of scholars, historians, and archaeological sources.

This work clearly emphasizes both scientific, religious, and in particular, oral sources on history. The fraternal Tajik, Kazakh, Kirghiz, Turkmen and Uyghur peoples all have immense respect for sacred sites associated with Hazrat 'Ali.

As we are unable to include all of the information contained in our sources in this article, we will continue to our research addressing related topics in future research. As our people have an inextinguishable reverence and undying interest in the person and life of Hazrat 'Ali, detailed and interesting works on the topic will follow in the future.

Bibliography

Abaeva, T. G. 1975. "Issledovaniya A. V. Stanishevskogo (Aziza Niallo) o Pamire" in *Strani i Narodi Vostoka. Vip. XVI. Pamir.*

Abashin S. N. 1999. "Shahi Mardan" in *Islam na territorii bivshey Rossiyskoy imperii. Enciklopedicheskiy slovar. Issue. 2.* Moskva.

Abashin S.N. 2006. "Shahi Mardan" in *Islam na territorii bivshey Rossiyskoy imperii.* Tom I. Moskva: Vostochnaya Literatura.

Abd ar-Rashid al-Bakuvi 1971. *Kitab talhis al-asrar va adzhaib al-malik al kahhar.* Moskva: Nauka.

Abdulakhatov, N. U. 2006. "Ziyoratgohlar va O'zbek mental tafakkurining shakllanishi" in *FDU. Ilmiy khabarlar.* № 4: 44.

Abdulakhatov, N. and O. Eshonboboev 2007. *Kokhna Marghilon ziyoratgohlari.* Farghona.

Abdulakhatov, N. and V. Azimov 2005. *Oltiariq ziyoratgohlari.* Toshkent: Sharq.

Abdulakhatov, N. and Z. Khaydarova 2003. *Bibi Ubayda tarikhi.* Farghona.

Abdurasulov, A. 1997. *Khiva.* Toshkent: O'zbekiston.

Abu Tokhirkhozha 1991 *Samariya.* Toshkent: Kamalak.

Ahmetgaleeva, Ya. S. 1979. *Issledovanie tyurkoyazichnogo pamyatnika "Kisekbash kitabi".* Moskva: Nauka.

Alimukhamedov, A. 1966. *«Muqaddas» va «qadamjoylar»ning paydo bolishi va zararlari.* Toshkent.

Alisher Navoiy 1968. "Nasoyim ul-muhabbat" in *Selected works.* XV. Toshkent: Ghafur Ghulom Nomidagi Badiiy Adabiyot Nashriyoti.

Amir Temur ajdodlari. Toshkent, 1992.

Bartold, V. V. 1931. *Mo'ngullar davrida Turkiston.* Samarqand: O'zbek Davlat Nashriyoti.

Bartold V. V. 1965-66. *Sochineniia.* Vol. III, IV. Moskva.

Blochet E. 1925-1926. "La conquète des Etats nestoriens de l'Asie centrale par les Shiites. Les influences chretienne et bouddhique dans le dogme islamique" in *Revue de l'Orient chretien,* № V.

Bobo Ravshan qissasi. Toshkent: Yozuvchi, 1991.

Bobolardan qolgan naqllar, 1998.

Bobrinskiy, A. A. 1908. *Gortsi verhoviev Pyandzha.* Moskva.

Buryakov, Yu. F., Kasimov M. R., Rostovcev O.M. 1973 *Arheologicheskie pamyatniki Tashkentskoy oblasti.* Toshkent: Fan.

DeWeese, D. 1994. *Islamisation and Native Religion in the Golden Horde. Baba Tükles and the Conversion to*

Islam in Historical and Epic Tradition. Pennsylvania.

DeWeese D. 1990. "Yasavian Legends on the Islamization of Turkistan" in Denis Sinor (ed.) *Aspects of Altaic Civilization III: Proceedings of the 30th Meeting of the Permanent International Altaistic Conference, Indiana University, Bloomington, Indiana, June 1987*. Bloomington.

Diakonov, M. M. 1948. "Neskol'ko nadpisey na kayrakah iz Kirgizii" in *Epigrafika Vostoka*. XII. Moskva.

Dzhahonov, U. 1989. *Zemledelie tadzhikov doliny Soha v kontse XIX - nachale XX v*. Doshanbe: Donish.

Dzhamal al-Karshi 2005. *Al-Mulhakat bi-s-surah (Istoriya Kazakhstana v persidskikh istochnikakh. Vol.I.)* Almaty: Dayk Press.

Ermoliev, N. I. and N. I. Kovalev *Devyatnadcat' ognennikh let. Rostovna Donu*. Rostizdat.

Gornenskiy, I. 2000. *Legendy Pamira i Gindukusha*. Moskva: Aleteyl.

Gorshunova, O.V. 2000. "Zhenskoe palomnichestvo k svyatim mestam (po materialam Ferganskoy dolini)" in *Itogi polevykh issledovanii*. Moskva.

Guliyanc, L. 2002. "Legendy i byli Shahi Mardana" in *Ferganskie zori*. 20.

Imomov, K. 1989. "Afsona" in *O'zbek fol'klori ocherklari*. Vol. II. Toshkent: Fan.

Ipak yo'li afsonalari. Toshkent: Fan, 1993.

Khasanov, F. 2001 *Tarikhi Mukhtasari dekhoti Isfara*. Dushanbe: Matbuot.

Khasanov, H. 1965. *O'rta Osiyo zhoy nomlari tarikhidan*. Toshkent: Fan.

Khatamov, A. 1979. *Hamza Shoximardonda*. Toshkent.

Khmelnitskiy, S. 2002. *Chorku Amir Hamza Hasti podsho. Drevneyshee derevyannoe zdanie Sredney Azii s reznim i skul'turnim dekorom*. Berlin - Riga.

Klimovich, L. I. 1962. *Islam*. Moskva.

Koran Translated by Academician I.Yu.Krachkovskiy. Moskva, 1990.

Latinin, B. A. 1961. "Nekotorie itogi rabot Ferganskoy ekspeditsii 1934 g" in *Arheologicheskiy sbornik*. Vypusk 3. Moskva: Izdatel'stvo Gosudarstvennogo Ermitazha.

Lidskiy, S. 1886. "Gornye okrestnosti Tashkenta." in *Turkestanskie vedomosti*. №48.

Magzuni 2007. *Fargana khandarinin tarikhi*. Bishkek.

Makhmud ibn Vali 1977 *More tayn*. Toshkent: Fan.

Mamadaliev, I. and D. Abdumalikova 1997. "Zhonodil-Maqotil qal'asi" in *Andizhonnoma*. № 41 (17311) 20 May, 1997.

Mandelshtam, A. M. and A. Z. Rozenfel'd 1960. "Kalai Imlok i Kalai Dzhamakhur v Karategine i svyazannie s nimi legendi" in Pamyati Mikhaila Stepanovicha Andreeva. *Karategine i svyazannie s nimi legendi* Vol. CXX.

Mankovskaya, L. and V. Bulatova 1978. *Pamyatniki zodchestva Xorezma*. Toshkent: Izdatel'stvo literatury i iskusstva imeni Gafura Gulyama.

Masalskiy, V.I. 1913. *Turkestanskiy kray*. St. Peterburg.

Masson, M. E. 1949. "Gorodisha Nisi v selenii Bagir i ikh izuchenie" in *Trudy YuTAKE*. Vol I. Ashhabad.

Masson M.E. 1963. "Iz proshlogo tigrov v Sredney Azii" in *Nauchnie trudi. Vipusk 200. Arkheologiya Sredney Azii*. VI. Toshkent.

Masson, M. E. 1976. *Iz vospominaniy Sredneaziatskogo arkheologa*. Toshkent: Izdatel'stvo literaturi i iskusstva imeni Gafura Gulyama.

Middendorf, A.F. 1882. *Ocherki Ferganskoy dolini*. Pribavlenie IV. A. XX. St.Peterburg.

Mirboboev, A. K. 1974. "Medrese Kanibadama i Isfari kak pamyatniki arkhitektury" in *Arkheologicheskie raboty v Tadzhikistane*, Issue XIV. Dushanbe: Donish.

Molla Musa Sayrami 2007. *Tarikhi hämidi*. Beijing: Millätlär Näshriyati.

Mollo Niyaz 1993. *Sanat digarsttar*. Bishkek.

Muhammad payghambar qissasi. Hadislar.Toshkent: Kamalak, 1991.

Muminov, A. K. 2000. "Die Erzählung eines Qožas über die Islamisierung der Länder, die dem Kokander Khanat unterstehen"in *Muslim Culture in Russia and Central Asia. Vol. 3: Arabic, Persian and Turkic Manusripts (15th-19th centuries)* (Islamkundliche Untersuchungen, Band 233), edited by Anke von Kügelgen, Aširbek Muminov, Michael Kemper, Berlin.

Muminov, A. K. 2003. "Kokandskaya versiya islamizacii Turkestana" in *Podvizhniki islama. Kult svyatykh i sufizm v Sredney Azii i na Kavkaze.* Moskva.
Nabiev, R.N. 1973. *Istorii Kokandskogo khanstva.* Toshkent: Fan.
Nalivkin, V. 1886. *Kratkaya istoriya Kokandskogo khanstva.* Kazan.
Narshakhiy 1991. *Bukhoro tarikhi.* Toshkent: Kamalak.
Nemtseva, N. B. 1995. "Mnogofunkcionalniy memorialno-kultoviy kompleks Khodzha Mashad na yuge Tazhdikistana" in *ONU.* 1995. № 5-6-7-8.
Ogudin,V.L. 2002. *Strana Ferghana.* Moskva: Centr Strategicheskikh i Politicheskikh Issledovaniy.
Ogudin,V.L. 2006. "Svyatye mesta v islame" in *Sredneaziatskiy etnograficheskiy sbornik.* Moskva: Nauka.
O'lmas Bahromzoda 2000. *Chodak (qishloq tarikhidan lavhalar).* Namangan: Namangan.
Pantusov, N. N. 1894. "Musulmanskie mazary v g. Uch-Turfane i ego okrestnostyakh" in *Zapiski RGO po etnografii.* Vol. 34.
Parfentiev, V. A. 1904. "Selenie Vuadil" in *Ezhegodnik Ferganskogo oblasti.* Vol III. G.Novyy Margelan.
Pisarchik, A. K. 1938. "Polevoy otchet po ekspedicii v Ferganskuyu dolinu" Arkhiv Glavnogo upravleniya po okhrane pamyatnikov kul'turnogo nalediya i ikh ekspluatacii ministerstva po delam kul'turi i sporta Respubliki Uzbekistan, № 1491.
Pisarchik A. K. 1956. "Nekotorye dannye po istoricheskoy topografii gorodov Fergani" in *Sbornik statey posvyashennih isskussttvu.* Stalinabad.
Pugachenkova, G. A. 1963. "K istoricheskoy topografii Chaganiana" in *Nauchnie trudi. Vipusk 200. Arheologiya Sredney Azii VI*. Toshkent.
Pulatov, U.P. 1975. *Chilkhudra.* Dushanbe: Donish.
Qoraev, S. 1970. *Geografik nomlar ma'nosini bilasizmi?* Toshkent: Ozbekiston.
Rahimov, N. T. 2002. *Mavzoley Hazrati Shoh.* Khudzhand: Nuri Ma'rifat.
Rakhman, H. U. 2000. *Khronologiya islamskoy istorii: 5701000 gg. ot R.H.* Translated from English D. Z. Hayretdinova. Nizhniy Novgorod.
Rakhmatulla Yusuf og'li 1998. *Bobolardan qolgan naqllar.* Nashrga tayyorlovchilar, so'zboshi va izohlar muallifi M. Zho'raev va U. Sattorov. Toshkent: Fan.
Rassudova, R.Ya. 1985. "Kultovie ob'ekti Fergani kak istochnik po istorii oroshaemogo zemledeliya." in *SE.* №4.
Rodoslovnaya Karahana 1899. "Patrona gor. Auliya ata" in *Protokoli zasedaniy i soobsheniya chlenov Turkestanskogo kruzhka lyubiteley arkheologii.* Toshkent.
Saidboev, T. S. 1984. *Islam i obschestvo.* Moskva: Nauka.
Saksonov, T. 1986. *"Muqaddas" joylar - hurofot va bid'at o'choghi.* Toshkent: Medicina.
Salim Muhtor, Karim Bobomurod. 1998 *Shofirkon tarikhi.* Toshkent: Yozuvchi.
Semenov, A. A. 1948. "Nadpisi na nadgrobiyakh Timura i ego potomkov v Guri emire" in *Epigrafika Vostoka.* № II.
Seydi Ali Rais 1963. *Mirhotul mamolik.* Toshkent: Fan.
Sheraliev, M. 1993. *Shohimardon haqida oylar.* Fargona: Fargona.
Snesarev, G. P. 1983. *Khorezmskiye legendi kak istochnik po istorii religioznikh kultov Sredney Azii.* Moskva: Nauka.
Spisok naselennikh mest Ferganskoy oblasti. Ot Ferganskogo oblastnogo staticheskago komiteta. Skobelev. 1909. 77.
Suhareva, O. A. 1960. *Islam v Uzbekistane.* Toshkent.
Sulaymonov, R. 2004. *Nahshab - unutilgan tamaddun sirlari.* Toshkent: Ma'naviyat.
Tokhtiev, Sh. 2006. "O'zbekiston hududida Hazrat Ali nomi bilan boghliq muqaddas joylar masalasi" in *Akademik Ubaydulla Karimov nomidagi yosh sharqshunoslar ilmiy konfrenciyasi tezislari.*
Troitskaya, A. L. 1968. *Katolog arkhiva Kokandskikh khanov XIX veka.* Moskva: Nauka.
TsGA Uz. Fund № I – 19. Op. № 1, D. 13965. l. 2.
TsGA Uz. Fund № I– 19. Op. № 1, D. 1821. l. 3
Usmonov, Y. 1995. *Jannat bogi.* Fargona: Farghna Nashriyoti..
Valikhonov, Ch. 1986. *Selected works.* Moskva: Nauka.

Vospominaniya komandira kaveskadrona. 113 kavpolka. 7 otd. Turk. Kavbrigada Bordadina V.V. (FOKM). KP. № 3235.

Zayniddinov, A. 1939. "Dnevniki BFK." Arkhiv Glavnogo upravleniya po okhrane pamyatnikov kul'turnogo naslediya i ikh ekspluatacii ministerstva po delam kul'turi i sporta Respubliki Uzbekistan. F 1487/ 021.

Zemlya i lyudi. 1892. *Vseobshaya geografiya. Aziatskaya Rossiya i Sredne-Aziatskie khanstva*. St. Peterburg.

Zho'raev, M. and R. Saidova 2002. *Bukhoro afsonalari.* Toshkent: Qodiriy Nomidagi Khalq Merosi Nashriyoti.

Zolotaya kniga Rossiyskoy imperii. Moskva, 1905.

Chapter Three

DOCUMENT STUDIES

The Waqf System and the Xinjiang Uyghur Society from the Qing Dynasty to the Republic of China Period

ZHANG Shicai

Introduction

The word *waqf* is Arabic word that means "to retain", "detain", "freeze", or "arrest" and is represented by several phonetic approximations in Chinese. The earliest use of the word *waqf* was in connection with land: "If the land is public property owned by all muslims, it is called 'fay', meaning 'spoils of war', *waqf*, or 'under permanent management.'"[1] In addition, a viceroy's foundation was also known as a *waqf*.[2] In the Southern Xinjiang where there is a high concentration of Uyghur communities, land is the most important part of a *waqf* endowment. An understanding of the *waqf* system from the Qing Dynasty through the Republican era is essential for gaining a deeper understanding of Uyghur social structure at the time.

Although there is still no textual proof of the earliest appearance of the *waqf* system along the southern routes of the Tianshan mountains, many scholars agree that "the Xinjiang *waqf* system appeared with its first mazar—the mazar of Satuq Bughra Khan.[3] The mazar is said to have appeared in Xinjiang in the 10th century; which was also when mazars began to become sites for worship. Jamal Qarshi's *Mulhaqat al-surah* provides support for this assertion in stating that Ali Arslan Khan and Abu Hasan b. Baytash Arslan Khan b. Satuq Bughra Khan were martyred at the end of the first month of the year 388 A.H. (998 A.D.). Thereafter, people reverently visited their graves in Kashgar.[4] Therefore it is likely that the *waqf* land system has had a long history in Xinjiang.

The political structure of Xinjiang went through great changes during the Qing Dynasty and Republican era. After the theocratic system of the "Khoja Period" (1680–1759) was dismantled, the Qing government implemented a strict policy of separation of church and state and initiated the transition away from the *waqf* land system as the principal pillar of the economy as changing relationship with the government and its land management strategies began to take place. An understanding and grasp of these changes will undoubtedly aid researchers in better understanding the social conditions of the Uyghur society during this period.

---

1 Hitti 1979, vol. 1: 198.
2 *Ibid.*: 261.
3 Maimaiti Sailai 1986: 95.
4 Hua Tao 2000, appendix 2. folio 37 verso: 222.

1. The *Waqf* System and its Transition

In the 24th year Qianlong's reign (1759), the Qing government quelled the rebellion of the Greater and Lesser Khojas (大小和卓), finally uniting the regions to the north and south of the Tianshan Mountains. As the religious leaders of the Ishan sect based in Southern Xinjiang, the Greater and Lesser Khojas used their religious position and accumulated family fortune to spur the people to rebellion. Their riches included income derived from the vast tracts of *waqf* lands that their families held. Obviously, the Qing government understood the value of this land and its religious significance, but its understanding was limited because it compared *waqf* lands to those owned and administrated by Buddhist temples in the Interior. Chinese documents at that time called *waqf* properties the "land where incense is burned" (香火地亩).[5] The Qing government dealt with *waqf* endowments according to the same administrative policies that it used to regulate land belonging to Buddhist temples in China proper. At the same time, the government also took into consideration the unique history and culture of the Uyghur communities of Southern Xinjiang.

Each time the Qing government quelled a rebellion in Southern Xinjiang, it would take "reconstruction and rehabilitation" (善后) measures that included confiscating the property of "traitors" (逆产); whether *waqf* land —or how much of it— was confiscated, is unclear in Chinese documents from the Qing Dynasty. But "even when the political situation was tumultuous, *waqf* land enjoyed relative stability because political compromise often required the new rulers to do their best to avoid touching *waqf* land. The same strategy for dealing with these lands was also followed during the rule of the Zunghar Khanate and the Apaq Khoja. When Ahmad Khoja was detained in Ghulja, the *waqf* land belonging to the Apaq Khoja Mazar remained untouched in spite of the change in political power.[6] Therefore, we have reason to believe that confiscation mainly involved the privately owned properties of the Khojas and their followers, while *waqf* land was reserved for religious use and remained untouched. We find an example of this in the second year after the unification of Xinjiang with the Interior when Emperor Qianlong decreed that the mazar of the Aqtaghliq sect be protected. In his imperial decree to Shu Hede (舒赫德), Counsellor of Kashgar, he wrote: "The traitors have betrayed imperial bounty and have done evil, they deserve their punishment. As for their ancestors, they have done no wrong. Now that all rebellions have been put down, people should be sent to guard all of the mazars of the Khojas of Kashgar, forbidding their desecration and repairing them accordingly. Officials should be appointed as their managers to show the government's leniency."[7] Following the imperial decree, Counsellor Aliqun (阿里衮) also stipulated that "the old Khoja mazars of Kashgar originally had thirty *patman* [one *patman* = 64 *mu*] of land with income from grain production, and with twelve Muslim families as their caretakers. This will remain unchanged, and the income will be used for the religious activities held at the mazars and for maintenance of the mazars themselves. The rest will go for the maintenance of

[5] *Xiyu tuzhi*, vol.39, The chapter of custom (风俗).

[6] Liu Zixiao 1985: 422.

[7] *GZSL* vol. 609: 6.

the caretaking families".[8] The reason the Khojas could oppose the Qing government was because "accumulating material wealth was an important component of the Khojas' power. The Khojas obtained large sums by leasing their property and, as religious leaders were also privileged to collect tithes." [9] But the Qing government was resolute in eliminating those ordered by the exiled Greater and Lesser Khojas to return and collect the gains from the *waqf* land, indirectly proves that the government had not confiscated the *waqf* land. For example, Samsaq, the son of Khoja Burhan al-Din (the elder of the two brothers), was "living in Samarqand, together with...ten other people who were reduced to beggary".[10] Another example was Jahangir, Samsaq's son, who earned his living by going from tribe to tribe reading the Qur'an and praying in exchange for food. [11] In 1759, the 24th year Qianlong, the exiled Khojas had no choice but to run the risk of sending people back to Xinjiang in the name of religious *ushr* and *zakat* (i.e. types of religious taxes) to collect what little they could in order to help them through their hard times, but in the end they were crushed decisively by the Qing Government. In 1784, the 49th year of Qianlong's reign, the government investigated and dealt with a case involving Samsaq, the son of Khoja Burhan al-Din, who had sent back letters to the *mullas* (i.e. Shiite clergy), begging Kashgar and Yengisar for silver; the government severely punished those involved.[12] In March of 1790, the 59th year of Qianlong's reign, a spy sent by Samsaq to collect materials and money was captured along with eight others, including Samsaq's son, Barat. They were tried, and subsequently executed.[13] In August 1811, the 16th year of the Jiaqing Emperor, Mulla Sufi (毛拉素皮), Ushur (乌舒尔), Omar (爱玛尔), and Shah Dost (? 沙朵斯) were captured for helping the descendants of the escaped traitors extort wealth by unfair means and for adding unlawful content to the *Qur'an*.[14] Because of the rebellious activities of Jahangir, son of Samsaq, the Qing government issued an ordinance in 1895, the fifth year of the Daoguang Emperor "strictly forbidding the return to Xinjiang for the purpose of gathering silver (money)".[15] Lattimore also notes that "the independent Khojas of the western oases frequently attempted to rebuild their power base in Xinjiang, especially in Kashgar. One of the main reasons [for this] was that the Apaq Khoja family mazar in Kashgar was an important source of alms giving."[16] These records reflect two possibilities: (i) the descendants of the Greater and Lesser Khojas continued to take advantage of the old system to acquire wealth and (ii) the Khojas retained control of *waqf* lands, but their use of the land was restricted.

The Chinese term "celestial tax"(天课) comes from the Arabic word *zakat* and originally meaning "cleanliness" and is one of the five duties of Islam. Chinese Muslims

[8] *GZSL* vol. 614: 2.
[9] Schwalz 1983: 133.
[10] *GZSL* vol. 1202: 2-4.
[11] *Xinjiang tuzhi*, vol.115.
[12] *GZSL* vol. 1215: 8-11.
[13] *GZSL* vol. 1351: 15-16.
[14] *RZSL* vol. 247 and 285.
[15] *RZSL* vol. 82: 9-10.
[16] Lattimore 2005: 118.

refer to it as "kegong"(课功). The celestial tax is a form of almsgiving in the name of Allah that is required by Islamic law to be given to aid the impoverished, thus distinguishing it from ordinary charity. As a result, *zakat* was strictly referred to as the celestial tax and changed from an ordinary form of almsgiving to a form of compulsory taxation based on one's wealth and a religious duty as well as a form of financial system.

Celestial tax collected on income derived from farm products and by-products, cattle, silver, gold, merchandise items, and mines was referred to as *ushr*, while the celestial tax collected on income derived from cattle, silver, and gold was referred to as *zakat*. The celestial tax levied on farm products is the heaviest and most common form of taxation and composes one-tenth of the yield from private lands; it is also sometimes referred to as a type of tithe. In 1759, the 24th year of the Emperor Qianlong's reign and before the unification of Northern and Southern Xinjiang, farmers tilling *waqf* lands were required to pay the celestial tax. "According to the old system of the Muhammadans, one-tenth of the yield of grain should be turned in as taxes, as it is written in the *Qur'an*. In Aqsu, in the public lands of the old Khans, the yield was halved between the farmers and the landowners, [and] the rest of the land was taxed on a tithe basis".[17]

After 1759, the descendants of the exiled Khojas began having financial difficulties and before long had no choice but to risk sending spies to gather small amounts sums of money in the name of religious *ushr* and *zakat* to survive. At the time, farmers tilling privately owned land paid the percentage originally taken by the celestial tax directly tithed to the Qing government. Therefore, the spies could only collect the celestial tax from the farmers who tilled *waqf* lands as they enjoyed tax-exempt granted by the Qing government. As a result, these spies were eradicated. According to Su Erde's *Huijiang zhi*, after the quelling of the Greater and Lesser Khojas' uprisings, the total amount of arable land administrated by cities in the Zunghar Basin was 21,470 *patman* of seeded land,[18] or 1,374,080 *mu*.[19] By 1772, the 37th year of Qianlong's reign, records showed that private land owned by Uyghur farmers totalled 600,000 *mu*, while the *beg*s of the region (i.e. secular officials) possessed 419,972 *mu*.[20] Together, the total amount of land came to 1,019,972 *mu*. By subtracting this figure from the estimate given by Su Erde, we can deduce that *waqf* land totalled 354,108 *mu*, or 25.77% of the total arable land in the region.

According to survey materials for Southern Xinjiang dating from soon after the Chinese Communist Party's consolidation of their control over the region:

> Typical survey statistics from fourteen villages in ten counties revealed that *waqf* land made up...about 20% of the total arable land in these places. [After accounting] for local differences, a conservative estimate shows that in the four prefectures of Southern Xinjiang, *waqf* land

[17] *Pinding Zhunga'er fanglue* vol.70: 265.

[18] *Hujiang zhi* vol.4: 194.

[19] According to Ji Dachun, there is no uniform value that can be associated with the term *patman*, but for the sake of convenience it can be assigned the value of 1 *patman* = 64 *mu*. See Ji Dachun 1991: 63.

[20] Saguch Toru 1983: 149.

> made up...15% of the total area of arable land. In other words, of the nearly 12,000,000 *mu* of arable land in Southern Xinjiang, nearly 1,800,000 *mu* was part of a *waqf* endowment.[21]

The above calculation is accurate. Although the Qing government did take measures to protect status of the *waqf* lands, it also confiscated *waqf* properties belonging to mazars, mosques, *khaniqa*, and other religious organizations that supported anti-Qing activities. For example, the *shaykh* and caretaker of Artush's Satuq Bughra Khan Mazar, Mir Amat Akhun, was an important figure that supported the Aqtaghliq sect during the Khoja rebellion. In 1875, the seventh year of the Xianfeng Emperor, he acted as an agent of Wali Khan and was captured and executed by the Qing army after instigating a rebellion. At that time, as a representative of the Aqtaghliq sect he was "the richest man in Kashgar." When he was executed in 1857 his possessions were confiscated and turned over to the national treasury. "He left behind vast stretches of land, several manors, and [an] enormous quantity of grain. The local residents said that he also had tens of thousands of silver ingots. Now, other mazar caretakers are prudent and guarded, leading frugal lives for fear that they will share the same fate as their counterpart."[22]

Although we do not know the exact amounts, we know that the government confiscated a certain amount of *waqf* land after each rebellion it quelled. After this, the land would be controlled by the *beg*s to discourage them from corruption. Therefore, changes in the proportion of *waqf* lands to arable lands differ over time but were generally insignificant.

Although the Qing government did not confiscate all *waqf* land, it did transfer the *yanchi* census from mosques to the populace so that the *yanchi* became subject to direct taxation by the Qing government. In the process of putting down the Khoja-led rebellions, 1,000 families of Dolan Muslims —5,000 people in total— sought refuge with the Qing army.[23] In addition, over 2,600 families totalling 8,300 Muslims, surrendered to the Qing army. The largest of these families were the Boderge (伯德尔格) and the Tarimchin (塔哩雅沁)."[24]

The Dolans were "the serfs of Khoja Jihan (系霍集占之农奴)" and the first volume of Su Erde's *Huijiang zhi* provides an extensive treatment of the Boderge and the Tarimchin.[25] These impulsive, unpredictable families were followers of the rebel chief, Khoja Jihan, who had lived in Ili for a long time. The Boderge were merchants, the Tarimchin were farmers, and the Ushaq (乌沙克) were warriors. These three groups were collectively known as the *taghliq* by the muslims." In total, there were over 8,000 serfs and 5,000 Dolans. According to Erde, by 1772, the 37th year of Qianlong's reign, the total population of the cities of the Tarim Basin came to 202,020.[26] The number of individuals who surrendered to the Qing army made up 5% of the Tarim Basin's total

---

21 Xinjiang Weiwuer Zizhiqu Bianjizu 1980: 108.
22 Valikhanov 1985: 163.
23 *GZSL* vol.601: 7.
24 *GZSL* vol.598: 18-19.
25 Bichang 1848: 4.
26 *Hujiang zhi* vol.3: 36.

population. The army settled these people in areas stretching from Kucha to Qarashahr to reclaim wastelands and allow them to support themselves.[27] They were no longer serfs of the Greater and Lesser Khojas, and the liberation of this portion of the population, which had been previously been directly dependent on the Khoja class, indirectly changed the land management model used along the southern routes of the Tian Shan.

These political upheavals only minimally affected *waqf* lands because of the relative stability of their claims; therefore, from 1759 to 1934, there was little change in the size of *waqf* properties and their usage. Under the rule of Sheng Shicai (盛世才), the rights to *waqf* lands were handed over to the cultural-promotion societies of the different muslim ethnic groups represented in the region. The majority of the income derived from these properties was then used for the development and promotion of cultural and educational programs.[28]

2. The *Waqf* System and Uyghur Society

2-1. The *waqf* system and changes in the social structure of Uyghur society

After the Mongols entered Central Asia and converted to Islam, they discovered the importance of religion in their military campaigns and governance. On the whole, Islam received preferential treatment as can be seen in the case of the lame conqueror, Timur. Politically, he divided society into 12 different categories. Because he was fervently religious, he grouped *sayyids*, preachers, and members of the *ulama* into the highest category, followed by the experienced, the virtuous, and those who were involved in fervent ascetic practices. The third class was composed of the generals, ministers, and friends of the monarch, and followed by scholars, doctors, literati, historians, theologians, clerics, and technicians who maintained weaponry. The final category included the travellers who had visited various countries.[29] He also deprived members of the nobility and royal household of their land and donated it to mosques.[30]

The Central Asian region had been in chaos and turmoil since the 13th century and the Muslim population was in urgent need of spiritual support. When the Ilkhanids sacked Bukhara, Samarqand, and Termez, muslims in the region began to waver in their faith and needed encouragement, especially from those seen as descendants of the Prophet Muhammad.[31] As "holy descendants", Khojas belonging to Sufi sects satisfied this needs. Sufis placed a special emphasis on the importance of having strong and independent financial power. Khoja Ahrar of the Naqshbandi Sufi order noted that the local *shaykh*s who depended on *waqf* lands had no choice but depend on whatever was given to them. He realized that he had to find his own means to support himself and his followers, and by doing so would he be able to wield greater influence than other *shaykh*s. His political

[27] *GZSL* vol.601: 7.
[28] Chen Huisheng (ed.) 1999: 366.
[29] Mazahéri 2006: 123.
[30] *Mengwuer shiji*, Vol. 141 (*Tiemuer chuan*: The Biography of Timur).
[31] Schwalz 1983: 122.

objective was to build his order into a financially independent and powerful organization that participated in politics and became influential through organizational reliability and centralized order.

To accomplish his goals, Khoja Ahrar first accumulated considerable wealth to ensure his political influence. He "owned 30 orchards and land in 64 villages as well as irrigation channels. In several cities he also owned commercial organizations and workshops."[32] "Islam Khoja [was] the owner of immense herds of horses, flocks of sheep, and herds of camels plus vast areas of arable land. [O]ver 300 conscripted [labourers worked] on his manors. For the purpose of keeping accounts, special offices were set up."[33]

During the Yarkand Khanate (1514–1680), great numbers of Sufi Khojas from Central Asia flocked to Xinjiang. They became interested in the region's land, water mills, and mines, and they accumulated great fortunes. During the Qing Dynasty, religious organizations and individuals were given donations in the form of *waqf* endowments. For example, document No. 074 from Wang and Li's *Collection of Contractual Documents of Uighur in Xinjiang* reads:

> 10 May 1914
> My name is Tokhti Akhun, son of Tokhti Yusuf Khoja of Qalaghacheghiz Village of Qarghaliq Township. To correct my ways, I have donated a piece of land [on] which can be sown half a *chengzi* of grain and which was redeemed with gold, to Hajji Nurmuhammad Ishan Khoja, and as he has accepted my donation I no longer have the right to that piece of land. Hereafter, if I or my descendants jointly bring a suit on the right of the land, it shall be considered null and void in religious court.
>
> The eastern side of the land borders the graveyard, with the wall as its demarcation; the southern edge of the land borders the graveyard and my land, [also] with the wall as its demarcating feature. The western side of the property borders the land of the descendants of Tokhti Akhun, with the wall as its demarcation; and the northern side of the land borders [both] the land of the descendants of Tokhti Akhun and the graveyard, with the wall as its line of demarcation.
>
> This document is given as proof.
>
> Witnesses: Imam Seley Akhun, Rozi Akhun, Kerim Hajji
> The 14th day of the sixth month of the year 1332 of the Islamic calendar (with the stamp of three seals of the religious court).[34]

Before the Qing government ruled the southern routes of the Tianshan Mountains, the Khojas, claiming to be of noble lineage, ruled Uyghur society. The secular officials, or *begs*, were completely dependent on them — Khojas decided everything, from changes in their official positions to whether they lived or died. Chun Yuan notes the following:

> On the day of *Ramadan*, drums were beaten and horns blown throughout the night. Hakim

[32] *Encyclopaedia of Islam*, supplement fascicules 1-2: 51.
[33] Gafurov 1985: 51.
[34] Wang & Li 1994: 51.

> Beg was arrayed in new clothes and wearing a hat woven with threads of gold and riding on a steed. [On] the backs of camels and horses were five to seven sets of lavishly decorated saddles, accompanied by waving flags and beating drums and people singing and dancing as they led the parade. The *begs* and *akhuns* were all wearing round white hats and stood on both sides, and with his armoured henchmen and other trusted ones in control, they entered the mosque. It was called entering the *id*. In the past, when Hakim Beg went to the mosque, the *akhuns* were there to decide whether he was virtuous or not. If he was, he could retain his position. They also judged if he was fair and just in his dealings. If they considered him otherwise, then the Muslim masses would ask to have him killed; therefore, Hakim Beg used soldiers for self-protection, although now the begs do not dare to use their military power at will. As of the old days, *Ramadan* is still celebrated with food and drink just like the Chinese celebrate the New Year.[35]

Choqan Valikhanov, in his personal observations on the social structure in Southern Xinjiang during the Qing Dynasty, noted that "the social position and influence of the inhabitants of Minor Bukhara...can be divided into three legal classes: the officials (*begs*), the clerics (*akhuns*), and the populace. People belonging to the first two classes were exempt from paying taxes. The third class, the populace, [was] divided into townspeople and farmers."[36] Valikhanov's observations concerning these three classes were primarily concerned with economic status.

The Qing government's rule over Southern Xinjiang began with its crushing of the Khoja class. The Qing government began by supporting Burhan al-Din Khoja of the Aqtaghliq sect in his return to Southern Xinjiang to wrest power from the Qarataghliq sect. After this, Qing sent out a large army to directly engage with the Greater and Lesser Khojas; these attacks greatly weakened the position of the Khoja class. After quelling the rebellion, the Qing government implemented "reconstruction and rehabilitation" measures, the most important of which was the confiscation of land, orchards, and other wealth belonging to the Khojas and their followers and greatly reduced the Khojas' influence. The *beg yanchi* land mainly originated from properties confiscated from former rulers (feudal lords) and turned over to newly appointed *begs*. The earliest record concerning this practice is in a report submitted by Zhao Hui (兆惠) after the army's suppression of the rebellions of the Greater and Lesser Khojas:

> General Zhao Hui and others who pacified the border submitted this report.... The land of the followers of the escaped traitors [has] been confiscated and handed over to the national treasury. They were required to pay three-fold; a sum totalling 1,200 *patman*. Before submission they should also hand over 13,000 *tenge*, to be converted to grain, as well as seven old orchards and the annual yield of grapes, to be dried. As the 13 orchards of Burhan al-Din are relatively new and have a limited yield, they will be kept for the enjoyment of the officers and soldiers of the army.[37]

The Qing army also confiscated rebel property in Yarkand: "Following the example set in Kashgar; we have confiscated the lands, houses, and orchards of the supporters of the

[35] Chun Yuan 1882, vol.4: 82.
[36] Valikhanov 1985: 162.
[37] *GZSL* vol. 593: 11-16.

escaped traitors and have turned them over to the national treasury."[38]

After putting down the rebellions of the Greater and Lesser Khojas and confiscating their property, the government gave part of the confiscated lands to the poor farmers, levying a 50% tax on them. According to Erde, after putting down the rebellions the Qing government confiscated 60 orchards in Kashgar and Yarkand, 18 water mills in Yarkand, and 1,770 *patman* of seeded land belonging to feudal lords and other supporters of the rebellion in Kucha, Aqsu, Kashgar, Yarkand, and other locations. At that time, the amount of total arable land in the Tarim Basin was around 21,470 *patman*,[39] thus the confiscated lands made up 8.4% of the total area. This figure would be larger if we included the properties confiscated from the Greater and Lesser Khojas of Khotan and Aqsu that originally belonged to the khans descended from Chaghatay. After quelling the Jahangir rebellion in 1828, the 8th year of the Daoguang Emperor, the property of the feudal lords who supported the rebellion was confiscated and sold for over 180,000 ounces of silver. Qing government contracts from 1832–1843 (12th to 23rd years of the Daoguang Emperor) recorded that one *patman* of seeded land was worth 50 ounces of silver. Of the 180,000 ounces of silver mentioned here, if half (90,000 ounces) came from the sale of houses and other confiscated goods, and the other half (90,000 ounces) came from land, then the total amount of confiscated land must have come to 1,800 *patman*. In other words, the land loss among feudal religious lords and their followers made up 8.38% of the total arable land in the Tarim Basin. These two large-scale land confiscations turned 16.78% of privately owned land into "official land" controlled by the Qing government.[40]

As mentioned above, the confiscation of vast tracts of land belonging to clerics, especially those in the Khoja class, led to a fall in their social standing, creating an opportunity for the Qing government to reshape Uyghur social structure in Southern Xinjiang as it saw fit. However, since the most prestigious social stratum in Southern Xinjiang —the *beg* class— had limited influence, the process of reshaping society did not move forward as planned. In fact, the waning social standing of professional clerics became a factor in clashes over social status in Southern Xinjiang. Thus, alternating waves of conformism and rebellion threw Southern Xinjiang into long-term social unrest.

In spite of this, the *akhuns* still possessed a great deal of prestige and influence in Xinjiang society, something *begs* still did not dare to encroach upon. Family affairs and disputes were settled by a word from the *akhun*, and no Muslim would oppose the decision.[41] Because of this, the Qing government purposely elevated the standing of the *begs*, but this did not prevent them from colluding with the *akhuns*. On the contrary, it promoted an alliance between the two groups as *akhuns* were nominated by the *begs*, thus "creating a hidden peril".[42]

---

[38] GZSL vol.598: 8.
[39] *Huijiang zhi* vol. 4: 64.
[40] Chen Huisheng (ed.) 1999, vol. 2: 4.
[41] Nayancheng 1932, vol. 77: 8932.
[42] *Ibid.*

It should be noted that professional clerics and *begs* enjoyed tax exemption and thus were both considered members of privileged classes. In addition, it was difficult to exclude professional clerics from secular power because, together with the *begs*, they enjoyed similar status in social activities. For example, in the countryside, "the administration of irrigation channels is organized by the villagers, and the person in charge is recommended by the villagers. Each irrigation channel has a channel official called the *Mirab Beg* [,] and all of the channels in a county [are] under the charge of the chief *akhun*. This shows the unity between agriculture and religion".[43]

2-2. The *waqf* system and Uyghur social education

The primary content of early Islamic education was theological, but over time it gradually began to develop into a unique educational system. These madrasa-type schools were built into mosques and provided free room and board for students. After the Qing government consolidated its rule over Southern Xinjiang, education among the local population continued in its original form — religious organizations remained in charge and theology was still the primary focus. There was no need for educational organizations to register or file records with the government and the government did not provide financial assistance as all daily expenses were provided for by income derived from *waqf* endowments.

Prior to the 19th century, the educational system in Southern Xinjiang was divided into two levels: *maktab*, or elementary education primarily consisting of *Qur'an* recitation; and *madrasa*, or higher education. To complete their higher education, a *mulla* needed not only a systematic knowledge of Islamic theology, but also proficiency in Arabic and Persian. During this period, Uyghur secular education did not part ways with Islam as Islamic theological education still continued to enjoy great prestige. In the late 19th century however, a change in the field of education occurred where leaders in Islamic education had reigned supreme, when a batch of secular schools appeared in Kashgar, Artush, Kucha, Ili, and other places with Uyghur communities. There was a sense that these schools somehow departed from traditional Islamic education in either issues of loyalty or curriculum.

The popularization of this new form of education in Uyghur society and changes in the *waqf* system are directly related. In December 1933, the Association for the Promotion of Uyghur Culture (维吾尔文化促进会, hereafter: APUC) was established. This was the product of a rising new form of Uyghur cultural education that was organized on the basis of the *okap* (奥卡甫) of Kashgar.[44] After its establishment, APUC used *okap* organizational funds that had accumulated over the years from income derived from the *waqf* endowments, to expand and build new schools. In Kashgar, funds were raised to build Norbeshi Elementary School, Qonaqbazar Elementary School, Enjanreste Elementary School, and Tumanboyi Elementary School. When they reached the appropriate age for matriculation, children entered the schools and their teachers

[43] Fu Xiruo 1948: 958.
[44] *Kaxi wenshi ziliao* vol.5: 86.

from the *maktab* came to the new schools together with them.

The continual appearance of new schools and ever-increasing number of students led to a severe shortage of teachers and prompted the APUC to hold short-term teacher-training classes while actively preparing for the establishment of a teacher training school. In April 1934, construction of the Kashgar Teacher Training School began using funds from the Kashgar Orda-ishik Royal Household Maktab that the APUC had accumulated from the income generated by the *waqf*. The school began enrolling students and started classes when construction finished in September of the following year. In 1937, a Women's Teacher Training School was built in the courtyard of Abla Baywechchi on Enjan Kocha. The APUC covered all expenses associated with the training classes and refresher courses, including the teachers' pay and the students' living expenses. On 30 July 1939, Ubaydullah, deputy director of the APUC, signed and approved an order giving 106 participants in the rotating training class a month's pay in the form of 200 ounces of provincial currency, coming to a total of 21,200 ounces. In addition, the 23 teachers who taught the classes were together paid 70,829 ounces.

On 28 December 1940, the Kashgar branch of the APUC convened its 13th plenary and decided to start a training class in accounting. As before, the APUC covered all the expenses involved. In 1946, the APUC sent 200 students to the Urumqi Teacher Training School as well as other institutions to study, with the APUC providing all living and travel expenses.

In addition to reforming traditional education, the APUC went to great pains to eradicate illiteracy among the populace. The fervour of its literacy program affected all levels of society. It was said that even the conservative chief of the Islamic Ishan sect, Tayhan Khoja, brought his followers to participate in these classes.

2-3. *Waqf* endowments and serfdom in Uyghur society

Historically speaking, changes in the management of *waqf* land in Xinjiang occurred during two transitional periods: (i) the transition from serfdom, a system characterized by forced personal attachment to a piece of land, to a system of tenancy and (ii) the transition from shared-system management to the fixed-rent management.

The management of *waqf* varies with time and place, but Central Asia and Xinjiang are unique in several aspects, especially in the extensive use of serf labor during the Khoja period.

> *Waqf* land and its dependent farmers are not supposed to be transferable. However, because most *waqf* land belong[s] to the high ranking clerics whose positions are hereditary; the *waqf* land and its appended *yanqi* farmers have become the hereditary property of a handful of families. ...Not long after the Qing Government unified Southern Xinjiang, it [included] in its census the commoners who worked *waqf* land [in] so that they became subjects who paid their taxes directly to the Qing Government. [The government] did not touch the *waqf* land itself or its auxiliary water conservation facilities.[45]

[45] Liu Zixiao 1985: 533.

Records have yet to show whether *waqf* land was farmed by those identified as *yanchi*, but according to Petrovshefskii, who wrote about the Ilkhanate in Iran during the 13th and 14th centuries, "this type of land can be included in the land of the *yanchi*, meaning the land a Khan has given to a religious society or charity organizations as *waqf* lands, and they are under the protection of Khan. Rarely do the *yanchi* use the property as state-owned land to collect taxes".[46] In this statement, this "rare" possibility is difficult to ignore.

In the densely populated areas of Central Asia, most land was irrigated and belonged to a *waqf* endowment, thus falling under the control of Muslim religious circles that profited greatly from these holdings. The *waqf* property system is unique in its unusually heavy exploitation of farmers and its communal serfdom. For example, one must have special written allowances to lease *waqf* land and any changes to these allowances must be made during the first three days of the New Year.[47] In Central Asia, "the populace and their land can avoid difficulties if they have the protection [of] a ruler or a high official. Nawa'i says that in late 15th century in Khurasan, "the legally free people would often attempt to establish a *yanchi* relationship in order to avoid extortion and plunder."[48] *Waqf* land enjoys tax exemption, so the farmers of *waqf* land are likewise exempt from paying taxes to the government. Therefore, many farmers who wanted to evade taxes would voluntarily donate their land to mosques and become *yanchi* farmers—serfs under the protection of the mosque. Therefore, prior to the Qing government's unification of Xinjiang, it is possible that *yanchi* serfdom existed on *waqf* lands. *Yanchi* farmers of religious organizations were actually required to perform corvée labour, a long established practice in Central Asia. Medjardov, a scholar of the status of serfs in Ferghana, concluded that corvée labour had always existed in the khanates.[49] Lenin pointed out that the corvée labour system works in the following way:

> The land of the landlord is tilled by farmers from nearby villages using their own tools. The form the rent takes does not change the substance of the system—whether it is paid in currency (such as the shared system), or in goods (such as the halving of the yield) or in substitute farming (such as hired labour renting system), they are the same.[50]

Historically, it is possible that the land management model of feudal serfdom has always been the most popular. After Islam spread through Xinjiang, the *iqta* system, a manor-based economy with an element of serf labour under the control of feudal lords, became widespread. At that time, the pattern of land ownership consisted of large parcels of land, and because of this, the mosque economy adopted an organizational structure similar to that of medieval Europe.[51] Before the Qing government established

---

46 Petrushevskii 1960: 242.
47 *Istoriya Uzbekskoi SSR*, vol.2: 17.
48 *Zhongya wenmin shi*, vol.4: 112.
49 *Istoriya Uzbekskoi SSR*, vol.1: 17.
50 *Lienin xuan ji*, vol.3: 17
51 Ge Jinfang proposes that Byzantine and the Islamic countries of the Middle Ages had land grant

its rule over Southern Xinjiang, we are not sure whether *waqf* lands there used the tenancy system or feudal serfdom. But judging from the material we do possess, it is likely that feudal serfdom was more prevalent.

Concluding Remarks

The rise of the *waqf* endowments was not the result of natural economic development, but was instead an artificially established phenomenon. The large increase in *waqf* land greatly reduced the opportunity of land ownership, which further intensified the population's dependence on the land. This was particularly true in Southern Xinjiang where the population was dense and arable land limited. The primary reason for the widespread existence of serfdom at the time was the supra-economic personal appendage relationship in Uyghur society that was created and reinforced these land rights. Those with high positions in the Islamic religious hierarchy were able to preserve their vested interests with their great wealth. The existence of the *waqf* endowments helped to reinforce and maintain religious unity and was a strong economic means of spreading religious ideology and ethics.

Bibliography

Bichang 璧昌 1848. *Ye'erqiang shoucheng jilue* 叶尔羌守城纪略 [A record of the defense of Yarkand], in *Zhongguo minzu shidi ziliao congkan* 中国民族史地资料丛刊 27, Beijing: Zhongyan Minzu Xuayuan.

Bosworth, C.W. and M.S. Asimov E. 博斯沃思，M. S. 阿西莫夫(eds.) 2010. *Zhonhgya wenmin shi* 中亚文明史 [*History of Civilizations of Central Asia*], tr. by Liu Yingsen 刘迎胜, Beijing: Zhongguo Duiwai Fangyu Chuban Gongsu.

Chen Huisheng 陈慧生(ed.) 1999. *Zhongguo Xinjiang diqu Yisilanjiao shi* 中国新疆地区伊斯兰教史 [The history of Islam in Xinjiang region of China], 2 vols, Urumqi: Xinjiang Renmin Chubanshe.

Chun Yuan 椿园 1882. *Xinjiang yutu fengtu kao* 新疆舆图风土考 [Survey on the geography and folklore of Xinjiang], Shanghai: Dianshizhai.

Fu Xiruo 傅希若 1948. "Xinjiangde nongye shehui" 新疆的农业社会 [The agricultural society of Xinjiang], in *Xibei luntan* 西北论坛 1948: 1-6, reprint, Gansu Sheng Tushuguan Shumu Cankaobu 甘肃省图书馆书目参考部 (ed.) 1985. *Xibei minzu zongjiao shiliao wenzhai (Xinjiang fengce)* 西北民族宗教史料文摘 (新疆分册), Lanzhou: Gansu Sheng Tushuguan, vol.2.

Gafurov, B.G. 加富罗夫 1985. *Zhongya Tajike Shi* 中亚塔吉克史 [History of Tajiks (<*Istoriya Tadzhikskogo Naroda*)], tr. by Xiao Zhixing 肖之兴, Beijing: Zhongguo Shehui Kexue Chubanshe.

Ge Jinfang 葛金芳 1998. *Tudi fuyi zhi* 土地赋役志 [History of Taxes and Corvee] Shanghai: Shanghai Renmin Chubanshe.

GZSL: Da Qing lichao Gaozong shilu 大清高宗实录 [Veritable records of the successive reigns of the Qing dynasty: Qianlong reign].

Hitti, Philip K. 希提 1979. *Alabo tongshi* 阿拉伯通史 [*History of the Arabs*], Beijing: Shangwu Yinshu Guan.

Hua Tao 华涛 2000. *Xiyu lishi yanjiu: 8 zhi 10 shiji* 西域历史研究：八至十世纪 [Study of history of Western region: from 8th to 10th century], Shanghai: Shanghai Guzhi Chubanshe.

Istoriya Uzbekskoi SSR [History of Uzbek SSR], Tashkent: AN Uzbekskoi SSR, 1955-56.

---

models that were similar to the models of their respective fiefdoms; the former's land system was called *pronoia*, while the latter's land system was known as *iqta*. See Ge Jinfang 1998: 75.

Ji Dachun 纪大椿 1991. "Weiwuerzu duliangheng jiuzhi kaosuo" 维吾尔族度量衡旧制考索 [Research on the old system of measurements of the Uyghurs], in *Xiyu yanjiu* 西域研究, 1991-1.

Lattimore, Owen 拉铁摩尔 2005. *Zhongguode Yazhou Neilu Bianjiang* 中国的亚洲内陆边疆 [Inner Asian Fontiers of China], tr. by Tang Xiaofeng 唐晓峰, Nanjing: Jiangsu Renmin Chubanshe.

Lenin 列宁 1954. *Lienin xuan ji* 列宁选集 [Collected Works of Lenin], Beijing: Renmin Chubanshe.

Liu Zixiao 刘志霄 1985. *Weiwuerzu lishi* 维吾尔族历史 [History of the Uyghurs] , Beijing: Minzu Chubanshe, vol.1.

Maimaiti Sailai 买买提·赛来 1986. "Xinjiang de maza chaobai: Xinjiang Yisilanjiao diyi tesi zhusheng" 新疆的麻扎和麻扎朝拜：新疆伊斯兰教地域特色初探 [Mazar worships in Xinjiang: Introduction to the features of Islam in Xinjiang], in *Shijie zongjiao yanjiu* 世界宗教研究, 1986-4.

Mazahéri, Aly 阿里·玛札海里 2006. *Sichouzhilu-Zhongguo Bosi wenhua jiaoliu shi* 丝绸之路—中国波斯文化交流史 [La Route de la Soie], Urumqi: Xinjiang Renmin Chubanshe.

Nayancheng 那彦成 1974. *Nawen yigong zouyi* 那文毅公奏议 [Memorials of Nayancheng], in *Jindai Zhongguo shiliao congkan* 近代中国史料丛刊 21, Taipei : Wenhai Chubanshe.

Petrushevskii, I.P. 1960. *Zemledelie i Agrarnye Otnosheniya v Irane VIII-XIV vekov* [The agriculture and land relationship in 8th -14th century Iran], Tashkent: ANSSSR.

Pinding Zhunga'er fanglue 平定准噶尔方略 [Millitary history of the pacification of the Zunghars], in Yinjing 印景 2008. *Wenyuange Siku Quanshu* 文渊阁四库全书, Taipei: Taiwan Shangwu Yinshu Guan, vol. 359.

RZSL: *Da Qing lichao Renzong shilu* 大清仁宗实录 [Veritable records of the successive reigns of the Qing dynasty: Jiaqing reign].

Saguchi Toru 佐口透 1983. *18-19 shiji Xinjiang shehuishi yanjiu* 18-19 世纪新疆社会史研究[Study on the Social History of Xinjiang in the 18th through the 19th Centuries], tr. by Ling Songchun 凌颂纯, Urumqi: Xinjiang Renmin Chubanshe.

Schwalz, Henry G. 施瓦茨 1983. "Xinjiang de Hezhuo" 新疆的和卓 [The Khwâjas of Eastern Turkestan]" tr. by Zhong Meizhu 钟美珠 in *Xibei shidi* 西北史地 1983-3.

Tuji 屠寄 1983. *Mengwuer shiji* 蒙兀儿史记 [History of the Mongols], Beijing: Shijie Shuju.

Valikhanov, Ch. Ch. 1985. *Sobranie Sochinenii v Pyati Tomakh* [Collected Works of 5 Volumes] tom 3, Alma-Ata: AN Kazakhskoi SSR.

Wang Shouli 王守礼, Li Jinxin 李进新 1994. *Xinjiang Weiwuerzu qiyue wenshu ziliao xuanbian* 新疆维吾尔族契约文书资料选编 [Collection of Contractual Documents of Uighur in Xinjiang], Urumqi: Xinjiang Shehui Kexueyuan.

Xinjiang Weiwuer Zizhiqu Bianjizu 新疆维吾尔自治区编辑组 1980. *Nanjiang nongcun shehui* 南疆农村社会[Rural society of southern Xinjiang], Urumqi: Xinjiang Renmin Chubanshe.

Xiyu tuzhi 西域图志 [Gazetteer of the Western Region] in Yinjing 印景 2008. *Wenyuange Siku Quanshu* 文渊阁四库全书, Taipei: Taiwan Shangwu Yinshu Guan, vol. 500.

XZSL: *Da Qing lichao Xuanzong shilu* 大清宣宗实录 [Veritable records of the successive reigns of the Qing dynasty: Daoguang reign]

Yong-gui 永贵 and Su'erde 苏尔德 1968. *Huijiang zhi* 回疆志 [Gazetteer of muslim region], Taipei: Chengwen Chubanshe.

Zhongguo Renmin Zhengji Xieshang Huiyi Kashi shi Weiyuanhui Wenshi Ziliao Yanjiu Weiyuanhui 中国人民政治协商会议喀什市委员会文史资料研究委员会(ed.) 1990. *Kaxi wenshi ziliao* 喀什市文史资料 [Material on the History of Kashgar], Kashgar.

A Holy Place and Its Shaykh in the XIX Century History of Southern Kazakhstan

Ashirbek MUMINOV

Foreword

The relations between the Qoqand (Khwāqand) Khanate (1798-1876) and its subject tribes of Southern Kazakhstan found little reflection in official Qoqandian historiography.[1] A few studies have shown quite well that these relations were complex; [2] however, new information is required in order to give full representation to Qoqand–Southern Qazāq relations.

In 2004 we discovered one document that can provide fundamentally new information about these relations.

Information about the Document's Owner

The document's owner was Ṣābir-Khwāja Sayyid-Khwājayev who died on August 14, 2011, a former resident of Suleymen Tileubayev street, section 2, Tashkent farm, Tashkent *tuman,* Tashkent *vilāyat,* to the north of the capital of the Republic of Uzbekistan. It was inherited by his son Bakhtiyār-Khwāja Ṣābir-Khwājayev. One may note that this location is along the border with the Republic of Kazakhstan (the Sarï-Aghash region of the South-Kazakhstan oblast'). We were assisted in examining and photographing the document by the Ph.D-student in Arabic and Islamic studies Muslim-Khwāja Ātayev, a relative of Ṣābir-Khwāja Sayyid-Khwājayev. Muslim-Khwāja's father, Rikhsī-Khwāja (Rizqī-Khwāja) ibn Sayyid-Khwāja ibn Āta-Khwāja (died in January 9, 2004) was Ṣābir-Khwāja's younger brother. However, due to a rivalry between the brothers concerning the ownership of the document, we had no opportunity to see it for a long time. This was because Ṣābir-Khwāja attempted to keep his *murīds* from the Ramadan tribe of the Junior Horde of Kazakhs around him by holding on to the document. After Rikhsī-Khwāja's death, this rivalry disappeared.

---

[1] Vakhidov 1998; Beisembiev 2009.

[2] Maduanov 1992.

Family Legends

Ṣābir-Khwāja Sayyid-Khwājayev received the document from his mother. His father Sayyid-Khwāja (died in April 17, 1967), had suffered repression as an observant Muslim. His mother wrapped the document up in its cloth cover and preserved it by keeping it next to her body. Ṣābir-Khwāja knew only the following about his descent:[3] Ṣābir-Khwāja ibn Sayyid-Khwāja ibn Āta-Khwāja ibn 'Azlar-Khwāja ibn 'Azīz-Khwāja.

Sayyid-Khwāja's father Āta-Khwāja lived in the vicinity of Tashkent and was a *pīr* among the Kazakhs of the Junior Horde. He died in 1907 and was buried in the Ramadan cemetery near Tashkent. The first person buried in this cemetery was the saint known as Sad-Qara. A red flag has been set up over Āta-Khwāja's grave, and many people come to perform *ziyārat* on the spot.

The ancestor of these men was Zhalaŋ Ayaq Qozha, known as "Barefoot 'Azlar." He belonged to one of the Kazakh *khwāja* (*qozha*) lineages, the Dīwāna (Duana, the branch Zhalaŋ Ayaq Qozha). The family does not know much at all about him, only they believe he is buried near the present-day city of Taraz, Kazakhstan (formerly Zhambul, Sozāq rayon of the South-Kazakhstan oblast' (See the photos below on the page 153 by Eralï Ospanov, citizen of Shïmkent).

According to the first story preserved by the family, Khudāyār-Khān's tax agents (*zakātchī*) began robbing the population to excess, so at the people's request Yalang Āyāq-Khwāja acted as a mediator and got into an argument with the *zakāt* collectors. When they spoke insultingly to him, the *khwāja* shouted out the war-cry "Alash!"[4] and the people all came together, beat the Qoqandians, and drove them off.

According to a second story, Khudāyār-Khān later had Yalang Āyāq-Khwāja caught and brought to Qoqand. When he entered the palace in chains, the *khān* got up from his seat and left. To the courtiers' questions the *khān* replied, "Don't you see? He has two lions at his side." After some conversation Khudāyār-Khān agreed to lower the taxes.

About the Document

The document is written on cream-colored locally handcrafted paper. The full size of the paper is 109 x 54 cm, and it is made up of three layers. The oldest part is the genealogy, which measures 50 x 30 cm. Two sheets of paper were glued to this part later. The first is a piece of heavy cream-colored locally handcrafted paper added to the back of the genealogy sheet. Later a piece of European paper was attached underneath this for reinforcement. As a result, the document came to consist of three sheets in layers.

A cover was created for the document out of coarse, undyed cotton cloth measuring 30 x 138 cm. While the document was being hidden, the cover could be wrapped around a person's body. The length of its cord is 227 cm.

---

[3] Henceforward, for purposes of continuity with the past, transliterations will follow usual philological conventions rather than modern Uzbek spelling.

[4] This war-cry was the common one for all nomadic tribes in this region – Kazakhs, Qara-Qalpāqs, Qirghīzs, and Quramas against Qoqand. They were known as "Altï-Alash" (Six Alashes): three Kazakh Hordes, Qara-Qalpāqs, Qirghīzs, and Quramas.

The text also consists of three parts. Each part is written in a different hand.

The first text occupies an area of 54 x 24 cm. and is made up of 20 lines of writing, of which the genealogy takes up 12 lines. The author's name is *kamīna-yi mukhliṣ-i mawrūthī* Sayyid Amānallāh ibn Sayyid Raḥīm-Tūra ibn Sayyid Nādir-Khwāja ibn Sayyid Muḥammad-Khwāja-yi Kāsānī. The date of writing is 4 Rabīʿ II 1242/5 November 1826. The person who commissioned the work could be any of Gadāy Khwāja-yi ʿAzīzlar ibn Ḥājjī Khwāja-yi ʿAzīzlar's three sons: Shāh-Muḥammad-ʿAzīzlar, Sārī-Khwāja, or Nazar-Khwāja. Gadāy Khwāja-yi ʿAzīzlar ibn Ḥājjī Khwāja-yi ʿAzīzlar's grandfather is Īr-Khāl-Muḥammad-ʿAzīzlar (*laqab*: Yalang Āyāq ['Barefoot'] Khwāja) ibn Ṣūfī Khwāja-yi ʿAzīzlar ibn Sayyid Manṣūr Khwāja. So we may know the full name of Yalang Āyāq-Khwāja: Īr-Khāl-Muḥammad-ʿAzīzlar ibn Ṣūfī Khwāja-yi ʿAzīzlar ibn Sayyid Manṣūr Khwāja. Among the estimated persons who commissioned this work may also be reckoned Sārī-Khwāja's son Jīyān-Khwāja.

A text of 22 lines has been added to the first text. The area written upon measures 33 x 29.5 cm.

To the edges of the two texts described above have been added 16 paper tags, with a total area of 109 x 24 cm. on the left side and 27 x 6.5 cm. on the right, with a total of 183 lines.

Bakhtiyār-Khwāja Ṣābir-Khwājayev and his family. Photo by Eralï Ospanov, July 2, 2013.

Contents of the Document

The first text gives the genealogy of Khwāja Aḥmad Yasavī (d. 1166-1167), beginning with Hāshim ibn 'Abd Manāf (the prophet Muḥammad's great grandfather) and ending with Khwāja Aḥmad Yasavī. There are two peculiar features here. The first is that a name new to the published genealogies – Tīmūr-Āta – is mentioned as Ibrāhīm-Āta's great-grandfather. This is the first time such a feature has been noticed among the numerous genealogies of Khwāja Aḥmad Yasavī.[5] The second peculiarity is that the name Jalīl-Āta has been added next to that of Isḥāq-Āta in a different, later hand. The reason for this must be that Yalang Āyāq-Khwāja and his progeny are descended not from the famous hero Isḥāq-Bāb (mentioned here as "Isḥāq-Āta"), the ancestor of Khwāja Aḥmad Yasavī, but from his younger brother, 'Abd al-Jalīl-Bāb (mentioned here as "Jalīl-Āta").

At the beginning of the document a *ḥadīth* of the prophet Muḥammad is quoted: "Whenever you are amazed by affairs of this world, seek aid at the tombs of the saints (from the people of the graves); they shall never die."[6] It is unknown whether this refers to the mazār of Khwāja Aḥmad Yasavī or the *mazār* of Yalang Āyāq Khwāja.

Five *fatwas* are quoted in the first piece of added text, four in Arabic and one in Persian. They are taken from well-known books of the Ḥanafī *madhhab*: *al-Khulāṣa* by Burhān al-Dīn al-Bukhārī (d. after 1074-1075), the *Fatāwā Qāḍīkhān* by Fakhr al-Dīn Qāḍīkhān (d. 1196), and the *Mukhtaṣar al-wiqāya* by 'Ubaydallāh ibn Mas'ūd al-Maḥbūbī (d. 1346). They deal with matters of profession of faith (*shahāda*), and affirm that testimony given by aggressors and robbers is not to be accepted.

In the texts added after this, the names of the tribes of the *murīds* of Yalang Āyāq Khwāja are given: Ramadan, Chumuchli, Balghali, Aq-börik, Qara-börik, etc.

It is indicated that the last information to have been included in this part is dated Muḥarram 1255/March-April 1839.

Significantly, after the name of each tribe and its *batïrs* and *biys* is given, there is an additional statement that they are accompanied by their troops (*cherīk*). In all, the names of more than 50 tribes, *batïrs,* and *biys* are cited here. However, because the names are written in an unprofessional hand, and in some places text has been lost due to wear, establishing them all remains a matter for the future. In a number of instances addressing these questions will require intensive labor in comparing archival documents and other narrative works, and in conducting interviews in the regions of Suzaq, Taraz (Zhambïl), and Tashkent.

The document is furnished with 37 seal impressions. However, it should be noted that some of the impressions have been cut out of other documents and affixed to this one. The reasons why this was done are among the problems that await future clarification.

[5] Muminov et al. 2008: 278-285.

[6] See also: Muminov and Nurmanova 2009: 182.

Mausoleum and tomb of Zhalaŋ Ayaq Qozha, Sozaq rayon of the South-Kazakhstan oblast', Photos by Eralï Ospanov

Conclusion

It follows that this document provides information about a rebellion by Kazakh tribes in Southern Kazakhstan against the Qoqandians in 1839. The rebellion arose over a matter of *zakāt,* and in several respects Islamic ideology played a considerable role in the conflict. The Qoqandians robbed pastoral peoples with the justification that they were adhering to the rules of *sharīʿa,* and as a consequence touched off a serious protest. Local *khwājas* played an active role in the ideology of the resistance. The name of Khwāja Aḥmad Yasavī and the tombs and descendants of saints figured prominently in the dispute. This document provides us with important information about features of the economic and ideological policies employed by the Qoqand Khanate.

Bibliographical references:

Beisembiev, Timur K. 2009. *Kokandskaia istoriografiia. Issledovanie po istochnikovedeniiu Srednei Azii XVIII–XIX vv.* Almaty: TOO Print-S.

Maduanov, Seitqali M. 1992. *Istoriia kazakhsko-uzbekskikh otnoshenii v XIX – nachale XX vv.* Turkestan.

Muminov, Ashirbek, Anke Kuegelgen, Devin DeWeese, and Michael Kemper (eds.) 2008. *Islamization and Sacred Lineages in Central Asia: the Legacy of Ishaq Bab in Narrative and Genealogical Traditions. Vol. 2: Genealogical Charters and Sacred Families: Nasab-Namas and Khoja Groups Linked to the Ishaq Bab Narrative, 19th-21st Centuries.* Almaty, Bern, Tashkent, Bloomington: Daik-Press.

Muminov, Ashirbek K. and Aytzhan Sh. Nurmanova 2009. *Shaqpaq-Ata: Inscriptions of the Underground Mosque and Necropolis* / Editor B.M. Babajanov. Almaty: Daik-Press.

Vakhidov, Shadman Kh. 1998. *Razvitie istoriografii v Kokandskom khanstve v XIX – nachale XX vv.* Dissertatsiia na soiskanie uchenoi stepeni doktora istoricheskikh nauk. Tashkent: Institut vostokovedeniia im. Abu Raikhana Beruni (unpublished).

Seals

1

2

3

4

5

6

7

8

9

10

11

12

13

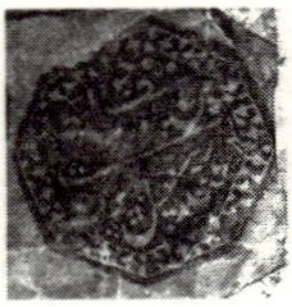
14

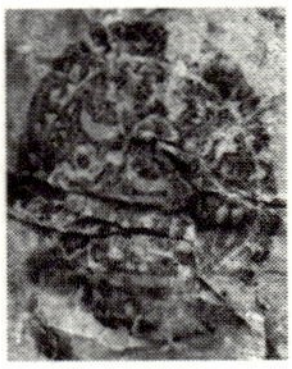
15

16

17

18

19

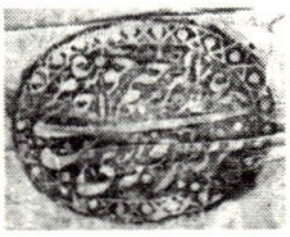
20

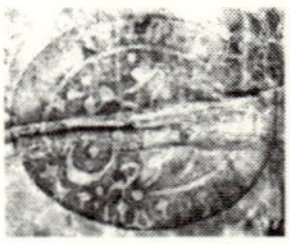
21

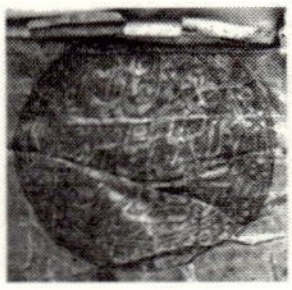
22

23

24

25

LIST OF THE SEALS ON THE DOCUMENT

1. Qāḍī Maḥmūd-Khwāja ibn Jān-Khwāja Ṣiddīqī, 1270/1853-1854;
2. Kenzhe-Khwāja ibn ʻAlī-Aṣghar-Khwāja
3. Qāḍī ... ibn Muḥammad
4. Muḥammad-Shāh ibn Muḥammad-Amīn Aʻlam-i ʻaṣrash bi-luṭf-i Ṣāḥib-i sharʻ-i matīn, 12..
5. Aʻlam Dāmullā Sulṭān ibn Dāmullā Bāltū-Bāy
6. Qāḍī ʻUmar-Khwāja Īshān Khān ..., 1270/1853-1854
7. Muftī Qārī Yūnus bi-luṭf-i jalīl ...
8. Aʻlam Khān-Khwāja ibn Aṣghar-Khwāja
9. Aʻlam Shādī-Khwāja ibn Muḥammad-Khwāja Ḥasanī, 1231/1815-1816
10. Muftī Muḥammad-Badal-Shāh ibn Mullā Muḥammad-Amīn-Shāh, 1240/1824-1825
11. Qāḍī Khān-Khwāja ibn Mullā Shāh-Niʻmat-Khwāja ʻUmarī
12. Muftī Shādī-Khwāja ibn Muḥammad-Khwāja Ḥasanī al-mutawakkil ʻalā-l-Lāh al-Ghanī
13. Qāḍī ʻĪsā-Khwāja ibn Yūnus-Khwāja
14. ʻAbd al-Rasūl-Khwāja ibn Yūsuf-Khwāja
15. Muftī...
16. Muftī Mullā Mīr Yaʻqūb-Makhdūm ibn Mullā Mīr Ṣāliḥ-i Marḥūm, 1270/1853-1854
17. Aʻlam Mullā Mīrzā Aḥmad ibn Jān-Khwāja, 1270/1853-1854
18. Aʻlam Muḥammad-Khān ibn ... al-ʻAlawī al-Ḥanafī ..., 1251/1835-1836
19. ʻAzīzlār-Khwāja ibn ʻAbd al-Raḥīm-Khwāja ʻUmarī, 1270/1853-1854
20. ʻAzīzlār-Khwājagī ibn ʻAbd al-Raḥīm-Khwāja ʻUmarī
21. ... -Khwāja ibn ... -Khwāja
22. Qāḍī-Kalān ... ...-Khwāja Īshān panāh ..., 1241/1825-1826
23. Qāḍī ...
24. Muftī Mullā Mīr ʻAzlār ibn Mullā Raḥīm-Khān, 1269/1852-1853
25. Kenzhe-Khwāja ibn ʻAlī-Aṣghar-Khwāja

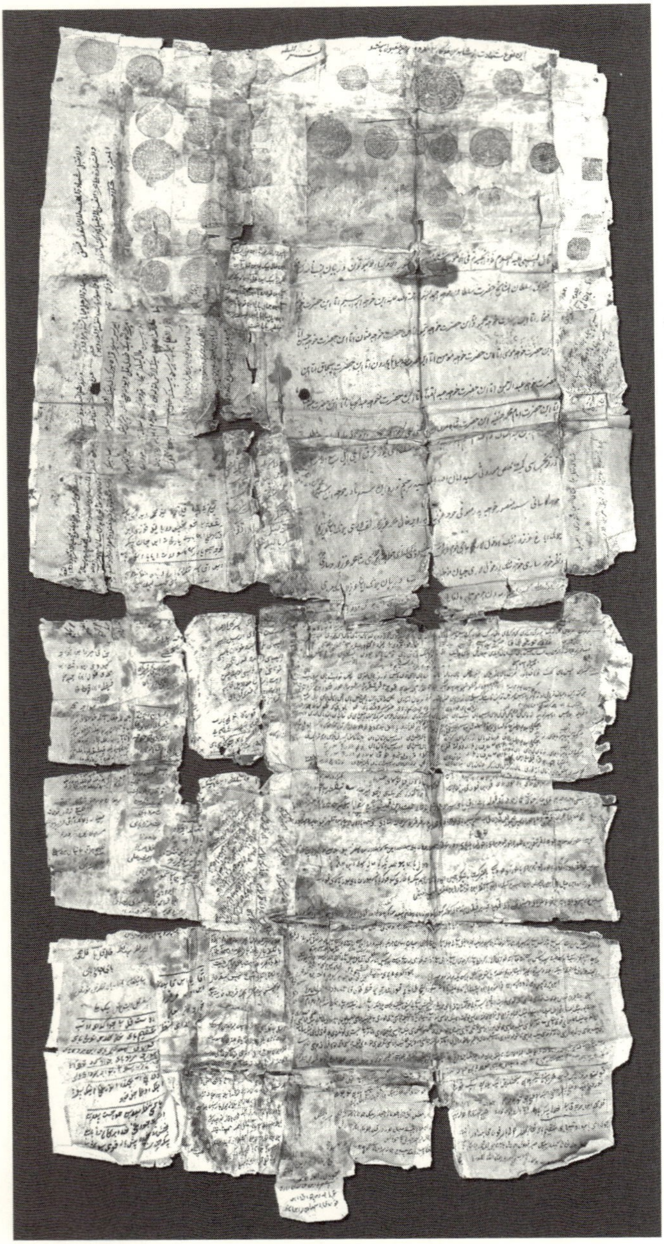

General View of the Document.

Upper Part of the Document with the Seals.

Part of the Document with the Khwāja Genealogy.

Section added to the First Text with the Names of Kazakh Tribes, their Biys and Batirs.

Lower Part of the Document with the Other Kazakh Names.

Opal, a Sacred Site on the Karakoram Highway

A Historical Approach Based on Mazar Documents

SUGAWARA Jun

Introduction

Opal (乌帕尔) is a small township located 47.5 km west of Kashgar where nature flourishes and clear streams are surrounded by mountains of parched rock. It is here that Highway Route 314 (Sino-Pakistan, or Karakoram Highway), extending out from Kashgar, is interrupted by the highlands and veers away to the south. This road connects to the Khunjerab Pass in the Karakoram Range, and eventually reaches the North Western Frontier Province of Pakistan.

Today Opal is famous as the burial site of Mähmut Qäshqäri (Maḥmūd al-Kāshgharī), author of *Dīwān Lughāt al-Türk* (*Compendium of the Languages of the Turks)* completed ca. 1077.[1] In *Xinjiang Gailan* (新疆概览; An *Overview of Xinjiang*), a semi-official guidebook for the Xinjiang Uyghur Autonomous Region, the "Mausoleum of Mähmut Qäshqäri (马赫穆德・喀什噶里陵墓)" is introduced as "a scenic spot (风光名胜)", and listed as respect as the mausoleum of "An outstanding national scholar and linguist of China's Uyghur nationality (我国维吾尔族杰出的学者，语言学家)"[2]. Now, Opal seems inextricably linked with this "scenic spot", and even the local authorities place a high degree of emphasis on tourism at the Mausoleum of Mähmut Qäshqäri and other spots such as the "Spring with Forty-Eyes (四十眼泉)" as well as agriculture and cattle breeding.[3]

The fact is, however, that besides Mähmut Qäshqäri, there are many mazars that stand at the edge of this valley, all of which somehow share legendary stories or historical motifs. The village of Opal is surrounded by so many mazars that it is as if it were "embraced by a dragon".[4] As one can imagine, the entire Opal valley can be viewed as a vast sacred complex.[5]

With this view in mind, in this paper I will explore several mazars from a historical

[1] Barat 1994: 77.

[2] *Xinjiang Gailan* 2001: 304.

[3] http://www.xjsf.gov.cn/lywh/ly/2014/10726.htm (last accessed November 22, 2015). An Introductory column on tourism by the People's Government of Sufu County (疏附县人民政府).

[4] Sidiq 1985: 47.

[5] Sugawara 2007b: 78.

perspective. More specifically, I will use the description of seven "mazar documents" found within the newly discovered material of the "*Compilation of Kashghar Waqf Documents*" (*CKWD*), to examine each mazar's socio-economic features such as the property size, social organization, relationship with the government, thus positioning the entire Opal valley historically.

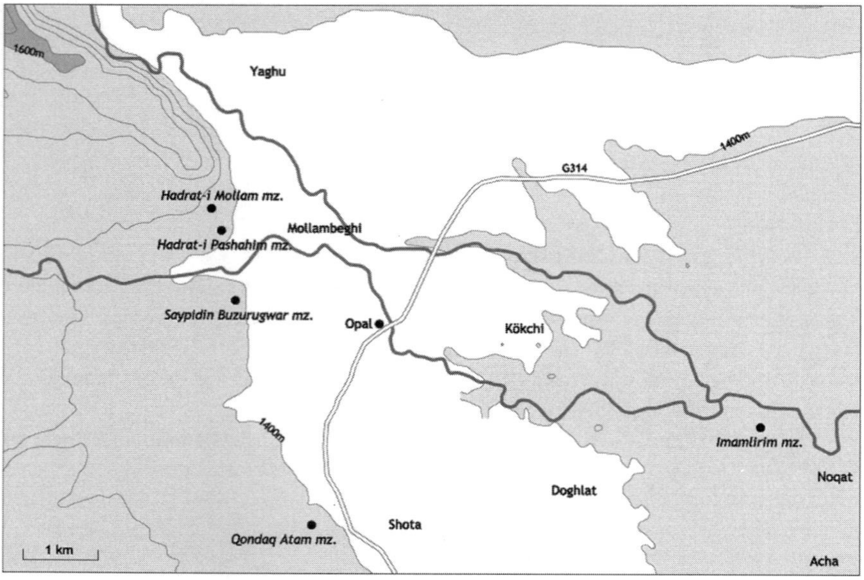

Map: Opal Township and the mazars.

1. *The Compilation of the Kashghar Waqf Documents* [CKWD]

This study makes use of material found in a volume of Turki manuscripts tentatively called The *Compilation of the Kashghar Waqf Documents* (*CKWD*). This volume circulates among certain groups of Uyghur Intellectuals in Xinjiang, and was acquired in photocopy during a period of text collection conducted by the "Mazar Document Project" and sponsored by The Toyota Foundation (2005-2008).[6]

The original page size of the *CKWD* is approximately 200 x 260mm assuming the original photocopy had not been enlarged or compressed. The first three pages of the *CKWD* contain a table of contents as well as the document numbers and titles of the listed texts, possibly an addition of the unknown compiler. The length of the documents

[6] The research project *Preservation, Compilation, and Annotation of Mazar Documents in Xinjiang and Ferghana* was headed by Jun Sugawara and sponsored by The Toyota Foundation (トヨタ財団), 2005-2008. For more information regarding this research project, see Jun Sugawara "INTRODUCTION: Towards a Study of Mazar Documents" in Sugawara & Kawahara 2006: 13-18.

found in the *CKWD* varies; some documents are only half a page while others are several pages long. In certain instances two short documents have been inserted into a single page. The collection contains a total of 131 texts in 197 pages.[7] The texts were copied by hand from the originals.

To use this material as a historical source, we must first examine them critically and decide whether they are authentic. Upon evaluating the texts I concluded that their trustworthiness is relatively high. Some of the content of the documents in the *CKWD* contain details that correspond to other historical sources or present day oral testimonies as will be shown in this paper.

At the moment, I do not have any information on the compiler or collection methods used in the creation of the volume. Therefore it is very difficult to make assumptions based on the content alone. It is unlikely, however, that the work of collecting 131 *waqf* documents and compiling them was performed by one individual. Thus, this collection should be seen as the result of an organized effort of a group of people. If we consider the fact that (1) texts in the *CKWD* were produced in the Kashgar region, and (2) the latest text dates from 1935, we arrive at the possibility that this material was compiled as part of an official project to vilify the *waqf* properties and was carried out by the local Kashgar government in 1935.[8]

In this paper, I will use following documents related to mazars in Opal:

No.4 (p.8-9) "The *tauliya* (deed of trusteeship) on Buzrugwār Ḥaḍrat-i Mollām of Opal" (Ṣafar, 1285 = May-June, 1868).
No.5 (p.10) " The *tauliya* on Ḥaḍrat-i Mollām Buzrūgwār of Opal" (Rabīʿ 1 15, 1260 = April 4, 1844).
No.6 (p.11) "The *tauliya* on Ḥaḍrat-i Mollām of Opal"(Qurbān (=Dhū al-ḥijja) 23, 1186 = March 17, 1773).
No.7 (p.12-14) "The *tauliya* on Imāmlarim of Opal" (Safar, 1285 = May-June, 1868).
No.8 (p.15) "The *tauliya* on Buzrūgwār Khwāja Qontāq(*sic*) of Opal" (Shawwāl 21, 1276 = May 12, 1860).

---

[7] This material will be discussed in an upcoming paper.

[8] Gu Bao suggests that certain *waqf* lands were organically condemned by the Government in 1935-36. According to Gu, "by the demand of the Uyghur people and the progressive youth", Sheng Shicai's government made the decision to condemn *waqf* lands and put them under the control of the Association for the Promotion of Uyghur Culture (APUC, 维吾尔文化促进会) for their cultural and educational operations among the Uyghur nationality. Though this condemnation originally targeted waqf lands belonging to mazars, banned religious schools, or *waqf* lands providing for the purchase of supplies necessary for maintaining mazars such as candles (*chiraq*), Qur'ans, caldrons (*qazan*), and eating facilities (*ashkhana*). However, while *waqf* lands belonging to mazars had not been condemned effectually, by contrast, *waqf*-facilities with a high public profile such as bridges (*köwürük*) and ponds (*hauḍ*) which had not originally been the object of condemnation, were taken over. The management of these seized *waqf* lands was given to the Xinjiang Democratic Defense League (保卫新疆民主同盟) after the elimination of the APUC. (Deng & Gu 1953: 99-100). Shimizu suggests that under the strong leadership of Maḥmūd Muḥīṭī, ruler of Kashgar from July 1934 to May 1937, the Bureau for Modification of Schools and *Waqfs* was established and conducted surveys on *waqfs* belong to mazars, mosques and madrasas. (Shimizu 2007: 67).

No.9 (p.16) " The *tauliya* on Khwāja Qondāq Buzrūgwār of Opal" (Barat (=Sha'bān) 22, 1260 = September 6, 1844).
No.10 (p.17) " The *tauliya* on Khwāja Qondāq Mazār of Opal" (Safar qoshni ay (=Rabī'1) 28, 1263 = March 16, 1847).

2. Ḥaḍrat-i Mollām Mazar (or Mausoleum of Maḥmūd al-Kāshgharī)

A view of the Ḥaḍrat-i Mollām Mazar from a distance (2004).

2-1. The Ḥaḍrat-i Mollām Mazar today

As mentioned above, this mazar is currently a very popular spot for "tourism" as it contains the grave of Maḥmūd al-Kāshgharī. Since this site's recognition as a National Historic & Cultural Heritage Site Under State Protection (全国重点文物保护单位) of the People's Republic of China on May 2005, the mazar's reputation has been firmly established.[9]

This mazar's current fame has its roots in the site's "discovery" and "recognition" that took place in the 1980s. A handful of publications and articles recorded the details of this process, stating that the mausoleum of Maḥmūd al-Kāshgharī (Ḥaḍrat-i Mollām Mazar) had been rediscovered by members of project for "Exploratory Research on Mähmut Qäshqäri's Homeland and Burial Site" project in December 1982, and the following year the Xinjiang government approved its recognition as a Regional Historic Site & Cultural Heritage under State Protection in December 1983.[10] This process moved forward quickly in the liberal atmosphere that characterized the Post-Cultural Revolution era.

However, on the contrary, even though there have been great discoveries and historical research performed, material which provides information on the mazar's

---

[9] See the webpage of the XUAR Bureau of Cultural Heritage (新疆维吾尔自治区文物局), http://www.xjww.com.cn/news/show-6867.aspx (last access on November 22, 2015)
[10] For example, Sidiq 1985; Barat 1994; Sugawara 1999; Hamada 1999.

socio-economic situation from a historical perspective are minimal. In the early 20th century, C. P. Skrine introduced the legend of the "picturesque shrine of Hazrat Maulam" proving it's sacred status at the time.[11] But excepting this account, there is no historical information on the mazar. Although Mollā Mūsā Sayrāmī, a historian and native of Sayrām (in Xinjiang) who lived in the 19th-20th centuries, spends the final part of his text, the *Tārīkh-i Ḥamidī,* to introduce the sacred sites in South Xinjiang, in his section on Kashgar he makes no mention of the mazars in Opal including the Ḥaḍrat-i Mollām Mazar.[12] Even in the book *Mähmut Qäshqäri* (1985), a compilation including a series of articles on the site's "discovery", historical sources are limited to a handfull of oral accounts from Opal natives, and one document about the donation of a book entitled *Mäsniwi Shirip* (< *Mathnawī-yi Sharīf*), dated *Rajab* 14 of 1252 (October 25, 1835).[13] Thus, the three documents I will introduce here may provide valuable new historical information on this mazar.

2-2. CKWD document No. 6 (p. 11)

> Date: *ʿĪd-i Qurbān* (=*Dhū al-ḥijja*) 23, 1178 (June 13, 1765)
> Issuer: Ḥaḍrat Gong Ḥākim Beg
> Content: *Waqf*-settlement document in which the issuer donates approx. 63 *pātmān* of land located in Opal's (Ofāl) Doghālāt (*sic*) Village and appoints the following individuals as its caretakers; Muḥammad Yūsuf as a *shaykh*, Moldechi Khwāja as a *sifārkhwān*, Qūrbān Ṣūfī as a *jārūbkesh* and Ibrāhīm Ṣūfī as a *yantaqchi.*

The contents of this document suggest three historical facts. First: though the description of the document clearly states that the Ḥaḍrat-i Mollām Mazar possessed "63 *pātmān*" of *waqf* land in Ofāl's Doghālāt Village, this seems to be unusually large, and should not to be accepted if this sawing-area-measure "*pātmān*" corresponds to the usual value of 573.44 kg.[14] Thus, here all we can determine is that the *waqf* is located in Doghālāt Village (in present day, Doghlat).

Second: Since this document was issued by Ḥaḍrat Gong Ḥākim Beg, we can assume that chief Ḥākim was involved in matters concerning *waqfs* during the initial decades of the Qing rule over the *Hui-bu* (回部). This Ḥaḍrat Gong Ḥākim Beg is clearly identified as Gadāy Muḥammad (噶岱默特) the Gong Ḥākim Beg of Kashgar (d.1775) who governed Opal after 1759.[15]

Third: the text indicates the personnel roles of the mazar in this period. Though the usual composition consists of the *shaykh* (chief), *sifārkhwān* (scholar) and *jarubkesh*

---

[11] Skrine 1920: 181.
[12] Sayrami 1986: 640.
[13] Sidiq 1985: 39-70.
[14] On the measure *pātmān* in Xinjiang, see Wang & Li 1994: 11.
[15] *Wangguang biaozhuang*, v.16- *biao* 16. This comment was based on the suggestion by Professor Onuma Takahiro (The Tōhoku Gakuin University, Sendai). For more on *ḥākim* of Kashgar's supervison of Opal, see Ji 1994: 583.

(sweeper),[16] it is worth noting that in addition to these there was also the position of *yantaqchi* (camel-plant collector). Besides the physical act of cultivation, collecting *yantaq* must have been recognized as a source of revenue for *waqf* land in Opal.[17] This may reflect the geographical and botanical atmosphere of the time.

2-3. CKWD document No. 5 (p. 10)

Date: *Rabīʿ* 1 15, 1260 (April 4, 1844)
Issuer: Shāydūn Shaykh
Content: *Waqf*-settlement document in which the issuer donates a property of unknown size located in the village of Shātū.
Witnesses: Aʿlam Najm al-Dīn Akhund, Aḥmad Yüz Bashi, Mollā Ṣalāḥ al-Dīn Akhund Khwāja, Turdūsh Bay.

This document provides very limited information and appears to be a fragment as it lacks pieces of information such as the date, donator's name, and the exact location of the *waqf* land. The place name, Shātū Kent possibly corresponds to present day Shota Kent.[18]

2-4. CKWD document No. 4 (p. 8-9)

Date: *Safar*, 1285 (May-June, 1868)
Issuer: Aldāsh Beg Dādkhāh
Content: *Waqf*-confirmation document. By the order (*farmāyish*) of [Muḥammad Yaʿqūb Beg Ataliq Ghāzī], Alash Beg Dādkhwāh, as a part of his activities on several mazars in the Kashgar region, investigates the *waqf* (*auqāf*) and expenses (*maṣārif*) of the 15 *fātmān* and 4 *charäk* of *waqf* land belonging to [Ḥaḍrat-i Mollām Mazar] located at Mollām Bāgh in Opal (Ofāl). He assigns caretaking positions for the waqf such as *mutawallī*, *shaykh*, *sipārkhwān*, *jārūbkesh*, *imām*, *khaṭīb* and *mu'adhdhin*, fixes the distribution rate of revenue from the *waqf's* properties for them and for maintenance (including ceremonial expenses), and confirms the exact location of the five *waqf* properties.

This text is clearly one of the *waqf*-confirmation documents issued by Alāsh (Aldāsh) Beg Dādkhwāh, a Ḥākim Beg of Kashgar under the rule of Yaʿqūb Beg from 1867 to 1877.[19] This series of documents was issued around 1285-6 A.H. (1868-70) to several

---

16 For the meanings of these titles, see Deng & Gu 1953: 102.
17 For the meaning of *yantaq* and *yantaqchi*, see Jarring 1964: 148; UTIL-Q: 1393.
18 ShUARKhT: 187.
19 For more information on Aldāsh Beg Dādkhwāh, see Shinmen 1987: 19.

mazars in the Kāshgar region, 10 of which are included in the *CKWD.*[20] The Museum of Folklore at Xinjiang University (新疆大学民族民俗博物馆) possesses a *waqf* document produced in 1285 A.H. related to the Toghraghliq or Khwāja Isḥāq Walī Mazar located in Sarman (present day Sämän 色满) and is the same type of document as the one addressed here. As *waqf*-confirmation documents typically contain the same form and phrases, it is likely that they were issued around the same time.

Table A: Allotments from the revenue of waqf land in 1285 Ḥ.
(Ḥaḍrat Mollām Mazar, Mollābagh, Opal, in document CKWD no.4)

<table>
<tr><th>EXPENSES</th><th>ALLOTMENTS</th></tr>
<tr><td>mutawallī</td><td>1 sahm</td></tr>
<tr><td>shaykh</td><td>2 sahm</td></tr>
<tr><td>sipārkhwān</td><td>1 sahm</td></tr>
<tr><td>imām</td><td rowspan="3">1 sahm</td></tr>
<tr><td>khaṭīb</td></tr>
<tr><td>mu'adhdhin</td></tr>
<tr><td>jārūbkesh</td><td rowspan="2">1 sahm</td></tr>
<tr><td>yantaqchi</td></tr>
<tr><td>maintenance and ceremonial expenses</td><td>4 sahm</td></tr>
<tr><td>total</td><td>10 sahm</td></tr>
</table>

Document No. 4, contains two caret marks that possibly indicates personal name and the name of the mazar. Typically, the supplimentary words for the caret marks are placed in the header or margin of the documents.[21] In the CKWD, however, such supplements are not visible on any part of the document. In this case we can assume that the correspondences are ("Muḥammad Ya'qūb Beg Ataliq Ghāzī" and "Ḥaḍrat-i Mollām Mazar") from the information given in the *CKWD's* table of contents, and the equivalent section from the original documents kept in the Folklore Museum. The description of the mazar's location (Mollā Bāgh) given in the texts preserved at the Folklore Museum supports this conclusion.

In spite of the formal language and rhetoric of the document, the text contains three unique pieces of information. Firstly, the text indicates the location and total size of the *waqf.* As mentioned earlier, the document also suggests that the *waqf* pertaining to the

[20] The documents issued by Aldāsh Beg in the *CKWD* are as follows: [1]no.4(p.8-9) Ḥaḍrat-i Mollām Mazar (Mz. hereafter). [Opal] 1285/Safar, [2]no.7(p.12-14) Imāmlarim Mz.[Opal] 1285/Safar, [3]no.22(p.38-39) Sugallik Mz. [Sarman] 1285/Safar, [4]no.26(p.50-51) Toghraghliq (Khwāja Isḥāq Walī) Mz. [Sarman] 1285/Muḥarram, [5]no.28(p.53-54) Toghraghliq (Khwāja Isḥāq Walī) Mz. [Sarman] 1285/Safar, [6]no.48(p.95-97) Aqtam Khōja Mz. and Oyghaq Khōja Mz. [Sarman] 1285/Safar, [7]no.84(p.143-144) Qadīm Jāy Mz. [Mūsh] 1284/Muḥarram/2, [8]no.106(p.170-173) Sulṭān Qarasaqal Mz. [Tazghūn] 1285, [9]no.109(p.174-176) Ḥusayn Bughrā Khān Mz. [Shahr Qaraqir Darwaza] 1285/Safar, [10]no.129(p.195-196) Chokur Rashīd al-Dīn Mz. [Bäshkeräm] 1285/Muḥarram.

[21] About the manner of caret marks in documentary sources, Professor Kim Hodong refers on the case of some royal decrees of the 17th century Yarkand. See Kim 2010: p.78, f.n. 75.

Ḥaḍrat-i Mollām Mazar was located at Mollām Bāgh, contained a total of 15 *fātmān* and 4 *charäk* of land, and *waqf* was divided into four parts. The place name "Mollām Bāgh" may corresponds to present day Mollambeghi, where the Ḥaḍrat-i Mollām Mazar is currently located. Secondly, the text contains information on the caretakers and their positions as well as information on the allotments of revenue from *waqf* properties: these details can be found in table A.

And thirdly, the final part of the document lists the *waqf's holdings*. According to the text, the *waqf* consisted of five separate parcels of the following size: (1) 4 *fātmān*, (2) 4 *fātmān*, (3) 4.5 *pātmān* (*sic*), (4) 0.5 *pātmān* (*sic*), (5) 1 *ghalbīr*. Interestingly, the sum of *waqf's parcels given* here (13 *fātmān* and 1 *ghalbīr*) does not match the size given in the initial description (15 *fātmān*).

3. The Imāmlarim Mazar

The Imamlirim Mazar (2004).

3-1. The Imāmlarim Mazar today

While the Ḥaḍrat-i Mollām Mazar has achieved certain degree of popularity as a "tourism" spot with authorization and support of the government, the two mazars that I will introduce here, have little to do with the business of modern "tourism", and have preserved their traditional role as a sacred site. Since there is very little information on these mazars, even in Rahile Dawut's comprehensive work on mazars in Xinjiang,[22] I will discuss these mazars from a historical perspective with the results of my 2005 fieldwork[23] and the descriptions of *waqf* documents contained in the *CKWD*.

The Imāmlarim Mazar (in Modern Uyghur: Imamlirim Mazar) is located in the vast, hilly expanses approximately 5 km south-east of the Opal *bazar*. This mazar exhibits many of the typical features of a mazar complex such as a pond (*ḥauḍ*) and mosque with a stand of trees at the foot of a hill. But unlike other mazars, the mausoleum and cemetery stand on a desolate hill. Two tombs are arranged on the right side of the building and there is a place for religious activities(*khaniqä*) on the left. A lattice separates the mausoleum from the outside and there are several flags (*tugh*) placed between the two tombs. There is another tomb at the foot of the hill that people believe belongs to a saint named "Shah Tälip Zärmäs" who is said to have been a cook (*ashpez*) for the Twelve Imams.

Although there is no historical records that mention the mazar, there is a legend associated with it. According to an informant, Yasin Akhun (Shaykh), the legend states that there are two saints buried in this mazar: "Imam Malik Äjdäl" and "Imam Malik Äskär." These two saints had joined in the battle against the man-eating dragon led by a saint known as "Mahmut Qäshqäri", and died as martyrs from the dragon's poison.[24] As this legend closely resembles the legend of Ḥaḍrat-i Mollām recorded by C.P. Skrine in the 1920s, we may infer that these two mazars - Imāmlarim and Ḥaḍrat-i Mollām – share a common legend of origin.

3-2. CKWD document No. 7 (p. 12-14)

Date: *Safar*, 1285 (May-June, 1868)
Issuer: Aldāsh Beg Dādkhāh
Content: *Waqf*-confirmation document. By the order (*farmāyish*) of [Muḥammad Ya'qūb Beg Ataliq Ghāzī], Alash Beg Dādkhwāh, as a part of his activities on several mazars in the Kashgar region, investigates the *waqf* (*auqāf*) and the expenses (*maṣārif*) of the three *fātmān* of *waqf* land with yard (*höyla*), three stone (*tash*) of water mill (*tigürmen*) and two mortars (*soqä*) belonging to [Imāmlarim Mazar] located at the cliff-edge of Doghlāt Village in Opal (Ofāl). He assigns the caretakers of the *waqf* such as the *mutawallī*, *shaykh*, *khaṭīb*, *mu'adhdhīn*, *maqṣūrekhān*, *jārūbkesh* and *yantaqchi*, as well as fixes the distribution rate of revenue from the *waqf* land

[22] See Dawut 2001a and b.

[23] In the following section, the descriptions of the current situation of the Imāmlarim Mazār and Qondaq Atam Mazārs are based on author's visit to the sites in August 2005. For more details concerning this fieldwork, see Sugawara 2007a: 19-33 and Sugawara 2007b: 67-78.

[24] From an interview Yasin Akhun (73 years of age), a 7th generation shaykh of the Imāmlarim Mazar. According to Yasin Akhun, the genealogy of the *shaykhs* of Imāmlarim, his ancestors, is as follows: (1)Yüsüp(<Yūsuf), (2)Palta(<Fāltū), (3)Niyaz(<Niyāz), (4)Yantaq, (5)Tokhti(<Tokhtī), (6)Ibrahim(<Ibrāhīm). For the legend as related by Yasin Akhun is given on. see p.76-77 (transcription), p.77-78.

for them and for maintenance or ceremonial expenses. This document also confirms the exact location of the five *waqf* lands.

This is another example of a *waqf*-confirmation document issued by Alāsh (Aldāsh) Beg Dādkhwāh. Like *CKWD document* No. 4, there are two symbols which indicate specific personal names (i.e. Muḥammad Ya'qūb Beg Ataliq Ghāzī) and the name of the mazar (i.e. Imāmlarim Mazar).

In this text we again find three interesting pieces of information. First, this document provides the location and the total dimensions of the *waqf* endowment. The *waqf* attached to the Imāmlarim Mazar is located at "the cliff's edge in Doghlāt", and is comprised of "three *fātmān*" of land with a "yard, three water mills and two mortars" dividing the *waqf's* property into five parts. The text suggests that the *waqf* and mazar are located in the same place.

Table B: Allotments from the revenue of waqf land in 1285 Ḥ. (Imāmlarim mazar, Doghlāt, Opal, in document CKWD no.7)

<table>
<tr><th>EXPENSES</th><th colspan="2">ALLOTMENTS</th></tr>
<tr><td>mutawallī</td><td colspan="2">1 sahm</td></tr>
<tr><td>shaykh</td><td colspan="2">2 sahm</td></tr>
<tr><td>khaṭīb</td><td rowspan="2">3/4</td><td rowspan="3">1 sahm</td></tr>
<tr><td>imām</td></tr>
<tr><td>mu'adhdhin</td><td>1/4</td></tr>
<tr><td>sipārkhwān*</td><td colspan="2">1 sahm</td></tr>
<tr><td>jārūbkesh*</td><td colspan="2" rowspan="2">1 sahm</td></tr>
<tr><td>yantaqchi*</td></tr>
<tr><td>maintenance and ceremonial expenses</td><td colspan="2">4 sahm</td></tr>
<tr><td>tot.</td><td colspan="2">10 sahm</td></tr>
</table>

**plural*

Second, there is also information on the assignment of caretakers and their allotments from *waqf* revenues: these details are provided in table B. As mentioned above, revenue allotments are also shown in the case of the Ḥaḍrat-i Mollām mazar (Table A). The contents of both tables clearly indicate that both *waqf*s employ a similar allotment standard and that there is very little differences in between. It is worth investigating whether this rate was newly fixed by the Ya'qūb Beg government (Aldāsh Beg Dādkhwāh) for all mazars in the Kāshghar region, or simply followed a traditional standard for allotments for the area.[25]

[25] In Iran, it is said that the treasurer (*mutawallī*) of a mazar had rights to "one-tenth" of its revenue. The allotments at the mazars in question may have followed a similar standard. Kozlowski, G.C.; Peters, R.; Powers, D.S.; Layish, A.; Lambton, Ann K.S.; Deguilhem, Randi; McChesney, R.D.; Hooker, M.B.; Hunwick, J.O. "Waḳf (a.)." *Encyclopaedia of Islam*. Edited by: P. Bearman , Th. Bianquis , C.E. Bosworth , E. van Donzel and W.P. Heinrichs. Brill, 2008. Brill Online. TOKYO UNIVERSITY OF FOREIGN. 26 June 2008 <http://www.encislam.brill.nl/subscriber/entry?entry=islam_COM-1333>

Third, the final part of the document lists the *waqf's* properties. According to the description, this endowment consisted of five separate properties: (1) old *waqf* lands (*mauqūfa-i qadīm*) (no information on size is provided), (2) four *charäk* of land at Uruklik Atam, (3) land donated by ʻAbd Khalīk Beg (no information on size is provided), (4) 10 *pātmān* at Jutuk/Jotok, (5) and seven *charäk* donated by Ṣūfiya Khān. The sum of the dimensions of these properties also differs from the total given in the section's description.

4. The Qondāq Atam Mazar

Qondāq Atam Mazar (2004).

4-1. The Qondāq Atam Mazar today

Based on my fieldwork conducted in 2005, when compared with the two mazars mentioned above, the Qondāq Atam mazar pales in both size and comparison. This mazar is located at the edge of a hill 3km southeast from the Opal bazar. From the mausoleum it has a commanding view of Opal's lush valley, while the view in the opposite direction reveals a vast expanse extending to the far-off Alai Mountains. The mausoleum is a mud and brick construction with a lattice separating it from the outside similar to the Imāmlarim Mazar. Apart from the mausoleum and a small cemetery, there are no other facilities belonging to the mazar. It is said that the name of this mazar was derived from the Turkic verb *qonmaq* (to spend the night); because of a legend that claims a saint stayed there for a night while on a journey.[26]

---

[26] From an interview with Imin Dawut Qari (70 years of age), *khaṭīb* of the Qondaq Atam Mazar in 1995.

4-2. *CKWD* document No.9 (p. 16)

Date: *Barāt* (=*Sha'bān*) 22, 1260 (September 6, 1844)
Issuer: Abū al-Ḥasan Khwāja, 'Abd Allāh Ṣūfī, and Mollā Shahābdūn
Content: *Waqf*-settlement document in which Abū al-Ḥasan Khwāja and 'Abd Allāh Ṣūfī donate (*waqf-i muṭlaq*) four *charäk* of land in each, located in Dong Būstān of Opal (Ofāl). And Mollā Shahābdūn donates 20 *tenge* of money.
Witnesses: A'lam Najm al-Dīn Akhund, Ibrāhīm Bay, Turdūsh Bay Khwājam, Niyāz Durgha, Mollā Ismā'īl, 'Azīz Khwāja.

The only historical information we can glean from this text is that the mazar acquired eight *charäk* of land and the sum of 20 *tenges* in 1844. Though it is impossible to identify the place name "Dong Bustan", as no information is given on the western border of the waqf land in the description, we can assume that lands belonging to the endowment was located on the eastern side of the mausoleum itself.

4-3. *CKWD* document No. 10 (p. 17)

Date: *Safar qoshni ay* (=*Rabī' al-awwal*) 28, 1263 (March 16, 1847)
Issuer: Sharīna Aghacha of Opal (Ofāl)
Content: *Waqf*-settlement document in which the issuer donates (*waqf-i muṭlaq*) one *ghalbīr* of land located in of Opal's (Ofāl) Qarāngghū Yār.
Witnesses: A'lam Najm al-Dīn Akhund, Mollā 'Īsā Khaṭīb Akhund Yüzbashi, Mollā Ṣalāḥ al-Dīn Yüzbashi, 'Azīz Chong, 'Abd al-Bāqī Khwāja, 'Abd al-Raḥmān Shaykh, Abū al-Ḥasan Khwāja, Yūsuf Khwāja, Ibrāhīm Bay, Turdūsh Khwāja, Khudāyār Khwāja

This document indicates that this mazar possessed one *ghalbīr* of land in 1847 in a place known as Qarāngghū Yār. It is worth noting that there are several individuals with the titles "*shaykh*", "*khaṭīb*" and "*yüzbashi*" found in the witness section. Individuals with titles such as *shaykh* and *khaṭīb* were most likely caretakers of the mazar at the time.

4-4. *CKWD* document No. 8 (p. 15)

Date: *Shawwāl* 21, 1276(May 12, 1860)
Issuer: Tokhta Shaykh
Content: *Waqf*-settlement document in which the issuer donates (*waqf-i muṭlaq*) one-third of a *fātmān* of land which had originally been donated (*waqf*) to the mazar by his father. The *waqf* located at Shōtī Kent of Opal (Ofāl).
Witnesses: A'lam Mollā Sulaymān Akhund Yüz Bashi, Bāqī Chong, Mämät Sayyid Akhund, Imām Mollā Niyāz, Imām Mollā Tokhtasūn, Turdūsh Bay, Islām Yüz Bashi,

Sulṭān Khwāja, ʻAbd al-Ṣamad, Kafar Khwāja, Mollā Ṣādiq, Mollā Ḥalim, Mollā Rōzī.

In this text we also find three interesting pieces of information. First, this *waqf* settlement document is filled with many formulaic expressions. The first 9 of the text's 22 lines are written using formulaic expressions and convey little practical information. The latter part of the text also contains a great deal of flowery rhetoric. This choice of language may be due to the fact that the document was issued by a *shaykh*; an Islamic specialist responsible for supervising the mazar. In this regard, this document clearly distinguishes itself from the two documents discussed above.

Second, this document gives the names of several of the mazar's caretakers (*shaykh, imām*) and of local leaders (*aʻlam, yüzbashi*).

Third, the document's description reveals what appears to be a perplexing case of "double donation." According to the description, the issuer's father had donated a parcel of land to the mazar as a *waqf*[27]. But in the present document, the issuer divides this land into three parts and donates one-third of it to the mazar again. This case might indicate a particular kind of custom concerning the *waqf* land in this region.

Concluding Remarks

Through an examination of these seven documents, we have gained a slightly more nuanced understanding of mazars in the Opal region. The three mazars discussed in this paper were functioning as sacred sites in the 19th century at the latest, as they possessed *waqf* endowments that believers had donated to them. The descriptions of the documents clearly shows that the Ḥaḍrat-i Mollām mazar received support from Ghadāy Muḥammad Ḥākim Gong Beg of Kāshghar in the 18th century, and that Yaʻqūb Beg's government reconfirmed the *waqf* lands of the Ḥaḍrat-i Mollām and Imāmlarim mazars in the 19th century. These facts prove that the mazars of Opal traditionally had strong ties to Kāshghar.

Also, it is particularly important to note that some of the descriptions in these documents indicate clear arrangements made for the handling of *waqf* endowments in the region. The organization of a *waqf's* administration, specific information on its caretakers and their allotments found in these documents may provide valuable insights for future comparative studies on sacred sites not only in Kashgar or Xinjiang, but throughout the vast region of Central Eurasia.

[27] "I divided and acquired one-third from a *patman* of land which had originally been donated by my father to Qonghaq Buzurgwar at Opal's Shota Kent. And with God's help, I too donated it to Qonghaq Buzurgwar." (*atam Khwāja Qonghāq Buzrūgwārgha waqf qilghan bir fātmānliq yerning üch ḥaṣṣaning bir ḥaṣṣasini ayrip alip män häm taufīq ilahī yār bolup Khwāja Qonghāq Buzrūgwārgha fī-sabīl allāh waqf-i muṭlaq wa taṣdīq wa muaʻyyad qilip berdim.*)

Bibliography

Barat, Kahar 1994. "Discovery of history: The burial site of Kashgarli Mahmud", in Paksoy, H.B.(ed.) *Central Asia Reader*. Armonk, N.Y.: M.E.Sharp: 77-81.

Dawut 2001a: Dawut, Rahilä 2001. *Uyghur mazarliri*. Urumqi: Shinjang Khälq Näshriyati.

Dawut 2001b: Dawuti, Reyila 热依拉达吾提 2001. *Weiwuerzu maza wenhua yanjiu* 维吾尔族麻扎文化研究 [A Study on the Mazar Cultures of Uyghurs]. Urumqi: Xinjiang Daxue Chubanshe.

Deng Liqun and Gu Bao 邓力群, 谷葆 1953. "Nanjiang de Wahafudi wenti"南疆的瓦哈甫地问题 [The *waqf*-matters in South Xinjiang], in Xinjiang Weiwuer Zizhiqu bianjizu 新疆维吾尔自治区编辑组(ed.) *Nanjiang nongcun shehui* 南疆农村社会, Urumqi: Xinjiang Renmin Chubanshe, repr.1979: 96-109.

Hamada Masami 濱田正美 1999. "Seijia no haka wo mitsukeru hanashi" 聖者の墓を見つける話 [Discovery of the tombs of Islamic Saints], *Kokuritsu Minzokugaku Hakubutsukan Kenkyū Hōkoku Bessatsu* 国立民族学博物館研究報告別冊 No.20: 287-326.

Jarring, Gunnar 1964. *An Eastern Turki-English Dialect Dictionary*. Lund: CWK Gleerup.

Ji Dachun 纪大椿 (ed.) 1994. *Xinjiang Lishi cidian* 新疆历史词典[Xinjiang Historical dictionary], Urumqi: Xinjiang Renmin Chubanshe.

Kim Hodong 2010. "Eastern Turki Royal Decrees of the 17th Century in the Jarring Collection" in J. A. Millward et al. (eds) *Studies on Xinjiang Historical Sources in 17-20th Centuries (TBRL 12)*, Tokyo: The Toyo Bunko: 59-107.

Sayrami, Molla Musa 1986. *Tarikhi hämidi*. Beijing: Millätlär Näshriyati.

Shimizu Yuriko 清水由里子 2007. "Kashugaru ni okeru Uiguru jin no kyōiku undō 1934-37"カシュガルにおけるウイグル人の教育運動 1934-37 [The New Education Movement of the Uyghurs in Kashghar(1934-37)], in *Nairiku Ajiashi Kenkyū* 内陸アジア史研究 22: 61-82.

ShUARKhT 2005: Shinjang Uyghur Aptonom Rayonluq Ölchäsh-Sizish Idarisi (ed.) 2005. *Shinjang Uyghur Aptonom Rayoni khäritilär toplimi*. [A Collection of Maps of the Xinjiang Uyghur Autonomous Region], Bejing & Urumqi: Junggo Kharitä Näshriyati & Shinjang Pän-tekhnika Näshriyati.

Shinmen Yasushi 新免康 1987. "Yākūbu Begu seiken no seikaku ni kansuru ichi kōsatsu" ヤークーブ・ベグ政権の性格に関する一考察 [The Character of the Government of Ya'qūb Beg] in *Shigaku Zasshi* 史学雑誌 no.96-4: 1-42.

Sidiq, Muhämmät Zunun et al.(eds) 1985. *Mähmut Qäshqäri (Maqalilar toplimi)*[Mahmud Kashgari (A collection of articles)], Kashgar: Qäshqär Uyghur Näshriyati.

Skrine, C.P. 1920. *Chinese Central Asia: An Account of the Travel in Northern Kashmir and Chinese Turkestan*. repr. in New Delhi: Bhavana Books & Prints.

Sugawara Jun 菅原純 1999. "Sōshutsu sareru 'Uiguru minzoku bunka': 'Uiguru koten bungaku' no hukkō to bobyō no 'hakken'" 創出される「ウイグル民族文化」—「ウイグル古典文学」の復興と墓廟の「発見」 [Creation of "Uyghur national culture": Revival of "Uyghur classic literature" and "Discovery" of the mausoleums]. in *Intriguing ASIA (Ajia Yūgaku)* アジア遊学 no.1: 74-86.

Sugawara Jun 菅原純 2007a. "Kashugaru chihō ni okeru seichi chōsa"カシュガル地方における聖地調査 [Description of Sacred Places Surveyed in the Kashghar Region] in Sawada Minoru (ed.) *Islamic Sacred Places in Central Asia: The Ferghana Valley and Kashghar Region*. Nara: The Nara International Foundation: 19-34.

Sugawara Jun 菅原純 2007b. "Kashgaru chihō ni okeru seichi denshō" カシュガル地方における聖地伝承 [Mazar Legends in the Kashghar region] in Sawada Minoru (ed.) *Islamic Sacred Places in Central Asia*. Nara: The Nara International Foundation: 67-78.

Sugawara Jun and Kawahara Yayoi (eds) 2006. *Mazar Documents from Xinjiang and Ferghana (facsimile) 1*, Tokyo: Research Institute for Languages and Cultures of Asia and Africa, TUFS.

UTIL-Q: Shinjang Uyghur Aptonom Rayonluq Millätlär Til-Yeziq Khizmiti Komiteti Lughät Bölümi(ed.) 1999. *Uyghur tilining izahliq lughiti (qisqartilmisi)*. Urumqi: Shinjang Khälq Näshriyati.

Wang Shouli 王守礼, Li Jinxin 李进新 1994. *Xinjiang Weiwuerzu qiyue wenshu ziliao xuanbian* 新疆维吾尔族契约文书资料选编 [Collection of Uyghur contractual documents from Xinjiang], Urumqi: Xinjiang Shehui Kexueyuan.

Wangguang biaozhuang: Qinding waihan meggu guibu wangguang biaozhuang 欽定外藩蒙古回部王公表傳 in Bao Wenhan and Chao Ketu 包文汉，朝克图(eds.) 1998. *Menggu huibu wanggong biaozhuan* 蒙古回部王公表传, Huhehuote: Neimenggu Daxue Chubanshe,

Xinjiang Gailan : Liu Yusheng et al. & The Foreign Affairs(Oversea Chinese Affairs) Office of XUAR People's Government 刘宇生，新疆维吾尔自治区人民政府外事（侨务）办公室(eds) 2001. *Xinjiang Gailan* 新疆概览 [Overview Xinjiang], Urumqi: Xinjiang Renmin Chubanshe.

FACSIMILES

CKWD No.6 (p.11) "The tauliya on Ḥaḍrat-i Mollām of Opal"
(Qurbān (=Dhū al-ḥijja) 23, 1186 = March 17, 1773).

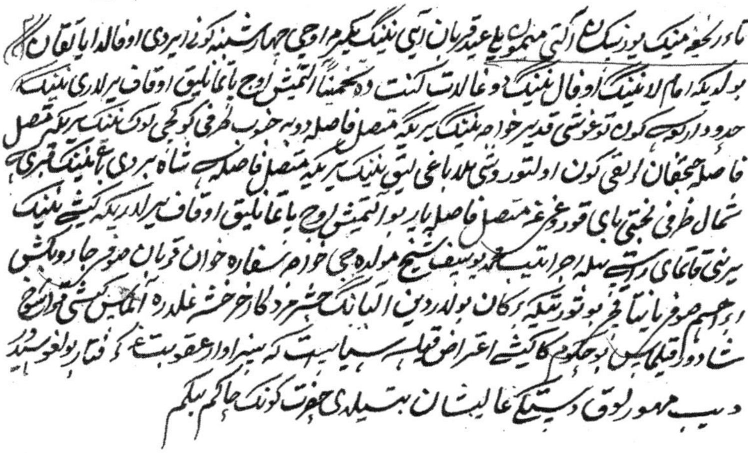

CKWD No.5(p.10) "The tauliya on Ḥaḍrat-i Mollām Buzrūgwār of Opal"
(Rabīʿ1 15, 1260= April 4, 1844)

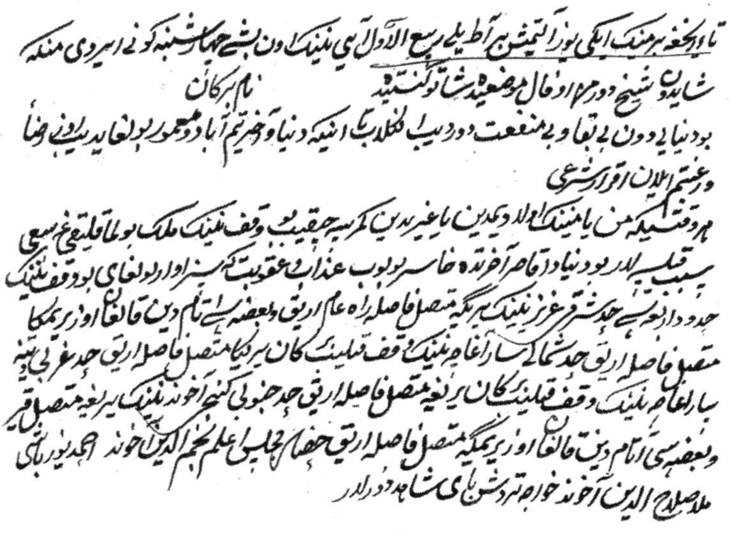

CKWD No.4 (p.8-9) "The tauliya on Buzrūgwār Ḥaḍrat-i Mollām of Opal"
(Safar, 1285 = May-June, 1868) -1/2.

CKWD No.4 (p.8-9) "The tauliya on Buzrūgwār Ḥaḍrat-i Mollām of Opal"
(Safar, 1285 = May-June, 1868) -2/2.

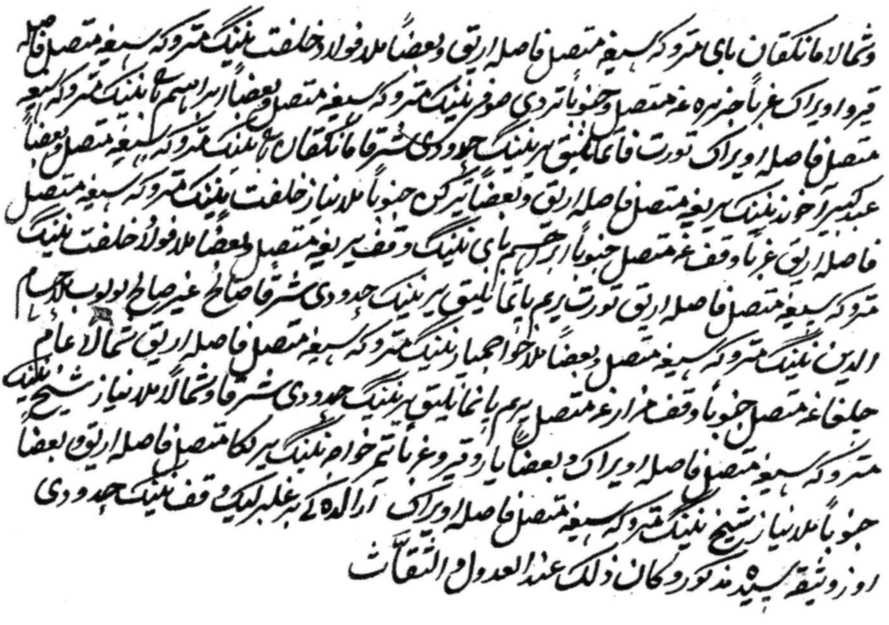
وشمالا مانکقان بای ملک و که سیغه متصل فاصله اریق و بعضا ملا فولاد خلفت ننینک ملک و که سیغه متصل فاصله
قیروا ویراک غربا جزیره غه متصل جنوبا تردی صوفی ننینک ملک و که سیغه متصل و بعضا ابراهیم ننینک ملک و که سیغه
متصل فاصله اویراک تورت فاتما تلیق بیر ننینک جدودی شرقا مانکقان ننینک ملک و که سیغه متصل و بعضا
عبد کبیر آخوند ننینک بیر یغه متصل فاصله اریق و بعضا تیرکن جنوبا ملا نیاز خلفت ننینک ملک و که سیغه متصل
فاصله اریق غربا وقف غه متصل جنوبا ابراهیم بای ننینک وقف بیر یغه متصل بعضا ملا فولاد خلفت ننینک
ملک و که سیغه متصل فاصله اریق تورت ریم باتما تلیق بیر ننینک جدودی شرقا صالح غیر صالح لودوب ملا حسام
الدین ننینک ملک و که سیغه متصل بعضا ملا خواجم بای ننینک ملک و که سیغه متصل فاصله اریق شمالا اعام
جلغا غه متصل جنوبا وقف غه ارغ متصل بیرم باتما تلیق بیر ننینک جدودی شرقا و شمالا ملا نیاز شیخ ننینک
ملک و که سیغه متصل فاصله اویراک و بعضا یار و قیر و غربا تیم خوام ننینک بیر یکا متصل فاصله اریق و بعضا
جنوبا ملا نیاز شیخ ننینک ملک و که سیغه متصل فاصله اویراک ارالده کی بر غلبر لیک وقف ننینک جدودی
روز وثیقه بیتیلدی مذکور و کان ذلک عند العدول و الثقات

CKWD No.7 (p.12-14) "The tauliya on Imāmlarim of Opal"
(Safar, 1285 = May-June, 1868) -- 1/3.

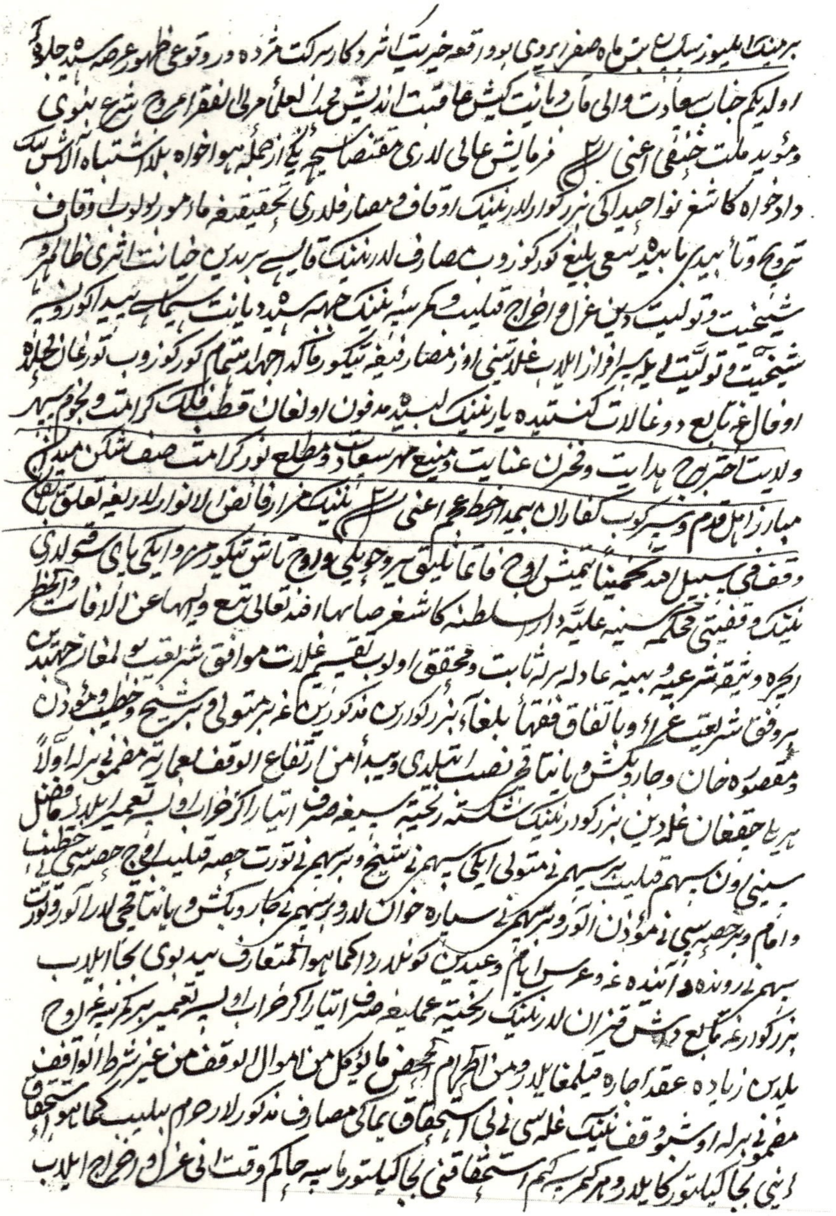

No.7 (p.12-14) "The tauliya on Imāmlarim of Opal"
(Safar, 1285 = May-June, 1868) -- 2/3.

اوزبیه باسعه مرد مندین لی نصب ایکایلدار سعادتمندیلم موقوفه مذکوره نلنیک آباد و [illegible] وقیعه سعی کوشش
قیلیلار دنیا و آخرتی آباد و معمور اولغای و مرشقاوتمند یکم موقوفه مذکوره نلنیک خرابلیغ نا تولوقیغه سبب
و باعث بولیلار دنیا و آخرتده اخوار دمقهور اولوب لعنت الله علیه کرفتار اولغای نعوذ بالله من شرور انفسنا
ومن سیئات اعمالنا بیز کوارین مذکورین غه تعلق موقوفه قدیملار نلنیک حد شرقی و شمالی قیزیل جیلغه
غربا طالب نلنیک یریکا و بعضا ملا یعقوب نلنیک متروکه سیکا متصل و بعضا عبد جان توبیک نلنیک متروکه سیغه
متصل فاصله یار و جنوبا ابوالحسن خوام نلنیک متروکه سیغه متصل فاصله یار و بعضا ازون نیاز نلنیک یریکه
متصل فاصله یار غربا کالشمال کما الله اوستنک و بعضا یعقوب نلنیک یریکا متصل عبد کریم عطار نلنیک
متروکه سی بعضا کنجیک بای و تردی آغا و تردی جونک لار نلنیک یریکا متصل فاصله اریق غربا تردی نیاز
نلنیک متروکه سیغه متصل فاصله اریق شمالا تاشقولاق نلنیک یریکا متصل و بعضا جوق خوام نلنیک متروکه سیغه
متصل فاصله اریق بعضا لجی لک نلنیک یریغه متصل فاصله عام اریق بعضا جوق نلنیک متروکه سیغه متصل
و بعضا قمر نلنیک بعضا توخته آخوند نلنیک متروکه سیغه متصل بعضا صوفی خوام نلنیک متروکه سیغه متصل
و بعضا تولک و بعضا قالتو و توخته و محمد [illegible] و الماس نلنیک متروکه سیغه متصل فاصله اریق غربا بابای
خوام نلنیک یریغه متصل فاصله اوراک جنوبا مام بای خوام نلنیک و بعضا آخوند جاق نلنیک و بعضا دروش
و قربان و صدیق بای نلنیک متروکه سیغه متصل و بعضا کنجه خوام نلنیک یریکا متصل فاصله اوراک قیر
و غربا آخوند جاق و عبد [illegible] لار نلنیک متروکه سیغه متصل و بعضا عباس خوام نلنیک متروکه سیغه متصل
و بعضا ملا موسی نلنیک یریکا و بعضا دروش نلنیک یریکا و بعضا ملا خوجش نلنیک یریکا متصل فاصله اریق
جنوبا خدایار نلنیک یریکا متصل و بعضا عدیل یار نلنیک یریکا و بعضا سعد آخوند نلنیک و بعضا تولک
عطار نلنیک و بعضا ملا یعقوب نلنیک متروکه سیغه متصل و بعضا ملا تولک بای نلنیک تیکو خوام اوستنکی
و بعضا ملا مقصود و نیاز صوفی نلنیک متروکه سیغه و بعضا صادق بای و آخوند جوغ انلنیک متروکه سیغه
متصل و بعضا لطف آخوند نلنیک مسجد یغه متصل و بعضا وقف و بعضا قدیر نلنیک متروکه سیغه متصل
و بعضا آخوند جاق نلنیک یریکا متصل فاصله اوستنک بعضه قیر و بعضه اوراک و بعضه اوستنک
بعضه قیر و بعضه اریق و شرقا توقت اوستلکی نلنیک قشور که سی شمالا قیزیل جیلغه اوراک ایکی تام دالی
تورت چارکلیک یر نلنیک تحدیدی شرقا ملا یوسف نلنیک متروکه سیغه متصل فاصله قیر شمالا غربا توباتلیک

No.7 (p.12-14) "The tauliya on Imāmlarim of Opal"
(Safar, 1285 = May-June, 1868) -- 3/3.

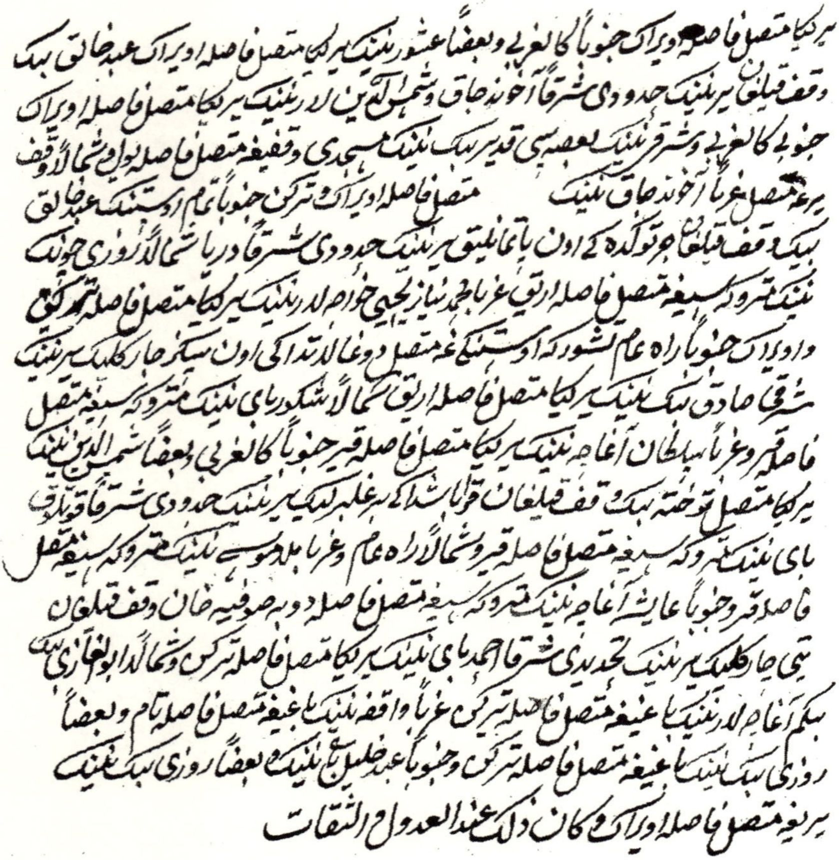
یر لیکا متصل فاصله اویراک جنوبا کالغربی و بعضا عشور ننکنک یر لیکا متصل فاصله اویراک عبد خالق بیک
وقف قیلغان یرننک حدودی شرقا آخوند حاجی و شمس الدین لار ننک یر لیکا متصل فاصله اویراک
جنوبی کالغربی و شرقی ننک بعضیسی قدیر بیک ننک مسجدی و تفیغه متصل فاصله یول و شمالاً وقف
یرغه متصل غربا آخوند حاجی ننک متصل فاصله اویراک و تیرکن جنوبا تمام اوستنک عبد خالق
بیک وقف قیلغان جو تو گده کی اون باتمانلیق یرننک حدودی شرقا دریا شمالاً روزی جونک
ننک تیر و کسیغه متصل فاصله اریق غربا محمد نیاز یحیی خواجه لار ننک یر لیکا متصل فاصله تیر کوچ
و اویراک جنوبا راه عام لشور که اوستنگغه متصل دو غالار تدا کی اون سیکز جارک لیک یرننک
شرقی حادق بیک ننک یر لیکا متصل فاصله اریق شمالاً اشکور بای ننک تیر و کسیغه متصل
فاصله قیر و غربا سیلطان آغاچه ننک یر لیکا متصل فاصله قیر جنوبا کالغربی و بعضا شمس الدین ننک
یر لیکا متصل توختة بیک وقف قیلغان قوراباشدا کی بر غلبر لیک یرننک حدودی شرقا قوتلوق
بای ننک تیر و کسیغه متصل فاصله قیر و شمالاً راه عام و غربا بلال موسی ننک تیر و کسیغه متصل
فاصله قیر و جنوبا عایشه آغاچه ننک تیر و کسیغه متصل فاصله دوبه صوفیه خان وقف قیلغان
تیجی جارک لیک یرننک تحدیدی شرقا احمد بای ننک یر لیکا متصل فاصله تیرکن و شمالاً ابو الغازی بیک
بیکم آغاچه لار ننک یاغیغه متصل فاصله تیرکن غربا واقف ننک باغیغه متصل فاصله تام و بعضا
روزی بیک ننک یاغیغه متصل فاصله تیرکن و جنوبا عبد خلیل بای ننک بعضا روزی بیک ننک
یریغه متصل فاصله اویراک و کان ذلک عند العدول الثقات

CKWD No.9 (p.16) "The tauliya on Khwāja Qondāq Buzrūgwār of Opal"
(Barat (=Sha'ban) 22, 1260 = September 6, 1844).

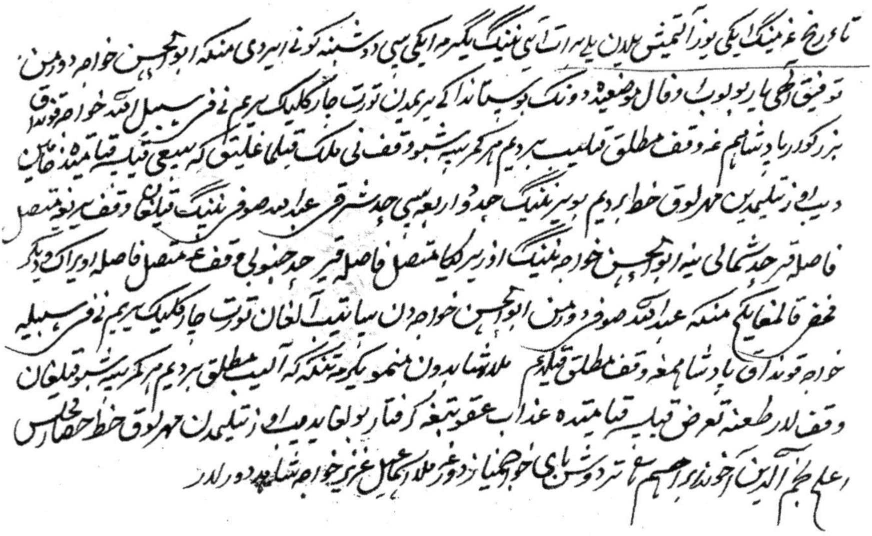

CKWD No.10 (p.17) "The tauliya on Khwāja Qondāq Mazār of Opal"
(Safar qoshni ay (=Rabī'1) 28, 1263 = March 16, 1847).

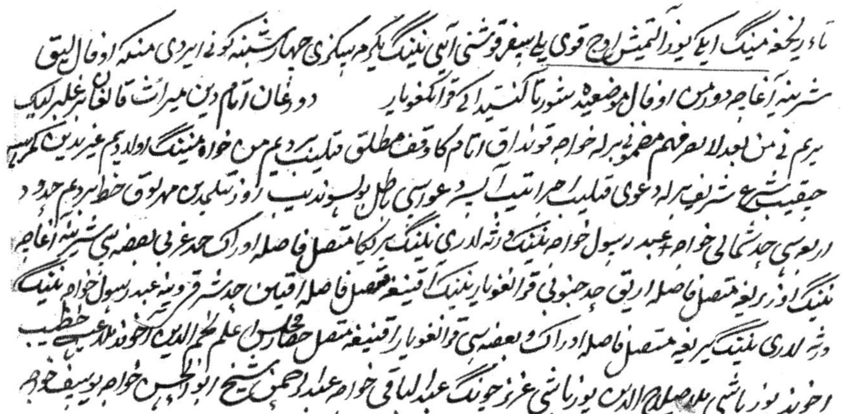

CKWD No.8 (p.15) "The tauliya on Buzrūgwār Khwāja Qontāq(sic) of Opal"
(Shawwāl 21, 1276 = May 12, 1860).

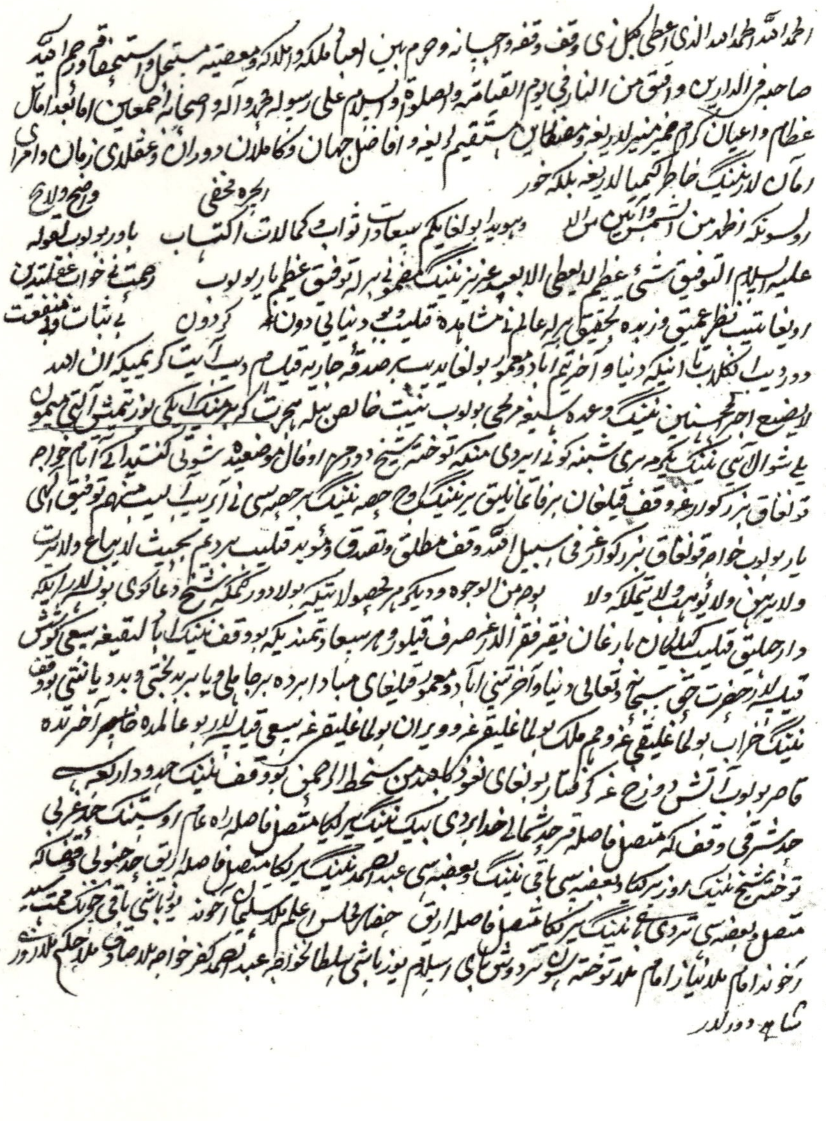

Chapter Four

STORIES OF CHILTÄN

The Historical Significance of Chiltän Mazar in Yarkand City

SHINMEN Yasushi

Introduction

There are many shrines, or mazars, of Islamic saints all over the Xinjiang Uyghur region—in cities, suburbs, rural areas, and deserts. They can be characterized by location. This paper aims to shed light on the historical relationships of the Chiltän Mazar inside the city of Yarkand with the city itself by investigating the historical aspects of the mazar and the character of its unique legend.

1. Chiltän Mazar and the City of Yarkand

1-1. Chiltän Mazar

The Chiltän Mazar is located in the city of Yarkand, inside the former city's walls,[1] which were destroyed by the government in the early period of the People's Republic of China.[2] The mazar is regarded as an important shrine to the Muslim people in Xinjiang. Its legend states that the shrine is a place where seven of the 40 saints called "Chiltän" (i.e., "Chihil tan" in Persian) arrived, stayed, and were buried.[3] This mazar is also called "Haft Muḥammadān" (i.e., seven Muḥammads) since it is the place where seven saints—all named Muḥammad—were buried.[4] The shrine is located in the cemetery at the northeastern side of Altun Mazar[5] in the city of Yarkand. At present, the Chiltän Mazar has a territory surrounded by walls, in which a mosque and the building of the shrine exist. There are seven forms of tombs constructed within the shrine (Rahilä Dawut 2001: 84-85). The present building of the mausoleum is believed to have been constructed in the 1289 AH (1872-1873) in the period of Ya'qūb Beg (Thum 2014: 98).

In the study of Hori Sunao, Yarkand city streets (*kocha*) that appear in the

---

[1] See De Filippi 1932: 477.

[2] The destruction of the city wall of Yarkand was carried out in 1958 (Hori 2006:20).

[3] With regard to a brief outline of the legend, see Thum 2014: 45-46.

[4] According to the manuscript preserved in the Jarring collection (Prov.414), the names of the seven saints are as follows: Muḥammad Fāḍil, Muḥammad Ibrāhīm, Muḥammad Qāsim, Muḥammad Rāzī, Muḥammad Sa'īd, Muḥammad Zāhid, Muḥammad Thābit (*Ḥaḍrat-i Khwāja Haft Muḥammadān Buzrukwārlarimning ismlari*).

[5] "Altun" is the mausoleum of the *khāns* of Yarkand Khanate. Xie Bin, an official of the Nanjing government, describes the shrine of "Altun" in his work (Xie 1923: 209-210).

descriptions of *Yäkän Nahiyisining Yär Namliri Khäritilik Täzkirisi* (Yäkän, 1996(?)) are clearly plotted and identified on the plan of the city. We can find the street named "Chiltänlirim kochisi" in the northwest part of the city on the plan made by Hori (Hori 2006: 15, 19). There is no doubt that the street is named after the Chiltän Mazar. It is needless, therefore, to say that the mazar is very familiar to the inhabitants of the city; its name is reflected in the name of the nearby street.

1-2. Chiltän Mazar and the inhabitants of Yarkand in history

Unfortunately, there are no materials that provide us with systematic information on the historical situations of the mazar. However, we must try to examine the various aspects of the relationship between the mazar and the city of Yarkand based on some fragmentary data that can be found in the various historical materials, such as literary works by the Uyghur authors, the texts of the legends of the mazar, and the records written by foreign visitors to the city.

It is evident that the shrine has been a relatively famous mazar in Yarkand history. As Rahilä Dawut points out, *Tārīkh-i Rashīdī* refers to this mazar as "Haft Muḥammadān" as follows: "The people of Yarkand believe that there lie [buried there] the Haft Muḥammadān." However, the author, Mīrzā Muḥammad Ḥaydar Doghlāt, did not mention the legend and adopted a skeptical attitude toward the truth of the historical origin of the mazar by pointing out that he did not remember having read about them in any history [Elias & Ross 1895: 299; Mīrzā Muḥammad Ḥaydar Doghlāt 2004: 430]. Undoubtedly, as late as the sixteenth century, this mazar was well known and widely believed in by the inhabitants of the city. Then, in the early eighteenth century, Zalīlī (Muḥammad Ṣiddīq Zalīlī), a famous Uyghur poet of Yarkand,[6] referred to the mazar in his work titled *Safar nāma* (Papas 2010: 153-54), and composed *Tadhkira-i Haft Muḥammadān* as a poetry work in 1147 AH (1734-35) (Zälili 1985).

Internal view of the shrine (Lundahl 1917: 212).

[6] With regard to Zalīlī , see *Uyghur Ädäbiyati Tarikhi*: 672-703; Li 1992: 198–202.

Most of the hagiographies and literary works on legends of the saints of the mazar, which include a work titled *Tadhkira-i Haft Muḥammadān,* written in 1815 [Sugawara, Orkhun 2007: 9], hold similar contents and motifs to Zalīlī's work. We cannot deny the presumption that Zalīlī's work was written based on the hagiography or oral tradition that had already existed since the previous period.[7] At any rate, there is no doubt that even in the eighteenth century, some of the city's intellectuals specially worshiped the mazar.

There is a lack of abundant material to provide credible evidence on the particular relationship between the mazar and the inhabitants of the city under the rule of the Qing dynasty after its conquest of Xinjiang in the mid-eighteenth century. However, we can investigate some aspects of the mazar in the nineteenth to twentieth centuries based on a few records written by foreign visitors to the region. At first, in the mid-nineteenth century, Valikhanov, a famous Kazakh scholar and officer of the Russian Empire who visited Kashgar and Yarkand under the rule of the Qing dynasty, described the largest temple in Yarkand, "Aftu-Moodan" — along with Altun Mazar, the mazar of Muḥammad Sharīf Pīr[8] and Mūy-i mubārak[9] — as representative religious institutions in Yarkand (Valikhanov 1985: 122). This "Aftu- Moodan" must be "Haft Muḥammadān."

Then, with regard to the circumstances of the Chiltän Mazar in the period of Ya'qūb Beg, who established the authority in the Muslim rebellion against the Qing dynasty in the second half of the nineteenth century, we can rely on the article written by a Swedish missionary. The members of the Swedish mission that expanded their activities in Xinjiang from the end of the nineteenth century not only engaged in missionary work in Kashghar, Yarkand, Yengi-Hisar, and Yengi-shahr of Kashghar but also conducted research on the Uyghur society with respect to their language, culture, and religion. Some of their findings were published in Sweden. Thus, we must pay attention to the descriptions of mazars by Gustaf Raquette, a doctor in the Swedish mission and a linguist who specialized in the study of Eastern *Turki,* mainly on the Chiltän Mazar (Lundhal 1917: 201–215).[10]

Raquette's descriptions present information on the historical situation of the mazar in the period of Ya'qūb Beg based on his interview. In particular, the descriptions mention the episode (legend) regarding the sacred tree that was cut down when the shrine was rebuilt in the period of Ya'qūb Beg. This tree was believed to be the one that

[7] Rian Thum argues that the legend was written in ca. 1690 to the mid-18th century (Thum 2014: 45).

[8] With regard to Muḥammad Sharīf, see Hamada 1991: 94–98.

[9] Generally speaking, a shrine that preserves the object which is called the "hair of Prophet Muḥammad" is named *Mūy-i mubārak.* The reference to the "Mūy-i mubārak" in Yarkand can be found in the work titled *History of Khotan* (Hamada 1980: 189).

[10] Raquette's descriptions of mazars are composed of three parts: the first part provides explanations of mazars in Xinjiang and interpretations of the nature of mazar worship; the second part presents details of the legend of the Chiltän Mazar; the third part presents information on the legend of Haft Muḥammadān based on his observation of the mazar and the historical situation in the period of Ya'qūb Beg based on his interview.

grew from the stick provided to the saints by the Prophet Muḥammad. "Ya'qūb Beg ordered that the sacred tree be cut down and used for building materials for the reconstruction. But some of the believers of the mazar cried out against such behavior as cutting down the tree. As a result, no one had the courage to approach the tree to cut it down. Finally, a great prince of Ya'qūb Beg had to carry out the order. However, anyone who touched the tree died immediately or a few days after that."

This episode indicates that the reconstruction of the mazar building in the period of Ya'qūb Beg acquired an important position in the history of the Muslims in Yarkand. It is known that Ya'qūb Beg patronized mazars in the territory of Yettä Shahr, which he governed, and rebuilt or repaired many mazars (Kim 2004: 130; Mulla Musa 1988: 502–503). According to Mullā Mūsā Sayrāmī, famous Uyghur historian, when Ya'qūb Beg advanced upon the city of Yarkand, which was seized by the authorities of Kucha *khwajas*, together with his army in 1866, he was quartered in the wide square in front of the mazar of Haft Muḥammadān (Mulla Musa 1988: 355; Pantusov 1905: 152). Probably he began to have connections with the mazar in the early stage of his regime, and then decided to reconstruct the building.

However, in considering the views of the people of the city of Yarkand regarding this mazar, it is interesting to note that in the episode on the reconstruction, the religious authority of the mazar displaying its magical power toward the activity of Ya'qūb Beg—who was, in a sense, an outside ruler from Khoqand—is emphasized. Further, the episode indicates the occurrence of a type of strain or friction between Ya'qūb Beg's policy toward the mazar and the local society that maintained the mazar.

Considering the points mentioned above, it can be argued that the Chiltän Mazar maintained an important position as one of the most representative mazars in Yarkand while Xinjiang was under the Qing rule. However, it is believed that it was in poor physical condition without repair or reconstruction under the rule of the Qing dynasty,[11] because in Raquette's descriptions, it is said that the mazar building was in decay before the period of Ya'qūb Beg. On the other hand, under Ya'qūb Beg's rule, it was reconstructed by the government through his patronization policy toward mazars, although it can be presumed that it produced a type of discord between the authorities and the local society of Yarkand, who supported the mazar.

As mentioned above, in the early twentieth century, after the recovery of Xinjiang by Qing, G. Raquette, the Swedish missionary who visited the Chiltän Mazar, described its situation at that time based on his observation (Lundahl 1917: 213): "The place where the (sacred) tree stood is still marked and is thought to be an especially holy point. There are a lot of skulls of wild sheep with monstrous large horns stacked in front of the entrance into the grave room, in which we can see the seven monuments in the form of sarcophagi which are decorated by lamps and flags of brocade silk." Moreover, the article includes three photographs of the Chiltän Mazar (presenting external and

[11] In the period of the Qing rule, it is known that some high ranking Uyghur local officials such as *junwang* of Turfan or *hakim beg*, reconstructed the building of mazars or donated facilities to mazars (Kim, Hodong 1992: 25-27; Jalilov, Kawahara, Sawada Shinmen, Hori 2008: 184), but there is no evidence that a protective policy was implemented in favor of the mazars by the Qing authorities.

internal views) (Lundahl 1917: 205, 209, 212).[12] It should be noted that the record of Raquette's observations and interview at the mazar provides us with information on the appearance and the interior of the mazar building at the time he visited it, and they serve as valuable materials that are useful for us to determine the historical appearance of the mazar in the early twentieth century, while hagiographies of Haft Muḥammadān contain little data on the mazar itself.[13]

It is regrettable that there are few materials that provide credible information on the mazar for eighty years after Raquette's descriptions; however, Sawada Minoru, a Japanese historian, visited to observe the mazar at the end of the twentieth century. He describes the Chiltän Mazar in his article about some mazars in the Tarim Basin, which he visited in August 1998, as follows: "(When I visited,) in this mazar we could see a few worshipers who were praying and one man who appeared to be a custodian was sitting at the entrance. There are the seven tombs, which the mazar is named after, inside the mazar building. They were decorated by flags and a lot of horns of goats." (Sawada 1999: 64) It is certain that in recent years after the establishment of the People's Republic of China, the mazar that was still attracting worshipers from Yarkand continued to exist as an active religious institution.[14] Moreover, it is very interesting to note that from the early twentieth century to the end of the century, there was no change in the way it was decorated using flags and horns of wild animals.

It can be considered that the religious authority of the Chiltän Mazar and the belief of the city's inhabitants in it through a few centuries, as mentioned above, relied on their ideas about the particular relationship of the city of Yarkand with the Chiltän Mazar. According to Rahilä Dawut's fieldwork reports from recent years, one of her informants, an old Uyghur man living at the city, told her that under the divine protection of some mazars inside and around the city, the most representative one of which is the Chiltän, the inhabitants could live in the city in peace and quiet without suffering from any serious natural disaster or famine (Reyila 2001: 47). Although it cannot be easily concluded that such a mentality was very popular among the inhabitants in historical situations, we can notice that the mazar continued to attract a lot of worshipers from the city of Yarkand, serving as a source of special religious power that was believed to keep the city safe.

1-3. Chiltän Mazar from the other oasis inhabitants' perspective

Mullā Mūsā Sayrāmī, a famous Uyghur historian, in his work *Tārīkh-i Ḥamīdī*, dealing with mazars as one of the main chapters, provides detailed information on the

[12] In the Fränne collection preserved at the National Archives of Sweden, we can find a few photographs of the mazar that were taken by Swedish missionaries (Riksarkivet, *Öst-turkestan samlingen*, 149: "Helgongravar" ark 8–9). See Jarring 1991a: 58–59.

[13] In general, most of the literature on mazars in Xinjiang written by the Uyghurs, such as hagiographies [Hamada 1990: 111–113], guidebooks of sacred places (For example, see Sugawara, Kawahara 2006: 115–147), or documents concerning mazars (For example, see Hamada 1991) include scant information on the objective situations of mazars.

[14] With regard to the situation of the shrine in recent years (2004-2009), see Rian Thum's vivid descripton based on his own observation (Thum 2014: 97-101).

representative mazars in Xinjiang in a systematic manner (Mulla Musa 1988: 636–703). As Sawada Minoru points out, Mullā Mūsā referred to "Haft Muḥammadān" as one of the major mazars in Yarkand with the mazar of Khwāja Muḥammad Sharīf and the Altun Mazar as follows: Since the mazar is called "Haft Muḥammadān" (i.e., seven Muḥammads), it must be the place where the seven saints whose names were Muḥammad were buried. I hear that they were from among the "Chiltän" (i.e., forty saints) (Mulla Musa 1988: 641; Pantusov 1905: 307; Sawada 1999a: 65).

The reference to the Chiltän Mazar in the descriptions of hagiography related to the other mazar should be more noted. The Kucha mausoleum of Mawlānā Arshidīn Walī, who, in his legend, is believed to have converted Tughluq Tīmūr Khān of the Moghūlistān Khanate to Islam (Hamada 1978: 81–83), is one of the most representative mazars in the Xinjiang Uyghur region (Shinmen, Sanada, Wang 2002: 193–194). In one of Arshidīn's hagiographies, it is stated that before Mawlānā Jalāl al-Dīn, Arshidīn's father, died, the Prophet Muḥammad appeared in his dream to tell him to let Arshidīn take up his residence in Kucha and to say that Muḥammad would give an offering of Kucha to Arshidīn, Ṣaḥāba Jānbāz, and Shaykh Niẓām al-Dīn; an offering of Turfan to Sulṭān Aṣḥāb al-kahf[15] and Ālif Ata;[16] an offering of Kashghar to Sulṭān Satuq Bughra Khān,[17] 'Alī Arslān Khān,[18] and Sulṭān Qarāstān; and an offering of Tartar (i.e., Yarkand) to Haft Muḥammadān [Hamada 2006: 56–57]. In this description, we can find the idea that in the oases region of the Tarim Basin, the saints unique to each oasis, who were said to have been buried at the mazar in the oasis—in other words, the custodians of the mazar—were allowed to be given the offering of the oasis by Prophet Muḥammad. In this context, Yarkand was said to have fallen only into Haft Muḥammadān's hands. Considering that the description is found in the hagiography of the mazar in the oasis far from Yarkand, it appears that some of the people in the oases region of the Tarim Basin at that time believed that the Chiltän Mazar held a dominant position in the religious authority among the Muslim inhabitants of Yarkand oasis and the city.

As mentioned above, the Chiltän Mazar, which has had a close relationship with the city of Yarkand since at least the sixteenth century, can be regarded as one of the influential shrines in Xinjiang.

2. Legend of Haft Muḥammadān

2-1. Contents of the Legend

In this paper, we throw light on nine versions of the legend of the Haft Muḥammadān or the Chiltän Mazar as follows: (A)*Tadhkira-i Haft Muḥammadān*, a poetry work composed by Zalīlī (18c.) (Zälili 1985); (B)*Tadhkira-i Haft Muḥammadān*, a poetry work in the so-called *Compilation of the Yārkand Mazār Hagiographies* (i.e., *Yärkän Mazar Tazkiriliri Toplimi* (YMTT)) (19c.) (Sugawara, Orkhun 2007: 69–59 (80b–90b)); (C)*Tadhkira-i Ḥaḍrat-i*

[15] With regard to the mazar of Aṣḥāb al-kahf, see Shinmen 2004.

[16] With regard to the mazar of Ālif Ata (Alp Ata), see Kim 1992.

[17] With regard to the mazar of Satuq Boghra Khān, see Hamada 1991; Sawada 1999: 55–57.

[18] With regard to the mazar of 'Alī Arslān Khān, see Shinmen, Sanada, Wang 2002: 173–76.

Haft Muḥammadān in prose in the Jarring collection (Prov.413, ff.75a-81b); (D)*Tadhkira-i Haft Muḥammadān* in prose in the Jarring collection (Prov.414, ff.1b-12a); (E)*Tadhkira-i Haft Muḥammadān Pādishāh* in prose in the so-called Jarring collection (Prov.13), which was brought to Sweden by Swedish missionaries; (F)*Tadhkira-i Ḥaḍrat-i Haft Muḥammadān Buzurgwār* in poetry and prose in the Jarring collection (Prov.414, ff.18b-35a); (G) legend presented by Raquette in his article mentioned above; (H) a version of the legend compiled by the Russian linguist Tenishev in the 1950s (Tenishev 1984: 67–68); and (I) another version compiled by Rahilä Dawut in recent years (Rahilä Dawut 2001: 85–88).

Chiltän Mazar (Lundahl 1917: 209)

Chiltän Mazar (photographed by Shinmen Y., Aug. 2011)

When comparing all the versions, we can find some interesting features of the legend of this mazar.

In the composition of the other motifs, there are no remarkable differences among the first seven versions, (A) to (G), although (F) and (G) have a part at the beginning that describes the circumstances in which the forty saints were born and how they were staying in the fourth sky (i.e., section (1) in the story mentioned below), while (A), (B), (C), (D), and (E) do not include such an episode.[19] And (A) to (F) possess more detailed contents of each motif with rhetorical expressions as compared to (G).

I would like to briefly introduce the main scheme of the motifs of this legend, according to (A) to (G):

(1) Since a man named Salmān-i Fārs (i.e., Salmān the Persian)[20] requested that the Prophet Muḥammad pray for a child, his wife bore forty sons. Although these babies were saints, Salmān, who was ignorant, put thirty-nine of them into a basket and threw them away in the desert. Then, the final son also joined them. When the Prophet Muḥammad went to meet them, the basket changed to a dome roof in the fourth sky, wherein the forty saints were living. [This section is included only in (F) and (G)]

(2) In Madīna, a beast appeared on a tree and called itself a "disaster from God." At the same time, Fāṭima (the Prophet's daughter) fell sick. The Prophet Muḥammad, with directions from Jabrā'īl, went to the place where the forty saints were staying. Seven of the forty saints descended upon earth and prayed for the recovery of Fāṭima. Then, she recovered entirely.

(3) The seven saints were not allowed to return to their place in the fourth sky and could not help but wander around the world. After the Prophet Muḥammad's death, they were given a stick by Muḥammad and told that they should wander the earth and that they should inhabit the place where the stick changes to a green herb. As they went to the land of Tatar (i.e., Yarkand), the stick changed to a green herb; thus, they settled down there. At that time, the place was a land of infidels.

(4) Later, during the period of King Abā Bakr, when Shāh Ṭālib Sermest of Bukhara made a pilgrimage with his forty disciples, he was instructed at the tomb of Prophet Muḥammad in Madīna by Muḥammad to head toward Yarkand to establish a mazar of the seven saints. In accordance with this instruction, Shāh Ṭālib went to Yarkand and established the mazar.

(5) Abā Bakr served him a dinner with cat meat as a *ḥarām* food to test him. Shāh Ṭālib saw through the trap and brought the cat back to life as a miracle. He was furious with the king (i.e., Abā Bakr) and left Yarkand. Abā Bakr regretted his actions and sent a mission to beg Shāh Ṭālib to forgive him. Moreover, Abā Bakr worshiped the mazar, contributed land to it, and appointed custodians of the mazar.

---

[19] (F) is a literary work that partly consists of poetry, which is very similar to the Zalīlī's work on the mazar, and partly consists of prose. The episode at the beginning of the story in prose (ff.20a-22b) is inserted in the poetry. At the end of the work we can find that it was written in 1290H (1872/73).

[20] Salmān-i Fārsī : one of the loyal companions of the Prophet Muḥammad, and the first Persian convert to Islam.

In contrast, the version (H) compiled by Tenishev includes the motif at the beginning of (A) and (E), which does not exist in (B), (C), (D), (F), and (G); however, it contains no episode on the discovery of the saints' tombs by Shāh Ṭālib and describes the episode of the resuscitation of a cat cooked for dinner as a miracle performed not by Shāh Ṭālib but by the seven saints themselves.

The version (I) compiled by Rahilä Dawut does not include the episode on the birth of the forty saints nor does it have an indication of the names of historical figures such as Abā Bakr (the king of Yarkand) or Shāh Ṭālib (a saint from Bukhara), although it includes an episode on the discovery of the saints' tombs. In other words, (A) to (G) put the discovery of the tombs and the formation of the mazars in actual historical context and describe the story as a historical fact, while we are under the impression that (I) appears to be more of a fable due to the lack of historical justification. Such story telling without a historical basis can also be found in (H) in the form of a legend. It is interesting to note that these two versions were compiled orally after the mid-twentieth century.

In short, principal parts of the legend in (A) to (G) comprise the common motifs, which have been handed down for a few centuries in the literary works.

2-2. Nature of the legend

Next, we would like to shed some light on the nature of the legend of the Chiltän Mazar.

Comparing the legend of the Chiltän with those of the other Islamic saints, we can find the following similar motifs: (1) The legend of Haft Muḥammadān can be related to the legend of *Chihil tan* in Central Asia about forty or forty-one saints wandering the world under the leadership of Khiḍr (Abashin 2001: 118–119; Chvyr' 2006: 150–151). The legend of Khiḍr, a saint who can control water, has been very popular among Muslims in Islamic areas (Yajima 1991: 121). (2) The image of the miraculous stick used by saints is also found in the legends of other types of Islamic saints, for example, in the *Tadhkira of Khwāja Muḥammad Sharīf Pīr*, translated into Japanese by Hamada (Hamada 2006: 159). (3) The legend of the Chiltän Mazar includes the important episode of the "discovery" of the tombs of the seven saints by Shāh Ṭālib, a Central Asian saint from Bukhara, who created the significant situation that the tombs of the saints were accepted by the ruler and other Muslim people in Yarkand, leading to the establishment of the mazar. Such an episode on the discovery of the sacred tombs is also found in other legends on the stories of the saints who discovered the tombs of great saints in the past, for example, Khwāja Muḥammad Sharīf, who is said to have discovered the tomb of Satuq Bughra Khān at Artush (Hamada 1999: 301–303). (4) With regard to small motifs such as the tale of the miracle that a killed and cooked cat was resuscitated, we can find a similar episode in the *tadhkira* of Ibad Allāh Khān Tora (i.e., so-called Kirgil Ata),[21] who was one of the Marghilan *toras*, who call themselves Makhdūmzādas (Kawahara 2005: 278). Considering the abovementioned points, it can be argued that the legend of Chiltän is skillfully composed, based on the legendary world popular among Muslims, and it

[21] He is said to be one of great grandsons of Khwāja Karāmat Allāh, a brother of Āfāq Khwāja.

incorporates episodes of miracles similar to those in other legends of Central Asia as motifs.

On the other hand, in this legend, the point that draws particular attention is that Prophet Muḥammad played an important role in almost all the motifs starting with the birth of the forty saints, their flight to the fourth sky, the advent and stay in this world of seven of the forty saints, their wandering around the world, and the discovery of their tombs by Shāh Ṭālib. Moreover, it was due to Muḥammad's direct instructions that the seven saints wandered around the world and inhabited Yarkand and that Shāh Ṭālib visited Yarkand to discover their tombs. In other words, it can be said that this legend is cast in the mold of the story that connects Prophet Muḥammad with the land of Yarkand through the seven saints and Shāh Ṭālib. The contents of this legend could influence the Muslims of Yarkand, who listened to legends that made them feel close to Prophet Muḥammad through his relationship with their land and exalted their consciousness as Muslims.

Concluding Remarks

The Chiltän Mazar, the mazar of Haft Muḥammadān, in the city of Yarkand, which has continued to hold a prominent religious authority among the inhabitants of the city and oasis since the sixteenth century, can be regarded as one of the major shrines in Xinjiang. The unique legend of Haft Muḥammadān enables us to get a glimpse of the mentalities of the Muslims or oasis people of Central Asia and the historical remembrances of the inhabitants of the city, which were reflected by the legend.

The relationship between the shrines of Islamic saints and oasis cities in Xinjiang suggests that further investigation on the aspects of mazars and the characteristics of this region could be beneficial. Further studies on the cases of shrines at other cities are expected.

References

HAN CHINESE

Li, Guoxiang 李国香 1992. *Weiwuer Wenxueshi* 维吾尔文学史 [History of Uyghur Literature], Lanzhou: Lanzhou Daxue Chubanshe.

Reyila Dawuti (Rahilä Dawut) 热依拉·达吾提 2001. *Weiwuerzu maza wenhua yanjiu* 维吾尔族麻扎文化研究 [A Study on the Mazar Cultures of Uyghurs], Urumqi: Xinjiang Daxue Chubanshe.

Xie, Bin 謝彬 1923. *Xinjiang Youji* 新疆遊記 [Xinjiang Travelogue], Shanghai: Zhonghua Shuju.

MODERN UYGHUR

Mulla Musa Sayrami 1988. *Tarikhi Hämidi*, Näshriga täyyarlighuchi: Änwär Baytur, Beyjing: Millätlar Näshriyati.

Rahilä Dawut 2001. *Uyghur Mazarliri*,Urumqi: Shinjang Khälq Näshriyati.

Uyghur Ädäbiyati Tarikhi: Shinjang Uyghur Aptonom Rayonluq Ijtima'i Pänlar Akademiyisi Millätlär Ädäbiyati Tätqiqat Oruni, *Uyghur Adäbiyati Tarikhi*, 2, Beijing: Millätlar Näshriyati, 2006.

Zälili 1985. *Zälili Diwani*, Näshgä täyyarlighuchi: Imin Tursun, Beyjing: Millätlär Näshriyati.

CHAGHATAY TURKIC

Pantusov, N. N. 1905. *Tarikh-i Emenie. Istoriya vladetelei kashgarii. Sochnenie Mully Musy ben Mulla Aisa*

Sajramtsa. Izbannaya N.N. Pantusovym, Kazan.
Tadhkira-i Haft Muḥammadān Pādishāh, Lund University Library, Jarring collection, Prov.13.
Tadhkira-i Ḥaḍrat-i Haft Muḥammadān, Lund University Library, Jarring collection, Prov.413, ff.75a–81b.
Tadhkira-i Haft Muḥammadān, Lund University Library, Jarring collection, Prov.414, ff.1b–12a.
Hazrat-i Khwāja Haft Muḥammadān Buzrukwārlarimning ismlari, Lund University Library, Jarring collection, Prov.414, f.18a.
Tadhkira-i Ḥaḍrat-i Haft Muḥammadān Buzurgwār, Lund University Library, Jarring collection, Prov.414, ff.18b–35a.

PERSIAN

Mīrzā Muḥammad Ḥaydar Doghlāt 2004. *Tārīkh-i Rashīdī*, 'Abbāsqulī Ghaffārī Fard ed., Tehrān: Mīrāth-i Maktūb.

EUROPEAN LANGUAGES

De Filippi, Filippo 1932. *The Italian Expedition to the Himalaya, Karakoram and Eastern Turkestan (1913–1914)*, London: E. Arnold.
Elias, N., Denison Ross, E. 1895. *A History of the Moghuls of Central Asia. Being the Tarikh-i-Rashidi of Mirza Muhammad Haidar, Dughlat*. London: Curzon Press, New York: Barnes and Noble, 1972 (First published 1895, Second edition 1898).
Hamada, Masami 1978. "Islamic Saints and Their Mausoleums," *Acta Asiatica*, No.34. Tokyo:Toho Gakkai, 79–98.
——— 1980. "*L'Histoire de Ḫotan* de Muḥammad A'lam (II): Un essai de traduction du text turc oriental," *ZUNBUN*, No.16, 173–208.
——— 1990. "Un apeçu des manuscrits Čaġatay en provenance du Turkestan Oriental," *Documents et Archives Provenant de L'Asie Centrale*, édité par Akira Haneda, Kyoto: Association Franco-Japonais des Étude Orientales.
Hultvall, J. 1981. *Mission och Revolution i Centralasien. Svenska Missionsförbundets mission i Östturkestan 1892–1938*, Stockholm: Gummessons.
Jarring, Gunnar 1991. "Eastern Turkestanica in the Swedish National Archives," *Central Asiatic Journal*, Volume 35, No.1–2, 55–61.
Kim, Hodong 1992. "The Cult of Saints in Eastern Turkestan: The Case of Alp Ata in Turfan", *Proceedings of the 35th Permanent International Altaistic Conference*, Taipei, 199–226.
——— 2004, *Holy War in China: The Muslim Rebellion and State in Chinese Central Asia, 1864–1877*, Stanford: Stanford University Press.
Lundahl, J.E. 1917. *På Obanade Stigar: Tjugofem år i Ost-Turkestan.* Stockholm: Svenska Missionsförbundets Förlag.
Orkhun, A., & Sugawara J.(eds) 2007. *Mazar Documents from Xinjiang and Ferghana (Facsimile) 2. (Studia Culturae Islamicae No.87).* Tokyo: Research Institute for Languages and Cultures of Asia and Africa, Tokyo University of Foreign Studies.
Papas, Alexandre 2010. *Mystiques et Vagabonds en Islam: Portraits de Trois Soufis Qalandar.* Paris: Les Editions du Cerf.
Shinmen Yasushi 2004. "The History of the Mausoleum of the *Aṣḥāb al-kahf* in Turfan," *Memoirs of the Research Department of the Toyo Bunko*, No.61, Tokyo: Toyo Bunko (Oriental Library), 83–104.
Sugawara, Jun & Kawahara, Yayoi (eds.) 2006, *Mazār Documents from Xinjiang and Ferghana (Facsimile) 1 (Studia Culturae Islamicae No.83)*, Tokyo: Research Institute for Languages and Cultures of Asia and Africa, Tokyo University of Foreign Studies.
Thum, Rian 2014. *The Sacred Routes of Uyghur History*. Cambridge, Mass.: Harvard University Press.

Riksarkivet (The National Archives of Sweden), *Öst-turkestan samlingen*, 149: "Islam" (ark 1–21), "Helgongravar" (ark 1–12).

RUSSIAN

Abashin, S. N. 2001. “Chiltan” in *Islam na territorii byvshei Rosiiskoi Imperii, Entsiklope-dicheskii slovar'*, Vyp. 3, Moskva: Izdatel'skaya firma “Vostochnaya literatura” RAN.

Valikhanov, Ch. Ch., *Sobranie sochnenii v pyat' tomov*, Alma-Ata, Tom 3.

Chvyr', L. A. 2006. *Obryaby i verovaniya uigurov v XIX-XX vv.*, Moskva: Izdatel'skaya firma “Vostochnaya literatura” RAN.

JAPANESE

Hamada, Masami 濱田正美 1991. “Satoku Bogura Han no bobyo wo megutte” サトク・ボグラ・ハンの墓廟をめぐって [Satuk Boghra Khan's Mausoleum in History] *Seinan Ajia Kenkyu*, 34, 89–112.

——— 1999, “Seija no haka wo mitsukeru hanashi” 聖者の墓を見つける話 [Discovery of Saints' Tombs], Matsubara Masatake, Konagaya Yuki, Sasaki Shiro (eds). *Yūrashia Yūbokusyakai no Rekishi to Genzai (Kokuritsu Minzokugaku Hakubutsukan Kenkyū Hōkoku Bessatsu No.20),* Senri: Kokuritsu Minzokugaku Hakubutsukan, 287–326.

——— 2006. *Higashi Torukisutan Chagatai go Seijaden no Kenkyū* 東トルキスタン・チャガタイ語聖者伝の研究[Hagiographies of Eastern Turkistan], Kyoto: Kyoto Daigaku Daigakuin Bungakukenkyuka.

Hori, Sunao 堀直 1987. “Kaikyo toshi Yarkando: Keikan fukugen no kokoromi” 回疆都市ヤールカンド——景観復原の試み [The City of Yarkand in *Huijiang* : An Attempt at Restoring the Historical Landscape] *Kōnandaigaku Kiyō: Bungakuhen* 63, 39–51.

——— 2006. “Yarukando no gaiku: Kyūjōnai no rekishiteki puran fukugen no kokoromi”, ヤルカンドの街区—旧城内の歴史的プラン復原の試み—[The Quarters of Yarkand : An Attempt at Restoring the Historical Plan of the Old City] *Kōnandaigaku Kiyō: Bungakuhen*, 144, 11–39.

Islamic Sacred Places in Central Asia: The Ferghana Valley and Kashghar Region (*Silkroadology* 28) 中央アジアのイスラーム聖地—フェルガナ盆地とカシュガル地方（シルクロード学研究 28：シルクロード学研究センター研究紀要）, Nara: Nara International Foundation, 2007.

Jalilov Amanbek, Kawahara Yayoi, Sawada Minoru, Shinmen Yasushi, Hori Sunao ジャリロフ・アマンベク, 河原弥生, 澤田稔, 新免康, 堀直 2008. *“Tārīhi Rashīdī” Tyurukugoyaku Fuhen no Kenkyū* 『ターリーヒ・ラシーディー』テュルク語訳附編の研究 [Addendum to *Tārīkh-i Rashīdī*: Translation and Annotation with Introduction and Indexes]. Tokyo: NIHU Puroguramu Isuramu Chiiki Kenkyū Tōkyōdaigaku Kyoten.

Kawahara, Yayoi 河原弥生 2005. “Kōkando Han koku ni okeru Marugiran no toratachi: Nakushubandei kyōdankei no seija ichizoku ni kansuru ichikōsatsu” コーカンド・ハーン国におけるマルギランのトラたち—ナクシュバンディー教団系の聖者一族に関する一考察—[Marghilan *Toras* in the Khoqand Khanate : Some Considerations on Sacred Family of Naqshbandī Order], *Nihon Chūtō Gakkai Nenpō*, 20-2, 269–294.

Sawada, Minoru 澤田稔 1999. “Tarimu bonchi shūenbu Isramu shiseki chosa hōkoku” タリム盆地周縁部イスラーム史跡調査報告 [Fieldwork at Islamic Historical Sites mainly in the Western Tarim Basin] *Tezukayama Gakuin Daigaku Ningenbunka Gakubu Kenkyū Nenpō Zōkangō*, 1, 49–70.

——— 2000. “Takuramakan sabaku nanpen no seibo” タクラマカン砂漠南辺の聖墓[Mausoleums in the Southern Periphery of the Taklamakan Desert] *Tezukayama Gakuin Daigaku Ningenbunka Gakubu Kenkyū Nenpō*, 2, 160–182.

Shinmen Yasushi, Sanada Yasushi, Wang Jianxin 新免康, 真田安, 王建新 2002, *Shinkyo Uiguru no Bazāru to Mazāru (Studia Culturae Islamicae No.70)*新疆ウイグルのバザールとマザール [The Bazaars and Mazaars of the Xinjiang Uyghur] Tokyo: Institute for the Study of Languages and Cultures of Asia and Africa, Tokyo University of Foreign Studies.

Yajima, Hikoichi 家島彦一 1991. “Musurimu kaimin ni yoru kōkai anzen no shinkō: Tokuni Ibun Battūta no kiroku ni miru Hizuru to Iriyasu no shinkō” ムスリム海民による航海安全の信仰：とくに Ibn Battūta の記録にみるヒズルとイリヤースの信仰 [Maritime Character of al-Khidr and Ilyas based on Ibn Baṭṭūṭa's *al-Rihla*] *Ajia Afurika Gengo Bunka Kenkyū*, 42, 117–135.

A Few Remarks on Muḥammad Ṣiddīq Zalīlī and His Tadhkira-i Chihiltan

Abliz Orxun

Introduction

Muḥammad Ṣiddīq Zalīlī is a poet who holds a special place in classical Uyghur literature. Aside from writing poems in a variety of forms over his lifetime, he also composed two works about mazars located in his hometown of Yārkand. In 1985, Mr. Imin Tursun collected all of Zalīlī's works that had been uncovered up until that time, including the two about mazars, and after editing them, published them under the title *Zäliliy Diwani* (Anthology of Zalīlī).[1]

The first work in the anthology is *Täzkirä'i Khoja Muhämmäd Shérip Pir Buzrukwar* (Legend of Great Master Khōja Muḥammad Sharīf). This work was originally written in prose form by an anonymous author in honor of the saint Khōja Muḥammad Sharīf, a tutor to 'Abd al-Rashīd Khān, the second sulṭān of the Sä'idiyä Khanate. Muḥammad Ṣiddīq Zalīlī took the story and rewrote it in poetic form in A.H. 1147 (A.D. 1734-1735).

The second work, the *Täzkirä'i Chiltän* (*Tadhkira-i Chihiltan*, or Legend of the 40 Bodies), was also originally a *tadhkira* written in prose form by an unknown author that Zalīlī later recreated in poetic form.[2] The Persian word *chihiltan* refers to a grouping of 40 magical, invisible, and inseparable souls often found in religious lore.

In this paper, I introduce the latter work briefly and clarify its value from a philological perspective through comparisons with similar materials.

The Story of Tadhkira-i Chihiltan

The events portrayed in the *Tadhkira-i Chihiltan* are of highly legendary character as they begin in Arabia and end in Yārkand. The story begins when a bird bearing disaster lands on a tree under which the Prophet Muḥammad is reclining. The tree's leaves turn yellow, fall and immediately afterwards the Prophet Muḥammad's daughter Fāṭima becomes gravely ill. The Prophet Muḥammad, thrown off balance by these events, prays and pleads with God.

God is moved to mercy and sends seven of the 40 heroes who reside at the fourth

1 Zäliliy 1986.

2 The manuscript is preserved in Lund University Library (Handskriftsavt, Prov. 13).

level of Heaven to help him. These seven warriors pray and praise God, thereby healing Fāṭima of her disease and ending the disasters that had since befallen the city of Medina. Following this, the seven take up residence in Medina, spending time with the Prophet Muḥammad and becoming his close friends. For this reason, these individuals are referred to as the *Haft Muḥammadān* (the seven friends of Muḥammad).

Before long, the Prophet Muḥammad dies. The seven remain in the city, but when they go to the Prophet Muḥammad's grave and ask where they should go and what they should do, the Prophet Muḥammad appears to them and calls on them to go to the Land of the Tatars (Yārkand). At this time, he also gives them a staff (*hasa*). They then journey to Yārkand and begin to cure people of sickness by praying and praising God. One day, they stick the staff in the ground, and it flowers. At this sign, they decide to make Yārkand their home, and all seven live out the remainder of their lives there.

Eight hundred years later, during the reign of the Yārkand ruler Mīrzā Abā Bakrī, Shāh Ṭalīb Seremes of Bukhārā took 40 disciples and went on the *ḥajj*, the pilgrimage to Mecca. When he visited the Prophet Muḥammad's grave, the Prophet appeared to him and told him to find the resting place of the seven heroes, raise a gravestone for them, and pray for their souls. Shāh Talīb Seremes followed the Prophet's instructions and after finding their grave and raising a gravestone for them, he built a mazar where he held a *dhikr* ceremony.[3]

When news of this reached Mīrzā Abā Bakrī, he decided to test Shāh Talīb and his disciples by sending them food prepared with cat meat. Greatly angered by this, Shāh Talīb left a disciple behind and returned home. Later, Mīrzā Abā Bakrī, regretting what he had done, assigned Mullā Ṣādiq to take custody of the mazar of the seven heroes. Bakrī also donated the *waqf* from a place called Qara Qum for its maintenance and had a lake dug there, causing the mazar to flourish.

Background of the Work

The reason that this work is sometimes known as the *Tadhkira-i Haft Muḥammadān* (Legend of the Seven Friends of Muḥammad) and other times known as the *Tadhkira-i Chihiltan* (Legend of 40 Bodies) is related to the two groups of men: the 40 angels of the fourth layer of heaven (referred to in the prose version of the work as 40 *mardan*, or heroes);[4] and the 40 individuals led by Shāh Talīb Seremes, as well as the seven among them who were sent to earth.

The *Täzkirä'i Chiltän* included in the *Zäliliy Diwani* as prepared for publication by Imin Tursun, begins directly with the reason for its composition: it was written at the request of Akhūn Khōja, the ruler of Yārkand at that time.

Recently, with the help of Mr. Muhämmätturdi Mirzähmäd, the editor of the Uyghur Language Division of the Shinjang Khälq Näshriyati (Xinjiang People's Press), we have been privileged to see a facsimile of the original manuscripts of Zalīlī's works (the

[3] A *dhikr* ceremony involves Muslim faithful sitting in a ring around a religious leader reciting the name of God or saints and prayers and praises to God in the saints' name.

[4] Zäliliy 19860: 4.

version referred to by Imin Tursun as the *Chong Diwan*, or Great Anthology). Zalīlī wrote that his work was 266 couplets long but the manuscript that Imin Tursun based his work on was only 259 couplets long, seven shorter than Zalīlī's work. During the text's preparation for publication, the first three sections, consisting of 26 couplets praising God and the Prophet as well as recounting the Prophet's genealogy, were abridged.[5] Even though a note is given in the foreword of *Zäliliy Diwani* mentioning the abridgement, it remains unclear exactly which areas were abridged and by how much.

It is also worth stressing that Imin Tursun added the above 22 lines of meterless verse to the end of *Täzkirä'i Chiltän*. Although this 22-line poem is related to the Seven Friends of Muḥammad (a panegyric (*qaṣīda*) written in a different meter), it cannot be considered part of the original *Tadhkira-i Chihiltan*.

As mentioned above, Zalīlī's *Tadhkira-i Chihiltan* was written in the year A.H. 1147 (A.D. 1734-1735). Thus, although it is clear that the original prose version of the *Tadhkira-i Chihilten* was written before Zalīlī's—that is, before the 17th century—a concrete date or author for the original text remains unknown.

Comparison

We are now in possession of a collection of five *tadhkiras* purchased in Kashgar in August 2006 which we introduced in our publication *The Compilation of the Yārkand Mazar Hagiographies* (*Yārkand Mazar Täzkiriliri Toplimi*, or YMTT), the second volume of the series *Mazar Documents from Xinjiang and Ferghana.*[6] The fourth legend in this collection is a poetic *tadhkira* similar to those found in the *Zäliliy Diwani*, entitled *Haft Muḥammadān Tadhkirasi* (Legend of the Seven Friends of Muḥammad). Although the third section of the work, which gives the reason for its composition, begins with "The reason for the poem Haft Muḥammadān is a secret," it ends by stating that "The reason was this, oh you have been with me at this feast: I have made the *Tadhkira-i Chihiltan* into a poem." [7]

For comparison's sake, we follow Mr. Imin Tursun's nomenclature below in referring to the *tadhkira* in *Zäliliy Diwani* as *Täzkirä'i Chiltän*. Although the version we possess refers to the work using two different names, for our purposes we will call it the *Haft Muḥammadān Tadhkirasi*.

The content of the work is exactly the same as the text found in the *Zäliliy Diwani*'s *Täzkirä'i Chiltän* described above; both works were written in the *remel* meter's *remeli museddesi meqsur* form. The manuscript on which Mr. Imin Tursun based his work and the *tadhkira* in the YMTT both follow Islamic tradition in beginning with praising Allāh, his messenger Muḥammad, and Muḥammad's companions. They also both have a regularized structure. The *tadhkira* in the YMTT has exactly 249 couplets, just 17 couplets less than Zalīlī 's work.

What attracts our attention most is the difference between the two works in terms of the reasons for and the time of the composition. It is more than clear that *Tadhkira-i*

---

[5] Copy of the *Chong Diwan*: 1-3.

[6] Orkhun & Sugawara 2007.

[7] *Ibid.*: 81.

Chihiltan was written at the behest of Yārkand ruler Akhūn Khōja in the year A.H. 1147. On the other hand, the reason for the writing of the *Haft Muḥammadān Tadhkirasi* remains unclear; the work simply states that "suddenly a wise man created it, these colorful heavenly works; I have accepted several of his requests. He said, 'make this work of prose into a poem, oh master.'" [8] It is surprising, however, that the date of authorship is given clearly: "Listen to this history, oh world, it was 1230." Here we see that there is an 83-year gap between the writing of the two works.

The manuscript of "comparison", Tadhkira-i Haft Muḥammadān, fol 80b-81a (Orkhun & Sugawara 2007: 69).

Concluding Remarks

We can see from a simple comparison of the two works mentioned above that both are variants of the original prose work that Zalīlī reinvented in verse form. However, it is clear that 83 years after Zalīlī's work appeared, an unnamed person claimed it as his own in the YMTT. We base this claim on the fact that both the information about the date of Zalīlī's writing and completion of the work and the section explaining the reason for writing the work were deliberately changed in the YMTT version.

References

Orkhun, A., & Sugawara J.(eds.), 2007. *Mazar Documents from Xinjiang and Ferghana (Facsimile) 2. (Studia Culturae Islamicae No. 87).* Tokyo: Research Institute for Languages and Cultures of Asia and Africa, Tokyo University of Foreign Studies.

Zäliliy, M.S. 1986. *Zäliliy diwani.* Prepared for publication by Imin Tursun. Beyjing: Millätlär Näshriyati.

[8] *Ibid.*: 91.

Mazar Pilgrimage

In the Footsteps of Swedish Missionaries in Eastern Turkestan

Patrick HÄLLZON

Introduction

At the end of the 19th and beginning of the 20th century, missionaries from the Mission Covenant Church of Sweden[1] were active in Xinjiang (1892-1938). They ran missionary stations in the oasis towns of Kashgar (including a station in Hancheng), Yengi Hissar and Yarkand. All of these stations, except the above mentioned mission in Hancheng which was devoted to the Chinese, served the Turki speaking population of Xinjiang.[2]

The Swedish missionaries were involved with a wide range of projects including schools, children's homes[3] and missionary hospitals.[4] In Kashgar, they also operated the region's one and only printing press.[5]

Just like their colleagues working in Congo, Central China and elsewhere, the missionaries in Eastern Turkestan regularly reported back home to Sweden about their personal experiences and observations on the mission field.

While one forum for disseminating information was the missionary journal *Missionsförbundet*, other reflections were brought forward in various monographs and extensive compilations such as the book *På Obanade Stigar: Tjugofem år i Östturkestan* [On Untrodden Paths: Twenty-five Years in Eastern Turkestan].

---

[1] The Mission Covenant Church of Sweden (Svenska Missionsförbundet) was founded in 1878. During the initial 30 years, missions were established in 9 countries. The most important intenational missions were in Congo, Central China and Eastern Turkestan. For a comprehensive survey about the history of the Swedish Mission in Eastern Turkestan, see Hultvall (1981s).

[2] Jarring 1991: 8. The Swedish missionaries as well as Gunnar Jarring referred to the local language as Eastern Turki (Uyghur). In addition the missionary sources most often refer to the region as Östturkestan and/or Ost-turkestan which can be roughly translated as Eastern Turkestan.

[3] For more information about the Swedish mission's children's homes see Hultvall 1981s: 88-90.

[4] For information about the Swedish Mission's activities within the field of healthcare see Hultvall 1981s: 73-81. Also see Jarring 1979a: 106-119.

[5] The printed material was mostly carried out in the Eastern Turki (Uyghur) language. While most of the missionary publications had a religious content, non-religious publications such as ABC-textbooks were printed as well. For a thorough study on the Swedish Printing office in Kashgar see Jarring (1991), *Prints from Kashghar*. Also see Jarring 1979a: 113-116.

These missionary reports contain numerous references to a wide range of topics concerning local day-to-day life, including religion. While the reports from Eastern Turkestan discuss different religious traditions, the emphasis clearly lies on various aspects of Islamic practice.

Some missionary material which deals with religious life in the region has already been made available in English by Swedish scholars such as Gunnar Jarring. However, a significant volume of the material collected by the missionaries has not been analyzed nor presented to an international audience.[6]

I suggest that it is of great importance to make this extensive material available to the greater community of non-Swedish speaking researchers and not the least to the people of Xinjiang.[7] I would hereby like to breach the linguistic gap and present some missionary material which to my personal knowledge has not been available in English until now.[8]

As mentioned above Gunnar Jarring collected and published material from missionary reports, some of which deals with mazars. In the article from 1979 entitled 'Matters of Ethnological Interest in Swedish Missionary Reports from Southern Sinkiang' he writes the following regarding the sources:

> I have [...] excluded moralizing passages which have no bearing upon the ethnological facts otherwise presented, but only reflect the missionary zeal of the authors.[9]

In contrast to Gunnar Jarring, who for his purpose excluded the "moralizing passages"[10] reflecting the "missionary zeal",[11] the present article includes the missionaries' personal reflections on mazars and the stories coupled with them.

My objective is twofold. On the one hand I intend to present the reader with 'new' material on mazars and the stories coupled with them and discuss its relevance for contemporary academic work.

On the other hand, I wish to provide the reader with a glimpse of 'how' culture and religion in Eastern Turkestan was presented to a Western audience a century ago. In this way, it is possible for us to learn both about the missionaries' own religious perceptions and of Islamic life in the region.[12]

---

[6] For ethnographically interesting examples see Högberg (1907a); Högberg (1907b); Högberg (1913); Palmberg (1915); Lundahl (1917); Törnquist (1926); Palmaer (1942).

[7] It is worth mentioning that Swedish Christian missionary groups currently are involved in a translation project of some of these sources. These translations are a welcome contribution since the immediate result of the translations is that it will make formerly 'unknown' material accessible in English. One book has already been published. See Ahlbert, 1934 (2009). For the original version in Swedish see Ahlbert, (1934), *Habil: En kristen martyr i Östturkestan*, [Habil: a Christian Martyr in Eastern Turkestan].

[8] Note that parts of the material which I present here also appears in Jarring (1979b). I have chosen to present my own translations with a reference to Jarring's publication.

[9] Jarring 1979b: 4.

[10] *Ibid.*

[11] *Ibid.*

[12] I would like to express my deep gratitude to Jonatan Habib Engqvist who has been more than

The Swedish Mission in Eastern Turkestan

As mentioned before, the Swedish Mission in Eastern Turkestan was active between the years 1892-1938. Gunnar Jarring points out that the decision to "open up a new mission field in Central Asia [was taken at] the general conference of the Mission Covenant Church of Sweden (Svenska Missionsförbundet) in Stockholm in 1893".[13] However, the missionary activities in the region can be traced back as far as 1892.

In 1891 the Swedish missionary Nils Fredrik Höijer left the town of Tiflis in Transcaucasia, and early in 1892 he arrived to Kashgar together with an Armenian companion called Mnatsakan and a formerly Muslim "man of Turkish origin"[14] called Johannes Avetaranian who had converted to Christianity.

After having stayed for eight days in Kashgar, Höijer and Mnatsakan (the Armenian) returned to Transcaucasia, whereas Johannes Avetaranian remained as a missionary in Kashgar. Avetaranian would stay there by himself until 1894 when the missionaries L. E. Högberg and his wife Sigrid Högberg as well as Miss Anna Nyström and the Persian physician Mirza Josef Messrur (Mirza Joseph Mässrur) arrived to join him in Kashgar on July 21, 1894.[15]

After establishing the first missionary station in Kashgar in 1894, three other missionary stations were opened in the area. In 1896 a station was opened in Yarkand, which was followed in 1908 by a facility in "Hancheng, the China-town of Kashgar".[16] Finally, in 1912, a fourth station was opened in Yengi Hissar. There existed plans to open a station in Khotan as well. However, those plans were never accomplished.[17]

The Swedish missionaries continued their work until 1938 when they were forced to leave the country.[18]

The Missionary View on Eastern Turkestan

In order to understand the background to the various mission fields established by *Svenska Missionsförbundet* during this time it is important to know within which context

---

helpful (and patient) in assisting me with valuable feedback on my translations. Many thanks also go to Äsäd Sulayman for his generosity in introducing me to so many aspects of Uyghur culture, for which I am most grateful. Appreciation also goes to Mrs. Katarina Thurell at the Mission Covenant Church of Sweden's archive in Stockholm (the rest of the staff at the archive also needs mentioning). In addition I want to thank Rahilä Dawut, Jun Sugawara, Ildikó Bellér-Hann, Devin DeWeese, Fredrik Fällman, Johan Fresk, Miriya Malik, Birgit Schlyter, Håkan Wahlquist and Ann Olsén. Many thanks also go to all friends, colleagues and family members not mentioned by name here. Finally, a special thanks to my dear wife and children. This study would not have been possible without your patience, love and support.

[13] Jarring 1991: 8.

[14] *Ibid.*

[15] Hultvall 1981s: 50-58; Hultvall 1991: 136-141; Jarring 1991: 8; Högberg, L. E. 1917a: 2.

[16] Jarring 1991: 8.

[17] Jarring 1979a: 107; Hultvall 1981s: 98.

[18] After leaving Eastern Turkestan, the Swedish Mission continued with its activities in India. For more information see Svärd (1979); Palmaer (1942). Also see Hultvall 1981s: 202-211, 219-225.

the movement was born. Wilhelm Östberg has pointed out that the last decades of the 19th century [and the early 20th century] was a time of Christian revivalism in Sweden.

It was also a time of social movements and of political rupture where people "who lived under meager circumstances gathered and worked together towards a brighter future"[19] both in Sweden and abroad.[20]

It was often ordinary people such as fishermen, farmers and dressmakers, who themselves had a limited income, that contributed economically to the missionary activities abroad. Being poor themselves, these people identified closely with the descriptions of poverty, injustice and harsh conditions of life that were brought forward by the missionaries at meetings and in publications.[21]

While books, articles and especially letters were the most important means for the missionaries to convey information from the field, it was also common for those missionaries who had returned to Sweden on furlough, to travel around the country and share their experiences from abroad at meetings with their congregations as well as at schools. At such meetings the missionaries would present the audience with different 'exotic' artifacts brought home from the mission field.

They would also show photographs and sometimes films. The visual element presented in publications and at meetings served to make the missionary experiences and observations more accessible for a public who had none or little knowledge about distant corners of the world such as Eastern Turkestan, China or Congo.[22]

Since the missionaries lived for long periods in the same place, they learned considerably about 'local' everyday-life, culture, customs and religious practices.[23]

In this context it should be pointed out that many of the Swedish missionaries were from modest backgrounds themselves, and practical issues were topics which they as well as their audiences in Sweden easily could relate to. This is reflected in the missionary sources (not only from Eastern Turkestan) that contain numerous references to how local people perform day-to-day tasks such as farm and construction work, as well as depictions of schooling, medicine and information about religion.[24]

For most people in Sweden, the information provided by the missionaries was their first and only acquaintance with Islam. The descriptions presented to the Swedish readers were all but favorable. Islam was portrayed as the root of more or less all evils found in Eastern Turkestan – a region which the missionaries' considered to be imbued with religious conservatism and fanaticism and an inherent resistance against any

---

19 Östberg 2002: 16.

20 *Ibid.*

21 *Ibid.*: 14-15.

22 Cf. Östberg 2002: 16-17. For further information about the use of lantern slides in the work of the Mission Covenant Church of Sweden, see Hällzon (2014).

23 The Swedish missionaries in Eastern Turkestan underwent comprehensive preparatory language training in Chinese or/and Eastern Turki and were required to study the content of the Holy Qur'an as well as popular religious literature such as *Qisasu'l anbiya* [Stories of the Prophets] and other classics. It was assumed that in order to speak with Muslims concerning religion, it was also necessary to know its fundamental principles (Ahlbert, G. et al. 1926).

24 For a missionary view regarding local medicine see Gustavsson (*sic*) 1917b: 245-249.

modern development.

Topics frequently discussed in the publications are people's ignorance, immoral behavior, women's low position in society, the widespread use of drugs, and people's belief in superstition and magic.

Especially disturbing for the missionaries was the peoples' belief in fatalism – a worldview, which according to the missionaries hindered development and left the people in misery, ignorance and poverty.

Where certain modern progress was to be found, the missionaries suggested that it was entirely thanks to European and Christian influence. In short, traits such as development, rational thinking, humanism and enlightenment were equated with Europe and Christian values, while Islam and its adherents were described as the unchanging bearers of a conservative and fanatic worldview.[25]

The missionary Ahlbert writes:

> During the approximate millennium that the country has been ruled by Islam, no significant development has been introduced through Muhammadan influence. It is true that, especially in Kashgar, rather significant progress may be observed in some fields, such as professionalism within the art of construction. But none of this [progress] has originated in Islam as it comes as a result of the [influence] that Christian civilization and Western culture has generated.[26]

In many respects, proselytizing, and the introduction of Western ideas was looked upon as the same thing. The missionary publications served to reinforce the idea of missionaries coming to underdeveloped regions in need of European assistance. Within this discourse, the missionaries' accounts frequently display examples of the orientalist view that was generally accepted practice in Europe and the Western World at this time, and thus not reserved for missionaries alone.[27]

Islam and its People

As Bellér-Hann has pointed out, many travelers to the region commented on what in their eyes was inadequate Islamic observance among the population.[28] Also in the missionary sources we encounter such views. It was suggested that while Islam may appear to be an impressive religion of rules, order, commitment and belief in one sole God, it is only a façade, since the 'superstitious' people in Eastern Turkestan believe in spirits and turn to a number of remedies that have no basis in the scriptures when they

---

[25] Cf. Peters 2010: 84-85.

[26] Ahlbert 1917d: 200. It is interesting that a similar discourse as the one about Muslim societies also is present in missionary articles dealing with non-Muslim missionary fields. See Olsson (2010).

[27] See Said (1978).

[28] Ildikó Bellér-Hann (2001: 10) writes that: "Over the last hundred years, many foreign observers have commented on the superficiality or inadequacy of Islamic observance among the settled oasis dwellers in Xinjiang".

become ill or find themselves in distress.[29]

This may for instance entail a pilgrimage to a mazar, the use of a *tumar* [30] for protection or calling on people who know the Qur'an to read prayers.[31]
The missionary Gottfrid Palmberg writes:

> Such superstition and disbelief flourishes among the Mohammedans in this country. [While] they carry a high confession of their faith in the one [almighty] God, they demonstrate [in their day to day life] a greater faith in spirits as well as trolls and all sorts of superstition.[32]

In a report from 1907, in the journal *Missionsförbundet*, the missionary L. E. Högberg brings forward a similar way of seeing things:

> In the life of the Kashgarian, there is hardly any kind of distress or difficulty in which he does not seek remedy in such kinds of witchcraft. When the woman is barren, when the man does not love his wife, when the wife has received a letter of divorce, when the cattle die from disease or starvation, when the rain won't fall or falls too exuberantly, at birth, weddings and death – Everywhere and in everything one encounters black magic.[33]

One missionary found it especially intriguing to report that some of the 'superstitious' practices observed among Islam's followers was due to the influence of 'pre-Islamic' religions.

> Various ideas, imported from the pre-Islamic religions, still survive in the shape of superstitious mindsets, customs and practices. Thus, [one can see that] there exist traces of the belief in reincarnation. Many [people] believe, for example, that if they hear a certain kind of fly come buzzing towards them; it is the spirit of some relative, who dwells in the insect and has come to visit them. The role which fire plays in people's superstitious beliefs also appears to be associated with some of the ancient religions. The sick are cured by fire which is swung around them. And by the means of bonfires which are lit on the year's final day, one is protected against illness throughout the coming year, etc.[34]

---

[29] Högberg, L. E. 1907a: 46-49. Cf. The following statement by missionary John Törnquist about the supposedly 'superstitious' people in Eastern Turkestan: "At Sirim's small village bazaar which is located 8 km outside Kashgar's Chinese city there is a holy shrine called Läglek Masar. Läglek is the word for stork and the masar or holy shrine has received its name from a stork nest which is located in a big poplar tree which stands at the side of the road. The large birds with their imposing costume are treated with superstitious reverence by the inhabitants. And nobody bothers them" (Törnquist 1926: 70). Note that I use the authors spelling for mazar ("masar") here.

[30] The *tumar* is a small bag which contains a paper with quotations from the Qur'an which is worn around the neck or sown into clothes for protection. For more on this, see Jarring 1979b: 9-10.

[31] This prayer reciter is referred to as *Duakhon*. In Jarring's words this is a "'prayer reader', soothsayer, magician" (Jarring 1979b: 5 n.10).

[32] Palmberg 1917: 189.

[33] Högberg, L. E., 1907b: 380.

[34] Ahlbert 1917c: 166. Cf. Bellér-Hann 2007: 136-137.

Saints as Intermediaries

Many reports from the region testify that people would regularly set out on pilgrimage to holy shrines. Through the mediation of a saint the pilgrim would find relief in his day-to-day life. According to the missionaries, this practice contradicted the Muslims' claim of believing in one God. The following comment by Gottfrid Palmberg serves as an illustrative example of the missionary discourse:

> In the midst of this bragging about their supposed pure worship of God, they are slaves under the cult of saints and purely heathen customs. They have a vague notion that the spirits of their holy men hover over their graves where their bodily remains are kept. Therefore great reverence is shown towards such graves. When passing by such a grave a prayer is often read and quite frequently candles are lit at the graves as a way to honor the saints.[35]

In order to understand the missionaries' aversion towards shrines and saints we have to take into account the religious background that may have shaped these attitudes.

In the book *Helgon och Helgonliv* [Saints and Saintly Life], Efraim Breim discusses some of these issues:

> When the reformists ruptured with the Catholic Church, and strove to return to the original ancient Christian ideal of piety, they also, as a consequence, ruptured with the saintly ideal such as it had developed, both theoretically and practically. Especially during the latter part of the Middle Ages, the cult of saints had taken wide proportions: the people did not only know father God as a distant and inaccessible power, but also the savior's own person had in the eyes of the majority of the people, come to acquire a kind of superior and unapproachable essence. Instead, people turned to the Madonna and the saints who they felt stood closer and whose love and sympathy they could be assured of, and called upon them for intercession with God. For the reformists with their strict Biblicism, this was pure heathendom, and Luther and Zwingli as well as Calvin did all they could to condemn this cult of humans. [Thus for the Protestants], neither the Pope or the saints or even the Madonna is an intercessor between God and man. In his despair of sinful behavior, the penitent must turn to God directly and become righteous through Jesus Christ's act of reconciliation.[36]

In Catholicism people resorted to the Madonna and the saints and had to listen to prayers in Latin instead of their mother tongue. In genuine reformist tradition the Swedish evangelical missionaries instead proposed a personal relation with God through Jesus Christ, without intermediaries. For them, the Muslim God was in the same way as within Catholicism, distant and inaccessible.[37] In this respect the following quote from Hultvall's book *Mission och Revolution* [Mission and Revolution] is quite

---

[35] Palmberg 1917: 190.

[36] Breim 1942: 203.

[37] It should be pointed out that similar critique was brought forward when evangelical missionaries discussed the liturgy of Orthodox Christianity and the 'Oriental' churches (e.g. the Coptic, Nestorian and Syrian churches). These churches were frequently described as 'spiritually dead' and in need of resurrection and truth, while its believers were criticized of being lost in superficial, empty and meaningless ceremonies as well as the 'cult of saints'. Cf. Hultvall 1991: 90; Högberg, L. E. 1925: 66, 216-217.

representative:

> [The missionary] Gunnar Hermansson once saw some 7 000-8 000 people gathered around the shrine of a local saint. He understands this saint cult as people's need for a mediator. Allah was so far away and so indifferent to the needs of ordinary people! People were looking for a link, someone close to them who could also reach God.[38]

Widespread engagement in religious practices such as pilgrimage to mazars was taken as a proof of that the Muslims in Eastern Turkestan wanted and longed for something 'closer', 'day-to-day' and less abstract than the legal and ceremonial aspects prescribed by Islam. Regarding shrine pilgrimage, L. E. Högberg makes the following conclusion:

> It is by no means an easy task to gather and then bring together from the depths of the people's minds, all those motifs and conceptions which motivate them to engage in this cult. Just like the Catholic who in his cult of Mary and the saints seeks intercessors and mediators, who will guide them, in this world and the next, along the narrow paths they must walk in order to reach the blessed eternal kingdom; it might seem that despite Islam's denial of the concept of reconciliation and mediation, [one could] interpret Islam's fumbling and searching for something which is unknown to the Qur'an, as an unconscious or deliberate quest for the mediator. This cult of tombs, saints and relics appears to have its origins in the deep dissatisfaction which the human soul [experiences] with the legal and ceremonial aspects of Islam. To the same account one may surely add the emergence of a great number of sects along with secret and public orders existing among the people of Islam.[39]

The missionary Palmberg brings forward a similar way of seeing things - For Muslims, God is distant and inaccessible. The saints are the mediators by which contact with God can be achieved.

> At the same time as they, in accordance with the Qur'an, claim that Muhammad is God's perfect apostle,[40] and hold in contempt the talk of reconciliation, especially Jesus' death of reconciliation, they demonstrate in many of their religious practices that they fumble for and seek something similar. In their sentiments of a necessity to appease the omnipotence and win its favors, they also loyally maintain a certain cult of offering.[41]

Day-to-Day Life at the Mazar

Albeit often biased in form, the missionary reports from Eastern Turkestan contain substantial information on various aspects of ritual at the mazars. The following description of the main features of mazars is in many ways valid also today.

> In Eastern Turkestan one encounters so-called 'saintly' graves everywhere. These usually have a relatively artistically designed cupola structure that has been erected over the place

---

[38] The quote in English is taken from Hultvall 1981e: 21. For the original text in Swedish see Hultvall 1981s: 36.

[39] Högberg, L. E. 1925: 66.

[40] Note the Christian terminology.

[41] Palmberg 1917: 191.

> where the "saint" (often a crook)[42] has been buried, and a larger or smaller mosque, as well as the living quarters of the person who is in charge of the holy place.[43]

In the report there are also references to the big rods (*tugh*)[44] that were brought to the shrine for the New Year's celebration.[45] Gottfrid Palmberg suggests that there was a common belief among the people of the region that with the exchange of flags from one place to the other, the intermediation of saints was made possible.

> The graves are also distinguished by a peculiar decoration of flags and rags in all kinds of colors. At the customary feasts for the New Year, these flags are carried from one shrine to the other. In their ignorance the people believe that the saints' visits to one another are intermediated.[46]

As is confirmed by the various sources from the period under discussion, shrines enjoyed great popularity among the people. Just like today there existed different types of shrines in the region.

> Just outside the city of Kashgar is the shrine of Häzrät-i-Afak. [The shrine] owns large domains and incomes and is a permanent place of pilgrimage, especially during the occasional reoccurring festivities that are held there.[47] There [also] exist other special shrines, where, for example all infertile women make a pilgrimage. In connection therewith should be mentioned relic-shrines, where for example, a bristle pertaining to the Prophet or similar things are kept, and also to these [shrines], there is a [constant] congregation.[48]

The Häzrät-i-Afak Mazar, close to Kashgar was described by the Swedish missionaries as the most important Muslim shrine in the region.[49] During the annual festivities the number of visitors would often reach the tens of thousands.

---

[42] Palmberg's portrayal of the saint as a "crook" is highly illustrative and reflects his personal view on shrines and pilgrimage.

[43] Palmberg 1915: 377.

[44] According to Jarring the big rods (*tugh*) that are brought to the mazars in the region, serve the purpose of keeping away *jin* (evil spirits). He explains: "The pilgrims consider it commendable to tear strips from their cloaks and to hang them up at the shrines. The wind makes the rags and cloths flutter and flap, and thus the evil spirits (*jin*) hovering round every grave are driven off" (Jarring 1935: 351).

[45] Palmberg writes "New Year" which probably refers to the *Ashure*. Cf. the book *Jolbas*, where L. E. Högberg mentions the Huschur Heit which he says is the equivalent of Äschur (< Ashure). He writes: "'äschur', a feast which in the Muslim World is celebrated at the beginning of the year's first month. Originally the Ashure has been celebrated as a memory of Noah's egress from the ark which is considered to have happened on the tenth day in the first month, but at present this feast has as its primary signification as a new year's celebration" (Högberg, L. E. 1913: 15). Here he is clearly referring to the Muslim month of *Muharram*.

[46] Palmberg 1915: 378.

[47] Regarding festivities at shrines in the region, Ahlbert (1917e: 234) writes about annual festivities in order to celebrate the Prophet's birthday. Everyone, both poor and rich were provided with food which was paid for with the revenue from the *waqf* foundation.

[48] Högberg, L. E. 1925: 65.

[49] For a more extensive missionary view on the *khoja*s see Raquette 1917a: 54-59.

> The holy shrines play an important role in the people's lives. At these places miracles occur through the power of the saints, who the people turn to with all their concerns. The saints are called upon since they are intermediates who present the distress of the people to Allah. People come in the tens of thousands to the more important saintly shrines. In this way flocks of people annually come to the shrine of Häzrät-i-Afak which is located right next to Kashgar and must be considered the most distinguished in the country.[50]

To stay close to a mazar for a longer period was believed to be especially beneficial for those hoping to receive help from the saints. Thus it was recommendable to stay there for as long as forty days.

> The most recommended for those wishing to receive help from the saints, is nevertheless to stay at the saints' tombs for an extended period which preferably lasts up to 40 days. The period is used for reading of the Qur'an and other acts of devotion. – A Mohammedan's final wish is also to be buried in the vicinity of a saint. However this is the prerogative of the rich, for such gravesites cost considerable sums of money.[51]

Many reports describe the mazar as a venue for people seeking remedy from their distress, many of which were women. Just like today, women in the region were not permitted to take part in the religious activities of the mosque.[52]

> Every week people make a pilgrimage to these graves. The sick go there in order to crawl under a log or the root of a tree, hoping in this way that they will be freed of their ailments by doing this, while childless wives go there and cry for hours in the expectation that they later on will be able to give birth to babies. If this does not help, a sheep or sometimes a horse is offered, slaughtered and prepared by the grave and distributed to the poor. The supervisor at the grave is usually also a so-called prayer man and sometimes people pay considerable amounts of money for his intercession.[53]

The missionaries often depicted a dark image of the spiritual conditions of the people among whom they were working. Especially shrines were described as a hotbed of sinful and superstitious elements. In one report the missionary Palmberg suggested that the extent of immorality which took place at shrines was so great that the Chinese authorities had been forced to intervene in order to stop what was going on there.

> Several of these holy places have become meeting points for such unworthy elements as the slaves of immorality. A sad testimony to the morals of Islam's adherents! It is significant, that

[50] Gustafsson 1917a: 227. Cf. Jarring 1979b: 15-16.

[51] Gustafsson 1917a: 228. Cf. Jarring 1979b: 15-16.

[52] Högberg, S 1917a: 221. There are interesting missionary reports from the region that deal with other topics than mazars. Sigrid Högberg for instance, has written quite a lot about women and their religious life. An interesting article is 'Khaneka' [Khaniqa], which deals with a religious meeting with only women involved (Högberg, S. 1917b: 451-454). Another article of interest regarding the missionary view on female life in the region is 'Den Ost-Turkestanska Kvinnan' [The Eastern Turkestanian Woman] (Högberg, S. 1917a: 216-223).

[53] Palmberg 1915: 377. Cf. Jarring 1979b: 16.

> the *heathen* Chinese authorities from time to time consider it advisable to intervene in order to prevent the practice of immorality that take place at the feasts of the Muhammadans [who gather] there. Depraved women are sometimes penalized in a radical way at the site, and prohibitions are issued for other women to make a pilgrimage there. But these bans soon become violated again.[54]

The author's comments regarding the visitors' dubious morals are of course open for interpretation. It could on the one hand be perceived as the occurrence of prostitution at shrines but it is also possible that the text is dealing with so-called temporary marriages, matchmaking or other types of behavior deemed immoral from the missionaries' perspective.[55]

Sacrifices

The missionary reports illuminate that shrines were visited for a varied number of reasons. While some mazars were visited by women only, shrines were also venues for social interaction which included whole communities.

As pointed out, shrines were visited on a regular weekly basis as well as during major festivals when whole communities were engaged in pilgrimage.[56] At the weekly gatherings animals were sacrificed and everyone was invited to share the sacrificial meal which was believed to have become blessed.

In a polemic article from 1917 the missionary Gottfrid Palmberg describes the procedure of sacrifices among the Muslims in the region. Although the following passage is quite long, I have chosen to present it in its entity due to its richness in detail.

> The [people] perform sacrifices in case of sickness as well as during other sorts of distress, and the sacrifice may, all depending on one's assets, consist in everything from a piece of bread to the most expensive camel. At times they sacrifice their most valuable possessions. A year ago or so, we received frequent visits to the hospital by a man who suffered from an incurable illness, which later ended his life. At these visits he came in the company of his son who rode on a very gallant and precious horse. When he sometime after his father's death, returned to us riding on a horse which was worse than the former, we asked him what had happened to the precious one and he answered: "We slaughtered it and swung the meat over our father, before he died". The most common proceeding when offering in this way usually

[54] Palmberg 1917: 190-191.

[55] During the period discussed here it was quite common with so-called temporary marriages. Many people in the region had been married (and divorced) on numerous occasions. For the missionaries such arrangements were no less than legalized prostitution. Thus, it is possible that the missionaries are speaking about this. For missionary views on this practice see Högberg, L. E. 1917c: 109-113; Högberg, S 1917a: 216-223. For a thorough discussion about marriage and divorce in the region also see Bellér-Hann 2008: 78, 266-278, 301.

[56] While the missionary reports consulted for this article do not specify which week day was most popular for visiting mazars, nor provide detailed information whether the weekly gatherings took place all year round or during a specific period of the year, they do as we can see, contain information about what was going on there. However, complementary sources clarify the picture. Bellér-Hann (2008: 350) suggests that it was the weekly market days that were especially popular for visiting shrines during this period.

is that firstly the animal is blessed by some spiritual leader. After this is done, it is slaughtered. The meat is then swayed over the person for whom the offering is made and then it is eaten by those invited or not invited who come there. Finally, everyone present engages in communal prayers.

Similar sacrificial acts are also carried out at the sacred tombs. At such tombs, which are meeting points for celebrations and crowds every week, the sacrifices usually take place in connection with such celebrations where one always finds participants who are willing to partake in the sacrificial meal. At other tombs the people who perform the sacrifice invite those living in the neighborhood and distribute the sacrifice to them. By this act, as well as the common prayers performed afterwards, they believe that they will benefit from the saint's merits, and thereby also receive preferences with Allah.

Within other aspects of the Mohammedans' saint worship, their need for mediators and protector is equally clearly discernible. Every profession has its powerful patron saint, embodied in some holy man, who according to tradition has been the first to practice this profession.[57]

People also search for mediators in living saints. Here and there in the country are men, who by their pretense of being descended from the Prophet's family as well as their zeal for the religion's commandments, have reached such a level of holiness, that they before God [almighty] are able to obtain merit for others as well [as for themselves]. The belief in these [holy men] and the sense of the need of their mediation is so widely spread, that amongst adult Mohammedans there are very few people who do not take advantage of their services.

The common procedure is to provide the holy man with a gift, which depending on the donor's assets ranges from a horse or camel, down to a thing worth a couple of pennies. Through the act of a simple ceremony, consisting of handshakes and prayers and a reminding of a few religious obligations, the "saint" adopts his new follower and protégé. The protégé now believes that through this relationship with the saint, he will in this present time share Allah's grace, but above all he safeguards himself by having received the saint as an advocate on the Day of Judgment. The Muslims pride themselves of being a "people of faith". Herein one also has to acknowledge that they are correct. However, as we have previously demonstrated, much of this belief must be assigned to pure superstition.[58]

Leisure and the Social Component of Mazar Visitation

As we have seen, the missionary reports contain frequent references to the therapeutic aspect of pilgrimage, the pilgrims' 'superstitious' activities, people's low moral standards as well as critical notes about the sacrifices and the role of mediators within Islam. The missionary sources consulted for this study also suggest that just as is the case today, pilgrimage was during the period of discussion indeed very popular among women. However, our discussion cannot merely approach mazar visitation as a female phenomenon or of pilgrimage consisting in solely instrumental prerogatives.

Regardless of religious tradition discussed, pilgrimage is a multifaceted practice which involves a number of components such as social interaction, economic issues,

---

[57] Palmberg is referring to the various patron saints (*pir*) of each profession. The *pir* system is mentioned by several authors such as Gustafsson 1917a: 229; Högberg, L. E. 1907a: 52-53, 1917b: 87; Ahlbert 1917b: 117. However, the most detailed account is provided by Bohlin 1917: 81-82.

[58] Palmberg 1917: 191-192. Note that parts of Palmberg's account also appear in Jarring 1979b: 13. However, I have chosen to present my own translation here.

and entertainment and so on. In this context, I find the following remark from 1917 by the missionary David Gustafsson illuminative, since it indicates that while many of the visitors to the shrine of Häzrät-i-Afaq surely did so for instrumental reasons, there were also many people who came 'only' for the "mere entertainment".[59]

> *Naturally there are many people who merely come for entertainment, but a large number of people come to find remedy in their suffering* [my italics]. To the latter also belong those who have not been blessed with an offspring. But here they have a saint who may help them and whom they try to affect by bitter lament. For these wretched people, there are many places where they can go to find remedy. At some of these sites it is possible for them to find out instantly whether their prayers have been heard. The proof of this is that they are able to lift quite heavy stones which are found at the site. It is also permissive to declare one's wish for a baby boy or girl. If a baby boy is wished for, which is the most common; the praying person should place a bow at a designated place.[60]

Also 'local' observations testify the "carnevalesque character"[61] of shrine visitation. The following exert is taken from Gunnar Jarring's publication 'Gustaf Raquette and Qasim Akhun's letters to Kamil Efendi', a reworking of a manuscript written by Gustaf Raquette based on mail correspondence between Qasim Akhun, a Kashgarian and his friend Kamil Efendi in Istanbul.

Qasim Akhun writes:

> A popular amusement which is very much appreciated is the big gathering of people at the shrines (*mazar*) in the spring and summer. Normally this would entail pious pilgrimages but little of that spirit is noticeable. Some people, or perhaps many, fulfil the demands of religious decency by crying for a while at the shrine of the saint in question or try to find some cure for their ailments but their chief motive is to have fun. And this includes that young people of both sexes use these occasions for meeting each other.[62]

Mazar Pilgrimage- Now and Then

When observing how *ziyarät* is performed among the Uyghur people today, one may discern a striking continuity with many aspects described in the missionary reports. Also today, some shrines are open for pilgrims all year round, while other holy places draw pilgrims mainly during festival time. Most of the smaller mazars scattered across the Xinjiang-region have no set date for pilgrimage. The pilgrims come whenever they need to and often the visits are quite brief.

Often the objective with the visit is of an instrumental character. The pilgrim prays

---

[59] Gustafsson 1917a: 227.

[60] *Ibid.*:227-228. Cf. Jarring 1979b: 15-16.

[61] This expression is used by Bellér-Hann 2008: 350.

[62] Jarring 1975: 18. Other sources point in a similar direction. Bellér-Hann writes: At saintly shrines, assistance was sought to make women, land and animals fertile, to prevent or cure sickness, to ward off pests and storms and to bring good luck. This last function also explains why the festivals organized around shrines had a carnevalesque character and included matchmaking (Bellér-Hann 2008: 350).

for good health, protection from evil, good luck in business, a stable family, good economy, to pass exams at university and so on. Among the Uyghur such short visits are called *mazar tawabiti* which literally means 'worship'.[63]

In contrast, a number of major mazars have fixed periods for visitation. These annual events which commonly are known as *mazar säylisi* (mazar festivals) sometimes attract tens of thousands of people simultaneously.[64] Just like pilgrimage festivals in other parts of the world, the *mazar säylisi* takes many dimensions and allows for both celebration and spiritual reflection.

For the pilgrim, participation at the shrine festivals on the one hand constitutes a religious act, but it also provides an opportunity for entertainment and social interaction.[65] This implies reinforcement of bonds between people living in oasis towns far from the shrine and also exchange of ideas (a feature also noted from the *hajj*).[66]

In addition, current research indicates that religious festivals often offer a valuable boost to the local economy through increased trade opportunities.[67]

At the mazar festivals food stalls are set up and a wide range of recreational activities take place such as different music performances, and the participation of storytellers (*mäddäh*), who tell stories about religion. Other activities at mazar festivals include "tightrope-walking, cock- and dog-fighting, and 'goat tussling' (*oghlaq tartish*)"[68]

As the Uyghur researcher Rahilä Dawut has demonstrated, the mazar festivals are events that include participation by entire communities. Young and old people, men as well as women, perform the *ziyarat* for a multitude of reasons.

> They come, some from far away, on trucks or donkey carts or on foot, to celebrate and mourn the saint. Old men come to pray; young people come to the Ordam to have fun and look for potential partners; women come to make a wish to the saint for a child. The sick come to bury themselves in the sand around the site, which is thought to have healing powers.[69]

---

[63] Harris and Dawut 2002: 102.

[64] Harris and Dawut 2002: 102; Dawut 2007: 151.

[65] Cf. Mernissi 1989.

[66] Morinis 1992: 24.

[67] Preston points out that: "Virtually every pilgrimage is associated with a field of economic exchange, as in fairs, carnivals, and permanent or temporary marketplaces. Materials are redistributed as pilgrims enter sacred places, then disperse" (Preston 1992: 43).

[68] Dawut 2007: 152-53. Also see Harris and Dawut (2002). For information about Uyghur music see Harris and Muhpul (2002).

[69] Dawut 2007:152. In the article 'Mazar Festivals of the Uyghurs: music, Islam and the Chinese State', Rachel Harris and Rahilä Dawut have correctly noted that historic reports on mazar festivities in the area are scarce (Harris and Dawut 2002: 102). However, some information is found in the form of a short booklet from 1913 written by the missionary L. E. Högberg. The original title of the book is *Jolbas: en kaschgargosses levnad, skildrad av honom själv* [Jolbas: The Life of a Kashgarian Boy, as Described by Himself]. One part of the book deals with what three school children are up to during their school break during Huschur (< Ashure) Heit when they decide to visit Ådapascha (< Ordam Padishah Mazar / Ordikhan Padishah Mazar) close to Kashgar. The story provides us with valuable information about a wide range of aspects concerning mazar festivities. For example the way the pilgrims make their way to the shrine, the food vendors, the many forms of entertainment

Authenticity of the Mazars and the *Täzkirä*

Whereas the focus up to now has been on the act of visitation, this section will deal with yet an important theme, namely the missionaries' own understanding of shrines and their development as well as the stories and/or legends coupled with mazars, often referred to as *täzkirä*.[70] These stories often contain detailed information about how the mazar originated as well as its originator (the saint).

L. E. Högberg, who prior to the establishment of the mission in Kashgar conducted missionary work in Persia, had several decades of experience with missionary work among Muslims. He was also a prolific writer and many of his books and articles deal with Islam.

With regard to the stories coupled with shrines, Högberg expressed that there was a natural explanation for their existence, and that they should not be understood as anything but made up legends.

> I have personally had the opportunity to observe the natural cause for the development of this cult [of Muslim shrines]. A poor wanderer succumbed on the long deserted paths of the Tianshan Mountains. Due to the dry climate and the intense heat of the sun, his body dried up and took the shape of a mummy. Above the mountain gorge, where [the mummy] lay, travelers now began to honor the dead by erecting poles with multi-colored flags and rags. With each [passing] year, these [poles and rags] increased [in numbers], just as [was the case with] the invented stories of the "saint's" feats.[71]

This skeptical attitude towards the 'authenticity' of mazars and religious lore is not isolated to L. E. Högberg, but can be observed in writings by other missionaries as well. Also the missionary Gottfrid Palmberg questioned the veracity of these stories, which he found both repulsive and abominable.

While the parts of Palmberg's article 'Helgongravar i Ost-Turkestan' [Saintly Shrines in Eastern Turkestan] that deal with shrine visitation and ritual have been discussed in a previous chapter; we will now examine what the missionary has to say about the stories coupled with mazars.

> Every saintly shrine is coupled with a long story about remarkable things that the deceased has done; how many infidels he has killed and so on. These often horrid stories are according to tradition passed from one generation to the other. There is no guarantee

available there such as story-telling, animal fights and wrestling as well as the spiritual element characterized by for example dervishes engaged in religious exercises such as the *zikr*.

[70] The missionary doctor Gustaf Raquette explains that a *täzkirä* (he spells this word "täzkir") is the written story or legend of a mazar and that the books containing the *täzkirä* usually are kept at the shrine. (Raquette 1917c: 202). Cf. Raquette (1917b: 132) where the missionary doctor writes that the "local literature which has emerged during the Muhammadan era, mainly consists of so-called "täzkir" [...], which should be understood as a description of the lives and fates of the holy men who are buried at the holy shrines." The missionary doctor also mentions other forms of literature produced during the Islamic era, such as novels, collections of songs (love songs), poetry and proverbs. However, the *täzkirä* is the form of literature which he mentions first when talking about Islamic literary production in the region (Raquette 1917b: 132).

[71] Högberg 1925: 65.

> that the contents are not altered in the same way as these people inherit the ability to fantasize and make up lies. Nevertheless, they believe just as blindly anyway.[72]

Material presented by both L. E. Högberg and Palmberg supports the idea that so-called 'relic shrines'[73] existed somewhere in the region. While L. E. Högberg mentions a hair pertaining to the Prophet,[74] Palmberg's story deals with the bristle of an unknown traveler.[75]

According to Palmberg, "[o]ne of these graves has emerged in the following way": [76]

> A man made a stop during his journey to perform his prayers. While the man performed his duty, the traveler's servant told the people what a great and holy man his master was. After the man had moved on, a bristle which had fallen from his beard when he had performed his regular ablution was found at the site. Thus the people agreed that it was sufficiently important to deposit a bristle coming from such a holy man at the same location where he had performed his prayers. While a sepulchral chamber with a cupola on top of it was built, as well as a mosque, the bristle was put in a bottle which was kept at the shrine. The site soon became one of the most important ones where people year after year prayed and gave alms. The supervisor of the tomb [certainly] knew how to tell wonderful things. If someone made a generous donation to the shrine, the bristle grew in length so that there was not enough room in the bottle, but if someone donated too little, the bristle would shrink. The people naturally believed all of this and a substantial amount of property was donated to the shrine.[77]

As to underline what he has expressed about this mazar, Palmberg states in yet another polemic passage of his article:

> A year ago it so happened that an Arab – a real extortioner and swindler who had lived in the area for a couple of years, passed away in an accident.[78] Then there was great commotion and the people feared the consequences of that a man from the land of the great Prophet had died here by accident. The people discussed amongst themselves and decided that the saintly shrine containing the holy bristle would be a sufficiently dignified place for receiving the remains of this holy man. Many people who earlier sighed under his tyranny, when he used to take their women by force and exhort their personal belongings; now believe that they ascribe merit by praying at the tomb of the "saint".[79]

---

[72] Palmberg 1915: 377.

[73] Cf. Högberg, L. E. 1925: 65. Relics are found in most religious traditions. Also today, shrines containing for example garments worn by the Prophet Muhammad or a hair of the Prophet's beard can be found across the Muslim world. Due to the scope of this article it is not possible to provide a comprehensive list of where these relics are kept.

[74] Högberg, L. E. 1925: 65.

[75] Unfortunately neither of the two specify in their respective articles, which shrines they are referring to.

[76] Palmberg 1915: 378.

[77] *Ibid.* Palmberg is clearly referring to a Muslim pious foundation, *waqf*. For a missionary view on the *waqf*, see Ahlbert 1917e, 'Vakf' [Waqf].

[78] The Arabs of Eastern Turkestan are described by the missionaries as being especially honored by the people (Gustavsson 1917c: 252-253). Cf. Jarring (1987).

[79] Palmberg 1915: 378.

As we can see Gottfrid Palmberg is of the opinion that the Muslim shrines in Eastern Turkestan have emerged under doubtful circumstances and should not be understood more than repositories of made up 'mumbo-jumbo'. In yet an attempt to 'prove' how fabled the stories coupled with mazars are, Palmberg brings forward the following example:

> One story that, at the most can be counted as a mere myth, tells that a servant of a supervisor and prayer man of a shrine, one day asked his master to provide him with equipment, since he wanted to travel the world. His master gave him a donkey on which he began his journey, but after covering a short while the donkey died. The servant buried it and sat down to weep by the grave. Some people, who were out traveling, found him in this condition. The servant told them that his only travel companion had died and that he now was planning to die too, and be buried with him. The people then decided to build a holy shrine and it did not take long until both rich and poor made their pilgrimage there. One day also the [aforementioned] prayer man arrived to the shrine and was astonished to find his former servant supervisor of the grave. In answer to the prayer man's question about which great saint this had been in his lifetime, the young man replied confidentially: "It was the donkey that you gave me." The young man then asked the prayer man: "But tell me, who was the saint that rests in the grave that you supervised?" The prayer man answered him: "[The saint] was the father of the donkey which I gave to you."[80]

The Role of Written and Spoken Literature in Daily Central Asian Life

Palmberg's story about the servant and prayer man is not really representative of the literature traditionally attributed to shrines. I believe that the author's objective with including it under such a heading as 'Saintly Shrines in Eastern Turkestan' was in fact to ridicule the tradition of shrine visitation itself, and not to present the reader with a real *täzkirä*.

While it should be pointed out that Palmberg's article clearly attempts to prove how invented and untrue the stories coupled with mazars are, it is however not entirely unlikely that such stories as the one discussed above were in circulation among people in Eastern Turkestan during our era of discussion. In fact, the story rather resembles a kind of 'Näsirdin Äpändi' tale: popular stories that are widely spread across Central Asia, Iran and Turkey.

It is of course possible that Palmberg had misunderstood the context of the story altogether. However, as pointed out earlier, the missionaries in Eastern Turkestan attended courses that dealt with the content of the Qur'an as well as popular religious literature.[81] From this we may suppose that it is unlikely that Palmberg would be totally unaware of the important role that popular literature played in Eastern Turkestan and other parts of Central Asia.

Besides the rich written literature mainly expressed in the Chaghatai language before the upheavals of the Russian conquest of Central Asia, the establishment of the Soviet

80 *Ibid.*

81 See Ahlbert, G. *et al.* 1926.

Union and the People's Republic of China, Central Asia was a treasury of oral literature which had acquired a multitude of dimensions.

Central Asian oral literature was traditionally expressed in short stories, poetry, proverbs[82], heroic and romantic epics (*dastan*) as well as religious texts.

In Eastern Turkestan and elsewhere in Central Asia, both religious and secular literature was during the period discussed here a shared experience. At shrines and bazaars stories were often read out loud by a storyteller (*mäddäh*) so that those who were illiterate could partake.[83] As Adeeb Khalid points out, it was not only oral literature *per se* which was recited. Also classical literature was read in various "informal settings".[84]

> Central Asia, of course, boasted a vibrant tradition of oral poetry, but oral transmission also extended to texts that could be read aloud in various formal and informal settings. Itinerant reciters and storytellers (*maddāhs, qissakhwāns*) were a common phenomenon in Central Asia, as were evenings (*mashrab*)[85] devoted to reading aloud from manuscript texts.[86]

Besides being a source of entertainment, the religious stories served as an important means for common people to attain detailed information regarding various religious concepts in an entertaining and easily understandable fashion. In addition the stories, especially those associated with shrines, served to link and place local communities' shrines within the larger general Muslim world. In fact, strolling around marketplaces, visiting mazars and partaking in *mäshräp* appear to have been some of the main forms of amusement among the people during the period discussed.[87]

We can thus see that the boundaries of where and how the transmission of religious and non-religious literature took place was blurred and not confined to definitions of explicitly religious places and vice versa, but woven into the social fabric of everyday life. During the period discussed here, large segments of the population were unable to read and write. These skills were reserved for the elite. However, this does not necessarily mean that 'common people' lacked general knowledge about literature. The Swedish missionary Gustaf Ahlbert provides the following colorful description of storytelling at the bazaar.

> We continue our way out to the open merchant site, where a bustling trading is going on. The baker sits on the ground with his bread basket, the water salesman promotes the sale of fruit syrup and water with ice cubes in it and the fruit vendor cuts slices from a large melon. But our attention is drawn to a group of people sitting on the ground, who despite the surrounding commotion, sit in reverence and listen to someone speaking. It is a

[82] For a list of popular proverbs in Eastern Turkestan see Ahlbert 1917a: 97-99.
[83] For a missionary description of bazaars see Nyström, (1917), 'Basarbesök' [Visits to Bazaars].
[84] Khalid 1998: 24.
[85] Cf. Jarring (1975: 15-18) who spells the word as *mashraf* (< *mäshräp*).
[86] Khalid 1998: 24. Cf. Laude Cirtautas (1980: 34-38) who informs us that in the early 20th century it was popular with gatherings in western Central Asia (Uzbekistan) referred to as *gap* (conversation).
[87] For information about bazaars, *mashraf* (< *mäshräp*), mazar visitation and other types of entertainment see Jarring 1975: 13-20, 27 (in English), 36-41, 50 (in Swedish).

> street-preacher, who tells wonderful stories from the lives of the prophets. [The preacher] also teaches his audience how they will consort to various life circumstances, such as how they should avoid swimming in cold water, and how they ought to exterminate rats and scorpions, and many more things. When the sermon is over, the audience is encouraged to engage in prayer. This is performed in such a fashion that the person raises his hands approximately on a level with his chin, says amen, and strokes his beard or, if it is not yet perceptible, the chin, where it should have its place. And then [having performed this procedure], the prayer has been done. Finally, an offertory takes place. While many people give a few pennies, some leave without offering anything at all. The latter are however informed by the zealous preacher, what kinds of people they are, in that they are cursed as being "donkeys", "pigs" and other even more descriptive epithets.[88]

The literature which Gustaf Ahlbert refers to in the above passage is without doubt the collection of stories commonly known as *Qisasu'l anbiya* [Stories of the Prophets], which was widely cherished by the people in Eastern Turkestan and other parts of Central Asia.[89]

In contrast to Ahlbert's scant information about this collection of stories, L. E. Högberg provides us with detailed accounts in the books *På Obanade Stigar* and *Islam och Evangeliet*.

As we have seen earlier, L. E. Högberg was of the opinion that the stories coupled with mazars were made-up tales which should be separated from 'real' historic events. When speaking of the veracity of *Qisasu'l anbiya*, his argumentation follows a similar logic.

According to L. E. Högberg, Muslim hagiography can be understood as no less than warmed up fables. He suggests that "the people that created the book Arabian Nights"[90] solely needed to use their lively imagination to invent stories where the Prophet performed a multitude of miracles or was involved in miraculous events.[91]

We can here observe that L. E. Högberg's viewpoint coincides with Palmberg's, who in his article about saintly shrines expresses that: "these people inherit the ability to fantasize and make up lies [and] believe blindly".[92]

The *Täzkirä* of Chiltän

In *På Obanade Stigar*, Gustaf Raquette discusses the *täzkirä* coupled with the mazar of *Tjiltän* (< Chiltän) in Yarkand.[93] While Raquette's article is far less polemic in nature

---

[88] Ahlbert 1917b: 117-118.

[89] As Jarring points out, in the early decades of the 20th century, the book market in Eastern Turkestan mainly consisted of so-called lithographs imported from Soviet Central Asia, as well as books copied by hand. The hand copied books in Eastern Turkestan often had a religious content. *Qissas ul-änbijá* (< *Qisasu'l anbiya*) held a prominent position as the most famous and popular of these books (Jarring 1979: 215, 216).

[90] Högberg, L. E. 1917d: 150. Note the 'orientalist' discourse used by the author. Cf. Said 1978.

[91] *Ibid.*

[92] Palmberg 1915: 377.

[93] The story recorded by Raquette is almost identical to the *Chilten Chronicle* by Muhämmäd Siddiq Zälili which is discussed in Abliz Orkhun's chapter in this volume. There are also other versions of this story. For more information on this shrine and the story (stories) connected with it see: Wei

than Palmberg's and L. E. Högberg's texts, also he casts doubt on the authenticity of Muslim shrines and the stories coupled with them.

Raquette suggests that the legacy of many Muslim shrines of Central Asia is pre-Islamic and that with the victorious spread of Islam, some of these focal points of veneration among the local populace, e.g. former Buddhist shrines, eventually were turned into Muslim holy places.

In his article, Raquette refers to a German archaeological expedition, which a few years earlier had undertaken excavations in the area. When the expedition explored a Muslim shrine in the desert, they initially found no indications of anything but a common Muslim shrine. But when they started digging in the sand, they found an ancient Buddhist temple below the surface.[94] Raquette writes: "The people's reverence had probably gradually moved from the lower to the upper temple".[95]

Although Raquette does not explicitly write that this is the case with the Chiltän Mazar, it is quite clear that that he wants to emphasize the connection between the pre-Islamic and Islamic period.

> All over Eastern Turkestan one comes across holy shrines in a variety of conditions where people go for pilgrimage; often without knowing who or which saint has been given his resting place there. Sometimes these graves actually do contain the remains of historically known personages such as for example Häzrät-i-Afak in Kaschgar and Sultan Satuk Mazar in the lower part of Artush; a village located a couple of [Swedish miles][96] to the northeast of Kaschgar.[97] It is possible that the people's reverence for some sites has been handed down from pre-Islamic times and these sites have merely been given names later on in accordance with the new religion and have arbitrarily been coupled with a more or less remarkable tradition.[98]

Raquette writes that there are two mazars in the Yarkand area that both claim to house one and same *täzkirä*. The Chiltän Mazar which is depicted in a couple of photographs in *På Obanade Stigar* is located in the town of Yarkand. The other shrine which goes by the name "Mazar of the Seven Mohammedans" is said to be in a village west of Yarkand called Kaltala.[99]

According to the *täzkirä* of Chiltän seven holy men are buried at the mazar. Raquette writes that the word *chiltän* means seven, while a correct etymological explanation of the word Chiltän instead would imply something which deals with the number forty.[100]

---

and Luckert 1998: 111-114; Dawut 2001: 83-88; Sayrami 2007: 591; Orxun and Sugawara 2007; 19-20. However, Raquette's version is the most extensive I have found so far.

[94] Raquette 1917c: 201-202.

[95] *Ibid.*: 202.

[96] A Swedish mile corresponds to 10 km.

[97] Raquette 1917c: 201. I have used Raquette's spelling here.

[98] *Ibid.*

[99] I visited Kaltala > Kaltila in 2014. There I learned that the shrine's name is 'Mazar of the Nine Mohammedans' (*toqquz muhammedan maziri*) and not 'Mazar of the Seven Mohammedans' as Raquette claims. The shrine is located in a village close to Kaltila called Toqquz Met = Abr. *toqquz muhammedan*.

[100] According to Basilov (1992: 15, the word *chiltän* (< *chiltan*) is constructed from Persian and

It would be surprising if Raquette, who was an authority on Eastern Turki, were unaware of the correct meaning of the word. It is difficult to know, but perhaps something was altered in the process of producing the book *På Obanade Stigar*.

The observant reader might now ask why seven men are said to be buried here and not forty as the name of the mazar implies. The answer to this question is found in the *täzkirä* recorded by Gustaf Raquette that initially deals with the wondrous birth of forty children (saints), but at a later stage deals with seven holy men.[101]

The Oral Version of the Story

Gustaf Raquette informs us that besides the 'official' *täzkirä* of Chiltän there exists a popular oral story. Also this story features the miraculous birth of forty children. According to Raquette the oral story is based on a historic event. Here, Salman Fares, a main character of the 'official' *täzkirä* has been exchanged for a person called Safvan ibn el- Mu'attab.

Raquette argues that it is undisputable that Salman Fares was included in the 'official' *täzkirä* as a way to insult believers of the Shiite group since he was a follower of Ali.

The missionary also claims that the oral version of the story is a combination of the story of the forty *chiltän* and the events described in the Qur'an 24:6,[102] and its following passages which reads:

> And for those who launch a charge against their spouses, and have (in support) no evidence but their own, - their solitary evidence (can be received) if they bear witness four times (with an oath) by Allah that they are solemnly telling the truth.[103]

The story and background to this 'oral' version, is as being told by Raquette, is as follows:

> When Muhammad on his sixth year after the refuge to Medina carried out an attack on the Mustalik tribe, his favorite wife Aischa (< Aisha) was left behind by coincidence. Thinking that somebody would miss her and soon and come to search for her, she sat down to wait.

---

means 'forty men'. However, the word has various connotations. Basilov explains that the *chiltan* is a category of mythological spirits found in both Turkic and Iranian speaking areas: He writes: "They are middle-aged or elderly saints who deliver people from misfortune and bring them happiness; they are the guardians of dervishes and of marriage and birth; of the young men and of success at fishing. In general, tradition ties them to orgiastic cults of antiquity. According to Uyghourian (*sic*) legend, they are the source of shamanism and protect shamans" (Basilov 1992: 15-16). It should be pointed out that Basilov's observations were influenced by the Soviet conceptual framework of associating so-called 'folk Islam' with shamanism. As Bellér-Hann points out, Soviet scholarship was "tailored to Soviet ideology, and insisted on a rigid division of pre-Islamic and Islamic layers" (Bellér-Hann 2007: 136 n.17). While I disagree with various analytical points in Basilov and other Soviet ethnographer's work, I agree with Bellér-Hann (2007: 136 n.17) who points out the utility of "the ethnographic raw material".

101 For the complete story, see the appendix.

102 Raquette 1917c: 214.

103 http://www.islamicity.com/mosque/QURAN/24.htm (Last accessed: March 3, 2015).

> Finally she fell asleep. Then Safvan came by on his travels and brought her back to camp where they arrived the following morning. Tongues hungry for scandal immediately started to gossip and slander of an illegal liaison having taken place between Aischa and Safvan. In particular, the party that was not in favor of the Prophet dealt with this matter with great amusement and the Prophet himself could for a period of a whole month not come over the suspicion that also had seized him.[104]

Raquette writes that Ali was of the opinion that Aischa was guilty and points out that although the Qur'an deems her innocent, the Shiite branch still adhere to the opinion that she was guilty. The continuation of the story as told by Raquette is as follows:

> The Chiltän legend states that Safvan had only found himself victorious in his great temptation by mutilating himself in a state of great despair. Nobody found out about this until later. But people noted that he did not take a wife to wed as is the common custom among Muslims. Finally Gabriel himself came and made the Prophet aware of this situation, and as a result Safvan was duly called for and then ordered to get married. But after some time had passed Gabriel returned and reproached the Prophet for not finding Safvan a wife. Safvan was summoned once again and experienced the Prophet's wrath for not having done as he had been instructed. Now the wretched man saw no other alternative but to confess the entire truth of the matter to Allah's messenger. But the command was irrevocable and the Prophet himself chose a wife for him and also arranged a wedding. Now it miraculously happened that his wife simultaneously gave birth to forty sons so that it would be manifested how great the richness of Allah's blessings are for the one who sacrifices himself for the sake of the merciful Prophet.[105]

Yet another interesting part in Raquette's article about the mazar of Chiltän which is related to the *täzkirä* is about a tree which used to grow just outside the mazar. According to Raquette, it was commonly believed that this tree actually grew from the cane that the seven holy men had planted in the ground.[106]

But, due to the poor state of the mazar, Yaqub Beg (r.1864-77) had ordered the people to cut down the tree and use the wood to repairing the shrine. However, because of the purported powers that that the tree inherited, local protest [against the cutting down of the tree] was immense. Nevertheless, the tree was finally chopped down.

The legend tells us that everyone involved in the cutting down of the tree either died immediately or shortly afterwards. The tree was gone, but the tree-stump continued to be considered holy by the populace.[107] Also the aforementioned article 'Helgongravar i Ost-Turkestan' [Saintly Shrines in Eastern Turkestan] contains an interesting account

---

[104] Raquette 1917c: 214.

[105] *Ibid.* : 214-215.

[106] The staff which turns into a tree is a symbolism which may be observed from other parts of Xinjiang as well. For example, at the famous Mahmud Kashgari Mazar in Opal there is a sacred tree called the *Häy Häy Teräk*. The pilgrims come and make a wish and drink the water from the holy well which is situated right beneath the *Häy Häy Teräk* (*teräk* means poplar in Uyghur) since they believe that the tree and the spring waters at the shrine have beneficial health qualities. According to the story associated with the tree, Mahmud Kashgari put his cane into the ground at this spot and a tree started growing incessantly. See Osman Hajim, M. and A. Äkhmidi 2005: 94-95.

[107] Raquette 1917c: 213.

regarding some sacred trees at a shrine which should not be cut down.

> At these graves there are usually also big trees that should not be touched until they rot on their own. It is widely told that once upon a time a branch from one such tree fell off and a cry of distress was heard from the tree and blood dripped from the place where the branch had grown.[108]

Discussion

This article has presented a selected corpus of missionary texts dealing with mazars and the stories coupled with them. As mentioned earlier, a significant portion of this material has not been available in English until now.

While the articles and books provide us with important first-hand accounts on how religious life was manifested in the region almost one hundred years ago, they also give us an opportunity to see how the West looked upon non-European civilization.

As demonstrated, the missionary articles were often written in a polemic fashion which would be unacceptable today. Moreover, the obvious attempts to show the superiority of Christianity versus Islam in all aspects of life and culture reflect the colonial underpinnings of the time when they were recorded.[109]

It should however be pointed out that the missionaries 'Eurocentric' way of seeing things, was not confined to them alone, but similar views may also be observed in contemporary reports ascribed to Western explorers active in the region.[110]

In many ways the missionary material is unique. In contrast to material written by European explorers, who often stayed in the area only for a limited time, these reports were written by people who spent many years in close contact with the local people. The missionaries became well informed about daily life, customs, rituals, and popular religious practices such as mazar pilgrimage. They also learned to speak the local language[s].

The detailed and frequent descriptions of 'mazar culture' found in the Swedish missionary sources indicate the important role of shrine pilgrimage and hagiography in the region. Why would the missionaries have devoted so much time to discuss these topics if it did not constitute core elements of 'Uyghur' religious practice?

Bearing in mind the turbulent history of Central Asia in the 19th and 20th century which brought about notable changes (not least politically), I suggest that these books and articles may indeed serve as part of an important 'anthropological encyclopedia' of the region. In addition, the sources consulted are valuable for understanding Christian attitudes towards Islam, Muslims and the society of Eastern Turkestan during the early decades of the 20th century.

A small portion of missionary material dealing with mazar pilgrimage has been presented here, but there is more to discover. This article is an initial contribution.

---

108 Palmberg 1915: 378. Cf. Jarring 1979b: 16.

109 It should be pointed out that Eastern Turkestan was not under European submission. It was the Chinese who were in power. However, the texts reflect ideas reminiscent of colonial discourse. Cf. Bellér-Hann 2008: 30-31.

110 For more information on this matter, see professor Shinmen's chapter in this volume.

Bibliography

Ahlbert, G.A. 1917a. "Ordspråk" [Proverbs], in Lundahl, J. E. (ed.), *På obanade stigar: Tjugofem år i Ost-Turkestan.* Stockholm: Svenska Missionsförbundets Förlag, 97-99.

——— 1917b. "Ur folklivet" [Images from Day-to-Day Life], in Lundahl, J. E. (ed.), *På obanade stigar: Tjugofem år i Ost-Turkestan.* Stockholm: Svenska Missionsförbundets Förlag, 116-119.

——— 1917c. "Islam i Ost-Turkestan 1" [Islam in Eastern Turkestan 1.], in Lundahl, J. E. (ed.), *På obanade stigar: Tjugofem år i Ost-Turkestan.* Stockholm: Svenska Missionsförbundets Förlag, 164-170.

——— 1917d. "Islam i Ost-Turkestan 4. Islam som kulturbärare" [Islam in Eastern Turkestan 4. Islam as a Conveyer of Culture], in Lundahl, J. E. (ed.), *På obanade stigar: Tjugofem år i Ost-Turkestan.* Stockholm: Svenska Missionsförbundets Förlag, 195-200.

——— 1917e. "Vakf" [Waqf], in Lundahl, J. E. (ed.), *På obanade stigar: Tjugofem år i Ost-Turkestan.* Stockholm: Svenska Missionsförbundets Förlag, 231-235.

——— Ahlbert, G. et al. 1926. *Studieplan för muhammedanmissionärer i Ostturkestan. Antagen av Ost-turkestankonferensen 1926.* [Study Plan for Islam-missionaries in Eastern Turkestan. Adopted by the Eastern Turkestan Conference in 1926], Kaschgar: Svenska Missionstryckeriet.

——— Ahlbert, Gustaf 1934. *Habil: En kristen martyr i Östturkestan*, [Habil: a Christian Martyr in Eastern Turkestan]. Stockholm: Svenska missionsförbundet Stockholm.

——— 2009 (1934). *Habil: A Christian Martyr in Xinjiang.* Translator: Gabriel. [Original title: Habil]. Stockholm: Swedish Covenant Church Press.

Basilov, Vladimir N. 1992. "Islamic Shamanism among Central Asian Peoples" in *Diogenes*, No. 158, 1992; 40; 5, 5-18.

Bellér-Hann, Ildikó 2001. "Making the Oil Fragrant: Dealings with the Supernatural among the Uyghurs in Xinjiang", in *Asian Ethnicity* 2-1, 9-23.

——— 2007. "Situating Uyghur Life Cycle Rituals between China and Central Asia." In Bellér-Hann, Ildikó et al. (eds) 2007 *Situating the Uyghurs between China and Central Asia.* Hampshire: Ashgate Publishing Limited. 131-147.

——— 2008. *Community Matters in Xinjiang 1880-1949: Towards a Historical Anthropology of the Uyghurs.* Leiden and Boston: Brill.

Bohlin, A. 1917. "Näringar och Skråväsen" [Livelyhood and Guild systems], in Lundahl, J. E. (ed.), *På obanade stigar: Tjugofem år i Ost-Turkestan.* Stockholm: Svenska Missionsförbundets Förlag, 66-82.

Breim, E. 1942. *Helgon och Helgonliv.* [Saints and the Life of Saints]. Berlingska Boktryckeriet. Lund: C.W.K. Gleerups Förlag.

Dawut, R. 2001. *Uyghur Mazarliri* [Uyghur Mazars]. Urumqi: Shinjang Khälq Näshriyati.

——— 2007. "Shrine Pilgrimage and Sustainable Tourism among the Uyghurs: Central Asian Ritual Traditions in the Context of China's Development Policies", in Bellér-Hann, Ildikó. et al. (eds.) *Situating the Uyghurs between China and Central Asia.* Hampshire: Ashgate Publishing Limited. 149-163.

Gustafsson, David 1917a. "Vidskepelse och Vantro" [Superstition and Misbelief], in Lundahl, J. E. (ed.), *På obanade stigar: Tjugofem år i Ost-Turkestan.* Stockholm: Svenska Missionsförbundets Förlag, 224-230.

Gustavsson(*sic*), David 1917b. "Inhemsk läkareverksamhet" [Domestic Medical Activity], in Lundahl, J. E. (ed.) *På obanade stigar: Tjugofem år i Ost-Turkestan.* Stockholm: Svenska Missionsförbundets Förlag, 245-249.

——— 1917c. "Tiggare" [Beggars], in Lundahl, J. E. (ed.), *På obanade stigar: Tjugofem år i Ost-Turkestan.* Stockholm: Svenska Missionsförbundets Förlag, 250-254.

Hällzon, Patrick 2014. "Med kameran i hand: betraktelser från Svenska Missionsförbundets arbete i Östturkestan" [With the Camera in Hand: Reflections from the work of the Mission Covenant Church of Sweden in Eastern Turkestan], *Kinarapport.* No 2. 2014. 4-13.

Harris and Dawut 2002. "Mazar Festivals of the Uyghurs: Music, Islam and the Chinese State", *British Journal of Ethnomusicology* vol. 11/I: 101-118.

Harris and Muhpul 2002. *Music of the Uyghurs.* British Academy Post-Doctoral Fellow, Music Dept.

SOAS, London. Available at: www.uyghurensemble.co.uk/en-html/nf-research-article1.html (Last accessed: March 3, 2015)

Högberg, L. E. 1907a. "Ett och annat från Kinesiska Turkestan (Västra Kina)" [This and That from Chinese Turkestan (Western China)], *Illustrerade Missionsskrifter* 4.

——— 1907b. "Kaschgarernas vantro: En bild från vårt verksamhetsfält i Turkestan" [The Misbelief of the Kashgarians: an Image from our Field of Work in Turkestan], *Missionsförbundet*. 15 december. N: r 24.

——— 1913. *Jolbas: en kaschgargosses levnad, skildrad av honom själv* [Jolbas: The Life of a Kashgarian Boy, as Described by Himself], *Missionsskriftserie* 7.

——— 1917a. "Inledning" [Introduction] in Lundahl, J. E. (ed.), *På obanade stigar: Tjugofem år i Ost-Turkestan*. Stockholm: Svenska Missionsförbundets Förlag, 1-6.

——— 1917b. "Bildbart material" [Educable Material] in Lundahl, J. E. (ed.), *På obanade stigar: Tjugofem år i Ost-Turkestan*. Stockholm: Svenska Missionsförbundets Förlag, 83-90.

——— 1917c. "Ur folklivet. 1. Ett bröllop" [From the Life of the People. 1. A Wedding] in Lundahl, J. E. (ed.), *På obanade stigar: Tjugofem år i Ost-Turkestan*. Stockholm: Svenska Missionsförbundets Förlag, 109-113.

——— 1917d. "Kristus och Muhammed enligt legenden" [Christ and Muhammad According to the Legend] in Lundahl, J. E. (ed.), *På obanade stigar: Tjugofem år i Ost-Turkestan*. Stockholm: Svenska Missionsförbundets Förlag, 150-163.

——— 1925. "Islam och Evangeliet" [Islam and the Gospel]. Stockholm: Svenska Missionsförbundets Förlag.

Högberg, Sigrid 1917a. "Den Ost-Turkestanska Kvinnan" [The Eastern Turkestanian Woman], in Lundahl, J. E. (ed.), *På obanade stigar: Tjugofem år i Ost-Turkestan*. Stockholm: Svenska Missionsförbundets Förlag, 216-223.

——— 1917b. "Khaneka" [Khaniqa], in Lundahl, J. E. (ed.), *På obanade stigar: Tjugofem år i Ost-Turkestan*. Stockholm: Svenska Missionsförbundets Förlag, 451-454.

Hultvall, John 1981s. *Mission och revolution i Centralasien: Svenska Missionsförbundets mission i Östturkestan 1892-1938* [Mission and Revolution in Central Asia: The MCCS Mission Work in Eastern Turkestan 1892-1938]. Stockholm: Gummessons.

——— 1981e. *Mission and Revolution in Central Asia: The MCCS Mission Work in Eastern Turkestan 1892-1938*. A translation by Birgitta Åhman into English of the original book, *Mission och revolution i Centralasien*. Stockholm: Gummessons. Available at: http://equmeniakyrkan.se/wp-content/uploads/2013/03/Hultvall-ENG.pdf (Last accessed: March 3, 2015)

——— 1991. *Mission och vision i Orienten: Svenska Missionsförbundets mission i Transkaukasien - Persien 1882-1921* [Mission and Vision in the Orient: The MCCS Mission Work in Transcaucasia - Persia 1882-1921]. Stockholm: Verbum Förlag.

Jarring, G. 1935. "The Ordam Padisha System of Eastern Turkestan Shrines". In *Geografiska Annaler, Vol. 17, Supplement: Hyllningsskrift tillägnad Sven Hedin*, 348-354.

——— 1975. *Gustaf Raquette and Qasim Akhun's Letters to Kamil Efendi: Ethnological and Folkloristic Materials from Southern Sinkiang*. (Scripta Minora Regiae Societatis Humaniorum Litterarum Lundensis 1975/76:1) Lund: CWK Gleerup.

——— 1979a. *Åter till Kashgar*. [Return to Kashgar] Stockholm: Bonniers Grafiska Industrier.

———1979b. *Matters of Ethnological Interest in Swedish Missionary Reports from Southern Sinkiang*. (Scripta Minora Regiae Societatis Humaniorum Litterarum Lundensis 1979/80:4) Lund: CWK Gleerup.

——— 1987. *Dervish and Qalandar: Texts from Kasghar. Edited and Translated with Notes and Glossary*. (Scripta Minora Regiae Societatis Humaniorum Litterarum Lundensis 1985/86:2) Stockholm: Almqvist & Wiksell International.

——— 1991. *Prints from Kashghar: The Printing-office of the Swedish Mission in Eastern Turkestan History and Production with an Attempt at a Bibliography*. Swedish Research Institute in Istanbul, Transactions. Vol. 3. Stockholm: Almqvist & Wiksell International.

Khalid, Adeeb. 1998 *The Politics of Muslim Cultural Reform: Jadidism in Central Asia*. Berkeley: University of California Press.

Koranen [The Qur'an], K.V Zetterstén's unabridged translation into Swedish in 1917 (reprinted in 1996).

Laude-Cirtautas, Ilse. 1980 *Chrestomathy of Modern Literary Uzbek*. Wiesbaden: Harrassowitz.

Lundahl, J. E. (ed.) 1917. *På Obanade Stigar: Tjugofem år i Östturkestan* [On Untrodden Paths: Twenty-five Years in Eastern Turkestan]. Stockholm: Svenska Missionsförbundets förlag.

Mernissi, F. 1989. "Women, Saints and Sanctuaries in Morocco", in Falk, Nancy Auer and Rita M. Gross (eds.), *Unspoken Worlds: Women's Religious Lives*. Belmon: Wadsworth, Inc, 112-121.

Morinis, Alan 1992. "Introduction" *in* Morinis, Alan (ed), *Sacred Journeys: The Anthropology of Pilgrimage*. Westport, Connecticut, London: Greenwood Press, 1-28.

Nyström, G. R. 1917. "Basarbesök" [Visits to Bazaars] in Lundahl, J. E. (ed.), *På obanade stigar: Tjugofem år i Ost-Turkestan*. Stockholm: Svenska Missionsförbundets Förlag, 434-442.

Olsson, Johan 2010. *Smuts och andligt förfall - Svenska Missionsförbundets Kina kring sekelskiftet 1900* [Dirt and Spiritual Decay: The Mission Covenant Church of Sweden's China at the Turn of the Century 1900], MA-thesis, Södertörn University. Available at: http://sh.diva-portal.org/smash/get/diva2:325192/FULLTEXT01.pdf (Last accessed: March 3, 2015)

Orkhun, Abliz and Sugawara Jun (eds) 2007. *Mazar Documents from Xinjiang and Ferghana (Facsimile) 2. (Studia Culturae Islamicae No 87)*. Tokyo: Research Institute for Languages and Cultures of Asia and Africa, Tokyo University of Foreign Studies.

Osman Hajim, M. and Äkhmidi, A. 2005. *Mähmud Qashgari Häqqidä Hekayätlär* [Stories about Mahmud Kashgari]. Qäshqär: Qäshqär Uyghur Näshriyäti.

Östberg, Wilhelm 2002. *När Afrika kom oss nära: Missionen och den svenska Afrikabilden.* [When Africa Came Close to us: The Mission and the Swedish View on Africa]. *Kulturperspektiv* 13. Skriftserie utgiven av Etnografiska Museet.

Palmberg, Gottfrid. 1915 "Helgongravar i Ost-Turkestan" [Saintly Shrines in Eastern Turkestan], *Missionsförbundet*, 377-379.

——— 1917. "Islam i Ost-Turkestan 3. Islam på Närmare Håll" [Islam in Eastern Turkestan 3: Islam Up Close], in Lundahl, J. E. (ed.), *På obanade stigar: Tjugofem år i Ost-Turkestan*. Stockholm: Svenska Missionsförbundets Förlag, 177-194.

Palmaer., G. (ed) 1942. *En ny port öppnas: från Svenska Missionsförbundets arbete i Östturkestan åren 1892-1938 och Indien åren 1940-1942* [A New Gate is Opened: Reports from the MCCS Mission Work in Eastern Turkestan During the Years 1892-1938 and India in 1940-1942]. Stockholm: Svenska Missionsförbundets Förlag.

Peters, Rudolph. 2010 (Original 2005). "Revivalist Movements in Islam from the Eighteenth to the Twentieth Century and the Role of Islam in Modern History: Anticolonialism and Nationalism", in Ende, Werner and Udo Steinbach (eds), *Islam in the World Today: A Handbook of Politics, Religion, Culture and Society*. Ithaca and London: Cornell University Press, 70-104.

Preston, James J. 1992. "Spiritual Magnetism: An Organizing Principle for the Study of Pilgrimage", in Morinis, Alan (ed.), *Sacred Journeys: The Anthropology of Pilgrimage*. Westport, Connecticut, London: Greenwood Press, 31-46.

Raquette, G. 1917a. "Ost-Turkestans Historia" [The History of Eastern Turkestan], in Lundahl, J. E. (ed.), *På obanade stigar: Tjugofem år i Ost-Turkestan*. Stockholm: Svenska Missionsförbundets Förlag, 43-65.

——— 1917b. "Ost-Turkiska Språket" [Eastern Turki, the language], in Lundahl, J. E. (ed.), *På obanade stigar: Tjugofem år i Ost-Turkestan*. Stockholm: Svenska Missionsförbundets Förlag, 127-137.

——— 1917c. "'Tjiltän': Historien om en helgongrav" [Chiltän: The Story of a Saintly Shrine], in Lundahl, J. E. (ed.). *På obanade stigar: Tjugofem år i Ost-Turkestan*. Stockholm: Svenska Missionsförbundets Förlag, 201-215.

Renard, J. 2008 *Friends of God: Islamic Images of Piety, Commitment, and Servanthood.* Berkeley, Los Angeles, London: University of California Press.
Said, Edward W. 1978. (reprint in Swedish 1997) *Orientalism.* Stockholm: Ordfronts Förlag.
Sayrami, Molla Musa. 2007 *Tarikhi hämidi.* Beyjing; Millätlär Näshriyati.
Svärd, Lydia. 1979. *Förbundskyrkan i Indien* [The Covenant Church in India]. Stockholm: Gummesson.
The Quran. Surah 24 verse 6, http://www.islamicity.com/mosque/QURAN/24.htm (Last accessed: March 3, 2015)
Törnquist, John. 1926. *Kaschgar: några bilder från innersta Asiens land, folk och mission.* [Kashgar: Some Images from Inner Asia's Countries, Peoples and Mission]. Stockholm: Svenska Missionsförbundet.
Wei, C. and Luckert, K. 1998. *Uighur Stories From Along The Silk Road.* Lanham. New York. Oxford: University Press of America.

Appendix

This wonderful story was recorded by the missionary doctor Gustaf Raquette in the book 'På Obanade Stigar' (1917). Raquette did not specify when the story was written or who the author of the story was and thus we can only speculate in this matter. However, the story is fascinating in a number of ways. Primarily because it is a good story of course, but it is also interesting since it is so multifaceted and detailed. For hundreds of millions of Muslims around the world the stories about the "friends of God"[111] *have not ceased to fascinate people. These holy figures stand as exceptional moral examples for ordinary people in their day-to-day life. However, many of the stories- both written and oral- that circulate in people's collective memory not only serve as giving moral guidance, but also to locate their town or village within the larger Muslim community.*
A good example is the story of Chiltän where a combination of local, regional and universal Muslim geographical settings and characters serve to place this story about a rather 'local' shrine into a wider universal Muslim framework. Thus while acknowledging its specific Central Asian location in Yarkand the shrine is described as an integral part within a sacred universal Muslim geography which includes for instance the Prophet's tomb at Medina . I would therefore like to argue that this story reflects local Islamic tradition but also displays continuity with mainstream universal Islamic hagiographical tradition in a very harmonious way.

Gustaf Raquette: *The Täzkir (sic) of Chiltän*

One day when the Prophet was sitting in the Holy Mosque, Salman Fares appeared before him in a crying state of mind and presented his desire:

"I am forty years old, and yet I have no children. I wish to see the face of my heir. Oh Prophet of Allah, I have prepared a sacrificial meal in my home. If his Holiness would be so kind to enter my home and pray for me, it would not be anything extraordinary if Allah would send me a successor because of a prayer like that."

Upon hearing this, the Prophet gathered thirty-nine companions and set off to Salman Fares' house where the forty men were offered the sacrificial meal. After having eaten, the Prophet prayed that Salman Fares would be granted an offspring, and all of the Prophet's companions said amen.

When exactly nine months, nine days and nine hours had come to an end, Salman Fares' wife gave birth to forty sons during a time period of three days. With the whole house filled with the cries of the forty babies, there was not even room enough for Salman Fares to set down his foot. Seeing the forty children made his mind stand still, and he thought to himself: "When I asked Allah

[111] Cf. Renard (2008).

for children, he has answered my prayers by giving me forty nuisances. If each one of them, but eats one loaf of bread a day, it will still be forty loaves of bread. Moreover, if they need clothes, it will be necessary to provide forty coats each time."

Pondering this way, he secretly named each one of them, but he regretted having asked Allah for an heir, and also felt ashamed for the people of Medina. After having kept the children hidden at home for three days and three nights, he decided one night to place thirty-nine of them in a large basket with a lid on top, proceeded to the desert on the outskirts of Medina where there were no people in sight, and left the children as well as the basket there. But as he returned home at dawn, he discovered that also the child that he had kept at home had disappeared. The child had escaped from him and had followed his thirty-nine brothers.

Salman Fares was ignorant of these children's highness, sanctity and position in regard to all important saints and was also unaware of their sacred value. Because of this, he from now on also became the laughing stock of the people of Medina. He could not show his face in the street, but was forced to hide in his home.

Then it so happened that the angel Gabriel appeared to the Prophet saying: "Ta Ha[112], Oh Muhammad, Allah greets you: 'Because of the prayer of my friend Muhammad and his thirty-nine companions, I gave forty high saints and godly people to Salman Fares through the absolute power invested in me. But he did not understand their true value. Instead he put them in a basket which he cast into the desert. But while Salman Fares rejects them, I do not. I am the God and owner of the Holy and the holy saints.'"

The Prophet then went with his companions into the desert, where they found the basket, now transformed into a green emerald dome, which had been elevated to the fourth heaven. From within of this dome there was a sounding as of prayer and crying, and a sparkling light emanated from it, embracing the throne of God. The dome hovered freely in space with nothing holding it from above and with no columns from beneath to support it.

The blessed heart of the Prophet became restless and tears came to his sacred eyes. In this state of mind, he returned to the holy mosque. He never again looked to Salman Fares and Salman Fares could never again show himself in public because of his shame and disgrace.

One day when the Prophet sat in the mosque in Medina a man by the name S'äd Maáz (< S'âd Maâz) appeared. The Prophet, who had noted the man's complexion had shifted color due to fright, asked him what was wrong. S'äd Maáz answered him: "Oh, messenger of Allah, upon returning from performing my prayers, I saw how an animal came and rested in the tree which you usually sit and rest against, and how this tree suddenly dried up and how its leaves fell off. When I saw this I was struck by horror and fled to you."

Upon hearing this the Prophet set off with a number of his companions to the tree in question and found that it to be the way S'äd Maáz had described.

The Prophet turned to the animal in the tree and asked: "Oh, animal, what kind of creature art thou?" The animal answered in his own language: "Oh, Prophet of Allah, I am the torment of the mighty God. According to Allah's commandment I have come to harm the people of Medina."

After having said this, the animal disappeared over Medina. When the people of Medina saw this, they wept and fell down at the Prophet's feet; calling and pleading: "Oh messenger of Allah! Would it not be good if you said a prayer so we might find salvation from this plague?"

At that very moment it was reported that the holy Fatima[113] suddenly had fallen ill. When the Prophet and his companions came to her, they found her in a dreadful state on the verge of death.

Just as the Prophet was going to start praying, the angel Gabriel appeared to him saying: "Ta ha! O, Muhammad! Your God greets you saying: 'tell me my dearest Muhammad: Will a knife cut its own shaft? In the fourth heaven there are forty men of God. Go to them and invite them so that they may come and pray. By so doing this plague will disappear.'"

---

112 According to Raquette (1917c: 206): "Ta Ha is the name of the Qur'an's 20th chapter. The expression commonly refers to the title or name of Muhammad".

113 Raquette (1917c: 207) writes: "The Prophet's daughter".

The Prophet set off alone to the fourth heaven, where he found an arched dome without a door or opening. Thanks to his knocking, the wall eventually collapsed and he saw forty men engaged in prayer. They were so united in each other so that when the Prophet pierced the finger belonging to one of them with a needle, blood began to pour from everyone's fingers. Out of those forty men, seven kept the Prophet company back to earth where they were instructed to cure his daughter through prayer, while the Prophet himself would say Amen.

They placed themselves in a circle around Fatima and prayed all night so that the whole of Medina was terrified. But Fatima recovered and the plague disappeared from the city.

The seven men now asked for permission to return to their place and their brothers in the fourth heaven. But the Prophet answered them saying: "Oh dervishes, permission will not be granted for this. Allah has replaced you with others. You will have to stay here on earth so that wherever you come across the ill, the weak and the miserable you may pray for their quick recovery, and that every place you might come to may turn green and life may be given to them who are afflicted by calamity and death."

For as long as the Prophet lived, these men roamed the earth. After the Prophet's death, they went to the Caliph Ali and prayed for liberation, asking him: "Where should we be?"

Ali answered them: "I am not the one who has the authority to set you free. Go to the Prophet and pray for your redemption."

Having received this answer they went to sit down by the Prophet's mortal remains. The Prophet gave them a staff saying: "Take this staff, roam the earth, and plant the staff into the ground every evening. And where it turns green, you shall settle down to live."

After a long walk through many countries they finally reached the land Tatar.[114] Here they placed their staff into the ground as they had gotten used to, and the following morning they discovered that it had turned green and taken root. And they decided to stay there. But in those days the people of Tatar were infidels and when they saw the seven men's worship of God they would not approach them at close hand but said: "These are Mohammedans."

When some of these people nevertheless came to mock them, they were punished by throwing up blood or tormented by some other infliction. After the death of these Holy men, people knew no more about them than that there had been seven Mohammedans living there for some years, but now they were dead and buried.

Thus, several centuries passed by up to the days of king Aba Bekr (< Abu Bakr) of Yarkand. At this time there was a divanä (mendicant) by the name of Schah Talib Särmäst who lived in Bokhara (< Bukhara). Together with his forty disciples he set off on a long walk to holy places, and thereby also arrived to the city of Medina. Schah Talib Särmäst stayed at the Prophet's grave for a period of forty days. After completing this period, he asked the Prophet for permission to withdraw. At that very moment, the Prophet appeared to him face to face. Schah Talib then approached him with his 40 companions and greeted him saying: "Oh king of the world, may God be praised because the honor of seeing your blessed beauty has been brought upon me!"

While all of them thus stood assembled in awe in the presence of his Holiness the Prophet, he said: "Well, dear Schah Talib, you have come at a good time. I have a word to entrust you. Undoubtedly you shall keep this word of mine. In the land of Tatar there are seven of our faithful. They belong to the forty. By calls of prayer we brought them down to earth, but after roaming the earth for the blessing of humanity, they now lay in the ground without name or sign. Tatar is now a Muslim land but no one knows about these seven. You shall now go there and build a memorial place and tell the people that they can make pilgrimages to the site and that by praying to Allah at this place, they will be delivered from disease and find relief from misery." Having said this, he told Schah Talib to leave.

Schah Talib immediately set off on a journey to Yarkand, where he together with his forty

---

[114] Raquette (1917c: 208) points out that: "The Jarkend (< Yarkand) area's older name is said to have been Tatar. It is said however, that the ancient city, which bore this name, was buried under the sands of the Taklamakan through the judgment of God".

companions stayed at this holy grave. There, they constructed an arched cupola over the heads of the holy men.

After completing this, the mendicants spent a period of forty days on the site. Their calls to prayer were heard all over the land so that everyone, high and low, old and young came to see.

After this, people started to bring sacrificial gifts and presents, and some came to believe. Finally also Aba Bekr became aware of these events. When he learned that people brought gifts to the grave in faith and worship, he meditated upon this very carefully, and concluded: "This has to be investigated thoroughly." Then he ordered that a cat should be fried and wrapped together with nine pieces of bread in a cloth, and then sent to this holy place. He said: "If they are real men of God they will not eat and otherwise they will. From this we will find out." And he ordered that it should be presented to the dervishes.

Schah Talib turned to Aba Bekr's messengers and said: "Oh, messengers, is your king in the habit of eating these kinds of things?" And look! At the same time as he reached his hand towards the tray, an angrily meowing black cat fled from it. Upon seeing this, the king's messengers fell down at Schah Talib's feet and prayed for forgiveness. They returned to Aba Bekr and told him what had happened. But Schah Talib became furious over how Aba Bekr had behaved and immediately set of with his companions to Andijan. But one in the party fell ill on the journey and the others left him behind saying: "You stay here as a reader of prayers."

Meanwhile, Aba Bekr sent two of his civil servants with rich gifts to Schah Talib. On their journey they came across a prayer cell by the roadside where a dervish lay. They asked him: "who are you and where have the others gone?"

The king's men were now carefully informed by the dervish of how the Bukharian, Schah Talib Särmäst had received the Prophet's command when he was in Medina, to go to the land of Tatar and construct the Tomb of the Seven, but that he had found himself forced to return to his native country due to the king's behavior. The messengers returned to their king and told him everything that they had heard. Mirza Aba Bekr now became utterly repentant and provided new messengers with bountiful gifts saying: "Go over yonder and wherever you may find him, present him with my gifts, pray for my forgiveness and bring him back here again."

They soon caught up with Schah Talib and his party at Schah Naz.[115] Here they asked for forgiveness for their king's sin and presented one gift after another. But despite their pleas for him to return, he would not concede to do this on any condition. Finally Schah Talib prayed a prayer that Yarkand never should come to an end and that the faith there stay pure and true, and then he encouraged the messengers to return home. These returned in hopelessness and told the king what had happened.

The dervish that had been left behind was appointed guardian of the holy place and the king honored the site by visiting himself. And his heart became soft and he found mercy, and he signed the documents, for a whole donation of land for the holy place. After this the king ordered that a huge pot was to be placed at the site. If someone was afflicted by sickness or distress he would place his sacrifice in this cooking pot to ease his burdens. And that is how it shall be to the day of resurrection.

The names of the high saints were Muhammad Fazil, Muhammad Ibrahim, Muhammad Kasim, Muhammad Razi, Muhammad S'aid, Muhammad Zahid, and Muhammad Sabit.

---

[115] Raquette (1917c: 212) writes: "The area around the village of Kizil, located a two days' journey north of Jarkend, is still today known as Shah Naz".

*Häzret Afaq. Photographer: missionary John Törnquist.**

Pilgrims on their way to Odäm>Ordam Padisha.
*Photographer unknown (possibly John Törnquist).**

*Unidentified mazar. Photographer: John Törnquist.**

*The lantern slide collection of the Mission Covenant Church of Sweden
(Svenska Missionsförbundet)
at The Museum of Ethnography, Stockholm.

Chapter Five

VOICES OF TADHKIRA

The Tale of Jānbāz Khoja

Pilgrimage and Holy War in a 19th-Century Tadhkira from Xinjiang

Devin DeWeese

The religious topography of Xinjiang may be said to be defined, in the Islamic period, by saints' shrines; while ethnographic study of these sites is invaluable for exploring their current roles and contemporary understandings of the region's history,[1] and especially religious history, there is still much to do in terms of studying the textual sources on the mazars of this region. Many such sources are relatively well known, including, in roughly chronological order, the travel account of Timur's embassy included in the work of Ḥāfiẓ-i Abrū, the invaluable account of holy sites in the *Tārīkh-i Rashīdī*, scattered references to various sites in the Naqshbandī hagiographies produced by the Isḥāqī and Āfāqī *khoja* lineages, and the extensive discussion of shrines in the region found in Mullā Mūsā Sayrāmī's *Tārīkh-i amanīya*. There are several less well-known works, however, with rich information on shrines.

These include, especially, little-studied hagiographical works such as the *Tadhkira*[2] of Zayn al-Dīn Qāghrāqī, a detailed hagiography of a saint of Üstün Artūch known popularly as "Ḥaḍrat-i Mullām" or "Khoja Mullām,"[3] or the *Tadhkira* of Abū Sa'īd Qūchqār Ata, which refers to the "900,000 saints, the twelve *imāms*, and the slaughtered *imāms*" (*imām-i zabīḥa-lar* [*sic*]), who lie buried in the region (with the first group, presumably, divided later into two groups, the 300,000 martyrs (*üch yüz ming shahīd-i jānbāz*) and 600,000 "soldiers of Islām" (*alta yüz ming lashkar-i islām*);[4] the work pays

[1] On shrines of the region, see the studies of Dawut 2001; Hartmann 1903; Pantusov 1909; Pantusov 1910; Trippner 1961; Hamada 1978; Hamada 2001; Gürsoy-Naskali 1985; Comneno 1993; Zarcone 1999; Zarcone 2001; Sawada 2001b; Shinmen 2003.

[2] I will adopt the 'standard' transcription, "*tadhkira*" (despite the pronunciation "*tazkira*"), for the term that is in fact more often written, in manuscripts from Eastern Turkistān, as "*tazkīra*" or "*tadhkīra*".

[3] This work, known from manuscripts preserved in Tashkent and St. Petersburg, pays considerable attention to *waqf* lands established to support the saint's shrine during the 15th century (judging from the location of the shrine of this Zayn al-Dīn, of which the popular names reflect a generic appellation, it would appear to be unrelated to the shrine of "Ḥaḍrat-i Mullām," now known as that of Maḥmūd Kāshgharī, discussed in Sugawara Jun's contribution to this volume). The hagiography also refers incidentally to other shrines, including mention of a tree that grew from the saint's staff, noting that people call it "Mazar Terek" ("shrine-tree") and regard it as a pilgrimage place" (*qadam-jāy*).

[4] MS St. Petersburg, Institute of Oriental Studies, C561 (described in Muginov 1962: 78, No. 107),

special attention to shrines of Khotan, including that of Imām Ja'far Ṭayrān, those of four saints who divided the city, in effect into directional quarters,[5] and that of Abū Sa'īd Qūchqār Ata himself.[6] Also of importance in this regard is the hagiographical work produced by the Katakī *khojas* of Kūchā, descendants of two famous Islamizing saints (Jamāl al-Dīn and Arshad al-Dīn), in which shrines of the region are discussed in connection with the story of the ancestral saints' role in the conversion of Tughluq Timur Khān.[7]

The present study will focus on another such text, preserved in an apparently unique manuscript produced late in the 19th century; the work, in Turkic, assigned the title *Tadhkira-yi Jānbāz Khojam*, is in fact not a hagiographical text like those mentioned above, focused on an individual saint who may be situated, at least plausibly, in a 'historical' context.[8] Rather, it combines a "shrine catalogue," in effect, that lists

---

ff. 21b-22a.

[5] I.e., Chūgh-lūq Ata in the North, Lāchīn Ata in the West, Majīd Ata in the South, and Yïlanchï Ata in the East (MS St. Petersburg, C561, ff. 18a-19a).

[6] It held special appeal, we are told, for the needs of "immature girls" (*nā-rasīda qïzlar*), and the site featured black fruits (evidently from a tree growing near the head of the grave) that would cure illnesses of the eyes and neck; it would thus be called the "Girls' Place" (*köz va boghuz aghrïghï-gha bashlarïda méva-yi siyāh bā'ith-i shifā-lïq-dur, va qïzlar jāyïgha ol-sabab-din atarlar*; MS St. Petersburg, C561, f. 25b).

[7] *Tadhkira-yi Mawlānā 'Arsh al-Dīn Valī*, MS St. Petersburg, C556, ff. 22b-24b; MS St. Petersburg, B736, ff. 15b-16b. Just prior to Arshad al-Dīn's journey to convert Tughluq Timur Khān, we are told, the saint was visited, while in contemplation, by the Prophet, the four Rightly-Guided Caliphs, and a host of other hallowed figures; they include various *imāms* and descendants of the Prophet and 'Alī, some Companions of the Prophet noted for the spread of Islam, several Islamizing figures from among the "Bughrā-khānid" ruler-saints, and a number of other saints linked with prominent Sufi traditions or with shrines, above all shrines in Eastern Turkistan (from one direction appear Ḥasan, Ḥusayn, Muḥammad-i Ḥanafīya, Baṭṭāl Ghāzī, Amīr Muṣayyab Ghāzī, "Abā Muslim," and Pahlavān Aḥmad Zamjī; from another direction appear Satūq Bughrā Khān, Yūsuf Qādir Khān, Sulṭān Qarāstān [*sic*], and 'Alī Arslān; from another direction appear Amīr Kulāl, Bahā' al-Dīn Naqshband, Burhān al-Dīn Qïlïch, the latter's descendant, called here "Khūja Abū Ḥafḍ-i Kabīr," and the twelve *imāms*; and from another direction appear Shaykh Niẓām al-Dīn Dihlavī, Ṣaḥāba-yi Jānbāz, Sulṭān Ālf Ata, "Sulṭān Sarīr Thaqatī," and "Sulṭān Khūja Aḥmad Yasavī"). More to the point, the Prophet instructs Arshad al-Dīn that, after his work of conversion is accomplished, he and his companions should dwell in Kūsan (Kūchā), inasmuch as the Prophet had granted the offerings (*niyāz*) from this region to Arshad al-Dīn, as well as to "Ṣaḥāba-yi Jānbāz and Shaykh Niẓām al-Dīn"; the Prophet further affirmed that he had given the offerings of Ṭūrfān to Sulṭān Ālf Ata; of "Ardavīl" (Aqsū) to Arshad al-Dīn and Imām Baṭṭāl Ghāzī; of Kāshghar to Sulṭān Satūq Bughrā Khān, Yūsuf Qādir Khān, and other Bughrā-khānids; of "Tārtār" to "the Seven Muḥammads" (*haft muḥammadān*); and of Mawarannahr to Amīr Kulāl, Bahā' al-Dīn Naqshband, Makhdūm-i A'ẓam, Burhān al-Dīn Qïlïch, and "Abū Ḥafḍ-i Kabīr" (i.e., Abū Ḥafṣ-i Kabīr, the famous Ḥanafī jurist of Bukhārā, cast in this work as an ancestor of Jamāl al-Dīn and Arshad al-Dīn). With the exception of the final group of saints, linked with Mawarannahr, the litany of names found here refers in nearly every case to prominent shrines of Eastern Turkistan, and the passage as a whole, beyond simply invoking various saints' prestige in sanctioning Arshad al-Dīn, amounts to a distribution of territories and their inhabitants among these shrines, with each shrine entitled to the offerings of the people of the designated regions.

[8] The text is, in addition, only incidentally linked with Sufism; several Sufi saints from outside the

27 holy places (most, evidently, in the vicinity of Kāshghar and Yārkand), with a narrative of Islamization and holy war linked to one of the saints featured prominently in the shrine catalogue, a Companion of the Prophet known as Ṣaḥāba Jānbāz Khoja[9] (assigned the additional appellation "'*alam-dār*," i.e., a "standard-bearer" in wars for the faith).

The apparently unique copy of this work is preserved in St. Petersburg, in the Institute of Oriental Studies (MS B731) and was catalogued by Muginov in 1962,[10] but so far as I know it has not attracted significant further study; aside from the catalogue description, I have traced only three brief references to the work, with no actual discussion of its contents in any instance (the date it gives for a 16th-century military campaign was noted briefly by V. P. Iudin and O. F. Akimushkin, while the late 19th-century date given in its colophon was mentioned by Hamada Masami [see below]). The description in Muginov's catalogue is itself quite brief and unhelpful: it assigns the work the title *Tadhkira-i Jānbāz Khojam*, characterizing it as an account of the life and martyrdom of Jānbāz Khojam, known also as Ṣaḥāba Jānbāz 'Alamdār Khoja (with no further particulars offered with regard to this figure's identity), and then notes that the anonymous work has "a long introduction in which are enumerated various graves and their visitation by pilgrims in 944/1537-38" (with no explanation of where or in what context this date appears in the work). The description incorrectly gives the folios on which the work appears,[11] and Muginov's account of the manuscript's date and copyist is also disappointing: it fails to give all the data included in the manuscript itself, inconsistent as it may be, regarding the date on which it was completed, in 1308/1891,[12]

---

region are mentioned along with those with local shrines, but the text cannot be clearly linked with any specific Sufi lineage or tradition.

[9] I use the form "*khoja*" here (except in direct quotations from the text) as a compromise between the 'correct' orthographic form (*khwāja*) and the spelling typically used in the manuscript itself (*khūja*), which indeed reflects the pronunciation "*khoja*."

[10] Muginov 1962: 69, No. 87, MS B731, ff. 119a-136a (see below). In the same catalogue (p. 140, No. 250) is described the first section of this manuscript (ff. 1b-37a), a fragmentary copy of an anonymous Turkic "*Sharḥ-i gulshan*," no doubt a commentary on the *Gulshan-i rāz* of Shabistarī (though Muginov does not mention this or offer further identification); this manuscript includes only the first two chapters (out of 22) of the full work. See also the brief description of MS B731 in Dmitrieva 2000: 222-223, No. 818, from which it appears that ff. 40b-118a comprise a copy of the Bughrā-khānid *ghazavāt-nāma* (on which see DeWeese 1995, and Rian Thum's contribution to the present volume).

[11] Muginov's catalogue erroneously says that the work appears on folios 113a-136a; the work actually occupies ff. 119a-136a (the correct folio range is given in Dmitrieva 2002), and, as we will see, it comprises two quite distinct sections, one on ff. 119a-125a and the other on ff. 125a-136a.

[12] The catalogue says only that it was copied in 1308/1890-91. The colophon at the end of the first section says that "this book was completed on Wednesday" (*īn kitāb rūzī chahārshanba tamām bolghan*, f. 125a); the colophon at the end of the second section (ff. 135b-136a) is more specific, however, affirming that it was completed on Wednesday, 6 Ramaḍān 1308, a Dog Year (*tārīkh-qa ming üch* /f. 136a/ *yüz sekiz īṭ yïlï māh-i ramaḍān-nïng alta-sï chahārshanba küni tamām bolghan īn tadhkīr-i ṣaḥāba jānbāz 'alamdār khūjām dérlär*). This corresponds to 15 April 1891, indeed a Wednesday; by the standard correspondence, this was not a Dog Year (on the discrepancies in the 12-year animal-cycle calendar as used in Eastern Turkistan, see most recently Hamada 1992 (287,

and offers a clearly unsatisfactory reading of the name of the copyist, who was evidently a native of Yangiḥiṣār.[13]

It is unfortunately impossible to judge when the text itself may have been written; it may have been compiled, on the basis of other works now lost, shortly before the time the unique manuscript was copied, in the late 19th century, or it may reflect an older textual tradition, going back, conceivably, as far as the 16th century, the period reflected in the part of the work of greatest interest to us. As we will see, parts of the work bear close parallels to a section from another Turkic *tadhkira* that also purports to reflect the 16th century, but was probably written somewhat later, perhaps as late as the mid-18th century. What is safe to say is that the work's compiler was clearly familiar with a wide range of shrine traditions, and probably with some other literary *tadhkiras* as well.

Insofar as the beginning of the text in effect places the work's subject, Jānbāz Khoja, on a par with Satūq Bughrā Khān, the celebrated Islamizing ruler-saint of the 10th-century Qarākhānid state, we might further argue that the text was intended to elevate the status of the shrine of Jānbāz Khoja to that of the famous shrine of Satūq near Kāshghar; however, the subsequent shrine catalogue, which appears in the form of an itinerary of shrine visits projected into the 16th century, allocates Jānbāz Khoja a special place among the saints visited, but hardly elevates him above all others, suggesting that the compiler, while perhaps indeed devoted to the shrine of Jānbāz Khoja, was not an 'interested' partisan of the shrine, but was instead simply intent upon recording what he could find about this saint's reputation and linking it with other holy sites of the region. What he produced, at any rate, was a quite strange work, and the sections we will consider below include some thoroughly enigmatic passages (their obscurity is often exacerbated by the low level of literacy evident in the manuscript).

As noted, the manuscript actually contains two distinct but related sections that differ considerably in content. The shrine catalogue appears first (ff. 119a-125a, or 13 pages in all), and though it alludes, in connection with one of the shrines, to the

---

No. 23 for the date given in this specific manuscript). It is likely that the first section was completed on the same Wednesday, and that the entire text was copied in 1308/1891.

[13] Muginov gives the Arabic-script version of the copyist's name as it appears at the end of the second section, and then simply transcribes it into Cyrillic; he read the name as "Ibn Yangiḥiṣār Livār-dīn ibn mullā Qurbān khalifat mullā Ibrāhīm Yangiḥiṣārī," without mentioning the earlier colophon at the end of the first section of the work, and without commenting on the problems his name presents. The copyist's two references to himself are indeed difficult to interpret. In the first case he appears to refer to himself as "the poor wretch Nūr al-Dīn [son of] Mullā Qurbān *khalfat* of Ūshtkir Street" (though the text actually reads, "*faqīr al-ḥaqīr-i bī-chāra l.wār.dīn* [?] *ūsh.t.k.r kūcha-sidin mullā qurbān khalfat* [f. 125a]; the strange graph read as "*l.wār*" appears to reflect the incorrect spelling of a long "*ū*" as "*wāw-alif*," as in some Arabic verbal forms, but this is far from certain). In the second colophon he writes, "the poor wretch, [known as] Ibn Yanghịṣār[ī], [namely] Nūr al-Dīn [?] the son of Mullā Qurbān, the lieutenant (*khalfat*) of Mullā Ibrāhīm Yanghịṣārī" (with the text reading, "*faqīr al-ḥaqīr ibn yanghịṣār l.wār.dīn* [?] *ibn mullā qurbān khalfat-i* [?] *mullā ibrāhīm yanghịṣārī*" [f. 136a]). Both readings are fraught with uncertainties and must be regarded as conjectural. Dmitrieva 2002: 223 identifies the copyist of MS B731 simply as Mullā Ibrāhīm Yangīḥiṣārī.

story of Jānbāz Khoja, the actual account of this figure's life occupies the second, longer portion of the text (ff. 125a-136a, approximately 22 pages), and is marked by a separate *bismillāh* and a separate colophon. Both sections were copied by the same person, as noted, and it seems clear that the second part was added as an explanation, in effect, of the high stature accorded Jānbāz Khoja in the first section (where he is praised by the Prophet himself).

The longer second section is worth reviewing here, before turning to the shrine catalogue that is our primary focus. The second section bears no title or heading, but turns at once, after praise of God and the Prophet, to an account of Jānbāz Khoja, who is immediately identified as an Islamizing saint, "the eraser of the rule of unbelief and rebellion, and the developer of the law of the last age" (*māḥī-yi amāratī* [*sic*] *kufr va ṭughyān, ravāj bergüchi-yi sharī'at-i ākhir-zamān* [f. 125b]). The account may be divided into three parts. In the first (ff. 125b-129a), we learn how Jānbāz Khoja came to join the Prophet and become a Muslim; the account refers to him here as "Muḥammad Khoja Jānbāz Khoja" or the like, but there is never any explanation, in either section of the manuscript, of the name "Jānbāz," which we may nevertheless assume is derived from his reputation as a valiant fighter in wars for the faith, and from his willingness to sacrifice his life in these struggles.

Jānbāz Khoja was a native, we are told, of the city of Vanj. This would appear to link him with the town, now called Vanch, in the lower reaches of the river bearing the same name, a right tributary of the Panj (i.e., the upper Amu Darya), in present-day Tajikistan; but to judge from a passage later in the account, on the saint's struggle for the faith in his native region, the geography of this area is only dimly reflected in the narrative, and it seems that Vanj was imagined to lie somewhere between Samarqand and Penjikent, or in the mountains along the Zarafshān valley (at the end of the story, moreover, the entire setting for the saint's struggles is transposed to western Xinjiang). According to the account, Jānbāz was summoned one day by his father, who asked why he brought back no game to the family; he explained that he was simply unlucky, and that when he set traps, no game fell into his snares, but in fact the real reason was his innate kindness toward animals: when he would go out hunting, he would treat kindly every creature that fell into his snares or his hands, because he would always think to himself that each one had a father, a mother, or a child who would suffer if the creature under his control should not return. This habit was counted as strange by his brothers, however, who prided themselves on their hunting skills, and who resented the fact that Jānbāz brought no game back; his habit was taken by them, for reasons that are not explained, as evidence that their brother would be likely to enter the religion of a man who, as they had heard, had recently appeared in Mecca, claiming to be a prophet through sorcery (*siḥrī jādū bilān payghāmbarlik da'vāsï qïlïb*) and attracting many ignorant people to himself. They told their father of their concerns, and described their brother's habit in more depth. Each day as Jānbāz went out to hunt, they said, a creature would come out of the sky and rub its head on his feet; he would pet the creature's back. Likewise, deer would come down from 'Twin Mountain' (*Ikiz Tagh,* evidently a proper name, as suggested below, and not merely "a high mountain" [*égiz tagh*]) and rub their faces and eyes on his feet; Jānbāz would stroke their foreheads (*manglaylari*) and let them go. The father was disturbed by this and gathered all his kinsmen together; they resolved that Jānbāz should be destroyed, for if they did not take this step, "he will destroy our religion" (ff. 126b-127a). They thus agreed to send him out to hunt, and to have someone follow him, kill him, and burn his body.

His mother and younger sister, however, did not agree with this plan, and his sister was instrumental in protecting him and warning him of the plot against him; God protected him as well, ensuring that his kinsmen were kept busy and thereby delaying their plan. Jānbāz, meanwhile, resolved to go to Mecca and to find this new prophet; if his religion was true, he told his sister, then this prophet would protect him from the plot of "these infidels" (f. 127a). When he wondered what sort of gift to take the Prophet, his sister suggested that nothing was purer or sweeter than water; they thus filled a bottle (*kūza-chāq*) with spring water, and he took it with him as he set off to find the Prophet (f. 127b). His kinsmen, at last ready to do away with him, hunted for three days in the mountains and deserts before realizing that Jānbāz was gone, and that what they had feared was indeed about to unfold (f. 128a). The account then turns to a rendering of the story about the Prophet splitting the full moon in response to the challenge of Abū Jahl; this miracle occurred just as Jānbāz reached the Prophet, we are told, and at once Jānbāz adopted the faith, became a Muslim, accepted Islam, and joined the Prophet's community (ff. 128b-129a).

The second part of this account (ff. 129a-134b) begins with the introduction of a new character: "Khūja Muḥammad Bashsharī" [*sic*], who is clearly the figure, cast as a Companion of the Prophet, for whom a famous shrine near Penjikent is named (he is typically called "Muḥammad Bashshārā").[14] This man, we are told, had set out from "a city called Māwarnaḥr" [*sic*] to ask for military aid from the Prophet; learning in "Baghdāt" of this prophet's appearance in Mecca, and of the way there, he set off at once and came to the Prophet's mosque (ff. 129a-b). The account that follows is clearly intended to explain how Jānbāz and this Muḥammad Bashsharī are joined together, the former as a champion in the army led by the latter; but the story becomes somewhat difficult to follow at this point, insofar as the text seems to conflate the arrival of

[14] On his shrine, see Voronina and Kriukov 1978; see also Brentjes 1983. The narrative recounted here, focused on Jānbāz Khoja, bears striking similarities to the account related in a versified Persian hagiography focused on Khoja Muḥammad Bashshārā, evidently produced in the Zerafshan valley and no doubt linked with the shrine ascribed to him, which was published in Cyrillic-script Tajik on the basis of a Persian manuscript dating, perhaps, from the 19th century: *Risolai Khoja Muhammad Bashoro*, ed. Kobilboi Jumaev (Khojand, 1993); I am indebted for this reference, and for an exposition of the Tajik work's contents, to Jo-Ann Gross, who is working on texts, documents, and oral tradition associated with the shrine of Muḥammad Bashshārā near Penjikent. The Persian account makes no mention of Jānbāz Khoja, but suggests a possible textual inspiration for the transfer of various narrative elements—the suspicion of the hero's father and brothers and their plan to kill him, his sister's warning, the trip to meet the Prophet, the Islamizing water-bottle—from the 'life' of Bashshārā to that of Jānbāz (the Persian text also recounts the martyrdom and dismemberment of a mighty warrior sent by the Prophet to accompany Bashshārā in his campaigns to Islamize the region of Penjikent, but assigns him a different name).

Muḥammad Bashshārī with that of Ṣaḥāba Jānbāz: we are first told that the Prophet sent his Companions out of the mosque to bring in the newcomer; then follows a passage in which the Prophet surmises that the newcomer is a stranger, while the newcomer affirms, "I was a stranger, but I came in order to become a friend" (*bīgāna édim, ashnā bolghalï keldim* [f. 130a]); this passage concludes with the newcomer adopting Islam and the Prophet congratulating him on his conversion; the Prophet then asks the man his name, and the man tells him it is Muḥammad; and when the Prophet asks what the man had brought him from "Māwarnaḥr," the man thrust his hand into the bosom of Ṣaḥāba Jānbāz Khūjām, brought out a bottle, and gave it to the Prophet. As the Prophet raised the bottle to his mouth in order to drink the water inside it, a voice came out of the water declaring it to be "the water of mercy" (*ichim-de-gi sū āb-i raḥmat sūyï dur* [f. 130a]); the Prophet drank it, and gave portions to his Companions, but then gave the bottle back to Jānbāz Khoja and told him to give the water from that bottle to every person he should meet, for "he who has drunk the water from this bottle will adopt the faith and accept Islam" (*shol kūza-chāq-nïng suyï-nï ichgän kishi īmān étib islām keltürür* [f. 130b]). Oddly enough, no further mention is made of this water, or of the bottle, during the remainder of the narrative, as this element, of interest in the context of conversion motifs, is simply dropped.

The account then turns to the impending military campaign. Muḥammad Bashshārī asked for an army "in order to summon the people to the faith;" the Prophet asked whether he needed one man or a thousand, and the reply was that he needed one man equal to a thousand men (f. 131a). The Prophet declared that "Khūja 'Alamdār Ṣaḥāba Jānbāz" was such a man (this marks the first occurrence of the epithet "'Alam-dār" in this portion of the text[15]), and sent him with Muḥammad Bashshārī, along with four other men, to "Māwarnaḥr," instructing them to recite the name of the Prophet in every city they reached, and to fight those who refused to adopt the faith (f. 131a). At this point the disjointedness of the text is again evident, as the Prophet is made to ask whether news of his prophet-hood had yet reached Māwarnaḥr, and then, when told that it had not, to ask how Jānbāz Khoja had heard of it; Jānbāz Khoja then recounted the story of the splitting of the 14-day-old moon, which he had witnessed there in "Māwarnaḥr" (ff. 131a-b; earlier the account said that the splitting of the moon occurred just as Jānbāz Khoja reached the Prophet).

What follows is a brief itinerary as Jānbāz Khoja and the four men—Muḥammad Bashshārī disappears from the story for awhile, but later reappears — ride toward Māwarnaḥr, reciting the name of the Prophet, "proposing" the faith (*īmān 'arḍ qïldïlar* [f. 131b]), and making war on the people who did not accept; their efforts yield some success, until they encounter the fierce resistance of Jānbāz Khoja's own family. The first place-name mentioned is recognizable as the Jayḥūn, i.e., the Amū Daryā, which they crossed, coming then to "an enormous city behind Kūhak mountain" where all the

[15] The title is consistently spelled "Alam-dār" in the first part of the text, while the second part uses this form as well as "'Alam-dār." Central Asian shrine lore knows many sites associated with figures to whose names the epithet "'Alam-dār" is attached; especially prominent shrines known by this name are found in Tashkent, Samarqand, and Sayrām.

people were infidels (*kūhak tāgh-nïng arqa-sïda bir chong shahr bar ékän, hamma khalq kāfir ékän* [f. 131b]; the reference to Kūhak suggests the vicinity of the upper Zarafshān valley); the ruler there accepted the faith, as did most of its people (the others were defeated and their property was seized [f. 132a]). They came next to the city of Vanj (no mention is made, at this point, of Jānbāz Khoja's birth there), which they passed, moving on to "Panj-kenti," where five people became Muslims; this figure was evidently inspired by the name of the town, suggesting that what seems to be a reference to the well-known site of Penjikent (well to the west and north of present-day Vanj) might refer to another place altogether (in any case, the other place names here remain unidentified). Then they came to "Jāv.rūt," where four persons adopted the faith. Next they came to "Panj-shahrī," and then, by a road called "Aq-nūr," to "Īkī-kenti," where a man came before them and recognized Jānbāz Khoja (*khūja-nï tūnūdï* [*sic*]); that man went and told Jānbāz Khoja's father, describing his son as "a tall man, from the people of 'Ajam, with a standard resting on his shoulder" (*arasïda bir uzun kishi bar, 'ajam khalq-dïn, bir 'alam öshni-sidä turadur* [f. 132a]; the latter element alludes to the title "'Alam-dār," which, as noted, is often attached to the name of Jānbāz Khoja). His father then reminded his sons of the warning he had given them, about ensuring that their brother Jānbāz be killed, and they all went out to fight Jānbāz Khoja and the other Muslims; not one of them adopted Islam, and after several days of fighting, the infidels were victorious, and the Muslims were left severely weakened (f. 132b).

In this state the Muslims crossed back over the "Jaḥyūn" [*sic*] and the infidels returned to their own towns; the Muslims planned to rest and return to the struggle. Before turning to the battle itself, the account affirms that "Khūja Alam-dār Ṣaḥāba Jānbāz Khūja" saw his own impending martyrdom in a dream, and so gave instructions to his companions; "the *kāfirs* will split me in two" (*kāfir-lär meni iki fāra qïladur* [f. 132b]), he declared, and so he explained what should be done with the two halves of his body. They had brought two camels, one with a red coat and one with a white coat, from Mecca; the two halves of his body should be placed onto a camel-litter (*bir käjäbä-gha salïb* [*sic*, for *kajāba* or *kajāva*]), the litters should be loaded on the camels, and the camels should be sent out toward the desert, with their stopping-places marking the sites where the two parts of his body should be buried (these instructions are here said to have been given to Muḥammad Bashshārī [f. 132b]).

On the next day, the battle was joined, and the infidels again were victorious (ff. 132b-133a); Jānbāz Khoja was martyred, and from the place where the tears his companions wept fell to the ground, a great tree grew up to mark the spot.[16] Following Jānbāz Khoja's instructions, Muḥammad Bashshārī and the other four companions placed the two halves of his body on the two litters, and placed the litters on the camels. The white camel stopped atop Twin Mountain (*ikiz tagh*), but the companions worried that a rushing stream would carry the camel-litter away, until, by the power of God and the *baraka* of Jānbāz Khoja himself (*khudāy ta'ālā-nïng qudra-ti* [*sic*]

---

[16] *ṣaḥāba khūja jānbāz khūjām-nïng dardī* [*sic*] *firāq-larïda yārānlarï-nïng köz yashï-larï* [*sic*] *mubārak közläridin aqa bashladïlar, ol yashdïn dirakht-i dāgh ünüb chïqtï paydā boldï* [*sic*] (f. 133a).

bilän khūja 'alamdār-nïng bara-kātïdïn [*sic*, f. 133b), the mountain was split into two parts (hence, undoubtedly, its name, though this is not stated explicitly), a pathway appeared (evidently between the two halves), and they were able to go up to the twin peaks; then a tree appeared, and it was there that they buried half the body of Jānbāz Khoja. His companions later followed the other half of his body and found it near Bukhārā; so they buried it there, and the account affirms that both sites are known by the name of "Khūja Alam-dār Ṣaḥāba Jānbāz Khūjām" (f. 133b).

Meanwhile, the infidels tried to capture Muḥammad Bashshārī, and pursued him up the twin mountain. When they came close and were on the verge of catching up with him, God "bent" the top of the mountain downwards (*tagh bashïnï éngishtürüb berdilär* [f. 134a]), allowing the fleeing saint to reach the top; then as the infidels again came close, by God's command, "that mountain returned to its former condition, and today they call that mountain Falla Tāgh" (i.e., "Stairstep Mountain:" *ol tagh yana avvalqï-dek boldï, ḥālā ol tagh-nï falla tagh dérlär* [f. 134a]). Thus saved from capture by the infidels, Muḥammad Bashshārī was nevertheless alone, separated from the slain Jānbāz Khoja and from his companions. Atop the mountain, hungry and hot, he went to where Jānbāz Khoja lay and placed a stick (*tayaq*) at the foot of his grave; then he lay down to rest awhile. The stick turned green and provided shade for Jānbāz Khoja's head; it became a huge tree, and water appeared at its base. When Muḥammad Bashshārī awoke, he saw the tree that had turned green, drank the water, and used it to perform his ablutions before his prayers; then he gave thanks to God. The tree, the account notes, is still there (ff. 134a-b; the 'greening' of a staff placed in the earth by a saint is a quite common hagiographical motif). Muḥammad Bashshārī then rejoined his companions, and they fought the infidels, returning to this place by night for worship; they did thus until Islam grew strong and the infidels became weak.

This marks the end of the narrative; the third part of this second section follows (ff. 134b-135b), comprising a collection of short comments that are of interest chiefly for referring occasionally to written sources. "It is said in books," we are told first, that for 13 years, Jānbāz Khoja performed his daybreak prayers in the village (*kent*) called Vanj; the writer notes that oral accounts about him are extensive, "but we have abbreviated" (*ularnïng manāqibat-läri* [*sic*] *tola déb durlar, ammā mukhtaṣar qïlduq*). Then we are told that "Khūja Muḥammad Bashshārī" was among the Companions of the Prophet; the account next mentions that on the top of a mountain three *farsang*s above the village of Vanj, there was (evidently the shrine of) a "*khāṭīb*" named "Khūja Isḥāq Imām," who was a great scholar from Samarqand (ff. 134b-135a), but stops short of linking this figure with a written account of Muḥammad Bashshārī. Rather, we are told, abruptly, that "the person who read and wrote down these events in the books about these [saints] was Abū Ḥafẓ [*sic*]-i Kabīr, of Balkh" (*bu vāqi'-larnï shularnïng kitāb-larïda oqughan va fütügän* [*f.tūkān*] *balkh-lïq ḥaḍrat abū ḥafẓ-i kabīr-ni fīqah* [*sic*, for *faqīh*]); the account adds that prior to this man, the title "*faqīh*" had never been assigned to anyone else (*ulardïn ilgeri hich kim faqīh āt qoymas érdi-lär va démäs édilär* [f. 135a]). Then follows a garbled passage that appears to refer to an Arabic inscription on the door of the mosque in Vanj identifying the aforementioned "Khoja Imām Isḥāq" as the mosque's *khaṭīb* (*vanj-ning masjid-ning* [*sic*] *éshik-lärige 'arabī lafẓ birle fütübdürlär, uvaysī khūja īmām* [*sic*] *isḥāq-nïng* [*sic*] *khāṭīb durlar*). This is followed by a brief comment, perhaps to be linked with this "*khāṭīb*," about the Prophet's reference to a city, beyond the "Jaḥyūn," called Samarqand, where was to be found the shrine of a pre-Islamic prophet (*anda bir mazār bar dur, ilgerigi payghāmbarlardïn*); there are 70,000 angels in Samarqand, the comment adds, and they protect the city's inhabitants from all afflictions.

At this point these disjointed comments return to a sort of summary of the accounts of the two saints, Jānbāz Khoja and Muḥammad Bashshārī. It is said "in some books" that oral accounts of "Khūja Muḥammadī Bashshārī" are extensive, but "we have abbreviated, so as not to fatigue those who read them and those who write them down and the devotees" (*ammā mukhtaṣar qïlduq, oquġuchï va fütügüchi va mukhliṣ-lar malāl bolmasundéb* [f. 135a]). This is followed by a disclaimer, "God knows best," that might signal the end of the text, but instead a citation, in effect, from a book about Muḥammad Bashshārī appears, summarizing the story of Jānbāz Khoja as follows:

> The account of Muḥammadī Bashshārī, may God have mercy upon him, [says further that] the holy Khūja Jān-bāz Khūjām, may God have mercy upon him, was evidently from the country (*yurt*) of Vanj, and was among the Companions of the Prophet . . . By his order and directive, he assembled an army and engaged in intense warfare in the deserts below the village of Saylïq, a dependency of Yangiḥiṣār; he himself and his companions and his army [were defeated?]. Muḥammad Bashshārī, may God have mercy upon him, placed half his body on a white litter and buried it in that desert; they call [his grave that of] Ṣaḥāba Jānbāz 'Alamdār Khojam. As for the other half of his body, Khoja Muḥammad Bashshārī, may God have mercy upon him, evidently placed it on a white litter and loaded it on a red camel; it evidently went to Bukhārā. His remaining companions went looking for it and found it in Bukhārā; they buried that half of his body in that place, and there they call [his grave that of] Ṣaḥāba Jānbāz Alamdār Khojam.[17]

The colophon begins immediately and runs on to f. 136a; following the colophon appear nine lines from a poem in praise of "Īrslān," i.e., 'Alī Arslān Khān.

The summary given above is of interest, beyond the apparent citation of written sources, for the geographical adjustment it seems to offer. The major narrative reviewed above implies that the wars for the faith conducted by Jānbāz Khoja and his companions, as well as his martyrdom and the burial of part of his body, took place in the vicinity of either Vanj (in Badakhshān) or Penjikent, perhaps in the upper Zarafshān valley; while it is not impossible that the localities of "Iki-kenti" and the mountains

[17] *va yana ḥaḍrat muḥammadī bashshārī raḥmatu'llāh 'alayhi-ning manāqibat-läri* [*sic*] *ḥaḍrat khūja jān-bāz khūjām raḥmatu'llāh 'alayhi vanj yurtïdïn ékänlär, ḥaḍrat muḥammad muṣṭafā ṣallā'llāh 'alayhi va sallama-ning ṣaḥāblarïdïn* [*sic*] *ékänlär, va buyrughan amri-läri-ni* [*sic*] *va īshārat-läri* [*sic*] *bilän lashkarlarni jam' qïlïb, yanghiṣārgha tābi' sāylïq dégän kent-ning tüfide-gi dasht-biyābānda jang-i sakht qïlïb, özläri yārānlarï lashkarläri bile* [. . . ?] *'shbu dashtda nim-tan-lärin muḥammadī bashshārī raḥmatu'llāh 'alayhi aq käjäbägha alïb dafn qïlïb ékän-lär, ṣaḥāba jānbāz 'alamdār khūjām deydürlär; yana qalghan nim-tan-läri mu khūja muḥammadī bashshārī raḥmatu'llāh 'alayhi aq käjäbägha alïb qïzïl téve-ge yükläb qoyab berib ékänlär, bukhārā barïb ékän-lär, qalghan yārānlar istäb barïb bukhārā-dïn taftïlar, shol nim-tan-läri-ni shol yerde dafn qïldïlar, anda mu ṣaḥāba jān-bāz alamdār khūjām deydürlär* (f. 135b).

referred to as Ikiz Tagh and Falla Tagh were understood to be well to the east of Penjikent and "Vanj," the full account implies a more westerly orientation for the mythic geography of these fights and flights. The summary, however, insists that the battles, and Jānbāz Khoja's martyrdom, occurred in the vicinity of Yangiḥiṣār, in western Xinjiang (the locality of Saylïq, north of this town, is specified);[18] this site, clearly, is the place understood as the mazar of Jānbāz Khoja in the list of shrines that precedes the narrative, to which we may now turn.

This first section, containing the shrine catalogue, bears the following title (written in the same hand as the text itself), in a kind of hybrid Persian-Turkic rendering: "*tadhkīra-yi ḥaḍrat-i khūja alam-dār* [*sic*] *ṣaḥāba janbāz* [*sic*] *khūjām-nïng tadhkīra-läri*" (f. 119a).

The text opens with a passage that will be immediately familiar to those acquainted with the better-known *Tadhkira* of Khoja Muḥammad Sharīf. The latter work, known from almost a dozen manuscripts,[19] and the object of scholarly attention for over a century,[20] celebrates the life of a saint who established himself in Yārkand in the middle of the 16th century and who is known, from other sources (including the historical work of Shāh Maḥmūd b. Mīrzā Fāḍil Churās) as a master of the Chaghatayid ruler ʿAbd al-Rashīd Khān (r. 939/1533-967/1560);[21] it includes an account of Muḥammad Sharīf accompanying the *khān* on a visit to a shrine (or several shrines, in some versions) in order to seek spiritual assistance and 'permission' prior to a punitive campaign against the Qïrghïz intended to avenge the death of the *khān*'s son, ʿAbd al-Laṭīf, who had been killed in the aftermath of a raid, initially successful, against the Qïrghïz. This campaign too is known from other sources, though many particulars about it remain unclear, including its date and the composition of the enemy forces that were fought, and, we are told, destroyed, by ʿAbd al-Rashīd Khān;[22] the work of Churās also mentions this joint 'quest' by the *khān* and the *shaykh*, specifying that they visited the shrine of Satūq Bughrā Khān in order to seek his aid for the campaign.

---

[18] This localization of Jānbāz Khoja's shrine may be further contrasted with the implication of the Katakī hagiography, cited above in note 7, that a shrine of Ṣaḥāba Jānbāz was to be found near Kucha.

[19] I have listed these in DeWeese 2011; they include, beyond those evidently used by Hamada Masami in his recent publication of the text (see the following note), a copy in Uppsala (MS Nov. 613, ff. 168b-180a, described in Zetterstéen 1935: 141, No. 720/7), and another (referred to here as "MS facs."), from Kashghar, that was recently published in facsimile in Orxun and Sugawara 2007: 120-147 (ff. 2b-30a).

[20] It was mentioned already in Ross 1908: 1, 4; a full Russian translation was published in Iudin 1987; a text edition was published by Hamada Masami (in Hamada 2006: 279-302); and an English translation with analysis and further discussion is now available (Eden 2015). On the misunderstandings surrounding the subject of this work, Muḥammad Sharīf (above all his supposed connection with an "Uvaysī" Sufi community in the 16th century), see DeWeese 1993: 7-11; DeWeese 1995: 104-109; and DeWeese 2011: 135-157, with a synopsis of the text.

[21] Akimushkin 1976: 155-156 (tr.), 11 (Persian text).

[22] On the campaign and the various problems surrounding it (including its date), see Akimushkin's discussion in his notes to the translation of Churās' work (Akimushkin 1976: 266-269, n. 58).

The account in the *Tadhkira* of Muḥammad Sharīf [23] focuses on the shrine-visitation by Muḥammad Sharīf and ʻAbd al-Rashīd Khān, and on the appearance before them of a host of saints who give their blessing for the campaign and in some cases resolve to accompany the *khān* into battle; but the various manuscript versions in fact give somewhat different accounts of where the *shaykh* and the *khān* went, and which saints they saw. The versions agree that the shrine visits, and the visions, began "on the eve of the 17th of Muḥarram" (*ʻāshūr āyi*), but the year is never indicated in the *Tadhkira* of Muḥammad Sharīf. In the work of interest here, focused on Jānbāz Khoja, however, we find a series of other shrine visits added to the basic account, to comprise a substantial itinerary of holy sites; at first glance we might be inclined to regard the work as, in effect, a variation on a section of the *Tadhkira* of Muḥammad Sharīf, but this text's departure from the latter work is quite substantial, even with regard to the campaign that prompts the shrine visits,[24] and there is no question that the *Tadhkira* of Jānbāz Khoja is an independent work, and not simply a variant of the other *tadhkira*.

The constants, shared by the *Tadhkira* of Jānbāz Khoja and the *Tadhkira* of Muḥammad Sharīf, include virtual echoes of certain passages in the latter work (e.g., accounts 'predicting' the fate of the Qïrghïz), as well as the element of the date on which Khoja Muḥammad Sharīf appealed to the saints on behalf of ʻAbd al-Rashīd Khān, namely the eve of the 17th of Muḥarram (spelled here "*ʻashūr āy*"), specified, in the tale of Jānbāz Khoja, as a Monday, and further specified by the inclusion of the year, 944 A.H., an element not found in copies of the *Tadhkira* of Muḥammad Sharīf. The mention of this year in the *Tadhkira* of Jānbāz Khoja was in fact the only feature of this work to have drawn scholarly attention in the past; both Iudin and Akimushkin mentioned the manuscript (B731), though without identifying the work, as giving this date for the campaign.[25] As both these scholars pointed out, the date is no doubt much too early for such a campaign; for present purposes what is significant is that however erroneous the date may be, it was apparently chosen with some care, insofar as 17 Muḥarram 944, corresponding to 26 June 1537, was a Tuesday, according to the standard conversion, placing the "eve" of this date on the preceding Monday.

If care was taken with the date, little was taken with the manuscript as a whole, or with the narrative it contains; as noted, the *Tadhkira* of Jānbāz Khoja is extraordinarily poorly written, in both orthographic and grammatical terms (to the point that one may question the degree of the copyist's literacy), and the narrative is often disjointed (the textual problems are in fact more pervasive in this first section of the work than in the narrative reviewed above). In any case, it begins by affirming that "on the eve of Monday, the 17th of Muḥarram (*ʻashūr ay*), in the year 944, Khoja Muḥammad Sharīf Pīr entered the mazar of the holy Yūsuf Qādir Khān and sought permission for ʻAbdī Rashīd Khān to go on campaign" [*ḥaḍrat-i yūsuf qādīr khān-nïng mazārïgha khūja muḥammad sharīf*

[23] Iudin 1987: 26-30 (with facsimiles of several pages); *Tadhkira-yi Khoja Muḥammad Sharīf*, MS facs., ff. 23a-25b; MS Uppsala, ff. 177b-178b.

[24] There is, for instance, no mention of or allusion to the death of ʻAbd al-Laṭīf Sulṭān, or any event that prompted the campaign against the Qïrghïz, in the *Tadhkira* of Jānbāz Khoja.

[25] Iudin 1969: 407, 518; Akimushkin 1976: 268, n. 58.

pīr kirib ʻabdī rashīd khān cherik-kä barurgha rukhṣat tilädilär]. The text then lists several saints, their names matching to some extent those mentioned in the *Tadhkira* of Muḥammad Sharīf as having appeared at the shrine; but here there is no actual mention of what they did, as the text veers off on a tangent and then returns to repeat, but adapt, the opening passage on the date of the visit.

The saints listed are "ḥaḍrat-i khūja Khiḍrī Bilāl" [*sic*]; the holy "Vays Qarān" [*sic*]; the holy "Shaykh Ḥasan Baṣrī;" the holy "Sulṭān Satūq Bughrā Khān;" and the holy "Sayyid Shahīd ʻAlī Arslān Khān" (his name is always written "Īrslān"). After these names, "the holy Abā Bakrī Ṣiddīq" is mentioned, and an enumeration of sorts follows: "second, the holy ʻUmar; third, the holy ʻUthmān; fourth, the holy Shāh-i Mardān Murtaḍā." This enumeration is then halted by a brief ʻcatechisticʼ digression: "If they ask how many Rightly-Guided Caliphs (*khulafā rāshidīn*) there are, answer that they are seven: first, ʻAbdullāh b. ʻAbbās; second ʻAbdullāh b. ʻUmar; third, ʻAbdullāh b. Masʻūd; (f. 119b) fourth, Zayd b. Shābit [*sic*, for Thābit]; fifth, ʻĀshīya [*sic*] Ṣiddīq; sixth, Abū'l-Mūsā Ashʻara [*sic*]; seventh, Muʻādh b. Jabīl. Here the text ends with a Persian phrase apparently affirming that one who does not recognize the Rightly-Guided Caliphs cannot serve as prayer-leader ("*khulafā rāshidīn-rā nadānad imāmatī dūst nabāshad*); the word *tammat* follows, seeming to signal the end of a textual digression; and the identity of all those named so far is evidently summed up by the phrase, "and these are the aforementioned holy saints" (*va madhkūr ḥaḍrat-i būzurgān-i dīn bu turur*).

The text then returns to the date but shifts from what we would expect, on the basis of the *Tadhkira* of Muḥammad Sharīf, by introducing the focus on Jānbāz Khoja, in connection with the first shrine visited.

(1)"On the eve of Monday, the 17th of the month of ʻAshūr [*sic*], in the year 944/1537, he sought assistance (*istimdād tilädilär*) at the ʻGardenʼ[26] of Yūsuf Qādīr Khān Ghāzī Pādshāh." There, we are told, the Prophet appeared, with "the four Prophetic Friends" (*chahār yārī payghāmbarī*), who are named and numbered, as well as "all the Companions" (*jamīʻ ṣaḥāba*). The Prophet said, "We have a Companion whose name is Ṣaḥāba Jānbāz Khūja; seek support from his shrine" (*bizning bir ṣaḥāba-miz bar dur, ularnïng āṭ-larï ṣaḥāba jānbāz khūja durlar, ularnïng mazārlarïdïn istimdād tilänglär*). The Prophet then explained further,

> I went on the *miʻrāj*; I saw the spirits of all the prophets and saints. I saw two spirits, brighter (*rawshan va tābān*) than the rest, atop the Throne (*ʻarsh üstide*); I asked the holy Jibrāʼīl, "Brother Jibrāʼīl, which prophet's and which saint's spirits are these?" The holy Jibrāʼīl said, "Muḥammad, this is not a prophet; this is not a saint. It is your community (*siz ummatingiz*): one of them is the spirit of Sulṭān Satūq Bughrā Khān, and one of them is the spirit of the Companion Jānbāz Khoja."

The Prophet then addressed these two as sons, and again instructed his hearers, "Seek support from the spirit of Ṣaḥāba Jānbāz Khoja" (*ṣaḥāba jānbāz khūja-ning rūḥ-larïdïn*

[26] *rawza-larïdïn*, corrected to *rawḍa* in the margin by a later hand. On the shrine of Yūsuf Qādir Khān, see Dawut 2001: 30-31.

istimdād tilänglär).

The account then adds another anecdote confirming the preceding one. On the night he returned from the *mi'rāj*, we are told, the Prophet began adding a personal appeal (*du'ā*) after every ritual prayer (*har namāz-dïn keyin bir du'ā-nï dhiyāda* [*sic*] *qïldïlar*); one day, Mu'ādh-i Jabal (one of his Companions) asked him why he did this, (f. 120b) and the Prophet explained,

> On that day when I ascended on the *mi'rāj*, in the fourth heaven I saw two spirits: one was the spirit of Sulṭān Satūq Bughrā Khān Ghāzī, [the other] was the spirit of one of my Companions, Ṣaḥāba Jānbāz Khoja. I pray on behalf of them.[27]

Thereupon all the Companions and all the saints took the hand of Ṣaḥāba Jānbāz Khoja, saying "This saint is the Khoja of all *khojas*" (*bu būzrūkvār hamma khūja-lar-nïng khūja-sïdurlar*).

This introduction thus ties in the second portion of the composite text with the account of the shrine visits that begins at this point; it evokes the familiar theme of the Prophet meeting, on the night of the *mi'rāj*, the spirit of a future saint (it is especially common in connection with Islamizing saints, and is evoked in connection with Satūq Bughrā Khān and Sayyid Ata, among others).

The shrine visits then follow (ff. 120b-125a, introduced simply by an indication that the author is returning to his main narrative, "*al-qiṣṣa*"); the typical format is for a saint to appear at each shrine, give a blessing to the *khān*, and affirm that it is incumbent upon him to go and "seize" the Qïrghïz.

First, evidently at the shrine of Yūsuf Qādir Khān (as in most versions of the *Tadhkira* of Muḥammad Sharīf), a group of saints appears and recites a blessing (*fātiḥa*) for the *khān*: listed here are Sulṭān Satūq Bughrā Khān; 'Abdī Rashīd Khān, thus placed among the saints already; 'Alī Īrslān Khān [*sic*]; Shaykh Junayd Baghdādī; "Shaykh Najmidīn Kubrāy," garbling the name of the famous saint; Sayyid 'Alī Hamadānī; and a saint whose name is regularly garbled (in the *Tadhkira* of Muḥammad Sharīf as well), written here "Shaykh 'āda-ba-i s.b.t.yān". The list here clearly reflects those named in the *Tadhkira* of Muḥammad Sharīf, though it is shorter than what appears in some versions of that work;[28] however, in that other work, it is typically Satūq, or Khiḍr, who then speaks, a role reserved in the *Tadhkira* of Jānbāz Khoja for the Prophet (who

---

[27] f. 120b: *olkünkim men mi'rāj-gha chïqqanïmda törtinchi asmānda iki rūḥ kördüm, biri sulṭān satūq bughrā khān ghāzī-ning rūḥï*, [*biri*, added in margin] *ṣaḥāba-i mening ṣaḥābam ṣaḥāba jānbāz khūja-ning rūḥï; shular ḥaqqïda du'ā qïladurmen.*

[28] In most versions, famous Sufi *shaykhs* predominate; in MS facs., those named are Khiḍr, Bilāl, Sulṭān Vaysī Qaran, Ḥasan Baṣrī, Sulṭān Satūq Bughrā Khān Ghāzī, Junayd Baghdādī, Najm al-Dīn Kubrā, Amīr Sayyid 'Alī Hamadānī, and "Shaykh-i 'alavīya Shībānī" (or "Shaybānī;" this *nisba* was read by Iudin as "Shabistānī"). Cf. MS Uppsala: Khiḍr, Bilāl, Vays Qaran, Ḥasan Baṣrī, 'Alī Arslān Khān Ghāzī, Yūsuf Qādir Khān Ghāzī, 'Uthmān Bughrā Khān Ghāzī, Qïlïch Bughrā Khān Ghāzī, Junayd Baghdādī, Shaykh Sarīr Saqaṭī, Khwāja Aḥmadī Yāsavī, "Shaykh-i 'alavīya Bastāmī (?); Shaykh Abū Yūsuf Hamadānī; Shaykh Najm al-Dīn Kubrā, Amīr Sayyid Hamadānī, and "Shaykh-i 'alavīya Shībānī."

evidently remained manifest at the shrine while the other figures were appearing). The Prophet said, evidently addressing Khiḍr, "From among the prophets, you go; from among the saints, let Yūsuf Qādir Khān Ghāzī go" (*payghāmbarlardi̇n sizlär bari̇ng, awliyā-lardi̇n yūsuf qādir khān ghāzī barsun*). Then he apparently spoke again, saying, "Let Shaykh Ḥasan Baṣrī, Shaykh Junayd Baghdādī, and Shaykh Najm al-Dīn Kubrāy, led by the holy Khiḍrī, go;" and so saying he (and evidently the rest of the saints as well) disappeared from the *khān*'s sight.

The text here does not make it clear, but what the Prophet is portrayed ordering is the specific group of saints who will accompany the *khān* on the campaign (as opposed to merely blessing it); the account, and the identities of who is saying what, and who is accompanying the *khān*, are only marginally clearer in some versions of the *Tadhkira* of Muḥammad Sharīf, in which it is the saints themselves, or Khiḍr, rather than the Prophet, who announce those who were to accompany the *khān*.[29] As this initial shrine visit ends, however, the parallels between the *Tadhkira* of Jānbāz Khoja and that of Muḥammad Sharīf begin to grow less frequent.

(2-3)"At dawn, on Monday," the account continues — and here it is clear that the text is departing from the depiction of Muḥammad Sharīf as the chief, or sole, visitor to the shrines —"the *khān* (f. 121a) came to the graves of Khoja Muḥammad Sharīf Pīr and Ḥusayn Faḍlullāh Khūjām and appealed to them; they appeared and recited a blessing for the *khān*, and [he received permission from them]."[30] This sets the stage for the stock sequence at each shrine; despite the reference here to the grave of Muḥammad Sharīf, we may note, there is one later appearance of a living Muḥammad Sharīf at a significant point in the narrative (see No. 16 below).

(4) Passing on from there, he came to the shrine of "Shaykh Ḥijjāz [*sic*] Khūja," which is said to be in a place called "Fākhtāk-lā" (I have not identified it);[31] the saint appeared there, and gave the *khān* a blessing.

---

[29] In the versions of the *Tadhkira* of Muḥammad Sharīf, it is most often Khiḍr who declares that he would accompany the *khān*, with three eminent Sufis usually mentioned as well (Ḥasan Baṣrī, Junayd Baghdādī, and Najm al-Dīn Kubrā). Cf. MS Uppsala: Khiḍr arose from the place of Yūsuf Qādir Khān Ghāzī and said that the two of them would accompany the *khān*, to whom they gave a sword; thereupon the *khān* and Muḥammad Sharīf left the shrine (and no other shrines are mentioned). In MS facs., Khiḍr affirmed that he would go, and then Satūq Bughrā Khān declared that Ḥasan Baṣrī, Najm al-Dīn Kubrā, and Junayd Baghdādī would go along; then these saints agreed to send "Shaykh-i ʿalavīya Shībānī." In Iudin's text (which he gives in facsimile), Satūq Bughrā Khān also spoke, but before mentioning the three shaykhs, he declared that "from among us" (evidently referring to his descendants, the Bughrā-khānid saints, collectively), "Yūsuf Qādir Khān Ghāzī will go."

[30] *tanglasi̇ dūshanba küni khān khūja muḥammad sharīf pīr ḥusayn fiḍlullāh* [*sic*] *khūjām-ni̇ng marqad-lärige kelib tavajjuh qi̇ldi̇lar, ular ḥāḍir bolub kelib khān-gha fātiḥa oqudi̇lar, āndi̇n rukhṣat berdi-lär* [*sic*]. On the shrine of Muḥammad Sharīf, near Yārkand, see Dawut 2001: 80-82; several photographs of the shrine appear in (and on the cover of) Orxun and Sugawara 2007. A shrine of "Ḥusayn Faḍl Khwāja" is mentioned already in the *Tārīkh-i Rashīdī* (Dūghlāt, tr. Thackston: 192), but is named among the shrines of Kāshghar.

[31] *andi̇n ötüb fākhtāk-lā-de-gī shaykh ḥijjāz khūja-ning mazāri̇-gha keldilär, ular ḥāḍir bolub, khān-gha fātiḥa oqudi̇lar, fātiḥa oqub rukhṣat berdilär.*

(5) Next he came to the mazar of "Khūja Ṣāliḥ Anwā'ī" [*sic*], who "became manifest" [*ẓāhir boldïlar*]; here a new element appears for the first time (variations on it appear in connection with several later shrines), with an enigmatic element: "He gathered the Qïrghïz and directed them to the ground they would press beneath their knees;" then, "saying, 'Let the *khān*'s sharp sword be like the breath of the saints,' he recited a blessing on the *khān*'s behalf."[32] The imagery appears to be that of the saint ordering the Qïrghïz to their knees prior to their slaying by the *khān*'s sword; visits to the next two shrines take this imagery further.

(6) The next shrine is a more familiar one, that of "Khūja Aḥmad-i Bī-ghamm," a figure prominent in the tales of martyrdom and holy war linked with the Bughrā-khānid *ghazavāt-nāma* cycle, and associated especially closely with 'Alī Arslān Khān; he too became manifest, "arranged the Qïrghïz in four rows, took out his sword, and cut off their heads."[33]

We may note here that several of the preceding shrines — Nos. 3, 4, 5, and 6 — appear also (with variants of their names) in the *Tadhkira* of Muḥammad Sharīf, where they are visited by the *shaykh* and the *khān* following the initial grand vision at the first shrine; one version of this work mentions Khoja Abū'l-Faḍl (paralleling "Ḥusayn Faḍlullāh," No. 3, in the Jānbāz text), Shaykh Ḥājjī Khoja (whose name, corresponding to "Ḥijjāz," No. 4, in the Jānbāz text, appears as "Ṣamājī" or "Ḥajjājī" or "Ḥ.mājī" in the text used by Iudin, and was read by him as "Simasi"); Ṣāliḥ Khoja (clearly No. 5 in the Jānbāz text), and "Khoja Bī-ghamm" (clearly No. 6).[34]

(7) The next shrine is that of "'Alī Īrslān Khān Pādshā[h],"[35] located, we are told, on the other side of the Tümen (i.e., the chief river of Kāshghar, its name spelled here *t.m.n*), near [the shrine of] Khoja Aḥmad-i Bī-ghamm.[36] This royal saint appeared as well, and, "arranging the boastful [?] Qïrghïz in three ranks, he took out his sword, and with that double-edged [?] sword,[37] (f. 121b) he struck all 3000 Qïrghïz. Then he put the sword in the *khān*'s hand, rubbed the *khān*'s back,[38] and three times raised the *khān* up and placed him back on the ground; then, saying 'May God most high give [you] strength,' he recited a blessing for the *khān*."[39]

---

[32] *qïrghïzlar-nï jam' qïlïb tizläri-ning āstïnda basïb yer-ge körgüzdïlär, khān-nïng tīghī burrā* [*sic*] *'azīz-lärning nafasi gūyā bolsun-déb, khān-nïng ḥaqda* [*sic*] *fātiḥa oqudïlar.*

[33] *qïrghïzlarnï tört qatār* [added in margin] *qïlïb qïlïch chïqārïb bashï-nï qïyar qalam qïldïlar.*

[34] Iudin's identifications for these saints (Iudin 1987: 39-40, notes 43-44) are doubtful.

[35] On the shrine of 'Alī Arslān Khān in particular, see Dawut 2001: 32-36, 45-53; see also Sawada 2001a, and the older work of Jarring 1935. The proximity of this shrine to that of Aḥmad-i Bī-ghamm reflects the pairing of these two figures as prominent martyrs in the Bughra-khānid cycle; see the excerpts translated in Shaw 1877: 336-337.

[36] Something seems to have been omitted from the description of the shrine's location; the text reads, "*ular tümen-ning ol yüzidä ularnïng maqām-larï khūja aḥmad-i bī-ghāmm-nïng bashïda durūr.*"

[37] Literally, "with that sword whose center was double" (*otrasï ikiz ol qïlïch bilän*).

[38] The phrasing here is the same used, in the actual story of Jānbāz Khoja, to describe how that saint treated the creatures that he captured (instead of taking them as game); when an animal was caught in his snare, or in his hands, the account says, Jānbāz would "rub its backside" (*uchalarïnï sïlab*), i.e., he would pet it.

[39] *qïrghïz-nāznï üch ṣaf qïlïb qïlïch chïqārdïlar, otrasï ikiz ol qïlïch bilän tamām üch ming qïrghïz-nï chaptïlar,*

This seventh shrine, and the account of what happened there, are likewise paralleled in the *Tadhkira* of Muḥammad Sharīf: in some versions of that work, we are told that Sulṭān ʿAlī Arslān Khān arrayed the Qïrghïz in three rows in front of the *khān*, cut off all their heads with his sword, handed the sword to the *khān*, rubbed the *khān*'s backside three times (*uchalarïnï üch martaba sïlab qoydïlar*, closely paralleling the language found in the Jānbāz text), and gave his blessing for the campaign. This, however, marks the last significant parallel between the *Tadhkira* of Muḥammad Sharīf and the Jānbāz text (until a faint echo of the result of the shrine visits, at the very end of the latter work).

(8) On Saturday, the narrative continues (without explicitly accounting for the intervening days, though in fact it seems one day is allotted for each shrine), the *khān* mounted and went to the mazar of "Quṭb-i ʿĀlam Khūja;"[40] the shrine of Quṭb-i ʿĀlam Khoja is mentioned already in the *Tārīkh-i Rashīdī* as a site near Kāshghar,[41] and the saint buried there is the subject of a Turkic *tadhkira* identifying him as Quṭb al-Dīn ʿIrāqī and recounting his journey, at the command of Khiḍr, from ʿIrāq via Bukhārā to Kāshghar.[42] Without further explanation (or identification), the text reads as follows, implying that Quṭb-i ʿĀlam Khoja was present, but focusing more on a saint who was, though temporarily absent, expected to join him:

> After a time, he appeared in the distance and approached, saying, "I, the holy Qarākhān Pādshāh,[43] have gone to the exalted Mecca, to the presence of the holy Prophet; we are on our way from there now." Within the hour, Qarākhān Pādshāh appeared as well, and, together with Quṭb-i ʿĀlam Khūja, the two of them stood together[44] and said, "The holy Prophet commanded that every one of the *shaykhs* of the country should go with the *khān* on campaign;" they went to the *khān* and recited a blessing for him. "There is no other way but to seize the Qïrghïz," the Prophet commanded.[45]

(9) Then the *khān*, or the *khān* and the accompanying shaykhs and/or spirits, went

---

qïlïch-nï khān-nïng qolïgha berib, khān-nïng uchasïnï sïlab, üch martaba khān-nï kötärib yerde qoydïlar, khudāy taʿālā quvvat bersün déb, khān-gha fātiḥa oqudïlar.

[40] The text first reads, "*ʿālam-nïng quṭb-nïng khūja-nïng* [*sic*] *mazārïgha bardïlar*, but later in the account he is referred to as "*Quṭb-i ʿĀlam Khūja*."

[41] Dūghlāt, tr. Thackston: 196; ed. Thackston: f. 144b.

[42] *Tadhkira-yi Khoja Quṭb al-Dīn ʿIrāqī*, MS St. Petersburg, B737 (described in Muginov 1962: 77, No. 104); the manuscript, evidently unique, runs to 68 folios, and was copied in 1306/1888-89. On this work, see now DeWeese forthcoming.

[43] On a shrine ascribed to "Qarakhan," see Dawut 2001: 102-103.

[44] The text includes here a word I have not been able to interpret, in the phrase, "*ikülän d.r.qām.tū turub*," i.e., "the two of them stood *d.r.qām.tū* (or *d.r.qāmītū*)" (perhaps a garbling of the Persian phrase *dar-qāmat*, i.e., they stood erect?).

[45] *furṣatdïn keyin yïraqdïn paydā bolub keldilär, ayttïlar kim men ḥaḍrat-i qarākhān pādshāh makka-i muʿaẓẓam-gä barïb ḥaḍrat-i payghāmbar (ṣallāʾllāhu ʿalayhi va sallama) qashlarïgha barïb aydïlar* [*sic*] *andïn kelädürmiz déb shol sāʿat qarākhān pādshāh ham paydā boldïlar, quṭb-i ʿālam khūja bilän ikülän d.r.qām.tū turub ayttï-lar kim ḥaḍrat-i payghāmbar (ṣallāʾllāhu ʿalayhi va sallama) ḥukm qïldïlar kim ölke mashāʾikhi-kī* [*sic*] *har biri khān bilän cherike* [*sic*] *barsun déb khān-gha barïb fātiḥa oqudïlar, qïrghïzlarnï almaqdïn almaq* [*sic*] *özge chāra yoq déb ḥaḍrat-i payghāmbar (ṣallāʾllāhu ʿalayhi va sallama) ḥukm qïldïlar.*

to "the shrine of 'Uthmān Bughrā Khān, which is in Āchïgh Būyā;" this saint appeared after a time, (f. 122a) "and went on campaign together with Yūsuf Qādīr Khān Ghāzī. Saying, 'I myself will come; there is no recourse but to seize the Qïrghïz,' he recited a blessing for the *khān*."[46]

(10) Next he went "to the shrine of their Imām" (*ularnïng imāmï-nïng mazārïgha bardïlar*); this figure is not further identified, but we are told that he was engaged, when they came, in reciting the Qur'ān, and had reached the verse (III.144) affirming that Muḥammad was simply a prophet, and that many like him had passed away before him;[47] this anonymous saint recited a blessing for the *khān*.

(11) He went then to the mazar of "Shām Pādshāh," who likewise appeared and recited a blessing on behalf of the *khān*.

(12) After that, he went to the mazar [of] "Mujāvir," which is in "Khūn-salā;" he too became manifest and recited a blessing for the *khān*. He said, "There is no recourse but to seize the Qïrghïz."[48] Who this "caretaker" is is not clarified, but this shrine seems to belong together with that of "his *imām*," both perhaps referring to figures known as confidants of 'Abd al-Rashīd Khān.

(13) Next he went to "the shrine of the Maidens, which is in Īṭ-yolï" ("Dog-Road"). The Seven Maidens (*yete qïz*) appeared and, declaring (in an echo of what the saint of the fifth shrine had said), "The breath of the saints will become like the *khān*'s sharp sword," recited a blessing for the *khān*.[49]

(14)"After that, he came to the village of Tārqūq; (f. 122b) it is in Upper Artūsh.[50] He went to the shrine of Mullā Nūr al-Dīn Khūja; he too appeared and recited a blessing for the *khān*."[51]

(15) From there, "upon the blessed directive of the holy Sulṭān" (presumably meaning Satūq?), he came to the mazar of "Ṭavvā Khūja" [*sic*], who likewise appeared and recited a blessing;[52] he is not further identified.

(16) At this point, the account turns to the first person (for this shrine, and partly for

---

[46] *men özüm yetib kelämen, qïrghïzlarnï almaqdïn özge chāra yoq déb, khān-gha fātiḥa oqudïlar.*

[47] *ol athnā-da qirā'at-kä mashghūl ékänlär, bu ayat-kä yetib ékänlär, "wa mā muḥammadun illā rasūlun, qad khalat min qablihi'l-rusulu"* (with the last three words written here, wrongly, "*min qabli'l-rasūli*").

[48] *andïn keyin khūn-salā-de-gi mujāvir mazārgha* [*sic*] *bardïlar, ular ham ẓāhir boldïlar, khān-gha fātiḥa oqudï-lar, qïrghïz-lar almaq-dïn özgä chāra yoq dédilär.*

[49] *andïn keyin īṭ yolï-de-gī qïzlar-nïng mazārïgha bardïlar, ol yerdin yete qïz paydā boldï, ol qïzlar aydïke 'azīzlärning nafasi gūyā khān-nïng tīghī burrā* [*sic*] *bolghay-déb khān-gha fātiḥa oqudïlar.* On the shrine of the Seven Maidens, see Dawut 2001: 238-239.

[50] As noted, the shrine of Zayn al-Dīn Qāghrāqī, known from the *tadhkira* referred to above, was in a locality of "Upper Artūch" (*üstün artūch*) near Kāshghar; Artuch has long been known as the site of the shrine of Satūq Bughrā Khān.

[51] *andïn keyin tārqūq kenti-ge keldilär, üstün artūshdä-dur, mullā nūr al-dīn khūja-nïng mazārïgha bardïlar, ular ham ẓāhir boldïlar, khān-gha fātiḥa oqudïlar.* There follows an obscure passage affirming that "At that time", the *khān* was at the border or limit of a certain place whose name has eluded interpretation (*ol vakhïtda* [*sic*] *khān b.jīrnār ḥaddïda érdilär*, with the questionable word perhaps to be read "*bejīz-nār*" or "*ba-baḥīr-i nār*").

[52] *andïn ḥaḍrat-i sulṭān-nïng mubārak īshārat-läri* [*sic*] *bilän ṭavvā khūja-ning mazārïgha bardïlar, ular ham ẓāhir boldïlar, ular ham khān-gha fātiḥa oqudïlar.*

the next). "After that, we went to the shrine of Shaykh Ḥabīb Khūja." While this site's location is indicated in the text in garbled fashion,[53] the shrine of Shaykh Ḥabīb, too, is known already from the *Tārīkh-i Rashīdī*, as a holy site of Artuch; the account mentions the circumambulation of the shrine by the Chaghatayid Sulṭān Sa'īd Khān as he was moving with his troops from the Farghāna valley to Kāshghar in 920/1514.[54] An account of this Shaykh Ḥabīb was also incorporated into the *Tadhkira-yi Bughrā-khānī*.[55] Here, in connection with this prominent site, the account in our text grows longer and more interesting; it is here, too, that Muḥammad Sharīf appears again as a living person:

> The *khān* went with the army [of] Islām; however it happened, the shaykh [i.e., Shaykh Ḥabīb] said, "One row of the *khān*'s men is faithful, the other is bad-intentioned; for that reason they are hesitating. We have appealed. [But] the irreligion and bad belief of the Moghūl *ṭā'ifa* are not small matters; they have been this way since ancient times." At that moment Khoja Muḥammad Sharīf Pīr grew zealous, and he said, "How would it be, Shaykh [Ḥabīb], if you were to show kindness and appeal to the *shaykhs*, (f. 123a) so that they would cast noble aspiration and strength into the hearts of those who have faithfulness, but cast fear and terror into the hearts of those who are opposed?" When he said this, the holy Shaykh [Ḥabīb] said, "Prophet of God!" He rose from his place, and declared, "Tomorrow at dawn I will go, join the *shaykhs*, and offer help." Then he said, "At first it was bad news that came; in the end good news will come." And so saying, he recited a blessing for the *khān*.[56]

(17) After that, on Wednesday, he (they?) went from Üstün Ārtūsh to the mazar of "Imām Ṣūfī," in a locality called "Yāgh Sū."[57] The exchange with this saint is thoroughly unintelligible (not in grammatical terms, but in its meaning in context); it again reverts to first-person, and seems to deal with a question about the campaign, but its import is quite unclear:

---

[53] It appears to read, "which is in Ayāsāq" (*ayāsāq-de-gi shaykh ḥabīb khūja-nïng mazārïgha barduq*), with the apparent place-name written unclearly (what is written looks like "*ayāq*" or "*ayāsāq*" with diagonal line inserted after "*yā*," to look like "*aykā*, then "*sāq*" or "*qāsā*").

[54] Dūghlāt, tr. Thackston: 193; ed. Thackston: 247 (f. 142b). The account refers to Shaykh Ḥabīb as one of the eminent saints of "Qumkand" (which Thackston vowels, in the translation, as "Qamkand"); it alludes to a miracle of Shaykh Ḥabīb in which he pulled and stretched one of the beams in his *khānqāh* that was too short. The shrine of Shaykh Ḥabīb, in Artuch, is mentioned also in the anonymous *Tārīkh-i Kāshghar*, from the late 17th century (Akimushkin 2001: 185/f. 55b).

[55] *Tadhkira-yi Bughrā-khānī*, ed. 'Ālam: 428-436; cf. Baldick 1993: 171-175.

[56] ff. 122b-123a: *khān islām cherike bardïlar, ne naw'ī boldï éken, shaykh aytïlar kim khān-nïng bir ṣaf kishi-si ṣādīq al-ikhlāṣ, özge bad-niyyat, ol sabab-din tarad-dūt* [sic] *qïlādūr-lar; 'arḍ qïldūq, moghūl ṭāyifa-nïng bī-diyānat va bad-'aqīda-ligi andak émäs, bular qadīmdin shūndāgh ékän-lär, shol dhamān-da khūja muḥammad sharīf pīr-ning ghayratï paydā boldï, ne bolghay, yā shaykh, siz 'ināyat qïlïb barïb mashāyikh-gha 'arḍ qïlsangïz,ol-ke ṣādīq al-ikhlāṣa-gī* [sic] *bar dur, ular-nïng köngli-ge himmat va quvvat salsa-lar, ol-ke mukhālīf-lar-nïng* [sic] *könglige khawf qorquncha* [sic] *salsa-lar, dégänidä, ḥaḍrat-i shaykh, yā rasūl-i khudā déb, ornïdïn qoptï, ayttïlar kim, men tangla ṣabāḥ barïb, mashāyikh-largha mulḥaq bolub, madad qïlalï, dédilär; ū aytïlar ke avval yamān khabar kelib-dur, ākhīr yakhshï khabar kelür déb, khān-gha fātiḥa oqudïlar.*

[57] Considering the localities mentioned, this is probably not to be connected with "Yāgh Būlāq" mentioned, near Keriya, in the history of Churās (Akimushkin 1976: 233).

> We asked him, "Where would the army be?" He said, "The *khān* has several viziers; if he does not consider what they say, he [?] will take [it?]." He is not agreeing with what they say, and for this reason, the *shaykhs* will help; probably they are doing it.[58]

(18) Next, as they were going to the mazar of "Khūja Muḥabbat Süzük," this saint appeared along with several others: Khiḍr, Quṭb-i 'Ālam Khūja, and "the holy Shāh-i Mardān" (i.e., 'Alī) were together with the *khān*, and they said, "Do not worry; God most high will give you the strength of the holy 'Alī and the fearsomeness of Zū'l-fiqār."[59]

(19) On Thursday, while going to the mazar of "Sulṭān Faqīh Ayyūb Khūja,"[60] in "Aqtur," in Yangiḥiṣār, this saint appeared together with 30 of his disciples; they brought a large loaf of bread and a vessel with 'juice', and recited a blessing, saying (again echoing two earlier saints), "Let the *khān*'s sharp sword be like the breath of the saints."[61] Then the account continues in another obscure passage: "they brought in two copies of the Qur'ān, written on deerskin with letters running in circular fashion in the middle;" the Khoja (i.e., Faqīh Ayyūb) brought in the large Qur'ān, with his 29 disciples, each of whom completed [apparently the recitation of] a smaller Qur'ān on behalf of the *khān*.[62]

The figure of Faqīh Ayyūb mentioned here is clearly the saint by this name whose story is incorporated into the *Tadhkira-yi Bughrā-khānī*;[63] one of the miracles recounted there involves Faqīh Ayyūb rescuing a caravan's goods from a raging river by ordering the waters below the site where they were lost to flow (*aq*) and ordering those above the site to halt (*tur*), and the account alludes to the naming of two villages based on these commands.

(20) Next they went, on Friday, to the shrine of "Khūja Ḥajākatu'llāh Khūja" [*sic*], in Chaghrï, where the saint appeared and recited a blessing.[64]

(21) The next shrine is, at last, that of Ṣaḥāba Jānbāz Khoja, here said to be in the

---

[58] *āndïn 'arḍ qïlduq, cherik qāydāgh bolghay, aytïlar kim khān-nïng bir muncha vazīrlarï bar, ular-nïng sözige baqmasalar, alurlar; ular-nïng sözige unamaydurlar, ol sababdin, mashāyikh-lar madad qïlur, alla iḥtimāl* [*sic*, apparently for *'alā'l-iḥtimāl*] *qïlādurlar*].

[59] *andïn keyin khūja muḥabbat süzük-ning mazārïgha barghanda, ular ham ḥāḍir boldïlar, ḥaḍrat-i khūja khiḍrī dhindah-lān, ḥaḍrat-i quṭb-i 'ālam khūja, va ḥaḍrat-i shāh-i mardān khān bile hamrāh, ne ghamm qïlasïz, ḥaḍrat-i 'alī-ning quvvatï-nï, zū'l-fiqār-nïng haybatï-nï khudāy ta'ālā sizge bergäy, déb* (123b) *takbīr aytïlar*.

[60] His appellation is spelled "*fiqa* [!] *āyyūb*".

[61] *fanjshanba küni, yanghiṣār-da aqturda sulṭān fiqa* [*f.y.qa*] *āyyūb khūja-nïng mazārïgha barghanda, ular ham ḥāḍir bolub, ular otuz shāgird-larï bilän paydā boldï, iki dast ulugh nān bir ṭarhïda sharbat āldurub keldilär, khān-nïng tīghī burrā* [*sic*] *va* [*sic*] *'azīzlarnïng nafasi giryān* [*sic*, for *gūyā*] *bolsun, déb, khān-gha fātiḥah oqudïlar*.

[62] *andïn keyin iki kilāmu'llāh alïb keldilär, kiyik teriside fütülgän* [*f.tūl.kān*] *otrada dāyir tartqan khaṭ-larï bar; ulugh kilāmu'llāh-nï khūja alïb, yigirm toquz shāh-girdläri* [*sic*] *bilän, har birlar bir saghāra* [for *ṣaghāra*] *kilāmu'llāh-nï khān-nïng ḥaqida tamām qïldï-lar*.

[63] *Tadhkira-yi Bughrā-khānī*, ed. 'Ālam: 365-371 (p. 369 for the miracle of the river); Baldick 1993: 151-153.

[64] *andïn keyin, azīna* [*sic*, for *ādīna*] *küni chaghrïda-gī khūja ḥajākatu'llāh khūja-nïng mazārïgha bardïlar, ular ham ḍāhir* [*sic*] *boldïlar, khān-gha fātiḥa oqudïlar*.

locality of "Sāylïq" (as mentioned in the 'summary' account from the second section of the text, noted above); together with him, the account affirms, again echoing the list of saints appearing at the first shrine (in this work and in the *Tadhkira* of Muḥammad Sharīf), were: Satūq Bughrā Khān; "the holy Qarākhān *ūsyāna*" (the latter term apparently masking "*uvaysīyān*"); Bilāl; Amīr Sayyid 'Alī Hamadānī; 'Abd al-Khāliq Ghijda-vānī [*sic*]; "the holy Shaykh 'Alī (f. 124a) Ḥajākatī" (?); "Shaykh 'Alāwu'l-Dīn Simnānī;" Khūja Aḥmadī Yasavī; and "the holy Khūja Mullā Rūmī." Following this list of names, the account adds this 'summarizing' comment, including an appellation (misspelled, as usual) for the chief saint that has not appeared in the text so far (outside the 'title' added later):

> These, and whatever saints were there, were evidently with the holy Khoja Alam-dār, Ṣaḥāba Jānbāz Khoja. All of them, following behind the holy Khoja Alam-dār, Ṣaḥāba Jānbāz Khoja, came in together and recited a blessing for the *khān*; they said, "There is no recourse but to seize the Qïrghïz."[65]

(22) The shrine of the 'title character' does not mark the end of the itinerary, however. From there they went on to the mazar of "the holy Ḥasan Bughrā Khān and the holy Esen Bughrā Khān," located in a place called "Jūshil" or "Choshul" (written *jūjūsh.l.de-gī*); these saints too became manifest and recited a blessing for the *khān*.[66]

(23) They next went to the shrine of "the holy Lady Chīn Tīrīm Anam" [*ḥaḍrat-i būbī jīn* (?, written above the line) *tīrīm anam mazārïgha bardïlar*]; her mazar, the account explains, is "attached" (*payvasta*) to the preceding shrine, of Sulṭān Ḥasan Bughrā Khān and the holy Sulṭān Esen Bughrā Khān. The saint declared, "I am the mother of the holy Khoja Aḥmad Yasavī," and recited a blessing for the *khān*.[67]

(24) From there they went to the shrine of "Mullā Ḥājjī Muḥammad Bakhtavī" (whose *nisba* is uncertain, and could be read in several different ways);[68] he too appeared and recited a blessing for the *khān*.

(25) After that, (f. 124b) they went to the mazar of "Khūja Jalīl Ūshī;" he too became manifest and recited a blessing for the *khān*.

(26) Next, they went to the mazar of "Sulṭān Sayyid Khūja Surkh," which is in Ūchār [? *ūjārde-gī*]; he too appeared and recited a blessing for the *khān*.

(27) After that, they went to the shrine of "Sayyid Ibrāhīm Madanī," which is in

---

[65] f. 124a: *bular har ne bar awliyā-lar, ḥaḍrat-i khūja alam-dār* [*sic*] *ṣaḥāba jānbāz khūja-nïng qashïlarïda* [*sic*] *ékän-lär, hamma-larï ḥaḍrat-i khūja alam-dār ṣaḥāba jānbāz khūja-nïng ārqa-larïdïn érgäshib, bā-ittifāq kirib khān-gha fātiḥa oqudïlar, qïrghïzlarnï almaqdïn özge chāra qalmadï dédilär.*

[66] These two saints are known from the Bughrā-khānid *ghazavāt-nāma* cycle; on the shrine, see Dawut 2001: 54-59.

[67] *ḥaḍrat-i khūja aḥmad yasavī-ning analarïdur-men déb khān-gha fātiḥa oqudïlar.* This shrine may be the one discussed in Dawut 2001: 65-66 (with no reference to Aḥmad Yasavī or his mother); in this connection also note the story, mentioned by a 19th-century traveler, that ascribes a shrine near Yangï-ḥiṣār to the martyred wife of Ḥasan Bughrā Khān, identified as a "cousin" of Aḥmad Yasavī (see Bellew 1875: 366-367).

[68] The *nisba* may be read *b.khīvī, n.jīvī, naḥbavī*, etc.

Chamālūn [*j.mālūn.d.gī*];[69] he too became manifest and recited a blessing for the *khān*.

This is essentially the last shrine mentioned as such, but the account concludes with a final passage that reassembles some saints already mentioned and introduces another one; the passage is typically enigmatic, but closes with the Prophet's own blessing and promise of support to the "Moghūl" ruler:

> After that, Khoja Khiḍr, with 200 of his disciples, with the exalted disciples of the holy Khoja Aḥmad Yasavī, and with 500 *shaykhs*, as well as all sorts of [saints] with their own companions, recited a blessing for the *khān* and then went before the *khān*. The *khān* seized the Qïrghïz and came to Yārkand. All the saints who were present came, together with Alf Ata,[70] who is in Qïzïl, and 600 companions, all bare-headed; the companions remained outside the court, while Alf Ata came forward, bare-headed, and entered inside. The Uvaysī [saints] [?] addressed Alf Ata and said, "You make the oppressors be your followers, make them bow their heads, and arrange for them to give you offerings;" thus they pardoned [their] fault, placed turbans on their heads, and recited the *takbīr*. The holy Prophet (may God bless him and keep him) appeared, and established the shrine-dwelling for Khoja Muḥammad Sharīf Pīr along the Shār [M.thār?] irrigation channel in Yārkand. He recited a blessing for the *khān*, and then said to the *shaykhs* of the land of Kāshghar, "I too will aid the Moghūl prince down to the time of the Resurrection; you all help him as well." Then the Prophet of God set off for Madīna.[71]

This last passage is followed at once by the colophon, discussed above.

We may note here, with regard to this text's divergence from the *Tadhkira* of Muḥammad Sharīf, that the Jānbāz Khoja text pays virtually no attention to the battle that (in the other work) followed the appeals to the saints, or to the fate of the Qïrghïz; indeed, this text appears to envision the pardoning of the Qïrghïz, who are forced to submit and pay "offerings," rather than the wholesale slaughter and exemplary punishments inflicted on the Qïrghïz in some versions of the *Tadhkira* of Muḥammad Sharīf.[72] The Jānbāz text can hardly be called 'sympathetic' to the Qïrghïz, but,

---

[69] Chamālūn is mentioned in the history of Churās (Akimushkin 1976: 225), and is identified as a village east of the road linking Yārkand and Yangi-ḥiṣār (see p. 314, n. 299).

[70] On this saint of Turfan, whose shrine there is mentioned in hagiographical sources focused on Isḥāq Khwāja from the beginning of the 17th century, and whose name may be read as "Alif" or "Alp" Ata, see Kim 1993.

[71] *andïn keyin, khūja khiḍrī iki yüz murīd-läri bilän, ḥaḍrat khūja aḥmadī yasavī-ning a'lā murīdläri bilän, besh yüz mashāyikh-lär bilän, har qaysï-larï öz aṣḥāba-larï* [*sic*] *bilän khān-gha fātiḥa oqub, andïn keyin khān-nïng āldïgha bardïlar; khān qïrghïzlarnï alïb, yārkand-gä keldilär; har ne bar jamī' awliyā-lar qïzïl-de-gī alf ātā alta yüz aṣḥāba-lar* [*sic*] *bilän yalāng-bash keldilär, aṣḥāba-lar bargāh-dïn tashqarï qaldï, alf atā yalāng bash īlgeri kelib ichkeri kirdi-lär; ūsyān* [*uvaysīyān?*] *khiṭāb bile alf atā-nï sen ẓālim-larnï özüng-gä muqtadī qïlïb, bash chaldurub, naẓrī niyāz* [*sic*] *qïldurub tüzüb ala-sen déb* [as catchword only] (f. 125a) *taqṣīr-nï mu'āf qïlïb, bashïgha dastār qoyub, takbīr aytï-lar; ḥaḍrat-i payghāmbar ṣallā'llāhu 'alayhi wa sallama ḥāḍir boldïlar, khūja muḥammad sharīf pīr-ning mazārïnï manzīl-lärini yārkande shār* [*? m.thār*] *ayrïqï-nïng* [*sic*] *boyïda qarār tabturdïlar; khān-gha fātiḥa oqub, kāshghar-dhamīn-de-gī mashāyikh-largha aytïlar kim moghūl tūra-sige* [app., but the *sīn* is written in such a way that it appears to read "*k.y.ka*," with two dots but two *markazes*] *tā dawrī qiyāmat-ghacha, men ham madad qïlur-men, sizlar ham madad qïlïnglar, déb payghāmbarī khudā madīn-ge* [*sic*] *'azm qïldïlar.*

[72] In MS facs., we are told that of the Qïrghïz fought by the *khān*'s army, 20 were taken alive, 50 escaped and saved themselves, and all the rest were slain (the 20 captives were divided into two

compared with the other work, it ignores the reason for the campaign against them, repeatedly mentions "seizing" them rather than slaying them, and alludes to their incorporation back into the fold of subjects duly submissive to the Moghūl ruler and the saints who sustain him.

* * *

Such is the list of shrines in the first part of the text. The actual story of Jānbāz Khoja that follows is, as we have seen, not unlike many other accounts of essentially ahistorical Islamizing warrior saints, who come from the center of the Muslim world to fight for the faith and spread it in a far-off region, that have been transmitted orally, and recorded in written *tadhkiras*, in Xinjiang and throughout Central Asia (and beyond). The initial short work, however, is quite unlike anything else I have found among the *tadhkiras* of this region; other such works typically focus on a single saint, and a single shrine, and while they may mention other holy sites, the long list assembled here, and linked, however awkwardly, with a historically-remembered pilgrimage, appears to be unique.

More broadly, however, in combining a shrine catalogue with a story of Islamization, the *Tadhkira* of Jānbāz Khoja resembles a work I have studied earlier, focused on the shrines and sacred history of Sayrām;[73] and insofar as it seems to project an itinerary of shrine visits onto a 'historical' pilgrimage by a noted figure — in this case, the Chaghatayid ruler 'Abd al-Rashīd Khān — we may suggest that it most closely resembles the account of the shrines of the Volga-Ural region, or "Bulghār," and their visitation by Timur, as studied by Allen Frank.[74] In any event, like the latter work, the *Tadhkira* of Jānbāz Khoja was undoubtedly based on earlier materials, but is most valuable for offering historical evidence on shrine traditions of Xinjiang prominent in the late 19th century, when we know the lone surviving copy was produced; and as such it may contribute, in conjunction with earlier sources and later ethnographic surveys, to a better understanding of the religious geography of Xinjiang.

groups, one sent to Kāshghar and one to Yārkand, where they were flayed and killed). The version translated by Iudin mentions the 20 left alive, and the killing of all the others; MS Uppsala, meanwhile, includes mention of the two groups of ten captives sent to the two cities, but specifies that their captors killed them, "pulled off their skins, stuffed them with straw, and hung them in the market-square" (*tere-sini soyub, saman tïqïb, chahārsū-gha astïlar*).

[73] DeWeese 2000.

[74] Frank 1996.

References

Akimushkin, O. F. (ed. & tr.) 1976. *Shāh Maḥmūd ibn Mīrzā Fāẓil Churās, Khronika.* Moscow: Nauka; Pis'mennye pamiatniki Vostoka, XLV.

Akimushkin, O. F. 2001. *Tārīkh-i Kāshġar: Anonimnaia tiurkskaya Khronika vladetelei Vostochnogo Turkestana po konets XVII veka.* Facs. ed. O. F. Akimushkin. St. Petersburg: Peterburgskoe Vostokovedenie; Pamiatniki kul'tury Vostoka, VIII.

Baldick, Julian 1993. *Imaginary Muslims: The Uwaysi Sufis of Central Asia.* New York: New York University Press/London: I. B. Tauris.

Bellew, H. N. 1875. *Kashmir and Kashghar: A Narrative of the Journey of the Embassy to Kashghar in 1873-74.* London: Trübner.

Brentjes, B. 1983. "Das Grabmal des Muḥammad Boššaro - ein Vorläufer timuridischer Baukunst." in D. Sturm (ed.) *Ibn Ḫaldun und seine Zeit,* Halle: Martin-Luther Universität, 17-23.

Comneno, M. A. L. 1993. "La necropoli dei Wensu nel Xinjiang: considerazioni a un peculiarità dell'Islām centro-asiatico." in *Islàm: Storia e Civiltà,* 12/42: 19-33, 71, 73.

Dawut, Rahilä 2001. *Uyghur mazarliri.* Urumqi: Shinjang Khälq Näshriyati.

DeWeese, Devin 1993. "An 'Uvaysī' Sufi in Timurid Mawarannahr: Notes on Hagiography and the Taxonomy of Sanctity in the Religious History of Central Asia." in *Papers on Inner Asia,* No. 22, Bloomington: Indiana University, Research Institute for Inner Asian Studies.

DeWeese, Devin 1995. "The *Tadhkira-i Bughrā-khān* and the 'Uvaysī' Sufis of Central Asia: Notes in Review of *Imaginary Muslims.*" in *Central Asiatic Journal,* 40: 87-127.

DeWeese, Devin 2000. "Sacred History for a Central Asian Town: Saints, Shrines, and Legends of Origin in Histories of Sayrām, 18th-19th Centuries." in Denise Aigle (ed.) *Figures mythiques des mondes musulmans.* Paris; *Revue des mondes musulmans et de la Méditerranée,* 89-90: 245-295.

DeWeese, Devin 2011. "The 'Competitors' of Isḥāq Khwāja in Eastern Turkistan: Hagiographies, Shrines, and Sufi Affiliations in the Late Sixteenth Century." in İlker Evrim Binbaş and Nurten Kılıç-Schubel (eds), *Horizons of the World: Festschrift for Isenbike Togan/Hududü'l-Alem: İsenbike Togan'a Armağan,* Istanbul: İthaki Press, 133-215.

DeWeese, Devin. forthcoming: "An 'Uvaysī' Hagiography from Eastern Turkistān: The Tadhkira of Quṭb al-Dīn 'Irāqī," in *Etudes orientales: Revue culturelle semestrielle* (Paris, forthcoming).

Dmitrieva, L. V. 2002. *Katalog tiurkskikh rukopisei Instituta vostokovedeniia Rossiiskoi Akademii nauk.* Moscow: Vostochnaia literatura.

Dūghlāt: Mīrzā Muḥammad Ḥaydar Dūghlāt, *Tārīkh-i Rashīdī.* 2 vols. Ed. and tr. W. M. Thackston, *Mirza Haydar Dughlat's Tarikh-i-Rashidi: A History of the Khans of Moghulistan* (Cambridge, Massachusetts: Harvard University, Department of Near Eastern Languages and Civilizations, 1996; *Sources of Oriental Languages and Literatures,* 38, ed. Şinasi Tekin and Gönül Alpay Tekin, *Central Asian Sources* II-III).

Eden, Jeffrey 2015. *The Life of Muhammad Sharif: A Central Asian Sufi Hagiography*; with an appendix by David Brophy and Rian Thum, Vienna: Verlag der Österreichischen Akademie der Wissenschaften [Veröffentlichungen zur Iranistik].

Frank, Allen J. 1996. "Islamic Shrine Catalogues and Communal Geography in the Volga-Ural Region: 1788-1917," in *Journal of Islamic Studies,* 7: 265-286.

Gürsoy-Naskali, Emine (ed. and tr.) 1985. *Aṣḥābu'l-Kähf: A Treatise in Eastern Turki.* Helsinki: Suomalais-Ugrilainen Seura; Suomalais-Ugrilaisen Seuran Toimituksia/Mémoires de la Société Finno-ougrienne, 192.

Hamada Masami 1978. "Islamic Saints and Their Mausoleums." in *Acta Asiatica,* 34: 79-98.

Hamada Masami 1992. "Rupture ou continuité: Le calendrier des douze animaux chez les musulmans turcophones du Turkestan Oriental," in Jean-Louis Bacqué-Grammont and Rémy Dor (eds), *Mélanges offerts à Louis Bazin par ses disciples, collègues et amis,* Paris: Éditions l'Harmattan, 285-291.

Hamada Masami 2001. "Le mausolée et le culte de Satuq Bughrâ Khân." in *Journal of the History of Sufism,* 3 (= *Saints and Heroes on the Silk Road*), 63-87.

Hamada Masami (ed.) 2006. *Hagiographies du Turkestan Oriental: Textes čaġatay édités, traduits en japonais et annotés avec une introduction analytique et historique*, Kyoto: Graduate School of Letters, Kyoto University.

Hartmann, Martin 1903. "Chademğai", in *Orientalistische Litteratur-zeitung*, 1903, No. 9 (April), cols. 361-367.

Iudin, V. P. 1969. (introduction and notes to the Russian translation of excerpts from the *Tadhkira* of Khoja Muḥammad Sharīf), in *Materialy po istorii kazakhskikh khanstv XV-XVIII vekov*, ed. S. K. Ibragimov, N. N. Mingulov, K. A. Pishchulina, and V. P. Iudin (Alma-Ata: Izdatel'stvo 'Nauka' Kazakhskoi SSR): 407, 518.

Iudin, V. P. 1987. "Anonimnoe tiurkoiazychnoe sochinenie vtoroi poloviny XVI v. iz Vostochnogo Turkestana 'Tazkira-ii Khodzha Mukhammad Sharif' (Istoriko-istochnikovedcheskoe vvedenie, perevod, kommentarii)" in *Voprosy istorii i kul'tury uigurov*, Alma-Ata: Nauka, 4-40.

Jarring, Gunnar 1935. "The Ordam-Padishah-System of Eastern Turkistan Shrines," in *Hyllningsskrift tillägnad Sven Hedin på hans 70-årsdag den 19 Febr. 1935* (= *Geografiska annaler 1935, Årg. XVII*): 348-354.

Kim, Ho-dong 1993. "The Cult of Saints in Eastern Turkestan: The Case of Alp Ata in Turfan," in *Proceedings of the 35th Permanent International Altaistic Conference* (September 12-17, 1992, Taipei, China), Taipei: Center for Chinese Studies Materials/United Daily News Cultural Foundation, 199-226.

Muginov, A. M. (ed.) 1962. *Opisanie uigurskikh rukopisei Instituta narodov Azii*. Moscow: Izdatel'stvo Vostochnoi Literatury.

Orxun, Abliz, and Sugawara Jun (eds) 2007. *Mazar Documents from Xinjiang and Ferghana (Facsimile)*, vol. 2 (Studia Culturae Islamicae, No. 87), Tokyo: Research Institute for Languages and Cultures of Asia and Africa, Tokyo University of Foreign Studies.

Pantusov, N. N. 1909. "Musul'manskie mazary v g. Uch-Turfane i okrestnostyakh ego (v kitaiskikh predelakh),"*Zapiski Imperatorskogo Russkogo geograficheskogo obshchestva po otdeleniyu ètnografii*, 34 (= *Sbornik v chest' semidesiatiletiya Grigoriya Nikolaevicha Potanina*,) 431-444 + 7 pl.

Pantusov, N. N. 1910. "Gorod Almalyk i Mazar Tugluk-Timur-khana" and "Legenda o Tugluk-Timur-khane," in *Kaufmanskii sbornik, izdannyi v pamyat' 25 let, istekshikh so dnya smerti pokoritelya i ustroitelya Turkestanskogo kraya, general-ad'yutanta K. P. fon-Kaufmana*, Moscow, 161-202.

Ross, E. Denison 1908. *Three Turki Manuscripts from Kashghar*. Lahore: Mufid-i-'am Press/Archaeological Survey of India.

Sawada Minoru 2001a. "A Study of the Current Ordam-Padshah System," in *Journal of the History of Sufism*, 3 (= *Saints and Heroes on the Silk Road*): 89-111.

Sawada Minoru 2001b. "Tarim Basin Mazārs: A Fieldwork Report," in *Journal of the History of Sufism*, 3 (= *Saints and Heroes on the Silk Road*): 39-61.

Shaw, R. B. 1877. "A Grammar of the Language of Eastern Turkistán," in *Journal of the Asiatic Society of Bengal*, n.s., 46: 242-368.

Shinmen Yasushi 2003. "The History of the Mausoleum of the *Aṣḥāb al-Kahf* in Turfan," in *Memoirs of the Research Department of the Toyo Bunko*, 61: 83-104.

Tadhkira-yi Abū Sa'īd Qūchqār Ata. MS St. Petersburg, Institute of Oriental Studies, C561 (described in Muginov 1962: 78, No. 107; cf. Dmitrieva 2002: 217, No. 787).

Tadhkira-yi Bughrā-khānī (Tadhkira-yi mashā'ikh-i Uvaysīya). Ed. Muḥammad Munīr 'Ālam. Islamabad: Markaz-i Taḥqīqāt-i Fārsī-i Īrān va Pākistān, 1376/1998.

Tadhkira-yi Jānbāz Khoja. MS St. Petersburg, B731 (described in Muginov 1962: 69, No. 87; cf. Dmitrieva 2001: 222-223, No. 818).

Tadhkira-yi Khoja Muḥammad Sharīf. MS Uppsala, Nov. 613, ff. 168b-180a (described in Zetterstéen 1935: 141, No. 720/7).

Tadhkira-yi Khoja Muḥammad Sharīf. MS facs., in Orxun and Sugawara 2007: 120-147 (ff. 2b-30a).

Tadhkira-yi Khoja Quṭb al-Dīn 'Irāqī. MS St. Petersburg, B737 (described in Muginov 1962: 77, No. 104; cf. Dmitrieva 2002: 222, No. 815).

Tadhkira-yi Mawlānā 'Arsh al-Dīn Valī. MS St. Petersburg, C556 (described in Muginov 1962: 89, No. 135; cf. Dmitrieva 2002: 220, No. 805 [wrongly called C856, corrected in the index on p. 599]); MS St. Petersburg, B736 (Muginov 1962: 91, No. 140; cf. Dmitrieva 2002: 221, No. 809).

Trippner, Joseph 1961. "Islamische Gruppen und Gräberkult in Nordwest-China," in *Die Welt des Islams*, N.S., 7: 142-171.

Voronina, V. L., and K. S. Kriukov 1978. "Mavzolei Mukhammeda Boshsharo," in *Drevnost' i srednevekov'e narodov Srednei Azii (Istoriya i kul'tura)*, Moscow: Nauka, 58-68.

Zarcone, Thierry 1999. "Quand le saint légitime le politique: le mausolée de Afaq Khwaja à Kashgar,"*Central Asian Survey*, 18 : 225-241.

Zarcone, Thierry 2001. "Le culte des saints au Xinjiang de 1949 à nos jours," in *Journal of the History of Sufism*, 3 (= *Saints and Heroes on the Silk Road*): 133-172.

Zetterstéen, K. V. 1935. *Die arabischen, persischen und türkischen Handschriften der Universitätsbibliothek zu Uppsala*, vol. 2. Uppsala.

A Sufi Travelogue as a Source for the History of Mazars in the Tarim Basin[*]

Alexandre PAPAS

Introduction

Compared to other historical fields—economic or social history for instance—there is no lack of sources for historians of Central Asian mazars. Although it is certainly more difficult to find mazar documents for periods prior to the 20th and 19th centuries, we find plenty of genealogies, hagiographies, *waqf* certificates and so on for pre-modern and medieval times. All of these sources are fundamental to the study of mazars, as recent discoveries by Yayoi Kawahara and Jun Sugawara have shown. The problem of such sources is that they, paradoxically or not so paradoxically, do not provide many details about the religious aspects of *ziyāratgāhs*, that is, the places themselves, people who visit them, rituals and general information about religious life in and around the shrines. From this perspective, one would expect that another type of text, pilgrimage guides (whether *ḥajjnāma*, *ziyārat* accounts or *faḍā'il* literature), would describe these different aspects, but this is not often the case. These sources not only belong to a rhetorical genre that limits original and personal observations, they also focus strictly on practical matters. Authors are naturally more interested in informing their readers about itineraries and travel conditions than in depicting sacred landscapes, holy cities and pilgrimage life.

Yet, there are always exceptions. Like famous examples from the Christian world—such as the anonymous *Otkrovennye razskazy strannika dukhovnomu svoemu ottsu*[1]for the Eastern Orthodox Church or *The Book of Margery Kempe*[2] and Pierre Favre's *Memorial*[3] for Catholics—several prominent Muslim mystics authored travel narratives that combine personal experience, ethnographic sketches and initiatic processes, the most celebrated example of which is probably 'Abd al-Ghanī al-Nābulusī's *Riḥlas*.[4] Regarding Central Asia, more precisely the Tarim Basin, we find an exceptional text within the works of the Sufi poet Muḥammad Ṣiddīq Zalīlī. In many respects, his

* I would like to thank Prof. Masami Hamada for his help during my reading of Zalīlī's *Safarnāma*.

[1] First published in Kazan in 1780, and then in 1881 in a more complete version. There is a French translation under the title *Récits d'un pèlerin russe*, traduits et présentés par Jean Laloy, 1963.

[2] Written in 1436, the critical edition was established by S.B. Meech and H.E. Allen in 1940.

[3] Composed between 1542 and 1545, and firstly edited in 1853 at the Collège Brugelette.

[4] See Sirriyeh 1985.

travelogue bears the same characteristics as the aforementioned writings. Highly sensitive to the spiritual atmosphere of places, prompted by a sort of inexhaustible pious curiosity, the *Safarnāma*, as it is called, appears as a unique source for the religious history of mazars in the Tarim Basin. This article offers an overview of Zalīlī's *Safarnāma* while comparing the descriptions given in the text with fieldwork observations performed in the nineteenth and early twentieth centuries, and in present-day Xinjiang.

A Short Biography of Muḥammad Ṣiddīq Zalīlī

The biography of Zalīlī is far from clear. As far as I know, the only biographical information we can find comes from his writings. This lack of sources is hardly surprising since the poet is not well known outside of Kashgaria; still puzzling is the fact that chronicles, hagiographies, and literary works issued from Kashgaria do not mention him. There is also a dearth of scholarly works on Zalīlī. Except in Xinjiang and Kazakhstan, we find few seminal publications: Zalīlī's *Dīwān*, which has been edited in Uyghur in 1985 by the great writer and scholar Imin Tursun;[5] a study of his travelogue by Abdushukur Turdi;[6] two studies on his works in general, published by Räjäp Yusup and Savut Mollaudov, respectively;[7] lastly, a curious popular novel written by Batur Rozi.[8] In his *Catalogue of publications in Uyghur on history and civilization*, Eziz Atawula Sartekin lists additional references; however, they seem less important and are often repetitive.[9]

---

[5] Tursun 1985.

[6] Turdi 1982.

[7] Yusup 1983; Mollaudov 1990.

[8] Rozi 2003.

[9] Sartekin 2004: 663-664. Here are the references (without pagination or place name): Zälili, 'Sheirlar' *Shinjiang ädäbiyat-säniti*, 1957-12; Muhämmäd Sidiq Zälili, 'Säpärnamä' *Bulaq*, 1980-1; A. Muhämmätimin, 'Muhämmät Sidiq Zälili wä uning ijadiyät roli' *Shinjiang ädäbiyati*, 1980-6; Muhämmäd Sidiq Zälili (Ömär Ismayil näshrgä täyyarlighan), 'Täzkirä khoja muhämmäd shirip buzurgwar' *Qädimki kitablar tätqiqat khäwiri*, 1984-1; Ghäyratjan Osman, 'Muhämmäd Sidiq Zälili wä uning ijadi paaliyätliri', *Uyghur klassik ädäbiyati tarikhidin tezis*, Shinjang Universiteti Näshriyati, 1987; Wahitjan Ghupur and Äsqär Hüsäyn, 'Muhämmäd Sidiq Zälili wä uning ijadi paaliyiti' *Uyghur klassik ädäbiyati tezisliri*, Millätlär Näshriyati, 1987; Mättokhti Ähmäd, 'Zälili wä säpärnamä' *Khotän ali pedagogika mäktipi ilmiy zhurnili*,, 1989-1; Ghäyratjan Osman, 'Zälili wä uning lirikliri', *Uyghur klassik ädäbiyatining qisqichä tarikhi*, 1992; Muhämmättokhti Ähmäd, 'Zälili wä säpärnamä dastani' *Qäshqär pedagogika instituti ilmiy zhurnili*, 1992-4; Zälili 'Ghäzällär' *Tängritagh*, 1993-2 and 1993-3; Abdushükür Muhämmätimin, 'Muhämmät Sidiq Zälili' *Uyhgur ädäbiyat tarikhi 3*, Shinjang Maarip Näshriyati, 1993; Ghäyratjan Osman, 'Zälili wä uning ijadiyiti', *Uyghur klassik ädäbiyatining qisqichä tarikhi 2*, 1996; Sharipidin Ömär, 'Zälili wä uning ijadi paaliyiti', *Ottura äsir uyghur kilassik ädäbiyati 2*, Shinjang Khälq Näshriyati, 1996; Iminjan Äkhmidi, 'Muhämmäd Sidiq Zälili', *Uyghur ädäbiyati tarikhidiki namayändilär*, Shinjang Khälq Näshriyati, 1996; Abduwäli Ayup, 'Zälili leriklirididiki insanpärwärlik wä wätänpärwärlik', *Tarim*, 2001-9; Ghäyratjan Osman, 'Muhämmäd Sidiq Zälili', *Uyghur klassik ädäbiyat tarikhi*, Shinjiang Khälq Näshriyati, 2001; Guljamal Mämtimin, 'Zälilining hayat paaliyätliri', *Uyghur klassik ädäbiyat tarikhi 2*, Shinjang Maarip Näshriyati, 2002; Guljamal Mämtimin, 'Zälilining lirikliri häqqidä', *Uyghur klassik ädäbiyat tarikhi 2*, Shinjang Maarip Näshriyati,

For the sake of clarity, I distinguish three periods of the life of Muḥammad Ṣiddīq Zalīlī:

Childhood and Early Adulthood

Muḥammad Ṣiddīq was born in Yārkand, probably in 1087 or 1091 *ḥijrī*, that is, 1676 or 1680.[10] Most biographies state that he came from a poor family of peasants, but nothing in his work confirms this supposition. Given the social conditions of this period, it is quite improbable that a peasant child could become a man of letters (*adib*). He spent his childhood and the first years of his adulthood in his hometown, the capital city of the declining Yārkand Khanate. The city was also a religious and intellectual capital, through, notably, the famous Khānlīq madrasa where Zalīlī was trained to become *'ālim* and *ākhūnd*.[11] There he learned classical Islamic sciences and languages (Arabic and Persian). Zalīlī would author 56 *ghazal* in Persian.[12]

Adulthood and Maturity

Seeking for further knowledge (*'ilm*) and mystical experience, namely love (*'ishq*), the young scholar decided to leave Yārkand and started a long initiatic journey. This is clearly in continuity with the Islamic tradition of the *ṭalab al-'ilm* and, more widely, of the *riḥla*, which was particularly active in the seventeenth and eighteenth centuries among Sufi groups throughout the Muslim world.[13] Yet what is interesting in Zalīlī's case is the fact that, unlike many others, he did not go to the main Muslim centres of knowledge or sanctity (such as Bukhara, Istanbul or Mecca). Instead, he travelled within the Tarim Basin. He remained in what was called Mughūliyya.

The Writing Period

His long journey took about fifteen years. Then, Muḥammad Ṣiddīq Zalīlī stayed in Khotan until his death in 1755 at the age of approximately 75-80.[14] This was the time of his intellectual production. As far as we know, Zalīlī composed only one *Dīwān*, almost entirely written in Chagatay Turkic. It contains poetry (*ghazal*, *rubā'ī*, *qaṣīda*, *mukhammas* and so on);[15] hagiographies such as the *Tadhkira-yi chihiltan* composed in 1736,[16] then

---

2002; Abdushükür Muhämmätimin, 'Zälili wä uning ijtimayi qarashliri', *Shinjang millätlärning pälsäpiwi idiyä tarikhidin ocherklar*, Shinjang Khälq Näshriyati, 2002.

[10] Tursun 1985: 2; Turdi 1982: 202. We find the date of 1674 in Yusup 1983: 74.

[11] Tursun 1985: 3-4; Yusup, 1983: 74 quotes Zälili considering the city of Yārkand as a 'garden of science and knowledge' and a 'garden of music and singing'. There is a wide range of Uyghur publications dealing with the cultural role of Yārkand; nevertheless, I would like to mention an unpublished work by Abdiqadir Dawut entitled *Yärkän tarikhi*, completed in 1982, which presents an interesting historical overview (pp. 89-110 in particular).

[12] Tursun 1985: 22.

[13] See, for instance, the introduction (more particularly the section devoted to the 'renouveau de la *rihla*') by Rachida Chih and Catherine Mayeur-Jaouen in Chih & Mayeur-Jaouen 2010.

[14] Yusup 1983: 75-76, 78 footnote 1. This author claims that Zalīlī was first buried in Khotan, and then reburied in a place called Altunluq (not to be confused with the well-known Altunluq shrine in Yārkand). His grave is marked *Muhämmät Siddiq Yärkänd Khälipäm qävrisi.*

[15] Tursun 1985: 8-9.

the *Tadhkira-yi khwāja muḥammad sharīf buzurgwar* written between 1742 and 1745. However, his first piece of writing (contained in the *Dīwān*) is the *Safarnāma*, which was completed in 1131/1718[17] in Khotan.[18] There are at least two manuscript copies of Zalīlī's *Dīwān*, and these are both preserved in the Xinjiang Museum in Urumqi. The first one is the so-called 'Major Divan' (*Chung Diwan*) that has been copied by a lineage of scribes: Mūnis Khwāja, Abū Shāhīm, Mullāh Qābil and Muḥammad Mīrad. The second manuscript is the so-called 'Minor Divan' (*Kichik Diwan*). Both contain the *Safarnāma*, but I was only able to access a copy of the second manuscript.[19] This manuscript consists of 130 folios, 9 lines per page and was written in late Nasta'līq style. The *Safarnāma* itself covers 64 folios—from [folio 56a] to [folio 119a]. It is composed entirely in verse, and it follows the *prosodic* characteristics of the mathnawī form.

Our author is obviously not the only writer at this time. Several other prominent East Turkestanese poets can be mentioned such as Nawbatī from Khotan or Muḥammad Amīn Khwājamqulī Ḥarakatī from Kāshghar.[20] Before and after Zalīlī, we find comparable figures, such as the well-known Bābāraḥim Mashrab and 'Abdullāh Nidā'ī Kāshgharī.[21] Clearly, the seventeenth and eighteenth centuries can be considered to be a prolific time for literature in the Tarim Basin. This is supplementary evidence—if need be—that the Khwāja rule, under the Mongol Zunghar suzerainty, was not the dark age so often depicted in Sino-Uyghur historiography.

Following the Path of Zalīlī

Although the *Safarnāma* raises many interesting questions—for instance, that of the *ḥajj* and its esoteric substitute via *ziyārat*, or the problem of the revival of Qalandar practices—I will deliberately leave them (and all the corresponding quotations) aside and focus on the historical value of this source, specifically on the physical information regarding mazars as well as the ethnographical observations made by Zalīlī and his companions on these mazars.

The Kāshghar area

If we follow Zalīlī's route, after his departure from Yārkand, he comes to the Kāshghar area and the mazar of Sulṭān Satūq Būghrā Khān. The pilgrim describes his arrival in the following verses:[22]

> I was roaming the roads until the afternoon prayer
> Beware when you pass through Bäghlär Tūgh!

---

[16] Yusup 1983: 76.

[17] Tursun 1985: 2.

[18] Turdi 1983: 211. It could also be 1720, according to Bahavidin, 1982: 301.

[19] I am particularly indebted to Jun Sugawara for giving me access to this rare document.

[20] Bahavidin, 1982: 296-298. See the various names given in Mämät, 2001: 3-61.

[21] For a detailed study of these three figures and their travelogues, see my book Papas, 2010.

[22] Muḥammad Ṣiddīq Zalīlī, *Dīwān*, Xinjiang Museum, Ms. 80b-81a; Tursun 1985: 594-595.

Without looking at my companions
I reached Chirmash *langar*

There I spent the night and left again at dawn
Without seeing that the day has risen

There was a crowd with drums and tambourines
That I met along the roads with poplar trees

I forgot my being and nothingness
I was then at the foot of Bughrāqūm

There, at this moment, I lamented
My lamenting face was like a wilted leaf

I shouted Āyā Ḥaḍrat-i Sulṭān Satūq
May the Lord open the door in this desert

I circumambulated your holy tomb
May my breast be purified by polishing it

(...)

Bughrāqūm became like Karbalā
In this desert, everything was sadness

Here the air is the most burning
Here the passion is the most passionate

It is impossible to locate the Chirmash *langar* since what remains of these refuges, when they still exist, rarely bears any name now. At least, what a historian can infer from this mention—and from many others as we shall see—is the existence of a relatively dense network of resting houses and basic accommodations. Such *langar*s were still functioning at the turn of the nineteenth and twentieth centuries as is shown by various expedition reports.[23] The ritual using musical instruments described here probably refers to a religious festival that could be the celebration of the saint's death.[24] Zalīlī himself performs the *ṭawāf* on the tomb. Lastly, our author compares Satūq Būghrā Khān's mazar with Karbalā, that is, to the place of Imām Ḥusayn's martyrdom, suggesting that the Qarakhanid khan was considered to be a martyr or that his shrine aroused an equivalent emotion among the pilgrims.[25] Even if the figure of Ḥusayn is

[23] See, at different periods, Grabczewski 1885: I, 131-132, 196, 207-210; Stein 1928: IV, maps n° 2, 12, 14, 17, 21, 30, 31.

[24] For material and historical details on this mazar, see Hamada, 2001; Dawut 2001: 1-6; Mäshhädi 2005: 21-23, 44-53, 70-74; Turan 2006: 175-176; Papas 2008. This mazar is now one of the most official and monumental shrines of Xinjiang, yet the cult is still active (personal observations in July 2008).

[25] Perhaps, there is also an allusion to a son of Satūq called Ḥusayn who died in 369/979-980 during *ghazāt* against Khotanese Buddhists. He is supposedly buried at Chüje Padishahim Mazar (5 kms

also venerated in Sunni Central Asia, its mention reveals a deep influence, and former presence, of Shiism in the Tarim Basin. The village (nearby Atush)[26] where Satūq Būghrā's mazar is situated is indeed called Mashhad/Mäshhäd:[27]

> At the other side of these mountains, was
> The limits of Satūq Būghrā Khān's territory
>
> From all directions, there were mountains
> The valley was composed of gardens
>
> In Mashhad, in summer as well as winter
> There are rivers flowing
>
> On Fridays, from morning to evening
> People gather to perform the circumambulation
>
> People fill up the saint's cemetery
> They parade like angels or stars
>
> Each one of them is a servant of Mashhad
> To make raise Mashhad
>
> One after the other, they light torches
> They are trembling like Sīmurgh's eggs
>
> They come to kiss the traces of the saint
> They come to harvest the seeds of knowledge
>
> To defend the religious rules
> To protect the weak and the fool
>
> The anchorites pray for the others
> The hermits ask for God's sake
>
> They attend the circumambulation
> They watch on the door of repentance

This valuable testimony confirms the vitality of the cult of Satūq. Asides from the description of the 'territory' of the saint bordered by mountains (probably the Tängritagh foothills), this excerpt attests to the popular practice of weekly *ziyārat*. The devotions include donations to *'ājiz ū ḥayrān* and blessings to pilgrims by solitary ascetics (*gūsha nishīnān, ṣawma'a dārān*). Zalīlī stays there three years and three months:

west of Yengisar). See Molla Haji 1988: 16. Nowadays, this shrine is mainly used by women to ask the saints' help in giving birth to a child. They repetitively crawl through a small arch made of wood and, sometimes, prepare small dolls (*qorchaq*) that represent a child, which they usually leave on the ground near the saint's grave (personal observations in July 2004).

26 For place names not mentioned in the text, I use modern Uyghur spellings. For the others, I use both when the toponym is identifiable today.

27 Muḥammad Ṣiddīq Zalīlī, *Dīwān*, Ms. 84b-85a; Tursn, 1985: 600-601.

Three years and three months, Zalīlī the poor / His face yellowed like a fall leaf.[28] In the meantime, between his first visit and this second long stay at Mashhad, Zalīlī travels to Kāshghar/Qäshqär. On the way, he uses two other *langar* (Chitlīq and Dungarlima), reaches Qarāqir (location of the future Kāshghar *yangī shahr*), crosses the Zanjīr River[29] and arrives in the suburb of Kāshghar. His aim is to worship the Khwāja holy tomb:[30]

After that, from there we started on our travel again
To take a look at Kāshghar

As the Almighty shows the way
Then appear the towns and the shrines

Until now, my eyes could not see the huge garden
Earth and heaven flooded with Divine grace

Its cells, its dome, its cupola, and its gate
The citadel was an arrow shooting far

In the *khānaqāh* and the cypress park
There, there are so many blessings

There the first grave causes suffering
It is covered by lapis-lazuli and banners

Here lies the Gnostic master of the *'ilm al-yaqīn*
The purity of religion, Khwāja Muḥammad Yūsuf

He is the one who grasped the Divine Law
He is the spiritual father of my master

(...)

The second grave is radiant
It is surrounded by numerous trees

Do not consider it a simple tomb, it is Mecca
Every day, many people come to see it

In the spiritual world, he is like the full moon
Khwāja-yi Āfāq is the king of men of the pen

He is the center of the circle of the pole of faith
He is from the spiritual chain of the Ḥaḍrat-i Makhdūm

(...)

---

28 Muḥammad Ṣiddīq Zalīlī, *Dīwān*, Ms. 85b; Tursun 1985: 601.
29 Muḥammad Ṣiddīq Zalīlī, *Dīwān*, Ms. 81b; Tursun 1985: 595.
30 Muḥammad Ṣiddīq Zalīlī, *Dīwān*, Ms. 82a-83a; Tursun 1985: 596-598.

He commented the beauties of the *Mathnawī*
The *Mathnawī-yi ma'nawī* of Mawlawī

He lifted from its face the imperceptible veil
He spread the pearls of wisdom

He opened his wings to the city of death
He reached the spiritual world

From his spiritual chain, then appeared
The illuminated Khwāja Yaḥya

The one at the service of Bahādūr Jahāngīr
Who, for the infidels' neck, was the sabre

On the mosque chair, this hero
Pronounced the *khuṭba* for the king

His name was Yaḥya, his surname Khān Khwājam
He was the sovereign of all the non-Arabs

This time, our author gives some material details of the architecture, gardens, adornments, the *tūghū 'alam* and so on. Moreover, he provides several pieces of biographical data about the saints by mentioning their genealogy (makhdūmī), intellectual and spiritual skills and politico-religious eminence—from Yūsuf to Yaḥya, who was exiled to India under Jahāngīr's reign. The surname of Mecca and the overall description of this mazar confirm the extent to which the Naqshbandī Khwājas were venerated at this time. Today, this mausoleum has become a museum, and Muslim pilgrims (including Huis) continue to go on *ziyārat*; the Friday Mosque within the complex is still in use.[31] The next stopover was Bishkiram/Bäshkeräm, 15 kilometres east of Kāshghar, where Zalīlī visits the tomb of Mīrzā Zīrak, a saint of the Qarakhanid dynasty from Chālīsh, whose *laqab* is Alif Atā, according to the *Safarnāma*.[32]

The Yārkand area

For unclear reasons, after a three-year stay in Atush, Zalīlī returns to his hometown Yārkand. However, this return is not a return to his former life. In Yārkand, the Qalandar Sufi—as he calls himself—stays only in mazars and lodges for two years:[33]

---

[31] Personal observations in June 2001, July 2004 and August 2008.

[32] Muḥammad Ṣiddīq Zalīlī, *Dīwān*, Ms. 83b-84b; Tursun 1985: 599-600. This is confusing since there is a well-known Qarakhanid saint named Alp Ata, whose mausoleum is located in Astana district near Turpan (see Qurbān 'Alī Khālidī 2b, 9b-13a; Kim 1993; Dawut 2001: 229-235; Wang 2004: 252-253). There is also a certain Mīrzā Mīrak who is buried at Bishkiram, see *Addendum to Tārīkh-i Rashīdī*, 2008, 403a.

[33] Muḥammad Ṣiddīq Zalīlī, *Dīwān*, Ms. 86b-88a; Tursun, 1985: 603-606.

Let's describe the city of Yārkand
Let's find the freshness of the gardens of Yārkand

The city was the place of the royal throne
The capital city of the whole Mughūliyya

It was a well-organized kingdom, a nice city
Compared to Āqsū and Kūchā

On one side runs the Yārkand River
If the year is wet, it overflows like a cauldron[34]

In front of the river is the cemetery of mystics
Where lies Khwāja Muḥammad Sharīf

The master of the masters of mystic lovers
The student of Sulṭān Satūq Būghra Khān

The city of Yārkand is always fresh
Where lies Khwāja Walī the jewel of Yārkand

Know that he was the master of kings and humbles
Know that he was a man of God

There is a high dome, also a *khānaqāh*
All travellers can shelter there

Each one hungry can be fed there
Each one naked can be dressed there

At nights from Thursday to Friday
People come on *ziyārat* there

But each day, they come for *nadhr* and *niyāz*
Whether Turks, Tajiks, Arabs or Persians

(...)

Let's present now the Seven Muḥammad
Let's describe this pure grave

Do not neglect the name of Seven Muḥammad
All are saints from the invisible world

This is why they are elected people
These saints are buried under the whirling dome

The outskirts of the graveyard are made of reed beds
The cemetery light comes from their graces

---

[34] This information is confirmed in Kerimi 2000: 172-173. The verse is ambiguous, it could mean: "If someone goes into ecstasies, he overflows like a cauldron".

Every people gather throughout the necropolis
On Thursdays and Fridays, one holds forty torches

Everywhere there are cells for spiritual retreat
Poles and banners are driven in tombs

The divine graces are not uncommon there
Those who do not circumambulate have a futile life

In this cemetery, the votive acts are not neglected
People do not come here without offerings

Men and women of Yārkand gather there
All their demands are satisfied

These rituals are performed mornings and evenings
Notables as well as common people come to celebrate

The strangers of the city stay in the *takiyya*
The poor of the city eat and drink there

Zalīlī evokes three major and quite well-documented shrines situated close to or within the city of Yārkand. Whereas the title of student or seeker (*ṭālib*) of Satūq Būghrā Khān regarding Muḥammad Sharīf alludes to the uwaysi initiation of the latter by the former, such a quotation shows a sort of continuity in the pilgrimage route of Zalīlī, which started at the first king converted to Islam and continued toward the main figures in the history of Islam in the Tarim Basin. Nowadays, the complex still encloses a *khānaqāh*, a mosque, and a *tilāwat khāna*, all of which are still active. The tomb of the Sufi saint is still regularly visited by devotees who will sometimes make a full day-tour of Yārkand's shrines by proceeding to Altunluq Mazar.[35] The description of that mazar is more precise: the so-called graves of the Naqshbandī shaykhs Khwāja Isḥāq and Khwāja Shādī (here Zalīlī repeats a common error about Isḥāq, who is probably buried in *Māwarānnahr* at Isfīdūk)[36] attract a large number of pilgrims every day. Interestingly, the author underlines the fact that the mazar's lodge welcomes many travellers (*musāfir*) and poor. At present, the *khānaqāh* no longer exists and the cemetery behind Altunluq still shelters many beggars during day time; at special occasions they benefit from collective charitable donations.[37] The third mazar, the Seven Muḥammad, better known today as Chihil Tan, seems to have not changed since Zalīlī's visit: the origin of the name that our author was not able to elucidate remains unclear (the seven shaykhs buried there are called Muḥammad, and they are said to be descendants from forty persons, *chihil tan*); the natural conditions, the crowd in the necropolis, the numerous ex-votos, poles and

[35] On Khwāja Muḥammad Sharīf Mazar, see Sawada 2001: 49-50; Dawut 2001: 80-82; personal observations in July 2004.

[36] On the problem of the localisation of his burial, see Sawada, 1996: 41-44.

[37] On Altunluq Mazar, see Dawut 2001: 72-76; Turan 2001: 130-131; personal observations in June 2001, July 2004 and August 2008.

banners, the cells (*ṣawma'a ḥujra*)—all this is still visible, while the ritual of the forty torches or the *takiyya* building have disappeared.[38]

The next stage of the trip is a short excursion outside Mughūliyya: following the path of a great Qalandar from Yārkand who left for *ḥajj*, Zalīlī crosses mountains and takes a caravan to a place named Sūsī. I believe this to be present-day Sust (in Upper Hunza), which was an old commercial outpost.[39] After a short stay, our traveller returns to Mughūliyya.

The road to Khotan

Zalīlī returns to his home region via Yārkand on the way to Khotan. This time, he travels with two companions:[40]

> I had two companions, two Sufis
> One was Dalīlī, the other was Mullāh Ghazal
>
> Us three, we were reading verses loudly
> We were wandering toward the walls of Yārkand
>
> This day, we left for the Yūlchāq river side
> The day after, we flew away from the water
>
> With Mullāh Ghazal and my younger brother Dalīlī
> We arrived in an instant at Pūskām
>
> Us three, we were like wild camels
> We spent that night at Yūsār
>
> Each of us, we were talking on a subject
> We quickly crossed the Tīznāb River
>
> If one goes out of the water, which city is this?
> The next city was Qārghālīq[41]
>
> We were going from town to town
> We could find supplies and food

---

[38] Dawut 2001: 83-88; Chvyr' 2006: 186. Here again, women ask God, by the intercession of the saints, to help with pregnancy or to solve marital problems in the home. They build miniature heaths from bricks and stones near the tomb and recite prayers (personal observations in June 2001, July 2004 and August 2008). The legend of the Haft Muḥammadān was well known to Zalīlī himself since he wrote a *Tadhkira-yi chihiltan*, on this question see Orxun & Sugawara 2007: 19-20.

[39] I thank Scott Levi for having given me this information. Yārkand was a departure/arrival point on the route linking Eastern Turkestan and Kashmir or Ladakh, see the report in Montgomerie, 1866.

[40] Muḥammad Ṣiddīq Zalīlī, *Dīwān*, Ms. 97b-100a; Tursun, 1985: 620-623.

[41] For a rare and interesting sketch of the old religious buildings of Qārghālīq and its region, see Khojähmät, 1983: 205-209.

Walking in the dust, we reached Luḥūq
On this fall day, it was surprisingly cold

On Saturday, we left Luḥūq
We took the road to Qūsh Chūlāq

(...)

During the day, the sun was burning us
At night, we were playing lute against the cold

In the sands, we suffered terribly
All the sufferings like Rustam

We reached Qūsh Langar
Almost lifeless, we lost consciousness

Unconscious, we laid on the grown of this *langar*
We stayed there until the afternoon prayer

The night slowly felt, we suddenly left
We walked on the road again

Morning has only just started
The rays of sunlight started to radiate

Evening has not yet hidden his face
The army of stars has not yet left

Then we were walking quickly
We saw the top of a tower[42]

There was a river but far from the desert
Alhtough we were thirsty, we were far from the Tangrī Lake[43]

(...)

We did not intend to stay in this refuge
Since the duty of the Qalandar is to be under way

It was an ancient *ribāṭ* in the wide world
Every people could spend the night and leave

Do not stay in this house, wise man
Free, I am drunk like ignorant people

Earth and heaven are the proofs of God
It was morning, we arrived at Gūmā

---

[42] Perhaps a stupa, the Turkic term is *tīm*.
[43] This lake is cited but not precisely located in Dutreuil de Rhins 1987-1898: III, 231.

(...)

After having passed this place
We visited the village of Mukūlyā

We passed Mūjī and a stony zone
Then appeared a place full of trees

We can say that at the end of this zone
It was a jungle like Māzandarān

But here, there was no plant growing
The name of this *langar* was Zangūyā

We implored God Above so much
We went to Piyālmā and spent the night

I have not been able to identify the Yūlchāq River and the town of Yūsār. The rest is easily recognizable from the contemporary toponyms in southern Xinjiang, the successive stopover towns follow an ancient caravan track: Pūskām/Poskam; Tīznāb/Tiznap River; Qārghālīq/Qaghliq; Luḥūq/Loq; Qūsh Chūlāq(/Qosh Dobä or Cholaq?); Gūmā/Guma; Mukūlyā/Mokoyla; Mūjī/Muji, Zangūyā/Zanguy and Piyālmā/Pialma. Here again, the network of *langars* and *ribāṭs* (small forts) along the desert road is worth noticing. Then, in the sands of the Taklamakan Desert, Zalīlī goes on pilgrimage to the famous mazar Qūm Rabāṭ Pādishāhīm that Jules-Léon Dutreuil de Rhins and Fernand Grenard,[44] and later Aurel Stein,[45] will visit 200 years later. As for the other shrines, Muḥammad Ṣiddīq provides short explanations of the identities and origins of the saints buried therein.[46]

We took a bit of rest there
We had discussions among men of God

We were then revived
We walked toward Qūm Rabāṭ

We took some steps forward
Before reaching the region, there was a tower

On the way, something magnificent appeared
There were also a *langar*, a *langarchī* and a mazar

All around there were only sand dunes
All around spread the fear of the lion

[44] Dutreuil de Rhins 1897-1898: II, 254.
[45] Stein 1907: I, 119-121. On the pre-Islamic holy place, see Sartekin 2005: 654-655.
[46] Muḥammad Ṣiddīq Zalīlī, *Dīwān*, Ms. 100a-100b; Tursun 1985: 623-624.

In the sand laid the master close to God
Ja'far-i Shākir the *imām* of religion

The stake of the love of God was pitched
As a tradition, numerous poles were tied

Ignore the links of his spiritual chain
Each member was a descendant of the Prophet

They came here to lead the holy war
They came to release this land from the infidels

At war, the infidel is full of tricks
Thus numerous *imāms* were martyred

They were buried in a spot of the desert
They were seventy to know this joy

The brief historico-legendary explanation given by our author is accurate. What is traditionally considered to be the first battle between Khotanese Buddhists and Muslims (then led by Imām Shākir) is indeed one the most famous stories of the Islamization of the Tarim Basin. Several versions of the episode of the *imāms*' martyrdom exist. The physical depiction (numerous *tūghs*, refuges and shelters) is quite interesting in so far as it complements the late pictures we find in nineteenth and early twentieth century Western travelogues. The Qūm Rabāṭ Mazar—also called Kaptar Mazar—is still renowned in Southern Xinjiang; local people recall the tragic story of martyred *imāms* and tend to apply it to the Cultural Revolution. However, the very remote location of the shrine results in a very difficult pilgrimage.[47] Zalīlī again takes to the road and continues his journey toward Qarāqāsh where he spends four months.[48] Unfortunately, he does not give much detail on this interlude. As a true vagrant mystic, he leaves again and goes to Lūp/Lop, then Dūl/Dol, using a *langar* called Reshme.[49] He finally reaches Chira/Chirä (90 kms east of Khotan).[50]

The Chira area

I was thirsty to go to Ja'far-i Ṣādiq
I was roaming in the desert

Becoming mad, I strayed from my path
I was like guided by the Prophet Khiḍr

---

[47] Personal observations in August 2004 and August 2008.
[48] Muḥammad Ṣiddīq Zalīlī, *Dīwān*, Ms. 100b-102a; Tursun 1985: 624-627.
[49] Muḥammad Ṣiddīq Zalīlī, *Dīwān*, Ms. 102b-103a; Tursun 1985: 627-628.
[50] Muḥammad Ṣiddīq Zalīlī, *Dīwān*, Ms. 103b-104b; Tursun 1985: 628-630.

Until I reached the town of Chira
After passing Chira, my intention was to reach Kīra

In this place, I was imploring while lamenting
When I came to Chira, it was time to sleep

Chira was a place of nice composition
Its climate reminded the paradise

(...)

Here saints make their appearance
As the bottle is full of wine

The saint Mīrzā like Mīrzā Rashīd
Was the key of the lock of Sufism

On the plank of loving heart, he was the *qalam*
Writing with the blood of liver

(...)

In the city of Chira, there was a place
Where stood the shrine of Ja'far-i Tayyār

The grave of Shāh was there indeed
Covered with blood from head to foot

He was the standard-bearer at the Uḥud battle
He was with the Prophet Muḥammad

Suddenly he brandished the standard with his right hand
Clouds begun to shake in the sky

His left arm held sword
He did not know anything about the situation

But he has not dropped his standard
He was repeating nothing but the name of God

Then happened the destiny decided by God
A dog of an infidel cut his head

Zalīlī considers Chira to be a source of the manifestation of saints such as Mīrzā Rashīd or Imām Ja'far-i Tayyār. The first one seems to be a local Sufi saint from Khotan, whereas the second is compared to or even identified as Muṣ'ab ibn 'Umayr, a well-known companion of the Prophet Muḥammad, who is considered to be the first missionary of Islam, and who died at the battle of Uḥud under dramatic circumstances. Today, the monumental shrine and its Friday mosque are quite busy. According to the legend, Imām Ja'far-i Tayyār was a cousin of Muḥammad who, in the year 8 of Hegira, passed away during a battle in Shām.[51]

The Kīra area

As he progresses on the southern route toward the East, the Qalandar pilgrim stays overnight in a hostel in Fūnāq. Afterwards, he arrives in Kīra/Keriya. After a brief visit to the town, he spends forty days at the mazar of a certain Khwāja Qamar:[52]

> Although Kīra did not contain any citadel
> One meets no one but *darwīsh*s
>
> The city's vicinity is full of gardens
> Widows' hip were plump
>
> Fresh and populated, the city was joyful
> People performed the oral *dhikrYā imām*
>
> From all sides of the city, there were mazars
> Here happened extraordinary events
>
> It was the home of all the *imām*s
> It was the abode of Khwāja Qamar
>
> It was a palace to accomplish the circumambulation
> Nobody would fail to come there

This mazar is, so far, not identifiable in the actual sacred landscape of Xinjiang. Nevertheless, a historian of Central Asian Islam can underline several elements from this passage of the *Safarnāma*: the practice of a *dhikr-i zabānī* performed collectively on this Sufi shrine; the invocation of *imām*s and *mazār,* which suggests a particular devotional subject referring to the proselyte heroes and the *lieux de mémoire* of the Islamization of the Tarim Basin rather than a Shiite legacy; lastly, also noticeable is the usual, ubiquitous ritual of *ṭawāf.*

The Niya area

Zalīlī does not stay long in Chira, and he travelled to Niya during the month of *muḥarram*.[53] He took the road of Yūqdū and crossed the bed of the Chāqtū river until he found the *qadamgāh* (halting-place of a saint) of Imām Ja'far-i Ṣādiq:[54]

---

[51] Dawut 2001: 150-154; personal observations in August 2008. In sources, Imām Ja'far-i Tayyār is also known under the name Ja'far-i Tahrān or Ja'far-i Tayrān, For further details on this shrine, see Sawada, 2012.

[52] Muḥammad Ṣiddīq Zalīlī, *Dīwān*, Ms. 105b-106a; Tursun 1985: 632-633.

[53] This particular month does not indicate a Shiite influence; it is also a propitious month for pilgrimage among the Sunnis.

[54] Muḥammad Ṣiddīq Zalīlī, *Dīwān*, Ms. 108a-111a; Tursun 1985: 635-640.

If, from far, one can see marvellous gardens
If one goes near, one sees forests of poplars

The dignity of all the poplars formed a park[55]
In the evening, I saw it by the light of a torch

Everywhere the sweet perfume of the Khotan musk
Everywhere the thorns of the straw of Khotan[56]

In all directions, were spiritual hunting grounds
Was the *qadamgāh* of Ja'far-i Ṣādiq

By the forest side, there was a river bed
The tomb was a wonderful place

Those who lay there were all martyrs
Heroes and men of God

(...)

Your slave came to circumambulate the *imām*
He came to repent and ask for your permission

Come God, powerful emperor
To the shrine of Imām Ja'far-i Ṣādiq

(...)

Up there I saw there were mazars
I saw there were miracles at Qarāsāy

The form of Qarāsāy was like a fallen hill
His surface was like black velvet

Poles and banners were countless
The king's grave was like a salt land

In front, ran a large river
Toward there, was a hermitage

On a pillar, there was an inscription
'Those who came here wrote their name'

Poles were laid out everywhere
This day, at the time of afternoon prayer

They played marches and tambourines
They shouted through the desert plain

---

[55] This description is almost similar to the one written in Stein, 1933: 74.
[56] This is a common evocation in classical Turko-Persian poetry; Khotan is historically famous for its musk trade. See King, 2007.

The birds stopped flying
The animals stopped grazing

Everywhere every time they screamed *hūy*
Clamours came out from nowhere

Ja'far-i Ṣādiq is the king of sea and earth
He is the guardian of the Kīra province

(...)

The thirteenth day I arrived at Qarāsāy
At what was called the Persian Mecca

I stayed in this place ten days long
I covered my face with sadness

How cannot be frightened in this place?
All around there was nothing but desolation

This famous shrine, according to Zalīlī, is a major holy site and a main pilgrimage site, which is remotely located in the Taklamakan Desert (70 kms north of Niya). Here, the *Safarnāma* confirms the account of other sources dealing with Khotan mazars, such as Mīrzā Muḥammad Ḥaydar's *Tārīkh-i Rashīdī.*[57] He reminds readers that only martyrs (*shuḥadālār* sic) are buried there. The remoteness, the hardships of the pilgrimage and the memory of the martyrdom gives this mazar a specific identity based on suffering and affliction. Clearly, the Ja'far-i Ṣādiq shrine is a main destination in Zalīlī's pilgrimage, yet it is not the last one. Zalīlī adds interesting material details on saintly tombs that are situated in Qarāsāy/Qarasay. Based on his geographical description and the present-day toponymy, he seems to be referring to the Qarasay located in the upper valley of the Ändir river at the foot of the Kunlun Mountains. There, the Sufi finds an ancient hermitage (*sawma'a*) and numerous ritual flags and poles; he even attends huge devotional ceremonies. This mazar is called the Persian Mecca or Mecca of Persians (*'ajam makkasī*), which may show a trace of Shiite influence, possibly the subsistence of a Shiite community.[58] I shall return to this point later. The title of Imām Ja'far-i Ṣādiq as 'the sentinel of the province of Keriya' (*kīra wilāyatīgha dūr huddagar*) refers to the territory patronized by the saint. It is also a literary transition to the follow-up of the travelogue, that is, the return to Khotan via Keriya.

The return to Khotan

Zalīlī leaves Qarāsāy and returns to Keriya. He then goes to Qambar Atā Mazar and stays

---

57 See Sawada 2012. Regarding this Mazar, see Dutreuil de Rhins 1897-1898: III, 27-31; Dawut 2001: 158-160; Sartekin 2005: 666-667. Additionally, see the pages devoted to Ja'far-i Ṣādiq *qadamgāh* in Mullā Mūsā Sayrāmī, 197b-198a.

58 For details about second Meccas in Central Asia, see Zarcone 2012.

overnight at Būghūz *langar* (the Boghâz Langar of Dutreuil de Rhins),[59] which is approximately 50 kms south of Keriya.[60] The Qambar Atā Mazar, situated 15 kms east of Keriya in the oasis of Oy Tughrak, honours the caretaker of the Duldul horse of 'Alī.[61] In the mountains around Būghūz *langar*, he meets many travelling Sufis (*fuqarā*), which means that they are on a pilgrimage. According to Zalīlī, the mountains contain the shrine of an *imām* composed of a *gumbadh-i 'ālī* and a *khānaqāh*; this region, says our author, is inhabited by *'ajam* people, which means non-Arabs (Persians, or probably Shiites since they are said to perform a nightly ritual for *imāms* using drums, cries, and lamentations). This group of people could correspond to the Abdals: Dutreuil de Rhins and Fernand Grenard, although they did not visit this area, collected 'information on an interesting group of population, the Abdals, isolated and despised, who still speak a corrupted Persian and who are blamed for being Jewish, though they profess Islam'.[62]

On his way back to Khotan, Zalīlī makes another detour, this time toward the north via Andira/Ändira:[63]

We did not see the mountain or the valley
We did not stay and went toward Andira

We were still far from Andira
We were in a place named Qobūrghā Būlāq

There lay a saint apparently
His name was Imām Hādī Ākhar-i Zamān

On both sides there was a huge mountain
There were a spring and a well

(...)

We made a pilgrimage to this mazar
We addressed thousands of praises to God

We visited the entire place
In a day and a night, we reached Archagha

Zalīlī stopped at a village called Qobūrghā Būlāq where a saint, Imām Hādī Ākhar-i Zamān, was buried. This mazar is possibly similar to Imām Mahdī Ākhar-i Zamān, although the location remains puzzling: Zalīlī indicates that he goes *ṭaraf-i andira*, whereas the mazar of Imām Mahdī Ākhar-i Zamān (the last *imām* in Twelver Shiism) is

[59] Dutreuil de Rhins 1897-1898: III, 22-23.

[60] Muḥammad Ṣiddīq Zalīlī, *Dīwān*, Ms. 111b-112b; Tursun 1985: 641-643.

[61] Chvyr' 2006: 191. There are actually several shrines dedicated to Qambar Atā in Xinjiang.

[62] Dutreuil de Rhins 1897-1898: I, 172. On the Abdals (their language mostly), see Ladstätter & Tietze, 1994.

[63] Muḥammad Ṣiddīq Zalīlī, *Dīwān*, Ms. 113b; Tursun 1985: 643-644. On the pre-Islamic vestiges of Andira, see Sartekin 2005: 589-592.

located south of Chira at the foot of the Kunlun range.[64] This is apparently the last *ziyārat* of our Sufi pilgrim, who then returns to Khotan where he stayed no less than seven years:[65]

I was suffering but I was happy
I was still walking when Khotan came into view

I entered the city to sojourn there
I became like a lake bird

I stayed seven years in this city
I was now rose now rosebud now thorn

I wended through the beauties of Khotan
I wended through the gardens and orchards

I was the nightingale of these rose gardens
I was the singer companion of the birds

At the service of all, lords, vizirs or poor
In the intimacy of all spiritual masters and saints

Conclusion: Using the *Safarnāma* as a Historical Source

Like other pilgrimage travelogues, the text of Zalīlī—partly used in my paper—provides numerous pieces of geographical data: it describes specific landscapes (desert zones, plains, mountainous areas, and rivers); it describes cities, towns and villages, mentioning various toponyms that we may still find today in Xinjiang. The sacred geography is the second major feature of this work: aside from the sometimes detailed descriptions of shrines, the author gives the name of inns attached to the shrines and the routes between them. All these are classical elements of *ziyārat* literature, although they are not so common regarding the Tarim Basin, where the medieval and early modern writing traditions of pilgrimages were much less represented than in other Islamic areas. The *Safarnāma* is also invaluable in that the spiritual journey takes place specifically in the Southern oasis of Xinjiang (except for a short trip to Hindustan); the author describes a sort of religious exploration of the sacred territories of Central Asia in verse. This characteristic may be a part of what Ron Sela epitomized as the 'Age of introspection' in the sense that Zalīlī's travelogue provides an original self-understanding of the religious space of the Tarim Basin. A hundred and fifty years later, the famous historian Mullā Mūsā Sayrāmī ended his chronicle, the *Tārīkh-i amniyya*, with a description of the Seven Cities (*yettī shahr*), including a systematic description of their mausoleums, as if they were the first—perhaps foremost—emblems of identity, emblems which are able to keep the land itself in the collective memoryof

[64] Sartekin, 2005: 674.
[65] Muḥammad Ṣiddīq Zalīlī, *Dīwān*, Ms. 114a-114b; Tursun, 1985: 644-646.

Turkestani people.[66] Based on Zalīlī's *Safarnāma*, this quasi-religious concept of 'Tarim territory' seems to begin as early as the eighteenth century.

Whether one studies *tadhkira*, *manāqib* or even *ḥajjnāma*, sources on mazars rarely deal with rituals and practices. Authors or actors of such sources are just not interested in explaining what they do on a day-to-day basis. It would be in vain to ask the texts the kinds of questions ethnographers ask their informants (a critique some ethnographers frequently, and pointlessly, direct to historians). However, the *Safarnāma* presents several accounts of the rituals performed on Muslim shrines: the usual *du'ā*, *ṭawāf* and *tūgh ū 'alam*-holding, but also processions, music performances, ascetic exercises, and so on. From a historical perspective, this is a precious testimony of the spiritual vitality of the mazars during this period. More than any other holy place, mazars were centres of religious activity and of local as well as regional sociability, at least for the pious segment of the population. Such vitality is mostly due to the role of the Sufis in promoting the cult of the saints, particularly in the auspicious visits to their shrines. This is, partly, the result of the Khwāja activities in the Tarim Basin from the late sixteenth century throughout the seventeenth century, when the Naqshbandī lineages strongly supported and promoted saints' mausoleums as social, political and religious symbols. Obviously, the cult of Muslim saints had already existed for a long time in this region; however, it turned into a central practice during this period. With Zalīlī's account, who was a Naqshbandī himself—although a specific kind of Naqshbandī Sufi, very close (if not simply similar) to the Qalandar model—we find additional evidence of this historical process.

References

Bahavidin, Mähämmättursun 1982. "17-äsirning akhiri vä 18-äsirning bashliridiki Uyghur ädibiyatining muhim namayändiliri" in *Uyghur ädibiyati toghrisida*, Beijing: Millätlär Näshriyati, 296-310.

Bonnemaison, Joël 1981. "Voyage autour du territoire" in *L'Espace Géographique* 4: 249-262.

Chih, Rachida and Catherine Mayeur-Jaouen 2010. *Le Soufisme à l'époque ottomane.* Cairo: Institut français d'archéologie orientale.

Chvyr', Lyudmilla A. 2006. *Obryady i verovaniya uigurov v xix-xx vv.* Moscow: Vostochnaya Literatura RAN.

Dutreuil de Rhins, Jules-Léon 1897-1898. *Mission scientifique dans la Haute Asie 1890-1895.* Paris: Ernest Leroux, 3 vol.

Grabczewski, Bronislaw 1885. *Kaszgarja. Kraj i ludzie. Podróż do Azji środkowej.* Warszawa: Nakład Gebethnera i Wolffa, 3 vol.

Kerimi, Niyaz 2000. *Shinjangning qädimki karwan yolliri.* Urumqi: Shinjang Khälq Näshriyati.

Khojähmät, Abdurishit 1983. "Qarghiliq nahiyisining 1926-yildin 1936-yilighichä bolghan 10 yilliq tarikhidin äslimä" in *Shinjang tarikh materyalliri* 12: 182-249.

Kim, Ho-Dong 1993. "The Cult of the Saints in Eastern Turkestan: the Case of Alp Ata in Turfan" in *Proceedings of the 35th Permanent International Altaistic Conference*, Taipei. 199-226.

King, Anya H. 2007. "The Musk Trade and the Near East in then Early Medieval Period", Ph.D. Dissertation. Indiana University, 320 p.

[66] Regarding this concept of territory, see the classical Bonnemaison, 1981.

Ladstätter, Otto & Tietze, Andreas 1994. *Die Abdal (Äynu) in Xinjiang*. Vienna: Österreichische Akademie der Wissenschaften.
Mämät, Abdulajan 2001. *Uyghur klassik ädäbiyati khäzinsi*. Urumqi: Shinjang Khälq Näshriyati.
Mäshhädi, Abdurehim Hashim 2005. *Atush (1)*. Kashgar: Qäshqär Uyghur Näshriyati.
Molla Haji 1988. *Bughrakhanlar täzkirisi*. ed. Abdurehim Sabit, Kashgar: Qäshqär Uyghur Näshriyati.
Mollaudov, Savut 1990. *XVII Äsir Uyghur poeziyasi (tätqiqat vä tekstilar)*. Alma Ata: Nauka Näshriyati.
Montgomerie, T.G. 1866. "On the Geographical Position of Yarkund, and Some Other Places in Central Asia" in *Journal of the Royal Geographic Society of London* 36: 157-172.
Muḥammad Ṣiddīq Zalīlī. *Diwān*, Ms Xinjiang Museum.
Mullā Mūsā Sayrāmī. *Tārīkh-i amniyya*, Gunnar Jarring Collection, Ms Prov. 478.
Orxun, Abliz & Sugawara, Jun 2007. *Mazar Documents from Xinjiang and Ferghana (Facsimile) 2*. Tokyo: Research Institute for Languages and Cultures of Asia and Africa, Toyko University of Foreign Studies.
Papas, Alexandre 2010. *Mystiques et vagabonds en islam. Portraits de trois soufis qalandar*. Paris: Cerf.
Qurbān 'Alī Khālidī. *Kitāb-i tārīkh-i jarīda-yi jadīda*, India Office, Ms Turki 2.
Rozi, Batur 2003. *Zälili (Tarikhi shäkhslär häqqida hekayilär 5)*. Urumqi:Shinjang Khälq Näshriyati.
Sartekin, Eziz Atawulla 2004. *Uyghurchä näshr qilinghan äsärlär katalogi (tarikh-mädäniyät qismi)*. Urumqi: Shinjang Universiteti Näshriyati.
Sartekin, Eziz Atawulla 2005. *Yadikarliqlardin mädäniyitimizgä näzär*. Urumqi: Shinjang Khälq Näshriyati.
Sawada, Minoru 1996. "Khwaja ke Ishaq ha no keisei XVII seiki zenhan no Tarim bonti seihen wo chūsin ni" in *Seinan azia kenkyū* 45: 39-61.
Sawada, Minoru 2001. "Tarim Basin Mazârs: A Fieldwork Report" in *Journal of the History of Sufism* 3: 39-61.
Sawada, Minoru 2012. "Pilgrimage to Sacred Places in the Taklamakan Desert: Shrines of *Imāms* in Khotan Prefecture" in Alexandre Papas, Thomas Welsford, Thierry Zarcone (eds.), *Central Asian Pilgrims. Hajji Routes and Pious Visits between Central Asia and the Hijaz*. Berlin: Klaus Schwarz.278-294.
Shinjang Uyghur Aptonom Rayoni khäritilär toplimi. Urumqi: Junggo Khäritä Näshriyati wä Shinjang Pän-Tekhnika Näshriyati, 2005.
Sirriyeh, Elizabeth 1985. "The Mystical Journeys of 'Abd al-Ghanī al-Nābulusī" in *Die Welt des Islams* 1985-25, 1/4: 84-96.
Stein, Aurel 1907. *Ancient Khotan. Detailed Report of Archaeological Explorations in Chinese Turkestan*. Oxford: Clarendon Press, 2 vol.
Stein, Aurel 1928. *Innermost Asia. Detailed Report of Explorations in Central Asia, Kan-su and Eastern Īrān*. Oxford: Clarendon Press, 4 vol.
Stein, Aurel 1933. *On Ancient Central Asian Tracks. Brief Narrative of Three Expeditions in Innermost Asia and North-Western China*. London: MacMillan.
Turan, Adil Muhämmät 2006. *Shinjang mädäniyät yadikarliq jäwärliri*. Urumqi: Shinjang Khälq Näshriyati.
Turdi, Abdushukur 1982. "Zälili ijadiyiti vä uning 'Säpärnamä' dastani" in *Uyghur ädäbiyati toghrisida*, Beijing: Millätlär Näshriyati, 202-216.
Tursun, Imin 1985. *Zälili Diwani*. Beijing: Millätlär Näshriyati.
Yusup, Räjäp 1983. "Muhämmät Sidiq Zälili vä uning ijadi paaliyiti toghrisida" in *Shinjiang Dashue Ilmi Zhurnili* 1983-2: 74-86.
Zarcone, Thierry. 2012. "Pilgrimages to the 'Second Meccas' and 'Ka'bas' of Central Asia", in Alexandre Papas, Thomas Welsford, Thierry Zarcone (eds), *Central Asian Pilgrims. Hajji Routes and Pious Visits between Central Asia and the Hijaz*. Berlin: Klaus Schwarz, 251-277.

Untangling the Bughrā-Khān Manuscripts

Rian THUM

In Eastern Turkestan, also known as the Southern Circuit of China's Xinjiang region, the word "Bughrā-khān" has long been much more than a defunct title from the Qarakhanid political hierarchy. Rather, it was and is intimately connected to the king who became, arguably, the most important local saint of Kashgaria, Sulṭān Satūq Bughrā-khān, and his immediate descendents. The reverence for Sulṭān Satūq Bughrā-khān stems from his reputation as the first king in the region to convert to Islam, while his children and grandchildren became famous for expanding the Islamic kingdom across the Tarim Basin through holy wars. Sulṭān Satūq Bughrā-khān's importance in the literary and religious traditions of Eastern Turkestan is hinted at by an episode in Mullā Ḥājī's *Tadhkirat al-Bughrā-khān*, when Satūq's son, Ḥasan, places his deceased father behind only God and the prophet Muḥammad in importance, sending his own child into battle with this blessing:

> "I have commended you first of all to God, second to His Holiness Muḥammad Mustafa, and third to my ancestor and noble father, His Holiness Sulṭān Satūq Bughrā-khān, Champion of the Faith."[1]

Sulṭān Satūq Bughrā-khān and two generations of his descendents were major figures in everyday devotional life in Kashgaria from the 18th century through the early 20th centuries. Veneration of the saints of Satūq's line took place at shrines in the town of Kashgar itself and in or around the nearby towns of Artush and Yengisar. These institutions controlled vast land holdings, managed sites of regular devotion for local residents, and attracted tens of thousands of worshippers from far and wide, especially during the annual pilgrimage festivals. It is not surprising then, that the saints of Satūq's line received much attention from local authors, and that their tales were among the most popular of local literary productions. Often authors and copyists gave these works titles that condensed the saints' names simply to "Bughrā-khān." For scholars outside of the tradition, such application of the title/name "Bughrā-khān" to any text dealing with Satūq's line has caused some confusion, and, in the catalogues of the world's best manuscript collections, sometimes obscured the differences between

---

[1] Mullā Ḥājī, *Tadhkirat al- Bughrā-khān*, in manuscript Prov. 73, f. 84a, Jarring Collection, Lund University Library. Manuscripts from this collection are hereafter indicated by the name "Jarring," plus the catalog number.

widely varied texts. Until now we have only outlines of the diversity of texts that circulated under the Bughrā-khān name.[2] It is hoped that this study, which is based on some (though by no means all) of the most important collections of the Bughrā-khān manuscripts from the 19th and early 20th centuries, will go some way to untangling these confusing texts and introducing their contents, especially in the case of works that still exist only in manuscript form.

Tadhkirah-i Ūwaysīya

The earliest known work under the Bughrā-khān name is the *Tadhkirah-i Bughrā-khān*, also known as the *Tadhkirah-i Ūwaysīya*, which is attributed variously to Aḥmad b. Sa'd al-Dīn al-Uzghanī al-Namanghāni or 'Abd al-Shahīd b. 'Abd al-Ḥamīd Samarqandī, and was likely composed in the 16th or 17th century.[3] To avoid confusion with later works, I will refer to this text as the *Tadhkirah-i Ūwaysīya*, but it should be noted that the text was more popularly known as the *Tadhkira-i Bughrā-khān*. Devin DeWeese has published a thorough study of the work's textual history and Julian Baldick has written a summarized translation, so I will not spend much space on the *Tadhkirah-i Ūwaysīya* here.[4] In its longest form, the work recounts the lives of seventy saints in forty chapters (*bāb*) and thirty sub-chapters (*faṣl*). Some twenty of these saints are connected in one way or another with Eastern Turkestan. The work is dedicated to Sulṭān Satūq Bughrā-khān and narrates his biography as chapter seven, between the biographies of his teachers, Abū al-Naṣr Sāmānī (chapter six) and Abu al-Fatāḥ (sub-chapter three). Following the *nisbas* of the possible authors, the *Tadhkirah-i Ūwaysīya* should perhaps be considered a work of Western Turkestani origin, but it was clearly more extensively propagated in Eastern Turkestan. It is closely connected in its style, format, and content to the wider Islamic tradition of Sufi hagiography in its Central Asian manifestation. Most significant in this regard is the work's arrangement as a biographical dictionary, a form that was abandoned thereafter by Eastern Turkestani authors in favor of hagiographical monographs that stuck to a single, connected narrative, even when treating multiple saints.

The *Tadhkirah-i Ūwaysīya* was originally written in Persian, but by the mid-18th century the vernacular, Eastern Turki (we might also call this language late Chaghatay or early modern Uyghur), had overtaken Persian in popularity as a vehicle for local literary production in Eastern Turkestan. At least two independent translations of the *Tadhkirah-i Ūwaysīya* are known. One of these is the work of Muḥammad Gadā of AH 1182 (1768-9), preserved in the St. Petersburg branch of the Institute of Oriental Studies of the Russian Academy of Sciences.[5] DeWeese suggests that a text in the British

---

[2] Best among these is Devin DeWeese's overview in DeWeese 1996: 87-127.

[3] *Ibid.*

[4] *Ibid.*; Baldick 1993: 266.

[5] D114, St. Petersburg branch of the Institute of Oriental Studies of the Russian Academy of Sciences. This collection was most recently catalogued by Lyudmila Vasil'evna Dmitrieva. See Dmitrieva 2002: 616. Manuscripts from this collection are hereafter referred to by the abbreviation

Museum is probably an independent translation. Another manuscript in St. Petersburg, SP D113, is also independent of the Gada translation, but I have not been able to compare it to the British Museum text to determine if the two are related.

Tadhkirah-i Ūwaysīya Extracts

The complete *Tadhkirah-i Ūwaysīya* was not a rare book – DeWeese has traced sixteen manuscripts in Persian along with six copies of Turki translations, and still-inaccessible Chinese archives likely contain more – but in Eastern Turkestan after the 18th century the work was far more widely known through extracts, most commonly of the chapters treating Sulṭān Satūq Bughrā-khān and his teachers (i.e. chapters six and seven, plus sub-chapter three). While these sections were the most popular, chapters about other saints without immediate connection to Sulṭān Satūq Bughrā-khān, and some without connection even to Eastern Turkistan, were also sometimes included.[6] Like all texts in Eastern Turkestan's manuscript tradition, the selected chapters appear in a wide variety of recensions, often heavily abbreviated. However, the vast majority, if not all, of such extracted versions seem to be descendents of the same translation, the anonymous work represented by SP D113. Some extracted recensions are nearly identical to the corresponding chapters in SP D113, while others fall within a range of variation that is normal for the heavy editing and abbreviation to which these texts were subjected in the process of copying.

With a few exceptions, the selected chapters are found bound together with other hagiographies, most often hagiographies of Sulṭān Satūq Bughrā-khān's descendants.[7] Sometimes the extracted chapters are manipulated to look like independent works by removing the chapter number and adding a title, such as "Sulṭān Satūq Bughrakhan's Tadhkirah."[8] In other cases copyists removed any indication that the separate works in a composite volume came from different texts, redacting the selected chapters of the *Tadhkirah-i Ūwaysīya* together with other hagiographies as though they all comprised a single work.[9] Some manuscripts preserved the chapter headings of the *Tadhkirah-i Ūwaysīya* but removed the chapter numbers, beginning simply "In this chapter...."[10] Where the chapter numbers have been included, they usually deviate from the numbering in the *Tadhkirah-i Ūwaysīya* translation represented by SP D113, counting Sulṭān Satūq Bughrā-khān's chapter ninth, and that of his teacher, Abū al-Naṣr Sāmānī , eighth (instead of seventh and sixth, respectively).[11]

"SP" plus their catalog numbers, the "new shelf-mark" of Dmitrieva's catalog.

6 Other popular choices included the chapters on Bahā' al-Dīn of Ghazna,'Allāmah Ḥuqqah Bāz, Abū al-Qāsīm of Farkhar, Faqīh Ayyūb, and Manṣūr of the Hijaz.

7 One such exception is SP A240, which consists only of the Sulṭān Satūq Bughrā-khān chapter, labeled as "chapter 2."

8 Jarring Prov. 413.

9 SP: C547, C549.

10 SP: A237, A238, C545, C546. Jarring: Prov. 148.

11 SP: B731, B4477, C544, C548. Jarring: Prov 73, Prov. 103, Prov. 143, Prov. 203, Prov. 504. ms. or. quar. 1303, Hartmann collection, Stadtsbibliotek, Berlin. See #106 in Hartmann 1904: 1–21.

Samarqandī's *Nasabnāmah*

One of the texts that often accompanied selected chapters from *Tadhkirah-i Ūwaysīya*, usually coming after them in a composite manuscript, was a genealogical work ascribed to a certain "Sayyid Qāsim Samarqandī."[12] This too, seems to be culled from a larger work, as many copies call it "the eighth chapter."[13] About half of this short work narrates the virginal conception of 'Alī Arslān-khān by 'Alanūr Khanim, a daughter of Sulṭān Satūq Bughrā-khān. The tale very briefly describes the miraculous circumstances of the pregnancy, the Sulṭān's investigation, and the child's descent from 'Alī ibn Abī Ṭālib.[14] The second part of the text is a list of the descendants of 'Alanūr Khanim's daughters and other women of the Sulṭān Satūq Bughrā-khān line. Usually the text ends with a genealogy (*nasabnāmah*) of Muḥammad Yūsuf Khwājam Pādshāh (father of the famous Āfāq Khwājah), traced through the eighth Imām, 'Alī ibn Mūsā al-Riḍā, and the prophet Muḥammad back to Adam, but this last section is often omitted or abbreviated.[15] Muginov listed the work here attributed to Samarqandī as the *Nasabnāmah-i Sulṭān Satūq Bughrā-khān*, though I have been unable to locate any manuscripts that include this title.[16] In at least one manuscript, the name "'Alanūr" is written in red above the "bismallah" much like a title.[17] However, Muginov's title is at least an appropriate description, and since the 'Alanūr designation seems to be the work of a lone copyist, there is little reason to change the designation.

SP C548

There is one manuscript, SP C548, that includes a text that begins very similarly to Samarqandī's *Nasabnāmah*, but is in fact quite a different work. Like the *Nasabnāmah*, it starts after the introductory praise by enumerating the children of Sulṭān Satūq Bughrā-khān, but whereas the Samarqandī extract focuses on the daughters and their descendants, this work also treats the sons. The story of 'Alanūr's conception of 'Alī Arslān-khān is also included in this work, but it is vastly different in its details. Muginov believed SP C548 to be a different recension of the *Nasabnāmah*, but the two versions of 'Alanūr's story diverge too much to be explained by editing, interpolation, scribal error, or abbreviation. Each version contains important elements that are lacking in the other. For example, SP C548 does not record the tradition presented in the *Nasabnāmah* that explains how 'Alanūr became pregnant when the angel Gabriel placed a drop of light in her mouth. At the same time, SP C548 presents a far more detailed description of 'Alanūr's relationship to 'Alī ibn Abī Ṭālib. In SP C548 this

---

[12] In many manuscripts, the work ends with "Sayyid Qasim Samarqandī composed [it]" (سید قاسم تصنیف قیلغان), including SP B731, B732, C732 Jarring Prov. 73, Prov. 143, Prov. 203, Prov. 504, among others.

[13] SP A238, B732, B4477, C544. Jarring: Prov. 143, Prov. 504.

[14] Most of this section of the work has been edited and translated in Shaw 1878.

[15] This genealogy differs markedly from that found in the *Tadhkirah-i Sayyid Āfāq Khwājam* (Prov. 22, Prov. 369), wherein the lineage is traced through the eleventh Imām, Ḥasan al-'Askarī.

[16] Muginov 1962.

[17] SP B732.

figure is not just mentioned as an ancestor of 'Alanūr's child, but appears to 'Alanūr in a dream with hands that resemble a tiger's paws, and tells her what to name the child. The tale stands out among Eastern Turkestani hagiographical literature for its unusual attention to the emotions of the characters:

> "One night she fell asleep. In her dream a tiger pressed 'Alanūr Khanim's organs. At this moment her heart became glad, and then she woke up in fright from the dream. In the morning she told her mother about what had happened. Her mother was astounded by this dream. Fatefully, month by month, day by day, the pregnancy became apparent to her as the child came into existence. She told her mother about it. The two of them cried together, becoming extremely melancholy and very ashamed. In particular they were distraught for fear of [the reaction of] her father, and in the nights they remained awake, weeping."[18]

The shared sadness of 'Alanūr and her mother, along with the intimate personal and familial relationships implied in this passage, are unusual subjects in Eastern Turkestan's locally produced literature, which is normally concerned with heroic or miraculous deeds.

In another departure from the *Nasabnāmah*, 'Alanūr is but one character among many to receive full narrative treatment in SP C548. Equal space is devoted to Qilich Bughrā-khān's noble qualities, Maryam Khanim's last stand against the unbelievers in battle, Ḥasan and Ḥusayn Bughrā-khāns' battles and martyrdom, 'Alī Arslān-khān's decapitation during the pre-dawn prayer, and Yūsuf Qādir Khān's alliance with Sayyid Jalāl al-Dīn Baghdādī. The character Qilich Bughrā-khān, presented here as Sulṭān Satūq Bughrā-khān's oldest son, is not recorded in other, related works. The *Nasabnāmah* and other works record the oldest son as 'Uthmān Bughrā-khān. Also special to SP C584 is the tale of Jalāl al-Dīn Baghdādī, a descendant of the prophet whose name appears in the *Nasabnāmah*'s genealogical section. In SP C584 we learn that when Yūsuf Qādir Khān visited Mecca, the spirit of the prophet Muḥammad told him to seek the *sayyid* Jalāl al-Dīn Baghdādī. The latter then joined Yūsuf Qādir Khān on his journey back to Kashgar and married into the Bughrā-khān line, providing later princes with the legitimacy of descent from the prophet. The tales of the remaining heroes are familiar from other works, especially Mullā Ḥājī's *Tadhkirat al-Bughrā-khān*. The backdrop for all of the stories is the holy war against the infidels of Khotan. The prose is simple and spare throughout.

Mullā Ḥājī's *Tadhkirat al-Bughrā-khān*

Within the typical composite manuscript, the text that often follows the *Nasabnāmah* is the most popular holy war text of the Bughrā-khān lineage, Mullā Ḥājī's *Tadhkirat al-Bughrā-khān*. The authorship and title of this work are clearly presented within the text of the preface, though sometimes the author's name is omitted[19] and in one

[18] SP C548, ff 28b-29a. Author's translation.
[19] E.g. SP B732.

manuscript the title is given as *Tadhkirat al-Abrār.*[20] The tale begins with the reign of Ḥasan Bughrā-khān, son of Satūq Bughrā-khān, and details the holy wars of Satūq's progeny against the Buddhists of Khotan and Yarkand. Over the course of the work, Satūq's children and grandchildren are martyred, one by one, in successive battles, until only Yūsuf Qādir Khān remains alive. The text bears obvious signs of oral transmission, and should probably be considered as a part of the Turkic epic tradition. Roughly the same story is repeated for each saint's death in battle, and epic formulae are encountered throughout. The establishment of a shrine ends each cycle of martyrdom, after which the surviving saints resume their struggle against the Buddhists.[21]

Questionable claims about Mullā Ḥājī's *Tadhkirat al-Bughrā-khān* were advanced in a modern Uyghur translation published in 1988 by the Kashgar Uyghur Press.[22] The editor, Abdurehim Sabit, worked from a manuscript that included chapters six and seven of the *Tadhkirah-i Ūwaysīya,* followed by the work described as Mullā Ḥājī's *Tadhkirat al-Bughrakhan* in the present study, and finally the story of Yūsuf Qādir Khān and the Four Sacrificed Imams, commonly known as the *Tadhkirah-i Türt Imām Ẕabiḥlar.* In the translation, Sabit considered all of these works together to constitute Mullā Ḥājī's *Tadhkirat al-Bughrā-khān.* This claim he based on Mullā Ḥājī's statement, just preceding the story of Ḥasan Bughrā-khān, that, "this collection, like the four elements that make up the body, I wrote with four sections, which are the muqaddam [*sic*], the two *maqālas*, and the *khātima.*"[23] Thus, Sabit presented chapter six of the *Tadhkirah-i Ūwaysīya* as the *muqaddima*, chapter seven as the first "*bab*" (a modern Uyghur translation of "*maqāla*"), Mullā Ḥājī's work proper as the second *bab*, and the *Tadhkirah-i Türt Imām Ẕabiḥlar* as the *khātima.* This arrangement is unlikely, as it places Mullā Ḥājī's introductory remarks, which clearly belong in a preface, in the second *bab.* Furthermore, many copies of the work label the preface just before the story of Ḥasan Bughrā-khān, "*amma muqadima*"(and so, the preface).[24] Thus, within the section that the editor calls the "second *bab*," we have the author's name, his presentation of the title, a description of the work, and the designation "*muqadima.*" It is clear that the manuscript used in preparation of the translation was a typical composite volume, with several works copied together, and that Mullā Ḥājī's claim of authorship only refers to the "second *bab*" of Sabit's manuscript. The conflation of these works as a single text is not uncommon in manuscript catalogues and other scholarly works. Nor is the phenomenon limited to scholars outside the tradition. Indigenous copyists sometimes grouped conglomerations of these texts under a single title, such as "*Tadhkirat al-Awliyā.*"[25]

Sabit also speculates that the text was written for a ruler-patron such as the Hakim

[20] SP B4477.

[21] For a longer overview of this text, see Thum 2014: 44–45. For translated selections, see Shaw 1878.

[22] Haji 1988.

[23] Jarring Prov. 143, f 20a.

[24] Jarring Prov. 148, f 135b, Prov 73, f 83a.

[25] Jarring Prov. 95.

Beg of Kashgar, based on Mullā Ḥājī's statement that "he/they requested of this poor man of little ability, me, Mullā Ḥājī, the bringing together of [records of the forefathers] in the Turki language."[26] Such patronage is possible, as elites were known in other instances to support hagiographical composition and the repairs of saints' shrines.[27] However, hagiographical works were also sometimes composed at the request of dead saints who appeared to the author,[28] so we cannot assume that Mullā Ḥājī's vague comments refer to a living patron.

Mullā Ḥājī's *tadhkirah* has appeared under additional alternate titles in more recent usage within Xinjiang. A 1983 carbon-copy manuscript in the author's collection includes both Mullā Ḥājī's *Tadhkirat al-Bughrā-khān* and Samarqandī's *Nasabnāmah* under the title "*Täzkirä Häzriti Soltan Säyd Äli Arislankhan,*" in modern Arabic-script Uyghur. Mullā Ḥājī's *tadhkirah* also appeared along with the *Tadhkirah-i Türt Imām Ẕabiḥlar*under the title *Yüsüp Qadirkhan Ghazi Täzkirisi* in a 1989 modern Uyghur translation.[29] These alternate titles suggest that two similarly titled manuscripts in Urumqi, which I was unable to access, may also contain Mullā Ḥājī's *tadhkirah.* They are a "*Täzkirä'i Säyid Äli Arslankhan Ghazi*" and a "*Täzkirä'i Yüsüp Qadirkhan,*" preserved in the Xinjiang Minorities Ancient Text Office.[30]

Abū al-Qāsīm's Versified *Tadhkirahs*

Versification of hagiographical works was common in the 18th and 19th centuries,[31] and the Bughrā-khān stories were not immune from such treatment. A manuscript in the Gunnar Jarring Collection contains a verse work called *Ūlūgh Tadhkirah-'i Bughrā-khān.*[32] The work follows the masnavi form and is divided into *dāstāns*, each of which begins with a short prose summary of its verse contents. A verse introduction precedes the first *dāstān* and the conclusion is missing, as the manuscript is defective, ending abruptly in the middle of the seventh *dāstān.* The *tadhkirah's* author identifies himself in the introduction as "Abū al-Qāsīm."[33] Sulṭān Satūq Bughrā-khān is the subject of the first two *dāstāns*, while the remaining sections treat his descendents, through Yūsuf

---

[26] Jarring Prov. 143, Prov. 148.

[27] Qäshqäri 1988: 2. An inscription on a wall of the tomb of Khwājah Muḥammad Sharīf in Yarkand records the patronage of Yūnus Ḥākim Beg.

[28] In his *Ūlūgh Tadhkirah-'i Bughrā-khān*, described below, Abū al-Qāsīm wrote that he composed at the behest of Sulṭān Satūq Bughrā-khān.

[29] Muhämmäd and Usman 1989.

[30] Xinjiang Weiwuer Zizhi Qu Shao Shu Minzu Guji Shouji, Zhengli, Guihua Chuban Lingdao Xiaozu Bangongshi [新疆维吾尔自治区少数民族古籍收集，整理，规划，出版领导小组办公室]. Numbers XĶQ 558 and XĶQ 821. Wäli 1986: 203, 205.

[31] Verse versions of popular prose *tadhkirahs* include Muḥammad Zalīlī's *tadhkirahs* of Khwājah Muḥammad Sharīf, the Haft Muḥammadān, and Sūt Būbī 'Azīz, (Jarring Prov. 76). The first two are available in a modern Uyghur version, Zalīlī 1985: 25, 663. In addition to Zalīlī's works there are verse *tadhkirahs* of the Türt Imām Ẕabiḥlar (MS # T-50, Library of the Nationalities Research Institute, Central University of Nationalities, Beijing) and the Aṣḥāb al-Kahf (Anonymous 2007: 39-48).

[32] Jarring Prov. 563.

[33] "فتوماكجى بولدى ابو القاسيم"; "ابو القاسيم بو خانلار اسمنى انديک بيان قلدى" Jarring Prov. 563, f 50b, f 49a.

Qādir Khān. Abū al-Qāsīm notes at several points that his work is a translation and abbreviation of a longer Persian original. I have been unable to trace any Persian work treating Sulṭān Satūq Bughrā-khān's descendants. It is likely that the original used by Abū al-Qāsīm is lost, though it would not be surprising if a copy were to eventually surface in Xinjiang.

Another verse *tadhkirah*, also in masnavi form, occupies the first half of the above-mentioned manuscript, before the *Ūlūgh Tadhkirah-'i Bughrākhān*. The introduction, which may contain clues about the work's authorship, is missing. However, based on its similarities to the *Ūlūgh Tadhkirah*, this work should probably be attributed to the same author. The date of completion is given in a chronogram at the end, corresponding to 1245 A.H. (1829-30), along with the month of Ramadan. This work also consists of long verse sections preceded by short prose summaries, though here the sections are called *bāb*, rather than *dāstān*. The content is devoted mostly to 'Alī Arslān Khān, though the tenth chapter relates the story of Khwājah Muḥammad Sharīf with little deviation from the tale known from the earlier *Tadhkirah-'i Khwājah Muḥammad Sharīf*.

The *tadhkirah* devoted to 'Alī Arslān-khān may be the same work mentioned by Sawut and Ablimit, as "Qasim's *Tadhkirah-'i Arslān-khān*, (1799)."[34] Abū al-Qāsīm's works are also closely related to (or probably the same as) two manuscripts described by Muginov, SP B734 and SP C543. Muginov reads a different author's name, "Ayman," in B734, which contains additional introductory material, and no author's name in C543.[35] The date of composition is given in C543 as 1245.

Jarring Prov. 358: *Tadhkirahs* in *Qaṣīdah* Form

Two additional verse *tadhkirahs*, both anonymous works loosely following the *qaṣīdah* form, are preserved in manuscript Prov. 358 of the Gunnar Jarring Collection.The first poem, titled *Ḥaẕrat Sulṭān Shahīd 'Alī Arslān-khān Ghāzī PādshāhimTadhkiralārī*, consists of 74 *bayts* (verses), two of which break with the *qaṣīdah* form by including three *miṣra's* (hemistiches). The refrain that ends each *bayt* is "Pādshāhim 'Alī Arslān-khān," a pattern which becomes awkward toward the end of the poem, when the focus of the narrative shifts to Maryam Khanim, as in the following *bayt*:

> "The girls stopped and stood together, against the Kafirs they fought together,
> martyrs they became together, Pādshāhim 'Alī Arslān-khān.[36]

For the most part, the poem represents a less detailed version of the tale familiar from Mullā Ḥājī's more popular *tadhkirah*, though it also mentions 'Alī Arslān-khān's pilgrimage to Mecca, which appears in Abū al-Qāsīm's work.

Immediately following the 'Alī Arslān-khān qaṣīdah is a similar poem called *Ḥaḍrat*

---

[34] Sawut and Ablimit 2001: 40. The authors do not report the location of the manuscript to which this title refers, nor do they cite a source for their date.

[35] Muginov 1962; 67, 152. The word Muginov reads as Ayman is, according to his catalogue,ايمنا.

[36] "قزلار توختاب توروشتی کافرلار بلان اوروشتی اخر شهید بولوشتی پادشاه علی ارسلان خان" Jarring Prov 358, f 38a.

Sulṭān Satūq Bughrā-khān Ghāzīning Tadhkiralārī, consisting of thirty two *bayts*. This work breaks from the *qaṣīdah* form only in the first *bayt*, which does not use the refrain in the first *miṣra'*. As in the previous work, the refrain is the name of the saint, here "Sulṭān Satūq Bughrā-khān." This work is a more general encomium, attending to the saint's qualities as much as his deeds, as in the following representative *bayt*:

> "Opening the door of Islam, spreading the light of faith,
> Taking respite in the mosque, Sulṭān Satūq Bughrā-khān.[37]

Like Abū al-Qāsīm's *tadhkiras*, the works in Jarring Prov. 358 reflect the general popularity of *tadhkira* versification in Eastern Turkestan, though they are somewhat shorter than most versified *tadhkiras*.

Chronology

A minority of Eastern Turkestani literary works, such as Abū al-Qāsīm's *tadhkirahs*, report the year of their completion. For the rest, we can only arrive at somewhat broad estimates based on other clues. Stories of local saints were set down in writing over a long period in Eastern Turkestan. The date and location of the composition of the Persian *Tadhkirah-i Ūvaysiya* is uncertain, but it may have been completed as early as the 16th century.[38] Among works with more certain roots in Eastern Turkestan, Persian stories and biographies of Makhdūmzāda Khojas first appeared no later than the 17th century. By the turn of the 20th century, when European collectors began exporting manuscripts, the most popular *tadhkirahs* were already widely distributed.[39] During this period, not only the copying but also the composition of *tadhkirahs* seems to have continued, as Mulla Musa Sayrami (1836-1917) is said to have written two such works.[40] The tradition has even resurfaced in more recent times. The loosening of publishing restrictions in the early 1980s allowed Ibrahim Qurban to compose and publish his *Yättä Qizlirim*, a verse tale of the Seven Maidens who are said to be buried at the main shrine in Uch-Turpan.[41]

The Bughrā-khān *tadhkirahs* described in this study, excepting the original Persian *Tadhkirah-i Ūvaysiya*, can be placed in a narrower date range, between the popularization of the vernacular in Eastern Turkestan as a language of composition, no earlier than the 1690s, and the earliest manuscript copy dates for each work, mostly in the mid 19th century. The rise of Turki as a language for composing books in Eastern Turkestan can be traced to the turn of the 18th century, around which time Mullā Mīr

---

37 "اسلام اشکنی اجقان ایمان نورینی ساجقان مسجد اجیدا یاتقان سلطان ستق بغراخان" Prov. 358, f 39a.

38 DeWeese proposes a date in the range of 1500-1700. DeWeese 1996; 96.

39 For example, by 1904 Grenard, Shaw, and Hartman had all acquired or studied Mullā Ḥājī's *tadhkirah*. Grenard 1900: 5-79; Shaw 1878; Hartmann 1904: 1-21.

40 Änwär Baytur lists a "*Täzkirätul Äwliya*" 1302 / 1885, and a "*Där Bayan Äshabul Kähäp*" of 1316 / 1898. Sayrami and Baytur 1986: 10.

41 Qurban1984.

Sālah Kāshgharī completed his history of Kashgar in Turki.[42] Throughout the 18th century, Turki gained prominence as local authors translated a host of Persian works into the vernacular.[43] Since the Bughrā-khān *tadhkirahs* in question are all Turki works, they were likely also set down in their current form during the 18th century or later. This is of course an imprecise method for estimating the chronology of these works, especially since Turki was popularized much earlier in Western Turkestan, but, in the absence of other evidence, it may be found suitable for establishing a provisional *terminus post quem*.

For the *Nasabnāmah* and Mullā Ḥājī's *Tadhkirat al-Bughrā-khān* we have a firm *terminus ante quem* in the year 1265 AH (1848-9), which is recorded as the copy date for both works in a composite manuscript in the Jarring collection.[44] Another Jarring manuscript provides an even earlier reference point for these works, though the date's connection to the works in question is somewhat less secure. Manuscript Prov. 504 was copied in 1930, yet also preserves in its colophon the date 1235 AH (1819-1820), presumably the record of an earlier copying. If, as is likely, the *Nasabnāmah* and Mullā Ḥājī's work were also included in the earlier manuscript to which the 1235 AH date refers, then the upper limit of the chronological range for these two works could be pushed back to 1820.[45]

SP C548 and the qaṣīdahs of Jarring Prov. 358 are harder to date, as they are known from manuscripts with no copying date. Given SP C548's stylistic and thematic connections to the *Nasabnāmah*, it was likely produced in the same period, i.e. the turn of the 18th century to the early 19th century. The Prov. 358 qaṣīdahs were likely composed by 1873-4, a date inscribed on the endpapers of the manuscript. Thus, the following chronology is proposed for the Bughrā-khān *tadhkirahs*:

- *Tadhkirah-i Ūwaysīya*:c. 1500- c. 1700
- Samarqandī's *Nasabnāmah*:turn of the 18th century to 1849
- Mullā Ḥājī's *Tadhkirat al-Bughrā-khān*:turn of the 18th century to 1849
- SP C548: turn of the 18th century to middle of the 19th century
- Abū al-Qāsīm's versified *tadhkirahs*: 1829-30
- *Qaṣīdahs* in Prov. 358: turn of the 18th century to 1874

As more manuscripts become accessible, earlier copying dates will likely surface, allowing us to further refine the chronology. It is important to emphasize that the dates proposed here refer only to the recording of the works in written form using the

[42] Akimushkin dates Kāshgharī's history to 1696 based on internal evidence. Anonymous 2001: 17.
[43] For example the independent translations of the *Tadhkirah-i Ūwaysiyya* and Muḥammad Ṣādiq Kāshgharī's translations of the *Tārīkh-I Rashīdī*, Ṭabarī's history, and the *Ādāb al-Ṣāliḥīn*. Hofman 1969: 23. Somewhat later is Shāh Muḥammad b. Khwājah Niẓām al-Dīn's 1837-8 translation of the *Shāhnāmah*. Dmitrieva 2002: 426.
[44] Prov 148.
[45] The 1930 manuscript is composed of 8 selections from the *Tadhkirah-i Ūwaysiyya*, the *Nasābnāmah*, Mullā Ḥājī's *Tadhkirat al- Bughrā-khān*, and the *Tadhkirah-'i Türt Imām Ẓabīḥlar*.

Turki language. Many of the *tadhkirahs* are likely based on much older vernacular oral materials and/or Persian written works. Such roots are certain in the case of Mullā Ḥājī's *Tadhkirat al-Bughrā-khān*, with its obvious oral epic characteristics, and in Abū al-Qāsīm's translation/versification of a Persian work which appears to be lost. Additional oral tales of the Bughrā-khāns never acquired a written form, and are known only from oral tales that have survived into the present.[46]

Manuscript Context

Except for the full *Tadhkirah-i Ūvaysiya* , the works described in this study rarely appeared alone. Instead, they were included in composite manuscripts that brought together several works in one book. The precise arrangements of hagiographical composite manuscripts varied widely in Eastern Turkestan, but most demonstrate a measure of geographical consistency, based on the locations of the tombs of saints described in the texts. Thus, *tadhkirahs* of the various Imams with shrines around Khotan and Keriya tend to be bound together, while the *tadhkirahs* of the Seven Muḥammads and Khwājah Muḥammad Sharīf of Yarkand are often found together. Following this tendency, the Bughrā-khān texts, all of which describe saints buried in or near Kashgar, including Yengisar and Artush, often appear together to make up the core of composite manuscripts. It is not rare for a small number of *tadhkirahs* related to more distant oases to appear alongside such a geographically concentrated collection, as in a manuscript in the Jarring collection with five Bughrā-khān-related *tadhkirahs*, a *tadhkirah* of Muḥammad Ghazālī (Keriya), and the *Tadhkirah-'i Khwājah Muḥammad Sharīf* (Yarkand).[47] However, one almost never encounters manuscripts with an even distribution of, for example, Khotan, Yarkand, and Kashgar-related *tadhkirahs*. Each composite manuscript appears to have a bias toward one geographical area. Within these tomb-based geographic clusters, no single arrangement represents a majority of the manuscripts.

The geographical clustering of *tadhkirah* anthologies likely arose in part from the use of these books in the practice of pilgrimage, and the importance of pilgrimage in disseminating knowledge about the saints. The shrines were geographically situated, and the *tadhkirahs* were closely linked to the shrines.[48] Western visitors to Eastern Turkestan in the early 20th century published reports that hinted at this strong connection between shrines and *tadhkirahs*. Some of these travelers actually acquired *tadhkirah* manuscripts from shrine's *shaykhs*; others documented the performance or preservation of *tadhkirahs* at the shrines.[49] In the introduction to his *Ūlūgh Tadhkirah-i Bughrā-khān*, Abū al-Qāsīm provides an insider's testimony of these practices. He

---

[46] See, for example, Ismayil 1995.

[47] Prov 73. This MS also includes additional biographical texts not connected to Eastern Turkestan.

[48] For extended treatment of this relationship, see Thum 2014.

[49] Hartmann and Mannerheim acquired manuscripts from shrines. Hartmann 1904: 1-21.; Raquette 1940: 3-15; Jarring 1935: 348-354.

writes that:

> "At the shrines the *tadhkirahs* are many
> In words the great *tadhkirah* is wealthy,
> The great shaykhs read out the *tadhkirah* together,
> Adding and joining to it words improper.[50]

Abū al-Qāsīm reveals a concern that the Persian language of the *tadhkirah* gave the *shaykhs* at the shrines inordinate control over the work's meaning, as most of the pilgrims understood only Turki. By recasting the *tadhkirah* in Turki verse he believed he could open the tradition to wide audience:

> "Thus, the story, in Turki and in verse was unfurled
> That they may hear it all, these people of the world.[51]

In light of Gunnar Jarring's report that tens of thousands gathered annually at the shrine where 'Alī Arslān-khān is said to have died, and that they recited there a *tadhkirah* of the Bughrā-khāns, Abū al-Qāsīm's hopes were probably not too far-fetched.[52] Though few in Eastern Turkestan could claim full literacy, many could listen to such public recitations in their own language, which continued from as early as the 18th century, until the great changes brought about by the government of the People's Republic of China. *Tadhkirahs*, through their connection to shrines and the practice of pilgrimage, gained a central place in the popular historical literature of Eastern Turkestan. At the same time, shrine recitations disseminated the *tadhkirahs* to a disproportionately local audience, a phenomenon mirrored in the composition of *tadhkirah* anthologies.

The number and diversity of distinct Bughrā-khān works suggest significant flexibility in the role of the written text in Eastern Turkestan's tradition of shrine devotion. While some texts enjoyed greater currency than others, no single text could boast exclusive orthodoxy. On the contrary, there was room for individuals such as Abū al-Qāsīm to compose new works that expanded the tradition. Authors would have found materials for new texts in the numerous oral tales that circulated alongside the manuscripts, especially in the vicinity of the shrines. Several literary conventions legitimized the production of such new works. Unspecified "traditionalists" or "narrators" were considered legitimate sources of information about the past, and they are frequently cited at the beginning of *tadhkirahs*.[53] These citations may represent

---

[50] "مزارلاردا بار کوب تولا تذکیره, اولوغ تذکیره سوزلاریدین بره, اولوغ شیخلار تذکیره اوقوشوب, موافیق ایماس سوز جالاسو قوشوب" Jarring Prov. 563, f 50b.

[51] "بولوب ترکی هم نظم بولدی بیان, تمام انکلاسون بو اهل جهان" *ibid.* f 50b.

[52] *Ibid.*

[53] For example, a copy of the *Tadhkirah-i Turt Imam Zebihlar* begins, "اما راویان اخبار ناقلان اثار انداغ ایتب دورلار کم ..." i.e.,"The narrators of histories and reporters of traditions say that..." Jarring Prov 327, 31b. Most copies of this *tadhkirah* are even more generic in their citations, saying simply "انداغ روایت قیلورلار کم..." i.e., "They tell such a narrative, that..."MSS using this phrase include MZXY: uncatalogued MS. Jarring: Prov 102, Prov 349.Mannerheim Collection,

explicit references to the oral tradition. Authors also had the option of presenting their compositions as the products of divine or saintly inspiration, as was the case for Abū al-Qāsīm and the author of the *Tadhkirah-i Ūwaysīya*. The trend of versification that appeared in the 18th century provided a further avenue for adding texts to the tradition. Finally, a tradition of adding personal verses to books may explain works like the *qaṣīdahs* in Jarring Prov. 358. Given such a range of opportunities for literate devotees of the saints to create their own *tadhkirahs*, it is likely that more Bughrā-khān works are waiting to be discovered, especially in the collections of Central Asia and China.

Bibliography

MANUSCRIPT COLLECTIONS (with their abbreviations):

Hartmann collection, Staatsbibliotek, Berlin
Jarring Collection, Lund University Library (Jarring)
Library of the Nationalities Research Institute, Central University of Nationalities, Beijing (MZXY)
Mannerheim Collection, National Library of Finland
St. Petersburg branch of the Institute of Oriental Studies of the Russian Academy of Sciences (SP)

Anonymous 2001. [c. 1696] *Tārīkh-i Kāshghar: Anonimnaya tyurkskaya Khronika vladetelei Vostochnogo Turkestana po konets XVII veka: Faksimile Rukopisi Sankt-Peterburgskogo Filiala Instituta vostokovedeniya Akademii Nauk Rossii* [Tārīkh-i Kāshghar: An Anonymous Turki Chronicle of the Rulers of Eastern Turkestan at the Beginning of the 17th Century: Facsimile of the Manuscript of the Saint Petersburg Branch of the Institute of Oriental Studies of the Russian Academy of Sciences]. Edited by O. F. Akimushkin. Sankt-Peterburg: Tsentr «Peterburgskoe Vostokovedenie».

Anonymous 1998. *Uyghur Khälq Riwayätliri: (Nam-Ataqlar Heqqidiki Riwayätlär)* [Uyghur Folk Tales: (Tales About Names)]. Edited by Osman Ismayil. Urumqi: Shinjang Yashlar-Ösmürlär Näshriyati.

Anonymous 2007. "Täzkirä'i Äshabul Kähf."in *Bulaq* 2, (2007): 39-48.

Baldick, Julian 1993. *Imaginary Muslims: The Uwaysi Sufis of Central Asia.* London: I. B. Taurus and Co. Ltd.

DeWeese, Devin 1996. "The Tadhkira-i Bughra-Khan and the "Uvaysi" Sufis of Central Asia: Notes in Review of *Imaginary Muslims*." in *Central Asiatic Journal* 40, no. 1: 87-127.

Dmitrieva, Lyudmila Vasil'evna 2002. *Katalog Tyurkskikh Rukopisei Instituta Vostokovedeniya Rossiiskoi Akademii Nauk.* [Catalog of Turkic Manuscripts on the Institue of Oriental Studies of the Russian Academy of Sciences], Moskva: Izdatel'skaia firma "Vostochnaia literatura."

Grenard, F. 1900. "La Légende de Satok Boghra Khân et l'histoire." in *Journal Asiatique* 9, no. 15: 5-79.

Haji, Molla 1988. *Bughrakhanlar Täzkirisi.* Translated by Abdurehim Sabit. Kashgar: Qäshqär Uyghur Näshriyati.

Hartmann, Martin 1904. "Die Osttürkischen Handschriften der Sammlung Hartmann." in *Mitteilungen des Seminars für Orientalische Sprachen an der Königlichen Friedrich-Wilhelms-Universität zu Berlin* 7, no. 2 (1904): 1-21.

Hofman, H. F. 1969. *Turkish Literature : A Bio-bibliographical Survey. Section III. Moslim Central Asian Turkish Literature.* Utrecht: University of Utrecht.

Ismayil, Osman, ed 1995. *Uyghur Khälq Riwayätliri: Nam-Ataqlar Häqqidiki Riwayätlär.* Urumqi: Shinjang Yashlar – Osmürlär Näshriyati.

Jarring, Gunnar 1935. "The Ordam-Padishah System of Eastern Turkistan Shrines." in *Geografiska Annaler 17, Supplement: Hyllningsskrift Tillagnad Sven Hedin,* (1935): 348-354.

National Library of Finland: II, V.

Muginov, A. M. 1962 *Opisanie Uigurskikh Rukopisei Instituta Narodov Azii.* [Description of the Uyghur Manuscripts in the Institute of the Peoples of Asia] Moskva: Izdatel'stvo vostochnoi literatury.

Muhämmäd, Abdurishit and Muhämmäd Usman 1989 "Yüsüp Qadirkhan Ghazi Täzkirisi." in *Qädimqi Kitablar Tätqiqati* 1989-1: 1-27.

Qäshqäri, Muhämmäd Sadiq 1988 *Täzkirä'i Äzizan.* Translated by Nijat Mukhlis and Shämsidin Ämät. Kashgar: Qäshqär Uyghur Näshriyati.

Qurban, Ibrahim. 1984 *Yättä Qizlirim* [The Seven Maidens]. Kashgar: Qäshqär Uyghur Näshriyati.

Raquette, G. 1940 "Collection of Manuscripts from Eastern Turkestan. An Account of the Contents." in *Across Asia from West to East in 1906-1908.* Edited by C. G. Mannerheim. Helsinki: Suomalais-Ugrilainen Seura, 3-15.

Sawut, Tursunmuhämmät, and Dil'ara Ablimit 2001. "Tilgha Elinmighan Täzkirilär." [Unmentioned Tadhkirahs] in *Shinjang Täzkirichiliki* 2001-1: 39-49.

Sayrami, Musa and Änwär Baytur 1986 *Tarikhi Hamidi.* Beijing: Millätlär Näshriyati.

Shaw, Robert 1878. *A Sketch of the Turki Language as Spoken in Eastern Turkistan (Kashgar and Yarkand).* Calcutta: Baptist Mission Press.

Thum, Rian 2014. *The Sacred Routes of Uyghur History.* Cambridge: Harvard University Press.

Wäli, Qurban (ed.) 1986. *Uighur, Özbek, Tatar Qädimki Äsärlär Tizimliki* [List of Old Uyghur, Uzbek, and Tatar Works]. Kashgar: Qäshqär Uyghur Näshriyati.

Zalīlī, Muḥammad 1985. *Zälili Diwani.* Translated by Imin Tursun. Beijing: Millätlär Näshriyati.

The Genealogy of Makhdūm-i A'ẓam and the Cultural Traditions of Mazars

SAWADA Minoru

Physical genealogy (*nisbat-i ṣūrī*) is thought to have been crucial factor for the descendants of Makhdūm-i A'ẓam to claim their spiritual legitimacy. The genealogy of the forefathers of Makhdūm-i A'ẓam (Aḥmad Kāsānī, d. 1542-43) has been studied by many scholars as regards its fabrication, borrowings from another sacred lineages such as the Shiite *imāms*, comparison with the genealogy of Kucha Khwājas (Katakīs), significance of heredity in *shaykh* succession.[1] As scholars specified already, the genealogy is not unitary and there are several genealogies in the hagiographies of Makhdūm-i A'ẓam and his descendents. But as I make clear in this chapter, a comparison of the source materials shows that there are two kinds of genealogies and the key character is Burhān al-Dīn Qïlïch, whose legends are also of two kinds. In addition, differences seen in the two kinds of genealogies and legends are closely connected with the mazar traditions of related provinces and periods.

1. Genealogies of Makhdūm-i A'ẓam

We can find the genealogy (bloodline) of Makhdūm-i A'ẓam, a renowned Sufi *shaykh* of Naqshbandiyya, in hagiographic literature from the 17th to 20th centuries. His genealogy seems to have been fabricated and there are some discrepancies between the hagiographies.

One of the earliest mentions of his genealogy is found in his biography *Jāmi' al-maqāmāt,* written by his grandson Abū al-Baqā' ibn Khwāja Bahā' al-Dīn in A.H.1026/1617-18.[2] This genealogy resembles other genealogies mentioned in later literature, such as the *Hidāyat-nāma* written by Mīr Khāl al-Dīn Kātib al-Yārkandī in

---

1 These studies are included in Shimada 1952, Schwarz 1976, Hamada 1978, Kim 1996, Papas 2007.

2 *Jāmi' al-maqāmāt*, Institut vostokobedeniya Akademii Nauk Respubliki Uzbekistan, Ms. No. 72, fol. 3a-b; *Jāmi' al-maqāmāt*, Bodleian Library, Ms. Ind. Inst. Pers. 118, fol. 3a-b. According to a study by B. Babajanov, Ms. No. 72 was copied in 1034/1624-25 (Babajanov 1999:6), while Ms. Ind. Inst. Pers. 118 was copied in 1130/1718 (Beeston 1954:12). Kim Ho-Dong used the manuscripts of Ms. Ind. Inst. Pers. 118 and Staatsbibliothek zu Berlin, Preussischer Kulturbesitz, Orientabteilung, Ms. Or. Oct. 1562 (Kim 1996:303, n. 52).

1143/1730-31,[3] the *Tadhkira-i ʻazīzān* written by Muḥammad Ṣādiq Kāshgharī about 1182/1768-69,[4] the *Majmūʻat al-muḥaqqiqīn*,[5] the *Tadhkira-i Sayyid Āfāq Khwājam*,[6] and the *Manāqib-i Ḥaḍrat-i Shaykh Maṣlaḥat al-Dīn Khujandī*.[7]

Another genealogy of Makhdūm-i Aʻẓam is found in the *Anīs al-ṭālibīn* written by Shāh Maḥmūd Churās in the late 17th or early 18th century[8] and in the *Tārīkh* written by the same author.[9] This genealogy fundamentally differs from the genealogy mentioned in the *Jāmiʻ al-maqāmāt* with regard to the names of the ancestors of Makhdūm-i Aʻẓam, as follows (see also List at the end of this chapter):

Jāmiʻ al-maqāmāt (Ms. No. 72)	*Anīs al-ṭālibīn*
Imām ʻAlī Mūsā RiḍāImām ʻAlī Mūsā Riḍā	
Ṭālib	Amīr Sayyid Ḥasan
ʻAbd Allāh	Sayyid Ṭāhir
ʻAbd Allāh al-Afḍal	Sayyid Qāsim
ʻAbd Allāh	Sayyid Burhān al-Dīn
Sayyid Aḥmad	Sayyid ʻAlāʼ al-Dīn
Sayyid Muḥammad	Sayyid Ḍiyāʼ al-Dīn
Shāh Ḥasan	Sayyid Ashraf al-Dīn
Shāh Ḥusayn	**Sayyid Jalāl al-Dīn**
Sayyid Jalāl al-DīnSayyid Kamāl al-Dīn Majnūn	
Sayyid Kamāl al-DīnSulṭān Burhān al-Dīn Qïlïch	
Sayyid Burhān al-Dīn Qïlïch	

---

[3] *Hidāyat-nāma*, British Library, Ms. Or. 8162, fol. 22b. Cf. Meredith-Owens 1968: 21.

[4] *Tadhkira-i ʻazīzān*, Bodleian Library, Ms. Turk d. 20, fol. 41b; Saint-Petersburg, Institute of Oriental Studies, Ms. D191, fol. 48a-b; Nurmanova 2006: 104-105.

[5] *Majmūʻat al-muḥaqqiqīn* (Staatsbibliothek zu Berlin, Preussischer Kulturbesitz, Orientabteilung, Ms. or. oct. 1680, pp. 23-24). This work is a Turki translation of *Jāmiʻ al-maqāmāt* with some additions. The translation was begun at Rajab 12, 1208 (February 13, 1794) and finished at Safar 20, 1235 (December 8, 1819) (Ms. or. oct. 1680, pp. 21, 154; See also Togan 1991: 475). Another copies of the *Majmūʻat al-muḥaqqiqīn* are preserved at Staatsbibliothek zu Berlin (Preussischer Kulturbesitz, Orientabteilung, Ms. or. oct. 1719) and British Library (India Office Library, Ms. Turki 7).

[6] *Tadhkira-i Sayyid Āfāq Khwājam*, Lund Universitetsbiblioteket, Gunnar Jarring Collection, Handskriftsavt, Prov. 22, fol. 3a-b.

[7] *Manāqib-i Ḥaḍrat-i Shaykh Maṣlaḥat al-Dīn Khujandī* (Islamabad, Markaz-i Taḥqīqāt-i Fārsī-i Īrān va Pākistān, Ms. No. 5703, pp. 83-84).

[8] *Anīs al-ṭālibīn*, Bodleian Library, Ms. Ind. Inst. Pers. 45, fol. 4a-b. Cf. Beeston 1954: 12-13.

[9] *Tārīkh*, Akimushkin 1976: 6.

This part of the genealogy mentioned in the *Anīs al-ṭālibīn* and slightly different in the *Tārīkh* resembles another genealogy of Burhān al-Dīn Qïlïch mentioned in the *Tadhkira-i Bughrā Khān* (or *Tadhkira-i Uwaysiyya*),[10] although he is not an ancestor of Makhdūm-i A'ẓam in the *Tadhkira-i Bughrā Khān*. The latter genealogy is as follows:

Tadhkira-i Bughrā Khān

Amīr Ḥusayn Madanī
|
Ṭāhir
|
Hāshim
|
Qāsim
|
Burhān al-Dīn
|
'Alā' al-Dīn
|
Ḍiyāv al-Dīn
|
Ashraf al-Dīn
|
Jalāl al-Dīn
|
Burhān al-Dīn (Qïlïchï)

Why do two genealogies (one in the *Anīs al-ṭālibīn* and the other in the *Tadhkira-i Bughrā Khān*) have common personal names such as Ṭāhir, Qāsim, Burhān al-Dīn, 'Alā' al-Dīn, Ḍiyā' al-Dīn and Ashraf al-Dīn, who are not mentioned in the genealogy of the *Jāmi' al-maqāmāt*? In this respect, the genealogy mentioned in the *Anīs al-ṭālibīn* is unusual also in comparison with those mentioned in other hagiographies of the descendants of Makhdūm-i A'zam, such as the *Hidāyat-nāma*, *Tadhkira-i 'azīzān* (see List).

The *Anīs al-ṭālibīn* contains accounts of many saints who have the material and spiritual lineage of Khwāja 'Abd Allāh ibn Khwāja Muḥammad Yaḥyā ibn Khwāja Isḥāq ibn Makhdūm-i A'ẓam, and it was composed during the reign of Dāniyāl Khwājam (great-grandson of Khwāja Isḥāq).[11] That is to say, Shāh Maḥmūd Churās, author of the *Anīs al-ṭālibīn*, is on the side of the Isḥāqī faction (Khwāja Isḥāq and his descendants) of the so-called Kashgharian Khwājas. The *Hidāyat-nāma*, a biography of Khwāja Āfāq (Hidāyat Allāh), who was a great-grandson of Makhdūm-i A'ẓam and a strong opponent of the Isḥāqī faction, mentions almost the same genealogy as that of the

---

[10] *Tadhkira-i Bughrā Khān*, Bodleian Library, Ms. Ind. Inst. Pers. 54, fol. 214b. According to the catalogue of Bodleian Library, the title of the manuscript is *Tadhkira i Uwaisīya* (Beeston 1954: 13-14), but we can find the title, *Tadhkira-i Bughrā Khān*, in the manuscript (fol. 3b). Baldick 1993: 133. On Baldick's book, see DeWeese 1996: 87-127.

[11] Beeston 1954: 12-13.

Jāmi' al-maqāmāt. The author of the *Hidāyat-nāma*, Mīr Khāl al-Dīn Kātib al-Yārkandī, wrote the biography in 1143/1730-31, not long after or before Dāniyāl Khwājam's death. It is possible to assume that the author of the *Anīs al-ṭālibīn* plagiarized the pedigree of the *Tadhkira-i Bughrā Khān* and fabricated a new genealogy for challenging the Āfāqī faction (Khwāja Āfāq and his descendants) of Kashgharian Khwājas.

In that case, why was the pedigree of Burhan al-Din Qïlïchï mentioned in the *Tadhkira-i Bughrā Khān* used for fabricating a new genealogy of the Isḥāqī faction? Khwāja Isḥāq (d. 1599), son of Makhdūm-i A'ẓam, faced strong opponents during his propagation in Kashghar and Yarkand, in the latter half of the 16th century. Representative of these opponents was an Uwaysī Sufi, Muḥammad Walī Ṣūfī, successor (*jā-nishīn*) of Khwāja Muḥammad Sharīf. Joseph Fletcher considers that Muḥammad Sharīf Pīr [=Khwāja Muḥammad Sharīf] founded the "confrérie Uwaysiyya" and died in 1555 or 1566,[12] although the actual conditions of the "confrérie" are not made clear. His mazar can still be seen in Yarkand today. The Chingizid sovereign of Moghūliyya (descendant of Tughluq Tīmūr Khān), 'Abd al-Rashīd Khān, was a disciple (*murīd*) of Khwāja Muḥammad Sharīf, and his son, 'Abd al-Karīm Khān, was a disciple of Muḥammad Walī Ṣūfī. But, eventually Khwāja Isḥāq of the Kashgharian Khwājas won the devotion of Muḥammad Khān, the younger brother of 'Abd al-Karīm Khān, and succeeded in propagating his religious order.[13] It is possible that an Uwaysī pedigree may have been incorporated into the genealogy of the Isḥāqī faction in the course of the confrontation with and overpowering of the Uwaysiyya by Khwāja Isḥāq. If so, about a century later, the author of the *Anīs al-ṭālibīn* possibly used the plagiarized genealogy.[14] In any case, it is noteworthy that the connection between two genealogies in the *Anīs al-ṭālibīn* and the *Tadhkira-i Bughrā Khān* was made through Burhān al-Dīn Qïlïch / Qïlïchï.

It may also be noted that the genealogies of Kashgharian Khwājas, which appear in the *Tadhkira-i khwājagān* (short version of *Tadhkira-i 'azīzān*) and *Xi-yu tong-wen-zhi* (『西域同文志』), resemble a genealogy of Kucha Khwājas (descendants of Arshad al-Dīn who converted Tughluq Tīmūr Khān to Islam).[15] In this pedigree of Kashgharian Khwājas, the personal names between Imām 'Alī Mūsā Riḍā and Burhān al-Dīn Qïlïch are almost the same as those in the genealogy of *Hidāyat-nāma*.

In a word, there are two kinds of genealogies of Makhdūm-i A'ẓam: one is found in *Jāmi' al-maqāmāt, Hidāyat-nāma,* and *Tadhkira-i 'azīzān* (*Tadhkira-i khwājagān*); the other is seen in *Anīs al-ṭālibīn* and *Tārīkh* of Shāh Maḥmūd Churās.

2. Legends of Burhān al-Dīn Qïlïch

Among the alleged ancestors of Makhdūm-i A'ẓam, the most important character is

---

[12] Fletcher 1985: 23.

[13] Sawada 1987: 66-70; see also Kim 1996: 308-314.

[14] Kim Ho-Dong examined the process of forging the genealogies of Makhdūm-i A'ẓam from a view point of struggles waged between Katakī Sufis and Kashgharian Khwājas (Kim 1996: 303-308).

[15] Hamada 1978: 90-91.

Burhān al-Dīn Qïlïch.[16] Legends of his birth and activities are included in the hagiographic literature, i.e., *Jāmi' al-maqāmāt, Anīs al-ṭālibīn,* and *Tadhkira-i 'azīzān*. The legend of Burhān al-Dīn Qïlïch according to the *Jāmi' al-maqāmāt*[17] may be summarized as follows:

> Ḥaḍrat-i Sayyid [=Sayyid Kamāl al-Dīn Majnūn] lived in Madīna [in Arabia]. He became attracted by God and reached Ūzkand, capital of Ferghāna province, to seek a saint (*ahl Allāh*). At the time, Ferghāna province was under the rule of Sulṭān Ilek (Ilik / Ilig) Māḍī. Sulṭān Ilek Māḍī was one of the perfect saints (*kummal awliyā'*) and an offspring of *amīr al-mu'minīn* Abā Bakr Ṣiddīq and one of the seven *sulṭāns* of God (*haft sulṭān-i Allāhī*). Before the arrival of Sayyid Kamāl al-Dīn, it was revealed by inspiration to Sulṭān Ilek Māḍī that a *sayyid-zāda* would come to the province. Ḥaḍrat-i Sayyid was welcomed and married a daughter of Sulṭān Ilek Māḍī. Ḥaḍrat-i Sayyid attended Sulṭān Ilek Māḍī for some time and obtained perfection (*kamāl*). Afterwards he returned to Madīna.
>
> When Ḥaḍrat-i Sayyid died, Sulṭān Burhān al-Dīn Qïlïch was in the womb of his mother. Before dying, Ḥaḍrat-i Sayyid made his will as follows: "It was revealed by inspiration to me that a son named Sulṭān Burhān al-Dīn would be born to me and he would be the owner of perfection (*ṣāḥib-kamāl*) and the pole (*quṭb*), and that from his offspring owners of perfection would emerge." After the death of Ḥaḍrat-i Sayyid, Sulṭān Burhān al-Dīn was born.
>
> His mother brought Sulṭān Burhān al-Dīn to his grandfather, Sulṭān Ilek Māḍī. Before dying, the latter set Sulṭān Burhān al-Dīn on the throne in his stead. For a while Sulṭān Burhān al-Dīn sat on the throne and governed well. But suddenly he became attracted by God and cast away the throne and crown as in the case of Sulṭān Ibrāhīm Adham. Sulṭān Burhān al-Dīn attended Shaykh Muṣliḥ al-Dīn Khujandī, who was the pole (*quṭb*) of that time, and attained perfection. After the death of Shaykh Muṣliḥ al-Dīn, Sulṭān Burhān al-Dīn returned to Ūzkand and guided the people to the right way, and he himself lived in honest poverty like Muḥammad (*ṭarīq-i faqr-i Muḥammadī*).

Almost the same story is found in the *Tadhkira-i 'azīzān.*[18] But the legend recorded in the *Anīs al-ṭālibīn* of Shāh Maḥmūd Churās[19] has some differences in details although the plot is the same. Of these differences, the following are the most important for us:

1) In the account of the *Anīs al-ṭālibīn*, "Sulṭān Ilek Māḍī was a grandchild (*nabīra*) of Satūq Bughr[ā] Khān Ghāzī [and] a paternal uncle's son (*'am-zāda*) of Yūsuf Qadïr Khān Ghāzī," whereas in the *Jāmi' al-maqāmāt*, Sulṭān Ilek Māḍī was an offspring of amīr al-mu'minīn Abā Bakr Ṣiddīq and one of the seven sulṭāns of God (*haft sulṭān-i Allāhī*).

2) The *Anīs al-ṭālibīn* does not mention Shaykh Muṣliḥ al-Dīn Khujandī, whereas according to the *Jāmi' al-maqāmāt*, Sulṭān Burhān al-Dīn cast away the throne and attended Shaykh Muṣliḥ al-Dīn Khujandī. In the account of the *Anīs al-ṭālibīn*, the Sulṭān [=Sulṭān Burhān al-Dīn] abandoned his throne and country and died between the age of sixty and seventy, and he was an Uwaysī.

---

[16] On his historical reality and legends of his cult, see Abashin 2003: 215-236, Hamada 2006: 40-41, n. 27.

[17] *Jāmi' al-maqāmāt*, Bodleian Library, Ms. Ind. Inst. Pers 118, fol. 3b-6a. Cf. Institut vostokovedeniya Akademii Nauk Respubliki Uzbekistan, Ms. No. 72, fol. 3a-5a.

[18] *Tadhkira-i 'azīzān*, Bodleian Library, Ms. Turk d. 20, fol. 11a-13a; Saint-Petersburg, Institute of Oriental Studies, Ms. D191, 13b-15b; Nurmanova 2006: 57-60.

[19] *Anīs al-ṭālibīn*, Bodleian Library, Ms. Ind. Inst. Pers 45, fol. 4b-7b.

What do these two differences in the legend of Burhān al-Dīn Qïlïch mean? I interpret these differences from the perspective of mazar cultures.

The *Jāmi' al-maqāmāt* describes Shaykh Muṣliḥ al-Dīn Khujandī as the spiritual guide of Burhān al-Dīn Qïlïch, while the *Anīs al-ṭālibīn* does not even mention the name of the shaykh. The *Jāmi' al-maqāmāt* was written by Makhdūm-i A'ẓam's grandson Abū al-Baqā' in the early 17th century, as mentioned above. Abū al-Baqā' is not a member of the so-called Kashgharian Khwājas. It is to be surmised that the legend of Burhān al-Dīn Qïlïch was formed in the religious tradition of Mawarannahr, especially Ferghana province.

In Ferghana province around the 17th century, reverence for Shaykh Muṣliḥ al-Dīn Khujandī and his mazar is thought to have been widespread. In historical sources, Shaykh Muṣliḥ al-Dīn Khujandī is also called Shaykh Maṣlaḥat Khujandī and the like.[20] According to a study by Devin DeWeese, "Shaykh Maṣlaḥat al-Dīn Khujandī [=Shaykh Maṣlaḥat] is mentioned in several sources from the 15th century, including Sharaf al-Dīn 'Alī Yazdī's history of Tīmūr, who in 792/1390 visited the *shaykh*'s shrine in Khujand; from this it is clear that Shaykh Maṣlaḥat's shrine, which still exists, was a pilgrimage site already in the second half of the 14th century, while the 15th-century guidebook to the shrines of Bukhara, the *Tārīkh-i Mullāzāda*, preserves an anecdote dating the *shaykh*'s death to the time of the first Mongol invasion of Central Asia...."[21] A Chingizid sovereign of Moghūlistān, Sulṭān Maḥmūd Khān, who was killed by a man of Shāhī Beg Khān (Shaybānī Khān) of the Uzbek on the river at Khujand in 914/1508-09, was buried at the mazar of Shaykh Muṣliḥ al-Dīn Khujandī.[22]

The *Anīs al-ṭālibīn* describes Sulṭān Ilek Māḍī as an offspring of Satūq Bughrā Khān Ghāzī, while the *Jāmi' al-maqāmāt* does not even mention the name of the khān. Elsewhere, the *Anīs al-ṭālibīn* also says that "Makhdūm-i A'ẓam was a descendant of Satūq Bughrā Khān and Sulṭān Ilek Māḍī, as first described in this book."[23] Clearly the *Anīs al-ṭālibīn* is asserting that Makhdūm-i A'ẓam is a descendant of Satūq Bughrā Khān through a daughter of Sulṭān Ilek Māḍī.[24] Why was Makhdūm-i A'ẓam linked to Satūq Bughrā Khān by a female lineage?

To answer this question, we have to consider the circumstances in which the Isḥāqī faction of Kashgharian Khwājas propagated their religious order. As mentioned above, Khwāja Isḥāq, a son of Makhdūm-i A'ẓam, overcame the influence of Muḥammad Walī Ṣūfī, a successor of Khwāja Muḥammad Sharīf, and propagated his teachings in Kashgharia. According to a study by Hamada Masami, Khwāja Muḥammad Sharīf was an

---

[20] Muṣliḥ al-Dīn Khujandī (*Tadhkira-i 'azīzān*, Bodleian Library, Ms. Turk d. 20, fol.12a), Shaykh Maṣlaḥat Khujandī (*Tadhkira-i 'azīzān*, Saint-Petersburg, Institute of Oriental Studies, Ms. D191, fol. 15a), Shaykh Maṣlaḥat / Muṣliḥ al-Dīn (*Bābur-Nāma*, Mano 1995: 7).

[21] DeWeese 2006: 34-35.

[22] Elias & Ross 1972: 209; Muḥammad Ḥaydar Dūghlāt, *Tārīkh-i Rashīdī*, British Library, Ms. Or. 157, fol. 163b.

[23] *Anīs al-ṭālibīn*, Bodleian Library, Ms. Ind. Inst. Pers 45, fol. 87b-88a.

[24] Cf. Hamada 1991: 100-101; Hamada 2001: 76-77.

Uwaysī of Satūq Bughrā Khān and rediscovered the mausoleum of Satūq Bughrā Khān and founded the waqfs for the mausoleum.[25] The author of the *Anīs al-ṭālibīn*, Shāh Maḥmūd Churās, also describes a visitation to the mazar of Sulṭān Satuq (*sic*) Bughrā Khān by Khwāja Muḥammad Sharīf and his disciple, 'Abd al-Rashīd Khān, in the *Tārīkh.*[26] At the time of propagation by Khwāja Isḥāq, the cult of the mazar of Sulṭān Satūq Bughrā Khān is thought to have been popular among Kashgharian people, at least among the khāns, and its cult was combined with Khwāja Muḥammad Sharīf. As the mazar of Khwāja Muḥammad Sharīf still survives and is maintained by people in Yarkand, the influence of Khwāja Muḥammad Sharīf must have continued after his death. It is to be assumed that the lineage connection of Makhdūm-i A'ẓam with Satūq Bughrā Khān through Burhān al-Dīn Qïlïch was fabricated in rivalry with the powers of Khwāja Muḥammad Sharīf and his successors.

Conclusion

To sum up, two kinds of pedigrees are found in the forefathers of Makhdūm-i A'ẓam, and legends of his ancestor, Burhān al-Dīn Qïlïch, also have two versions. The genealogy and the legend mentioned in the *Jāmi' al-maqāmāt* were formed on the cultural basis of Ferghana valley and had no connection with Kashgharian Khwājas. On the other hand, those mentioned in the *Anīs al-ṭālibīn* are closely concerned with the mazar culture of Kashgharia, especially with the mazar of Sulṭān Satūq Bughrā Khān. But the genealogy and the legend in the *Anīs al-ṭālibīn* were not taken over by later hagiographies written in Kashgharia, such as the *Hidāyat-nāma* and the *Tadhkira-i 'azīzān*. It is to be surmised that the later hagiographies had no need to support the Isḥāqī faction of Kashgharian Khwājas against Uwaysī Sufis in Kashgharia.

---

[25] Hamada 1991: 97; Hamada 2001: 72.

[26] *Tārīkh*, Akimushkin 1976: 11; Sawada 1987: 68-69; Hamada 1991: 96; Hamada 2001: 70.

List: The Genealogies of Makhdūm-i Aʻẓam and Kashgharian Khwājas, etc.

Jāmiʻ al-maqāmāt (No. 72, fol. 3a-b)	*Jāmiʻ al-maqāmāt* (Ind. Inst. Pers 118, fol. 3a-b)	*Hidāyat-nāma* (Or. 8162, fol. 22b)	*Tadhkira-i ʻazīzān* (Turk d. 20, fol. 41b)	*Majmūʻat al-muḥaqqiqīn* (or. oct. 1680, pp. 23-24)
			Muḥammad Muṣṭafā	rasūl
	ʻAlī b. Abī Ṭālib	ʻAlī	ʻAlī al-Murtaḍā and Fāṭima al-Zahrā	Būbī (*sic*) Fāṭima Zahrā
	al-Ḥusayn	Imām Ḥusayn	Imām Ḥusayn	Imām Ḥusayn
	ʻAlī	Imām Zayn al-ʻĀbidīn	Imām Zayn al-ʻĀbidīn	Imām Zayn al-ʻĀbidīn
	Muḥammad	Imām Muḥammad Bāqir	Imām Muḥammad Bāqir	Imām Muḥammad Bāqir
	Jaʻfar	Imām Jaʻfar Ṣādiq	Imām Jaʻfar Ṣādiq	Imām Jaʻfar Ṣādiq
		Imām Mūsā Kāẓim	Imām Mūsā Kāẓim	Imām Mūsā Kāẓim
Imām ʻAlī Mūsā Riḍā	**Mūsā al-Riḍā**	**Imām ʻAlī Mūsā Riḍā**	**Imām ʻAlī Mūsā Riḍā**	**Imām ʻAlī Mūsā Riḍā**
Ṭālib	Imām ʻAlī	Ṭālib	Sayyid Ṭālib	Sayyid Ṭālib
ʻAbd Allāh	five "mediators" (*wāsiṭa*)	ʻAbd Allāh Aʻraj	ʻAbd Allāh Aʻraj	Sayyid ʻAbd Allāh Aʻraj
ʻAbd Allāh al-Afḍal		ʻAbd Allāh Afḍal	ʻAbd Allāh Afḍal	Sayyid ʻAbd Allāh Afḍal
ʻAbd Allāh		ʻAbd Allāh	ʻUbayd Allāh	Sayyid ʻAbd Allāh
Sayyid Aḥmad		Sayyid Aḥmad	Sayyid Aḥmad	Sayyid Aḥmad
Sayyid Muḥammad		Sayyid Muḥammad	Sayyid Muḥammad	Sayyid Muḥammad
Shāh Ḥasan		Shāh Ḥasan	Shāh Ḥusayn	Shāh Ḥusayn
Shāh Ḥusayn		Shāh Ḥusayn	Shāh Ḥasan	Sayyid Shāh Ḥasan
Sayyid Jalāl al-Dīn		**Sayyid Jalāl al-Dīn**	**Sayyid Jalāl al-Dīn**	**Sayyid Jamāl al-Dīn**
Sayyid Kamāl al-Dīn	**Sayyid Kamāl al-Dīn Majnūn**	**Sayyid Kamāl al-Dīn**	**Sayyid Kamāl al-Dīn**	**Sayyid Kamāl al-Dīn**
Sayyid Burhān al-Dīn Qïlïch	**Sulṭān Burhān al- Dīn Qïlïch**	**Sayyid Burhān al-Dīn Qïlïch**	**Sayyid Burhān al-Dīn Qïlïch**	**Sayyid Burhān al-Dīn Qïlïch**
Mīr Dīwāna		Mīr Dīwāna	Sayyid Khwāja	Mīr Dīwāna
(Sayyid Burhān al-Dīn ////) Khwājam	Mawlānā Burhān al-Dīn Khāl	Mīr Khwāja		Sayyid Muḥammad Khwāja
Sayyid Burhān al-Dīn	three "mediators" (*wāsiṭa*)	Sayyid Burhān al-Dīn	Sayyid Burhān al-Dīn	Sayyid Burhān al-Dīn
Sayyid Jalāl al-Dīn	Mawlānā Jalāl Kāsānī	Sayyid Jalāl al-Dīn	Sayyid Jalāl al-Dīn	Sayyid Jalāl al-Dīn
Mawlānā Khwājagī (Aḥmad)	**Makhdūm-i Aʻẓam**	**Makhdūm-i Aʻẓam**	**Makhdūm-i Aʻẓam (Aḥmad Khwājagī)**	**Makhdūm-i Aʻẓam**
		Muḥammad Amīn	Khwāja Isḥāq	Khwāja Muḥammad Emīn Khwājam
		Khwāja Muḥammad Yūsuf	Khwāja Shādī	Khwāja Muḥammad Yūsuf Khwājam
		Khwāja Hidāyat Allāh	Khwāja ʻUbayd Allāh	Khwāja Hidāyat Allāh Khwājam
		Khwāja Mahdī	Khwāja Dāniyāl	Khwāja Yaḥyā Khwājam
			Khwāja Yaʻqūb (Khwāja Jahān)	Khwāja Aḥmad Khwājam
				Qïlïch Burhān al-Dīn Khwājam and Khwāja Jahān Khwājam

Tadhkira-i Bughrā Khān (Ind. Inst. Pers. 54, fol. 214b)	Shāh Mahmūd Churās, *Tārīkh* (ed. O. F. Akimushkin, p. 6)	*Anīs al-ṭālibīn* (Ind. Inst. Pers 45, fol. 4a-b)	*Tadhkira-i Sayyid Āfāq Khwājam* (Prov. 22, fol. 3a-b)	*Manāqib-i Hazrat-i Shaykh Maslahat al-Dīn Khujandī* (No. 5703, pp. 83-84)
			Muḥammad Muṣṭafā	
		ʿAlī Murtaḍā	ʿAlī and Fāṭima Zahrā	
		Imām Ḥusayn	Imām Ḥusayn	
		Imām ʿAlī Zayn al-ʿĀbidīn	Imām Zayn al-ʿĀbidīn	
		Imām Muḥammad Bāqir	Imām Muḥmmad Bāqī (*sic*)	
		Imām Jaʿfar Ṣādiq	Imām Jaʿfar Ṣādiq	
		Imām Mūsā Kāẓim	Sayyid Imām Mūsā Kāẓim	
		Imām ʿAlī Mūsā Riḍā	**Sayyid Imām Muḥammad ʿAlī Mūsā al-Riḍā**	**ʿAlī Mūsā Riḍā**
Amīr Ḥusayn Madanī	Amīr Sayyid Ḥasan Umdanī (? AMDNY)	Amīr Sayyid Ḥasan	Sayyid Imām Muḥammad Naqī	Sayyid ʿAbd Allāh Ṭālib
Ṭāhir	Sayyid Ṭāhir	Sayyid Ṭāhir	Sayyid Imām Muḥammad Taqī	Sayyid ʿAbd Allāh Afḍal
Hāshim	Sayyid Hāshim	Sayyid Qāsim	Sayyid Imām Muḥammad Ḥasan al-ʿAskarī	Sayyid ʿAbd Allāh
Qāsim	Sayyid Qāsim		Sayyid ʿAbd Allāh Aʿraj	Sayyid Aḥmad
Burhān al-Dīn	Sayyid Burhān al-Dīn	Sayyid Burhān al-Dīn	Sayyid ʿAbd Allāh Afḍal	Sayyid Muḥammad
ʿAlāʾ al-Dīn	Sayyid ʿAlāʾ al-Dīn	Sayyid ʿAlāʾ al-Dīn	Sayyid Shāh Ḥusayn	Shāh Ḥasan
Ḍiyāv al-Dīn	Sayyid Ḍiyā al-Dīn	Sayyid Ḍiyāʾ al-Dīn	Sayyid Shāh Ḥasan	Shāh Ḥusayn
Ashraf al-Dīn	Sayyid Ashraf al-Dīn	Sayyid Ashraf al-Dīn	Sayyid Jamāl al-Dīn	Sayyid Jalāl al-Dīn
Jalāl al-Dīn	**Sayyid Jalāl al-Dīn**	**Sayyid Jalāl al-Dīn**	Sayyid Kamāl al-Dīn	Sayyid Kamāl al-Dīn
		Sayyid Kamāl al-Dīn Majnūn	Sayyid Burhān al-Dīn	**Sayyid Burhān al-Dīn Qïlïch**
Burhān al-Dīn (Qïlïchï)	**Shāh Burhān al-Dīn**	**Sulṭān Burhān al-Dīn Qïlïch**	Sayyid Mīr Muḥammad Dīwāna	Mīr Dīwāna
	ten "mediators" (*wāsiṭa*)	Maulānā Burhān al-Dīn Khāl	Sayyid Qïlïch Burhān al-Dīn	Khwājam
		three "mediators" (*wāsiṭa*)		Sayyid Burhān al-Dīn
			Sayyid Jalāl al-Dīn	Sayyid Jalāl al-Dīn
			Makhdūm-i Aʿẓam	**Makhdūm-i Aʿẓam**
		Maulānā Jalāl Kāsānī		
	Mawlānā Khwājagī Kāsānī (Makhdūm-i Aʿẓam)	**Mawlānā Aḥmad Khwājagī Kāsānī (Makhdūm-i Aʿẓam)**		
	Khwāja Muḥammad Isḥāq	Khwāja Isḥāq		
	Khwāja Muḥammad Yaḥyā	Khwāja Muḥammad Yaḥyā		
	Khwāja Muḥammad ʿAbd Allāh	Khwāja Muḥammad ʿAbd Allāh		

References

Anīs al-ṭālibīn, Shāh Maḥmūd Churās.
Bodleian Library, Ms. Ind. Inst. Pers. 45.
Bābur-Nāma (Vaqāyi'), Zahīr al-Din Muhammad Bābur.
Mano 1995.
Hidāyat-nāma, Mīr Khāl al-Dīn Kātib al-Yārkandī.
British Library, Ms. Or. 8162.
Jāmi' al-maqāmāt, Abū al-Baqā' ibn Khwāja Bahā' al-Dīn.
Institut vostokovedeniya Akademii Nauk Respubliki Uzbekistan, Ms. No. 72.
Bodleian Library, Ms. Ind. Inst. Pers. 118.
Staatsbibliothek zu Berlin, Preussischer Kulturbesitz, Orientabteilung, Ms. or. oct. 1562.
Majmū'at al-muḥaqqiqīn.
Staatsbibliothek zu Berlin, Preussischer Kulturbesitz, Orientabteilung, Ms. or. oct. 1680.
Staatsbibliothek zu Berlin, Preussischer Kulturbesitz, Orientabteilung, Ms. or. oct. 1719.
British Library, India Office Library, Ms. Turki 7.
Manāqib-i Ḥaḍrat-i Shaykh Maṣlaḥat al-Dīn Khujandī.
Islamabad, Markaz-i Taḥqīqāt-i Fārsī-i Īrān va Pākistān, Ms. No. 5703.
Tadhkira-i 'azīzān, Muḥammad Ṣādiq Kāshgharī
Bodleian Library, Ms. Turk d. 20.
Saint-Petersburg, Institute of Oriental Studies, Ms. D191.
Nurmanova 2006.
Tadhkira-i Bughrā Khān (or *Tadhkira-i Uwaysiyya*)
Bodleian Library, Ms. Ind. Inst. Pers. 54.
Tadhkira-i Sayyid Āfāq Khwājam.
Lund Universitetsbiblioteket, Gunnar Jarring Collection, Ms. Prov. 22.
Tārīkh, Shāh Maḥmūd Churās.
Akimushkin 1976.
Tārīkh-i Rashīdī, Muḥammad Ḥaydar Dūghlāt.
British Library, Ms. Or. 157.
Elias & Ross 1972.

Abashin, S. N. 2003. "Burkhaniddin-Kylych: uchenyi, pravitel', chudotvorets? O genezise kul'ta svyatykh v Srednei Azii," in *Podvizhniki Islama. Kul't svyatykh i sufizm v Srednei Azii i na Kavkaze*, Moskva: Vostochnaya literatura RAN, 215-236.

Akimushkin, O. F. 1976. *Shāh Makhmūd ibn Mīrzā Fāzil Churās, Khronika, Kriticheskii tekst, perovod, kommentarii, issledovanie i ukazateli O. F. Akimushkina*, Moskva: Nauka.

Babajanov, B. 1999. "Biographies of Makhdūm-i A'zam al-Kāsānī al-Dahbīdī, Shaykh of the Sixteenth-century Naqshbandīya," in *Manuscripta Orientalia. International Journal for Oriental Manuscript Research* 5-2: 3-8.

Baldick, Julian 1993. *Imaginary Muslims: The Uwaysi Sufis of Central Asia*, London-New York: I. B. Tauris & Co Ltd.

Beeston, A. F. L. 1954. *Catalogue of the Persian, Turkish, Hindustani, and Pushtu Manuscripts in the Bodleian Library*, Pt. 3, Oxford.

DeWeese, Devin 1996. "The Tadhkira-i Bughrā-Khān and the 'Uvaysī' Sufis of Central Asia: Notes in Review of *Imaginary Muslims*,"in *Central Asiatic Journal* 40-1: 87-127.

DeWeese, Devin 2006. "'Struck in the Throat of Chingīz Khan': Envisioning the Mongol Conquests in Some Sufi Accounts from the 14th to 17th Centuries," in Judith Pfeiffer, Sholeh A. Quinn et al. (eds) *History and Historiography of Post-Mongol Central Asia and the Middle East. Studies in Honor of John E. Woods*, Wiesbaden: Harrassowitz Verlag, 23-60.

Elias, N. & Ross, E. Denison 1972. *A History of the Moghuls of Central Asia. Being the Tarikh-i-Rashidi of Mirza Muhammad Haidar, Dughlat.* London: Curzon Press, New York: Barnes and Noble, 1972 (first published 1895, second edition 1898).

Fletcher, Joseph 1985. "Les «voies» (turuq) soufies en Chine," in A. Popovic & G. Veinstein (eds.), *Les ordres mystiques dans l'Islam*, Paris, 13-26.
Hamada Masami 1978. "Islamic Saints and Their Mausoleums,"*Acta Asiatica* 34: 79-98.
Hamada Masami 濱田正美 1991. "Satoku Bogura Han no bobyō o megutte," サトク・ボグラ・ハンの墓廟をめぐって [Satuḳ Boghra Khan's Mausoleum in History], *Seinan Ajia kenkyū* 西南アジア研究[Bulletin of the Society for Western and Southern Asiatic Studies] 34: 89-112.
Hamada Masami 2001. "Le Mausolée et le culte des Satûq Bughrâ Khân," in *Journal of the History of Sufism* 3: 63-87.
Hamada Masami 濱田正美(ed.) 2006. *Hagiographies du Turkestan Oriental: Textes čaġatay édités, traduits en japonais et annotés avec une introduction analytique et historique* 東トルキスタン・チャガタイ語聖者伝の研究, Kyoto: Graduate School of Letters, Kyoto University.
Kim Ho-Dong 1996. "Muslim Saints in the 14th to the 16th Centuries of Eastern Turkestan," in *International Journal of Central Asian Studies* 1: 285-322.
Mano Eiji 間野英二 1995. *Zahīr al-Din Muhammad Bābur, Bābur-Nāma (Vaqāyi'). Critical Edition Based on Four Chaghatay Texts with Introduction and Notes,* by Eiji Mano バーブル・ナーマの研究 I 校訂本, Kyoto: Shokado.
Meredith-Owens, G. M. 1968. *Handlist of Persian Manuscripts 1895-1966*, [London]: The Trustees of the British Museum.
Nurmanova, Aytjan 2006. *Qazaqstan Tarikhï Turalï Türkí Derektemelerï IV tom. Mŭkhammed-Sadïq Qashghari, Tazkira-yi 'Azizan*, Almatï: Dayk-Press.
Papas, Alexandre 2007. "Shaykh Succession in the Classical Naqshbandiyya: Spirituality, Heredity and the Question of Body,"in *Asian and African Area Studies* アジア・アフリカ地域研究, 7-1 : 36-49.
Sawada Minoru 澤田稔 1987. "Hoja Isuhaku no shūkyō katsudō: toku ni Kāshugaru Hānke to no kankei ni tsuite" ホージャ・イスハークの宗教活動—特にカーシュガル・ハーン家との関係について [The Religious Activities of Khwaja Ishāq: With Special Reference to Relations with the Kāshghar Khānids], *Seinan Ajia kenkyū* 西南アジア研究 [Bulletin of the Society for Western and Southern Asiatic Studies] 27: 57-74.
Schwarz, Henry G. 1976. "The Khwājas of Eastern Turkestan,"in *Central Asiatic Journal* 20-4: 266-296.
Shimada Jōhei 嶋田襄平 1952. "Aruti-shahuru no wataku to kan to" アルティ・シャフルの和卓と汗と [The Khwājas and Khāns of Alty Shahr], *The Tōyō Gakuhō* 東洋学報 34-1/4: 103-131.
Togan, Isenbike 1991. "Chinese Turkestan. v. Under the Khojas," in Ehsan Yarshater (ed.), *Encyclopaedia Iranica*, vol. V, fascicle 5, Costa Mesa, California: Mazda Publishers, 474-476.

The external appearance of the mausoleum of Makhdūm-i A'ẓam in Samarkand (photographed by Sawada Minoru, September 2002).

The tomb of Makhdūm-i A'ẓam (photographed by Sawada M., September 2002).

The Mazar of Imām Mūsā Kāẓim of Khotan
—A Quest for Legends and other Cultural Elements

Omerjan NURI

Foreword

In Khotan's Buzaq Township, there stands a mazar that is believed to be that of Imām Mūsā Kāẓim, the seventh of the Twelve Imāms (*Ithnā 'ashariyyah*). This mazar is a very popular sacred site among the Muslims in Southern Xinjiang and has been mentioned in many travelogues throughout history. In this paper, I will examine the social and cultural roles of this mazar in local society by bringing together information from many sources, especially from a newly-discovered manuscript containing a *tadhkira* of the mazar current anthropological fieldwork.

1. A Manuscript

Mr. Memitimin Turdi of the Khotan Prefectural Bureau for the Collection and Publication of Ancient Texts Works of Minority Nationalities (*Khotän wilayetlik az sanliq millätlärning qädimki äsärlärni yighish, rätläsh, näshir qilishni pilanlashqa rähbärlik qilish guruppisi*) has in his possession a manuscript on 10×25 cm Khotan paper, 290 folios in length, and missing both the beginning and end [Fig. 1]. Each page of the text contains 13 lines in *ta'līq* script; many pages have become stuck together. On page 139 the title of the text is given as *Tadhkira-i tört imām dhabīḥullāh adkhal shahīdān dasht-i karbalā raḍiyallāhi anhu,* and in the left margin it is noted that the manuscript had been purchased by Bari Akhun b. Tokhta Akhun of Ayagh Budushiq Känt (i.e. Manglay Township of present day Qaraqash County) from A'ẓam Khalīfa in the year of 1345, the year of monkey, on the 10th day of *Muḥarram* (=July 21, 1926) for six *tin* and thirty *ful*. The manuscript contains the legendary *tadhkiras* of numerous *Imāms*, starting with Prophet Muḥammad, as and including works on 'Alī and Fāṭima, Imām Muḥammad Bāqir, Imām Ja'far Ṣādiq, Imām Aftah, the four Imāms Zebihullāhs, Imām Āzam Kufe Rejullāh, Imām Mūsā Kāẓim, Imām Qāsim, Imām Muḥammad, Imām Zeyn ul-'ābidīn, and Khaje Mujib Kohmar among others. The form of composition and the manuscript's descriptive style are similar to those of traditional mazar *tadhkiras* and are, as such, not free of superstitious exaggeration.

In the *tadhkiras* of the *Imāms* and holy men whose tombs are believed to be located in Khotan, legends of how they came from Mecca to Khotan to spread Islām and were later martyred in battle are commonplace. There are also stories that tell of how said figures came to be buried in Khotan.

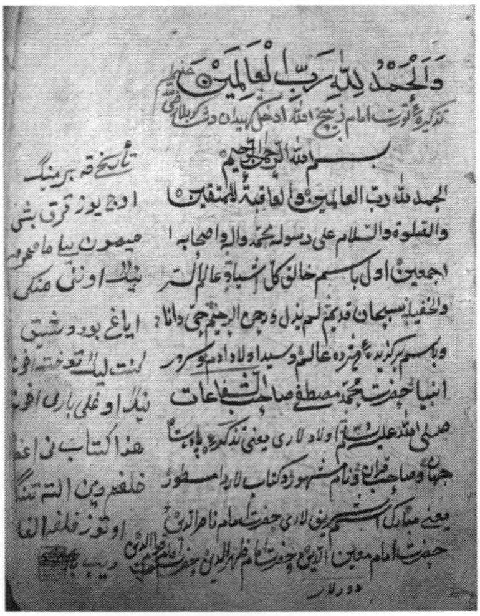

Fig. 1. *Tadhkira-i tort imām*, fol.72a.

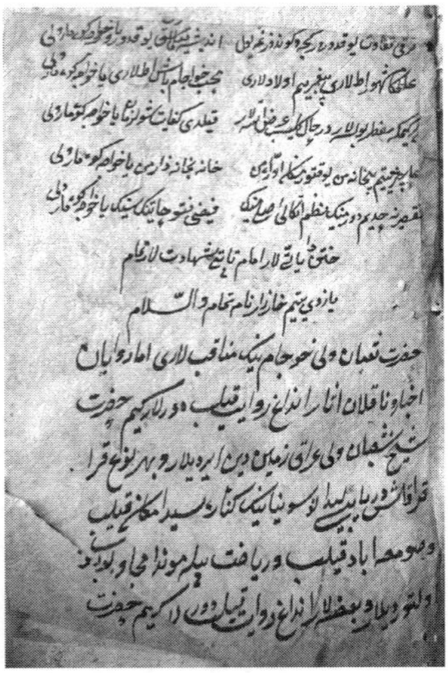

Fig. 2. *Tadhkira-i tort imām*, fol.146b.

2. The Author

We can see from this poetic conclusion in the middle of the 287th page that the original author of the tadhkira was Yitimī [Figure 3]:

> Khotanda yettilar Imām tapti shahādātlär tamām,
> yazdi Yitimī khār-zār nāme tamām wassalām

The name of the poet who used the *nome de plume* "Yitimī" was Qādirkhān (1900–16 August, 1964); a native of the Seziy Village (*Känt*) of Qarāqāsh. After his father Turdī Khalīfa Ḥājjī taught him to read, he continued his studies in Qarāqāsh and Qarghalīq. Although he is known to have composed the *Dīwān-i Yitimī*, *Chashma-yi Yitimī* and *Sapar Astaliq*,[1] there had been no previous indication that he had composed the *tadhkira* discussed here.

A comparison of the calligraphic style in Yitimī's *Diwān* and that of this *tadhkira* reveals two distinct hands; also, the note in the *tadhkira* stating that Tokhta Akhūn's son, Barī Akhūn, bought this book from Aʿẓam Khalīfa infers that Aʿẓam Khalīfa may have copied the *tadhkira* and sold it to Barī Akhūn.

---

[1] Mätqasim Äkräm, Muhämmät'imin Turdi n.d. show that Qadirkhan Yitimi's short biography (p.141) and other verses were dedicated to his master Ishan Khoja (p.142-151). Muhämmät'imin Qurban and Eziz Atawullah Sartekin 2005 introduce both his and his son, Ablät Qadir's, verses (p.293-302). However, Yitimi's biography in both publications are somewhat contradictory.

Fig. 3. The Mazar of Imām Mūsā Kāẓim in Khotan.

3. Contents of the *Tadhkira* Manuscript

Imām Mūsā Kāẓim's *tadhkira* is found on pages 72–75 of the manuscript. Although the content of this *tadhkira* is similar to that found in other manuscripts, it possesses handful of unique characteristics in terms of language, place of composition, and style.

There are several places where the manuscript makes unrealistic claims. For example, the claim that "Rūmning pādishahi Imām Mūsā Kāẓimning bābālari" ('The King of Rome is among Mūsā Kāẓim's ancestors') is obviously false; in reality, during the Abbasid Caliphate,Rome (Byzantium) was controlled by the Greeks. Imām Mūsā Kāẓim did not lead soldiers to Chin Machin (Khotan) to spread Islam nor was he martyred in Khotan. The people of Khotan in fact converted to Islam 200 years after the death of Imām Mūsā Kāẓim.

If this is the case, how are we to understand this *tadhkira* and mazar of Imām Mūsā Kāẓim? For this, we must first acquaint ourselves with Imām Mūsā Kāẓim's life, his mazar in Khotan, and the current state of his grave.

Fig. 4. The Grave of Imām Mūsā Kāẓim's Mother.

4. Imām Mūsā Kāẓim's Life

The seventh of the Shiites' "Twelve Imāms", Imām Mūsā Kāẓim was the second son of Ja'far Ṣādiq, the sixth Imām, and was born in Medina's Ebne Market. While he was still a child he learned *sharī'a* and *ḥadīth* from his father and studied at the famous madrasas of Medina, acquiring a thorough knowledge of both ethics and law. Since Imām Ja'far's oldest son, Ismā'īl, was given to alcohol, Imām Ja'far nullified his right to succeed him as Imām and instead announced that his second son, Mūsā Kāẓim, would succeed him as Imām. Dissatisfied by this, Imām Ismā'īl's followers broke off and established the Ismā'īlī sect after the death of Ismā'īl and Imām Ja'far. Members of this sect have historically been referred to as the Ismā'īlī or Sab'iyyah (Sevener) sect.[2] The Ismā'īlī sect later spread among Persian-speaking peoples.

After Mūsā Kāẓim inherited the position of Imām, the Abbasid Caliph Hārūn al-Rashīd became worried by the fact that Mūsā Kāẓim was a member of the Prophet's tribe and in addition to being a respected legal scholar, his political power was growing rapidly. The son of Mūsā Kāẓim's elder brother Ismā'īl, his nephew Muḥammad, took advantage of the situation and told Hārūn al-Rashīd that Imām Mūsā Kāẓim planned to seize control of the Caliphate. As a result, in 795 C.E., while Imām Mūsā Kāẓim was performing the Ḥajj, Hārūn al-Rashīd had him taken into custody and thrown into the prison at Baṣra; the next year, he was transferred to a prison in Baghdād. Imām Mūsā Kāẓim died in prison in 799 C.E. (some legends say he was poisoned).[3] Imām Mūsā

[2] *Zhungguo Yisilan Baike Quanshu*: 401-402 ; 698.

[3] İlhan 2005: 11-13.

Kāẓim's supporters among Shiites later formed the "12 Imām Sect." The members of this sect acted in opposition to the Abbasid Caliphate, thus incurring its wrath. The sect thus developed to the east of the Caliphate. In Iran, in the year 1501 C.E., the Safawids, a clan that claimed descent from Imām Mūsā Kāẓim, formed a state. After this, the influence of the sect became even greater.

Fig.5. The Main Gate of the Friday Mosque.

5. Maqami Mazar

This *tadhkira*'s claim that "the honorable Imām's tomb is in Khotan" is also found in other hand-written *tadhkiras* on Imām Mūsā Kāẓim. Sawada Minoru even mentions the existence of a hand-written manuscript about Imām Mūsā Kāẓim, acquired by Dutruil de Rhins and Grenard around 100 years ago, which claims that "Imām Mūsā Kāẓim was martyred in Khotan, and his corpse buried in Mecca."[4]

In fact, Imām Mūsā Kāẓim was not, as the manuscript claims, buried in Mecca, but instead was buried in the Kāzimayn near Baghdād. Given this piece of information, how should we deal with his mazar in Khotan?

The mazar of Imām Mūsā Kāẓim in Khotan is located in Buzaq Township's Aznä

[4] *Ibid.*

Bazar in present-day Khotan County. In addition to the tombs of Imām Mūsā Kāẓim and his mother, the mazar contains old tombs said to belong to the soldiers that Imām Mūsā Kāẓim brought with him, as well as innumerable graves of local people [Fig. 4, 5, 6]. The grounds of the mazar also include a large mosque, a prayer-house, a *sümä* (more on this later), among other sites. With the passage of time and other social factors, the current state of the mazar is significantly different from how it was described by European visitors.

The locals call the mazar "Imamuskazim" or "Muskazim" and visit it every Thursday morning to pray at the graves of their parents or relatives as well as at the graves of Imām Mūsā Kāẓim and his mother. Since local residents are convinced of the authenticity of the mazars of Imām Mūsā Kāẓim and his mother, they sometimes come from great distances to pray. Women usually pray at the tomb of Imām Mūsā Kāẓim's mother; and, although they do not enter the *sümä*, they stand equal with the men at Imām Mūsā Kāẓim's grave—some even stay to pray for days. Further, even if pilgrims are unaware of the sect or denomination to which they belong, indications of Sufi tendencies can be observed in their words and actions. It is fair to say that none of the pilgrims who worship at the site possesses formal religious education.

Each Friday, those who live near the mosque or even further a field gather in the prayer-house for Friday prayers. The *kaltä bazar* ('short market') is held in front of the prayer-house for two to three hours following prayers. For this reason, this place has been named "Aznä Bazar" (*aznä* is a corruption of the Persian word, *ādīna*, meaning 'Friday'). The mazar has been described in the works of mazar researchers, Ma Pinyan,[5] Rahile Dawut,[6] Sugawara Jun,[7] and Sawada Minoru as a "fake mazar" (假麻扎). Although this opinion is generally accepted, given that the term is rather inappropriate, it has not been accepted by those who worship at the mazar. Furthermore, because Shiites believe that a person's soul moves elsewhere after death, this particular belief has received special emphasis among the *tanāsukhīya sulūkī* and they thus accept that souls move on after death.[8] Therefore, Shiites may accept that a person's corpse is not physically present at a given mazar while continuing to emphasize that the person's soul has taken up residence there. Therefore, such mazars are referred to as *maqami* mazar or mazars where the titular saint's soul has come to rest. The word *maqam* (مقام) has the meaning of 'place', 'homeland', 'destination', 'rank', or 'level' in Arabic. Shiites refer to taking up residence in a new place as *mäqam ätmäk* ('to make a place' in modern Uyghur) or *muqam äylimäk* ('to do a place' in Chaghatay).[9] Therefore, according to this belief, the mazars of seven of the twelve Shiite Imāms, as well as some of the relatives of Imām Ghazzālī (in Keriyä), Shams al-Dīn Tabrīzī (in Khotan City), and other famous mystics, are located in Khotan Prefecture. Sunnis do not recognize this Shiite belief and Molla Musa Sayrami, after critically considering the mazars that the Uyghurs had been

---

5 Ma 1983.
6 Reyila Dawuti 2001: 155.
7 Sugawara 2001.
8 Zämir Säidullahzadä, Pärhat Ghappar 2002: 214-216.
9 *Chaghatay tilining izahliq lughiti*: 606.

venerating, when discussing the mazars of Khotan felt compelled, to note that "The Imāms of Khotan must be of those moving or disappearing high-level *talips* (religious scholars). Only the one God can know the truth or falsehood of this."[10] Even now, Sunnis cannot openly deny the legitimacy of this mazar.

Fig. 6. Sümä.

6. Sümä

In the body of research on mazars, one term that has remained unanalyzed is *sümä,* especially as used at the mazar of Imām Mūsā Kāẓim [Fig. 6]. Besides this, local people also refer to the tomb on top of the Kohmarim Mountain as *döng sümä* (hill *sümä*) and to the area around the grave of the unidentified martyr on the road from Langru Village's market to Pupuna Neighborhood as Süme Tüwi or Süme Chéqil. Ordinary people's graves and even the graves of those venerated non-martyrs are usually not referred to as *sümä*. This word, which has yet to be addressed in research on mazars, is considered by some to have been derived from Mongolian. Among the Yellow Uyghurs (a Buddhist Uyghur group in Gansu Province) the term is pronounced *seme* and means 'temple.'[11] However, on a stele commemorating the construction of a mosque for Uyghurs by decree of Emperor Qianlong, who was of the same faith as the Yellow Uyghurs, the word *sümä* is used in the Uyghur-language text to refer to Manchu temples, while the word *meschit* ('mosque') is used for the Uyghurs' place of worship.[12]

---

[10] Molla Musa Sayrami 1986: 644-645.

[11] Lei 1992: 320 and 324, even mosque is called "sart seme".

[12] In *Chijian libaisi beiji,* it appears inscriptions like "ansestors' *sümä* (*babalarimning sümäsi*)" for

Hence, because mazar worship is a tradition of Shiite origin, it is not likely that this word was derived from Mongolian. Since it is clear that most terms related to mazars are derived from Persian we may assume that this word also was adopted from Persian, probably from the Persian word *sum'e* (صومعه), meaning 'temple' or 'sheykh's quarters.'[13] In light of this, we can deduce that the Persian word *sum'e* is pronounced in Uyghur as *sümä*, and its usage has shifted from the original meaning to refer to the tomb of a martyr.

7. The Recording of *Mazar* Names

References to the mazar in historical documents are introduced in detail in an article by Professor Sawada Minoru, who reveals that although the name of the mazar is written many different ways in different records, in terms of the geographic location in question, they all refer to the mazar of Imām Mūsā Kāẓim. Mr. Sawada mentions that those who saw the mazar around 100 years ago recorded the mazar's name as follows: Dutruil de Rhins and Grenard, "Imām Musa Kasim"; Stein,"Imām Musa Qasim", and Mannerheim, "Nuzay Kazém."[14]

The "Kasim", "Qasim", and "Kazém" of these records are merely differences in transcription; that is, they are all simply variants of the word "Kāẓim." However, the inclusion of the term *nuzay* is worth further consideration. There is currently a famous neighborhood called "Nusüy neighborhood" about 6–7 kilometers to the southeast of Imām Mūsā Kāẓim's mazar, just below Kohmarim Mountain. The *nuzay* mentioned in Mannerheim's record may be related to this Nusüy because Mannerheim traveled from south to north, thus passing through Nusüy on the way to the mazar of Imām Mūsā Kāẓim, he may have recorded the mazar's name as "Nusüy Kāẓim." Another possibility is that Mūsā Kāẓim is written in most hand-written materials as Mosi Kāẓim. Perhaps, Mannerheim misheard "Mosi" as "Nosi." Moreover, how the term *nuzay* would be pronounced by a person from Finland is unclear to us.

Conclusion

Even if the stories of the Imāms and holy men mentioned in Yitimī's work do not conform to reality, the materials contained in these *tadhkira* must be examined since they are one of the sources for research on mazar culture. Therefore, I consider it appropriate to refer to the mazars of Imāms, holy men, and other mystics, as *maqami* mazar, and to understand the word *sümä*, as used to refer to the mazar graves of Imāms and holy men, as a term meaning 'the grave of a martyred person.'

Zuzoingsi(祖宗寺) in *l*.21; *sümä* which make all in peace (*barcheni tinch qiladurghan sümä*) for Puningsi(普宁寺) and "Ghulja *sümä*" for Guerzasi(固尔扎寺) in *l*.31.

[13] *Bosiyu-Hanyu cidian*: 1538.

[14] Saguchi 1995: 114-119; Sawada 2000: 160-182.

Bibliography

Bosiyu-Hanyu cidian 波斯语-汉语词典 [Persian-Chinese Dictionary], Beijing: Shangwu Yinshuguan, 1981.

Chaghatay tilining izahliq lughiti [Annotated Dictionary of Chaghatay Language], Urumqi: Shinjang Khälq Näshriyati, 2002.

Chijian libaisi beiji 敕建礼拜寺碑记 [Inscription of mosque established by imperial edict] Collection of the Cultural heritage bureau of Xicheng ward, Beijing city.

İlhan, Avni 2005. "İmam Mūsā Kāẓim, İmam Ali Riza, İmam Muhammed Taki" in *Türkiye Diyanet Vakfi Yayınları.*

Lei Xuanchun 雷选春 1992. *Xibu Yuguyu-Hanyu cidian* 西部裕固语-汉语词典 [Western Yugur-Chinese dictionary], Chengdu: Sichuan Minzu Chubanshe.

Ma Pinyan 马品彦 1983. "Nanjiang de maza he maza chaobai "南疆的麻扎和麻扎朝拜 [Mazar and Mazar Worships in Southern Xinjiang], in *Xinjiang shehui kexue*, 1983-3.

Mätqasim Äkräm, Muhämmät'imin Turdi(eds) n.d. *Bayaz.* Khotan: Khotän Wilayäylik Az Sanliq Millätlär Qädimki Äsärlärni Yighish, Rätläsh, Näshir Qilishni Pilanlash Rähbärlik Guruppa Ishkhanisi.

Molla Musa Sayrami 1986. *Tarikhi hämidi.* näshrigä täyyarlighuchi Änwär Baytur, Beijing: Millätlär Näshriyati.

Muhämmät'imin Qurban, Eziz Atawullah Sartekin (eds) 2005. *Qaraqash mädiniyät täzkirisi* [Cultural Accounts on Qaraqash], Urumqi: Shinjang Khälq Näshriyati.

Nizamidin Tokhti 2002. *Khotändiki Qädimki Izlar.* [Ancient Tracks in Khotän], Urumqi: Shinjang Khälq Näshriyati.

Reyila Dawuti (Rahile Dawut)热依拉・达吾提 2001.*Weiwuerzu Maza Wenhua Yanjiu.* 维吾尔族麻扎文化研究 [Study on Uyghur Mazar Cultures], Urumqi: Xinjiang Daxue Chubanshe.

Saguchi Tōru 佐口透 1995. *Shinkyō musurimu kenkyū.* 新疆ムスリム研究 [Studies on muslims in Xinjiang], Tokyo: Yoshikawa Kōbunkan.

Sawada Minoru 澤田稔 2000. "Takuramakan sabaku nanpen no seibo" タクラマカン砂漠南辺の聖墓 [Mausoleums in the southern periphery of the Taklamakan desert] in *Annual Report, Department of Human and Cultural Studies. Tezukayama-Gakuin University, Osaka* 2: 160-182.

Sugawara Jun 菅原純 2001. "Junkyōsha no kuni hotan" 殉教者の国ホタン [Land of martyr, Khotan] in *Tsushin* (ILCAA, Tokyo University of Foreign Studies) 101: 10-17.

Zämir Säidullahzadä, Pärhat Ghappar 2002. *Ottura Asiyadiki Islam mez'hepliri* [Islamic Sects in Central Asia], Urumqi: Shinjang Khälq Näshriyati.

Zhungguo Yisilan Baike Quanshu 中国伊斯兰百科全书 [Chinese Encyclopaedia of Islam], Chengdu: Sichuan cishu chubanshe, 1994.

APPENDIX(A): *Tadhkira of Imām Mūsā Kāẓim* (Transliteration)

تذکره امام موسی کاظیم

حضرت امام موسی کاظیم نیک بیانیدا بیشهٔ سوزنیک برابری دفتر فطرت نیک سخن ورلاری جواهرلاری فروش بازار معانی ئانداغ روایت قیلیب دورلار کیم، قعسهٔ پر غعسهٔی امام دین صاهب خروج کشور جین ملت ابن امیرالموئمنین امام موسی کاظیم // جراغ مجلیس امان و کاظیم // شهید کشور طوران و کاظیم // جراغ بزم // صادیق روشین اندین کلستان ختن ههم کلشن // اندین سرامد سرور اهل هدایت سخن پرداز // اقلمی فصاهت مسند خلافت کا قایم امیرالموئمنین // موسی کاظیم اول زمانیکه مسند خلافت کا اولتوردلهر. ولایت رومی نیک پادهشاهی امام موسی کاظیم نیک بابالاری بولور ایردی. امام غا هر کون مینک دینار خرج قیلغالی برور ایدی.اما،خدا و رسول نیک امرینی خلقغه خبر برور ایردی.نچه وقتین کین امام ایدیلار کیم:-ای سهابهلار، منکا ایمدی لازیم بولوب دورکه،مکه ملک، عجم مقبرئ ملک// اعظم کریم الاکرم پدر مشفق// و حضرت امام جعفر صادیق // و افتاب سبهع صادیق // پادهشاه حدود مشریق نی ذیارت قیلغالی سهابهلار بله بارسام- دیب ایدلهر. بابالاری ایدی کیم:-چن ماچن همه دین دین بیگانهدورلار، سیزلارکا جفا قیلورلار،الهال بارماسلهر-دیب منع قیلدیلار. حضرت امام اونامای، اخر الامر الته مینک مسلمانلار بله خروج قیلب چقتی لار. نچند کون منزل مراهل لار طی قیلب ولایت چن ماچن غه کلدیلار. سهابهلار ایدیلار کیم:-یا امام نیک بو ولایت نیک حاکمی ملک مظفر ابن توقوز خان دور،اول بی دین کافردور.زات شریف اتالاری هم امام جعفر صادیق شبولارنیک قولیدا شهید بولدیلار،موندین کجه بله اوتماک کرک-. حضرت:-خوب،بولور-دیب سهابهلار بله شب کر قیلب یوردیلار.اما،ملک مظفر حضرت امامنی استیب ایردکیم،التە مینک لشکر بله ولایت ختن کا داخل بولوب دورلار-دیب یکرمه مینک ترک خونخوار کافرلار بله حضرت امامنیک جست جوی لاریدا اطلانیب ایدی.تون یارمی ایدیکیم،لشکر حضرت امام موسی کاظیم نیک ارقهلاریدین یتی. مسلمانلار ناچار صف باغلادی.ایکی لشکر بر-برلاریدین واقف بولدیلار،ملک مظفر اطینی داب بریب میدانغه کردی.ایدیکیم:-ای ابو ترابیلار،بو کون پهلوانیک بولسه منک میدانمغه کرسون-دیب. حضرت امام اونک قول سول قولغه قرالادیلار،هچ کشی کرمابدور. ایدیلار:-اي مسلمانلار،بوکون بو میدان کربالاغه اوخشایدور، هرکیم بوکون شهید بولغودیک بولسه،ببام حضرت امام حسین نیک توغ لاری نیک استیندا مشهور بولور-دیدیلار.انداغ بر مرد جنک پهلوانلاری یوق ایردیکیم، میدانغه یالغوز کریب ملک مظفر بله روبرو بولغودیک لا علاج بیکباره.مسلمانلار حضرت امام موسی کاظیم بله اوزلارینی لشکر کافرغه اوردیلار-‹یا امام› دیب اوروشور ایردیلار.اندین انداغ جنک بولدیکیم،- حدسیز، حسابسیز اوچ کوندین کین سر حساب باردیلار:مسلمانلاردین اللیک-اتمیش جه کشی قالیب دور،اولار یرالیغ، حضرت امام نیک هم بدنلاری ده اللیک یردا زخم کاری بولوبدور. اما،‹یا حسین!› دیب اوروشور ایردیلار.ناکاه قتل ترك ارقهلاریدین کىلیب قلچ سالدی. اطدین اوچوپ توشتی لار.

ايدىلار كه:

-الهى پرويدكارا،منكا جديمنيک اياغ لاريدا كوشه‌پناه برسه‌نک-ديب مناجات قيلديله‌ر.

نظم

الهى عرش قلم حرمتى، الهى حوا و ادم حرمتى.
سندين ايرور بار جمله ثبات، كوردى سنيكدين همه ادم نيک حيات.
ال نبى حضرت احمد دومن، قيل نظرى اكر بدومن.
جسم صنعيغيم نى نهان ايلاكيل، رو-توراريمنى عيان ايلاگىل.
يروح امامِلارغه قاوشتور منى، ال نبى روح يتكور منى.

ديب درياى قان ايچره مناجاتنى تمام قيلماي توروب غايبدين بر صاندوق پيدا بولدى. حضرت امام اول صاندوقغه كريب،دارالفنادين دارالبقاغه سفر قيلديله‌ر. ملک مظفر بويروديكيم:- حضرت امامنينک جسدلارىنى تافينكلار.كافرلار هرچند جست جو قيلدى-تاپالمادى،يانيب قلعئ چينغه باردى.والله عالم.بر روايتدا حضرت امامنيک مقبره‌لارى ختن دادور-ديديلار.ينه بر روايتدا،شولزمان فرشته‌لار خداى تعالى نيک امر فرمانى بله مكه معظم اتا-ببالارى نيک اياغ لاريغه التيب قويديلار.قالوانااللهوانااليهراجعون.

نظم

شهيد اولدى امام اهل امان، شهادت تاپتى الته مينک مسلمان.
بياباني ختن دين اوندى لاله، هلال اولدى باشيدا جبرهاله.
قزيل كل هر طرفدين هم اچيلدى، قوياشنى توتى عالم بوزولدى.

APPENDIX (B): ***Tadhkira of Imām Mūsā Kāẓim*** (Translation in Modern Uyghur)

تەزكىرەئى ئىمام مۇسا كازىم

ھەزرەت ئىمام مۇسا كازىمنىڭ بەيانىدا پىشەئى سۆزنىڭ بەرابەرى دەفتەر فەترەتنىڭ سۇخەنۋەرلەرى جەۋھەرلەرى فۇرۇش بازار مەئانى ئانداغ رىۋايەت قىلىبدۇركىم، قىسسەئى پىر غۇسسەئى ئىمام دىن ساھىب خۇرۇچ كىشۋەر چىن مىللەت ئىبىن ئەمىرائىلمۇئمىنىن ئىمام مۇسا كازىم // چىراغى مەجلىس ئىمان ۋە كازىم // شەھىد كىشۋەر تۇران ۋە كازىم // چىراغى بەزم // سادىق روشەن ئاندىن گۇلىستان خوتەن ھەم گۇلشەن // ئاندىن سەرامەد سەرۋەر ئەھلى ھىدايەت سۇخەن پەرداز // ئىقلىمى فەساھەت مەسنەدى خىلافەتكە قايىم ئەمىرائىلمۇئمىنىن // مۇسا كازىم ئول زەمانىكى مەسنەدى خىلافەتكە ئولتۇردىلەر. ۋىلايەت رۇمنىڭ پادىشاھى ئىمام مۇسا كازىمنىڭ بابالارى بۇلۇر ئېردى. ئىمامغا ھەر كۈنى مىڭ دىنار خەرج قىلغالى بىرۇر ئىدى.ئەمما،خۇدا ۋە رۇسۇلنىڭ ئەمرىنى خەلقغە خەبەر بىرۇر ئېردى.نىچە ۋاقىتتىن كېيىن ئىمام ئېيدىلاركىم:-ئەي ساھابەلەر،ماڭا ئەمدى لازىم بۇلۇبدۇرلەركى،مەككە مىلىك،ئەجەم مەقبەرئى مىلىك// ئەئزەم كەرىملئەكرەم پەدەر مۇشفىق// ۋە ھەزرەتى ئىمام جەئفەر سادىق// ۋە ئافتاب سۇبھى سادىق// پادىشاھ ھۇدۇدى مەشرىقنى زىيارەت قىلغالى ساھابەلەر بىلە بارسام-دىب ئېيدىلەر.بابالارى:-ئېيدىكىم چىن ماچىن ھەممە دىندىن بىگانەدۇرلەر،سىزلەرگە جەفا قىلۇرلار،ئەلھال بارماسەلەر-دىب مەنئى قىلدىلەر. ھەزرەتى ئىمام ئۇناماي، ئاخىر ئەلئەمىر ئالتە مىڭ مۇسۇلمانلار بىلە خۇرۇج قىلىب چىقتىلەر. نىچەند كۈن مەنزىل مەراھىللەر تەي قىلىب ۋىلايەتى چىن ماچىنغا كەلدىلەر. ساھابەلەر ئېيدىلەركىم: - يا ئىمام، بۇ ۋىلايەتنىڭ مىلىكى مۇزەففەر توققۇز خاندۇر، ئول بى دىن كافىردۇر. زاتى شەرىف ئاتالارى ھەم ھەزرەتى ئىمام جەئفەر سادىق شۇبۇلەرنىڭ قولىدا شەھىد بولدىلەر، مۇندىن كېچە بىلە ئۆتمەك كېرەك. ھەزرەت: - خوب، بۇلۇر- دىب ساھابەلەر بىلە شەبگەر قىلىب يۈردىلەر. ئاما، مىلىك مۇزەففەر ھەزرەتى ئىمامنى ئىستەب ئېرۇركىم، ئالتە مىڭ لەشكەر بىلە ۋىلايەت خوتەنگە داخىل بۇلۇبدۇرلەر- دىب يىگىرمە مىڭ تۈرك خۇنخۋار كافىرلەر بىلە ھەزرەتى ئىمامنىڭ جۇست جۇيىلارىدا ئاتلانىب ئېدى. تۈن يارىمى ئېدىكىم، لەشكەر ھەزرەتى ئىمام مۇسا كازىمنىڭ ئارقەلەرىدىن يەتتى. مۇسۇلمانلار ناچار سەف باغلادى. ئىككى لەشكەر بىر-بىرلىرىدىن ۋاقىف بولدىلەر، مىلىك مۇزەففەر ئاتىنى داب بىرىب مەيدانغا كىردى.ئېيدىكىم:-ئەي ئەبۇ تارابىيلار،بۇگۈن پەھلىۋانىڭ بولسا مېنىڭ مەيدانىمغا كىرسۇن- دىب. ھەزرەتى ئىمام ئوڭ-سول قولغە قارالادىلار، ھىچكىشى كىرمەبدۇر. ئېيدىلەر: -ئەي مۇسۇلمانلار، بۇگۈن بۇ مەيدان كەربالاغا ئوخشايدۇ، ھەركىم بۇگۈن شەھىد بولغۇدەك بولسە، بابام ھەزرەت ئىمام ھۇسەيىننىڭ تۇغلارىنىڭ ئاستىدا مەشھۇر بولۇر- دېدىلەر. ئانداغ بىر مەرد جەڭ پەھلىۋانلىرى يوق ئېردىكىم، مەيدانغا يالغۇز كىرىب مىلىك مۇزەففەر بىلە روبەرۇ بولغۇدەك لائىلاج بىكپارە.مۇسۇلمانلار ھەزرەتى ئىمام مۇسا كازىم بىلە ئۆزلەرىنى لەشكەرى كافىرغە ئۇردىلەر-‹يا ئىمام› دىب ئۇرۇشۇر ئېردىلەر.

ئاندىن ئانداغ جەڭ بولدىكىم، -ھەدسىز، ھىسابسىز. ئۈچ كۈندىن كېيىن سەرھىساب باردىلەر: مۇسۇلمانلاردىن ئەللىك-ئاتمىشچە كىشى قالىبدۇر، ئۇلار يارالىغ، ھەزرەت ئىمامنىڭ ھەم بەدەنلەرىدە ئەللىك يەردە زەخمەكارى بولۇبدۇر. ئاما، ‹يا ھۇسەيىن› دىب ئۇرۇشۇر ئېردىلەر. ناگاھ قەتل تۈرك ئارقەلەرىدىن كىلىب قىلىچ سالدى. ئاتدىن ئۈچۈپ تۈشتىلەر. ئېيدىلەركى: - ئىلاھا پەرۋەيدىگارا، مەڭا جەددىمنىڭ ئاياغلارىدا كۆشەپەناھ بەرسەڭ - دىب مۇناجات قىلدىلەر.

نەزم

ئىلاھا ئەرشى قەلەم ھۆرمەتى، ئىلاھا ھەۋا-ۋُ-ئادەم ھۆرمەتى.
سەندىن ئىرۇر بار جۈملەئى سۇبات، كۆردى سېنىڭدىن ھەمە ئادەمىڭ ھەيات.
ئەل نەبى ھەزرەت ئەھمەد دۇمەن، قىل نەزرى ئەگەر بەددۇمەن.
جىسىم سۈنئىغىمنى نىھات ئەيلەگىل، يەرۇ-تۇرارىمنى ئەيان ئەيلەگىل.
روھ ئىماملەرغە قاۋۇشتۇر مەنى، ئەل نەبى روھ يەتكۈر مەنى.

دىب دەريايى قان ئىچرە مۇناجاتنى تامام قىلماي تۇرۇب غايىبدىن بىر ساندۇق پەيدا بولدى. ھەزرەت ئىمام ئول ساندۇقغە كىرىب، دارىلفەنادىن دارىلبەقاغا سەفەر قىلدىلەر. مىلىك مۇزەففەر بۇيرۇدىكىم: -ھەزرەتى ئىمامنىڭ جەسەدلارىنى تافىڭلار. كافرلەر ھەرچەند جۇستىجۇ قىلدى-تافالمادى، يانىب قەلئەئى چىنغە باردى. ۋەللاھۇ ئەئلەم. بىر رىۋايەتدە، ھەزرەت ئىمامنىڭ مەقبەرەلەرى خوتەندەدۇر -دېدىلەر. يەنە بىر رىۋايەتدە، شۇلزەمان فەرىشتەلەر خۇدايى تەئالانىڭ ئەمىر فەرمانى بىلە مەككە مۇئەززەم ئاتا-بابالەرىنىڭ ئاياغلارىغە ئىلەتىب قويدىلار. قالۇئىننالىللاھى ۋە ئىننائىلەيھى راجىئۇن (بىز ئەلۋەتتە ئاللاھنىڭ ئىگىدارچىلىقىدىمىز، چوقۇم ئاللاھنىڭ دەرگاھىغا قايتىمىز. ‹سۈرە بەقەر،156.ئايەت›)

نەزم

شەھىد ئولدى ئىمام ئەھلى ئىمان، شەھادەت تاپتى ئالتە مىڭ مۇسۇلمان.
بەيابانى خوتەندىن ئۈندى لالە، ھىلال ئولدى باشىدا جەبىرھالە.
قىزىل گۈل ھەر تەرەفتىن ھەم ئاچىلدى، قۇياشنى تۇتتى ئالەم بۇزۇلدى.

APPENDIX (C): ***Tadhkira of Imām Mūsā Kāẓim*** (Facsimile)

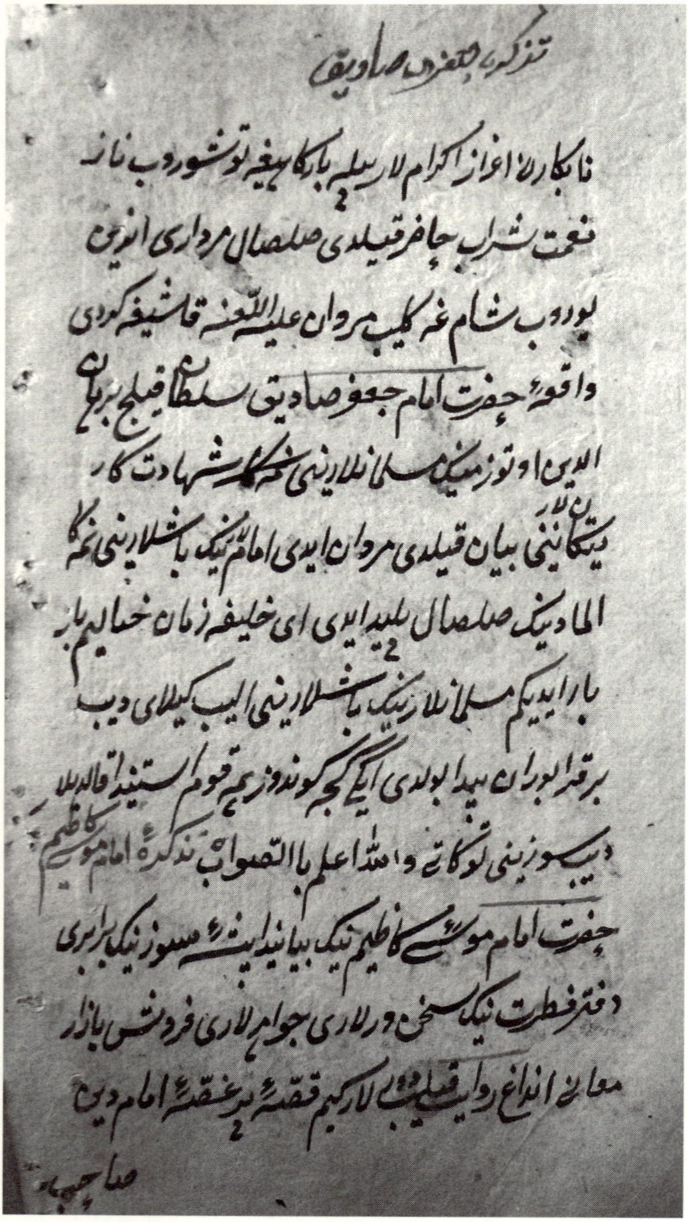

fol. 36b

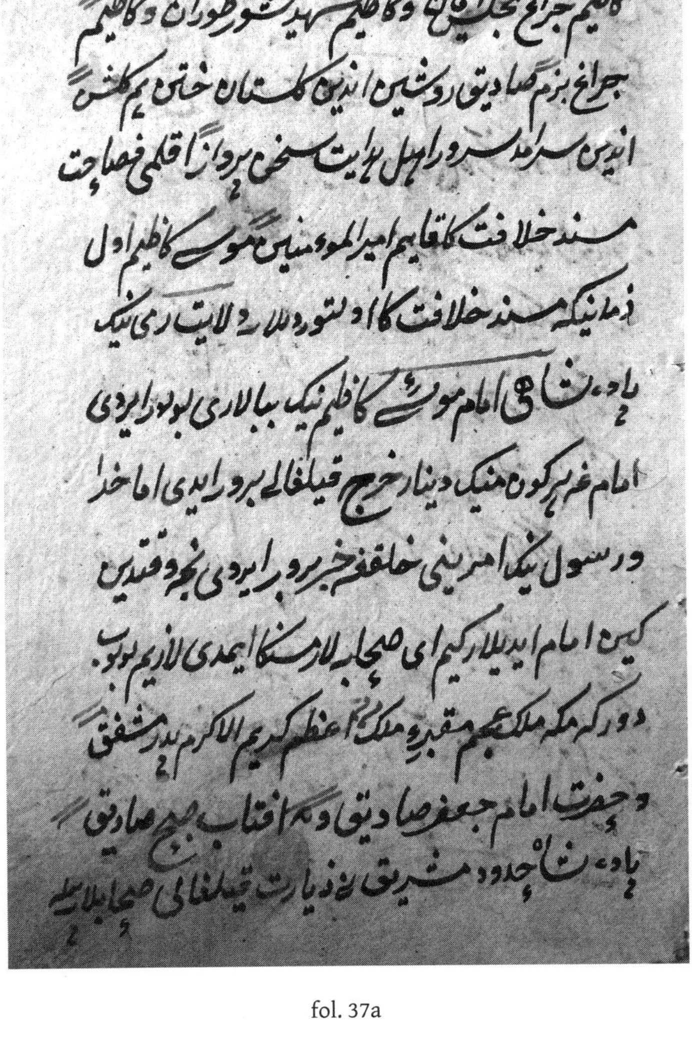
تذکره موسی کاظم

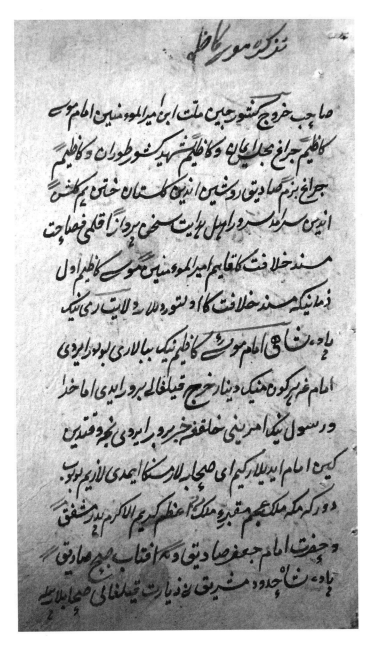

صاحب خروج کشور چین ملت ابن امیر المؤمنین امام موسی
کاظم چراغ مجلس ایمان و کاظم شهید کشور طوران و کاظم
چراغ بزم صادیق روشین اندین گلستان ختن هم گلشن
اندین سرآمد سرو راهل هدایت سخن پرداز اقلیمی فصاحت
مسند خلافت کا قایم امیر المؤمنین موسی کاظم اول
زمانیکه مسند خلافت کا اولتوردیلار ولایت ری نینک
پادشاهی امام موسی کاظم نینک بابالاری بولور ایردی
امام غره کون مینک دینار خرج قیلغالی بیرور ایردی اما خدا
و رسول نینک امرینی خلقغه خبر بیرور ایردی نیچه وقتدین
کین امام ایدیلار کیم ای صحابه لار مینگا ایمدی لازیم بولوب
دور کیم مکه ملک عجم مقبره ملکه اعظم کریم الاکرم بدر مشفق
و حضرت امام جعفر صادیق و هم افتاب صبح صادیق
پادشاه جدود مشریق نی زیارت قیلغالی صحابه لار

fol. 37a

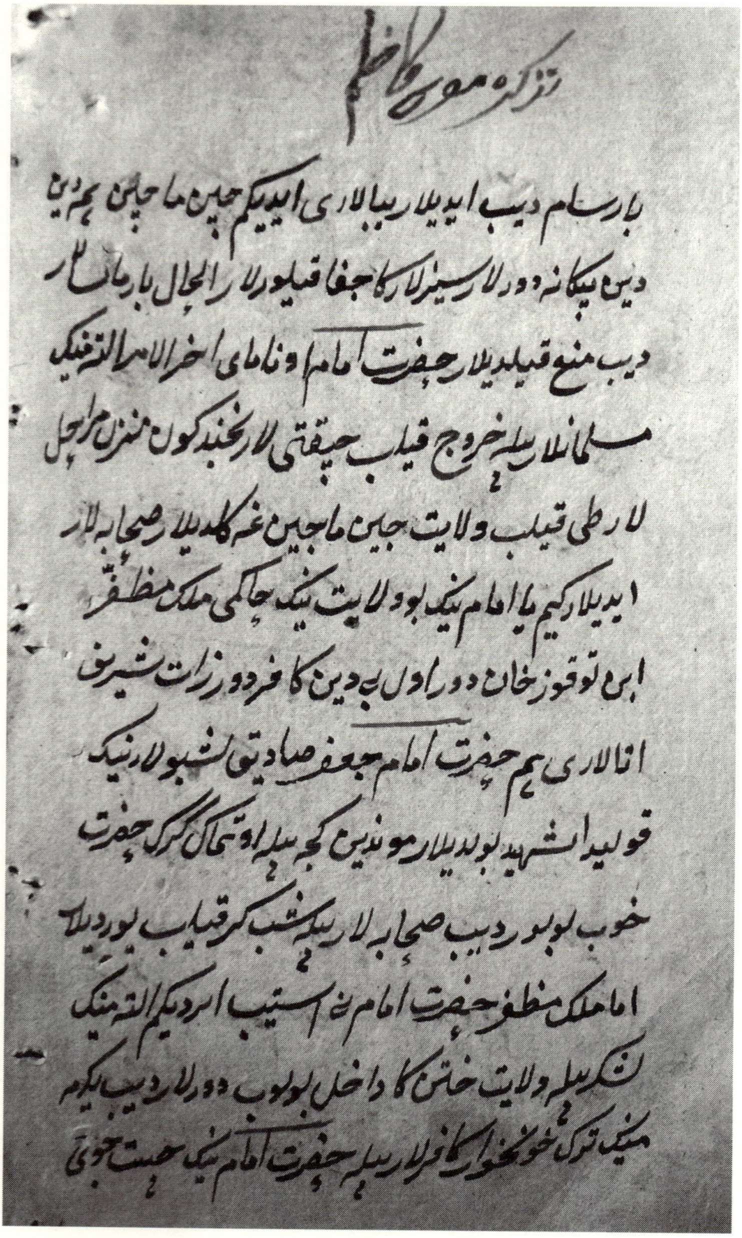
تذکرۂ موسی کاظم

بار اسلام دیب ایدیلار ریبالاری ایدیکیم چین ماچین هم دیب
دین بیگانه دورلار سیزلار کا جفا قیلیورلار الحال بار مانسالار
دیب منع قیلدیلار حضرت امام او نامای اخر الامر الله نینگ
مسلمانلار بیله خروج قیلیب حقیقتی لار خجند کون منزل مراحل
لار طی قیلیب ولایت چین ماچین غه کلدیلار صحابه لار
ایدیلار کیم یا امام بیگ بو ولایت نینگ حاکمی ملک مظفر
ابن توقوز خان دور اول بی دین کافر دور زات شریف
اتالاری هم حضرت امام جعفر صادق لشبولار نینگ
قولیدا شهید بولدیلار مونینگ بیله او تماکن گرک حضرت
خوب بو بور دیب صحابه لار بیله نشب کیر قیلیب یوردیلار
اما ملک مظفر حضرت امام نی استیب ایردیکیم الله نینگ
لشکر بیله ولایت ختن کا داخل بولوب دورلار دیب بلکیم
مینگ تورک خونخوار کافرلار بیله حضرت امام نینگ جست جوی

fol. 37b

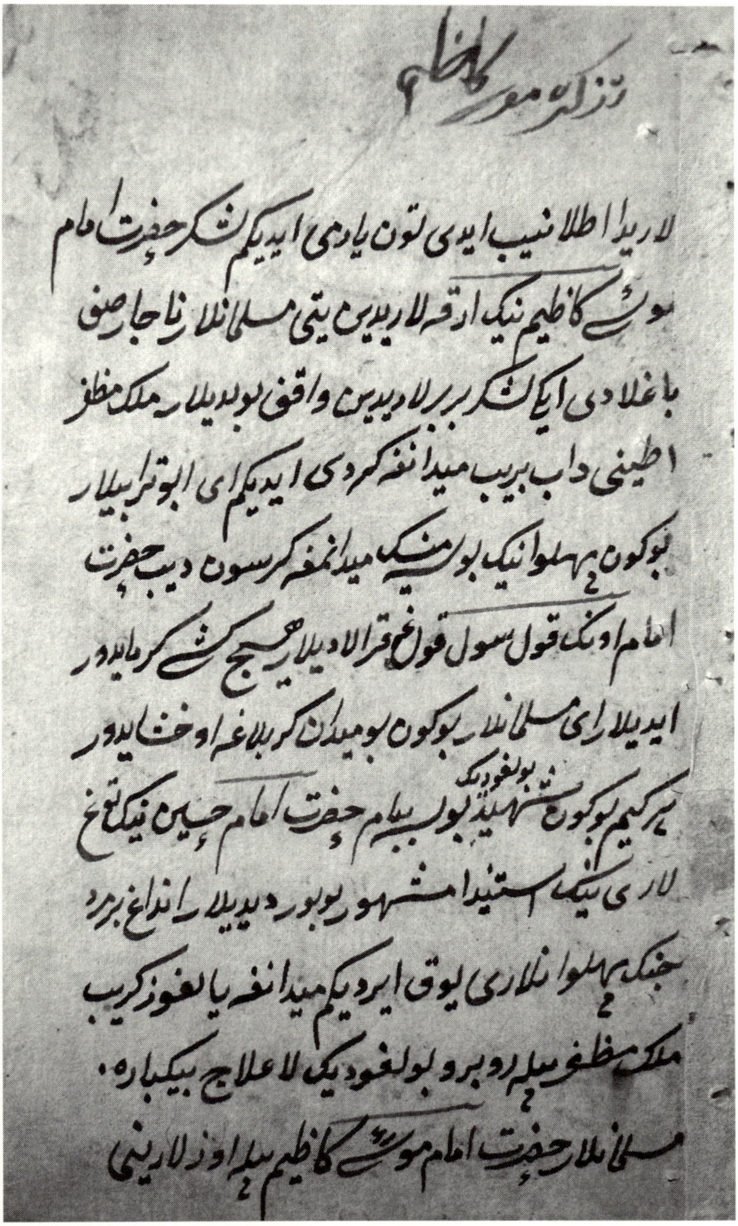
تذکره موسی کاظم

لاریدا اطلانیب ایدی توتون یادمی ایدیکیم لشکر حضرت امام
موسی کاظیم نینک ادقه لاریدین بیتی مسلمانلار تاجا صنف
باغلادی ایکی لشکر بربرلادیدین واقف بولدیلار ملک مظفر
اطینی داب بریب میدانغه کردی ایدیکیم ای ابوتراب بیلار
بوکون پهلوانینک بورمنینک میدانمغه کرسون دیب حضرت
امام اونک قول سول قولغ قرالادیلار هیچ کشی کرمایدور
ایدیلار ای مسلمانلار بوکون بو میداندا کربلاغه اوخشایدور
بولغودیک
هر کیم بوکون شهید بولسه بیله حضرت امام حسین نینک توغ
لاری نینک استیدا مشهور بولور دیدیلار اندااغ بربرد
جنک پهلوانلاری یوق ایردیکیم میدانغه یالغوز کریب
ملک مظفر بیله دبرد بولغودیک لاعلاج بیکباره،
مسلمانلار حضرت امام موسی کاظیم بیله اوذلارینی

fol. 38a

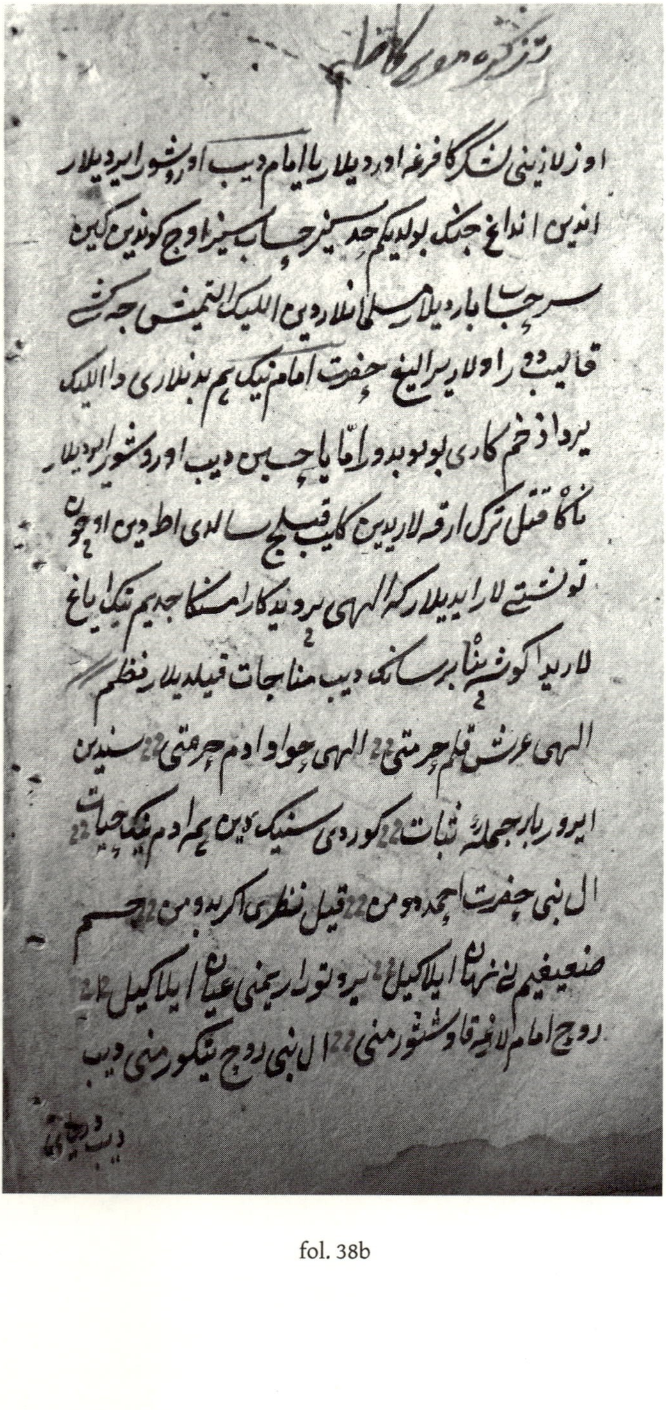
اوزلارینی لشکر کافرغه اوردیلار یا امام دیب اوروشور ایردیلار
اندین انداغ جنگ بولدیکم حد سیز حساب سیز اوچ کوندین کیین
سر حساب باردیلار مسلمانلار دین الیک التمیش جه کشی
غایب دیب راد لار یر الیغ حضرت امام نینک هم بدنلاری و الیک
یر داغ زخم کاری بو بو بدور اما یا حسین دیب اوروشور ایردیلار
نا کافر قتل ترک ارقه لاریدین کلیب قیلیچ سالدی اطدین اوچون
تونستی لار ایدیلار که الهی یردید کار اسنکا جدیم نینک یاغ
لاریدا کونینکا بر سانک دیب مناجات قیلدیلار نظم
الهی عرش قلم حرمتی الهی حوا و ادم حرمتی سیندین
ایرور بار بارجمله ثبات کوردی سنینک دین هم ادم نینک حیات
ال نبی حضرت احمد من قیلی نظری اکر بدو من حسم
ضعیفیم نی نهانی ایلا کیل یردو تولا رحمنی عیانی ایلا کیل
روح امام لا عیقاو شوری منی ال نبی روح نینک کورمنی دیب

fol. 38b

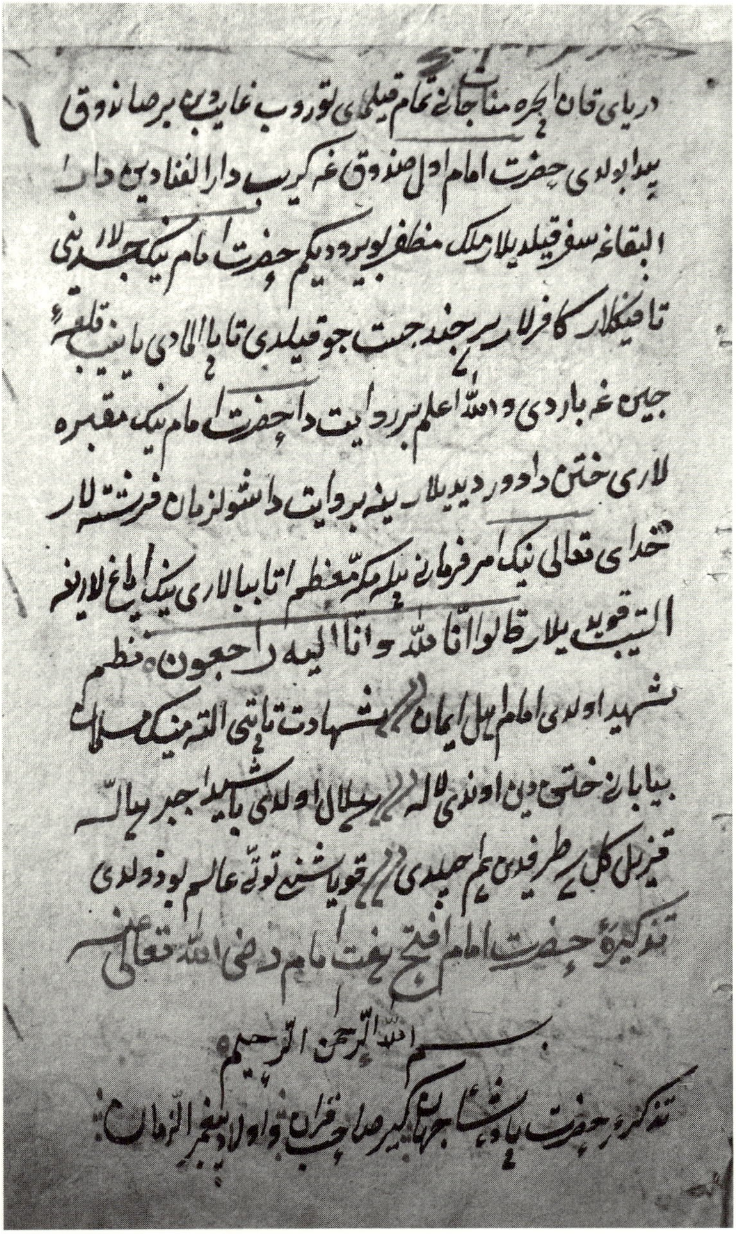
دریای تحان ایچره مناجاتنه تمام قیلمای توروب غایب بر صاندوق
پیدا بولدی حضرت امام اول صندوق غه کیریب دار الفنادین دار
البقاغه سفر قیلدیلار ملک مظفر بویرودیکیم حضرت امام نینک جسدلارینی
تاپیکلار کافرلار سر جند جست جو قیلدی تاپالمادی یانیب قلعه
چین غه باردی والله اعلم بر روایت دا حضرت امام نینک مقبره
لاری ختن دا دور دیدیلار بینه بر روایت دا شول زمان فرشته لار
خدای تعالی نینک امر فرمانی بیله مکه معظم اتا بابالاری نینک ایاغ لاری غه
الیتیب قویدیلار قالوا انا لله و انا الیه راجعون نظم
شهید اولدی امام اهل ایمان در شهادت تاپتی القه مینک مسلمان
بیابان ختن دین اوندی لاله در بیلال اولدی تا شهیدا جبر بیاله
قیزیل کل هر طرف دین بیم حیلدی در قیو یاشین توتی عالم بوزولدی
تذکره حضرت امام افتح بغت امام رضی الله تعالی عنه
بسم الله الرحمن الرحیم
تذکره حضرت پادشاه جهانگیر صاحب قران و اولاد پیغمبر الزمان

fol. 39a

Remarks on the Tazkira-yi Awliya in the Uyghur Script

SUGAHARA Mutsumi

Introduction

As is well known, there was a kind of "revival" of the Old Uyghur script in the Timurid period (fifteenth century). In cities such as Herat, Samarqand, and Yazd, several manuscripts of Turkic literary and religious texts were produced in this script. To our great regret, the reason and the background behind its use in this period remain unknown.

In this paper, we deal with one such manuscript titled *Tazkira-yi awliya*, which is contained in the manuscript Supplément turc 190 (Paris, Bibliothèque Nationale).[1] It is a Middle Turkic translation of *Tadhkirat al-awliyā'* (Memorial of the saints), written in Persian by the famous mystic Farīd al-dīn 'Aṭṭār (d.1221?). According to the colophon,[2] the manuscript was completed in Herat in 1436. In spite of the unique position it holds among the Central Asian Turkic prose literature, the text itself has been little investigated since A. Pavet de Courteille's publication of its French translation in 1889.[3] A fuller study of it naturally lies outside the scope of this paper, and we limit the discussion here to (1) the Uyghur orthography employed, (2) its relation to the original Persian text, and (3) several remarks on the language of the text.

1. The Orthography

The orthography employed in this manuscript contains notable differences from the

---

[1] The first 68 folios of this manuscript contain the text of *Mi'rāj-nāma*, written in almost the same language as the *Tazkira-yi awliya*. See Scherberger 2003 for details.

[2] *tarix säkiz yüz qïrqta at yïl jumadiya-l-axir (cwm'dyy'l-"qyr) ayniŋ onïta Haruta Haru* (?) *Malik baxšï bididim* 'on 10 Jumadiya-l-axir 840 (= 20th December, 1436), year of horse, in Herat, I, Haru (?) Malik baxšï wrote this' (TA 264v13-17). Subsequent quotations from this work are taken from the text edition published in 2007, with a slight modification in transcription. Note that the transcription is a tentative one and does NOT contain any claim on the actual phonology of the relevant language. Persian and Modern Turkic examples are rendered in basically phonemic notations.

[3] Among the recent contributions Sertkaya (2007, 2015) should be mentioned. Unfortunately I was not able to consult them before finishing this paper.

traditional Uyghur orthography of the pre-Islamic period. For example, word-initial *a* and *ä* are both spelled with a double aleph (''), while in the traditional orthography, the latter is spelled with a single aleph (').[4]

a = ''- : *''dlyġ* (*adlïġ*) 'named'; *''ryġ* (*arïġ*) 'pure'; *''y'q* (*ayaq*) 'foot'
ä = ''- : *''rm'z* (*ärmäz*) 'is not'; *''mk'k* (*ämgäk*) 'labor'; *''dkw* (*ädgü*) 'good'
cf. traditional spelling: *'rm'z* (*ärmäz*); *'mk'k* (*ämgäk*); *'dkw*(*ädgü*)

The use of *-wy-* (as opposed to *-w-*) for *ö/ü* in the first syllable of the word is not consistent. In other words, front vowels *ö/ü* and back vowels *o/u* (which are always spelled with *-w-*) are not always distinguished in spelling.

ö/ü = *-wy-* : *kwyk* (*kök*) 'sky'; *swyz* (*söz*) 'speech'; *kwyn* (*kün*) 'day'
ö/ü = *-w-* : *twp'* (*töpä*) 'hill'; *twrlwk* (*türlüg*) 'various'; *'wcwn* (*üčün*) 'for'
ö/ü = *-wy-* or *-w-* : *kwyrdy* / *kwrdy* (*kördi*) 'he saw'; *'wysk'* / *'wsk'* (*özgä*) 'other'; *'wyz-'*/ *'wz-'* (*üzä*) 'upon'

Defective writing of the first-syllable vowels *ä/a* in certain words, which is a feature of the traditional orthography, is not employed.

''rsl'n (*arslan*) 'lion'; *y'rlyx* / *y'rlyq* (*yarlïġ*) 'decree, revelation'; *t'nkry* (*täŋri*) 'God'
cf. traditional spelling: *'rsl'n* (*arslan*); *yrlyx* (*yarlïġ*); *tnkry* (*täŋri*).

The orthographic features given above are, in fact, commonly observed in most of the Uyghur manuscripts of the Timurid period.[5] From this viewpoint, we may say that these manuscripts were not primarily meant for those familiar with the traditional Uyghur writing convention. In other words, the use of the Uyghur script in this period was neither a simple revival nor a continuation of the former use of it.

It must be noted, however, that spellings of individual words may vary slightly among different manuscripts. Let us compare three manuscripts, namely: (a) a collection containing *Maḥabbat-nāma, Mas'ala kitābï* and other prose and verse texts, (b) the Herat manuscript of *Qutadhghu Bilig (Kutadgu Bilig)*, and (c) the Samarqand manuscript of *'Aṭabat al-Ḥaqā'iq.*[6]

As Table 1 indicates, both *Tazkira-yi awliya* and the Herat manuscript of *Qutadhghu Bilig* use the letter aleph (') for the first-syllable vowel in such words as *ber-*, *kečä,* and *yeti*, but in the other two manuscripts the corresponding vowel is written with yod (*y*) as in the traditional orthography.[7] The two groups of manuscripts differ also in their

[4] There is no reason to suppose that the front/back oppositions of the vowels had been neutralized in this variety of Middle Turkic.
[5] In some of the manuscripts, the use of *-wy-* for the first-syllable *ö/ü* is even rarer.
[6] Facsimiles used are contained respectively in: Gandjeï 1957 and Sertkaya 1975, 1976 (a); QBH (b); Arat 1951 (c).
[7] It seems unlikely, though possible, that the use of *aleph* instead of *yod* in these examples reflects a

spelling of several words of Arabic and Persian origin. It is possible to say that the forms found in manuscripts (a) and (c) are more faithful to the original *spelling* in the Arabic script,[8] while those in the *Tazkira-yi awliya* and manuscript (b) bear traces of the actual pronunciation of these words. cf. Uyg. (dial.) *dʒuva:b* 'answer, reply'(Jarring 1964:92) ; Krg. *duba*, *duwa*[9] 'molitvoslovie s pozhelaniyami blagopoluchiya' (Yudakhin 1965:200); Uzb. *qoġoz* 'paper'.

Table 1 Spelling in Different Manuscripts

	TA (Herat 1436)	(a) (Yazd 1431)	(b) (Herat 1439)	(c) (Samarqand 1444)
ber- 'to give'	*p'r*	*pyr*	*p'r*	*pyr, p'r*
kečä 'night'	*k'c-'*	--	*k'c'*	*kyc'*
yeti 'seven'	*y'ty,y'dy*	*yyty*	*y'ty, y't-ty*	--
anbiyā' 'prophets'	*''mpyy-',''npyy-'*	*''npyy-'*	*''mpyy-'*	--
jawāb 'answer'	*cww'p*	*c'w'p*	*cwv'p*	*c*[ ]
du'ā' 'prayer'	*twx-', tww-'*	*twq-'*	*twx-', tww-'*	*twx-'*
hēč 'any'	*''c*	*'yc*	*''c*	*'yc*
kāġaḏ 'paper'	*q'q't, k'q't*	*k'q'z*	*x'q't, q'x'z*	--

We can see from these examples that two distinct varieties of Uyghur orthography were in use in the fifteenth century Timurid cities. The Uyghur manuscript of *Tazkira-yi awliya*, together with the Herat manuscript of *Qutadhghu Bilig*, represents the "Herat type" orthography, which is characterized by the use of aleph instead of yod in some words, a reflection of the actual pronunciation rather than the original spelling of borrowed words, and possibly other features. How these different types of orthography came into being, however, is a question that needs further investigation.

2. Comparison with the Original Persian Text

Now let us compare the Turkic text of the *Tazkira-yi awliya* with the original Persian text. The Turkic text contains biographies of the 72 saints, as in the Persian original, beginning with Ja'far Ṣādiq and ending with Ḥallāj.[10] The relation between the translated text and its Persian original is, however, quite complicated: in some cases the translator reproduces the original text rather faithfully, while in others (s)he omits

sound change such as *e>ä*. I leave the matter open here.

[8] Note that the nasal consonant in the word *anbiyā'* is pronounced as *-m-* instead of *-n-* both in Arabic and Persian.

[9] Since the word-internal Arabic ' (*'ayn*) is normally written with the Uygur letter *x/q* in these manuscripts, spellings such as *twq-'* or *twx-'* should be considered as the regular reflections of the Arabic form *du'ā'*. Modern forms with *-ġ-* (e.g. Kazakh *duġa*), therefore, are irrelevant here.

[10] This name is given in the text as Mansur-i Halaj, not as Ḥusayn Manṣūr-i Ḥallāj or Ḥusayn bin Manṣūr.

several paragraphs altogether. Sometimes the translatoreven tries to reproduce the formal characteristics of the original at the expense of the meaning. This is observed when the original is written in rhymed prose.

ol 'alimlarnïŋ ***sultanï****, ol šari'atnïŋ* ***imamï****, ol tariqat išin* ***qïlġan****, ol haqiqat sirrin* ***bilgän****, ol xulqï barčatïn* ***yägräk****, ol 'Abdulla-yi* ***Mubarak*** *rahmatu-llayi 'alayi* (TA186v 1-3)
'the sultan of the learned, the imam of the Law, who fulfilled the duties of the Path, who knew the secrets of the Truth, whose nature is better than anyone else, 'Abdulla-yi Mubarak, the mercy of God be upon him'

cf. *ān zayn-i* ***zamān****, ān rukn-i* ***amān****, ān imām-i sharī'at u* ***ṭarīqat****, ān dhū al-jihādayn ba* ***ḥaqīqat****, ān amīr-i qalam u* ***balārak****, 'Abdullāh bin* ***al-Mubārak*** *raḥmatu Allāhi 'alayhi* ('Aṭṭār:211.2-3)
'the adorning of the time, the pillar of the peace, the imam of the Law and the Path, the possessor of two jihads to the Truth, the commander of pen and sword, 'Abdullah bin al-Mubarak, the mercy of God be upon him'

In the original Persian text *zamān-amān*, *ṭarīqat-ḥaqīqat*, and *balārak-Mubārak* are rhyming words, while in the corresponding Turkic text *sultanï-imamï*, *qïlġan-bilgän*, and *yägräk-Mubarak* constitute rhymes, and thus the contents of both texts differ greatly.

In terms of syntactic structure, there is a tendency to prefer the verb-final word order in the Turkic translation. Thus, it is often observed that when the original Persian sentence has a post-predicate element, the translator either moves it forward or adds a finite verb phrase at the end of the sentence.

anïŋ bir ***körklüg*** *qïzï bar ärti* (TA 99v13-14)
'He had a beautiful daughter.' (his - a **beautiful** daughter - existed)

cf. *dukhtarē dāsht, sakht* ***ṣāḥib-jamāl*** ('Aṭṭār:50.15-16)
'He had a very beautiful daughter.' (a daughter - he had - very **beautiful**)

öz boyïnï ***täŋri ta'ala säwmägän išlärtin****<u>saqlaġay</u>* (TA 96v11-12)
'One should guard his own body from the deeds which God the most high does not like.' (his own body - **from the deeds which God the most high does not like** - <u>he should guard</u>)

cf. *a'ḍā-yi khʷad nigah dārad* ***az har chi xashm-i khudāy 'azza wa jalla dar ān bāshad*** ('Aṭṭār:44.15)
'One should guard his body parts from everything upon which the wrath of God the most high will be.' (his body parts - he should guard - **from everything upon which the wrath of God the most high will be**)

sän burun özüŋni 'ilaj qïlġïl, ***andïn soŋra özgälärni****<u>'ilaj qïlġay sän</u>* (TA 87v9-10)
'You should first cure yourself; after that you should cure others.' (you - first - yourself - cure - **after that** - **others** - <u>you should cure</u>)

cf. *tu nukhust khʷadrā 'ilāj kun,* ***pas dīgarānrā*** ('Aṭṭār:33.16-17)
'You should first cure yourself, then others.' (you - first - yourself - cure - **then** - **others**)

In the following examples, on the other hand, the Turkic sentences contain grammatical constructions closely parallel to those found in the corresponding original Persian sentences, yielding a kind of "literal translation":

bolġay kim *Täŋri ta'ala maŋa rahmat qïlġay* (TA163r3-4)
'Perhaps God the most high will have mercy upon me.'

cf. ***bāshad ki*** *Khudā-yi ta'ālā bar man raḥmat kunad* ('Aṭṭār:147.8-9)

na *učmahqa mayil qïltïlar* ***na*** *tamuġtïn qorqtïlar* (TA159r7)
'Neither did they aspire to the heaven, nor did they fear the hell.'

cf. ***na*** *ba bihisht mayl kardand wa* ***na*** *az dōzakh tarsīdand* ('Aṭṭār:141.3)

bizlär ***bir hafta turur kim*** *ol sawabnï üläšip ...* (TA 155r2-3)
'It has been a week that we are splitting that reward.'

cf. ***yak hafta ast tā*** *mā thawāb-i ān qismat mē-kunīm* ('Aṭṭār:133.15-16)

Since these patterns occur rather consistently, one may say that such usages were fixed ones in translating Persian texts.

Very little is known about the stages of development of translation activities from Persian into Turkic. Without doubt, *Tazkira-yi awliya* holds an important position as a representative of translated texts of the earliest period, along with works such as the translation of Niẓāmī's *Khusraw u Shīrīn* by Quṭb (1341/42) and the translation of Sa'dī's *Gulistān* by Sarāyī (1391). Detailed comparison of these three texts with their originals on the one hand, and comparison among them on the other, will therefore contribute much to our understanding of the translation activities in this period.

3. The Language of the Text

In this section, several linguistic features of the *Tazkira-yi awliya* are compared with those of two varieties of Middle Turkic: the language of the fourteenth-century sources (so-called Khwarazmian Turkic) and the language of the fifteenth-century sources (Chaghatay in a narrow sense).[11]

In the *Tazkira-yi awliya*, locative case is used before the postposition *soŋra* 'after,' e.g. ***ämtitä*** *soŋra* 'from now on,' (TA 99r14) along with the ablative, e.g. *ämtitin soŋra* (TA 117r3). Examples of locative case before the postposition *soŋ* or *kedin* (both meaning 'after') are attested in Middle Turkic texts of the fourteenth century: *saqyš-syz* ***anda*** *soŋ erkäk tiši-lär* 'After that (there were) numberless men and women' (Quṭb:194); *aḫşam* ***bolmışta*** *kėḏin* 'after evening came' (NF 29.17). In the fifteenth-century Chaghatay, on the other hand, the corresponding forms *soŋra*, *soŋ* and *keyin* are all used with ablative noun phrase (Eckmann 1966:126; Bodrogligeti 2001:82).[12]

Additionally, the *Tazkira-yi awliya* uses the postposition *üzä* 'above, upon' also as a

[11] Information on the latter is chiefly based on Eckmann 1966 and Bodrogligeti 2001. Note that Bodrogligeti 2001 includes also the fourteenth-century variety in its scope.

[12] Bodrogligeti 2001:83-84 gives several examples of *keḏin* and *song* used with the locative case; but none of these examples are taken from the Chaghatay proper.

noun, e.g. *Tabaristan mulkinda učup bir jinaza* ***üzäsindin*** *ödti* 'He flied over a funeral procession and passed away in the region of Tabaristan' (TA 174v14-15). Supplied with the third-person possessive suffix *-si(n)* and the ablative case suffix *-din*, the word *üzä* is used here as a noun meaning 'space over'. Examples of similar usage are: ***üzäsingä*** *sačyŋyz sansyz altun* 'Scatter a countless amount of gold upon him' (Quṭb:212); *Yūsufnı téwe* ***üzesinde*** *qoydılar*'They put Yūsuf on a camel' (NF 358.12). In the fifteenth-century Chaghatay *üzä* is used only as a postposition (Eckmann 1966:124; Bodrogligeti 2001:78). However, at least one example of *üzä* as a noun is found in the divan of Sakkākī, a Chaghatay poet of the Pre-classical period: *'ālem* ***üzesinde*** 'over the universe' (SD 220). Compare the use of *üzä* and *üzäsintä* in Old Turkic (Erdal 2004:332, 400, 408).

The conditional of the definite past has a contracted form in *-dïsa* (<*-dï ärsä*), in *qačan kim wafat* ***boldïsa***'when he deceased' (TA 156r5). Examples of the contracted form: *ägär* ***soldysa*** *ol bir gül ne qaḏγu / čičäk-lär bar bāġynda andyn äḏgü* 'Though that rose wilted there is nothing to grieve about; there are flowers better than that in the garden' (Quṭb:190); *kim* ***ḳıldı-sa*** *müşāhade dünye ġarāibin* 'if one has witnessed wonders of the world' (Sayf 198.6). The corresponding form in Chaghatay is *-di e(r)sä* (Eckmann 1966:160; Bodrogligeti 2001:193).[13] An example of the contracted form is found in the divan of Luṭfī, another Chaghatay poet of the Pre-classical period: *körklüg kişi (...)****tüştise****ẓālım* 'if a beauty has turned into a tyrant' (LD 1241).

The perfect participle in *-miš* used as a verbal noun before *käräk*'(is) necessary': *bukün Hasan-i Basrini* ***sïnamïš*** *käräk*'Today it is necessary to test Hasan Basri' (TA 88r17). In the same construction verbal nouns in *-mäk* and *-gü* are used as well: *qopup* ***köčmäk*** *käräk*'It is necessary to rise up and set out' (TA 130r9-10); *anï* ***nädgü*** *käräk*'What should we do with it?' (TA 111v3). The form *-miš käräk* is rarely attested in Middle Turkic sources.[14] In Old Turkic, on the other hand, *-miš kärgäk* is quite common as an expression of necessity (Erdal 2004:525).

The *Tazkira-yi awliya* uses the conjunction *ärkän*'while' as it is used in Old Turkic: *bu hale oğlan* ***ärkän*** *mundağ turur*'While still being a small child, he is (as clever) as this' (TA 202v6). cf. *bu jaŋlyγ 'išrät ičrä* ***erkän*** *ol šāh / jetildi jel-teg ol Šāvur nāgāh* 'While the king was enjoying himself in this way, Šāvur suddenly arrived like the wind' (Quṭb:82); *bir kün ol ġār içinde olturur* ***erken*** *bir kimerse peydā boldı*'One day, while he was sitting in that cave someone appeared' (NF 7.14). The corresponding Chaghatay form *e(r)kän* is used mostly as a sentence final particle expressing supposition (Eckmann 1966:183-184), although examples of the conjunction *erkän* (transcribed as *irken* in the editions) are attested in the divans of Sakkākī and Luṭfī: *hīç yoḳ****irken*** *yazuḳum mini giriftār eyleme* 'Don't take me captive while I have no guilt at all' (SD 497); *uyḳuda* ***irken*** *meger zülfüngni tağıttı ṣabā* 'Perhaps the morning breeze scattered your locks of hair while asleep' (LD 441).

The sentence final particle *ärki*, expressing doubt or hesitation, is also used as in Old Turkic (Erdal 2004:276, 350): *yämäk ičmäk qaydïn tapar* ***ärki*** 'From where does he get food and drink, I wonder?' (TA 157r9-10). cf. *qaju arslan elingä tüštüŋ* ***ärki*** 'By which lion have

[13] All examples of the contracted form *-disä* given in Bodrogligeti 2001:193 are from Sayf (fourteenth-century).

[14] Examples are given in Brockelmann 1954:263 and Shcherbak 1962:147-148.

you been caught, I wonder?' (Quṭb 65); *mäniñ tañrïm bu mu* ***ärki*** 'Is this really my God?' (Rbġ. 38v7). In Chaghatay the sentence final particle used for this purpose is, as shown above, *e(r)kän.*

In regard to the lexicon, the following items are especially noteworthy.

käz 'time, turn' in *yäti käz* 'seven times' (TA 236r3). Although not attested in Chaghatay,[15] this word occurs in some of the fourteenth-century sources: e.g. *bu* ***käz*** 'this time' (Quṭb:39); *bir* ***kez*** 'once' (Sayf 34.7). It is also found in the *Codex Cumanicus*, a Middle Kipchak source of the fourteenth century (Grønbech 1942:142).[16]

küy- 'to wait' as in *kämä kälgäy täp* ***küyüp*** *turur män* 'I have been waiting for a ship to come' (TA 110v6-7). This use is not attested in Chaghatay.[17] cf. *biz munça vaqıtdın* ***küyüp*** *erdük qaçan çıqġay tėp* 'We had been waiting for such a long time, wondering when he would appear' (NF 80.6); *tän vä ǯān birlä vaṣlyŋ-ny* ***köjar****män*(to be read *küyär män*) 'With my body and soul I am waiting for a meeting with you' (Quṭb:177). It is also found in the *Codex Cumanicus* (Grønbech 1942:157).

quw (spelled as *qww*) 'dry; dried-up': *yolda bir kišiniŋ* ***quw*** *bašïnï tapdï* 'He found a man's skull (lit. dry head) on the way' (TA 167v5). It is not attested in Chaghatay. cf. Kirgiz *qū baš* 'vysokhshii cherep' (Yudakhin 1965:454). Along with the modern Kipchak forms such as Kirgiz *qū*, Tatar*qu* and Kazakh *qu*[18] (all meaning 'dry, dried up'), we find *quv aġač* 'dead tree' in the *Codex Cumanicus* (Grønbech 1942:205).[19]

taŋda 'the following (day)' as in ***taŋdasï*** *kün* 'the following day' (TA 109r2-3). It is attested in Sayf (e.g. 211.10) and in the *Codex Cumanicus* (Grønbech 1942:234). Note that the corresponding Chaghatay form *taŋla* does not occur in the text of *Tazkira-yi awliya.*

tapla- 'to be pleased (with)' as in *män siziŋ üč qïlïqïŋïznï körüp* ***taplamayïn*** *musulman bolmaz män* 'I have seen three of your behaviors which I am not pleased with. That's the reason why I won't become a Muslim' (TA 92v17-93r1). It is not attested in Chaghatay. cf. *sojurqady kimin* ***tablab****ẖarāǯyn* 'He rewarded anyone whose tribute he was pleased with' (Quṭb:127).

All these linguistic features prove clearly that the language of *Tazkira-yi awliya* has more in common with the Turkic language of the fourteenth-century sources than with Chaghatay Turkic of the fifteenth century. It must be recalled here that most of the fourteenth-century sources mentioned above originate from such regions as Khwarazm, the area of the Golden Horde or Mamluk Egypt. This fact, together with the Kipchak trait observed in the lexicon (e.g. *käz, quw, taŋda*), provide an important clue about the linguistic situation in which the Uyghur manuscript of *Tazkira-yi awliya* was produced.

The Uyghur manuscript of *Tazkira-yi awliya* is supposed to be a copy[20] and the exact

---

[15] Pavet de Courteille 1972:458 lists *g(ä)z* 'fois' without quoting any authorities. On the other hand, what the editor has read as *her kez* in LD 1435 should be *hergiz* (*hargiz*), a Persian word meaning 'ever, never'.

[16] For the examples of *käz* in other Middle Kipchak sources see Karamanlıoğlu 1994:106.

[17] The cognate form *küt-* has only the meaning 'to lead (animals)' in Chaghatay.

[18] Both Tat. *qu* and Kaz. *qu* can be represented phonologically as */quw/.*

[19] Translated by the editor as 'ein hohler Baum', i.e. 'a hollow tree'.

[20] There are several scribal errors such as: *"w'l* (93r1) for *'wl* (*ol* 'it'); *m'l"lt* (254r9) for *m'l'm't* (*malamat* 'censure'), *"dyz* (82r10) with the Arabic subscript *H* instead of *Ḥ* (*ḥadis* 'hadith'), etc.

date and place of its translation has so far not been confirmed. It follows naturally that we cannot give a definite answer as to the origin of the linguistic features mentioned above: they may be due to either the translator or the copyist(s). Whichever the case may be, however, the text was certainly written down in its present form in Herat. This strongly suggests that there were linguistic contacts between Herat and the Khwarazmian-Kipchak Turkic areas in the first half of the fifteenth century. As is well known, the court of Herat played a leading role in the development of the Classical Chaghatay language and literature in the following period, especially in the reign of Timurid Sulṭān Ḥusayn Bayqara (1469-1506). How the 'non-Chaghatay' elements, that is, elements proper to Khwarazmian and/or Kipchak Turkic were sifted out from the language in the process is a question that lies outside the scope of this paper.

Concluding Remarks

The Uyghur manuscripts of the fifteenth century have so far been utilized mainly as (often inferior) materials for establishing the critical texts, and little attention has been given to the linguistic characteristics in themselves. These manuscripts, however, provide valuable information not obtainable from those written in the Arabic script on the historical development of the Central Asian Turkic languages. For this reason, I would like to emphasize that each of these manuscripts merits a separate study.

ABBREVIATIONS

'Aṭṭār = Farīd al-dīn 'Aṭṭār, *Tadhkirat al-awliyā'*.
  edition: Shaykh Farīd al-dīn 'Aṭṭār Nīshābūrī, *Tadhkirat al-awliyā'*. bar-rasī, taṣḥīḥ-i matn, tawḍīḥāt u fahāris az Dr. Muḥammad Isti'lāmī. Tehran 1379h.[11]

LD = Luṭfī,*Dīwān*.
  edition: *Lutfî Divanı. Giriş - metin - dizin - tıpkıbasım*, ed. by Günay Karaağaç. Ankara: Türk Dil Kurumu 1997.

NF = anonymous, *Nahj al-farādīs* (ca. 1350).
  edition: *Nehcü'l-Ferādīs. Uştmaẖlarnıng Açuq Yolı (Cennetlerin Açık Yolu)* II. Metin. çevriyazı: J. Eckmann, yayınlayanlar: S. Tezcan - H. Zülfikar. Türk Dil Kurumu.

QBH = *Kutadgu Biliğ*, Tıpkıbasım I, Viyana Nüshası. İstanbul: Türk Dil Kurumu 1942.

Quṭb = Quṭb, *Khusraw u Shīrīn* (1341/42).
  edition: Zajączkowski, Ananiasz 1958 *Najstarsza Wersja Turecka Ḫusräv u Šīrīn Quṭba* I. Tekst. Warszawa: Państwowe Wydawnictwo Naukowe.

Rbġ. = Nāṣir al-dīn al-Rabghūzī, *Qiṣaṣ al-anbiyā'* (1310).
  edition: Al-Rabghūzī, *The Stories of the Prophets (Qiṣaṣ al-anbiyā'). An Eastern Turkish Version* I. ed. by H. E. Boeschoten, M. Vandamme and S. Tezcan. Leiden: E. J. Brill 1995.

Sayf = Sayf-i Sarāyī, *Gulistān bi-l-turkī* (1391).
  edition: Seyf-i Serâyî, *Gülistan Tercümesi (Kitâb Gülistan bi't-Türkî)*, ed. by A. F. Karamanlıoğlu. Ankara: Türk Dil Kurumu 1989.

SD = Sakkākī, *Dīwān*.
  edition: *Mevlâna Sekkâkî Divanı*, ed. by K. Eraslan. Ankara: Türk Dil Kurumu 1999.

TA = *Tazkira-yi Awliya*.
  facsimile: *Tezkereh-i evliâ, manuscrit ouïgour de la Bibliothèque Nationale, reproduit par l'héliogravure typographique*, Paris 1890.

edition: Sugahara Mutsumi 2007. *Tazkira-yi Awliya in the Uyghur script: Part I. Introduction and text in transcription.* Kobe: Kobe City College of Nursing (菅原睦 2007.『ウイグル文字本『聖者伝』の研究Ⅰ. 序論と転写テキスト』, 神戸:神戸市看護大学).

REFERENCES

Arat, Reşid Rahmeti 1951. *Atebetü'l-Hakayık.* Ankara: Türk Dil Kurumu.

Bodrogligeti, András J. E. 2001. *A Grammar of Chagatay.* Muenchen: LINCOM Europe.

Brockelmann, Carl 1954. *Osttürkische Grammatik der Islamischen Litteratursprachen Mittelasiens.* Leiden: E. J. Brill.

Eckmann, János 1966. *Chagatay Manual.* Bloomington: Indiana University.

Erdal, Marcel 2004. *A Grammar of Old Turkic.* Leiden: Brill.

Gandjeï, Tourkhan 1957 "Il "Muḥabbatnāma" di Ḫōrazmī" in *Annali dell'Istituto Universitario Orientale di Napoli,* N. S. 6: 131-161 + Facsimile.

Gandjeï, Tourkhan 1970. "The <Laṭāfat-nāma> of Khujandī" in *Annali dell'Istituto Universitario Orientale di Napoli,* N.S.10: 345-368; plate I-XXV.

Grønbech, Kaare 1942. *Komanisches Wörterbuch, Türkischer Wortindex zu Codex Cumanicus.* København: Munksgaard.

Jarring, Gunnar 1964. *An Eastern Turki-English Dictionary.* Lund: CWK Gleerup.

Karamanlıoğlu, Ali Fehmi 1994 *Kıpçak Türkçesi Grameri.* Ankara: Türk Dil Kurumu.

Muḥammad ibn Ibrāhīm Farīdu'ddīn 'Aṭṭār, ed. by Reynold A. Nicholson 1905/1907. *Tadhkiratu'l-Awliyā* ("Memoires of the Saints") I/II. London: Luzac & Co.

Pavet de Courteille, Abel 1972. (reprinted) *Dictionnaire Turc-oriental.* Amsterdam: Philo Press.

Scherberger, Max 2003. *Das Mi'rāğnāme, Die Himmel- und HöllenfahrtdesProphetenMuhammad in der osttürkischen Überlieferung.* Würzburg: Ergon Verlag.

Sertkaya, Ayşe Gül 2007. "Ferîde'd-dîn-i 'Attâr'ın Tezkire-i Evliyâsının Doğu Türkçesi çevirisi üzerine bazı görüşler" in *Türk Dilleri Araştırmaları* 17: 305-318.

Sertkaya, Ayşegül 2015. *Tezkire-i Evliyâ'nın Çağatay Türkçesi Çevrisi: Arap ve Uygur Harfli Yazmaların Transkripsiyonlu Metni.* İstanbul: Çantay Kitabevi.

Sertkaya, Osman F. 1975. "Uygur harfleri ile yazılmış bazı manzum parçalar II" in *İÜTDED* 21: 175-195 + I-XII.

Sertkaya, Osman F. 1976. "Uygur harfleri ile yazılmış bâzı mensur parçalar I" in *TM* 18: 245-268 + I-XII.

Shcherbak, A. M. 1962 *Grammatika Starouzbekskogo Yazyka.* Moscow-Leningrad: Izdatel'stvo Akademii Nauk SSSR.

Sugahara Mutsumi 2004. ""Devrik Cümle" in Middle Turkic" in Fujishiro Setsu (ed.), *Approaches to Eurasian Linguistic Areas.* 1-13, Kobe: Kobe City College of Nursing.

Sugahara Mutsumi 菅原睦 2008. *Tazkira-yi Awliya in the Uyghur script: Part II. Japanese translation with notes.* ウイグル文字本『聖者伝』の研究Ⅱ. 日本語訳および註, Kobe: Kobe City College of Nursing.

Sugahara Mutsumi 2011. "*Kutadgu Bilig*'in Herat (Viyana) nüshası ve XV. yüzyıl Türk dili" in Musa Duman (ed.), *Doğumunun 990. Yılında Yusuf Has Hacib Ve Eserleri Kutadgu Bilig Bildirileri, 26-27 Ekim 2009.* Ankara: Türk Dil Kurumu: 471-478.

Yudakhin, K. K. 1965. *Kirgizsko-Russkii Slovar'.* Moscow: Izdatel'stvo Sovetskaya Entsiklopediya.

INDEX

Abā Bakr / Abā Bakrī Ṣiddīq / Abu Bakr as-Siddik, 99, 184, 185, 190, 239, 293
Abā Bakrī, Mīrzā, 190
Abā Muslim, 228
Abay Qunanbayev, 67
Abbasid, 103, 303, 304
'Abd al-Karīm Khān, 292
'Abd al Khāliq Ghijda-vānī, 247
'Abd al Laṭīf (Sulṭān), 237, 238
'Abd Allāh al-Afḍal, 290, 296
'Abd al-Rashīd Khān / 'Abdī Rashīd Khān, 189, 237, 238, 240, 244, 249, 292, 295
'Abdallah b. 'Ali → Imam Abdullah Bahir
Abdals, 271
Abdulaziz-Bab, 67
'Abdullāh b. 'Abbās, 239
'Abdullāh b. Mas'ūd, 239
'Abdullāh b. 'Umar, 239
Abdullah Bahir → Imam Abdullah Bahir
Abdurahman Khan, 78, 83
Abla Baywechchi, 137
Abū al-Baqā' b. Khwāja Bahā' al-Dīn, 289, 294, 298
Abu 'Ali Dakkak, 106, 107
Abū al-Qāsīm / Abulqasim, 83, 98, 114, 277, 281-286
Abū Ḥafṣ-i Kabīr / Abū Ḥafḍ-i Kabīr / Abū Ḥafẓ-i Kabīr, 228, 235
Abū'l Mūsā Ash'ara, 239
Abū Sa'īd Qūchqār Ata, viii, 227, 251
Abū Shāhīm, 256
Äbu Talip, 91
Adam, 67, 278
adib, 255
Āfāq / Afaq / Apaq / Appaq / Afak / Hidāyat Allāh, Khwaja, vii, 4, 8, 12, 22, 28, 29, 39, 40, 128, 185, 201, 202, 205, 212, 223, 252, 259, 278, 290, 291, 296- 298
Āfāqī, 227, 292
Afghanistan, 76, 95, 102-105
Aftah → Imam Aftah
Aftu- Moodan → Chiltän
Aghïntay, 67
Aḥmad b. Sa'd al-Dīn al-Uzghanī al-Namanghāni, 276
Aḥmad Kāsānī → Makhdūm-i A'ẓam
Ahmad Khoja, 128
Aḥmad, Sayyid → Sayyid Aḥmad
Aḥmad Yasavī → Yasavī
Aḥmad Zamjī, Pahlavān, 228
Ahrar, Khoja, 132, 133
Aisha, 213
'ajam, 234, 270, 271
Akhtam Sahaba, 99
akhun / ākhūnd, 49, 53, 134-136, 255
'Alā' al-Dīn, Sayyid → Sayyid 'Alā' al-Dīn
'alam, 229, 234, 237, 247, 260, 273
'Alanūr Khanim, 278, 279
Alastau, 70
Aldāsh / Alāsh Beg Dādkhāh, 158, 161
Alexander the Great, 101, 106, 120
Alf Ata / Ālf Ata / Ālif Ata / Alif Atā / Alip Ata, Sulṭān, 38, 182, 228, 248, 260
'Alī / Äli, 77, 80, 81, 85, 91-93, 117, 147, 246, 247, 260, 271, 274, 278, 290, 292, 294, 296, 297, 301
'Alī Arslān / Äli Arslan / Ali Arslan / Īrslān, 4, 5, 7, 27, 30, 31, 127, 182, 228, 236, 239, 240, 242, 243, 278, 279, 281, 282, 286
'Alī b. Mūsā al-Riḍā / Äli Musa Riza / Ali Riza, 78, 85, 117, 278, 290, 292, 296, 297, 309
'ālim, 255
Aliqun, 128
Almatï, 69, 299
Al-Mulhakat bi-s-surah, 96, 122
Altïnsarin, 67
Altishahr, viii
Altun / Altunluq Mazar, 27, 177, 179, 182, 255, 262
amanat, 68, 71
Amat Akhun, Mir, 131
Amu-Darya, 120
Andijan, 100, 101, 107, 222
Ändir river, 270

Andira, 271
animal-cycle calendar, 229
Anīs al- ṭālibīn, 290-295, 297, 298
Apaq Khoja → Āfāq
Appaq → Āfāq
Aptah → Imam Aftah
Aq Mazar, 37, 117
Aq Ul, 64, 65
aqqu, 65, 66, 69-72
Aqsaray, 77, 87
Aqsu / Āqsū / Aqsū / Ardavīl, 110, 130, 134, 228, 261
Aqtaghliq, 128, 131, 134
Aqtam Khōja Mazar, 159
Aqtam Village, 77
aqtïq, 69, 71
Arab, 47, 59, 76, 95, 98, 107, 208
arbakesh, 71
Archa Mazar, 108
Ardavīl → Aqsu
Arïstan-Bab, 64-67, 72
Arshad al Dīn / Arshidīn Walī / Arshidin Khoja, 182, 292
Arshdin Khoja Mazar, 22
Artush / Atush / Artūch / Artuch, vii, 4, 18, 35, 37-43, 131, 136, 185, 212, 227, 244, 245, 255, 258, 260, 274, 275, 285
arwah, 66, 70, 72
Asaf b. Burhiya, 97
Aṣḥāb al-kahf / Äshab al-kähf, 6, 182, 187, 250, 251, 281, 287
Āshīya Ṣiddīq, 239
Ashraf al-Dīn, 290, 291, 297
Asht, 105
Ashura, 7
Asim → Imam Asim
Association for the Promotion of Uyghur Culture (APUC), 136, 137, 155
Ata Zholï, 64-72
'Aṭabat al-Ḥaqā'iq, 322
'Aṭṭār, Farīd al-dīn, 321, 324, 325, 328, 329
Atush → Artush
axis mundi, 27, 28
ayan, 64, 66
Ayman, 282
Aysha-Bibi, 64-66
Aytu-Bi, 67
Ayyub, 96, 118
Āzam Kufe Rejullāh, Imām, 301

Baba Akhtam, 99
Baba Qambar, 99
Baba-yi Khorasan, 99
Badakhshān, 236
Baghdad / Baghdād / Baghdāt, 16, 19, 232, 304, 305
Baghdādī, Sayyid Jalāl al-Dīn → Sayyid Jalāl al-Dīn Baghdādī
Baghdādī, Shaykh Junayd , 240, 241
Bahā' al-Dīn Naqshband, 228
bakhshi, 23, 24, 31, 36-44, 106
Baku, 105
Balasaghun, 4
Balkh, 116, 235
Balpïq-Bi, 67
Bamiyan, 7
banner, 9, 10, 24, 31, 100, 259, 262, 263, 269
Bao'an, 55
Baq Sögöt Atam Mazar, 38, 41
baraka / barakat, 25, 53, 234
Baraq-Ata, 67
Barat, 7, 30, 129, 153, 156, 165, 173
Barbar, 103, 106, 116
Bäshkeräm / Bishkiram, 5, 159, 260
Baṣra, 304
Bastāmī, Shaykh-i 'alavīya, 240
bata, 65-67, 71, 72
Batkent, 116
Baṭṭāl Ghāzī, Sayyid → Sayyid Battal Gazi
Baydibek-Baba, 65, 66
beg, 130, 131, 133-136, 185
Beishangen, 58, 59
Beizhuang, 48
Beket-Aulie, 67
Bel Mazar, 108
Bes Ata, 64, 66
Besharik Uchkuprik, 98
Bijiachang, 48-50
Bilāl, 239, 240, 247
Bobrinskiy, A. A., 121
Boderge, 131
Bogouddin, 109
Bögü Khan, 26
Buddhism, 3, 6, 7, 10-12
Buddhist, 4, 6-8, 11, 75, 77, 128, 212, 307
Bughrā-khān, 275, 276, 279, 281, 283, 284-287
Bughrā-khān, Esen → Esen Bughrā Khān
Bughrā-khān, Ḥasan → Ḥasan Bughrā Khān, 247, 280
Bughrā-khān, Ḥasan and Ḥusayn → Ḥasan and Ḥusayn Bughrā-khān
Bughrā-khān, Satūq → Satūq Bughrā Khān
Bughrā-khān, Uthmān → Uthmān Bughrā-khān

Bughrā-khānid, 228, 229, 241, 242, 247
Bukhara / Bukhārā, 4, 76, 96, 106, 109, 132, 134, 184, 185, 190, 221, 228, 235, 236, 243, 255, 294
Bukhārī / al-Bukhārī, Burhān al-Dīn, 144
Bulgaria, 67
Bulghār, 249
Burhan al-Din, Khoja, 129, 134
Burhān al-Dīn Qïlïch, 289-297
Burhān al-Dīn al- Bukhārī → Bukhārī
Büwi Märyäm, 5, 15

Caliph, 99, 103, 221, 304
Caspian Sea, 105
Caucasus, 102
celestial tax, 129, 130
Central Asian Muslim Religious Board (SADUM), 63
Central State Archives of Uzbekistan, 98
Chaghatay, 135, 186, 276, 299, 306, 309, 325-328
Chaghatayid, 237, 245, 249
Chakka Tama, 117
Chālīsh, 260
Chāqtū river, 268
Chashma-yi Yitimī, 302
Chekende Mazar, 40-42
Chengdu, 52, 83, 309
Chengqing Caigu Huijiao Menhuan, 49
Chihil Tan → Chiltän
Chilantoo Mazar, 38, 39
Chilkhujra, 102
Chiltän / Chihil Tan / Haft Muḥammadān / Aftu- Moodan, x, 83, 177-183, 185-187, 189-192, 211-214, 218, 219, 255, 262, 263
Chimion, 115
Chīn Tīrīm Anam, 247
Chinar, 41, 77
Chinese Communist Party, 130
Chingizid, 292, 294
Chin-Machin, 86
Chinzhou, 50
Chira, 78, 79, 81, 91, 93, 94, 266-268, 272
Chokur Rashīd al-Dīn Mz., 159
Christian, 6, 194, 196, 197, 199, 200, 215, 216, 253
Churās, Shāh Maḥmūd b. Mīrzā Fāḍil, viii, 237, 245, 248, 250, 290-293, 295, 297, 298
cloth, 5, 6, 9, 40, 69, 71, 79, 142, 222
Compilation of Kashghar Waqf Documents, 154
Compilation of the Yārkand Mazar Hagiographies, 191
corvée labour, 138
cradle, 9, 20, 118
Cultural Revolution, 156, 266
Cyprus, 67

Da Gongbei, 50, 52
Dal Zal, 103
dalïchï, 36
Dalīlī, 263
Dalverzin, 103
dance, 26, 31, 32
Dāniyāl Khwājam, 291
Daoguang, 129, 135, 140
daotang, 47, 50, 60
darïmchï, 36
darvazakhana, 97
Dasht-i Qipchak, 99
dastan / dāstān, 210, 281, 282
Datong, 50
Dawan Gongbei, 51
Dawantou, 50
Daxiangbaba, 59
Denau, 103
dervish / darwīsh, 221, 222, 268
dhikr → *zikr*
Dihlavī, Shaykh Niẓām al Dīn, 228
divana, 120
Dīwān-i Yitimī, 302
Dīwān Lughāt al-Türk / Divanu Lughat-it-Türk, 5, 22, 153
Ḍiyā' al-Dīn / Ḍiyāv al-Dīn, Sayyid → Sayyid Ḍiyā' al-Dīn
Dolan, 131
doll, 9
Domalaq-Ana, 65
domchu, 36
Dongchuan Gongbei, 51, 52
Dongxiang, 50, 55, 61
du'ā, 273, 323
Dūl, 266
Duldul Ata Mazar, 101
Duldul horse, 271
Duva festival, 26

Eastern Turki, 33, 34, 166, 179, 188, 193, 196, 213, 218, 227-229, 250, 251, 276, 277, 287, 288, 328, 329
eesi, 39
Eidgah Jami, 32
Ellik Paysaki, 116, 117
emchi, 36
Enjan Kocha, 137

Enjanreste Elementary School, 136
Er Hubbi, 120
Ergongjinjiao Laorenjia Gongbei, 51
Erkurgan, 103
Erliugong Gongbei, 51
ermanli, 52-54
Esen Bughrā Khān, 247
Essenqoja-Ata, 67
Ethiopia, 67
Eziret Bigim Mazar → Ḥaḍrat-i Mollām Mazar
Ezsultunum Mazar → Satuq Bughra Khan Mazar

faḍā'il, 253
fake mazar, 75, 306
Falla Tāgh, 235
Faqīh Ayyūb Khūja, 246
Farghāna → Ferghana
Fatāwā Qāḍīkhān, 144
Fatima / Fatimä / Fāṭima, 86, 184, 189, 190, 220, 221, 296, 297, 301
Faxian, 6
fay, 127
Fengmen, 49
Ferghana / Ferghāna / Farghāna, ix, 4, 95-100, 103, 105, 107-110, 113-120, 123, 138, 154, 166, 187, 188, 191, 192, 218, 245, 251, 274, 293-295
fiqh, 81
flag, 9, 10, 64, 91, 142
four great menhuan, 56
Fragrant Concubine → Xiang Fei
Fukang, 52
Fūnāq, 268

Gadāy Muḥammad, 157
Gansu, 23, 47-50, 52, 54, 62, 139, 307
Gazatname-i Shah Jarir, 108, 109
genealogy, 104, 107, 111, 142-144, 161, 191, 260, 278, 289-292, 295, cf. *nasabnāmah*
Genghis Khan, 104, 115
ghazal, 255
ghazavāt-nāma, 229, 242, 247
Ghazzālī → Imam Ghazzālī
Ghulja / Ili, 9, 20, 21, 51, 128, 131, 136, 308
Giyaskhodja, 114
Golden Horde, 121, 327
gongbei, x, 47-50, 52-54, 62
Great Game, The, ix
Greater and Lesser Khojas, 128-130, 132, 134, 135
Guanghe, 57
Gūmā, 264, 265
Gumayunruy, 102
gumbäz, 7, 107
Gur-i Emir, 104
Guyuan, 47, 48, 50, 52, 54, 57- 62

Ḥabīb Khūja, Shaykh, 245
Hādī Ākhar-i Zamān → Imam Hādī Ākhar-i Zamān
hadith / *ḥadīth*, 81, 96, 327, 144, 304
Ḥaḍrat-i Makhdūm, 259
Ḥaḍrat-i Mollām / Ḥaḍrat-i Mullām / Eziret Bigim, 37, 155-162, 165, 167-169, 227, cf. Mahmud Kashgari
Ḥaḍrat Sulṭān Satūq Bughrā-khān Ghāzīning Tadhkiralārī, 283
Ḥāfiẓ-i Abrū / Hafiz-i Abru, 104, 227
Haft Muḥammadān → Chiltän
hagiography → *tadhkira(h)*
Haiyuan, 50
Ḥajākatī, 247
hajj / *ḥajj*, 22, 47, 190, 206, 256, 263
Ḥājjī Khoja, 242
Ḥājjī Muḥammad Bakhtavī, Mullā, 247
ḥajjnāma, 253, 273
ḥākim / *hakim*, 134, 157, 180, 280
Ḥallāj, 323
Hamadānī, Amīr Sayyid 'Alī → Sayyid 'Alī Hamadānī, Amīr
Hamadānī, Shaykh Abū Yūsuf, 240
Hami → Qumul
Han (Chinese), 35, 49, 53, 55, 186, 188, 299
Ḥanafī, 144, 147, 228
Ḥarakatī, Muḥammad Amīn Khwājamqulī, 256
Hārūn al-Rashīd, 304
Hasan / Ḥasan / Häsän → Imam Hasan
Ḥasan and Ḥusayn Bughrā-khān, 279
Häsän Äsqäri → Imam Häsän Äsqäri
Ḥasan Baṣrī, Shaykh, 239-241
Ḥasan Bughrā Khān / Hasan Bughra, 4, 247, 280
Hasan Nuri, Khoja, 98
Hāshim, 144, 291, 297
ḥauḍ, 161
Haydar, Mirza Muhammad, 75, 250
Haydarkan, 118
häzrät säylisi, 8
Hazrat Shah, 98, 108
Häzrät-i-Afak → Āfāq
Hebei, 50

Heilongjiang, 35
Hezhou, 49- 51
Hidāyat-nāma, 289- 292, 295, 296, 298
Ḥijjāz Khūja, 241
Hindu, 6
Hindu Kush, 105
Hindustan, 272
Hong Yang, 48
Honggangzi Gongbei, 51, 52
Hua Mosque, 49
Hualong, 50
Huasi Gongbei, 50
Huazhe Abdu Donglaxi, 50
Hui, 23, 47- 55, 57, 61, 134
Hui-bu, 157
Huihu, 10
Huijiang zhi, ix, 26, 27, 130, 131, 134, 140
Humen Gongbei, 51
Hunza, 263
Husayn / Ḥusayn / Hüsäyin → Imam Husayn
Ḥusayn Bayqara, 328
Ḥusayn Bughrā Khān, 159
Ḥusayn Faḍlullāh, 241, 242
Ḥusayn Madanī, Amīr, 291, 297

Ibad Allāh Khān Tora, 185
Ibrāhīm Adham, Sulṭān, 293
Ibrahim Qurban, 283
Ibrahim-Ata, 67
Ichang Kala, 106
Ikhwani, 54
Ilek Māḍī, Sulṭān, 293, 294
Ilgar, Khoja, 99
Ili → Ghulja
Ilkhanate, 138
'ilm al-yaqīn, 259
imam / imām, 49, 65, 81-83, 158, 159, 162, 165, 227, 244, 266, 268, 269, 271, 301, 302, 324
Imam Abdullah Bahir / 'Abdallah b. 'Ali, 97-99
Imam Aftah / Aptah, 19, 75, 78-80, 83, 87, 301
Imam 'Ali → 'Alī
Imam Äskär → Imam Hasan Eskeri
Imam Asim, 31, 76, 80
Imam Ata → Imam Zayn al-Abidin
Imām Āzam, 301
Imam Ghazzālī, 306
Imam Hādī Ākhar-i Zamān, 271
Imam Hasan / Ḥasan / Häsän, 80, 92, 93, 164, 228, 239-241, 247, 275, 278-280, 290, 296, 297
Imam Hasan Eskeri / Häsän Äsqäri, 78, 79, 84-86, 297
Imam Husayn / Ḥusayn / Hüsäyin, 7, 77, 78, 80, 81, 86, 92, 97, 98, 228, 257, 279, 290, 296, 297, 323
Imām Isḥāq, Khoja, 235
Imām Ismā'īl, 304
Imam Jaffar Sadiq / Imām Ja'far Ṣādiq, viii, 22, 29, 30, 75, 78, 79, 86, 99, 266, 268-270, 296, 297, 301, 304, 323
Imām Ja'far Ṭayrān / Ja'far-i Tahrān / Imām Ja'far-i Tayyār, viii, 81, 228, 267, 268
Imām Mahdī Ākhar-i Zamān / Mahdi / Mähdi, 76, 79, 80, 82, 83, 87, 91-94, 271
Imam Malik Äjdäl, 161
Imam Malik Äskär, 161
Imam (-related) mazars, 22, 76, 80-83
Imam Muhammad / Imām Muḥammad, 120, 301
Imam Muhamamd Ansari, 81
Imam Muhammad Baqir / Imām Muḥammad Bāqir / Imam Muhämmäd Baqir, 78, 86, 97, 98, 296, 297, 301
Imam Muhammad Hanifa / Muhammad b. al-Hanafiya, 80, 99
Imam Muhamamd Naqi, 78, 79, 85, 86, 297,
Imam Muhammad Taqi, 78, 79, 85, 86, 297
Imam Musa Kazim / Mūsā Kāẓim / Musa Qasim, x, 75, 78, 79, 85, 296, 297, 301, 303-310, 312, 314
Imam Qasim / Imām Qāsim, 78, 79, 83, 177, 282, 297, 301
Imām Shākir, 266
Imām Ṣūfī, 245
Imám Zabiha / Zabija, 75
Imam Zayn al-'Abidin / Imam Zäydin Abid / Imam Ata, 78, 86, 97-99
Imāmlarim, 155, 159-163, 165, 170, 172, 296, 297, 301
iman / īmān, 81, 233
Independent Muslims' Board of Kazakhstan (DUMK), 63
Ipar Khan → Xiang Fei
iqta, 138
Iran, x, 95, 138, 162, 209, 305
Iraq, 76, 95, 103
'Irāqī, Quṭb al Dīn, 243
irik, 38
Īrslān → 'Alī Arslān
Isbid Bulan / Safed Bulan, 96
Isfīdūk, 262
ishan, 79, 128, 137

Isḥāq Walī, Khwāja, 159, 250, 262, 291, 292, 294-297
Isḥāq Imām, Khūja → Imām Isḥāq
Isḥāq-Āta, 144
Isḥāq-Bāb, 144
Isḥāqī, 227, 291, 292, 294, 295
Ishkashim, 101
Ishqol säylisi, 8
Islam Khoja, 133
Islamic ideology, 145
Islamic law, 11, 47, 63, 69, 79, 130
Islamization, 63, 122, 145, 229, 249, 266, 268
Ismāʻīlī, 304
Ismāʻīl, 164, 304
Istanbul, 12, 205, 217, 250, 255
Istaravshan, 99, 102
Ithna-ʻashariyyah, 77
Izbaskan, 100

Jaʻfar Ṣādiq / Jaʻfar-i Ṣādiq → Imam Jaffar Sadiq
Jaʻfar-i Shākir, 266
Jaʻfar-i Tahrān → Imām Jaʻfar Ṭayrān
Jabrāʼīl, 184
jada tash, 36
Jahangir / Jahāngīr, Khoja, 129, 135, 260
Jahriyya, 48- 50, 52
Jalāl al-Dīn, Mawlānā, 182, 290, 291, 296, 297
Jalāl al-Dīn Baghdādī, 279
Jalalabad, 96, 118
Jalīl Ūshī, Khūja, 247
Jamal Qarshi, viii, 96, 97, 127
Jāmiʻ al-maqāmāt, 289-296, 298
Janadil-Makatil, 101
Jānbāz Khoja, 227-242, 246-249, 251
jārūbkesh, 157-159, 161, 162
Jay Atam, 38-40
Jay Döbö, 38-40
jaychï, 36
Jayḥūn, 233
Jew, 271
Jiaqing, 129, 139
jihad / jihād, 4, 324
Jihan / Jahān, Khoja, 131, 296
Jilanduu Mazar, 38
Jilanjay Mazar, 38
Jilin, 48, 50, 52
Jilu Suu Mazar, 39
jin, 31, 166, 201
jönchü, 36
Josef Messrur, Mirza, 195
Judaism, 12

Kabil, 102
kadamdzhay → *qadamjay*
Kafiristan, 105
Kaifeng, 52
Kakhkakha, 101
Kala-i Dev-i Safid, 103
Kala-i Imlak, 103
Kala-i Jamahur, 103
kalima, 66
Kamāl al-Dīn Majnūn, Sayyid → Sayyid Kamāl al-Dīn Majnūn
Kampir Ravat, 118
Kangle, 50
Kao Futang, 57, 59
Kaptar Mazar → Qūm Rabāṭ Pādishāhīm
Karatepa Qishlaq, 106
Karbala / Karbalā, 7, 257
Kāsānī, Aḥmad → Makhdūm-i Aʻẓam
Kashgar / Kāshghar / Kashghar / Kaschgar, vii, viii, 4, 5, 8-10, 12, 15, 20-22, 24, 27, 28, 32, 33, 35, 38-40, 76, 102, 127, 128, 131, 134-136, 137, 140, 153-155, 157-159, 162, 166, 179, 182, 188, 191, 193, 195, 197, 198, 201, 202, 206, 207, 212, 216, 217, 219, 229, 230, 237, 242, 243, 245, 248, 250-252, 256, 259, 260, 274, 275, 279-281, 284, 285, 287, 288, 292
Kashgar Orda-ishik Royal Household Maktab, 137
Kashgar Teacher Training School, 137
Kāshgharī,ʻAbdullāh Nidāʼī, 256
Kāshgharī , Maḥmūd / Mahmud Kashgari / Mähmut Qäshqäri, 26, 32, 153, 156, 157, 166, 214, 218
Kāshgharī, Muḥammad Ṣādiq, 290, 298
Kāshgharī, Mullā Mīr Sālah, 284
Kashgaria, 254, 275
Katakī, 228, 237, 292
katput, 100
Katta Mazar, 117, 118
Kazakh, 35, 55, 63-65, 67, 70, 115, 121, 142, 145, 151, 152, 179, 323, 327
Kāzimayn, 305
kegong, 130
Kekilik Mazar, 39
Kempe, 253
Kengirbay-Bi, 67
Keriya / Keriyä, 78, 81, 245, 268, 270, 285, 306
keruen, 67, 69-71
keruen-basï, 71
keruen-saray, 67, 69-71
Khaje Mujib Kohmar, 301

khanaqah / *khānaqāh* / *khaniqa* / *khaniqä*, vii, 23, 50, 78, 131, 161, 259, 261, 262, 271
Khaqan, 86
khaṭīb, 158, 159, 161-164, 235, 236
Khaybar, 116
Khiḍrī Bilāl, 239
Khiva / Khiwa, 76, 105, 106, 121
Khizr / Khiḍr, 120, 185, 240, 241, 243, 246, 248, 266
khoja / *khwāja*, vii, 79, 142, 227, 229, 254, 256
Khoja Mullām → Ḥaḍrat-i Mullām
Khoja Period, 127
Khojikent Qishlaq, 103
Khoqand → Qoqand
Khorasan / Khurasan, 76, 99, 107, 138
Khotan, viii, x, 4-10, 12, 14-19, 21, 22, 30, 31, 34, 35, 43, 55, 75-83, 91, 94, 135, 179, 195, 228, 255, 256, 263, 266, 267, 269-272, 274, 279, 280, 285, 301, 303, 305, 306, 309
Khotani, Molla Niyaz, 78
Khudayar / Khudāyār-Khān, 110, 112, 142
Khufiyya / Khufiya, 48-50, 52, 59
Khūja Aḥmadī Yasavī → Yasavī
Khūja Ḥajākatu'llāh Khūja, 246
Khujandī, Shaykh Muṣliḥ / Maṣlaḥat al-Dīn, 290, 293, 294, 297, 298, 329
Khulāṣa, 144
Khunjerab Pass, 153
khuṭba, 260
khwāja → *khoja*
Khwāja Walī, 261
Khwarazmian Turkic, 325
Khwarezm, 76
Kichik Mazar, 116, 117
Kipchak, 327, 328
Kīra, 267, 268, 270
Kirghiz / Qïrghïz, x, 35-41, 43-55, 121, 237, 238, 240, 242-244, 247, 248, 327
Kiyiktuz Atam, 39
Kizilsu, 35-39, 41, 42
Kokand → Qoqand
Kokhmarim, 6
Kökönïshïq Mazar, 38, 40
Koktash, 116

Kubrā / Kubrāy, Shaykh Najm al Dīn / Najmidīn, 240, 241
Kubrawiyya, 48-50
Kucha / Kūchā / Kūsan, 21, 22, 132, 134, 136, 182, 223, 228, 237, 261
Kucha Khwājas, 180, 289, 292
Kūhak mountain, 233
Kükürt Mazar, 38
Kulāl, Amīr, 228
Kunlun mountain, 270, 272
Kūsan → Kucha

Lāchīn Ata, 228
Lamaism, 11
lamp, 7
langar / *längär*, 5, 257, 259, 264-266, 271
Langar Khoja Ishan, 114
Langzhong, 50
Lanzhou, 48, 50-52, 56-60, 139, 186
Lenin, 138, 139
Lesser Mazar, 117, 118
lieux de mémoire, vii, 268
Lingmingtang Gongbei, 51, 52
Lintiao Beixiang, 49
Linxia, 48, 50, 57-59
Liumen, 48
Lop / Lūp, 76, 78, 266
Luḥūq / Loq, 265
Luṭfī, 326, 328

Ma Hasan, 58, 59
Ma Lingming, 56, 59
Ma Renpu, 57, 59
Ma Xianzhong, 49
Machin, 80, 86, 91, 92, 303
Madaminbek, 112
Madanī, Sayyid Ibrāhīm → Sayyid Ibrāhīm Madanī
māddāh, 206, 210
Madīna / Medina, 77, 79, 92, 98, 107, 109, 116, 117, 184, 190, 213, 219-222, 248, 293, 304
madrasa / *madrasah*, 97, 136, 255
Maḥbūbī,'Ubaydallāh b. Mas'ūd, 144
Mahdi / Mähdi → Imām Mahdī Ākhar-i Zamān
Mahmud Kashgari / Maḥmūd al-Kāshgharī / Mähmut Qäshqäri → Kāshgharī
Maḥmūd Khān, 294
Mahmud Khoja, 114
Mahsum, 112, 113
Majīd Ata, 228
Majmū'at al-muḥaqqiqīn, 290, 296, 298
Makdisi, 96
Makhdūm-i A'ẓam / Aḥmad Kāsānī, x, 143, 289, 290, 292, 294-298, 300
Makhdūmzāda, 283
Makhzuni, Ziyavuddin Makhdum, 110
maktab, 136
Mamluk Egypt, 327

manāqib, viii, 273
Manāqib-i Ḥaḍrat-i Shaykh Maṣlaḥat al-Dīn Khujandī, 290, 298
Manichaeism, 6, 11
Marghilan / Margelan, 102, 111, 113, 115, 123, 185, 188
Mariyam-Ana, 67
martyr → *shahid*
Mashhad / Mashad, 96, 97, 116, 123, 258, 259
Mashhad Maydan Buva, 97
Mashhad Maydan Mazar, 97-99
Mashrab, Bābāraḥim, 256
Masjid Imam, 81
Maṣlaḥat al-Dīn → Khujandī, Shaykh Muṣliḥ
mathnawī, 260
Mathnawī-yi Sharīf, 157
Mawarannahr / Māwarānnahr / Māwarnaḥr, 76, 86, 96, 111, 115, 228, 232, 233, 250, 262, 294
Māzandarān, 265
mazar säylisi, 206
Mazar-i Sharif, 76, 103, 104
Mazartagh, 83
Mecca, 4, 22, 65, 67, 68, 71, 86, 92, 109, 117, 190, 231, 232, 234, 243, 255, 259, 260, 270, 279, 282, 301, 305
Medina → Madīna
menhuan, x, 49, 50, 56, 62
Middle Turkic, 321, 322, 325, 326, 329
Minhe, 50
Miralī-Ata, 67
Mission Covenant Church of Sweden, 193, 195, 196, 216, 218, 224
Moghūl, 245, 248, 249
Moghūlistān, 182, 294
Moghūliyya / Mughūliyya, 255, 261, 263, 292
Mohammad Emin → Muḥammad Amīn
Mojiang, 52
moldo, 38, 39
Mongol, 256, 294, 298
mosque, 7, 22, 32, 48, 49, 52, 59-61, 78, 80, 81, 95, 97, 100, 108-113, 133, 138, 161, 177, 201, 202, 208, 213, 219, 220, 232, 235, 260, 262, 267, 283, 306, 307, 309
Mu'ādh b. Jabīl, 239
mu'adhdhīn, 161
mufti, 49
Mufti Gongbei, 50
Mughūliyya → Moghūliyya
Muḥabbat Süzük, Khūja, 246
Muhammad / Muḥammad / Muhämmäd, Prophet, 59, 64, 68, 77, 82, 85, 86, 91, 92, 95, 96, 99, 106, 109, 118, 122, 132, 144, 180, 182, 184-186, 189-191, 200, 208, 211, 213, 217, 220, 228, 232, 267, 296, 297, 301
Muḥammad, Sayyid → Sayyid Muḥammad
Muhammad, Sultan, 107
Muḥammad Amīn / Mohammad Emin, 28, 296
Muhammad Baqir / Muḥammad Bāqir / Muhämmäd Baqir, Imam → Imam Muhammad Baqir
Muḥammad Bashshārā / Muḥammad Bashshārī, Khūja, 232
Muḥammad Gadā, 276
Muḥammad Ghazālī, 285
Muḥammad Ḥaydar Doghlāt, Mīrzā, viii, 178, 187, 250, 270, 294, 298
Muhammad b. al-Hanafiya, 98, 99, 111
Muḥammad Khān, 292
Muḥammad Mīrad, 256
Muhammad Naqi / Muhämmäd Näqi → Imam Muhamamd Naqi
Muḥammad Ṣādiq Kāshgharī → Kāshgharī
Muhammad Shakir, 112
Muḥammad Sharīf Pīr / Muhammad Sherip, 22, 179, 182, 185, 189, 237-243, 245, 247, 248, 251, 261, 262, 281, 282, 285, 292, 294
Muhammad Taqi / Muhämmäd Täqi → Imam Muhammad Taqi
Muḥammad Walī Ṣūfī, 292, 294
Muḥammad Yūsuf, 259, 278, 296
Muḥīṭī, Maḥmūd, 155
Mūjī, 265
mukhammas, 255
Mukhtaṣar al-wiqāya, 144
Mukūlyā / Mokoyla, 265
Mulhaqat al-surah, viii, 127
mulla / molla, 23, 136
Mullā Ḥājī, 275, 279-285
Mullā Mīr Sālah Kāshgharī → Kāshgharī
Mullā Ṣādiq, 190
Mulla Sufi, 129
Mullāh Ghazal, 263
Mullāh Qābil, 256
Mullah Shakir, 112
Mūnis Khwāja, 256
Muradbakhsh, 120
murid / murīd, 48, 52, 248, 292
murshid, 47-50, 52, 53
Musa Kazim / Mūsā Kāẓim → Imam Musa Kazim
Muṣayyab Ghāzī, Amīr, 228

music, 26, 206, 255, 273
mutavalli / mutawallī, 114, 115, 119, 158, 159, 161, 162
Mūy-i mubārak, 179

Nābulusī, 'Abd al-Ghanī, 253, 274
nadhr, 261
Najaf, 76, 95, 101, 103
Namangan, 98, 100, 123
Namatgul Qishlaq, 105
namaz, 22, 27, 30, 32, 91, 107
Namazgoh Mosque, 107
Naqshbandi / Naqshbandī / Naqshbandiya, 63, 132, 188, 227, 260, 262, 273
Narshakhi, 96, 123
nasabnāmah, 278
Nasabnāmah-i Sulṭān Satūq Bughrā-khān, 278
Nasabname-i Turki, 111
National Historic & Cultural Heritage Site Under State Protection, 156
Nawa'i, 138
Nawbatī, 256
Nestorian, 11, 199
Nidā'ī Kāshgharī → Kāshgharī
Ningxia, 47-50, 52, 54, 57, 59, 62
Nisa, 107
nisbat-i ṣūrī, 289
Niya, 29, 78, 79, 268, 270
niyāz, 228, 248, 261
Niẓām al-Dīn, Shaykh, 182
Norbeshi Elementary School, 136
Nūr al Dīn Khūja, Mullā, 244
Nur Ata, 106

obo, 5, 11
offerings, 4, 6, 8, 9, 11, 19, 27, 38, 86, 118, 119, 228, 248, 262
oghlaq tartish, 206
Oghuz Khan, 26
Oghuznama / Oghuznamä, 10, 12, 26
okap, 136
Old Turkic, 326, 329
Old Uyghur script, 321
Omar, 109, 129
Opal, 5, 37, 153-159, 161-165, 167-170, 172-174, 214
orda, 66, 68, 72, 91
Ordam Padishah, 4, 206
orthography, 321-323
Osh, 97, 106, 118
Otin, 70
Oy Tughrak, 271
Oyghaq Khōja, 159

På Obanade Stigar, 187, 193, 211-213, 218, 219
Padichim Mazar, 38
Pahlavān Aḥmad Zamjī → Aḥmad Zamjī
Pakhtaabad, 101
Pakistan, 63, 153
Palvan-Ata, 109
Pamir, 101, 121
Panj, 231, 234
Pap, 98
parïz, 66
Parsinshah, 111, 117
patron saint, 36-43, 82, 204
Pa-yi Duldul, 99
Paykend, 103
Paytug Qishlaq, 100
pende, 65
Penjikent, 231, 232, 234, 236
Persians, 261, 270, 271
peshtak, 97
Petropavlovsk, 65
Ping Huizhi, 49
Pingliang, 50, 52
pir / pīr, 40, 63, 118, 142, 204, 239, 241, 245, 248
Pirimkulov, Sultan, 102
protected cultural sites, 75
Pūskām, 263, 265

Qabïlissa-Ata, 67
qadamgāh, 268-270
qadamjay, 76, 77, 81, 99, 108, 116, 118
Qāḍīkhān, Fakhr al-Dīn, 144
Qadīm Jāy Mazar, 159
Qadiriyya, 48-50, 52, 59
Qādirkhān, 302
Qāghrāqī, Zayn al Dīn, 227, 244
Qalandar, Mirza, 112, 187, 217, 256, 260, 263, 264, 268, 273
Qalday Mazar, 38
Qamar, Khwāja, 268
Qambar Ata / Qämbär, 45, 92, 93, 99
Qara Suu Mazar, 40
Qara Yazi baba, 98
Qarajul Atam Mazar, 39
Qarākhān Pādshāh, 243
Qarakhanid, 4, 5, 7, 10, 43, 104, 230, 243, 257, 260, 275
qaralïq, 72
Qaraqash / Qarāqāsh, 28, 76-80, 83-85, 87, 266, 301, 302, 309

Qarāqir, 259
Qarasaqal Mazar, Sultan, 159
Qarasay / Qarāsāy, 67, 269, 270
Qarashash-Ana, 67
Qarāstān, Sultan, 182, 228
Qarasuu Mazar, 39
Qarataghliq, 134
Qara-Tash, 99, 106
Qaratau, 68
Qarghalīq / Qārghālīq, 263, 265, 302
Qarshi, 97, 103, 127
qaṣīda(h), 191, 255
Qasim / Qāsim, Imam → Imam Qasim
Qasim Akhun, 205, 217
qawm, 48, 52-54
Qazan Bulaq Mazar, 39, 46
Qazāq, 141
Qazïghurt, 64, 67
Qianlong, 4, 12, 128, 130, 131, 139, 307
qibla, 119
Qijiachang, 49
Qïlïch Bughrā Khān (Ghāzī), 240, 279
Qing, ix, 3, 27, 49, 62, 127, 128, 130, 131, 133-140, 157, 179, 180
Qinghai, 47-50, 53, 54, 62
Qïrghïz → Kirghiz
Qïrghïz Mazar, 38
Qirmish Ata, 28
Qizil Jilghin Mazar, 37
Qizil Khoroz Mazar, 37
Qobūrghā Būlāq, 271
Qonaqbazar Elementary School, 136
Qondaq / Qondāq / Qontāq, Khwāja, 23, 155, 156, 161, 163, 173, 174
Qonïr-Aulie, 67
Qoqand / Kokand / Khoqand, 97, 103, 109, 110, 141, 142, 145, 180, 188
Qoqand–Southern Qazāq relations, 141
Qoyjol Mazar, 46
Qūchqār Ata → Abū Sa'īd Qūchqār Ata
Qūm Rabāṭ Pādishāhīm / Kaptar Mazar, 265, 266
Qumul / Hami, 8, 21, 57-61
Qur'an, 30, 86, 129, 136, 155, 196, 198, 200, 202, 209, 213, 214, 218, 220
Qūsh Chūlāq, 264, 265
Qushnaguch Ata, 99
Qustanay, 67
Qutadhghu Bilig, 322, 323
Qutayba(h) b. Muslim, 76, 96, 107
quṭb, 243, 246, 293
Quṭb-i 'Ālam Khoja, viii, 243, 246
Ramadan, 7, 134, 141, 142, 144, 282
Rashīd, Mīrzā, 267
rayyis, 60
Red Army, 113
Republic of China, 35, 127, 156, 177, 181, 210, 286
ribāṭ, 264
riḥla, 255
ritual, 6, 9, 21-23, 26, 29-33, 42, 44, 52, 53, 55, 60, 63, 65, 67, 71, 200, 207, 240, 257, 263, 268, 270, 271
Rohman, 28
rubā'ī, 255
Rūmī, Khūja Mullā, 247
Russia, 67, 122
Rustam, 80, 120, 264

Sä'idiyä Khanate, 189
Sab'iyyah, 304
sacred tree, 9, 10, 22, 32, 77, 179, 180, 214, 215
sadaqa, 66
SADUM → Central Asian Muslim Religious Board
Safarnāma, viii, x, 253, 254, 256, 260, 268, 270, 272, 273
Safed Bulan, 96, 98
Ṣaḥāba Jānbāz ('Alamdār) Khoja, 229, 236, 239, 240, 246, 247
Sa'īd Khān, 245
Sakkākī, 326, 328
Salahiddin Ishan, 114
Salar, 55, 99
salat, 81 cf. *namaz*
Ṣāliḥ Khoja, 242
Salim, 59
Salman Fares / Salmān-i Fārs, 184, 213, 219, 220
sama, 31
Sāmānī, Abū al-Naṣr, 276, 277
Samarqand, 76, 104, 121, 129, 132, 231, 233, 235, 321-323
Samarqandī, 'Abd al-Shahīd b. 'Abd al-Ḥamīd, 276
Samarqandī, Sayyid Qāsim → Sayyid Qāsim Samarqandī
Samsaq, 129
Sanga 'Ali / Sangi 'Ali, 105
Sapar Astaliq, 302
sarbaz, 72
Sarīr Saqaṭī, Shaykh, 240
Sarīr Thaqatī, Sulṭān, 228

sartarash, 102
Satuq Bughra Khan / Satūq Bughrā Khān / Satūq Bughrā-khān, viii, ix, 4, 5, 37, 40, 127, 131, 212, 228, 230, 237, 239-242, 244, 247, 275-278, 281-295
Saudi Arabia, 63
sawma'a, 270
Sayid Ishan, 114
sayil, 118
Sayrām, 157, 233, 249, 250
Sayrami, Molla Musa / Sayrāmī, Mullā Mūsā, 75, 83, 106, 122, 157, 166, 180-182, 186, 212, 219, 227, 270, 272, 274, 283, 288, 306, 307, 309
sayyid, 279, 293
Sayyid Aḥmad, 290, 296, 297
Sayyid 'Alā' al-Dīn, 290, 291, 297
Sayyid 'Alī Hamadānī, Amīr, 240, 247
Sayyid Battal Gazi / Baṭṭāl Ghāzī, 98, 228
Sayyid Ḍiyā' al-Dīn / Ḍiyāv al-Dīn, 290, 291, 297
Sayyid Ibrāhīm Madanī, 247
Sayyid Jalāl al-Dīn Baghdādī, 279, 290, 296, 297
Sayyid Kamāl al-Dīn Majnūn, 290, 293, 296, 297
Sayyid Muḥammad, 143, 290, 296, 297
Sayyid Qāsim Samarqandī, 278, 290
Sayyid Ṭāhir, 290, 291, 297
Schah Talib Särmäst → Shah Talib
serf, 137, 138
Seven Muḥammad, 228, 261, 262
Sha Baoqing, 57, 59
Shabistānī, 240
Shabistarī, 229
Shādī, Khwāja, 147, 262, 296
Shah Abdurahman, 111
Shah Akhtam, 99
Shah Dost, 129
Shah Hakim Halis, 108
Shāh Maḥmūd Churās → Churās
Shah Mansur, 111
Shah Qutayba Mazar, 107
Shah Talib / Shāh Talīb Seremes / Shāh Ṭālib Sermest / Shah Tälip Zärmäs, 99, 111, 116, 117, 161, 184-186, 190, 221, 222
shahāda, 144
Shah-i Mardan, 76, 95, 99, 101, 103, 105, 106, 108, 110-119, 121, 122
Shah-i Zinda 'Ali Mazar, 98
Shāhī Beg Khān / Shaybānī Khān, 294
shahid / *shehit* / martyr, 4, 24, 79, 86, 95, 111, 194, 216, 257, 307-309
Shahid Maydan, 97
Shahname, 80
Shahqadam, 102
Shahr-i Barbar, 103, 116
Shahr-i Kalach Khojend, 116
Shahristan, 102
Shakarim, 67
Shakir Mingbashi, 112
Shakir Naib, 112
Sham / Syria, 95, 116, 268
Shām Pādshāh, 244
shaman, 26, 36-38
Shamanism, 34, 216
Shan Zijiu, 56, 57, 59
Shandong, 50
shari'a /*sharī'a*, 47, 50, 59, 145, 324
Shaybānī, 240
Shaybānī Khān → Shāhī Beg Khān
shaykh / *sheykh*, vii, 24, 28, 29, 79, 80, 115, 117, 131, 157-159, 161, 162, 164, 165, 237, 238, 241, 242, 245, 289, 294, 308
Shaykh Abū Yūsuf Hamadānī → Hamadānī
Shaykh Junayd Baghdādī → Baghdādī
shehit → *shahid*
Sheng Shicai, 132, 155
sheykh → *shaykh*
Shi'ite, x, 7, 11, 12, 76, 79, 81-83, 129, 213, 214, 268, 270, 289, 304-306, 308
Shībānī, Shaykh-i 'alavīya, 240, 241
shïmïldïq, 72
Shïmkent, 67, 142
shïraq, 66, 70, 72
Shoqay-Aulie, 67
Shorbulaq Mazar, 39
Silk Road, 5, 34, 47, 80, 219, 250-252
Simnānī, Shaykh 'Alāwu'l Dīn, 247
Sīmurgh, 258
sïnchï, 36
sipārkhwān / *sifārkhwān*, 157-159, 162
Sogd Oblast, 98, 116
Sokh, 99-101, 118
Solikur, 100
song, 41, 42, 325
Soviet, 70, 100, 102, 112, 113, 209, 211, 213
Sredne-Chirchik, 102
Stein, Aurel, 6, 12, 22, 28, 34, 75, 83, 257, 265, 269, 274, 308
stupa, 7, 264
Su Erde, 130, 131
Sufi, 12, 21-27, 29, 31, 34, 47-50, 52-56, 58-63, 83, 129, 132, 133, 228, 237, 240, 250, 253,

255, 260, 262, 267, 268, 270, 272, 273, 276, 289, 292, 298, 306
Sūt-Bībī, viii, 281
Sufi order → *tariqa*
Sugallik, 159
Sui Shu, 10
Suiding Gongbei, 51
Sulayman / Suleyman, 39-42, 80, 83, 97, 106, 118, 120, 195
sümä, 306-308
Sunna / Sunni, 7, 59, 76, 81, 82, 258
sunqar, 65, 66, 69, 70-72
Surkh, Sulṭān Sayyid Khūja, 247
Surkhan-Darya, 103
Suunun Bashï Sulayman Mazar, 39-42
Syr-Darya, 99
Syria → Sham

Tabïlghï Mazar, 38
Tablighi Jama'at, 63
Tabrīzī, Shams al-Dīn, 306
tadhkira(h) / *täzkirä* / hagiography, viii-x,78, 80, 179, 182, 185, 189, 191, 207, 209, 211-215, 227, 230, 232, 237, 238, 243, 244, 273, 276, 281-283, 285, 286, 301-303, 305, 308
Tadhkira-i Chihiltan / *Täzkirä'i Chiltän*, 189-191
Tadhkira-i Ḥaḍrat-i Haft Muḥammadān, 182
Tadhkira-i Haft Muḥammadān, 178, 179, 183, 186, 187, 190, 192
Tadhkira-i Ḥaḍrat-i Haft Muḥammadān Buzurgwār, 183
Tadhkira-i Haft Muḥammadān Pādishāh, 183
Tadhkira-i Jānbāz Khojam, x, 229
Tadhkira-i khwājagān, 292
Tadhkirah-'i Arslān-khān / *Täzkirä Häzriti Soltan Säyd Äli Arislankhan*, 281, 282
Tadhkirah-i Bughrā-khān / *Tadhkira-i Bughrā Khān* / *Tadhkirat al-Bughrā-khān*, 275, 276, 279-281, 284, 285, 291, 292, 297, 298
Tadhkirah-'i Khwājah Muḥammad Sharīf / *Täzkirä'i Khoja Muhämmäd Shérip Pir Buzrukwar*, viii, 189, 282, 285
Tadhkirah-i Sayyid Āfāq Khwājam / *Tadhkira-i Sayyid Āfāq Khwājam*, 278, 290, 297, 298
Tadhkirah-i Türt Imām Ẓabiḥlar / *Täzkiä-i Töt Imam*, 78, 280, 286
Tadhkirah-i Ūvaysiya / *Tadhkirah-i Ūwaysīya* / *Tadhkira-i Uwaysiyya*, 276, 277, 278, 280, 283-285, 287, 291, 298
Tadhkirat al-Abrār, 280
Tadhkirat al-Awliyā / *Tazkira-yi awliya*, x, 280, 321-323, 325-327
taghliq, 131
taharat, 66-68, 72
Ṭāhir, Sayyid → Sayyid Ṭāhir
Tajik, 55, 121, 232
Tajikistan, 98, 101, 103, 105, 116, 231
takbīr, 246, 248
Takht-i Suleyman, 106, 118
Taklamakan, 5, 188, 221, 265, 270, 274, 309
Tal Mazar, 108
ṭalab al-'ilm, 255
Taldïqorgan, 67
Tangrī Lake, 264
Tängritagh / Tianshan, 127, 128, 133, 207, 254, 258
Taraz, 142, 144
Tārīkh-i Ḥamidī, 157
Tārīkh-i Mullāzāda, 294
Tārīkh-i Rashīdī, viii, 178, 187, 188, 227, 241, 243, 245, 250, 260, 270, 294, 298
Tarim Basin, 12, 131, 135, 181, 182, 188, 251, 253, 255, 256, 258, 262, 266, 268, 272-275
Tarimchin, 131
tariqa / Sufi order, 23, 25, 47-50, 56, 58, 59, 61, 63, 132
Tartar / Tārtār, 182, 228
tasbih, 52
Tash Mazar, 108
Tashkent, 102, 120, 139, 141, 142, 144, 145, 227, 233
Tash-Salar, 99
Tatar, 55, 184, 221, 222, 288
tauliya, 155, 156, 167-170, 172-174
Ṭavvā Khūja, 244
ṭawāf, 257, 268, 273
tawhid, 66
Tayhan Khoja, 137
Ṭayrān / Tayyár → Imām Ja'far Ṭayrān
Täzkiä-i Töt Imam → *Tadhkirah-i Türt Imām Ẓabiḥlar*
täzkirä → *tadhkira(h)*
Täzkirä Häzriti Soltan Säyd Äli Arislankhan → *Tadhkirah-'i Arslān-khān*
Täzkirä'i Chiltän → *Tadhkira-i Chihiltan*
Täzkirä'i Khoja Muhämmäd Shérip Pir Buzrukwar → *Tadhkirah-'i Khwājah Muḥammad Sharīf*
Täzkirä'i Yüsüp Qadirkhan, 281
Tazkira-yi awliya → *Tadhkirat al-Awliyā*
Tegirmeti, 37-39, 41, 42, 46
Tengri, 10
Termez, 120, 132
Termez Ata, 120

Tianshan → Tängritagh
Tianshui, 52
Tibetan, 53
tilāwat khāna, 262
Timur, Amir, 104, 115, 132, 227, 249
Timurid, 250, 321-323, 328
Toghraghliq Mazar, 159
Toghuz Bulaq, 41
Tolebi Ata, 65
tölgöchü, 36
Tongxin, 50
Toroq Bulaq Mazar, 39
Töt Imam, 78, 79, 83
Toudaohezi Gongbei, 51
Toyoq, 6, 16, 28
Toyoq Thousand Buddha Caves, 6
travelogue, 254, 270, 272
tugh / tūgh, vii, 31, 161, 201, 273
Tughluq Tīmūr Khān, 182, 228, 292
Tuktibay-Ata, 70
Tul, 100, 101
tumar, 92, 198
Turab, 99
Turan, 106, 257, 262, 274
Turfan / Ṭūrfān / Turpan, 6, 8, 16, 21, 51, 62, 106, 180, 182, 187, 228, 248, 251, 260, 273, 283
Turk Khaganate, 10
Turkestan, 12, 68, 71, 99, 102, 103, 106, 108, 139, 145, 166, 187, 193-198, 200, 207- 212, 214-218, 250, 251, 256, 263, 273-277, 279, 283, 285-288, 299
Turkey, 6, 63, 209
Turki, 111, 154, 166, 179, 193, 196, 213, 218, 250, 251, 274, 276, 277, 281, 283, 285-288, 290, 298, 329
Turkmenabad, 105
Turkmenbashi, 102
Turks, 10, 12, 153, 261
Turpan → Turfan
Tushuqtagh, 28
Tuya-Tash, 99
Twelve Imams, 7, 76-83, 84, 161, 227, 271, 301, 304, 306

Ubaydullah, 137
Uch Turfan / Uch-Turpan, 106, 283
Uchtur Khälipä, 8
Uḥud, 267
Üjmä, 6, 22
Ukkasha-Ata, 66, 68
ulama, 132
Ulïtau, 67
Ulkan-Toytepa / Ulkan Toytyube, 102
Ūlūgh Tadhkirah, 281, 282, 285
umra, 47
Ura-Tyube, 102
Urumqi, 51, 137, 256, 281
Ushaq, 131
ushr, 129, 130
Usta Umrzak, 113, 114
Ust-Kamenogorsk, 65
Üstün Artūch, 227
'Uthmān Bughrā-khān, 244, 279
Uvaysī / Uwaysi, 237, 248, 250, 262, 298
Uways, 60
Uwaysiyya, 291, 292, 298
uyezd, 115
Uyghur script, 321, 322, 329
Uzbek, 55, 139, 142, 218, 288, 294
Uzbekistan, 4, 70, 76, 98, 100, 103, 105, 106, 108, 114, 121, 123, 124, 141, 210, 289, 293, 298
Ūzkand, 293

Vanj, 231, 234-236
Vays Qaran / Vaysī Qaran, Sulṭān, 240
Volga-Ural region, 249
Voodoo, 10, 11
Voruh, 101
Vuadil, 114, 116, 123

Wali Khan, 131
Wang Shoutian, 48, 57, 58
waqf, x, 97, 113, 127, 128, 130-133, 136-139, 155, 157-166, 190, 201, 208, 227, 253
Women's Teacher Training School, 137
Wujiazi, 35
Wuxingping, 57-61
Wuzhong, 48, 50, 52

Xianfeng, 131
Xiang Fei / Ipar Khan / Fragrant Concubine, 4, 12
Xiaxiyuan, 56-59
Xihaigu, 50
Xiheba, 57-59
Xiji, 50
Xining, 50, 62
Xi-yu tong-wen-zhi, 292
Xiyu tuzhi, ix
Xuanhuagang Gongbei, 51
Xuanzang, 6
Xunhua, 50

Yāgh Sū, 245
Yalang Āyāq Khwāja, 144
Yalghuz Oghul Mazar, 76, 80
yanchi, 131, 134, 138
Yang Zengxin, 49
Yangiḥiṣār → Yengisar
Yangiqurgan, 100
Yangmen, 48
yantaqchi, 157-159, 161, 162
Yaqub Beg / Ya'qūb Beg, 158, 159, 161, 162, 165, 166, 177, 179, 180, 214
Yardan, 111, 112, 119
Yarkand / Yārkand, ix, x, 8, 10, 21, 22, 24, 26, 27, 31, 133, 134, 139, 159, 177-182, 184-186, 188-191, 193, 195, 211, 212, 219, 221, 222, 229, 237, 241, 248, 249, 255, 256, 260-263, 280, 281, 285, 288, 292, 295
Yarkand Khanate, 133, 177
Yārkand Mazar Täzkiriliri Toplimi, 191
Yārkandī, Mīr Khāl al-Dīn Kātib, 289, 292, 298
Yasavī / Yasawi / Aḥmad Yasavī, Khoja, 65, 67, 144, 145, 228, 247, 248
Yasawiya, 63
Yasï, 68
Yättä Qizlirim, 283, 288 cf. yete qïz
Yazdi / Yazdī, Sharaf al-Dīn 'Alī, 104, 294
Yengisar / Yengi Hissar / Yengi-Hisar / Yangiḥiṣār, 10, 38, 40, 129, 179, 193, 195, 230, 236, 237, 246, 258, 275, 285
Yengi-shahr, 179
Yesbol-Ata, 67
Yeskeldi-Bi, 67
yete qïz, 244
Yettä Shahr, 180
Yïlanchï Ata, 228
Yinchuan, 50, 54, 62
Yitimī, 302, 308
Yūlchāq river, 263
Yunnan, 48, 50, 52
Yūqdū, 268
yurt, 44, 236
Yūsār, 263, 265
Yusuf Khass Hajib, 5
Yūsuf Qādir Khān / Yüsüp Qadirkhan, 228, 238-241, 279-282, 288
Yüsüp Qadirkhan Ghazi Täzkirisi, 281, 288

Zabiha, Imám → Imám Zabiha
zakat / *zakāt*, 129, 130, 142, 145
zakātchī, 142
Zalīlī, viii, x, 178, 179, 182, 184, 189-192, 253-260, 262, 263, 265-268, 270-274, 281, 288
Zäliliy Diwani, 189-191
Zangūyā / Zanguy, 265
Zara Khatime, 23
Zarkul, 102
zawiya, 50
Zayd b. Shābit, 239
Zayn al-'Abidin → Imam Zayn al-'Abidin
Zayniddinov, 105, 124
Zhambïl / Zhambul, 64, 70, 142, 144
Zhangjiachuan, 50, 51
Zhangmen, 48
Zhanïs-Ata, 67
Zhao Hui, 134
Zhazï-Bi, 67
Zholbarïs-Ata, 67
Zhou Shu, 10
zikr / *dhikr*, 23, 24, 31, 49, 50, 53, 190, 207, 268
Zīrak, Mīrzā, 260
Zirk Mazar, 100, 108
ziyara / *ziyarat* / *ziyarät* / *ziyārat*, 21-24, 27, 29-32, 48, 52-54, 63, 64, 68-72, 142, 205, 206, 253, 256, 258, 260, 261, 272
Zoroastrian, 6
Zulfikar, 102
Zunghar Basin, 130
Zunghar Khanate, 128

Contributors (in alphabetical order, by SURNAME)

Nodirjon ABDULAHATOV,	*O'qituvchilarning Malakasini Oshirish Instituti, Ferghana, Uzbekistan.*
Rahile DAWUT,	*Xinjiang University, Urumqi, Xinjiang, China.*
Devin DEWEESE,	*Indiana University, Bloomington, Indiana, USA.*
Gulbahar GHOJESH,	*Xinjiang Normal University, Urumqi, Xinjiang, China.*
Patrick HÄLLZON,	*Stockholm-Istanbul Program for Central Asian and Turkic Studies (SIPCATS), Stockholm, Sweden.*
Ashirbek MUMİNOV,	*L.N.Gumilyov Eurasian National University, Astana, Kazakhstan.*
Omerjan NURİ,	*Khotan Education Institute, Khotan, Xinjiang, China.*
Aitzhan NURMANOVA,	*R.B. Suleimenov Institute of Oriental Studies, Almaty, Kazakhstan.*
Abliz ORXUN,	*Millätlär Näshriyati, Urumqi, Xinjiang, China.*
Alexandre PAPAS,	*Centre National de la Recherche Scientifique , Paris, France.*
SAWADA Minoru,	*University of Toyama, Toyama, Japan.*
SHİNMEN Yasushi,	*Chuo University , Hachi'ōji, Tokyo, Japan.*
SUGAHARA Mutsumi,	*Tokyo University of Foreign Studies, Fuchū, Tokyo, Japan.*
SUGAWARA Jun,	*Tokyo University of Foreign Studies, Fuchū, Tokyo, Japan.*
Rian THUM,	*Loyola University New Orleans, Louisiana, USA.*
WANG Jianxin,	*Lanzhou University, Lanzhou, Gansu, China.*
WANG Ping,	*Xinjiang Normal University, Urumqi, Xinjiang, China.*
Ablimit YASİN,	*Xinjiang University, Urumqi, Xinjiang, China.*
ZHANG Shicai,	*Xinjiang University, Urumqi, Xinjiang, China.*
ZHOU Xijuan,	*Willamette University, Salem, Oregon, USA.*